OFFICIAL

HTML Publishing for Netscape

WINDOWS EDITION

OFFICIAL

HTML Publishing FOR Netscape

WINDOWS EDITION

An imprint of
Ventana Communications
Group

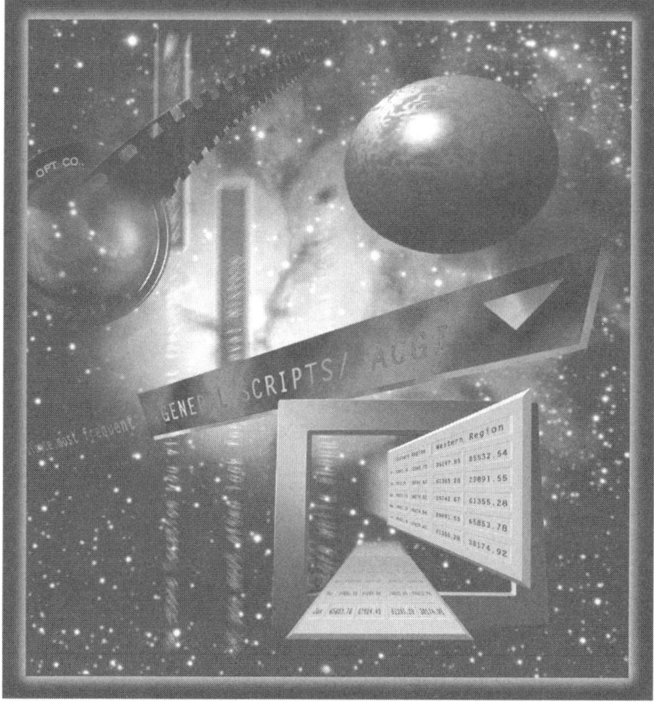

Stuart Harris
Gayle Kidder

Official HTML Publishing for Netscape

Library of Congress Cataloging-in-Publication Data

Harris, Stuart (Stuart H.)
HTML publishing for Netscape : your guide to online design & production / Stuart Harris & Gayle Kidder. — 1st ed.
p. cm.
Includes index.
ISBN 1-56604-288-7
1. HTML (Document markup language) 2. Netscape. 3. World Wide Web (Information retrieval system) I. Kidder, Gayle. II. Title.
QA76.76.H94H372 1995
005.75—dc20 95-50052
CIP

First Edition 9 8 7 6 5 4 3 2 1

Printed in the United States of America

Published and distributed to the trade by Ventana Communications Group, Inc., P.O. Box 13964, Research Triangle Park, NC 27709-3964 919/544-9404 FAX 919/544-9472

Limits of Liability and Disclaimer of Warranty

The authors and publisher of this book have used their best efforts in preparing the book and the programs contained in it. These efforts include the development, research, and testing of the theories and programs to determine their effectiveness. The authors and publisher make no warranty of any kind, expressed or implied, with regard to these programs or the documentation contained in this book.

The authors and publisher shall not be liable in the event of incidental or consequential damages in connection with, or arising out of, the furnishing, performance or use of the programs, associated instructions and/or claims of productivity gains.

Trademarks

Trademarked names appear throughout this book. Rather than list the names and entities that own the trademarks or insert a trademark symbol with each mention of the trademarked name, the publisher states that it is using the names only for editorial purposes and to the benefit of the trademark owner with no intention of infringing upon that trademark.

PRESIDENT/CEO
Josef Woodman

VICE PRESIDENT OF CONTENT DEVELOPMENT
Karen A. Bluestein

PRODUCTION MANAGER
John Cotterman

TECHNOLOGY OPERATIONS MANAGER
Kerry L. B. Foster

PRODUCT MARKETING MANAGER
Diane Lennox

ART DIRECTOR
Marcia Webb

ACQUISITIONS EDITOR
Cheri Robinson

DEVELOPMENTAL EDITORS
Tim Mattson
Katherine Murray

PROJECT EDITOR
Judith F. Wilson

COPY EDITOR
Ellen Strader

ASSISTANT EDITOR
JJ Hohn

TECHNICAL REVIEWER
Dick Cravens

DESKTOP PUBLISHER
Lance Kozlowski

PROOFREADER
Marie C. Dobson

INDEXER
Bob Richardson

COVER ILLUSTRATION
Laura Stalzer

About the Authors

Gayle Kidder is a journalist and editor with 20 years of experience in books, magazines, newspapers, and documentary television. She has published more than 500 articles in magazines and newspapers on topics as diverse as science, theater, art, travel, fiction, and computers. She currently maintains an online column of cultural events for the city of San Diego at http://www.zoomsd.com.

Stuart Harris is the author of *The irc Survival Guide* (Addison-Wesley) and numerous articles about the Internet in national magazines. He works as an Internet consultant and is leader of his local computer society's Internet special interest group. He has also been involved in technical editing and TV documentary production. Stuart enjoys communicating complex ideas to a mass audience.

Kidder and Harris are the coauthors of *Netscape Navigator Quick Tour (Windows and Mac versions), and HTML Publishing With Internet Assistant,* both published by Ventana. Other joint projects have included TV documentary production, journalism, software product management, and a type of live theater on the Internet. Gayle and Stuart work in the classic "electronic cottage" near the beach in San Diego and are on the Net every day of their lives.

Acknowledgments

Writing a book about the Web today is rather like trying to jump onto a moving train. Legs pumping and hearts racing, we toss our rucksacks full of half-finished ideas into an open boxcar, and leap over a blur of disappearing track. If it weren't for the many hands held out to us from inside, we don't think we'd ever make it.

Being conscientious, we make every effort to ensure the accuracy of our text, and we have at least one tech editor to back us up. So you can trust what you read here, pretty much—the fact that this material goes out of date five times before breakfast every day is beyond our control, alas.

You should be profoundly suspicious, however, of much of what you find in our figures when they depict invented Web sites. We make no claim whatsoever to expertise on the subjects of, for instance, Mayan culture or Monarch butterfly migration. The sites that depict these things are totally fanciful. We acknowledge the following, who helped make our imaginary sites look plausible (we hope):

There's a very fine and absolutely genuine Mayan Adventure on the Web, created by the Science Museum of Minnesota. It's at http://www.ties.k12.mn.us:80/~smm/, and Mike Petrich kindly gave us permission to make use of some of the traditional textile patterns.

There's also a fine and genuine Monarch Watch site—http://129.237.246.134. This is run by Professor Orley "Chip" Taylor of the University of Kansas Department of Entomology. Professor Taylor took the time to look at an early draft of our imaginary Monarch data-gathering form, and corrected some obvious blunders.

The genuine Philately page is done by the West Coast Stamp Collectors' Association at http://www.adnetsol.com/stamps/stamps.html. We thank Eli Eisenberg for permission to rearrange some of his GIFs (stamps are more valuable when reused, aren't they Eli?).

That monstrous mathematical equation in Figure 7-8 is the work of Gail Bamber of the San Diego Supercomputer Center. We thank her and Webmaster Joshua Polterock for permission to reproduce it.

For the JavaScript we use as a teaching aid in Chapter 8 and that is provided on the CD-ROM, we have Patrick Taylor to thank. It's based on original work by Daniel Wyszynski. For the VRML example we're indebted to Mark Pesce and his own excellent book on VRML, which we recommend to VRML enthusiasts.

"Abigail's Dream" is, of course, entirely the work of the Dutch computer programmer who is known by the name of Abigail to numerous members of newsgroups and mailing lists on Web topics. She's a tireless promoter of good HTML who generously shares her knowledge, while never failing to remind people of the high-minded uses to which the Web can be put. We commend her dedication and thank her for allowing us to share her piece with our readers in Chapter 1.

Under the heading of "People Who Taught Us a Lot" come Martin Reddy of the University of Edinburgh (images), Eric Olson of Silicon Graphics (marvelous Perl that didn't end up in the book but *really* taught us a lot), Harold Carey (Server-side Includes), Craig Kanarick of M.I.T. (server redirection), and Ed Hott of Intersé Market Focus (site visit analysis). Those whose Web pages and FTP sites on Perl and cgi-bin in general were helpful are too numerous to mention individually, but we've included most of them in Appendix D.

Not too numerous to mention, as ever, is our sysadmin and pal Mark Burgess of http://www.thegroup.net. We've all come a long way since public Internet access was a new idea and Netscape was a gleam in Marc Andreesen's RAM. This time around, we'd also like to pay tribute to our *other* sysadmin, Steve Froeschke of esnet. Steve went the distance and further in reconfiguring things so that our experiments would work "as advertised."

Those who contributed to the accompanying CD-ROM get their thanks in that medium, appropriately enough—but one cross-over is Martine Gingras of the University of Quebec. Some of the background textures she contributed to the disc collection also made incidental appearances in our figures. Merci, Martine.

We've shared a lot of campfires along the way and picked up a lot of stories, and sometimes it's hard to remember who said what and who to thank. If we've forgotten anyone here, we hope we'll have the chance to return the favor on the next trip.

Stuart Harris
Gayle Kidder

Contents

Introduction

Computer people, we've discovered, come from all walks of life. One of the major delights of life online for us has been the diversity we've encountered there. We often chuckle to ourselves when we read another so-called Internet marketing expert or business writer telling us that the Internet is largely made up of young males from 18 to 39.

A 10-year-old boy who asks all the right questions with unabashed directness regularly shows up at our local Internet users' group, as does a retired woman whose age we wouldn't think of asking but whose career in international politics has spanned the globe. There are military electronics experts, people with small businesses, and retirees who now have the time to keep up with all the new things they've been telling themselves they would for years. Our Net acquaintances and e-mail contacts include a wide range of people of all ages and professions—business people, teachers, librarians, university professors and their students, and cybertravelers from around the world.

The one thing they all have in common is curiosity and a thirst to expand their horizons and continue learning, which is what we assume you share in picking up this book. We assume no special computer background, just a working familiarity with your own computer.

It doesn't matter to us if you want to get on the World Wide Web to make money, find a new job, publish your book, or to share your family news with family and friends around the globe. Just bring your curiosity and come with us; we hope we'll have fun together showing you how to fulfill your Web ambitions.

What's Inside

Since not all readers will be coming in with the same level of knowledge, we've structured the material so that you can dive in at the appropriate place for you. Begin at the beginning, or start right in on the things that interest you.

Although this book focuses on what you can do with Netscape Navigator, the most popular and versatile browser on the Web, we've tried to cover the entire range of HTML as it exists as an international standard today. We want you to continue to use this as reference even after you've learned what you need to write your first Web pages. For that reason, whenever we discuss an HTML tag for the first time, we give a complete definition that is set apart in clear definition boxes for easy reference.

Chapter by chapter, here's what we cover:

For those of you who are new to the world of the Web, we provide some background in Chapter 1, "Media for a New Millennium," on the evolution of the Internet and the Web. If you're confused about how these things relate, this should help you sort it out and give you some idea of how it's organized and how it all works. But even some old hands at life online should find some inspiration in *Abigail's Dream*, one Web denizen's optimistic view of the future of the Web.

Chapter 2, "Getting Down to Work," starts by covering the essential applications you'll need as you clear your desk and get ready to start your new career as a Web author. We'll talk about how to organize your Web site as a whole. Then we'll ease into the topic of HTML by showing how you can build a Web page with just 10 easy tags. Everything you need to know about simple file structure and the elementary HTML tags is in this chapter.

Chapter 3, "Links, Links & More Links," goes into detail about the all-important business of hypertext links, the glue that holds the Web together. We'll talk about how this relates to your site structure as a whole and how you can avoid the "Back button blues." We'll show how, with the right type of links, you can reward visitors quickly with the information they want, and they'll be grateful to you for it. And if you thought hypertext just meant dishing up one HTML document after another, you'll have a surprise in store when you discover the other kinds of information you can link to using protocols other than HTTP.

If you've ever looked at a site full of wonderful graphics and wondered "How do they do that, anyway?" Chapter 4, "All About Images," will give you the answers. We'll start with a necessary primer on computer color display so you'll know what to expect, before going on to talk about sizing and placing images and using color wisely. We'll show you how you can speed up loading time by using different image formats, interlacing, and low-source images. We'll discuss the "hot topic" of active images. You'll learn how to make those clickable image maps that turn smart graphics into hot links—a task that's probably easier than you think.

Chapter 5, "Getting Stylish," discusses the many ways you can add a flourish to your pages. This includes using different fonts and colors, as well as some clever layout tricks using both decorative and invisible tables. Then we'll get into that great Netscape 2.0 invention, frames, and explain how you can make multiple frames and coordinate them to work on your Web page.

Then take a look at Chapter 6, "Design Tips: Learning From the Pros." Wonder how they created those spectacular effects? We'll tell you their secrets. This chapter is a fun and interesting side tour of some outstanding Web sites. We've chosen them to illustrate some design concepts from which even the novice can learn—starting with the easiest of techniques anyone can do with no special knowledge, all the way up to ambitious animations with Java and cgi-bin programs.

If you're the orderly type, you're going to love Chapter 7, "The World of Tables & Equations." It shows you in several simple examples how to use HTML tables to organize and display material in a clear and sensible fashion. And if numbers are your game, you'll learn how to deal with mathematical elements and equations on Web pages.

Chapter 8, "Multimedia & the Web," is a chapter for all you multimedia jockeys out there who just love to play with your sound editors and movie players—you'd make your computer sing and dance if only you could. We'll not only be explaining the basics of creating sound and animation for the Web, we'll show you some of the latest geewhizzery coming down the Internet pike, including Java, virtual reality, and live broadcasting via the Web. We guarantee you'll have fun trying out some of the simple tutorials we've provided in Java and VRML.

Chapter 9, "Forms, Feedback & cgi-bin," will be your guide to getting feedback of all kinds from your Web site. We'll explain how to design effective user feedback forms and how to capture the incoming data from the server. For the really daring, we'll offer a little elementary Perl programming and a look at the cgi-bin interface between HTML pages and the binary programs that serve them. Even if you aren't bold enough to take the step of writing programs yourself, the explanations will set you up for understanding the ways you can make use of the data you collect from forms and how to monitor the visitors to your site.

Chapter 10, "Databases, Web Servers & Search Engines," will take this one step further by showing you what to do with all that data you collect. You'll learn how to turn the information you retrieve into the kind of useful statistics that marketing people love—like how many people visited your site and where they spent their time. Then we'll take you on a little tour into the heart of a Web server and talk about how you can set up your own Web server if you're so inclined. And finally, we'll discuss how to publicize your Web page and get yourself into those all-important Web search databases.

The appendices include easy reference to all the HTML tags, a guide to online resources and lists of special characters, standard icons, and a color table. And don't forget to take advantage of the Online Companion, which includes these and a lot of other helpful resources, including most of the software mentioned herein.

Another note: We've written this book with a Windows bias, but we think you'll find it very useful even if you're working on a Mac or a Sun workstation. HTML and the Web, after all, were designed to transcend operating systems and computer platforms. If some of the software you might use is different, the principles will be the same.

Quick Start

When learning a new topic, some people take the methodical approach and others just can't stay in their seats for two minutes. We realize that some of you will just want to cut to the chase (we're kind of like that ourselves). So here's your advice for the fast track.

If you're new to HTML but you're the impatient type and you've already got your HTML project in mind, boot up your computer and open this book to Chapter 2 on your desk. Follow along with our 10-tag HTML primer and we guarantee you'll have a Web page in just an hour or two.

If you've already got a Web page but want to know more about using images or adding special effects, jump ahead to Chapters 4 & 5 to learn all the things no one ever tells you about computer images and how to put real style in your pages.

If multimedia's your passion, skip on to Chapter 8 and learn how to add sound and animation to your Web pages. And if you're puzzled about how to get feedback and monitor accesses to your site, Chapters 9 & 10 are where you'll find some explanations and answers.

NEXT STOP: THE WEB

Well, the bus is pulling out of the station now, and as one of our favorite pop legends of the '60s used to say, "You're either on the bus, or you're off the bus."

We hope you're on the bus with us, because it's going to be an interesting trip. The tour will include a lot of the highlights of the World Wide Web we've discovered in our wanderings. But the best part will be the new roads you'll forge yourself, as you build your own piece of the World Wide Web.

Stuart Harris
Gayle Kidder
San Diego, California

1

Media for a New Millennium

Everybody's talking about it. The newspapers are full of stories about the World Wide Web. It's the buzz of the nineties: the reinvention of the media. The last nail in the coffin of the printing press. The imminent death of TV as we know it. Last year a business card with no e-mail address was totally unhip. Now adding a Web address as well promises to get you invited to all the right parties. You're ready to catch the wave of the future and get on the Web. But how do you cut through all the hype? Before getting started, find out how much you already know about the Internet.

Here's a quick little multiple choice test:

The Internet is owned and operated by:

1. The United States government.
2. A consortium of U.S. and international universities.
3. A consortium of telephone and cable companies.
4. Michael Ovitz and Stephen Spielberg.

The World Wide Web is:

1. Just another name for the Internet.
2. A rival system to the Internet.
3. The European contribution to the Internet.
4. The business and entertainment section of the Internet.

If you chose anything in either of the above lists, you are wrong —with the exception, perhaps, of number four on both lists, to which the only safe answer is, "not yet!" But all of the above answers are viable common misconceptions about the Internet and the World Wide Web.

We assume that since you've picked up this book, you have already had some exposure to the Internet and the World Wide Web. You may even be quite familiar with what's available there. But even quite accomplished Web surfers are often confused about exactly what this resource *is* that they're tapping into. The confusion is justifiable, since the nature of the Web, and the face of the Internet in general, has changed vastly in the last few years. And even more radical changes are appearing even as this book is going to print.

A Little Background, Please

Before we tap into the great publishing resource of the Web, let's try to put the Web phenomenon in perspective. In this chapter, we'll give you a feel for what the Web was designed for, where it is right now, and where it's going. Later in the book, we'll talk about some exciting prospects in the Web's near future, some of which you'll be able to participate in right away.

But first, let's start with a basic understanding of what HTML is, how it and the Web came about, and how the Web fits into the wider universe of the Internet. Then we'll talk about what you need to launch yourself into Webspace. Finally, we'll explain how to start organizing your desktop and get on your way to being a Web author.

Anyone Here Speak HTML?

HTML, short for HyperText Markup Language, is the basic language of the World Wide Web. As languages go, it's probably the easiest one you'll ever learn. Its roots are English, its vocabulary is made up of basic mnemonic abbreviations, and its syntax is based on something you probably learned in high-school English: simple document structure.

HTML was invented as recently as 1989 by Tim Berners-Lee, a young software engineer at the European Laboratory for Particle Physics (or CERN, as it's commonly known from its French initials) in Switzerland. It was based on a language called SGML—for Standard Generalized Markup Language—and remains a subclass of that very powerful language. SGML's original purpose was to make it possible to share documents created on one computer with entirely different computer systems without having to take into account all the idiosyncrasies of different hardware and software. The idea was to embed code tags in the text that would describe the elements of a document. Then each computer could make its own decisions about how to display it, while preserving the original format. And unlike much of the software you buy today, an SGML document's lifetime is meant to outlast the computer system on which it is written.

SGML is still alive and well. It is particularly appropriate for certain types of documents for which sophisticated search techniques might be useful, such as dictionaries, technical documentation, catalogs, academic journals, or highly annotated works. In Figure 1-1, you see a section of a play that's part of the works of Shakespeare available in SGML on the Web shown in the free SoftQuad Panorama viewer for SGML, which can be installed as a helper application for Netscape Navigator.

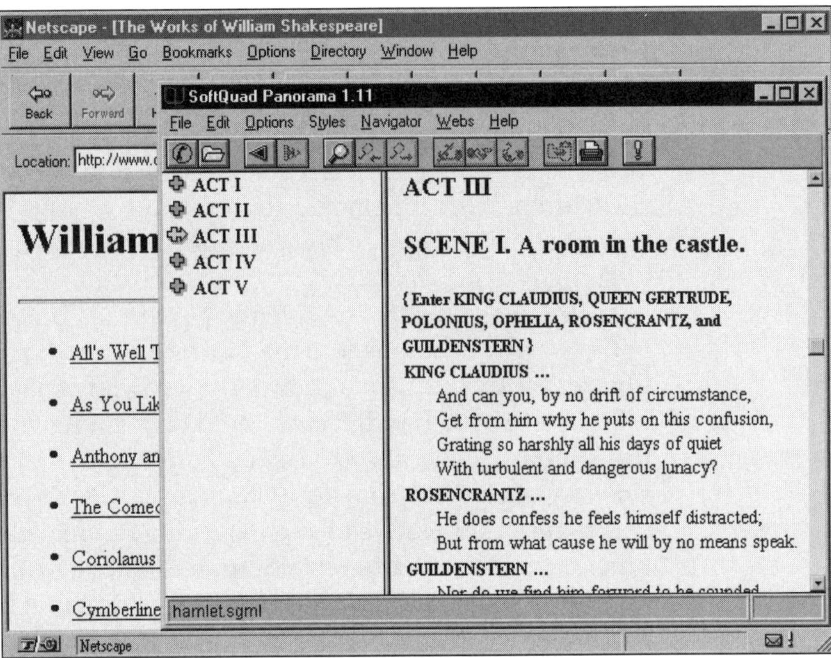

Figure 1-1: Hamlet *in SGML, viewed with Panorama.*

TIP

If you're interested in SGML and the SGML viewer Panorama, you can get more information about them on the Web at: ***http://www.ncsa.uiuc.edu/SDG/Software/Mosaic/WebSGML.html.*** *Get the free Panorama viewer at* ***ftp://ftp.ncsa.uiuc.edu/Web/Mosaic/Windows/viewers/panofr10.exe.*** *A Pro version is also available from SoftQuad. See* ***http://www.sq.com.*** *Shakespeare in SGML can be found at* ***http://www.oclc.org:5046/oclc/research/panorama/contrib/Shakespeare/.***

HTML is actually a simplified version of SGML. Since its invention in 1989, it has far outstripped its predecessor for general, wide applications. Although simpler, it adds one crucial powerful idea: hypertext. This simple point-and-click concept for traveling from one piece of information to another has become so common in applications today that it hardly needs any introduction. The help system for Windows (or dozens of other pieces of software you might have) is full of examples. The idea of applying hypertext to the Internet, however, was revolutionary. It meant one no longer had to enter complex UNIX commands to search and retrieve each new piece of information.

SGML and HTML documents are simple ASCII text files with presentational tags embedded within them. HTML is not even a real computer language at all, but a sort of "computerese." The first version contained little more than 30 codes—or "tags"—that needed to be embedded within any existing document to make it readable with a Web browser. The next generation version, HTML 2.0, soon improved on the original by adding a few more tags. Its most useful advance was the ability to make interactive forms. As more people have come onto the Web, more ideas have sprung up on how to improve on the original.

In 1995, a formal proposal for the next-generation code—known as HTML 3.0—was drafted by the WWW Consortium and generously discussed, both on and off the Net. But as Netscape and others preempted discussion by selectively implementing the HTML 3.0 proposals, it dawned on the Consortium that they were trying to build a house on shifting sands, and HTML 3.0 was allowed to expire, to be replaced by a whole host of fragmentary proposals and subcommittees. So HTML 3.0 does not officially exist as this book goes to press—but we and other writers still use the term as shorthand for the next-generation version of HTML markup.

HTML still remains highly accessible to the average computer user, though. There are still less than a hundred basic HTML tags in the latest proposed version, and it's possible to do most of the things one would want to do with far fewer than that.

New versions of HTML have not necessarily made the original 1.0 language obsolete; they have merely added more power and flexibility to it. "Backwards compatibility" is the watchword in Web development, as in software development, so HTML 1.0 documents are still perfectly readable by browsers of the HTML 3.0 generation. In fact, many documents claiming to be HTML 3.0–compliant really use little more than the original 30 or so codes.

A Web browser is simply the software tool (Netscape Navigator is an example) that interprets all that code for you and turns it into a pretty little page on your screen, complete with buttons, logos, beeps, and fill-out forms (and no doubt its share of sassy error messages).

THE DAWN OF HTML EDITORS

Anybody here remember the early days of word processors when you used to be able to see the formatting codes all over the screen? Whoa! Look at all those hands! So much for those who say the Internet is full of under-25-year-old geeks. (For the rest of you, just take our word for it that formatting codes were a fact of life for the computer literate in the 1980s.)

Obviously, since those bad old days, word processors have made a lot of progress toward becoming transparent interfaces where "what you see is what you get." With less than 100 basic codes, you might think it would then be an easy task to design an editor for HTML that would be a simple transparent interface. Well, yes and no. While a word processor only has to concern itself with how your document looks on the one particular operating system it's designed to work on, an HTML editor has to be concerned with how the document may look on any of the dozens of Web browsers circulating about cyberspace, and on several different operating systems.

Complicating the problem is the fact that HTML is still an evolving language (as the HTML 3.0 debate has shown), and standards are still being hashed out to make sure it maintains its basic principle of being cross-platform. New tags are being introduced regularly to answer new needs or whims, and HTML editors are having a hard time keeping up with it all.

One day, after the blood of many a young startup company who went the wrong direction has been mopped up from the floor, you can be sure that writing a Web page with an HTML editor will be as easy as writing a memo with your word processor (and probably indistinguishable from it). For now, as good as any particular HTML editor may be, the smart Web designer needs to understand the underlying code, not just to tweak what resists being automated but also to implement *right now* what the editing software might not catch up with for a few months.

We'll have more to say about HTML editors a little later.

Netscape & HTML

Since Netscape hit the cyber-market in late 1994, it has swept across the Web like Coca-Cola on a hot day in Sinaloa. Its ability to cache and retrieve documents quickly, its superior image display, and its complete package of Internet tools have made it the slickest and easiest way to look at the Internet.

In line with Netscape's policy of staying ahead of the competition and on the cutting edge of Web development, Netscape Navigator 2.0 incorporates a number of the tags included in the HTML 3.0 proposal. In the rapidly moving field of Web design, these will in all likelihood soon be generally recognized. Navigator also has several added custom features that allow more control over document presentation. These features are considered "Netscape extensions" to HTML. This means that, as a Web author, you can exert a high degree of control over the look of your document in Netscape Navigator, which is by far and away the most popular browser used on the Web (estimated to account for about 70 to 80 percent of all Web accesses). However, as a Web author, you should also bear in mind that some of these features may not always be preserved in non-Netscape browsers—an admonition you're going to see repeated many times in this book.

To put the maximum power in *your* hands, we've chosen in this book to clearly mark any HTML codes that are Netscape extensions. We'll also point out, when appropriate, some HTML 3.0 additions expected to be implemented in the near future. You can then decide for yourself what features suit your own Web presentation and expected audience.

In order to decide, you should bear in mind the audience you hope to reach. If you're preparing a slick marketing interface for the Web or playing with the latest avant-garde multimedia applications, you'll be yearning to walk on the wild side, and you'll find these Netscape-added tools the cat's meow. But if you're planning to present important public information or instructional tools, you might prefer to be a bit more conservative in your authoring to ensure you reach the widest possible Internet public. (For example, a Web page on information for diabetics would cut off a crucial section of its potential audience if it did not take into account those with vision problems, which is a common side effect of diabetes.) We'll talk a little bit more about this later as we get ready to design pages.

THE HTTP PROTOCOL

When Tim Berners-Lee first invented HTML, it was not in order to talk in code to some secret society of visionaries in pointed purple hats. Quite the contrary. He had in mind a project that would allow people all over the world to share documents and information easily. HTML was only one piece of the puzzle—the piece that handled document presentation.

Another piece of the puzzle was how to use the already existing Internet to transmit these documents. To do this, it was necessary to establish a new "protocol." Protocols are just technical specifications invented to facilitate information exchange over the Internet. During the last 20 years, several protocols have been developed for different types of information exchange requirements on the Internet. These include:

NNTP (Network News Transfer Protocol): The protocol used for accessing Usenet news articles.

SMTP (Simple Mail Transfer Protocol): The protocol that handles your e-mail.

FTP (File Transfer Protocol): A method of posting and retrieving files from a remote computer on the Internet.

Gopher: A menu-driven system of searching for and displaying documents that are available on other computers on the Internet.

Telnet: A way to connect to a specific remote computer on the Internet system and execute commands just as if you were on that system.

WAIS (Wide Area Information Searching): A way to search Internet databases for information using keywords.

Each of these protocols has its own language and methods of searching and transferring information.

The World Wide Web, a project that was born with a modest six months' funding, established a new protocol—HTTP, short for HyperText Transfer Protocol. HTTP has become such a powerful method of exchange that many kinds of information that previously depended on other protocols like Gopher and WAIS have either been rewritten for the Web or are presented quite transparently on it. Many browsers today, including Netscape Navigator, allow you to send mail and read the Usenet news without thinking about the protocol you're using. And today's generation of Web browsers all generally allow you to use FTP to download files or access a Gopher menu the same way you go to another Web page—by clicking on a link. So it's no surprise that many Web users are often unfamiliar with what these protocols mean.

The World Wide Web grew quietly for a couple of years after Berners-Lee's successful little project. By 1992 there was a nice but contained little Web of 50 HTTP servers around the world, and a useful little virtual library of material available on it, which was overwhelmingly scientific in nature. But all of this material was primarily text-based, as were the browsers used to access it. Then that same year, the National Center for Supercomputing Applications (NCSA) in Illinois released Mosaic, the first graphical Web browser. This added a second critical ingredient, after hypertext, to the Web—images. Suddenly the drawbridge was down and the mob rushed into the Internet castle.

Since then the Web's growth has been nothing short of explosive, as you can see in Figure 1-2. Since the Web now embraces so much of the information on the Internet, the terms *Web* and *Internet* are often used interchangeably. But as you can now understand, the Web is only one very young and rebellious country in the Internet empire, although a very large and growing one.

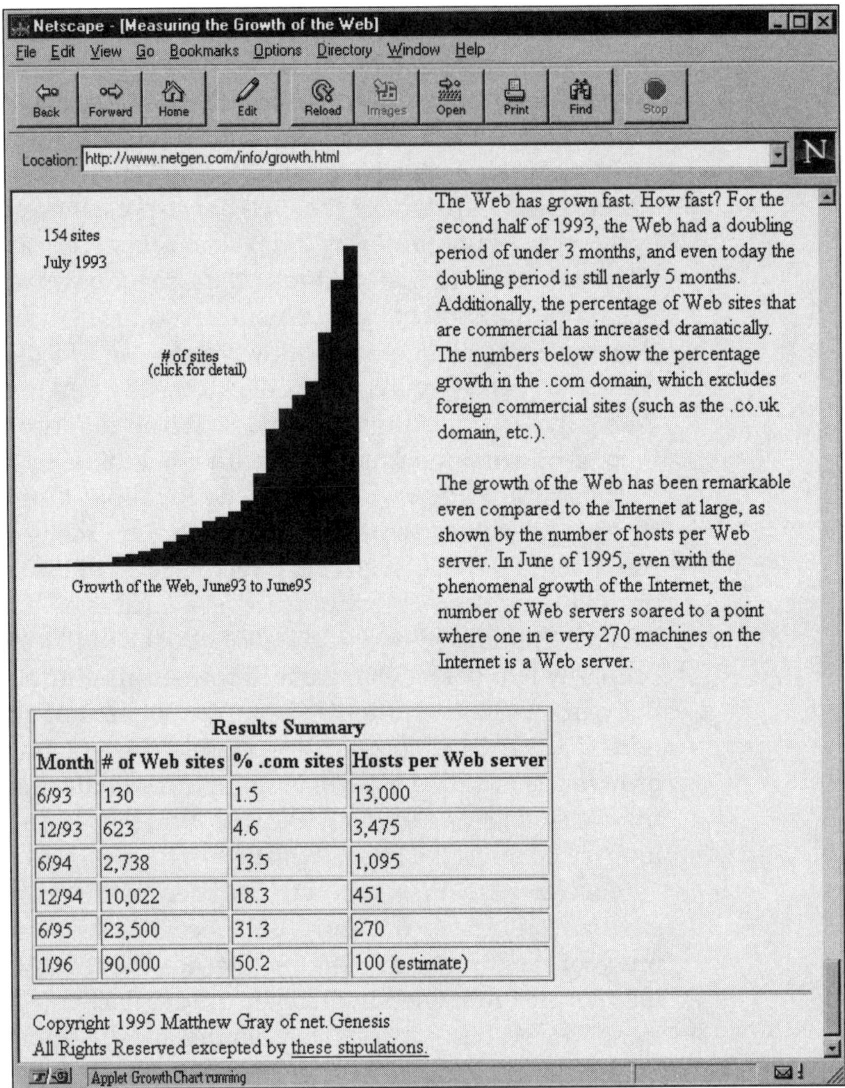

Netscape - [Measuring the Growth of the Web]
File Edit View Go Bookmarks Options Directory Window Help
Back Forward Home Edit Reload Images Open Print Find Stop
Location: http://www.netgen.com/info/growth.html
154 sites
July 1993
# of sites
(click for detail)
Growth of the Web, June93 to June95
The Web has grown fast. How fast? For the second half of 1993, the Web had a doubling period of under 3 months, and even today the doubling period is still nearly 5 months. Additionally, the percentage of Web sites that are commercial has increased dramatically. The numbers below show the percentage growth in the .com domain, which excludes foreign commercial sites (such as the .co.uk domain, etc.).
The growth of the Web has been remarkable even compared to the Internet at large, as shown by the number of hosts per Web server. In June of 1995, even with the phenomenal growth of the Internet, the number of Web servers soared to a point where one in e very 270 machines on the Internet is a Web server.
Copyright 1995 Matthew Gray of net.Genesis
All Rights Reserved excepted by these stipulations.
Applet GrowthChart running

Results Summary

Month	# of Web sites	% .com sites	Hosts per Web server
6/93	130	1.5	13,000
12/93	623	4.6	3,475
6/94	2,738	13.5	1,095
12/94	10,022	18.3	451
6/95	23,500	31.3	270
1/96	90,000	50.2	100 (estimate)

Figure 1-2: *Matthew Gray's ongoing study charts the explosive growth of the World Wide Web.*

THE INTERNET: WHAT COUNTRY .SYS THIS?

If you've ever tried to explain to a newbie what the World Wide Web is, you've undoubtedly come up against the question, as we have, "What's the difference between the Internet and the Web?" It's an understandable confusion.

Let's go back to the first question in our multiple choice questionnaire at the top of this chapter: Who owns and operates the Internet? The answer is simple: nobody and everybody. While the Internet *began* as a U.S. government project, it has long ago outgrown national and political boundaries, as well as its original intentions. Those original intentions were first military, and secondarily academic.

When the first four universities hooked up their computers to talk to one another in September 1969, no one knew that they were really creating the first organic matter of a new mass communication tool. That little four-celled organism born that autumn morn divided and multiplied until it had grown to include thousands of computers at hundreds of organizations and businesses around the world. Today that's been added to by millions of PCs in home offices, schoolrooms, and techno-cubbyholes around the world.

The Internet is quite literally this vast architecture of computers, cables, phone lines, and satellite dishes over which information can be exchanged at any time of day around the world. Your computer is part of it, whether you dial into it via an online service or private access provider or plug straight into the system via a large business or other organization. And everyone who plugs into it helps operate it and contributes to its development. Needless to say, some people own bigger pieces of it—like phone lines and satellites—and are in the business of selling access to the rest of us. But nobody owns and operates the whole thing.

But surely, you say, *someone* runs it. In fact, several organizations have had a hand in it. On a national scale, the U.S. military, who established the initial computer network in the late '60s, handed over its development to the National Science Foundation in the mid-'70s. At the beginning of 1995, the NSF in turn handed over its role of supporting the ever-expanding infrastructure in the United States to private development—all of which raised more questions than it answered about how the network was to be managed. Many of these issues are discussed vociferously on the Electronic Frontier Foundation's home page at: **http://www.eff.org** (see Figure 1-3).

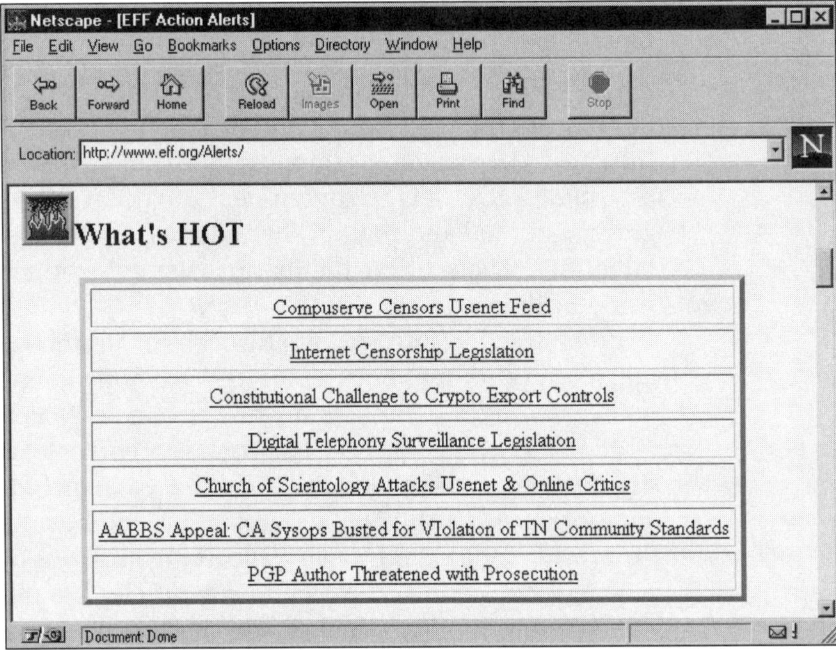

Figure 1-3: *A provocative page from the Electronic Frontier Foundation, a Web watchdog organization.*

In the equally important international arena, the Internet Society (ISOC) was established in 1992 to try to impose some order on, and promulgate international standards for, this fast-growing medium. The ISOC soon assumed oversight of work by the Internet Engineering Task Force (IETF), a loose group of computer and industry experts who had been meeting regularly for several years to hash out the myriad technical details and standards needed to keep the whole thing functioning smoothly. While the group's working core includes a lot of heavyweights in the computer business, Internet Society membership is open to anyone who wants to join. You can get information about it on the ISOC Web site at:

http://www.isoc.org.

The IETF is an open international community of network designers, operators, vendors, and researchers concerned about the evolution and smooth operation of the Internet. Its meetings, held three times a year, are open to anyone who has two cents to contribute to the topics at hand. But the real work is done in the working groups, which are divided into eight different areas of interest:

- Applications
- Internet
- IP: The Next Generation
- Network Management
- Operational Requirements
- Routing
- Security
- Transport & User Services

If you're interested in the working mechanics and politics of the Internet, it's worth taking a look at the IETF Web site at: **http://www.ietf.cnri.reston.va.us/home.html.**

The W3 consortium is another group whose voice is often heard in Internet debates. An industry consortium set up under Tim Berners-Lee's guidance as a collaborative project between the Massachusetts Institute of Technology and CERN, it has both a European and a U.S. base. Its expressed mission is to try to promote standards and encourage interoperability between products designed for the World Wide Web, and to establish a repository of information for Web developers and users.

It's easy to understand the importance of all these groups in the continuing development of the Web. Given its essentially anarchic nature and its many disparate pieces, the Web could become a Tower of Babel and quickly fall apart without some agreed-upon standards.

Organizing Your Desktop

In the rest of this chapter we'll talk about what you need—besides your dreams—to get your own Web project underway.

Fortunately, you need not set out for your local computer software store armed with a forklift and a U-Haul. Preparing to write a Web page is simple enough with the tools you probably already have on hand. And those you don't, you can get for free or as shareware from the Net or on the Companion CD-ROM. If you're fairly meticulous and somewhat detail-oriented, you really don't need anything other than an ASCII text editor (Windows Notepad or Write is perfectly adequate) and a Web browser to view your work as you go. However, as with any endeavor in which detail counts, a few aids can make your work a lot easier. And as you begin to add style and depth to your pages, you'll find yourself relying on them more and more.

When you're ready to set up your Web shop, these are the basic tools you'll find necessary:

- An HTML editor.
- A Web browser.
- A graphics program to manipulate images.

If you have Netscape Gold, you'll already have your browser and editor in one piece. You'll find a couple of useful graphics programs on the Companion CD-ROM to this book.

For work you expect to distribute widely on the Web, it's also a good idea to have more than one Web browser on hand, since different Web browsers display things differently. If you're planning on wide distribution on the Web, you'll want to check the appearance of your pages to non-Netscape viewers. This will depend on the number of stylish features you intend to use and the audience you intend to reach.

If you're posting your pages on a remote server, you may also find an FTP program useful for transferring files to your host computer. You can use Netscape Navigator's built-in FTP feature for this purpose (or Netscape Gold's Publish feature), but for a large number of files you'll probably find a dedicated FTP program handy. (WSFTP and WinFTP are two good ones for Windows.) Again, Netscape Gold users will find that the "one-button publishing" feature will take care of this for them quickly and easily.

A Closer Look at HTML Editors

A few words are in order about HTML editors in general. Many Web authors prefer at first to work in their familiar word processing program and create macros to do their most common coding tasks. If your Web authoring needs are light, this approach may suit you just fine. The only extra requirements will be a meticulous mind and a keen eye to spot your own mistakes. But if you intend to produce a large number of pages or do regular updates, you'll soon find a dedicated HTML editor to be both a timesaver and a headache preventative.

HTML editors come in various flavors, similar to word processing software—and it must be remembered that they are really nothing more than text-based word processors with a mission. It seems to be a fact of human–computer interactions that people get inordinately attached to their word processing software. Since most people would rather change spouses than switch word processing software, a number of add-on programs to familiar software programs like Microsoft Word and WordPerfect have come out in the last few years. One advantage of these add-ons is that they allow you to use the familiar features of your word processor, including the spell-checking and thesaurus resources. But if you don't use these features all that much and don't feel irrevocably wedded to your word processor, a stand-alone HTML editor may be less of a drain on computer memory and make more sense.

Among stand-alone HTML editors, there are the basic variety that do nothing more than automate the placement of HTML tags for you with simple macros. Then there are self-checking editors, which won't let you put in anything that isn't deemed correct, or will let you know if you try to do something illegal. These can be very helpful to a novice. One problem with self-checking editors, however, is that HTML is still an evolving language, and you may wish to use coding that is not strictly legal—perhaps to produce an effect you can't create otherwise or because your audience is limited and how it may appear in various other browsers is irrelevant.

Finally there are WYSIWYG editors, which attempt to show your page during composition as it will finally appear in a Web browser. This obviates the need to be constantly switching back and forth from your editor to your Web browser to check the display of your page. It's wise to keep in mind, however, that your WYSIWYG editor is showing you only what your pages look like on one particular browser, with its own set of conventions; it can't show how all browsers will display your document.

NETSCAPE GOLD: A COMPLETE PACKAGE

Netscape Gold is an all-in-one package that will simplify your Web authoring needs greatly. The HTML editor incorporated in the package, shown in Figure 1-4, is a WYSIWYG editor, which lets you know exactly how your page will look in Netscape Navigator as you compose. So there's no need to switch back and forth between your editor and browser. In addition, Netscape Gold's Publish feature allows you to post your pages on a remote server when you're done, right from within the program.

If you have Netscape Gold, it's likely the only other tool you'll need, until you're ready to tackle multimedia elements, is a graphics editor—with one caveat: Later in this book we'll be talking about some sophisticated HTML techniques and some new elements just appearing on the frontier, like new Netscape plug-ins still in development. These may require you to use specific code that may not be possible yet with Netscape Gold or with any other HTML editor. For these things you'll just have to roll up your sleeves and get down to the code level to accomplish what you want.

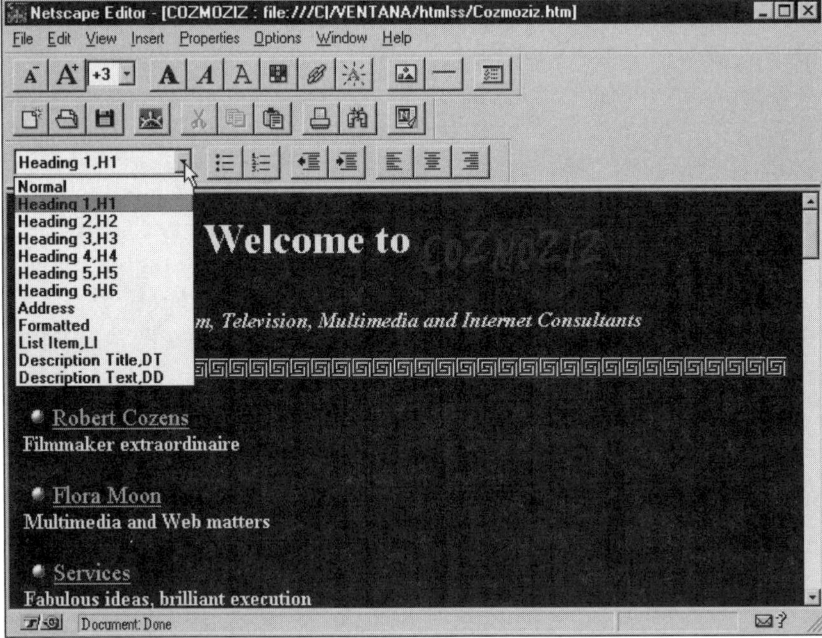

Figure 1-4: *Netscape Gold's editor shows you how your page looks as you compose and edit.*

Graphics Editors

Text is only one part of what Web page design is about, of course. It's the ability to incorporate images that has made the Web take off in the last few years. If you're coming to Web design with a professional design background, you may think you already know it all and can skip this section. That may not be entirely true.

If you already have a good graphics editor like Adobe Photoshop or CorelDRAW!, you do indeed have everything you need to design and manipulate images for the Web. However, graphic design for the Web has its own rules and inherent limitations, so you may have to learn a few new ways of doing things. All of this will be discussed in detail in Chapter 4.

If you don't have one of these top-of-the-line graphics programs, and don't need the other features in them, there's no reason to max out your credit card limit acquiring one. There are only a few image formats that are widely accepted on the Web, so you need only have a program that recognizes and will work with these common types—not the full suite of image types available for print media in the full graphics packages. Several good graphics software programs for Web design use are available online.

A good standard one is LView Pro (see Figure 1-5), which allows you to resize images, manipulate color, and save your images in GIF 87a and 89a or JPEG format. (You'll find explanation of image formats in Chapter 4.) You can get LView Pro on the Companion CD-ROM with this book or online at:

http://world.std.com/~mmedia/lviewp.html.

Another good shareware graphics program for Web work is Paint Shop Pro, which you'll also find on the Companion CD-ROM.

Figure 1-5: *A JPEG image being readied for a Web page in LView Pro.*

If you're doing a lot of graphics work, a scanner is definitely a desirable tool. A scanner allows you to convert photos, transparencies, and print images to digital format. With your graphics editor, you can then manipulate them—crop them, resize them, edit the colors, and save them in an appropriate format for Web presentation. Scanners are a major hardware investment, however. For a limited amount of work, you can use commercial services to scan photos and images into digital format at a very reasonable price. Many photo processors and even a number of corner copy shops will do this for you for less than $10.

Your CD-ROM Extras

We've simplified your Web authoring needs greatly by providing a lot of the pieces you need to get started on the Companion CD-ROM.

Besides the basic software tools, we've included some extras that'll allow you to start adding pizzazz to your pages right away. The package includes:

- Graphics editors: Take your choice of LView Pro or Paint Shop Pro.
- Mapedit, a tool for making image maps (see Chapter 4).
- A clip-art library with a variety of images, and an assortment of textured backgrounds.
- RTFtoHTML, a program to convert documents in Rich Text Format to HTML.
- Web Forms, a program that will help you create HTML forms easily and quickly (see Chapter 9).
- Sound editors for creating or editing sound files: Take your choice of Cool Edit or Gold Wave.
- Adobe Acrobat Reader for viewing files in PDF format.

All you need to do is load the programs you choose in your computer, click on your Netscape icon, hang onto your hat, and we're off.

But before you begin to enter the exciting world of Web publishing, we'd like to give you one Web contributor's version of what the Web could be, both as an inspiration and an introductory lesson.

Abigail's WWW Dream

Springfield, some state, USA

The hospital Rebecca works in has just opened its WWW pages. They look flashy. A background colour in the house-style, pictures of the hospital itself, and a sound file from one of the doctors, stating that it is a fun hospital and children should not be afraid. Some silly games to play, and links to other hospitals in the country. Rebecca clicks with her mouse, and sees again a page mostly containing pictures, this time of room C212. *Nice pictures,* she thinks, *but who cares?* She takes a deep breath. *This could not have been the intention of WWW,* Rebecca thinks. *Where is the useful information?* All she could find were the opening hours of the gift shop.

Rebecca leans back and looks at her bookcase. A huge pile of files looks back. They are the notes she made when she studied children's diseases in Africa. For two years she travelled through the continent, talking to native doctors. She inventoried the different diseases, taking notes how the doctors cured them with the available means. It was only partially put on computer disk yet, mostly to write some articles with it. She is well-known for her work, but she feels sorry she cannot give the material to those who need it.

Suddenly, she sits straight, and stares at her screen, still showing the picture of room C212. *Should I?* she thinks, *Could I?*

The death of a child

Africa, generic village

Mtshali mourns. He is the doctor in a small African village. This morning he witnessed how a young child died in the arms of its mother. The nearest hospital is five days walking; the child would never had made it. Despite a whole life of experience, Mtshali was powerless; he never saw the symptoms the child had before.

In the light of the setting sun, Mtshali sits alone, staring at the horizon. *Someone must know!* he thinks, *If only I could reach him.* Mtshali realizes it could take many deaths if he has to find a cure all by himself.

The work

Rebecca did not hesitate much. She designed a strict format all files should follow, so people could benefit from its consistency, and the files could be searched by a search engine. She found a programmer willing to assist her.

It took many weeks to type in all the files, and to convert what was already on disk to the new format. She spent many evenings working until midnight. Everyone wondered how she had the energy to do it. *There are no graphics!* they said, *It is only dull science; people want cheesy backgrounds and silly sounds!* But Rebecca works on, often side-by-side with the programmer.

And one day, it is finished, and Rebecca opens her database on diseases of African children to the world.

The saving of a child

Mtshali walks. He left his village at four in the morning, and it is a seven hour walk to the nearest school. His thoughts are with the young girl who has the same symptoms as the child that died a few months ago. He felt powerless, not knowing what to do to save the child. But he has heard of the new thing they have at the school. It should know many answers. Mtshali does not know what it is, or how it works; it even scares him a little. But he is desperate, and willing to find out whether it can help.

When Mtshali arrives at the school, he talks with the head of the school, explaining his problem, and that he had heard of this device knowing a lot of answers at the school. *Would the school master help him?* The school master assigns a girl of the highest grade to assist Mtshali in finding the information about the disease.

The girl takes Mtshali to the school's computer corner. Next to the electricity generator stands an old PC and an old VT100. Both were used in the early eighties at a European university, and donated to the third world when it upgraded to graphical workstations. The girl switches the computer on, and the monitor slowly comes to life. Mtshali holds his breath as the letters appear on the screen. The girl takes the radio device next to the computer, and makes a short wave connection to a server a few hundred kilometers away. That server has a 2400 baud modem connection to a machine in the capital, from which the rest of the Internet is reached via satellite. But Mtshali does not know that. All he sees are the messages from the server coming on the screen, letter by letter.

The clear voice of the girl makes Mtshali stop pondering. *You have a sick child, and do not know what to do with it, do you?* Mtshali nods and starts talking about the symptoms. The girl politely interrupts Mtshali, *We can only do one thing at a time.* The girl logs in to the remote server and starts a simple, text-based browser. Mtshali sits down next to the girl, fascinated with what is happening. The girl, who obviously has some experience, connects to one of the web search tools, and after a few tries, she finds Rebecca's database. *Maybe we can find your answer here,* the girl says, letting Mtshali read the screen as well. Mtshali can only nod.

They find the search tool Rebecca and the programmer developed, and with the help of the girl, Mtshali enters the relevant data. A push on a button, and slowly the pages describing various diseases and their cures appear on the screen. Mtshali reads and reads and reads, making mental and paper notes, while the girl navigates. The setting sun forces them to stop.

The next morning, Mtshali walks back to his village, but this time filled with hope.

Epilogue

Some weeks later, Rebecca receives a letter from Africa. She has some trouble reading the handwriting. It is from an old doctor, thanking her and explaining how the database saved the life of a child. It also contains a description of how the disease affected the child, and what else the doctor did beside what was mentioned in her pages.

The same night, Rebecca updates her pages.

MOVING ON

Even if your Web plans aren't as grand as Rebecca's, you can rightly have a sense of being part of the history of this new communications medium as you go on to develop your own Web site in the rest of this book. We hope we've given you a pretty good overview of the Web universe and the basis of HTML in this chapter.

So clear your desk. In the next chapter, we'll move straight on to designing a Web site and starting your first Web page. We'll start by building a Web page using just 10 simple tags. By the end of the next chapter, you'll have a thorough grounding in the terms and conventions of HTML and be ready to start putting your Web publishing plans in action.

2

Getting Down to Work

Now that you have your virtual desktop all organized, it's time to roll up your sleeves and get down to work. In this chapter, we'll first talk a bit about the basics of Web site design and document layout. Then, beginning with the 10 most common HTML tags, we'll show you how to build a Web page in only a single session that meets all of the requirements for posting with a Web server.

Then we'll go into more detail on other elementary HTML tags you'll quickly find a need for as you develop your Web site. As each new tag is introduced, we'll provide a complete definition, since we anticipate you'll be referring back to these definitions frequently as you discover new things you can do and get new ideas for your pages. Don't worry if you don't understand all the terms the first time through. By following our examples, you'll be able to put them all to use quickly in simple form. In later chapters you'll discover ways of refining your pages and adding more style.

Lastly, before you run off to post your masterpiece to the world, we'll talk about how to check your page to ensure it will stand up to rigorous Web use.

BASIC WEB SITE DESIGN

The initial home page is the basic unit of Web design. Every site has one. It's the front door into the site, the entry point, presumably, for all other adventures. Of course each page has its own unique Web address (in the form of its URL), so it's perfectly possible for visitors to enter your site by going directly to any of your other pages if they have the correct address. Regular visitors with an agenda will learn to sidestep the front door and slip in the side to avoid any unnecessary download time. But by and large they'll come in through your home page and that's where your welcome mat should be. You need to clearly establish your identity there.

ORGANIZE YOUR SITE

The information you intend to present should be organized clearly and thoughtfully before you set out compiling all those wowser graphics and flash effects. Web pages have a way of growing like mushrooms in the dark. As you get more into the fun of creating your own site, you'll undoubtedly have new ideas about things to add or new ways to present your information. If you've got your HTML pages and graphics organized neatly to begin with, it will be much easier to revamp your presentation than if you have to go back and redo links and paths that you didn't get right the first time. It helps if you have a clear idea of what you want to present, of course.

If you're planning a Web site for a network that will have both private information (for company use) and public information (for outsiders), you should pay particular attention to your site structure before starting. It's advisable to consult with your systems administrator and possibly involve the MIS department as early as possible in the planning stages to ensure your site structure has both secure and public areas. This is particularly important if you want to include existing bulletin boards or databases.

CHOOSING YOUR FILENAMES

When you start to create Web pages, choose your filenames carefully. Don't use anything too long or too obscure. Remember, you'll be making links to these files, and so will others, you hope. The simpler they are, the less room for error.

It's also important to know the conventions of the server on which you intend to post. Many will not allow long filenames or filenames with spaces or other special characters in them, and they may or may not be case-sensitive. Some will accept the extension .HTM, others require .HTML. (If you're constrained to three-character extensions on your system, you'll have to change the filenames after you post.) Check with your Webmaster first if you don't know the conventions, and you'll save yourself the headache of redoing all your links later.

Planning Your Site Structure

Pyramid Design. Once you decide on the pages that will be part of your overall site design, you should think about how you anticipate people moving through your site, from one Web page to the next. A sketch that shows the "walk-through" of your site will help you plan your links as you go. We've culled some examples from real-live Web sites here to give you an idea of possible ways to organize your site.

In a classic pyramid design, subsequent pages link from the home page to a second level comprised of one or more pages, each of which may then link to third-level documents and so on. The XYZ Corporation that does business online may, for example, have links to Product Information, Company Profile, and Stockholder Information. From Product Information one might go to different product lines, product descriptions, ordering information, and so on. Chances are that a visitor who is principally interested in finding a particular product won't care to wander around through your company profile and stock reports, and will be annoyed if he or she has to. Your file structure should allow visitors to cut to the chase.

The Web site for a computer services company shown in Figure 2-1 provides a site plan so that visitors can easily find their way to what they want. If you're looking for software reviews or goodies to download or the latest Web contest, you can see where to go to get it immediately. Guess it takes a computerized mind to be this organized!

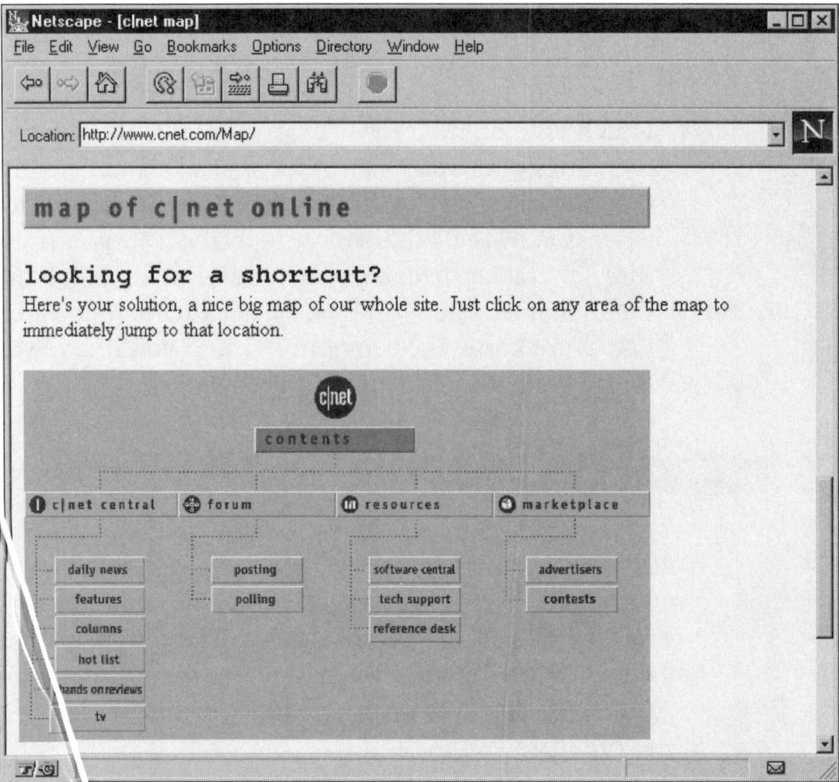

Figure 2-1: *This well-organized site for a computer services company includes a map of the site structure.*

The Web Wanderer's Site. Another site design might be a series of pages, any of which might lead to any other, depending on the visitor's interest. For example, take a series of pages for a major music festival, such as in Figure 2-2. Site visitors are liable to be interested in any of several different areas—the schedule, the performers, the food, the tickets—and there's no telling quite how their interests will lead them through the site. It's best to allow them to wander at will and consider that all roads lead to Rome. This site is basically one level deep, with everything linking to everything else.

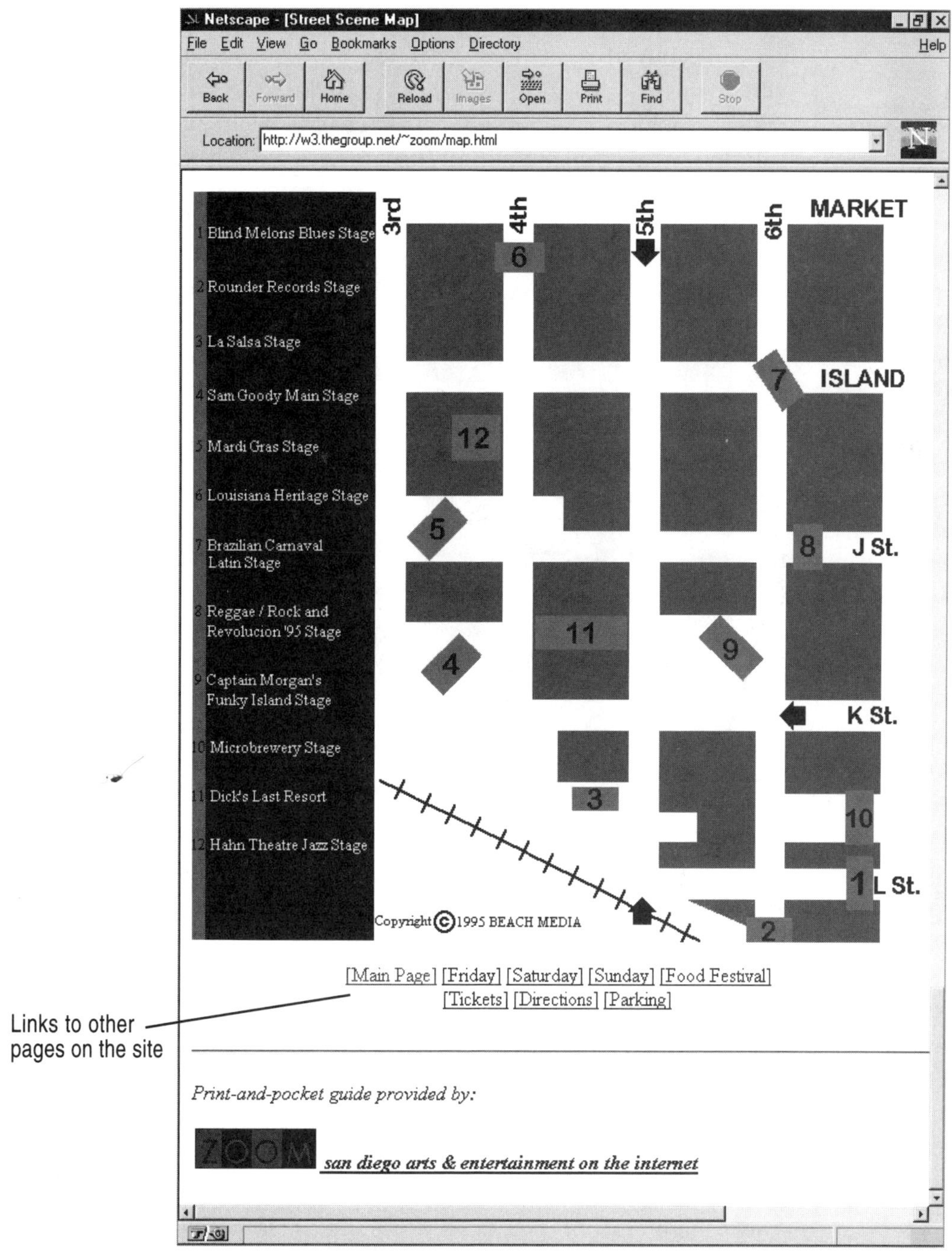

Figure 2-2: *On this multipage site for a music festival everything links to everything else.*

The Guided Tour. On the other hand, you might wish to prompt your visitors along a predetermined course through your site, to ensure that they see what you want them to see in some orderly fashion. Of course Web surfers can be an independent-minded lot, so this plan might not always work (and may in fact irritate some visitors), but at least it reassures the public relations department. Figure 2-3 shows such a design for a Web services company, where choices on the main menu simply lead you through an informational loop back to the home page.

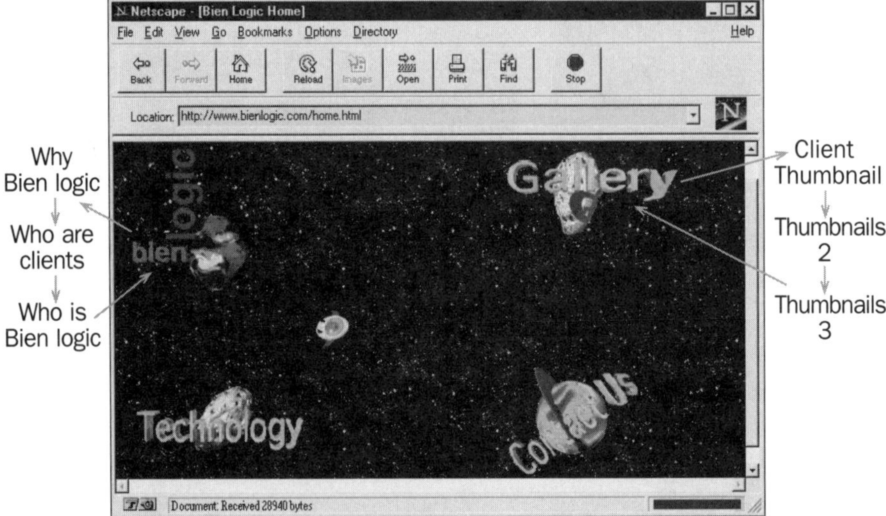

Figure 2-3: *This company's site, which features an animated space ship on the home page, includes two information "loops."*

The Labyrinth. You can find a much more complex file structure at MCI's Gramercy Press site (http://www.mci.com/gramercy) (see Figure 2-4). At this site, visitors are encouraged to snoop around the "offices" of various characters portrayed in an ongoing Web soap opera by clicking on objects in the picture. You're encouraged, in particular, to click on the computer screen so you can read each character's personal e-mail and schedule files. MCI doesn't care where visitors go in the site as long as along the way, sometime or other, they notice that what's on the character's computer screen is an MCI product, which they're fairly certain to, sooner or later. While this may feel rather random to a visitor, it's actually a very deliberate and carefully planned site.

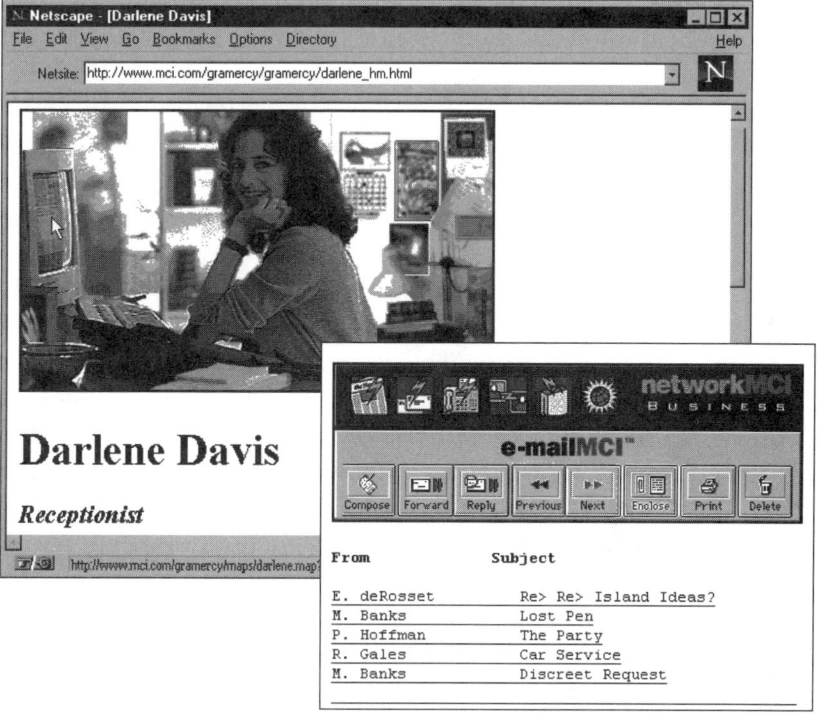

Figure 2-4: *Click on Darlene's computer, and you'll soon see the method behind MCI's clever Web advertising scheme.*

The way all of these structures work, of course, is through links. We'll go into the art of linking in detail in Chapter 3, "Links, Links & More Links." But for now, if you envision several interlinked pages on your site, it's a good idea to sit down and sketch out a little flow chart for yourself. Develop a Hollywood-style storyboard, especially if you'll have to explain the site proposal to others (e.g., a client). Try to imagine all the possible ways people might go through your site, and make it easy for them to find what they want.

BREAK DOWN YOUR INFO

A basic fact of Web life is that every byte of information takes time to download. We wish we could offer authoritative research figures on how long the average Web cruiser will wait for information to download and what the ideal size of a Web page should be. Unfortunately (or perhaps fortunately), the Web is too new to have produced its authoritative pundits on this issue, although there is no lack of opinions.

Much depends, of course, on the type of information you're presenting and the kind of Web surfer you expect to attract. But if you wouldn't wait five minutes for a 150K document to download, don't expect your visitors to, either. Better to break down your text and give them the document in, say, 50K chunks. Graphics are additional elements that take time to download—we'll be discussing these in Chapter 4, "All About Images," and giving you some suggestions on how to reduce their size and make them more user-friendly. One suggested measure might be what it takes to print out your page. A good rule of thumb is that an average "Web page" when printed out should take no more than three or four printed pages. Again, this does not take into account the file size when graphics are included, so is no measure of download time, but is a fair measure of what is required of your reader in onscreen scrolling.

Although standards in the computer business are constantly improving in the direction of speed, it's safe to assume that the average computer user is at least a few years behind the current state-of-the-art. At the moment, designers of Internet applications assume that the average target user has a 486 computer with 8MB RAM and a 14.4 baud modem, connected to a standard phone line (not a high-speed connection, such as ISDN). Speed may be highly variable according to the type of connection, the load on the server, and the mood of the Net on any given day, in any given place. But on average, it's safe to assume a download speed of about a second or two per kilobyte of information.

In general, small bites of information are easier to digest. But don't break things down so much that you frustrate readers. It can be equally irritating to have to work your way through several pages of choices before ever reaching the information you've come for. To the impatient Web surfer, this experience is like being offered a constant series of menus but never a thing to eat. Or like those frightful voice mail menus that offer everything except what you need.

Try to achieve a balance between the size of your graphics, the content offered on each page, and the size of the document. It's safe to assume that people who wait for a large document to download will want to find it worth waiting for, in terms of information. If they wait for a large image file to download, only to find they have to download an equally large one on another page before getting to anything substantial, they're liable to wander off in search of a little more instant gratification.

For example, if you've got a 300K graphic at the top of a page that's only an introduction to the topic at hand with a menu of choices of where to go next, you'll be wasting your visitor's time, and you should consider either a smaller graphic or more information on the page (and probably both). On the other hand, if you're presenting a really good magazine article on the page and want to entice your readers with some great graphics to go with it, you can feel more justified in larger file sizes, since what they're getting should be worth the wait.

Fortunately, if you're designing a Web site for an internal network you needn't be as concerned with file size as you should be for a general Web site. You can design for larger files and more complex graphics and be generally assured they'll come to everyone on the network just as fast as they do to you, with one caution: Don't forget the users stuck with old computer systems in that underfunded department! Be nice to them and check out your files on the slowest equipment in the house.

HTML Document Structure

Once you have your information organized, you're ready to start designing pages. Each HTML document, or "page," is simply an ASCII text document with formatting codes inserted. The Web browser interprets these codes and decides how to display the document within the given parameters of the platform.

Understanding The Code: Tags & Attributes

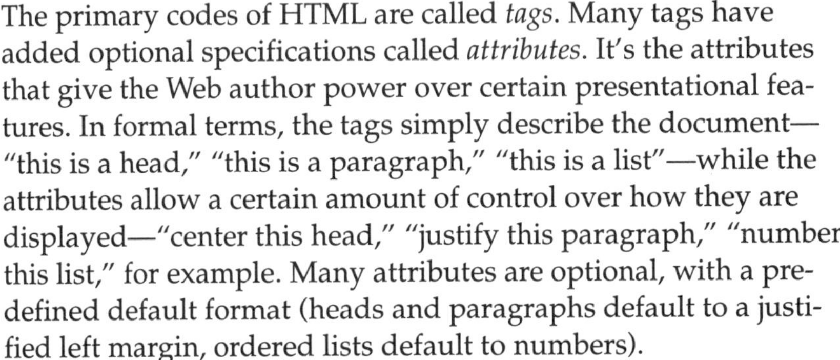

The primary codes of HTML are called *tags*. Many tags have added optional specifications called *attributes*. It's the attributes that give the Web author power over certain presentational features. In formal terms, the tags simply describe the document—"this is a head," "this is a paragraph," "this is a list"—while the attributes allow a certain amount of control over how they are displayed—"center this head," "justify this paragraph," "number this list," for example. Many attributes are optional, with a predefined default format (heads and paragraphs default to a justified left margin, ordered lists default to numbers).

Netscape Navigator's color-coded document source view makes it easy to distinguish between coding elements and document text. Call up any Web page in your Web browser and select View | Document Source. (See Figure 2-5.) The HTML code immediately stands out from the rest of the page, with tags in one color, attributes in another, and attribute values in yet a third. You'll also notice that HTML tags are always enclosed in angular brackets (< >), and any attributes are placed after the initial tag, within the brackets. The codes (both tags and attributes) may appear in either upper or lowercase. For purposes of illustration, we use uppercase in this book because it is easier to distinguish from surrounding text, but you're free to suit yourself.

A

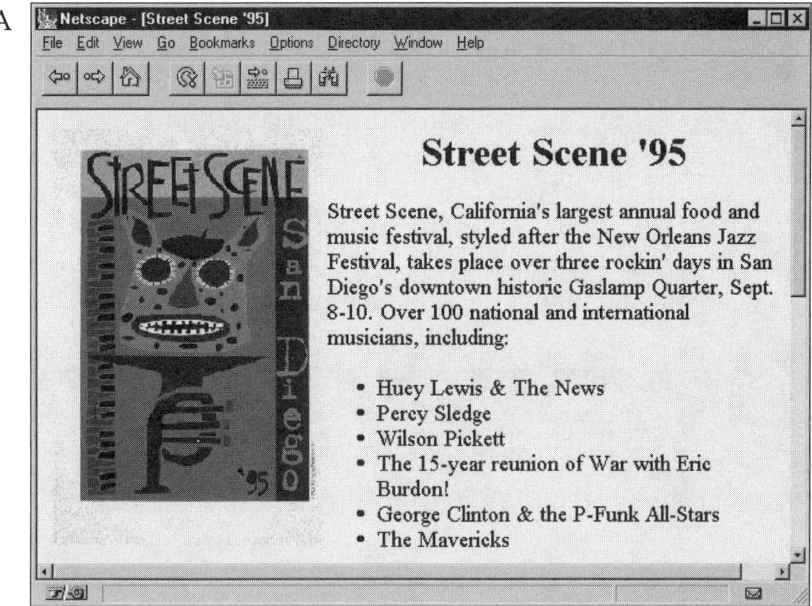

B

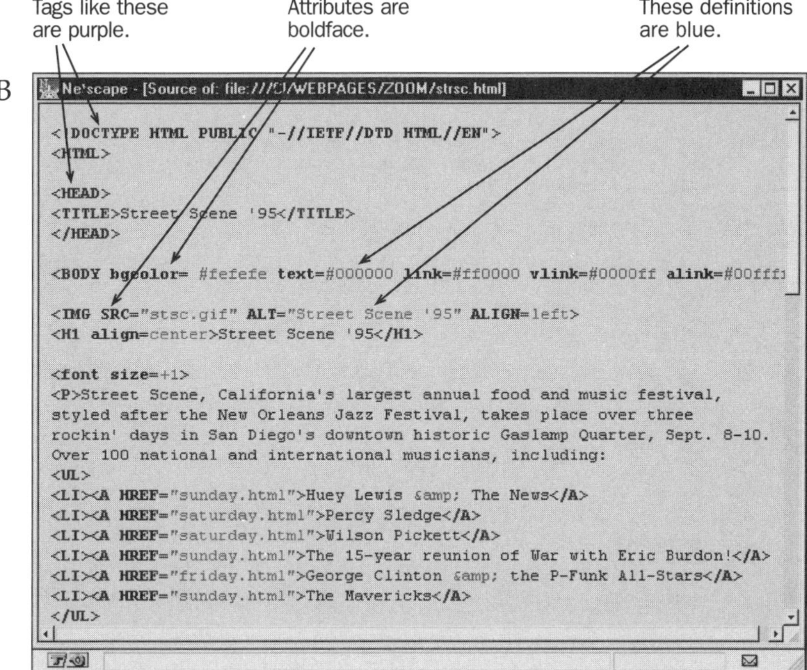

Figure 2-5 A&B: *The Document Source View for this HTML page uses color coding to clearly distinguish between HTML code elements and text.*

As shown in Figure 2-6, spaces other than those between words are ignored, and carriage returns are interpreted simply as a space between words. Extra spaces, including those implied by tabs, are automatically discarded (except in text that appears between the <PRE> and </PRE> tags, which we discuss later). An advantage of this is that you may use spaces and indents to clarify sections of your document for yourself (for instance, to show a list indented), and it will not affect the final display of the document in the Web browser.

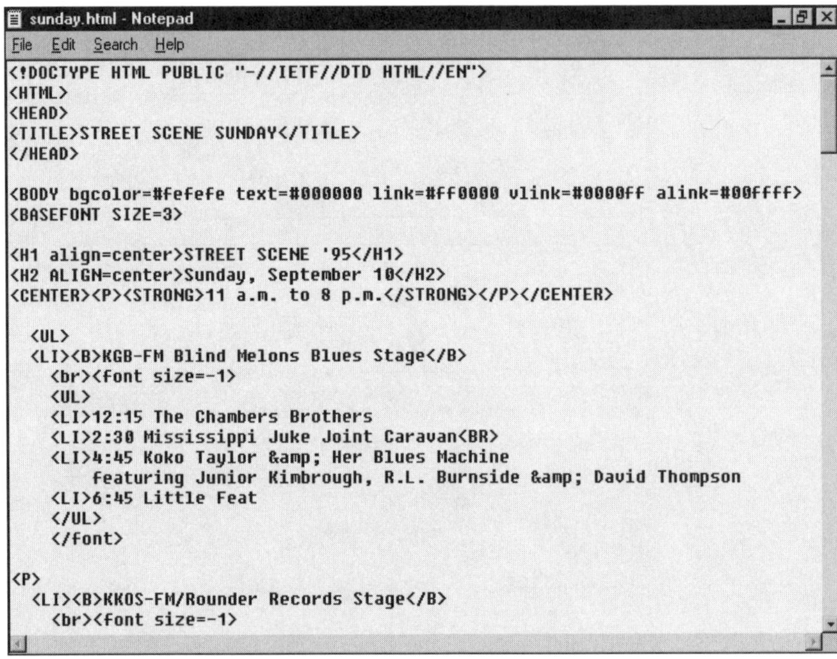

```
<!DOCTYPE HTML PUBLIC "-//IETF//DTD HTML//EN">
<HTML>
<HEAD>
<TITLE>STREET SCENE SUNDAY</TITLE>
</HEAD>

<BODY bgcolor=#fefefe text=#000000 link=#ff0000 vlink=#0000ff alink=#00ffff>
<BASEFONT SIZE=3>

<H1 align=center>STREET SCENE '95</H1>
<H2 ALIGN=center>Sunday, September 10</H2>
<CENTER><P><STRONG>11 a.m. to 8 p.m.</STRONG></P></CENTER>

  <UL>
  <LI><B>KGB-FM Blind Melons Blues Stage</B>
    <br><font size=-1>
    <UL>
    <LI>12:15 The Chambers Brothers
    <LI>2:30 Mississippi Juke Joint Caravan<BR>
    <LI>4:45 Koko Taylor &amp; Her Blues Machine
        featuring Junior Kimbrough, R.L. Burnside &amp; David Thompson
    <LI>6:45 Little Feat
    </UL>
    </font>

<P>
  <LI><B>KKOS-FM/Rounder Records Stage</B>
    <br><font size=-1>
```

Figure 2-6: *The extra spacing and indentations in this page of code make it easier to read, but they will be ignored by the browser.*

TIP

If you're working in a group environment, you may want to define a standard format for Web page coding, including spacing and upper/lowercase codes, to maintain consistency and make it easier for different people to work with the Web pages on the site.

The 10 Most Useful HTML Tags

Many people are surprised the first time they create an HTML page how little it really takes to make a perfectly respectable page and send it on its way to China—or Budapest or Chicago (it's all the same on the Web). As a matter of fact, you can do most things you want to do on a Web page with only 10 simple tags. In the subsequent section we'll show you how. Here they are:

1. <HTML> identifies the document type.
2. <HEAD> encloses technical information about the document.
3. <TITLE> gives your document a name.
4. <BODY> encloses the actual document content.
5. <H1> through <H6> define headings in the document.
6. <P> defines a paragraph.
7. <UL> and <LI> define a list.
8. <A HREF="..."> sets up a hyperlink.
9. <IMG SRC="..."> inserts a graphic.
10. <PRE> defines "preformatted text."

The first four of these tags are "document structure tags," which provide the foundation for the document. Most of the rest define different ways of handling text—specifying heads, paragraphs, lists, and preformatted text—and are therefore considered "containers" or "block elements" for the text. Add a tag for making hypertext links and one for inserting images, and you've got a Web page faster than you can shake-and-bake a chicken.

In the rest of this chapter and throughout the book, formal tag definitions will be separated from the text for easy reference purposes. For ease of reading, you can skip the definition boxes if you prefer—the tags will be explained in more casual terms in the text.

DOCUMENT STRUCTURE TAGS

At its most basic, a Web document has four elements to define it.

- A "start" tag to tell the server what kind of document it is: <HTML>
- A "head" tag, which signals the beginning of identifying information about the document: <HEAD>
- A "title" tag, which gives an identifying name to the document: <TITLE>
- A "body" tag, which signals the beginning of the document itself: <BODY>

Each of these is a "container" tag—that is, it encloses information, and therefore requires a matching end tag to signal the end of the information it encloses. All other tags belong either within the head or the body of the document. There should be nothing outside of these two sections (with one exception we'll get to shortly).

The <HTML> Tag. The Web document needs an identifier to tell the computer handling it what kind of document it is. The tag <HTML> at the beginning of the document accomplishes this task. The matching </HTML> tag signals the end of the document.

HTML Tag

<HTML> .... </HTML>

The HTML tag occurs at the beginning and end of an HTML document and signifies the document type to the server. The HTML 3.0 proposal would permit the omission of this tag, which *in most cases* should be interpreted by the MIME type, but it is always safest to include it for the sake of older browsers.

The only thing that may precede the <HTML> tag is a "comment string," which is customarily used at the beginning of the document to identify the version of HTML the document conforms to. It looks like this:

```
<!DOCTYPE HTML PUBLIC "-//IETF//DTD HTML 2.0//EN">
```

What the line above means is that this is a publicly distributed HTML document that conforms to the HTML 2.0 document type definition (DTD) standards developed by the Internet Engineering Task Force (IETF). A list of all the accepted DTD strings and their proper syntax can be found at:

http://www.webtechs.com/html-tk/sre/lib/catalog

Including a comment line is optional, although generally a good idea. It can be helpful to older browsers or to programs that might want to request documents of a certain HTML vintage only. And it will help you in checking your document for conformity to a particular standard with the online HTML validation services we discuss at the end of this chapter.

The <HEAD> Tag. The document itself is divided into two parts: the HEAD and the BODY, both of which have matching end tags. The HEAD contains basic information relevant to the host computer that serves up the document on request from viewers. It also contains information useful to searchers and robots that may attempt to reference the document.

HTML Tag

<HEAD> .... </HEAD>

The HEAD tag contains general information about the document, corresponding to the top of a memo or message. Information within the HEAD may also be useful to searching or indexing tools.

The following tags *only* are allowed within the head: BASE, ISINDEX, LINK, META, and TITLE. Of these, only TITLE is required. (The others will be discussed in subsequent chapters.) Two more attributes are proposed for HTML 3.0, RANGE and STYLE, which refer to style sheets.

The HTML 3.0 proposal would also allow for the omission of the <HEAD> tag, but it is always safer to include it for the sake of older browsers. <TITLE> is *always* required and can stand alone. But if you're using any of the other tags that belong within the HEAD, use the HEAD tag as well.

The <TITLE> Tag. Only one element in the HEAD is actually visible to the viewer and displayed by a Web browser, and that is the TITLE. This is the line that normally appears in the title bar of a graphical Web browser as a label for the window displaying it. (See Figure 2-7.) It does *not* appear in the main screen as part of the document. It is the only element that is *required* in the HEAD; all other elements are optional.

The TITLE is used by searchers and robots, as well as by browsers in the history list, and so should accurately but briefly reflect the content of the document. Bear in mind that a generic title such as "Introduction" is meaningless out of context. Introduction to what? Far better to have something specific to the topic, such as "Poison Control HotWeb," to which you might add the subhead "Introduction" if you want to qualify it.

HTML Tag

<TITLE> .... </TITLE>

The TITLE tag identifies the contents of the document generally. Every HTML document *must* contain a TITLE (and only one is allowed). The TITLE is placed within the head tags of the document.

The TITLE may not contain anchors, paragraph tags, highlighting, or any other special marks. No attributes are allowed within the TITLE tag.

The <TITLE> .... </TITLE> elements are entirely contained within <HEAD>....</HEAD>. The length of the title is not limited, but since long titles are likely to be truncated, they should be kept to fewer than 64 characters.

The <BODY> Tag. After the HEAD comes the BODY. This is the content area of the Web document—the whole of the document that will appear in the viewing screen on a graphical Web browser.

HTML Tag

<BODY> .... </BODY>

The BODY tags contain and surround the actual content of the document. The <BODY> tag occurs directly after </HEAD>. The end tag </BODY> occurs at the end of the document just preceding </HTML>.

HTML 3.0 allows for the omission of the <BODY> tag, which should be implied by the start of any other body element after <TITLE>, but it is always safest to include it for the sake of older browsers.

Only one BODY tag is allowed within a document. Attributes include:

BACKGROUND="image.gif"—Defines an image to be used as a document background, which will be tiled in, if it is smaller than the full-screen area.

BGCOLOR="#rrggbb"—Defines a background color for the document.

TEXT="#rrggbb"—Defines the color of normal body text.

LINK="#rrggbb"—Defines the text color for a hypertext link.

VLINK="#rrggbb"—Defines the text color for a "visited link."

ALINK="#rrggbb"—Defines the text color for an "active link" (the color that briefly flashes when link text is clicked).

These attributes are all current Netscape extensions whose use has spread to several other browsers.

Note: In a Netscape Frames document, there is no BODY tag as the FRAMES tag replaces it.

While the HEAD is limited to a very few technical elements, the BODY contains many different elements that describe the appearance of the text. Within the <BODY> tag, you can also specify a background color or background image file and text colors. For example:

```
<BODY BGCOLOR="#ffffff" TEXT="#000000" LINK="#ff0000"
VLINK="#0000ff" ALINK="#00ff00">
```

The above describes a document with a white background, black text, red links, and blue visited links. It also specifies that a green flash will appear when a link is clicked. (For a full description of RGB color codes, see Chapter 4, "All About Images." Hexadecimal color codes can be found in Appendix F.)

A Basic Document Template

Using the four tags we've discussed so far, you can create the skeleton of your document:

```
<HTML>
<HEAD>
<TITLE>This Is the Title</TITLE>
</HEAD>
<BODY>

[This Is the document.]

</BODY>
</HTML>
```

Most HTML editors provide a template with minimal HTML code to start a document. Figure 2-7 shows a basic document template supplied with Netscape Gold's editor. By the time you get through this chapter, you'll understand all of these codes and more, so that you can write your own starter template. As you go on to establish your own style for your documents, you can alter this starter template to contain the elements you normally use—say, for instance, a certain background and color definition, a signature and address at the bottom of the page, or a graphic you use regularly as a logo on your pages. You can drop text directly into the body portion of the document and proceed to set up the codes to display it. You'll have a document ready to go in minutes.

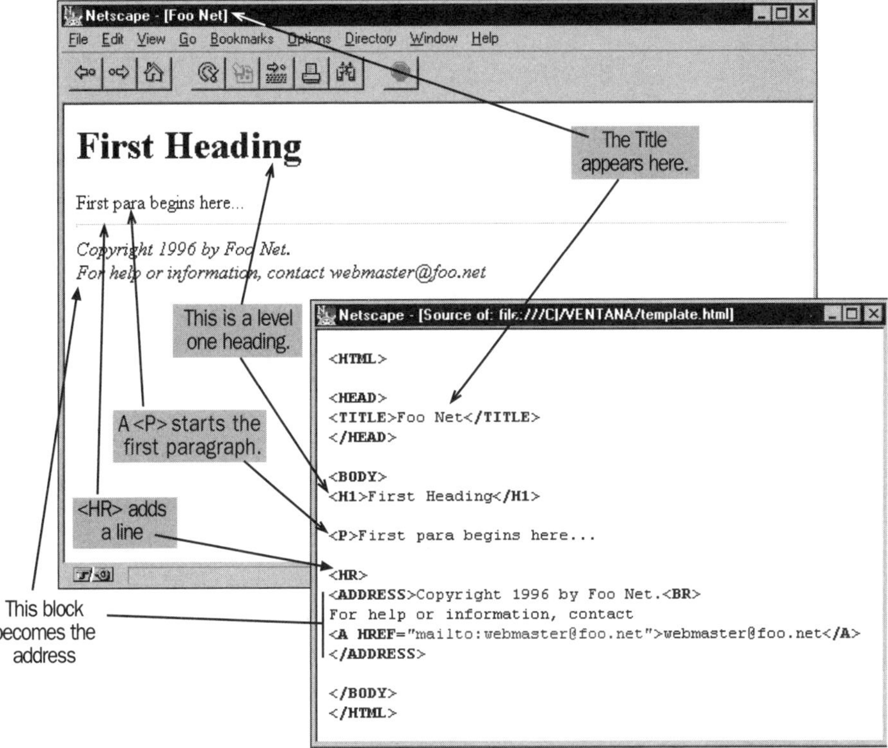

Figure 2-7: *This document template has minimal HTML code inserted and is ready for the addition of content.*

Making Headings With <H1>

All of the document structure elements above can be considered the foundation of the virtual house you're about to build on the Web. Now that you've got the four corners and the basic foundation, you're ready to start putting up the frame.

Usually the first thing you'll want is a title for your document. Don't confuse this with the formal TITLE element above. This is called a heading or header. Headings can be designated in six levels (logically enough, <H1> through <H6>). Each heading tag must have a matching end tag to cancel it.

HTML Tag

<H1> .... </H1> Through <H6> .... </H6>

These tags define text to be separated out and displayed more prominently than normal body text as document "headings." Six levels are allowed, with H1 being the highest (the largest font) and H6 the lowest (the smallest font). A paragraph break is implied before and after a header, and word wrapping is in effect unless turned off. (See NOWRAP and NOBR below.)

The HTML 3.0 ALIGN attribute is recognized by Netscape for aligning heads on a page.

ALIGN="left/right/center"—Align the head with the left or right margin or center. ("Justify" is also allowed in HTML 3.0 but is not generally recognized by browsers.)

Other HTML 3.0 attributes, which are not currently recognized by Netscape but may eventually be incorporated are:

CLEAR="left/right/all"—Move the head down until the margin(s) is (are) clear or there is sufficient room before displaying. You may also specify a certain number of ens or pixels, such as CLEAR="40 pixels", meaning move down until 40 pixels are free.

NOWRAP—Disables word wrapping for the head.

*Instead of the NOWRAP attribute, Netscape uses the tag <NOBR> .... </NOBR>, which can contain any number of text containers (such as headers, paragraphs, and lists).

DINGBAT="icon"—Specifies a standard icon to appear preceding the head. Standard icon entity names are given in Appendix G.

SRC="image"—Specifies an image to appear preceding the head.

SEQNUM=n—Assigns a specific sequence number to a heading level. A sequence number is associated with each level of head from H1 to H6. This resets the current element to a given number, e.g. SEQNUM=10, which can then be controlled by a style sheet for rendering.

SKIP=n—Increments the sequence number a specified number for rendering. This is used when heads are out of sequence. For instance, SKIP=3 advances the number past three omitted items. Also meant to be used in conjunction with a style sheet.

The important thing to realize is that the manner of display of the heads—the font and font size—is not entirely under your control. The display fonts and font sizes are strictly browser-dependent, and often user-dependent as well, since many Web browsers allow the user to choose display fonts from whatever is available on the system. As you design for Netscape, you may be inclined to treat the header tags as just a suite of fonts available to you. You may choose to do so for the average Netscape viewer who will be using default settings, but you should be aware that your text may not always appear to others as it does to you.

If you're presenting technical information in a logical outline style, you should adhere to the basic rule of header sequencing, which is: A header should never be more than one level down in descending size order than the previous header. An H2 follows an H1, an H3 follows an H2, and so on. When you signal an <H1> or any higher level head than the previous one, the previous sequence is canceled, just as if you were following a strict outline format. You can see how the intent translates in the outline of a document shown in Figure 2-8.

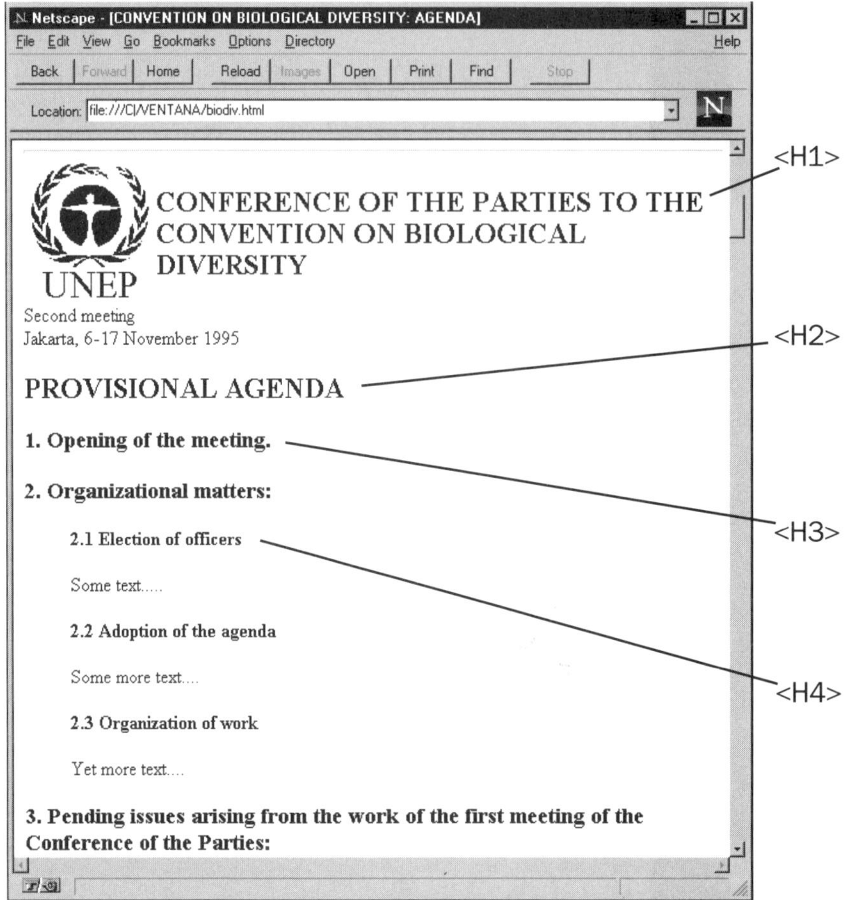

Figure 2-8: *A technical document using headers for a logical outline.*

Defining a Paragraph With <P>

The most basic text container element, and the most frequently used tag, is <P>, which is used to start a paragraph.

HTML Tag

<P>

The P tag defines a paragraph. The end tag </P> to close the paragraph is optional. A </P> will be implied by a new paragraph tag or any other text container element such as a list or header tag.

The HTML 3.0 ALIGN attribute is recognized by Netscape for aligning paragraph text.

ALIGN="left/right/center"—Make paragraph flush left, flush right, centered, or justified, if possible. Paragraphs are usually rendered flush left if alignment is not specified. ("Justify" is also allowed in HTML 3.0 but is not currently recognized by browsers.)

Other HTML 3.0 attributes, which are not currently recognized by Netscape but may eventually be incorporated are:

CLEAR= "left/right/all"—Move paragraph down until the margin(s) is (are) clear or there is sufficient room before displaying. You may also specify a certain number of ens or pixels, such as CLEAR="40 pixels", meaning move down until 40 pixels are free.

NOWRAP—Disables word wrapping. If you want to specify explicit line breaks at particular spots, you can use the <BR> tag.

*Instead of the NOWRAP attribute, Netscape uses the tag <NOBR> .... </NOBR>, which can contain any number of text containers (such as headers, paragraphs, and lists).

The end tag is not strictly necessary as any other text container tag, such as a new <P> or a list element, automatically signals the end of the previous paragraph. Normally, a carriage return and line feed are generated in the display, and paragraphs are not indented, but the exact rendering is up to the individual browser. If you really want indented first lines, Chapter 4 suggests how to do this with a "picture of an indent."

Adding a List With <UL>

It's likely that on your very first Web page, you'll find some occasion to use lists, especially given that hypertext links to other documents are most commonly displayed as a menu of choices on a list. The simplest and most common form of a list in HTML is <UL>, for an "unordered list." This *doesn't* mean it's an untidy list, just that it's a list with no particular sequence required (apples, oranges, and bananas might as well be bananas, apples, and oranges) and contains no numbering or other sequential indicator.

HTML Tag

<UL> .... </UL>

The UL tags define an unordered list, which is usually displayed indented. The start tag is followed by an optional list header <LH> and then by the first list item <LI>. The </UL> end tag is required to signal the end of the list and cancel indenting. An unordered list is by default "bulleted" with a standard typographical symbol in front of each list item.

A Netscape extension to the UL tag is:

TYPE=[disc, circle, square]—Specifies the bullet type to use for the list.

HTML 3.0 also allows the following attributes within the <UL> tag, which are not currently recognized in Netscape:

CLEAR="left/right/all"—Move list down until the margin(s) is (are) clear or there is sufficient room before displaying. You may also specify a certain number of ens or pixels, (e.g. CLEAR=40 pixels), meaning move down until 40 pixels are free.

PLAIN—Specifies that no bullets be used.

DINGBAT="icon"—Specifies a standard icon to appear preceding the list item, in place of the usual bullet. (Use the IMG tag for this in Netscape 2.0.) The complete set of standard icons can be found in Appendix G.

SRC="image"—Specifies an image to display instead of a list bullet. (Use the IMG tag for this in Netscape 2.0.)

WRAP="vert/horiz"—Used for multicolumn lists. WRAP="vert" arranges the items down the page before wrapping to the next column. WRAP="horiz" (less common) arranges the items across the page. The number of columns is up to the browser.

COMPACT—Indicates that the list should be displayed as compactly as possible by reducing the space between items. This has no effect in Netscape, but you can achieve the same effect more precisely using Netscape font size changes.

Instead of numbers, an unordered list usually uses "bullets" or standard typographical symbols before each list item. Discs, circles, and squares are the default symbols used in Netscape, applied in that order as the list level descends—that is, outline-style, as lists are embedded within lists. (In practice, "circle" actually produces an open box in Netscape, while "square" produces a filled box.)

Using the tags we've discussed so far, we're going to start creating a Web page for the French artist Henri Matisse. One of the first things we'll need is a list, to categorize his works that we intend to show and discuss. In Figure 2-9, we've made a two-level list by embedding one list within another.

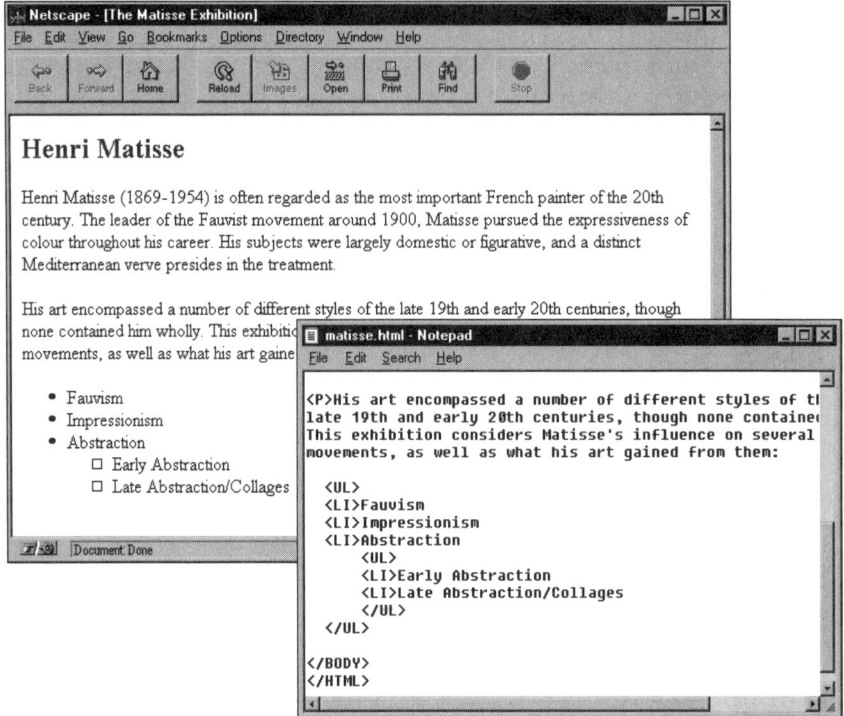

Figure 2-9: *One list is embedded within another to make a two-level list in the beginning of this Matisse page.*

The other face of <UL> is <OL>, which produces an ordered (sequential) list. Corresponding attributes control the way a list displays and what kind of ordering it uses—Arabic numbers, alphabetic characters, or Roman numerals. Since lists are so commonly used, and there are yet other kinds you can invoke, we'll go into those in greater detail later in this chapter under "List Types & Tags."

List Structure and List Items. Every <UL> requires a matching end tag to signal the end of the list and cancel indentation. An optional list header (like a caption for the list) can be added with the <LH> tag. Each item in the list is then specified with the tag <LI> for "list item."

HTML Tag

<LI>

The LI tag is used within the <UL>....</UL> tags and denotes an item in a list. An <LI> tag may have a matching end tag, </LI>, but if the end tag is absent, it will be implied by the next list tag.

Netscape extensions for the LI tag are:

TYPE="disc/circle/square/1/A/a/I/i"—Changes current typographical symbol for this item and those following. Types are disc, circle, and square for a bulleted list. Ordered list values are *1* (for numbered), *A* (alphabetic uppercase), *a* (alphabetic lowercase), *I* (Roman numerals, uppercase), and *i* (Roman numerals, lowercase).

VALUE=n—Changes current sequential number or alphabetic order value for an ordered list <OL>.

We hope you'll forgive us for considering UL and LI one tag. Like a horse and carriage (and like love and marriage years ago), you can't have one without the other.

Strictly speaking, <LI>, like <P>, should have a matching end tag. But the occurrence of the next <LI> tag or the end tag for the list </UL> implies the end of the previous list element, so it's permissible to omit it, and many Web authors do.

Making a Link

So now you've got a list, which in all likelihood is meant to be a menu of choices leading viewers to other documents, such as the one in Figure 2-9. The next thing you need to know is how to turn those list elements into hypertext links. That's done with the most common version of the anchor tag.

HTML Tag

<A HREF="file.html"> .... </A>

The A element indicates an anchor for a piece of text or image which serves as a hypertext link. The A element must have either an HREF or a NAME attribute.

<A HREF="file.html">...</A> is the most common form of hypertext link, where "file.html" is the filename or complete URL referenced. *file.html* is usually another HTML document, but it may also be an image, an audio or video file, or another resource.

<A NAME="..."> .... </A> specifies a link destination. It may surround text or be "empty" (serving as a reference point) but the end tag is required. We cover links in detail in Chapter 3.

To turn a word or phrase into a hypertext link, place <A HREF="file.html"> before the anchor text and </A> after it.The hypertext link will appear underlined and highlighted. Clicking on the link takes you to the file specified with HREF=.

We'll turn all the list items in our Matisse page into hypertext links with this code:

```
<UL>
  <LI><A HREF="fauvism.html">Fauvism</A>
  <LI><A HREF="impress.html">Impressionism</A>
  <LI><A HREF="abstract.html">Abstraction</A>
      <UL>
      <LI><A HREF="earlyabst.html">Early Abstraction</A>
      <LI><A HREF="lateabst.html">Late Abstraction/Collages</A>
      </UL>
</UL>
```

If the file you are linking to is another file on your site, all you'll need is the complete file name, as above; if it's in a different directory, you'll need the path as well (although you may use the complete URL). If it's on a remote computer, you'll need the complete URL. The different types of links you can make with the anchor tag are explained in detail in Chapter 3. For now, note how we turned our list items into hypertext links in Figure 2-10.

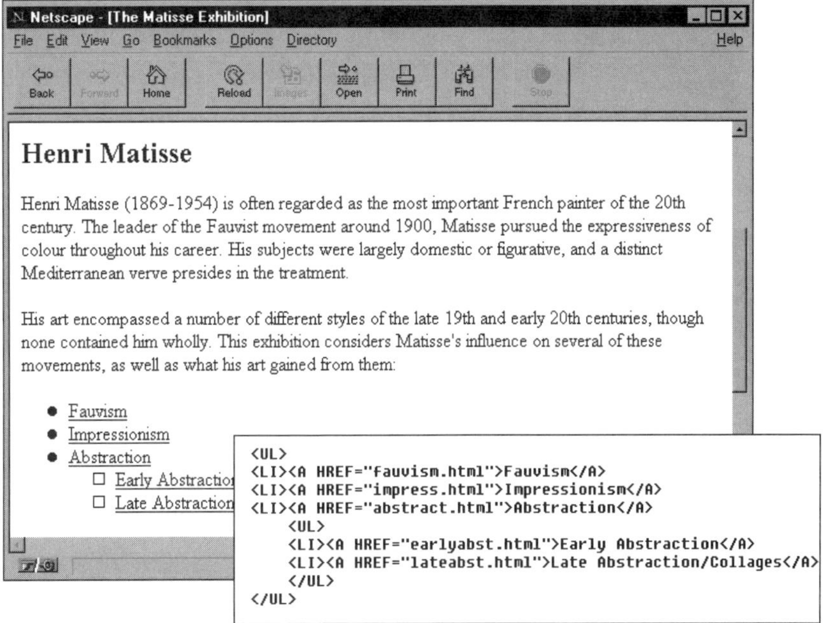

Figure 2-10: *Our list items are now hypertext links.*

Inserting an Image With <IMG>

The many wonders of the Web that have appeared in the last few years have a lot to do with its burgeoning graphical capabilities. And while it's not strictly necessary (nor even always a good thing) to insert graphics, they are so common today that most Web page authors would no more post a page without a graphic or two than they'd go naked to the office party.

To dress your page up graphically, all you need is (1) a graphic and (2) the image tag <IMG>. The GIF and JPEG formats are the ones most commonly recognized by graphical browsers, so in general it's wise to stick to these image formats. We'll go into this in a lot more detail in Chapter 4.

HTML Tag

<IMG >

The IMG tag defines an image file to be inserted. The attribute SRC is necessary to define the source file for the image. The minimal code for an image tag is thus:
<IMG SRC="file.gif">
where "file.gif" is the name of the image file, which may be a .GIF, .JPG, or any other acceptable image format. It may include a full URL. There is no IMG end tag.

The IMG tag may have any of several other attributes, including ALIGN, WIDTH, HEIGHT, BORDER, VSPACE, HSPACE, ALT, USEMAP, and ISMAP (A more complete definition of IMG and its attributes is given in Chapter 4).

The IMG tag tells the browser to place an image in this position in the document. Its attributes allow you to specify how it should be placed there and how text should be displayed around it. The options for specifying text alignment and spacing are shown in Figure 2-16, as we insert an image using the Netscape Gold editor. If no alignment is specified, the first line of the text will align with the bottom of the image, providing there's room. Several images can be placed alongside one another as long as space allows and no break is specified. That's what we've done in our Matisse page now, as it appears in Figure 2-11.

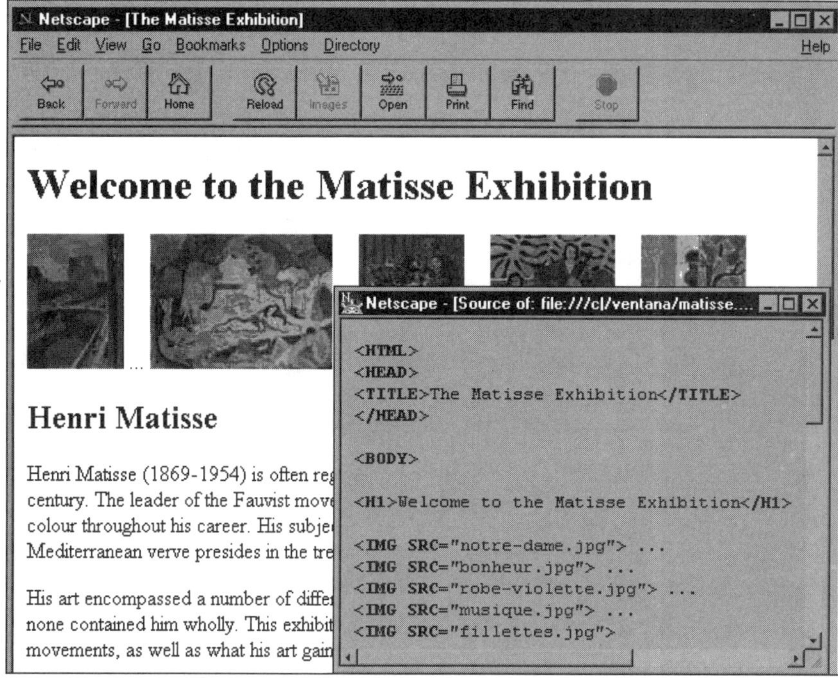

Figure 2-11: *The image tag is used to insert several pictures in our Web page here.*

Web Pages in a Hurry with <PRE>

Allowing for a little cheating on the header and list tags, we have room for one more tag in our "10 most useful" list. If you have a lot of text that you want to get up in a hurry, you'll find this tag very convenient. It's also useful if you haven't figured out yet how to make certain areas of text, such as tables, do what you want in HTML. We're talking about the PRE tag.

HTML Tag

<PRE> .... </PRE>

The PRE tag defines text that is "preformatted," indicating that the text enclosed within the tags is to be presented exactly as entered, preserving spacing and line breaks. Preformatted text is usually displayed in a fixed-width, typewriter-style font. The text must be in ASCII format.

The PRE tag simply tells the browser to display the text enclosed between <PRE> and </PRE> exactly as it's entered. The text has to be basic ASCII text, of course. Since the HTML document will be saved as an ASCII text file, it won't preserve fancy formatting from a sophisticated word processor, but it will preserve spacing. Unlike ordinary HTML text, PRE treats spaces as characters and not simply as word dividers, which is why it is sometimes useful in displaying tables.

You could theoretically post a document on the Web with nothing more than the first four document structure tags—HTML, HEAD, TITLE, BODY, and PRE. You can see how we used PRE to set off a block of text in Figure 2-12.

Many, many Web documents use nothing more than the 10 tags we've described above. In Figure 2-12, we show a complete Web page that uses just these basic tags, and in Figure 2-13, you can see the code that went to make it.

Note that we used a simple little "trick" to space the pictures out, just a series of ellipses. If we were only concerned with how this looked in Netscape, we could use the HSPACE attribute (for horizontal space) in the IMG tag to give a defined amount of space to the left and right of each picture (as shown with the Netscape Gold editor in Figure 2-16). It's part of the evolving nature of HTML, however, that this very useful attribute is not yet universally recognized. In Chapter 4, you'll learn how to create the same effect more elegantly in a way all browsers will recognize, but inserting the ellipses isn't a bad quick solution to the problem.

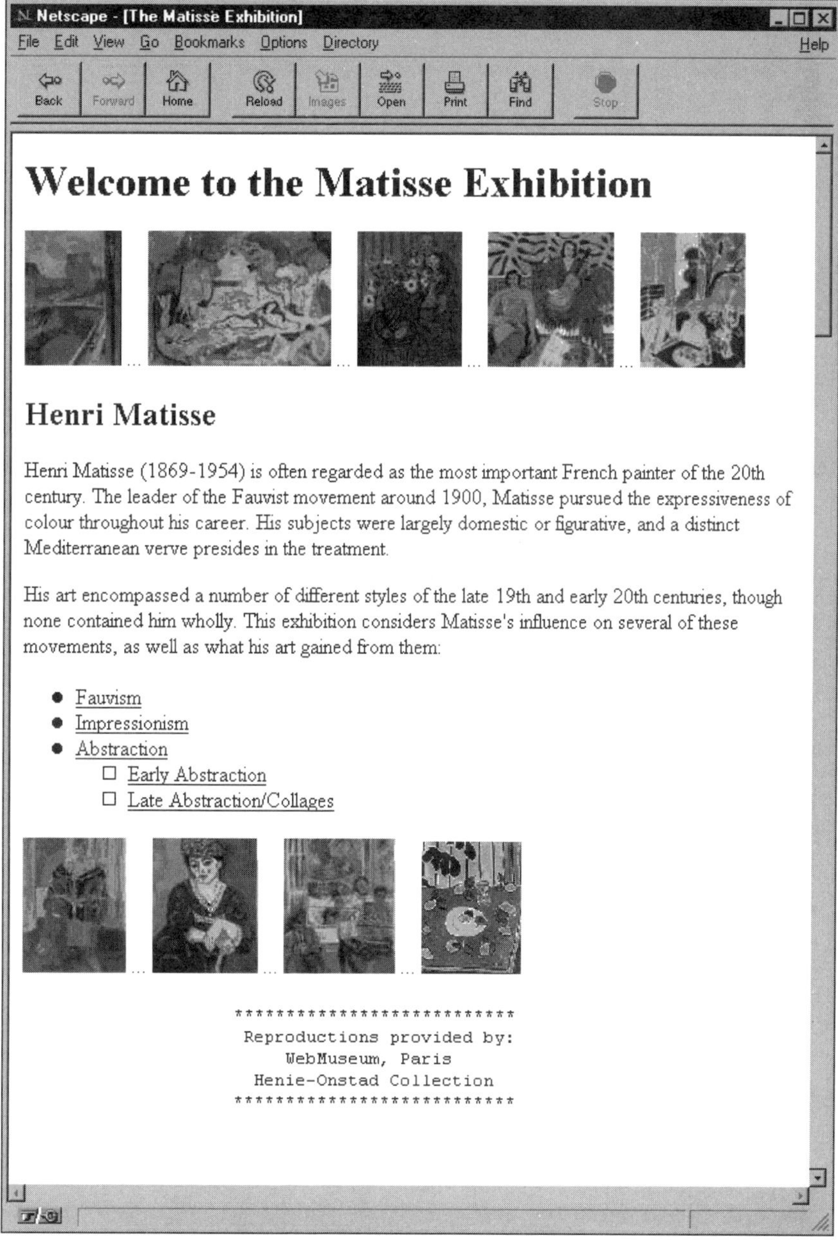

Figure 2-12: *We're already Web artists with this document, which was created with nothing more than the 10 most common HTML tags.*

Netscape - [Source of: file:///C|/VENTANA/matisse.html]

```
<HTML>
<HEAD>
<TITLE>The Matisse Exhibition</TITLE>
</HEAD>

<BODY>

<H1>Welcome to the Matisse Exhibition</H1>

<IMG SRC="notre-dame.jpg"> ...
<IMG SRC="bonheur.jpg"> ...
<IMG SRC="robe-violette.jpg"> ...
<IMG SRC="musique.jpg"> ...
<IMG SRC="fillettes.jpg">

<H2>Henri Matisse</H2>

<P>Henri Matisse (1869-1954) is often regarded as the most important
French painter of the 20th century. The leader of the Fauvist movement
around 1900, Matisse pursued the expressiveness of colour throughout
his career. His subjects were largely domestic or figurative,
and a distinct Mediterranean verve presides in the treatment.

<P>His art encompassed a number of different styles of the
late 19th and early 20th centuries, though none contained him wholly.
This exhibition considers Matisse's influence on several of these
movements, as well as what his art gained from them:

  <UL>
  <LI><A HREF="fauvism.html">Fauvism</A>
  <LI><A HREF="impress.html">Impressionism</A>
  <LI><A HREF="abstract.html">Abstraction</A>
      <UL>
      <LI><A HREF="earlyabst.html">Early Abstraction</A>
      <LI><A HREF="lateabst.html">Late Abstraction/Collages</A>
      </UL>
  </UL>

<IMG SRC="rifain.jpg"> ...
<IMG SRC="mme-matisse.jpg"> ...
<IMG SRC="lecon-musique.jpg"> ...
<IMG SRC="lemons.jpg">

<PRE>
                    ***************************
                     Reproductions provided by:
                         WebMuseum, Paris
                      Henie-Onstad Collection
                    ***************************
</PRE>

</BODY>
</HTML>
```

Figure 2-13: *The code that produced our Matisse page.*

MATISSE WITH NETSCAPE GOLD

Let's create the same Matisse page using Netscape Gold and you'll see how easy it is to put all of the HTML you've learned so far in practice—and even add some of those confusing attributes to make your presentation smarter.

From the main Netscape Navigator screen, click the Edit button to get the Editor. Start your document by choosing Document from the Properties menu. Choose the General Properties tab and enter the Title of your document and your name as Author, if you wish (see Figure 2-14). The Title line corresponds to the HTML <TITLE> tag. The Author and any other information about your document you enter in the boxes here will be stored in a <META> tag in the HEAD. We'll discuss this tag and its uses in Chapter 3.

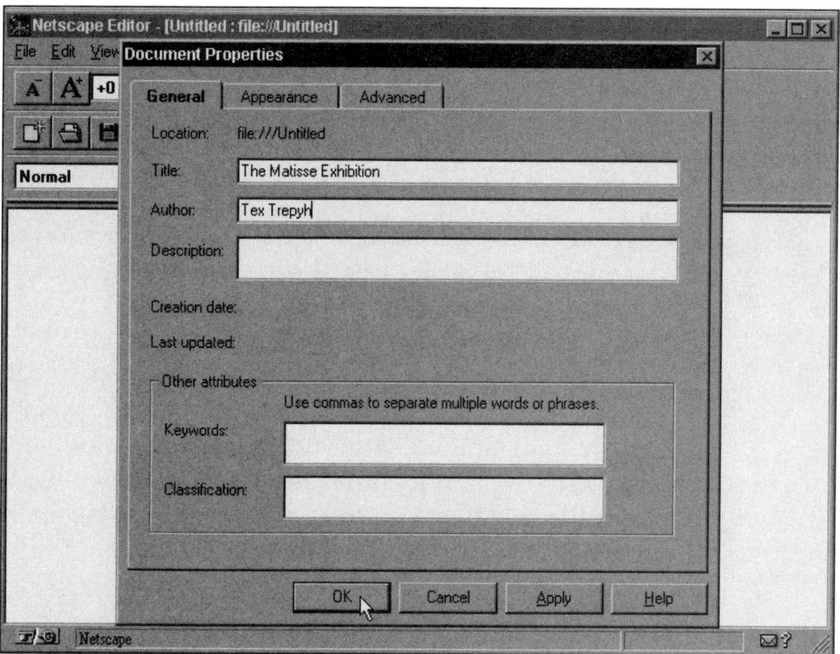

Figure 2-14: *Choose Document from the Properties menu, and enter document HEAD information in this box.*

Type in your first heading and then choose Heading 1 from the pull-down menu, as shown in Figure 2-15. In practice you can type your information in first and then format it, or format it as you go.

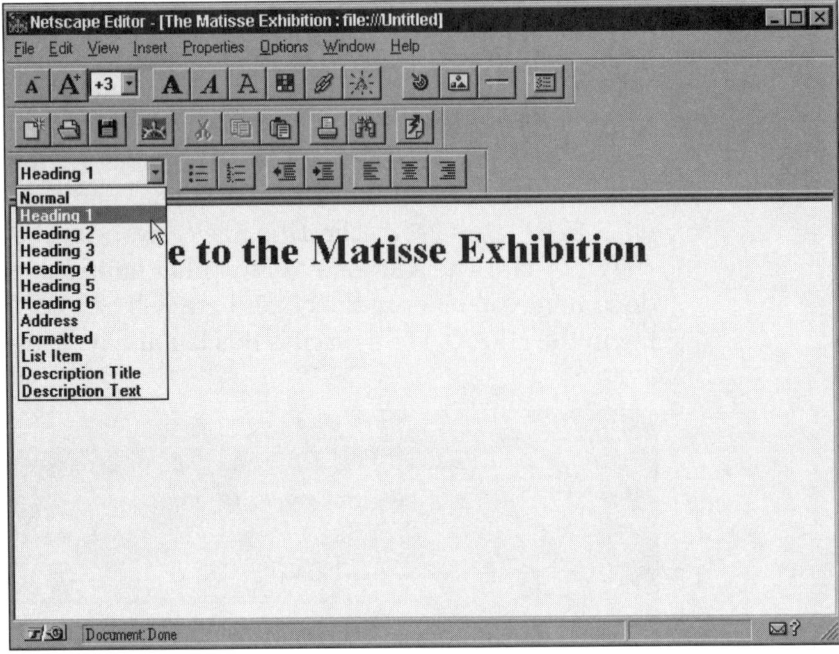

Figure 2-15: *Choose a Heading size from the pull-down list.*

Next, we'll insert an image. If you click the image button, you'll be prompted to save your file first. This is so that Netscape can preserve the path to your image file and make the correct link to it. Make sure that the images you insert have the same relation to your file that they will have on the final Web site. In other words, if your HTML documents will be in the main directory and your images in a subdirectory named "images" off this, see that images are in a subdirectory of the same name and location in your local setup. Alternatively, you can take the Copy option and copy the file to the same directory as your HTML file.

Once you've saved your document you can click the image button again, or choose Insert/Image from the menu. Enter the

Image file name or browse your directories to find the image you want to insert. (See Figure 2-16.)

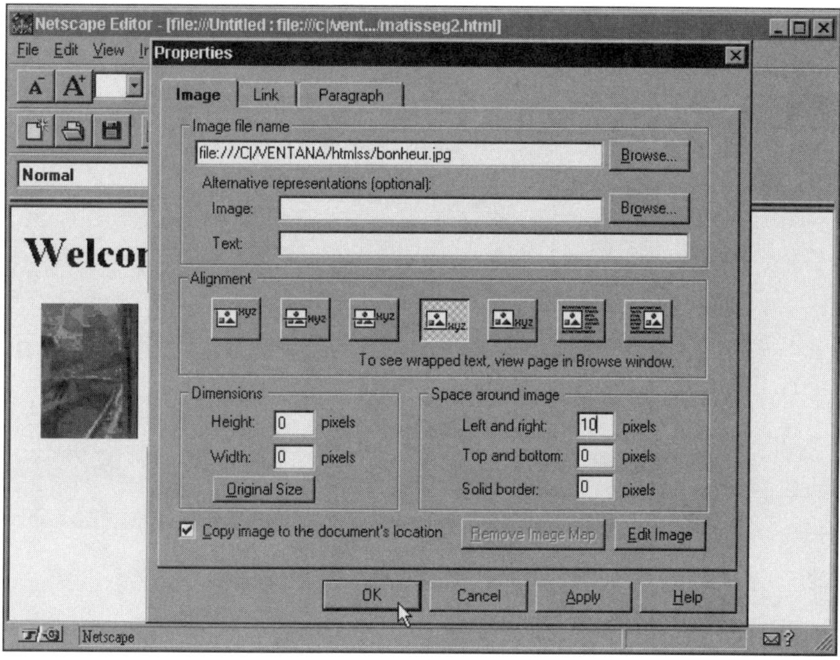

Figure 2-16: *Click the Image button to insert an image. Choose text alignment and spacing in the Link Properties box.*

In the Text box you can enter any ALT text you want to appear if images are not displayed. Choose text alignment by clicking any of the illustrated examples. The Alternative Image box is for designating a "low source" image, a topic we'll cover in Chapter 4. You can ignore that for now.

You needn't enter anything in the Dimensions box (if you're using the original size of the image, which is 99% of the time), as Netscape will automatically calculate that for you when it inserts the image. Designate space around the image by entering a figure in the appropriate boxes. Since we want to space out several images on a line without crowding, we've entered a figure of 10 pixels to the left and right of the image.

After you've inserted your images, you can begin a paragraph by entering text directly into the screen. Choose your text style before entering from the pull-down menu, or afterwards by highlighting it and choosing your code as in Figure 2-17.

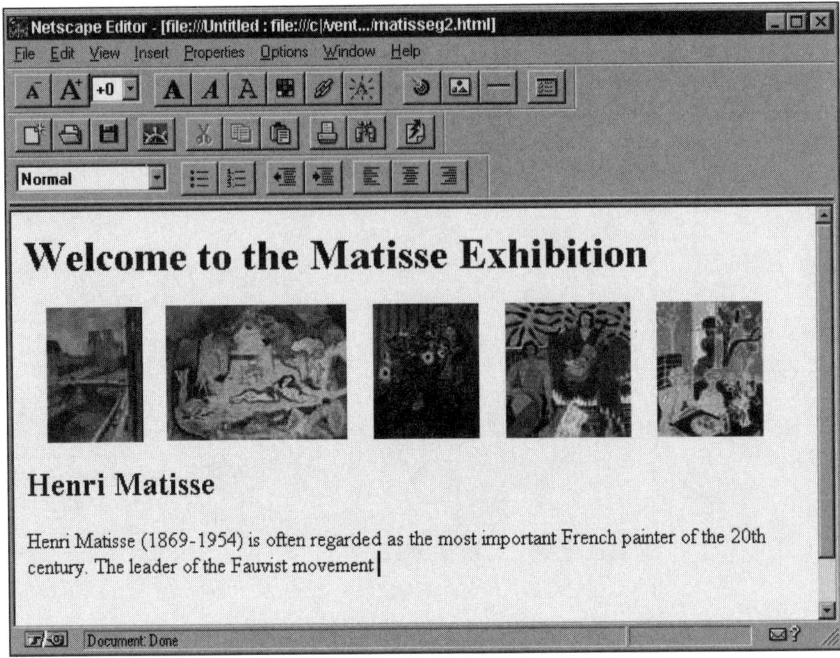

Figure 2-17: *Choose Normal text style and type your paragraph text directly into the window.*

Use the bulleted list button to make an unordered list (<UL>). The simplest way is to enter your text, outline it, then click the Bullet List button (see Figure 2-18). You can also click the List button as you go and enter your items. When you're done with the list, click the List button again and you'll be returned to normal text.

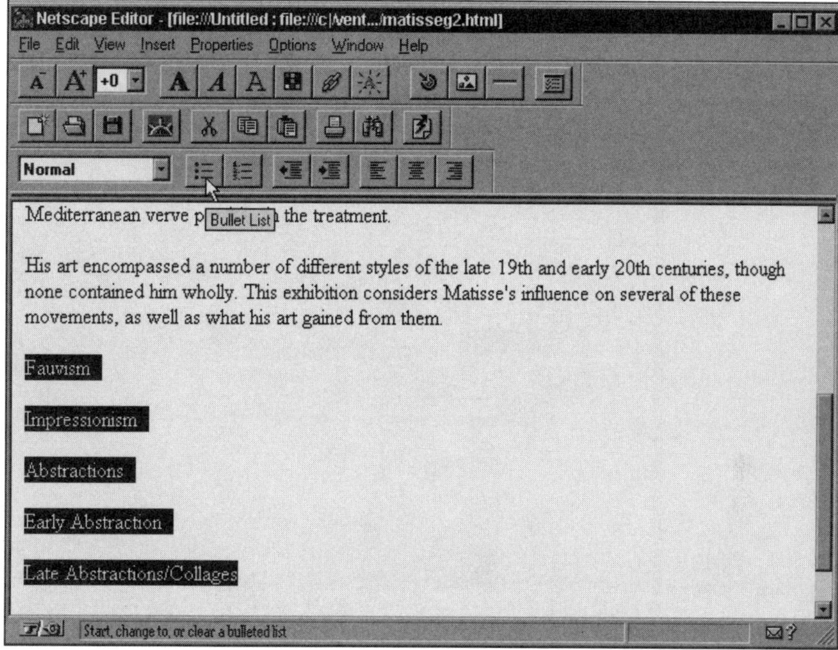

Figure 2-18: *Making a bulleted list: Outline your text and click the Bullet List button.*

Making a hypertext link is as easy as selecting the anchor and clicking on the Link button. Enter the page (the local file) you want to link to, or the complete URL of a document on another computer site. See Figure 2-19.

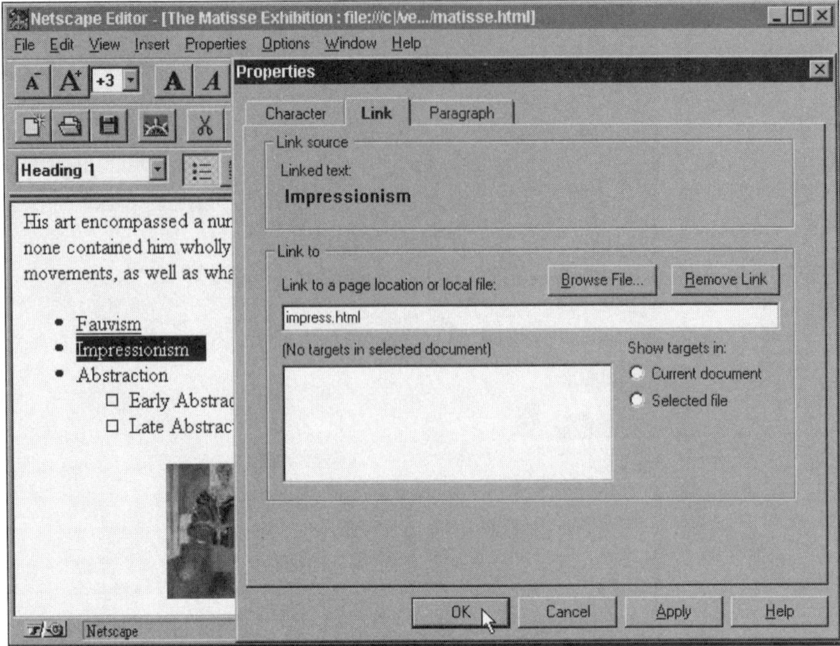

Figure 2-19: *Outline your text then click the Link button to create a hypertext link.*

We don't really need the <PRE> tag anymore, since it's easy to align text as we want it using the formatting toolbar buttons. It's just as easy to pick a different font style—bold, italic, or fixed width—with the font buttons. We want to keep the style we originally created, so we'll choose a fixed width font and center it.

In Figure 2-20, we're picking a fixed width font, using the appropriate font button on the editor. Other font buttons (indicated with an A) allow you to choose bold or italic, or to decrease or increase font size.

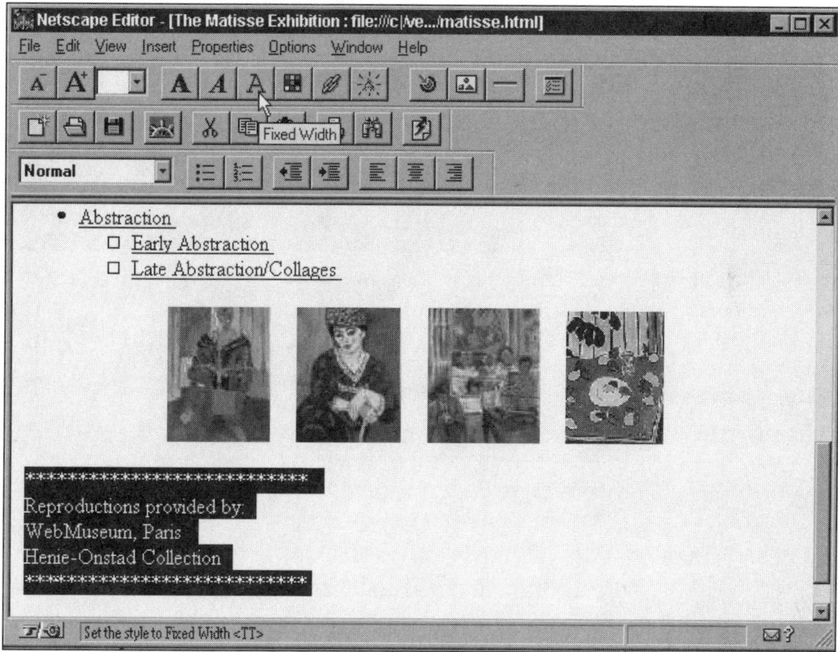

Figure 2-20: *Choose a fixed width font for this text by selecting it and clicking the Fixed Width font button.*

In Figure 2-21, we're centering the text using the Center button. You can just as easily justify text left or right or indent it using the toolbar buttons.

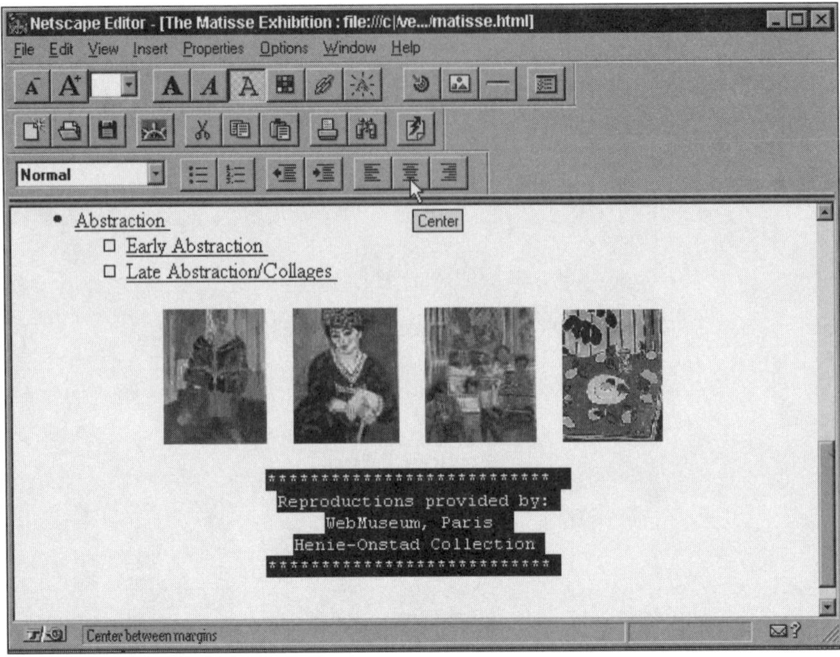

Figure 2-21: *Just click to center a block of text.*

Note how easy it is to change styles on your Web page and see the effect immediately. Changing your mind is just a click or two away.

LIST TYPES AND TAGS

In the previous section, we illustrated the most common type of a list used on the Web, the "unordered list." Now we'll talk about the other types of lists you can create. These include:

- Ordered List (also known as a numbered list)
- Definition List (for longer items or a list without symbols)
- Directory List (for a short list with shorter display)
- Menu List (for more compact list display)

We'll also cover the various attributes of the list tag, so that you can make your list look exactly like you want it to.

Ordered Lists With <OL>

The ordered list is the type of list tag you need if you want a sequential order, whether numerical or alphabetical. With the <OL> tag you do not need to enter the sequence (1,2,3,…)—it will be supplied when displayed by the browser.

HTML Tag

<OL> …. </OL>

The OL tag defines an ordered list, which is usually displayed indented. The opening tag is followed by an optional list header, <LH>, and then by the first list item, <LI>. The end tag is required to signal the end of the list and cancel indenting. An ordered list is by default numbered. Netscape extensions to the OL tag are:

TYPE="1/A/a/I/i"—Specifies the sequential type to use: numbers, upper or lowercase letters, upper or lowercase Roman numerals.

START=n—Set the starting sequence for the first item. (Same as SEQNUM in HTML 3.0.)

HTML 3.0 also allows the following attributes to the OL tag, which are not recognized by Netscape:

CLEAR="left/right/all"—Move the list down until the margin(s) is (are) clear or there is sufficient room before displaying. You may also specify a certain number of ens or pixels, (e.g. CLEAR="40 pixels"), meaning move down until 40 pixels are free.

SEQNUM=n—Set the starting sequence for the first item, such as <OL SEQNUM=15>.

CONTINUE—Don't restart the sequence number (continue where previous list left off), (e.g. <OL CONTINUE>).

COMPACT—Indicates that the list should be displayed as compact as possible by reducing spacing between items. This has no effect in Netscape, but you can achieve the same effect more precisely using Netscape font size changes.

For a simple ordered list, you need nothing more than the OL tag combined with <LI> for list items. For example, the following ordered list code:

```
<OL>
<LI>The Executive Branch
<LI>The Legislative Branch
<LI>The Judicial Branch
</OL>
```

displays as:

1. The Executive Branch
2. The Legislative Branch
3. The Judicial Branch

A variety of options are available, however, which allow you to choose the sequence style and manner of display.

Numbering Options

Netscape extensions allow you to specify with the TYPE attribute whether you want numbers (1, 2, 3) or letters (A, B, C *or* a, b, c). You can also specify Roman numerals (I, II, III *or* i, ii, iii). If a type is not specified, numbers will be used.

HTML 3.0 proposes handling sequence types with a style sheet, which would be advantageous with large or frequently updated documents, making it unnecessary to spec each list individually. Since the style sheet mechanism is not yet available for all platforms, Netscape allows you to do this with Netscape extensions. Since style sheets are liable to be an important option in the future, we'll discuss style sheets later in Chapter 5, "Getting Stylish."

Another Netscape extension that has the same effect as a proposed HTML 3.0 tag is START. You can use START to specify whether you want the sequencing to begin with something other than 1 (or the first unit in the chosen TYPE). START=7 would display as either 7, G, g, VII, or vii, according to the specified TYPE.

The HTML 3.0 syntax is SEQNUM=n, with the TYPE defined in a style sheet. Both the Netscape extension and the HTML 3.0 attribute are relatively new, so you should check how this will appear in any non-Netscape browsers that are important to you.

In Figure 2-22 you can see how we used the START attribute when we wanted to pause a list to add a paragraph, then start a new list that picks up where the previous list left off. This can also be useful if you anticipate adding steps to a sequence in later drafts, such as in updating or rewriting a manual. You can "skip" the missing numbers with START and not upset your outline.

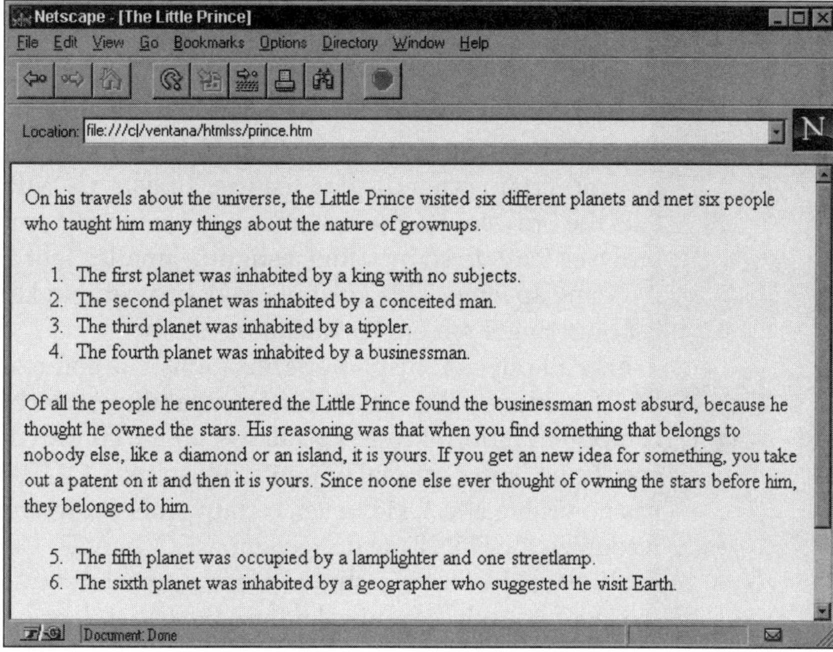

Figure 2-22: *You can change the starting number for a list using the START attribute.*

The coding that produced the lists in Figure 2-22 follows:

```
<P>On his travels about the universe....
<OL>
  <LI>The first planet....
  <LI>The second planet....
  <LI>The third planet....
  <LI>The fourth planet....
</OL>
<P>Of all the people he encountered....
<OL START=5>
  <LI>The fifth planet....
  <LI>The sixth planet....
</OL>
```

Display Options

The HTML 3.0 attributes COMPACT and CLEAR allow you to control certain other display features of lists. COMPACT simply tells the browser to display the list as compactly as possible. The browser may do so by using a slightly smaller font and/or by reducing spacing. This attribute may be useful in keeping a long list on a single screen, for instance.

Like all physical display specifications, the end result of COMPACT is entirely dependent on the capability of the browser and the computer platform. Netscape allows you to control the display by specifying larger or smaller font sizes, so the COMPACT attribute has no visible effect. However, certain other browsers that do not recognize the FONT tag do recognize COMPACT. Use both and you'll have the best of both worlds, since each browser will ignore the tag it doesn't recognize and use the one it does.

The CLEAR Attribute

An indispensable addition to the careful designer's arsenal is the CLEAR attribute. This allows you to make sure that items that should be distinct on the page do not "run into" each other.

When text flows around a figure or table in the margin, you may want to start a header, a paragraph, or a list below the figure rather than alongside it. Even if you manage to make things fit nicely on your own screen, it's not always possible to tell whether the browser will respect this layout, since a different size font or a wider screen size can throw off your careful design.

CLEAR is an attribute that is common to most block-like elements in HTML 3.0. Figure 2-23 shows how inserting a figure in the file in Figure 2-22 affects the list display. The HTML 3.0 fix is to include the CLEAR attribute in the OL tag thus:

```
<OL CLEAR="left" START=5>
```

The problem is that few browsers recognize this as yet. Netscape has implemented CLEAR as an attribute of the <BR> tag (line break) only. So the appropriate fix is to add <BR CLEAR> after the paragraph and before starting the list. (The code can be seen in Figure 2-26.)

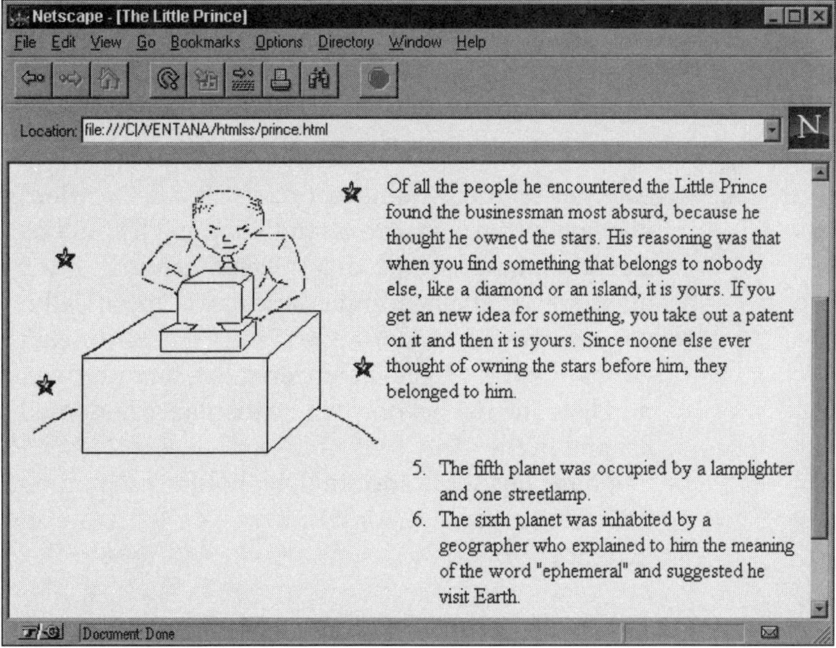

Figure 2-23: *An image aligned with text interferes with the display of a list...*

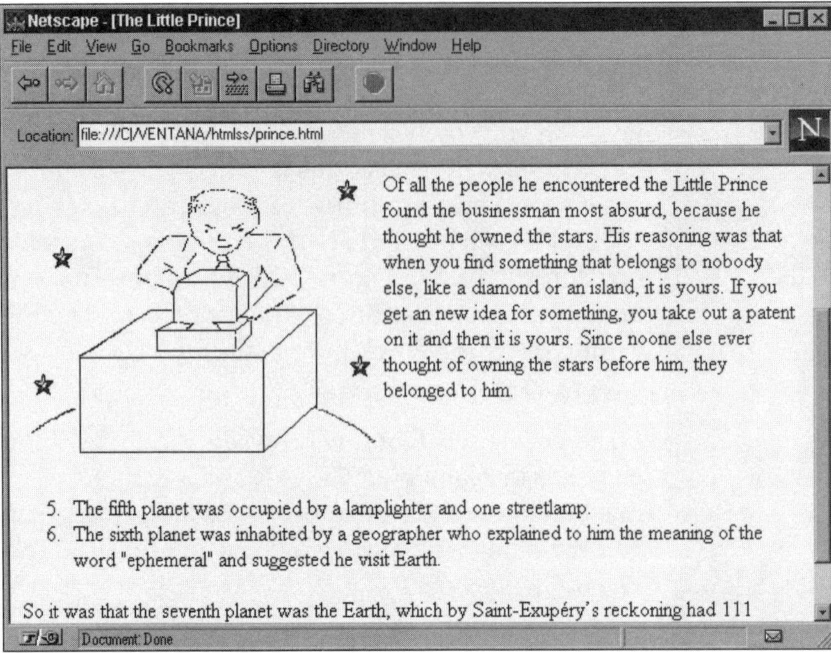

Figure 2-24: *...but <BR CLEAR> fixes the problem.*

List Header <LH>

Another optional element for a list is a list header. This is largely a display option, as more often than not a list will be introduced by a preceding paragraph or a selected heading. But if you wish to make sure that a heading is associated specifically with the list, you can use the <LH> tag to signify a list header. This can be used with any type of list—an ordered list, an unordered list, or definition list. The list header will be displayed indented along with the list and in the same font as the list.

If a list header is specified, it should come immediately after the list start tag (UL, OL, or DL).

HTML Tag

<LH> .... </LH>

The LH tag defines the optional list header. <LH> follows a UL, OL, or DL tag and precedes the list elements.

Definition Lists With <DL>

Another type of list is the *definition list*. This is typically used when a short list item might be followed by a longer explanatory paragraph. A simple example appears in Figure 2-25.

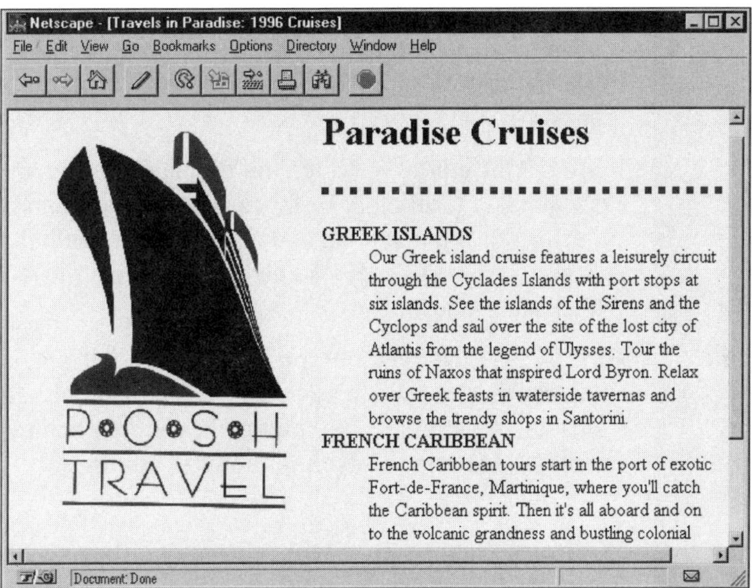

Figure 2-25: *A definition list allows for descriptive paragraphs to follow unnumbered list items.*

The coding for the list in Figure 2-25 reads:

```
<DL>
<DT>GREEK ISLANDS
<DD>Our Greek Island cruise features....
<DT>FRENCH CARIBBEAN
<DD>French Caribbean tours start in the exotic port of....
</DL>
```

HTML Tag

<DL>

The DL tag defines a definition list. List terms <DT> are unnumbered and unbulleted and allow for longer descriptive paragraphs (definitions) <DD> to follow each item. A <DD> must be preceded by a <DT>, but a <DT> may exist without a <DD>.

HTML 3.0 allows the following attributes, which are not recognized in Netscape:

CLEAR="left/right/all"—Move the definition list down until the margin(s) is (are) clear or there is sufficient room before displaying. You may also specify a certain number of ens or pixels, such as CLEAR="40 pixels", meaning move down until 40 pixels are free.

COMPACT—Indicates that the list should be displayed as compactly as possible by reducing spacing between items. This has no effect in Netscape, but you can achieve the same effect using Netscape font size changes.

Definition lists are by nature plain—neither numbered nor bulleted. However, it's possible to decorate them with your own "bullets" by inserting an image of your choice next to each item using the IMG tag. For that reason, the definition list has often been used in place of the unordered list when the author wished to use a colored ball or totem icon next to list items instead of the standard "disc/circle/square" display.

The definition list has the same proposed HTML 3.0 attributes as the unordered and ordered lists: COMPACT for more economical display and CLEAR to clear space taken up by any prior figures before displaying. Neither of these works currently in Netscape, however.

As you can see from the coding for Figure 2-25 above, there are two subsequent elements after the <DL> tag for the definition list, in place of the one <LI> for ordered and unordered lists. The <DT> tag signifies the "definition term"—the term to be defined, and <DD> the "definition" itself (which is often more like an expansion or explanation).

HTML Tag

<DT>

The DT tag defines a "definition term," the term to be defined or amplified. It does not require an end tag.

HTML Tag

<DD>

The DD tag is the "definition definition"—a definition or explanatory paragraph to follow a definition term (<DT>). A <DT> is required before any <DD>.

<DD> does not require an end tag.

```
<H2>Company Policy: Leave Procedures</H2>
<DL>
<DT>Leave of Absence
<DD>Unpaid leave of absence will be granted on a case-by-case
basis. A written request should be submitted to the Supervi-
sor...
...
</DL>
```

The definition list would then be rendered as:

Leave of Absence

Unpaid leave of absence will be granted on a case-by-case basis. A written request should be submitted to the Supervisor...

DIRECTORY & MENU LISTS: <DIR> AND <MENU>

Two other types of lists you may encounter on the Web are the *directory list* (<DIR>....</DIR>) and *menu list* (<MENU>....</MENU>). These list types are on their way to becoming obsolete, to be replaced by new proposed list attributes available in HTML 3.0. Like the unordered and ordered lists, these list types are used in conjunction with the list item tag, LI.

The directory list is meant to be used for a list of short items, which a browser could, if it chose, display in columns across the screen, like so:

• apples • oranges • bananas • pears

instead of:

- apples
- oranges
- bananas
- pears

Other, more reliable ways for specifying column display are available using the TABLE tag and the VALIGN attribute. Chapters 5 and 7 discuss these options.

A menu list is virtually identical to an unordered list. It is meant to be used with a list of items no more than a sentence long, which the browser could format in a more compact manner, similar to the effect of <UL COMPACT>.

Since Netscape does not treat either of these list forms any differently than an unordered list, we'll skip over them. Their use is not recommended, since support by other browsers is unreliable.

Other Common & Useful Tags

As you hone your Web authoring skills, it won't be long before you'll be casting about for a few more useful tags to make your Web page behave the way you want it to. In the rest of this chapter, we'll present the tags you're most likely to need in the beginning. The complicated and fancy stuff will be saved for more detailed chapters. Everything else here you should find easy to implement and immediately useful in designing the layout and display of your pages.

Dividers: Horizontal Rules & Bar GIFs

The tag for a horizontal rule is so common that it probably deserved a place in our "top 10" list. It was nudged out of the running only to give priority to tags more essential to content. The <HR> tag simply draws a rule of preset thickness across the page—a very useful and common way to divide sections of text.

HTML Tag

<HR>

The HR tag inserts a divider line in the document, usually used after a header or between sections.

Netscape extensions to the HR tag include:

SIZE=x—Specifies a thickness (in pixels). (The standard is 2.)

WIDTH=x—Specifies the horizontal width of the rule. Can be a number (interpreted as pixels) or a percent (interpreted as a percentage of the display screen.

ALIGN="left/right/center"—Specifies whether the rule should align with the left or right margin or center (useful with rules that are less than the width of the page).

NOSHADE—Allows for a solid bar, with no shading.

HTML 3.0 also allows for these attributes, which are not recognized in Netscape:

CLEAR="left/right/all"—Move horizontal rule down until the margin(s) is (are) clear before displaying rule. Used to ensure that the rule is positioned below an image, figure, or table. You may also specify any number of pixels or ens (for example, CLEAR="40 en" means move down until there is at least 40 en units free).

SRC="image.gif'—Specifies a custom image to be used for a rule.

How the HR tag displays the line depends on the background of the page. On a white background, it appears as a bar outline in beige. On a standard gray background, it appears as a darker gray shaded line. Netscape allows you to turn off the shading with the NOSHADE attribute, which will cause the rule to display as a solid bar. You can control the thickness of the rule with the SIZE attribute, and its length across the page with WIDTH (600 is normal 100% width). (Note that WIDTH refers to the width of the screen, not the thickness of the line.) Since you may wish a shorter rule to be centered, for instance, or prefer your rule adjusted to the right margin instead of the left, you can also specify this with the ALIGN attribute.

With some backgrounds (chiefly dark backgrounds), the horizontal rule will not show up at all. Partly because of this, and partly for decorative reasons, it has become common to use the IMG tag to replace the horizontal rule with bars of various colors, in the form of GIFs, such as:

```
<IMG SRC="redbar.gif">
```

Because this practice has become so common, HTML 3.0 allows for a "source file," by means of the SRC attribute, to replace the standard rule only if the browser is capable of displaying it. So, the code

```
<HR SRC="redbar.gif">
```

would produce the colored bar (redbar.gif) if the browser is capable of displaying it, and a horizontal rule if it is not. This would assure that a line is displayed instead of an uninformative (and rather misleading) GIF icon. Unfortunately, this is not supported by most browsers, including Netscape, but it's one of the HTML 3.0 attributes you might want to check for in future.

Block Tags for Special Text Treatments

Many of the tags for handling text that we've discussed so far are known as "block elements"—that is, they act as containers for text and allow for special formatting requirements in documents.

Besides headings, paragraphs, and list items, there are a few other requirements you might have for setting apart sections of text. Two common ones are "block quotes" (often used for long quotations) and "address" (used to identify bottom-of-the-page information).

The <BLOCKQUOTE> tag. The Blockquote tag allows you to set off a block of text as a quote. A block quote is usually shown as an indented block of text.

HTML Tag

<BLOCKQUOTE> .... </BLOCKQUOTE>

The <BLOCKQUOTE> .... </BLOCKQUOTE> tag is used for extended quotations. In HTML 3.0, the equivalent proposed tag is <BQ> .... </BQ>. HTML 3.0 allows the following attributes for BQ (which are not recognized in Netscape):

CLEAR="left/right/all"—Move the block down until the margin(s) is (are) clear before displaying rule. Used to ensure the rule is positioned below an image, figure, or table. You may also specify any number of pixels or ens (for example, CLEAR="40 en" means move down until there are at least 40 en units free).

NOWRAP—Don't wrap lines. Use if you don't want the browser to automatically wrap lines. You can specify explicit line breaks with <BR>.

*Instead of the NOWRAP attribute, Netscape uses the tag <NOBR> .... </NOBR>, which can contain any number of text containers, including BLOCKQUOTE.

Here's a useful tip about BLOCKQUOTE: It can be nested, so that every time you add another BLOCKQUOTE tag inside the first one, the indent increases.

The <ADDRESS> Tag. It is generally good practice to sign all your Web pages and to give visitors a way to contact you. The address tag allows you to do this by specifying a section of text as the "address." Netscape displays the ADDRESS in italics, as do most browsers. You can theoretically put anything you like in an address tag. But, as designed, the tag has more than cosmetic purposes. It is also a searchable element that could be useful to search engines and robots looking for your site. So keep that in mind when you compose your ADDRESS text.

HTML Tag

<ADDRESS> .... </ADDRESS>

The ADDRESS tag specifies information such as address, signature, and authorship for the document, typically placed at the top or bottom of the document. The address will be set off like a paragraph with breaks before and after. HTML 3.0 allows the following attributes, which are not recognized in Netscape:

CLEAR="left/right/all"—Move address down until the margin(s) is (are) clear before displaying rule. Used to ensure the rule is positioned below an image, figure, or table. You may also specify any number of pixels or ens (for example, CLEAR="40 en" means move down until there are at least 40 en units free).

NOWRAP—Don't wrap lines. Use NOWRAP if you don't want the browser to automatically wrap lines. You can specify explicit line breaks with <BR>.

*Instead of the NOWRAP attribute, Netscape uses the tag <NOBR> .... </NOBR>, which can contain any number of text containers, including ADDRESS.

Physical & Informational Styles

Physical and informational style tags are useful to highlight text in various ways and convey emphasis. The chief effect all these tags have is to produce text in a different font: usually bold, italics, or a fixed width font ("typewriter style"). Sticklers for precise HTML are careful to distinguish, however, between the tags that are merely physical font specifications and those that are meant to convey different types of information.

This difference is probably too fine a point for most users, but technical writers may appreciate the distinction. For example, TT and KBD generally cause most browsers to render text in the same fixed-width font. A technical writer who is writing a manual, however, may wish to distinguish KBD as something to be entered by a user at the keyboard, whereas TT might represent something else, say a memo. While they may appear identical on the Web, if the text were translated back into a printed document, the difference could be respected. Browsers can be made to recognize this difference and display these tags differently.

Similarly, <B> and <STRONG> both produce bold type and <I> and <EM> both produce italics, and they are often used interchangeably. <STRONG> and <EM> are older forms carried over from HTML 1.0, so for that reason are preferred by conservative HTML writers who wish to be considerate of older browsers. However, they are rapidly being replaced in common usage with the newer tags <B> and <I> (not surprisingly, since they're easier to type). But an argument can be made that there is a difference between a phrase to which you want to add strong emphasis in a document, such as **Never drink and drive!,** and a desire simply to render something in bold to stand out from surrounding text as a reference, such as "featuring **Henry IV, Part I** starring Kenneth Branagh." Similarly, you might use <EM> to emphasize some point such as "*Important: Use no more than 1 part acid to every 3 parts solution,*" which does not convey the same meaning as "The highlight of the evening was the performance of Debussy's *Afternoon of a Faun*." In the latter example, one is simply following a convention for putting a title in italics, while in the first instance the italics are used for important emphasis.

In Table 2-1, we distinguish between the physical and informational style tags, for reference. Whether the distinction is meaningful to you is entirely dependent on the nature of your document.

Physical & Logical Style Tags	
Physical Styles	
*<B> .... </B>	Bold.
*<I> .... </I>	Italic.
*<U> .... </U>	Underline (not widely supported).
*<STRIKE>....</STRIKE>	Strikethrough, in Netscape. See below.
<S> .... </S>	Strikethrough, as proposed in HTML 3.0. (Display text with horizontal line through, as deleted text.)
*<TT> .... </TT>	TeleType (display in fixed pitch typewriter font).
*<BIG> .... </BIG>	Large typeface (increase font size, as available).
*<SMALL>....</SMALL>	Small typeface (decrease font size, as available).
*_{....}	Subscript (display if possible in smaller font or as otherwise treated by browser).
*^{....}	Superscript (display if possible in a smaller font or as otherwise treated by browser). (Both <SUB> and <SUP> may take the ALIGN attribute, but it is only meaningful within the <MATH> element, as discussed in Chapter 7.)
Logical Styles	
*<STRONG>....</STRONG>	Strong emphasis; usually rendered in bold.
*<EM> .... </EM>	Emphasis; usually rendered in italics.
*<KBD> ....</KBD>	Keyboard; indicates text typed by the user (as in an instructional example).
*<SAMP>....</SAMP>	Sample; indicates a sequence of literal characters.
*<CODE>....</CODE>	Indicates an example of code (usually shown in a monospaced font).
*<CITE>....</CITE>	Specifies a citation; usually rendered in italics.
<INS>....</INS>	Used for inserted text (as in a legal document).
<DEL>....</DEL>	Used for deleted text (as in a legal document).

Table 2-1: *Special character styles for HTML. Those supported by Netscape are asterisked.*

ACCENTS & SPECIAL CHARACTERS

HTML, it must be remembered, is an international language. Although the syntax of HTML may be based on English usage, the Web is both multilingual and cross-cultural. Therefore, a number of conventions and special characters have been established for dealing with languages other than English.

This includes accented characters and other special characters, like monetary symbols and copyright symbols, which are so common as to become necessary quite quickly in Web authoring. This is particularly so if you're creating a business site and want to indicate trademarks and copyrighted information.

Two different formats for special characters are recognized in HTML. All accented letters plus a few special symbols may be represented as *entities*. Entities are a special character combination that will be interpreted by the browser as a single special character. These are fairly easy to remember; for example, the format *é* to represent *é* is intuitive once you get the feel for it. A larger set of symbols is represented by numeric character references that are far from intuitive and are not much used if an entity is also available for the symbol needed.

Besides the extended characters, four keyboard characters have special meaning in HTML and therefore need to be encoded as entities if the intention is to display them literally, unless they're between <SAMP>...</SAMP> containers. Since the angle brackets are used to indicate tags, their use in the document itself can be confusing to a browser. Likewise, quotation marks and ampersands are used in coding, so when used in the text they need to be indicated as literal or numeric characters. Their proper representation in HTML is shown in Table 2-2.

Char.	Literal	Num.	Description
<	<	<	Less than sign
>	>	>	Greater than sign
&	&	&	Ampersand
“	"	"	Double quote sign

Table 2-2: *Keyboard characters that need special coding in HTML.*

In addition, HTML allows an extended set of symbols, based on the International Standards Organization's ISO-8859-1 characters, known as the *Latin-1* set. If you use Microsoft Word, you'll recognize these as the lower half of the table you see when you use Word 6.0's Insert Symbol option.

A complete table of all special characters and entities can be found in Appendix E. Some of the more common ones are listed in Table 2-3.

Char	Literal	Num.	Description
ˆ		ˆ	Circumflex accent
–		–	En dash
—	&emdash;	—	Em dash
™		™	Trade mark symbol
¡		¡	Inverted exclamation mark
¢		¢	Cent sign
£		£	Pound sterling
¥		¥	Japanese Yen
¦		¦	Broken vertical bar
§		§	Section sign
¨		¨	Umlaut (dieresis)
©	©	©	Copyright symbol
-			Soft hyphen
®	®	®	Registered trademark

(Continued)

Char	Literal	Num.	Description
^{2}		²	Superscript two
^{3}		³	Superscript three
´		´	Acute accent
¸		¸	Cedilla
^{1}		¹	Superscript one
$^{1}/_{4}$		¼	Fraction one-fourth
$^{1}/_{2}$		½	Fraction one-half
$^{3}/_{4}$		¾	Fraction three-fourths
¿	&#	191;	Inverted question mark
Ç	Ç	Ç	Capital C, cedilla
à	à	á	Small a, grave accent
á	á	á	Small a, acute accent
ç	ç	ç	Small c, cedilla
è	è	è	Small e, grave accent
é	é	é	Small e, acute accent
ì	ì	ì	Small i, grave accent
í	í	í	Small i, acute accent
ñ	ñ	ñ	Small n, tilde
ò	ò	ò	Small o, grave accent
ó	ó	ó	Small o, acute accent
ô	ô	ô	Small o, circumflex accent

Table 2-3: *Special characters and the code necessary to create them in a Web page.*

The © and ® strings are Netscape extensions and may not be recognized by all browsers.

To see how these special characters appear in an HTML document, we need only take a look at the coding for the Little Prince page we did a while back. Figure 2-26 shows the coding for this page. For the accented *e* and the quotation marks we used entities; for the em dash we used a numeric entry, because experience has shown that it is more universally recognized by browsers than the corresponding literal entity.

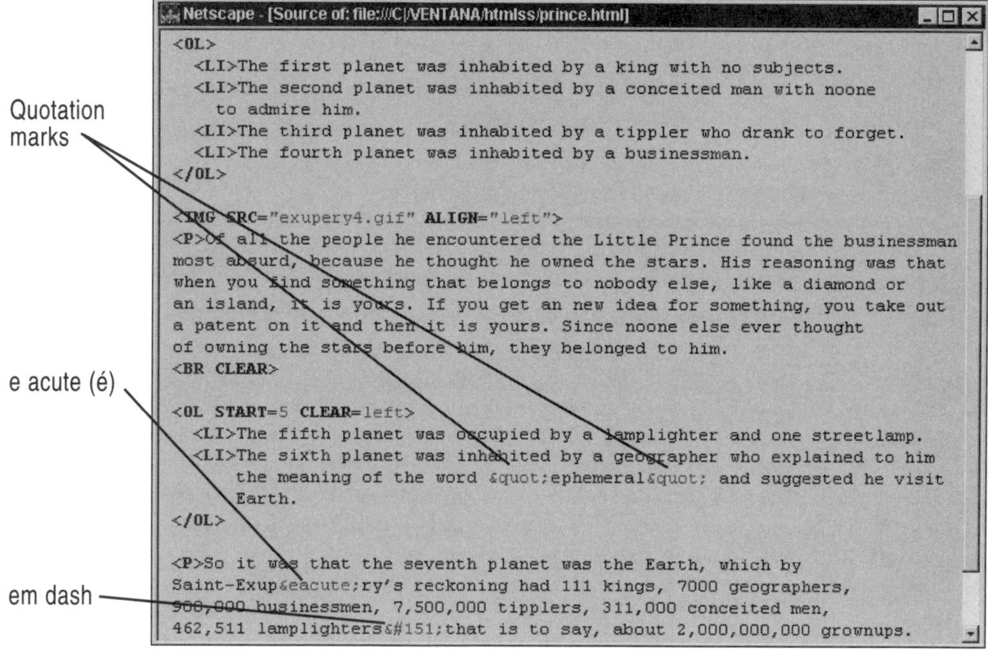


```
<OL>
  <LI>The first planet was inhabited by a king with no subjects.
  <LI>The second planet was inhabited by a conceited man with noone
    to admire him.
  <LI>The third planet was inhabited by a tippler who drank to forget.
  <LI>The fourth planet was inhabited by a businessman.
</OL>

<IMG SRC="exupery4.gif" ALIGN="left">
<P>Of all the people he encountered the Little Prince found the businessman
most absurd, because he thought he owned the stars. His reasoning was that
when you find something that belongs to nobody else, like a diamond or
an island, it is yours. If you get an new idea for something, you take out
a patent on it and then it is yours. Since noone else ever thought
of owning the stars before him, they belonged to him.
<BR CLEAR>

<OL START=5 CLEAR=left>
  <LI>The fifth planet was occupied by a lamplighter and one streetlamp.
  <LI>The sixth planet was inhabited by a geographer who explained to him
      the meaning of the word &quot;ephemeral&quot; and suggested he visit
      Earth.
</OL>

<P>So it was that the seventh planet was the Earth, which by
Saint-Exup&eacute;ry's reckoning had 111 kings, 7000 geographers,
900,000 businessmen, 7,500,000 tipplers, 311,000 conceited men,
462,511 lamplighters&#151;that is to say, about 2,000,000,000 grownups.
```

Figure 2-26: *The coding for our Little Prince page (Figure 2-24) shows several special characters.*

ADDING COMMENT LINES

Every computer language allows the programmer to add comments or "remarks" that have absolutely no effect on the program's function, but help a mere human to understand what's going on. Assembly language is so cryptic that programmers in that obscure shorthand are taught to add a comment after every line of code.

HTML is nowhere near that bad, but comments are nevertheless helpful. Here's the correct way to insert one:

```
<!- Uploaded 4.4.96, next rev. 5.2 ->
```

DOCUMENT CHECKING

HTML authoring is a bit like gardening—there's always something you should be doing. Gardeners are quite reconciled to the idea that even when they're done they're not done, and HTML authors need that same philosophical attitude if they are to create really successful pages.

When you finish your Web page, with all its paragraph breaks, horizontal rules, and ordered lists looking spiffy, you're not done because you've only ever seen that document from one point of view—namely, from a local file loaded into your own Netscape Navigator. It's a common error to assume that everyone is using Netscape—the *majority* of your readers are, to be sure, but it isn't in your interest to disregard the 20 percent who use some version of Mosaic, nor to totally ignore the 7 percent who access your pages with the text-only Web browser *Lynx* or one of the other browsers incorporated in various online services.

TIP

The WebMaster's Page is a good place to check to keep up on the latest browser stats. Bob Allison publishes running statistics on browser usage and other Web statistics, among many other useful pieces of information, here at http://gagme.wwa.com/~boba/masters1.html.

THOSE HARD-TO-SPOT ERRORS

Figure 2-27 shows a page that appears to be finished for Netscape. Now see Figure 2-28, which shows what you get when you load that page into Mosaic.

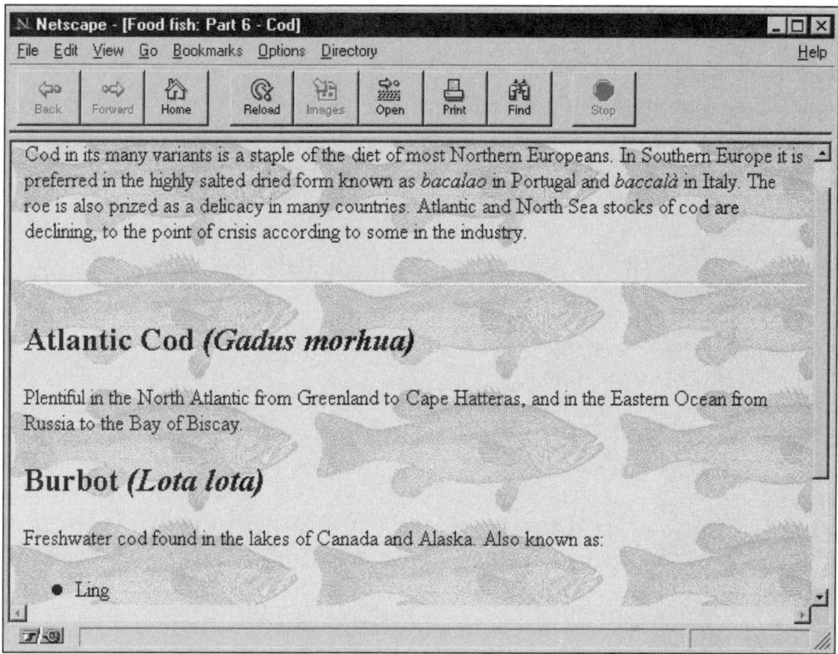

Figure 2-27: *The codfish page: Is it ready to go?*

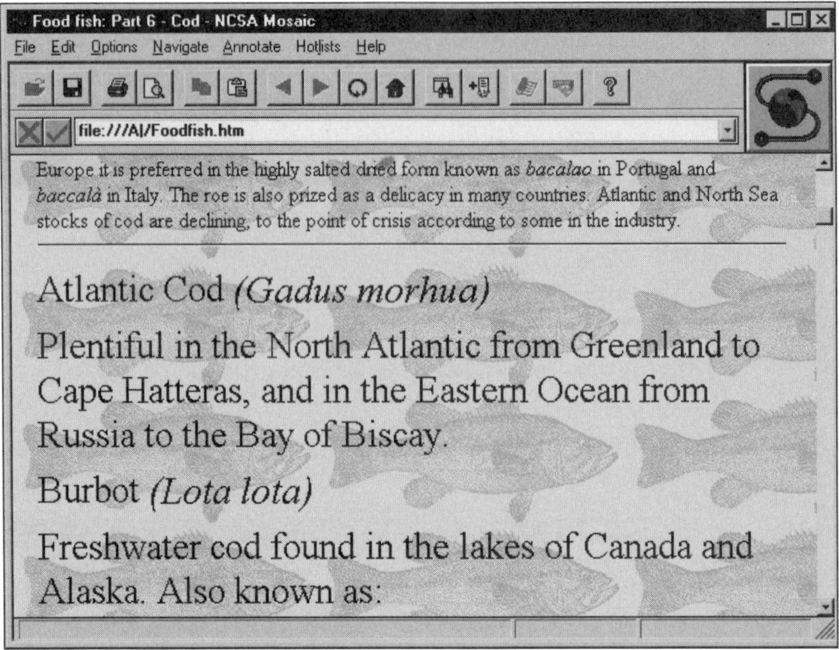

Figure 2-28: *Not according to Mosaic!*

The problem? Here's the source code (see if you can spot it):

```
<HTML>
<HEAD>
<TITLE>Food fish: Part 6 - Cod</TITLE>
</HEAD>
<BODY>
<P>Cod in its many variants is a staple of the diet of most
Northern Europeans. In Southern Europe it is preferred in the
highly salted dried form known as <I>bacalao</I> in Portugal
and <I>baccal&agrave;</I> in Italy. The roe is also prized as
a delicacy in many countries.
Atlantic and North Sea stocks of cod are declining, to the
point of crisis according to some in the industry.
</P>
```

```
<HR>
<H2>Atlantic Cod <I>(Gadus morhua)</I></H3>
<P>Plentiful in the North Atlantic from Greenland to Cape
Hatteras, and in the Eastern Ocean from Russia to the Bay of
Biscay.</P>
<H2>Burbot <I>(Lota lota)</I></H2>
<P>Freshwater cod found in the lakes of Canada and Alaska.
Also known as:</P>
<UL>
<LI>Ling</LI>
<LI>Eel pout</LI>
<LI>Lawyer fish</LI>
<LI>Lotte de rivi&egrave;re</LI>
</UL>
</BODY>
</HTML>
```

You could stare at this all morning and not spot the fact that the start and end tags of one of your headings do not match—the <H2> tag for "Atlantic cod" is followed by a </H3>.

Pre-flight Checks

Before you get your "finished" page on the Web, there are a few things you can do to guard against errors. First, obviously, you can look the code over *just one more time* to see if you can spot any errors. Then, you can make use of the built-in error-checking routines of your editor. Netscape's ordinary Document Source View often can reveal errors. Bad code that causes the browser to scratch its head will "blink" in the source code window.

If you're lucky enough to have a color card that allows several screen resolutions, check your pages at all widths—we'll be talking more about the effect of screen resolution on Web pages in Chapter 4.

TIP

If you have a color card that allows it, you can change your screen resolution in Windows 95 by double-clicking on "Display" in the Control Panel, then choosing Settings. (Or right click anywhere on the desktop and select Properties.) Adjust the control slider in Desktop Area. If there's no Desktop Area control slider, or if it has no effect even when you reboot the computer, then you have no choice of screen resolution.

Another recommended check before "publishing" is to view your page in whatever other Web browsers you have available, such as any of the various flavors of Mosaic, Microsoft's Internet Explorer, and *Lynx*, too, if possible. When you use Netscape extension tags, it's imperative to cross-check your pages with a different browser because they are guaranteed to look different, and you need to know *how* different. This cross-checking is a good habit to establish even when you're dealing with relatively "penny plain" pages.

HTML Validation Services

Another good way to check your Web pages is to use one of the several online HTML validation services. These services provide a Web address that offers you a form field where you can enter the URL of your page. A program at the remote site then downloads and parses your code line by line, reporting any syntax problems it finds. These invaluable services used to be no good until your page was published and you had a URL to refer them to, but the best of them have now added a generous input window for unpublished code. Just pop your entire source code—or just a section you wish to validate—onto your clipboard, call up the validation service, and drop it into the window (as you see in Figure 2-29). Don't worry—the parser can take far more code than the size of the input window seems to indicate before getting indigestion.

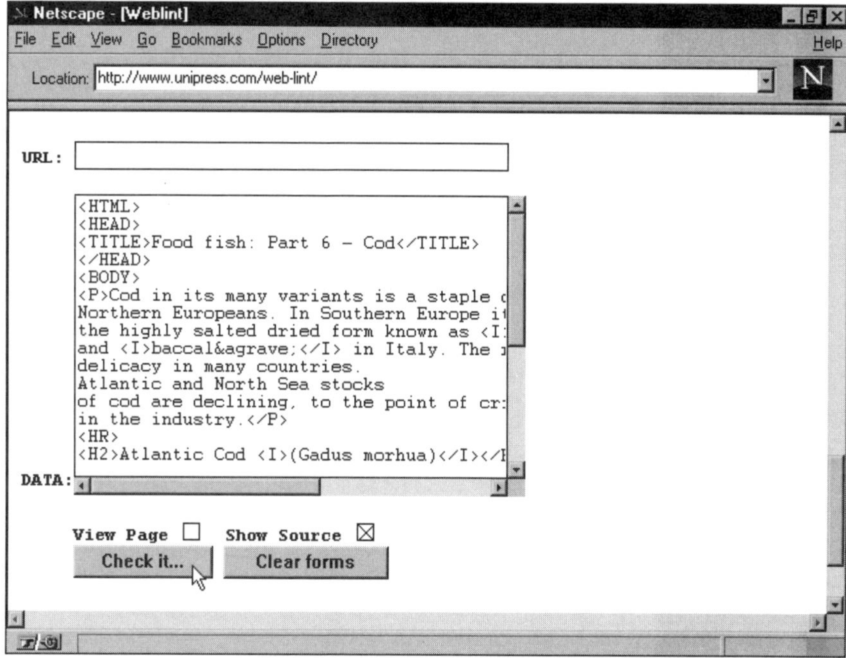

Figure 2-29: *The codfish code ready to submit to WebLint.*

Send It to the WebLint Cleaner

Perhaps the best known validation service is WebLint—a fine user interface designed by Clay Webster, making use of a code parser written by Neil Bowers. WebLint is at:

http://www.unipress.com/Web-lint

and it currently performs the following checks:

- Is basic document structure correct?
- Are there any unknown elements or element attributes?
- Do tags appear in the proper context within other elements?
- Do any elements overlap improperly?
- Does the document have a TITLE in the HEAD?
- Do IMG elements have ALT text?

- Are there any illegally nested elements?
- Are there any mismatched tags (e.g., <H1> ... </H2>)?
- Are any elements left unclosed (e.g., <H1> ...)?
- Are elements repeated that should only appear once?
- Are there any obsolete elements?
- Are the right number of quotation marks present in tags?
- Are headings ordered properly?
- Does any markup appear within comments (this can confuse some browsers)?
- Are tags used where attributes are expected (e.g., anchors)?
- Do all local anchor targets exist?
- Are there any potentially unsupported HTML 3.0 elements, such as TABLE, MATH, FIG, and the rest?

In addition, it will flag the case of tags if you wish, so your code can remain consistent with your house style. And just because it's somebody's pet peeve, it will also whine if you use anything like "click here" in anchor text.

Figure 2-30 shows WebLint's diagnosis of the coding error we presented earlier in this section. It took about 15 seconds.

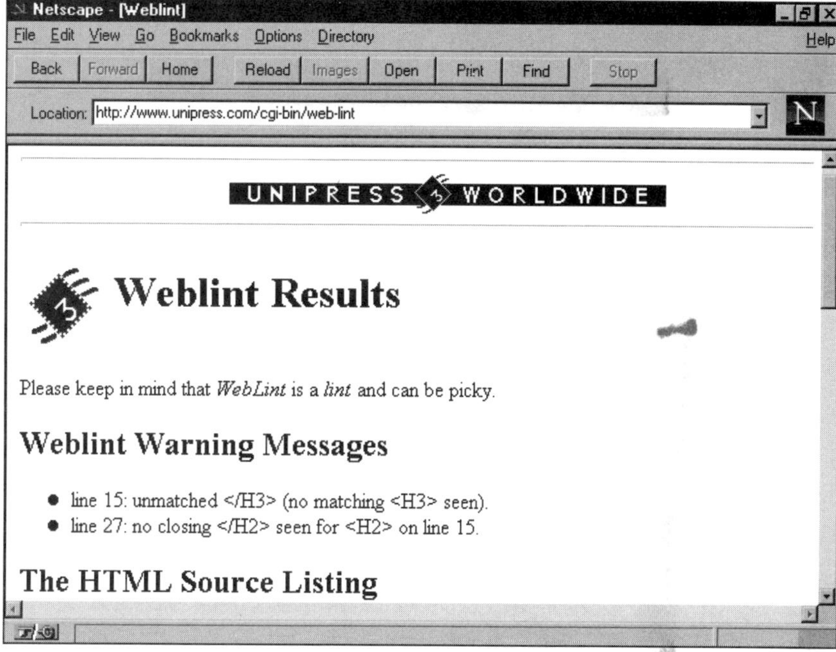

Figure 2-30: *WebLint finds the problem.*

Hold the Presses!

Once your code is up on the server and available for all the world to see and criticize, it's still worth checking. Web design is not like newspaper or book publishing, where you may have to live with your mistakes for a very long time. On the Web, correcting a little error is probably as simple as a three-minute FTP session.

Once you have a *bona fide* URL for your work, you can enter that into a validation service form field and have it checked. For pages that need very frequent updates, like events listings or school class schedules, the HaLSoft validation service has a suggestion for you.

HaLSoft, maintained by Mark Gaither of HAL Computer Systems, is at:

http://www.webtechs.com/html-val-svc

and its main page is essentially identical to WebLint's. But HalSoft will also accept correctly formatted input directly from your own page and use it to launch its code parser according to your hidden instructions. To make use of this service, add the following code to your page:

```
<FORM ACTION="http://www.hal.com/hal-bin/html-check.pl"
METHOD="POST" >
<INPUT NAME="recommended" VALUE="0" TYPE="hidden">
<INPUT NAME="level" VALUE="2" TYPE="hidden">
<INPUT NAME="input" VALUE="0" TYPE="hidden">
<INPUT NAME="esis" VALUE="0" TYPE="hidden">
<INPUT NAME="render" VALUE="0" TYPE="hidden">
<INPUT NAME="URLs" VALUE="YOUR URL HERE" TYPE="hidden">
<INPUT TYPE="submit" VALUE="Check my code">
</FORM>
```

If you're a newcomer to HTML, that may look like gobbledygook because this book doesn't get to forms until Chapter 9, "Forms, Feedback & cgi-bin." The fact is that, because practically every form field defined in that code fragment is designated "hidden," all you will see is a rectangular button on your page bearing the words "Check my code." Click on it, and the full power of HaLSoft will put your code to the test. Go to the HaLSoft page and click on "About" to get further information about how you can use the fields labeled "recommended," "level," "input," "esis," and "render" to customize the validation process.

TIP

As a general rule, it's unwise to incorporate blocks of code that you don't properly understand just because someone such as a book author told you it was a great idea. So if you don't understand the above code, perhaps it's prudent to hold off until you do.

Moving On

We've covered a lot of ground in this chapter, but if you've been trying things out as you go, you've probably discovered your learning curve beginning to make a sharp upward turn. By now you should have a solid background for everything else you'll learn in this book.

In the next chapter, we'll concentrate on the art of linking. Keeping in mind the idea of a complete Web site structure we introduced at the beginning of this chapter, we'll talk about how to lead visitors through your site with links, and how to link to different types of information available on the Internet.

3

Links, Links & More Links

Without links, the Web would lose most of its point. After all, the "HT" part of "HTML" is hypertext, and hypertext *is* links. It's possible, of course, to find plenty of examples of Web pages that do nothing but act as public billboards declaring some author's existence or yet-to-be-realized intentions. But personally we think these are as dry as yesterday's toast. The most interesting link out of there is usually the Back button.

In the last chapter we covered site design without being too specific about how to make the necessary links between the pages that make up your site. This chapter is your complete course about links. First we'll explain the anchor tag and its various attributes. Then we'll talk about making links between the files on your site and to other sites, being creative with your links, and about including other interesting resources on the Web using some specialized links.

Creating Links With the Anchor Tag

Because hypertext must link *from* somewhere *to* somewhere, it almost goes without saying that a link has to have two parts: a *source* and a *destination*. The essential HTML tag used to define a link's source and destination is <A>, the anchor. You use it to specify the word, phrase, or picture that is the source of your link, and also to identify where the link points to. The destination can be simply a different paragraph in the same document. Very often, it's a different file on the same site—but it can be an object that has no idea that it's the target of your link, such as a document on a different computer, a picture, an audio file, a movie, or some Internet object quite outside the Web. This chapter covers all of these possibilities.

HTML Tag

<A> ... </A>

The anchor tag is *essential* in defining a link's source and destination. What is placed between the <A> and the </A> becomes the active part of the user's screen—a word, a phrase, or an image to click on (or activate by choosing some other way) in order to hyperlink to the destination. The anchor tag must have either an HREF or NAME attribute. Other attributes are optional.

The attributes of <A> are:

HREF="[link destination]"—Hypertext REFerence: the file or resource to be accessed, in the form of a filename or complete URL

NAME="[bookmark]"—Link destination marker; used to identify a bookmark destination within a file

TARGET="[frame label]"—Identifies the window or frame this link should be sent to, when several diffferent browser windows or frames are known to be active (see Chapter 5, "Getting Stylish") (This is a Netscape extension, not yet recognized by other browsers.)

TITLE="[destination object description]"—An identifier for the object targeted by the link

The <A> tag is meaningless without at least one attribute, and it also requires the </A> end tag to close the statement. The TITLE attribute is not yet supported by Netscape, but may become important one day as a way of "popping up" a quick thumbnail description of the destination document. We'll get to NAME a bit later in this chapter, under "Bookmarks." The syntax you need to remember, and that you'll be inserting into your page code time after time, is:

```
<A HREF="destination">source</A>
```

The effect of that on your page is that "source" is visually identified as a hyperlink. The link style (how it is displayed) is user-dependent, but typically the source will be in a different color than regular text, and underlined.

If you use a dedicated HTML editor such as Netscape Gold, you won't have to worry about it because the code will be done for you. If you don't use a dedicated HTML editor, write that line on your wall in felt-tip pen, or scribble it on your monitor in grease pencil. Better still, have it tattooed on your left wrist. You're going to need it.

In Figure 3-1, we're using Netscape Gold to set up a text link to another file. The procedure is the same whatever the file type (image, sound, movie, or other): Position the cursor where you want the text to appear, choose the Link button, then type the link text directly in the box provided. Alternatively, you can type the text in the page first and format it as you please. Then select it and click the Link button. The Link Properties box will appear with the text already filled out, as in Figure 3-2.

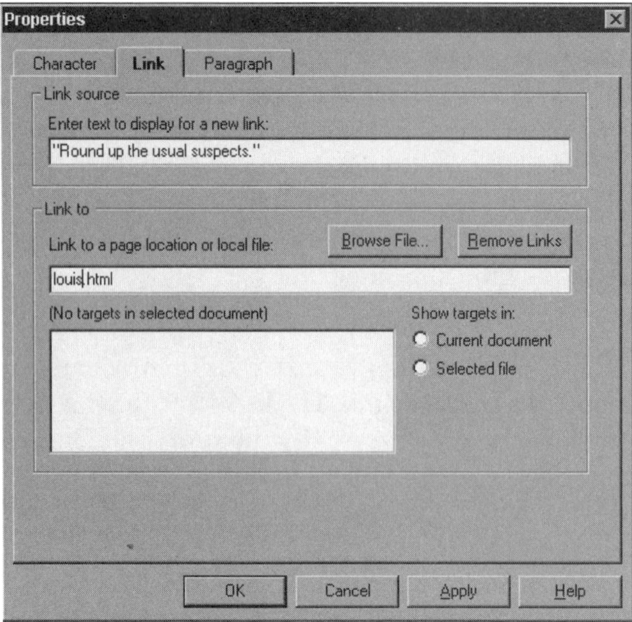

Figure 3-1: *Click the Make Link button to display a dialog box and set up a hyperlink in Netscape Gold's Editor.*

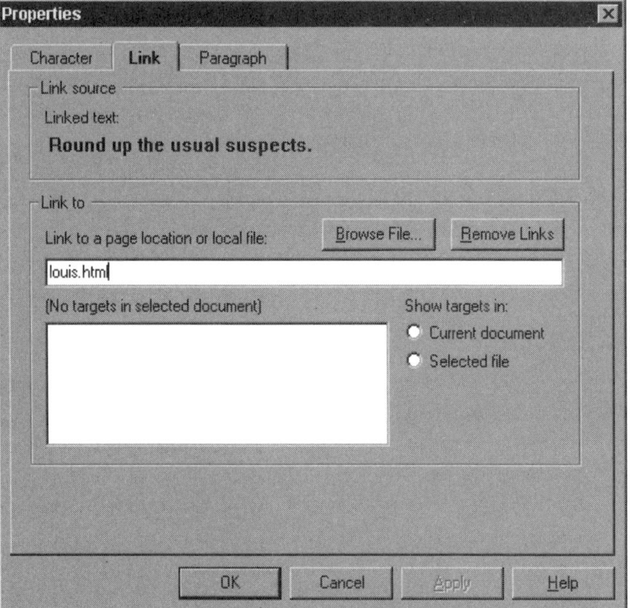

Figure 3-2: *Highlight existing text in your file, then choose the Link button, and you need only enter your link destination.*

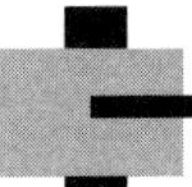

Link Source Types

The source of a link is, obviously, the items on your page that create the link. Since this can be words or pictures or both, let's consider link sources to be in three forms:

- **Text.** A word, phrase, or section of text forms an active link.
- **Pictorial.** An image is an active link.
- **Hybrid.** A combination of words and pictures makes the active link.

We'll explain each of these types separately.

Text Links

By far the most common type of link is the text link, where the source is a word or phrase. Almost anything is permissible here, from the economical...

```
<P>In case anybody wants to offer me a job, I've also in-
cluded my <A HREF="../margaret/resume.htm">C.V.</A>
...to the verbose...
```

```
<P>Another of our publications on this topic was <A
HREF="tv91.htm">Behavioral Problems Observed in Teenage
Inmates at the San Marcos Treatment Facility Attributable to
Exposure to Television Crime Stories.</A> This paper was
initially published... blah blah blah...
```

Note what we did with the spaces in the above example. The spaces between "was" and "Behavioral" and between "Stories." and "This" were kept outside the anchor. If they are inside, they normally get underlined along with the link source text, which looks ugly. If "...Crime Stories.</A>" ended a line, there would be no need to add an extra space. The normal space that HTML assumes at a line break would be correctly positioned outside the link source.

Link sources can become very minimal. At the FringeWare site, seen in Figure 3-3, each comma is a hyperlink source—and their destinations are surprising!

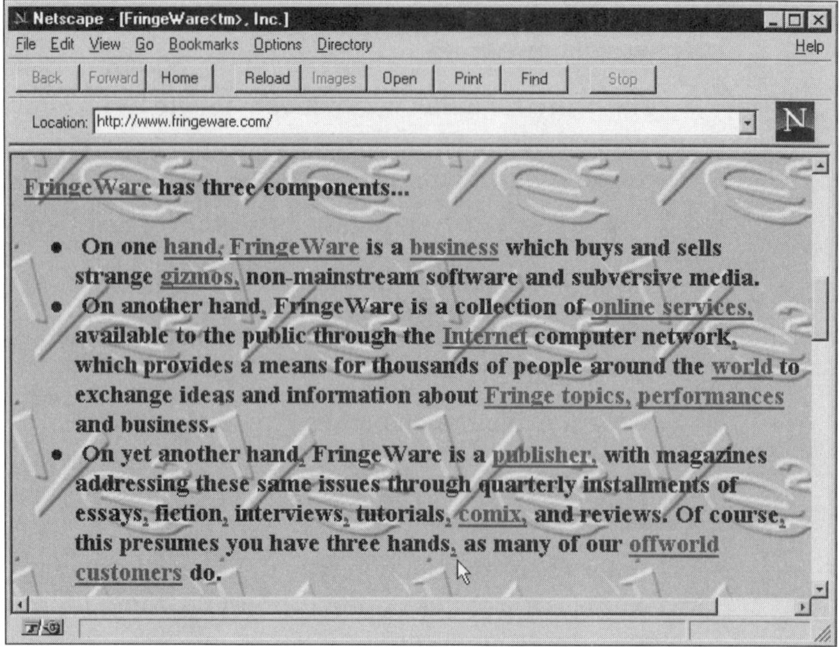

Figure 3-3: *Click on the commas on this iconoclastic Web page and you'll launch an audio file.*

One usage that is definitely considered lame is:

```
<P>To see my C.V., click <A HREF="../margaret/
resume.htm">here.</A>
```

It's scorned not only because it's trite, but because not everybody who uses your page will be clicking anything. There are in fact a few Web browsers that allow selection of hyperlinks with the keyboard.

Pictorial Links

The active part of your screen can be an image just as easily as a word or a phrase. Figure 3-4 shows an example of a link whose source is a *thumbnail* image—of a dinosaur, in this case:

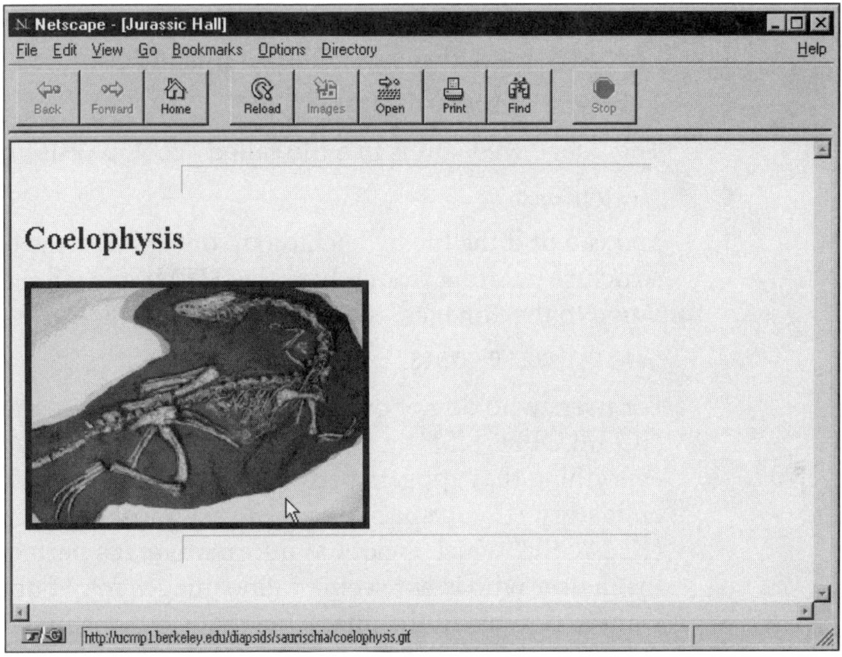

Figure 3-4: *"Thumbnail" image used as a link to a higher quality version of the same picture.*

The code can end up looking a bit scary because there's no text involved, but it's perfectly logical if you just keep in mind the basic structure of a link.

```
<A HREF="http://ucmp1.berkeley.edu/diapsids/saurischia/
coelophysis.gif">
<IMG SRC="../images/coelophysissmall.gif"
ALT="[COELOPHYSIS]"></A>
```

This code represents a very common situation in Web page design, in which a small "thumbnail" version of a picture is a link to a much bigger and better version of the same picture. The user gets a quick low-quality preview of what's available and can take the time to download the high-quality file if he or she chooses. Onscreen, the small image is normally surrounded by a border indicating that it's a link, and the border is whatever color has been assigned to links. Let's unpack that code piece by piece, starting in the middle.

```
<IMG........>
```

That's the piece that says, "Put an image here."

```
SRC=......coelophysissmall.gif
```

The image we want is in a file called "coelophysissmall.gif."

```
../images/
```

You can find the file by backing up one level in the directory structure (starting from where this HTML file is), then going back down to the "images" subdirectory.

```
ALT="[COELOPHYSIS]"
```

For users who do not or cannot view images, use the word "[COELOPHYSIS]" as the link source instead. The ALT text is everything that appears between the quotation marks, which are obligatory. (If you specify no ALT text, most browsers default to "[IMAGE]," which is not too informative. It's perfectly plausible that a user who is not seeing inline images might nevertheless want to download the image file that's the destination of this link.)

```
<A ......>.....</A>
```

That's the top-and-tail that says, "This is a hyperlink source."

```
HREF="http://ucmp1.berkeley.edu/diapsids/saurischia/
coelophysis.gif"
```

This is the destination of the link, just as for a text link. In this case, the destination is a much bigger version of the same picture, on a Web server at UC Berkeley.

The overall effect of that structure is that when a user selects the pictorial link, the high-quality image is sent, either for immediate display or for saving to a file in the user's own computer. The little thumbnail image is said to be *inline* because it's intended to be part of the page along with the text, but the bigger image is called an *external* image.

TIP

You need to exercise care when constructing an image link followed by text that is not part of the link source. All will be well if you abut the text immediately to the ">" closing the link tag—but if you allow a space or even a line break *to intervene, Netscape will often include a space as part of the link, resulting in an unwanted blue underline character on many users' screens.*

A whole different type of image link, in which different areas of the same image are links to different destinations, is called an *active image*. We'll be discussing active images at the end of Chapter 4, "All About Images."

Making an Image Link With Netscape Gold

Once you put an image into your file, it's easy to create an image link with Netscape Gold's Editor. Here's how:

First use the right mouse button to click on the image, and choose "Create Link" from the pop-up menu shown in Figure 3-5.

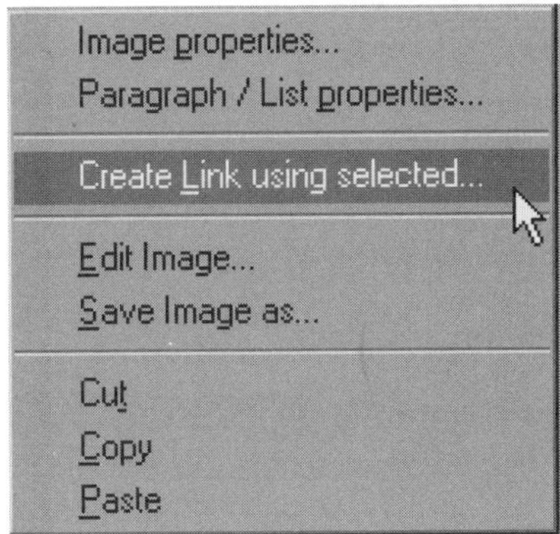

Figure 3-5: *Setting up an Image Link in Netscape Gold.*

The dialog box shown in Figure 3-6 pops up, ready for you to enter the link destination either as a local file path/name or as a full URL.

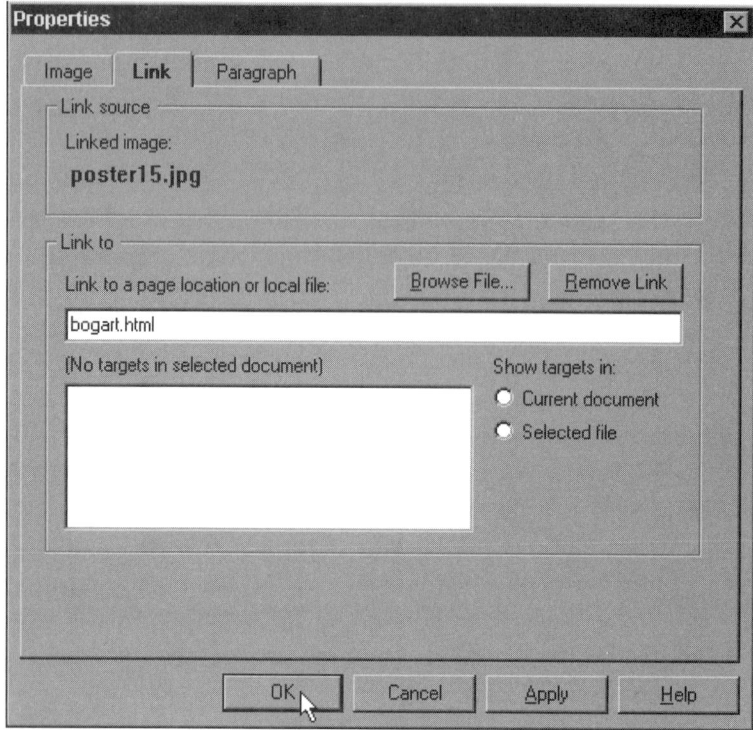

Figure 3-6: *Fill out the link destination in the dialog box.*

HYBRID LINKS

The source of a hyperlink can be both an image *and* a piece of text. Here's a piece of code from a recipe listing page—the mouth-watering picture and the recipe name in Figure 3-7 are equally valid links to the page containing the actual recipe, and both are rendered in link color style on the user's screen.

```
<P><A HREF="stgrpep.htm"><IMG SRC="/cook/pix/bifstek.gif"
ALT="[ILLUS.]"> Steak with green pepper sauce</A>
```

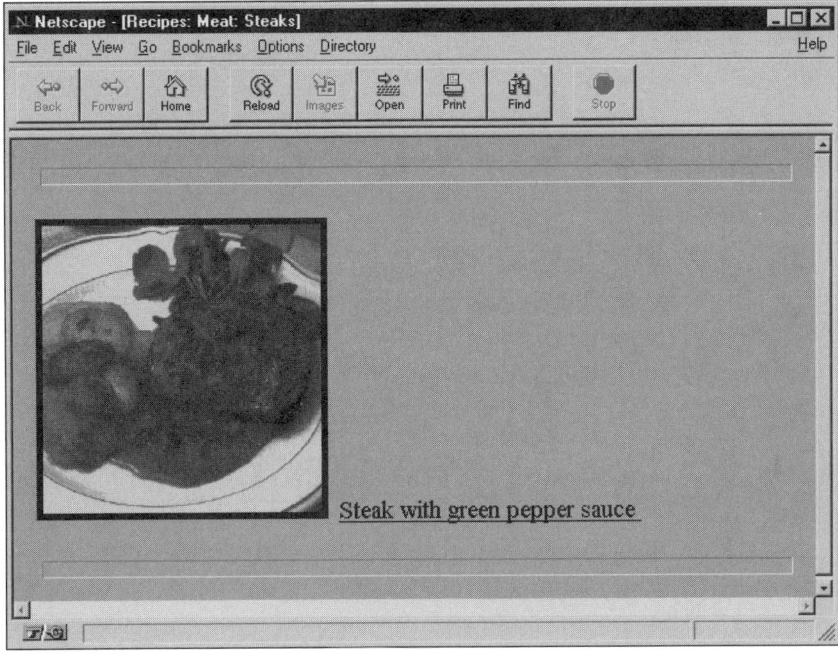

Figure 3-7: *Hybrid link to a recipe. The link destination would be the same whether the mouse cursor was on the picture or the link text.*

TIP

When you create a hybrid link like that, Netscape actually considers the entire rectangular area enclosing the image and the phrase as "active." Other browsers only activate the space actually occupied by the image and the words.

Link Colors: Who's in Charge?

A Netscape user can select his or her own color rendering for straight text, links, and followed links in the Preferences | Fonts dialog box. It's extremely useful to have a color code for followed links, so that in a complex search through many Web pages you can easily see which roads you've already traveled.

In the "Backgrounds & Text Colors" section of the next chapter we explain how the Web page designer can set his or her own style for the color of text, links, visited links (just another name for followed links), and active links. Never forget, however, that the user has the last word on this! Even if you specify these colors, user-set preferences can override your design.

All of the links we've described so far are assumed to be "one-way" links—that is, the user hits a dead end when he arrives at Margaret's résumé, the sociology paper, the dinosaur, the Bogart page, or the steak recipe. The only way out is the Back button on the browser.

AVOIDING THE BACK BUTTON BLUES

Successful Web site design is a little like successful architecture. A really well-functioning site allows people to move through it as easily and logically as they move from room to room of a well-designed house. They must be able to find a way in, a way out, and ways to move from one place to another. Simply relying on people to use the Back button to move around is like expecting them to walk backwards out of the room. That's why doors and hallways were invented. On the Web, you can make magic hallways that take you from basement to attic in a single step—but they mustn't be overused or the whole logic of the house will break down.

The doors and hallways of your Web site are the links. Naturally on your first page, the home page, you'll include links to the other pages on your site you want people to visit. But many page designers forget to give visitors the same or similar options on subsequent pages.

Link destination types come in four basic varieties:

- **Relative link.** A link to another document on the same site or host computer.

- **Bookmark link.** A link to specific destinations within the same or a different document (usually but not necessarily on the same site).

- **External link.** Link to a file on another site at a remote computer.
- **Link to a different protocol.** Includes links to Internet services other than the Web, such as FTP, Gopher, and Telnet.

We'll look at all of these separately, paying special attention to links within your own site.

Relative or Local Links

Relative links are the links you make to other files on your site or on your host computer. If you've got a clear outline of the file structure on your Web site, as we discussed in "Basic Web Site Design" at the beginning of Chapter 2, making relative links to the other files on your site will be easy. Let's deal with the mechanics first, and then go on to some more artistic concerns you should keep in mind.

The Mechanics of Local Links

Besides an overall flow chart for your Web site, you need to keep in mind the directory structure for your files. If your files are all in one directory, your relative links will be easy: You need only use the filename, as in:

```
<A HREF="file.html">anchor text</A>
```

This is the simplest case, in which the page containing the link and the file that's the destination of the link are both in the same directory, the "current" directory. Of course, the "file.html" in the above example might as easily be "image.jpg" or "soundbite.au" or "movie.qtw" (but more on those latter types in Chapter 8, "Multimedia & the Web").

In a larger Web site, you may find it convenient to break down your files into different directories and subdirectories. Or on a local network you may link together resources that reside in different places on the network. In that case, link paths will be specified in relation to the current directory.

When creating a Web site on your own computer that you intend to transfer to a host computer for publishing on the Web, you should create the same directory structure on your computer that you will use on the host computer. Then when you transfer everything to the host computer your links will all work the same as they did on your desktop.

Now let's review the forms the anchor command can take.

If the file is in a subdirectory of the current directory, the link will look like this:

```
<A HREF="path/filename.html">anchor text</A>
```

Path specifies the directories that define the location of the file. In the above example, it represents a single directory below the current directory, but the file you are linking to could be several directory levels down.

If the file is not located in a subdirectory of the current directory, your link might look like this:

```
<A HREF="../path/file.html">anchor text</A>
```

This tells the server to back up one level in the directory structure and follow the given path to the correct subdirectory to find the file.

You can direct the server to go back each level necessary to reach the branching point or the root (each "../" backs up one level), then give a complete path to the target file, as in:

```
<A HREF="../../path/file.html">anchor text</A>
```

The above example directs the server to back up two directories, to follow the given path. Instead of using relative links like this, you could use a complete URL to the file (an absolute link), as you would for an external link, which is probably the safest way to avoid confusion but usually incurs a performance penalty.

Here are some general tips about making links on your site:

- Make your filenames clear and simple.
- Know the file naming conventions in effect on your server (whether you're restricted to eight characters and which extension is required, .HTML or .HTM).

- Make sure you include the full path to your file if it's in a different directory.
- When in doubt, use a complete URL.

TIP

There's another point to consider when deciding whether to use a relative path to the file you're linking to or an absolute link in the form of a complete URL. Many browsers, including Netscape, allow for saving graphics along with Web pages, but the resulting links will not function correctly if the browser does not automatically convert relative links. Absolute links may be a better choice if you want to allow for easier downloading.

The Aesthetics of Local Links

Back in Chapter 2, we discussed the advisability of keeping your files relatively small for loading convenience. This is generally good practice, but like all rules, it's made to be broken. The fact is that probably 80 percent of the visitors to most sites never get beyond the first page, and "hits" diminish considerably after that. Why this is so may have to do with the peripatetic nature of Web surfers. Or the lack of appeal of most home pages. Or impatience. Or whatever you might imagine.

The nature of the information you're presenting and your own sense of the type of people who will be accessing your site should dictate how you present your information. Most people who are not trained writers or marketing experts are not accustomed to keeping in mind their audience. So what we have to say about this can be summed up succinctly: Put yourself in your audience's shoes.

Do you have information that's liable to appeal to different groups of people? Then break it up and give them a choice. Do you just want people to stay at your site long enough to be impressed by your graphics and subliminal (or not so subliminal) marketing message? Then put as much as you can, and certainly all the important stuff, up front, and let your supplementary pages be for those surfers with more curiosity and time.

. Are you presenting instructional or other material that has a clear hierarchy? It might lend itself naturally to being broken down into smaller files. But consider also whether you expect people to download or print out the material. Downloading and printing out many small files can be a big nuisance. You might even consider breaking down your files for easy online reading, but making a larger, comprehensive file available for downloading and printing, so your visitors can choose. This would be particularly considerate of those whose online time might be limited for one reason or another.

TIP

Everyone knows that an online habit can be expensive if you're paying by the minute, but many people don't know that in some parts of the world this is exacerbated by high phone charges and/or long-distance requirements. If you're thinking of reaching an audience in Europe or other parts of the world, you'd do well to consider this: Many people will dash online simply to grab the files they want, then read them offline.

SOME DOS & DON'TS OF LINKS

Now, remember what we said about some people using a side door or a back door to your site, if they find some part of it that's useful? Let's consider the Web page shown in Figure 3-8.

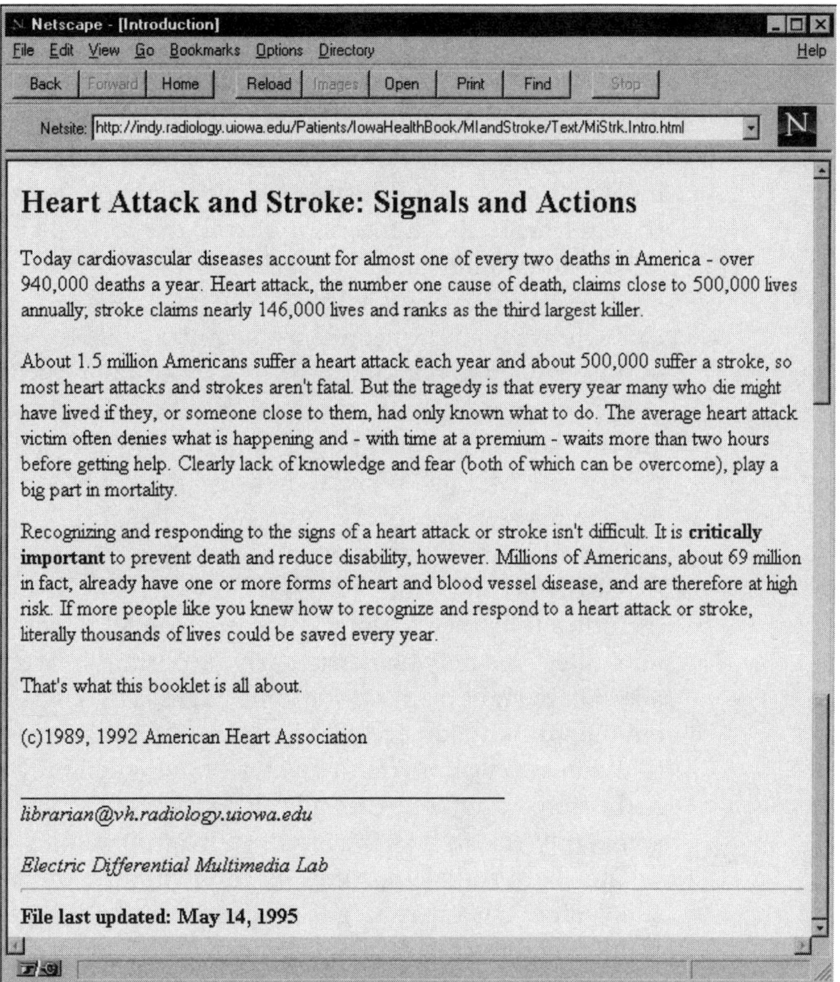

Heart Attack and Stroke: Signals and Actions

Today cardiovascular diseases account for almost one of every two deaths in America - over 940,000 deaths a year. Heart attack, the number one cause of death, claims close to 500,000 lives annually; stroke claims nearly 146,000 lives and ranks as the third largest killer.

About 1.5 million Americans suffer a heart attack each year and about 500,000 suffer a stroke, so most heart attacks and strokes aren't fatal. But the tragedy is that every year many who die might have lived if they, or someone close to them, had only known what to do. The average heart attack victim often denies what is happening and - with time at a premium - waits more than two hours before getting help. Clearly lack of knowledge and fear (both of which can be overcome), play a big part in mortality.

Recognizing and responding to the signs of a heart attack or stroke isn't difficult. It is **critically important** to prevent death and reduce disability, however. Millions of Americans, about 69 million in fact, already have one or more forms of heart and blood vessel disease, and are therefore at high risk. If more people like you knew how to recognize and respond to a heart attack or stroke, literally thousands of lives could be saved every year.

That's what this booklet is all about.

(c)1989, 1992 American Heart Association

librarian@vh.radiology.uiowa.edu

Electric Differential Multimedia Lab

File last updated: May 14, 1995

Figure 3-8: *This Web page would be even more useful with the addition of a link.*

We found this site by doing a search for heart attack information on the Web. But without a link, it's difficult to figure out where we are. The only recourse is to knock the filename and maybe a directory or two off the end of the URL to see if we can get to the root.

In fact, this page is one of five on heart attack and stroke information, which is part of the extensive online patient informational materials on the otherwise excellent Virtual Hospital site posted by the University of Iowa. (We've had occasion to recommend this site before.) It could have been improved if there were a couple of links at the bottom of this page to point people back to the main page for heart attack information and the Virtual Hospital home page—and an internal link on the words "signs of a heart attack or stroke" would be very helpful.

There are many conceivable examples of Web pages that might tempt viewers to bookmark them so they can return directly later. People often pick up interesting URLs through a reference on another site or a Usenet newsgroup, or they may be referred to a page while using a Web searcher, and it's not always the home page that's referenced.

To avoid the "Oz syndrome"—the sense you've been picked up by a tornado and dropped who knows where—it's wise to always include a reference to your home page on all the other pages on your site. This may be particularly important if you're worried about copyright or credit for your pages. There's nothing to stop anyone from making a link to any one of your pages that appeals to them, and visitors don't always know when they've left one site and entered another. After all this work, you wouldn't want somebody else to take the credit (or blame), would you?

The "Labyrinth syndrome" is another common failing of Web site design. On a very large and complex site, where you envision visitors' interests diverging in various ways, you don't want to present too many choices at once, but at the same time you don't want visitors to feel trapped in a labyrinth from which it seems there's no exit. It can be very frustrating to wend your way down into the basement of a site and then want to go back to an interesting page you saw and not be able to find your way back. Consider including a site directory, which you can link to repetitively, or place links to major branches at strategic places.

Another technique that is becoming popular on the Web is an active image that serves as a banner for your site, which you can click to access other areas of the site. We'll be talking more about making active images in Chapter 4, "All About Images."

The San Jose Mercury News (Figure 3-9) goes one better than this by providing a pull-down menu by which you can access different "sections" of the online newspaper. This is actually a very simple version of a form, which we'll show you how to do in Chapter 9, "Forms, Feedback & cgi-bin."

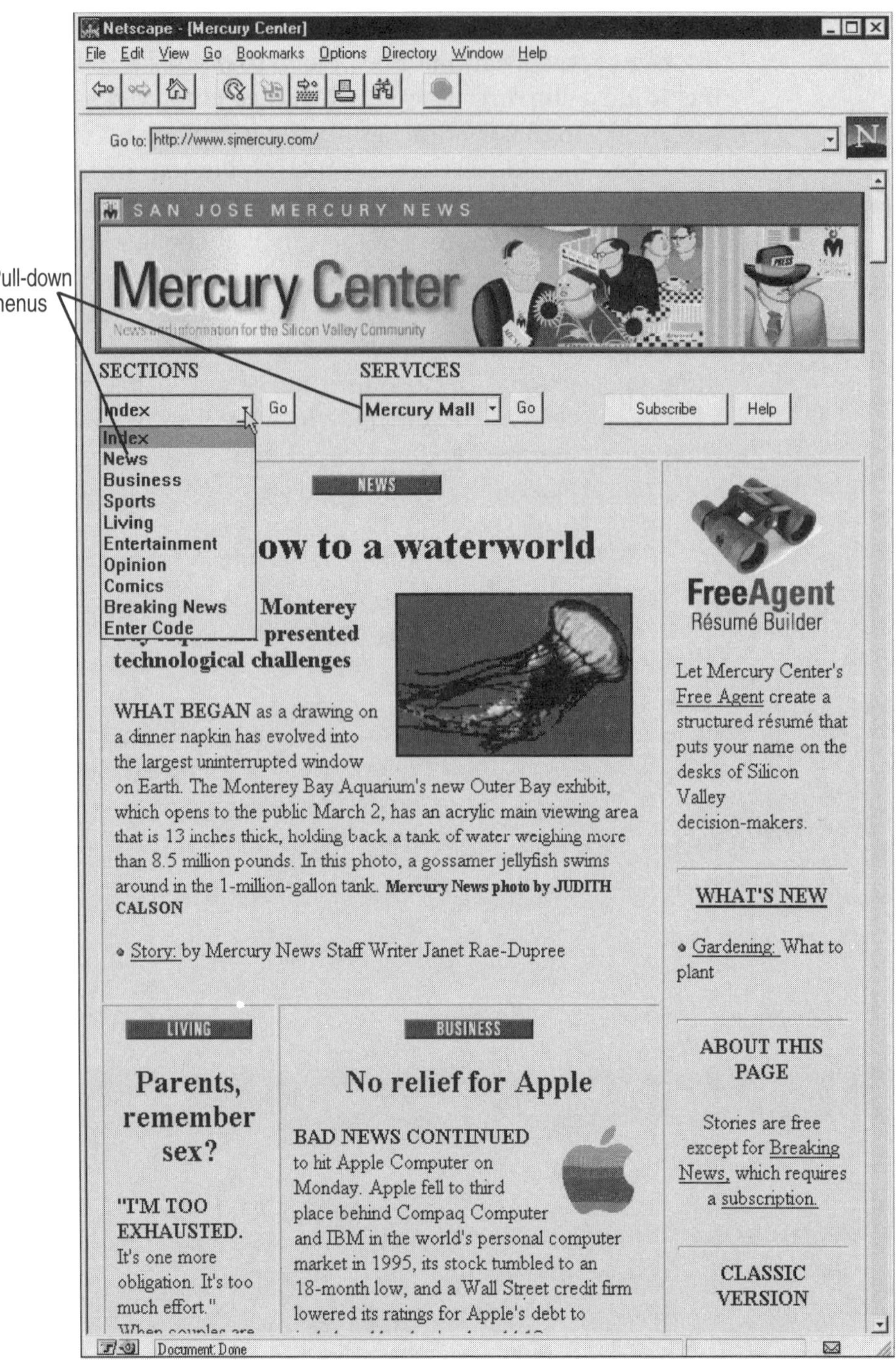

Figure 3-9: *Pull-down menus at the San Jose Mercury News Web site allow you to choose where you want to go.*

Once you have your site laid out and most of your pages done, try doing a walk-through as if you were visiting it for the first time. Think about what your visitors are liable to want to do from any point, and provide the appropriate links.

Here's a list of useful tips to keep in mind as you design your site links:

- Always give your visitors someplace to go—at the very minimum, a Home button.
- Make sure your visitors have choices, but don't overwhelm them with too many at once.
- Clearly indicate where links go (unless mystery is your deliberate policy).
- If your site is very complex, try to give visitors an idea of the overall structure as they go through it.
- Sign or otherwise clearly identify all your pages.

Bookmarks

Bookmarks are convenient links you can make to particular points in your documents. They can be very useful when you have a large file that you don't want to break up into smaller ones, or when you want to cross-reference information in different documents.

The Mechanics of Bookmarks

Bookmark links require two components: first, the source link, and second, a destination marker. The source link is the same as any other relative link, with one addition: a hash mark (#) followed by the name you give to your bookmark. The # is what's known technically as a *fragment identifier,* and whatever follows it is a *URL fragment*. Let's take an example:

```
<P>The <A HREF="treatment.html#sideeffects">side effects</A>
of this medication can be of concern with older patients.
```

The destination of this link is a section on side effects in a file called "treatment.html." So, the destination is marked by placing a corresponding tag, or bookmark, in the target file. Here's how the bookmark is marked up, followed by a "ready reference" to bookmark mechanics.

```
<A NAME="sideeffects"></A>
<P>Side effects may include sleepiness, loss of concentration,
and mild nausea.
```

HTML Tag

<A HREF="[target file]#fragment">bookmark text </A>

The source link is a typical link, with the addition of a hash mark (#) and fragment to reference the bookmark destination. If the bookmark destination is in the same file as the source link, the source link will simply contain "#fragment" as the HREF; as in, <A HREF="#fragment"> .... </A>. If the bookmark destination is in a different file from the source link, the # and fragment are added to the end of the filename.

<A NAME="bookmark"> ... </A>

The bookmark itself identifies a target point in a document for a hyperlink, which may or may not enclose text, but requires the end tag.

The end tag </A> is required, even if, as in the above case, the bookmark contains nothing, but only marks a point in the file. The bookmark may, however, contain any amount of text (we could as easily have put the </A> after the sentence), but it's not particularly useful for the bookmark to wrap around a large amount of text, because the browser will simply be directed to the point at which it finds the start tag. And any other bookmarks within this block would not work properly.

It is perfectly possible to create a link to a bookmark in a file at another site, if there's a convenient bookmark in the file. (You might discover this when looking at the source code.) However, if the page is not under your control there's always the possibility it will be changed or deleted without your knowing about it. In general, if the browser does not find the bookmark, it does not signal the user but simply presents the last screenful of information from the file as it finishes its search.

The Aesthetics of Bookmarks

Bookmarks are obviously convenient if you decide to keep a substantial amount of information together in one file. You can create a "table of contents" at the top of the file with bookmark links allowing the reader to jump to each section.

But bookmarks can also be used quite creatively within your site to cross-reference material. With a little clever bookmark management you can significantly reduce repetition and clutter on your Web site. Why say something three or four times, when you can say it once and provide convenient hyperlinks to that information whenever appropriate?

Figures 3-10 and 3-11 show setting up bookmark links in two files of an entertainment calendar. From the current schedule of theatrical events in Figure 3-10, visitors can access a season schedule in the file shown in Figure 3-11. The bookmark anchor tag takes them directly to the part of the file they're interested in.

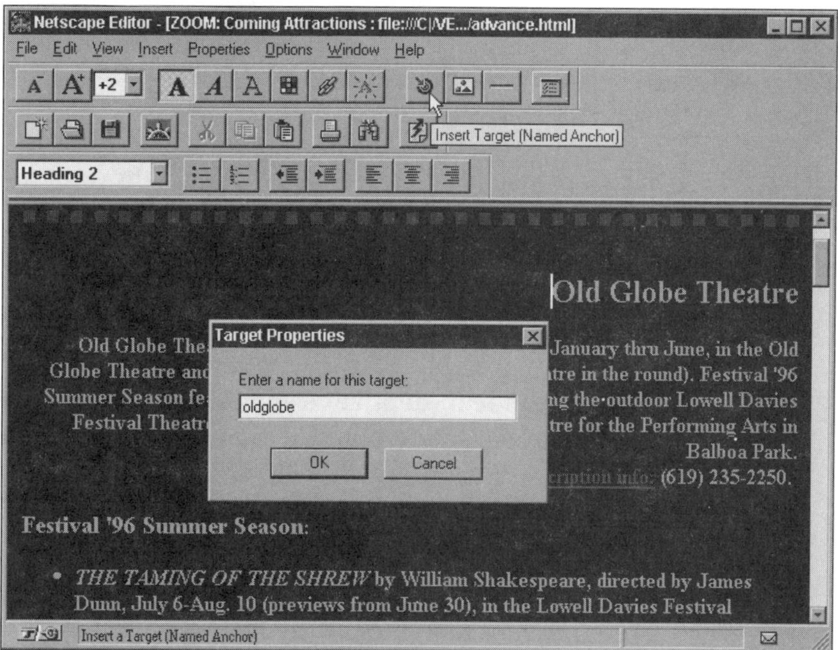

Figure 3-10: *Using Netscape Gold's Editor, we make a target in this file...*

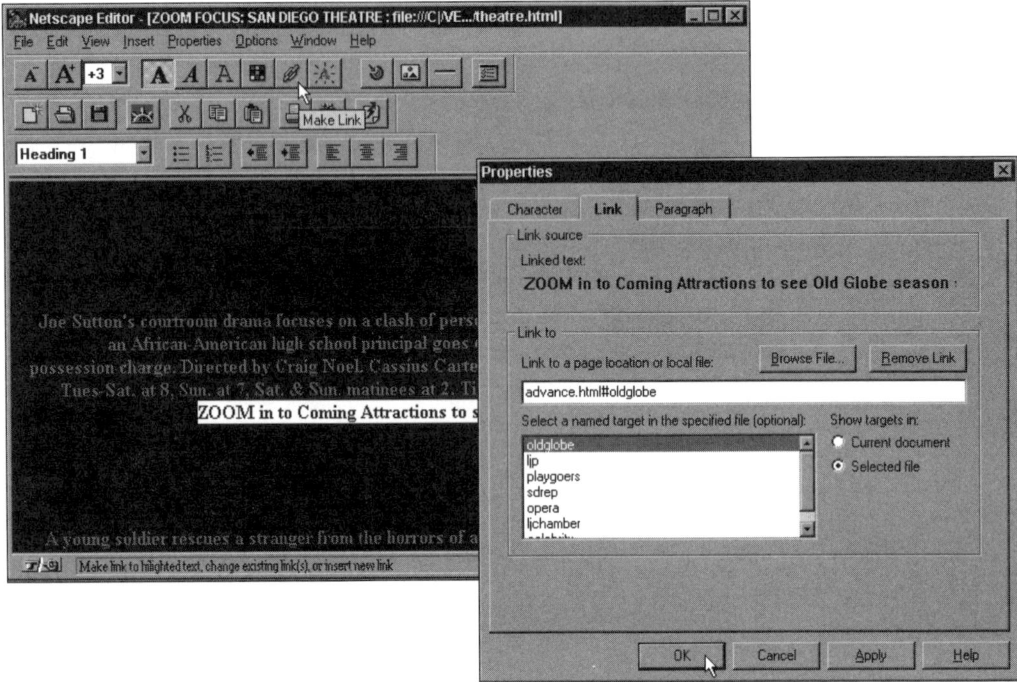

Figure 3-11: *...and set up a bookmark link to the target in this file.*

Here are just a few creative uses you might want to make of bookmarks:

- Create an easy index to material in one file or several files.
- Cross-reference material.
- Provide "jumping off points" for different uses or interests.
- Provide in-depth explanations or subsidiary material (similar to footnotes) without cluttering up your files.

EXTERNAL LINKS

External links are the links you make to other resources on the Web. The most common form of external link is to another Web page. But the destination of a link can also be a special resource like an FTP site or a Gopher menu. The mechanics are the same, although the URL addresses will differ.

The Mechanics of External Links

By way of introduction to this section, it's perhaps worth reminding ourselves about the anatomy of a URL. The complete address of a Web document, such as...

```
http://meteora.ucsd.edu:80/~norman/paris/index.html
```

...is in five parts, as follows:

```
http://
```

The protocol. In the section on "Specialized Links" we'll describe what else besides HTTP this might be, but for now we'll stick with HTTP.

```
meteora.ucsd.edu
```

The hostname of the computer where the document is stored. This address is registered by the site administrator with the Network Information Center so that it can be located by other servers on the Net. InterNIC assigns a numeric address to the site, which is the actual form that other computers use. So far as other computers are concerned, the address might be something like 199.2.50.5, and you could substitute that "IP address" in the URL without invalidating it. There is *no* obligation for sysadmins to use the "www" prefix for a Web server's address—it's just a convention. Often when the address is aliased through a registered domain name the "www" component is missing, as the host computer will interpret the domain name into the full address. The hostname must include no spaces, and certain other symbols are prohibited also.

```
:80
```

The port number on the host computer for information exchange. Eighty is the default for HTTP data, so it is usually omitted. You will see other port numbers occasionally, like :8000 and :8080, and if you have difficulty connecting to an http address it will *sometimes* help to add that redundant ":80".

```
~norman/paris/
```

The directory path to the document. The tilde ("~"), which you see very often in URLs, is a UNIX shell feature invoking a shortcut to a user area. Most Web servers interpret this, correctly, as a request to cross-link from the server's own directory tree to the users' area of the standard UNIX structure. From that point on, the directory structure is under a user's personal control—in this case user "norman." Many NCSA-type servers are set up to link direct to the subdirectory *public_html*.

```
index.html
```

...is, at last, the actual filename of the document.

When you make a link from your Web page to another document, you need all of the above information in the form of a complete URL, for example:

```
<P>Get the latest stats and game info for the<A HREF="http://
www2.nando.net/baseball/bbs/bbhome/lad.html">Los Angeles
Dodgers.</A>
```

There's an exception to that rule, however; often, when you're accessing a site's home page, you can leave out the filename, as in the following:

```
<P>See <A HREF="http://www.movielink.com/">Movielink</A> for
movie listings in your area.
```

This is because the Web server has a defined default file (usually "index.html" or "default.htm,"depending on the type of server). If the home page for the site takes this default filename, the server will deliver this file if no other file is specified. In our main example, since the file we want is "index.html" we can simply enter:
http://meteora.ucsd.edu:80/~norman/paris/
and we'll be served the right file. When using a URL without a filename you may have occasionally come across a page called "Index of ...." and a list of files that looks like an FTP directory. This is because the person responsible for that site failed to provide a default file.

TIP

Notice the final forward slash we added following "paris." The slash serves as a "terminator" to the address. Technically, any URL that does not end in an actual filename must *end in a slash—but Netscape and most other Web browsers no longer insist on it in practice.*

The Aesthetics of External Links

Links are the very engine of evolution on the Web. They're also the equivalent of conferencing and networking, a way of joining an International Association of Like-Minded Individuals for which you pay no dues and swear no loyalty oath.

We've all seen those obligatory pages of "cool sites" and "hot links" full of the author's whimsy, so let's make it clear that we're not talking about that kind of page. We're talking about using related resources that can enhance your Web site by pointing people to places where they can get complimentary information.

Spend a little time before or after you design your Web page (preferably before) to search for other pages and information related to your project. You might find that someone else has already done the hard work in cataloging something you were dreading doing, so you can just make a convenient link and save yourself the work. If *Enya* lyrics are your passion, for instance, you'll find that listing them on your page is like re-planting a garden that's already fully flourishing elsewhere. Or maybe you'll find that everybody's just waiting for you to do it—and once you've done your investigation you'll know where to go to get people to link back to your site.

Just as a matter of courtesy, it's polite to drop e-mail to the author of any page you're planning to reference. Later you'll be hoping people will do the same for you, so you can keep track of where your visitors are coming from and make sure those links are updated when necessary. Which brings us to one more important point: Check those external links regularly! Outdated links begin to smell after a month or two. And once people discover your links don't work, they may start distrusting the rest of the information on your site.

Tacking on Search Data

One more "optional extra" of an HTTP URL is a *query string* specifying a shortcut to a data page that a user would not normally arrive at without filling out a form (see Chapter 9, "Forms,

Feedback & cgi-bin"). A query string is preceded by a question mark, tacked onto the end of a URL. For example, "http://www.dealernet.com" is a very interesting page that links auto dealers all over the USA. (See Figure 3-12.) The page offers a whole series of form fields and check boxes, by which users can zero in on their particular area of interest. If you know what you're doing, all of those decisions can be "pre-made" with a query string such as:

```
http://www.dealernet.com:80/cgi-bin/
texhtml?form=models.one&modno=383&modmanu=Land+Rover&modhome=/
cars/95/land-rover/l_rover.htm
```

That example will take you straight to a list of 1995-model Land Rovers.

The sure way to get such a complicated URL right, of course, is to use the forms on the page you're interested in to go all the way to the final page. Then the whole URL including the query string will be available in your location window for copying and pasting via the Windows clipboard. If you're using Netscape Gold, you can drag and drop the destination straight into the editor to create a hyperlink.

If you choose to include that type of pre-searched URL in one of your Web pages, check its validity *frequently.* Sites that feature user-choice pathways like DealerNet are liable to change their pathways around quite often. They have no way of knowing that your page references their data, and would certainly feel no obligation to inform you of changes even if they did know.

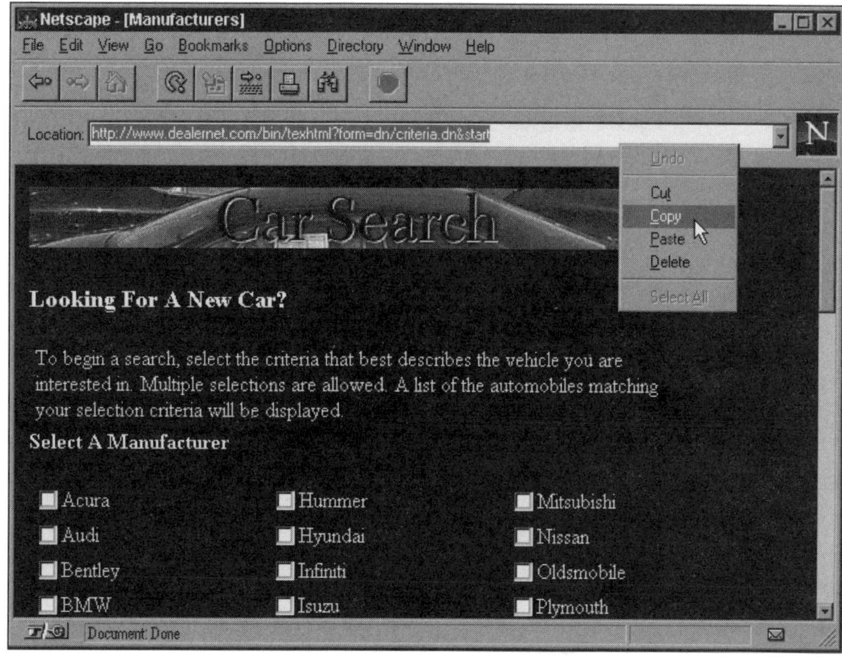

Figure 3-12: *Search for your dream car on DealerNet, then copy the URL string that makes the search in anticipation of that big check.*

This kind of link can be especially useful when you want to include information from a wide database, while narrowing it down to a particular area, such as local resources instead of national ones. One example might be a national movie database that allows you to search for movies playing in your area. If you wanted to link to this resource for just your area, you could search for "Boston," for example, then copy that search string into a link.

Links to Other Protocols

Ninety-nine percent of external link destinations are to other documents on the Web, using the Web's own protocol, HTTP. A Universal Resource Locator (URL), however, does its best to live up to its rather presumptuous name by allowing you, a Web page author, to reference Internet resources other than HTTP documents in your links. If you know how, you can in fact address most Internet resources directly from a Web page, and several more indirectly via so-called "gateways" to such resources as Finger and Archie. The only Internet resource that's unreachable by URL is Internet Relay Chat (IRC)—and even that can be brought to the Netscape screen through a kind of gateway.

FTP

Including a link to an FTP site is a good way to provide your Web site visitor access to files of interest. Figure 3-13 shows the correct way to make a hyperlink to an FTP resource.

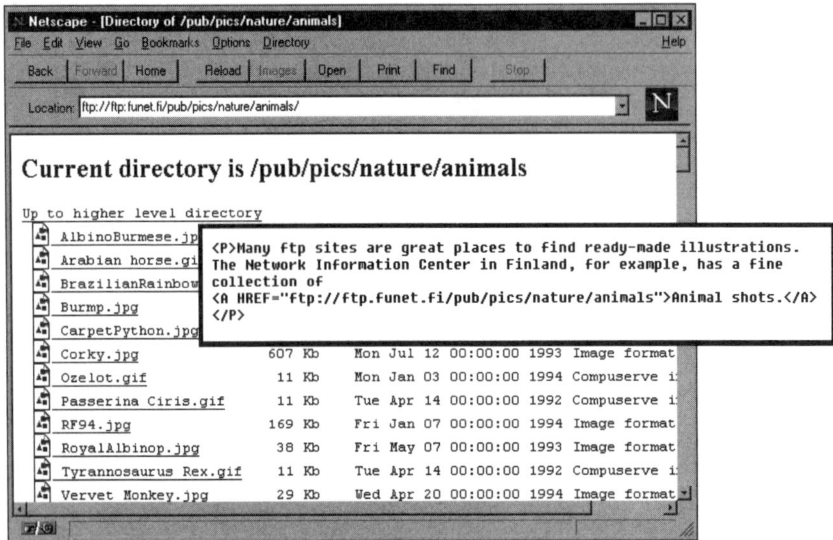

Figure 3-13: *Resource brought into the Netscape window by anonymous FTP, with the code that invoked it.*

In this example, the intention is to link to a directory and allow the user to make his or her own choice, but the URL could be extended to an actual file, such as:

```
ftp://ftp.funet.fi/pub/pics/nature/animals/Whale_flukes.gif
```

In that case, the response would be to display the actual picture in the Netscape content window. Other binary file types would be handled in whatever way the user's preferences were set.

A URL with the ftp:// protocol is a possible use of the login:password@ option. That way, a successful hyperlink could be made to a non-anonymous FTP server—but the password would then be public!

That might not be as crazy as it sounds. Not all sites are configured for anonymous FTP login, so the password might be just a formality needed to satisfy site procedure rather than security. Commercial sites might want to provide several possible login:password combinations, in order to deal with different classes of visitors in different ways, without any of them being actually secret. At any rate, the way to write a passworded URL is:

```
ftp://login:password@ftp.thissite.com/path/file.ext
```

Dragging & Dropping Links

The type of complicated URLs you're liable to run across when making links to other protocol are a perfect example of something that the Netscape Gold Editor makes easy for you. You can drag and drop a link directly from one document to another. Click and hold down the mouse cursor, drag the mouse to the location you want it in the new document, then release. The link code and text will be inserted intact in the new document. If you like, you can edit the link text onscreen. Simply click to put the cursor on the text and make your changes.

Gopher

When hyperlinks are made to FTP resources, the Netscape browser makes its best guess at the type of file that's being transferred, and automatically selects the ASCII or binary transfer protocol as apparently needed. A URL with the gopher:// protocol, however, can actually contain coded information about the file type in the form of a *resource identifier (RI) code.* This can be important because the variety of possible file types that may be accessed via Gopher servers is very great, and includes transfers to other services such as Telnet.

Following the RI code, a *selector string* is usually appended to a Gopher URL, which will auto-select from the first Gopher menu accessed. The following URL will access the Gopher server at the National Institutes of Health in Bethesda, MD, shown in Figure 3-14, and display the directory of Cancernet, an information service and database about cancer research. The RI code 11 means a directory, and the selector string takes this URL down the same path you would follow if you logged on to the Gopher and manually made the directory choices "clin" and "cancernet."

```
gopher://gopher.nih.gov/11/clin/cancernet
```

The next example includes the port number (70 is the default for a Gopher server), and the RI code for a binary file, and brings the user the latest weather satellite picture of North America.

```
gopher://spinaltap.micro.umn.edu:70/I9/Weather/Maps/
NorthAmericaMapvis
```

Finally, a query string can be tacked on the end, preceded by a question mark. The search keyword or words are then passed to the Gopher search resource. In the following example, the inquiry "phg" is passed to the genetic code database at *Genbank,* and the result is a readout of all Genbank records listing the gene sequences of bacteriophages. The RI code 77 denotes a database search.

```
gopher://gopher.nih.gov:70/77/gopherlib/indices/
genbank/index?phg
```

Note: If more than one search keyword is needed, they are separated by + symbols, *not* spaces. If, for some reason, a + symbol is required as part of a URL other than a separator, encode it as %2B.

TIP

Most of the prohibited symbols can be encoded as their ASCII hex values prefixed by %. This includes a space, which is permitted in a Macintosh filename and may be rendered %20 in a URL.

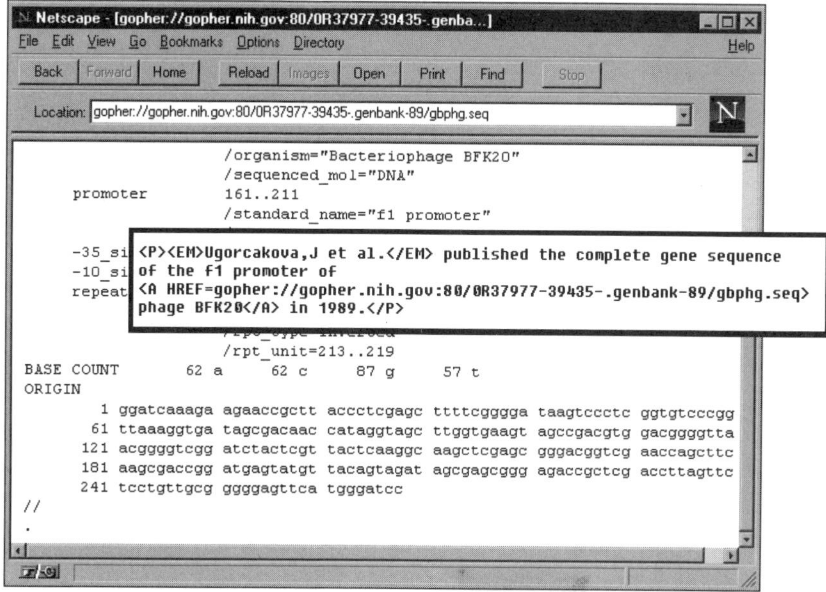

Figure 3-14: *Resource brought into the Netscape window by Gopher, with the code that invoked it.*

The RI codes are not as standardized as the Internet community would like them to be, and they vary from Gopher server to Gopher server. Before you add a Gopher hyperlink to your code, visit the site yourself and make sure you get it right by transferring the exact address string to your own file with a copy- and-paste operation. If you're using Netscape Gold, you can drag and drop the destination straight into the editor to create a hyperlink.

Telnet, TN3270, Rlogin, WAIS

Telnet://, tn3270://, rlogin://, and wais:// are all legitimate URL prefixes that theoretically open doors to the named Internet resources. However, they are used extremely rarely as HTML hyperlinks, for two good reasons.

First, all of them require that resources external to Netscape—sometimes known as proxies—be present on the user's computer and correctly configured to be launched ("spawned," as Netscape calls it) when the user activates a hyperlink. This may be a fairly safe bet for the minority community working in UNIX, but for the PC/Mac majority it's very far from reliable.

Secondly, almost all such resources require a login procedure, often quite a complex one, and this *cannot* be built into the URL in the form "login:password@". Neither will search instructions appended to the URL following ? meet with much success in general.

We use a Telnet URL, however, very often—and probably many other HTML authors do the same. It's the one that's in our Netscape bookmark file, which enables us to set up a Telnet link into the UNIX directory at our Web sites, for last-minute adjustments to HTML and cgi-bin text files right there on the server. (This is especially useful if you're trying to make a cgi-bin script work and need to try out different versions.) The UNIX directory pops up in a separate window, and we can see the effect of adjustments immediately in the main window. The Telnet application we use is called QVTNET, and the URL we type to reach the desired directory is simply (for example) telnet://access.thegroup.net.

There are several sites that allow access to the fabulous richness of WAIS-searchable data without using the wais:// protocol as such. Take a look at WAISGATE, for instance—it's still classed as "experimental", but it provides more than enough data to satisfy most queries, and if you complete a WAISGATE search, you could take the complete URL that comes attached to the search result page, copy it to your clipboard and use it as a hyperlink destination in an HTML document.

TIP

A Scandinavian cooperative venture called Nordinfo *has created another "experimental" WWW-WAIS interface that is very powerful. Morten Nielsen has configured a server to accept WAIS queries without needing a WAIS proxy. The required syntax is explained at http://www.dtb.dk/w4/w4.html, and the Nordinfo page is at http://www.ub2.lu.se:80/auto_new/UDC.html.*

Newsgroups & E-mail

The last two external protocols are the basis of what we have to call "pseudo-URLs" because they also depend on correctly configured resources external to the Web server. However, the vast majority of Netscape users can be relied upon to have access to news and e-mail servers, and to have configured their client software to exchange data with those servers.

URLs in the form news:[name.of.newsgroup] are fairly common. (*Note the absence of the double forward slash.*) You can see one such link in Figure 3-15.

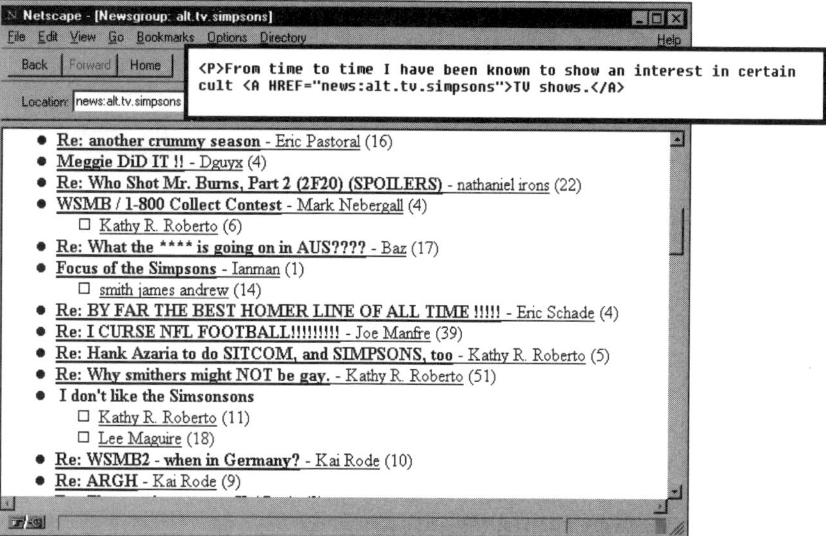

Figure 3-15: *Usenet newsgroup brought into the Netscape window, with the code that invoked it.*

Use of pseudo-URLs beginning "mailto:" went almost overnight from "never" to "ubiquitous" when Netscape implemented it in 1994. It's such a convenient way of inviting users of your page to send you feedback that it's hard to resist—and the syntax is a no-brainer (see Figure 3-16).

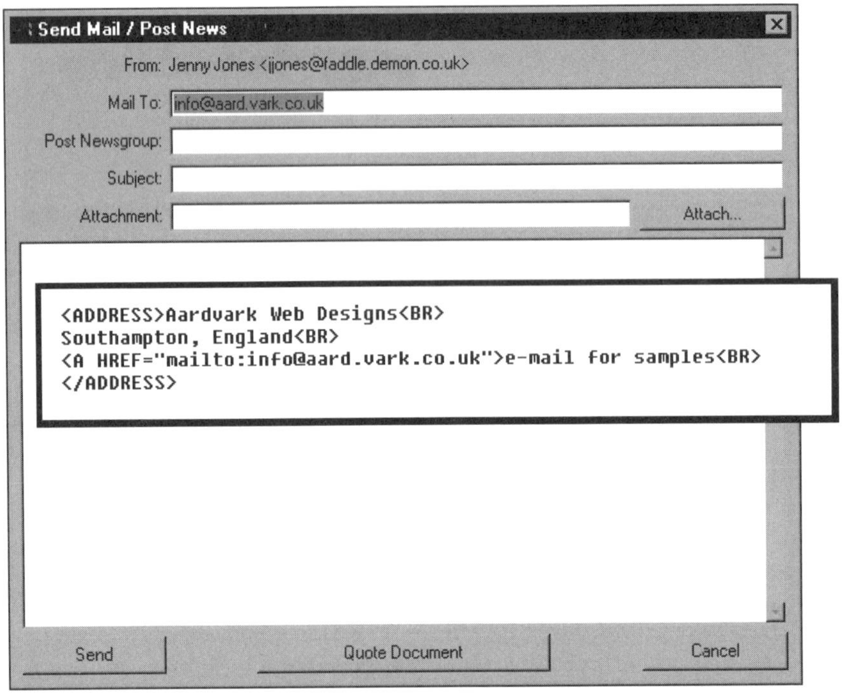

```
<ADDRESS>Aardvark Web Designs<BR>
Southampton, England<BR>
<A HREF="mailto:info@aard.vark.co.uk">e-mail for samples<BR>
</ADDRESS>
```

Figure 3-16: *E-mail blank invoked by a "mailto:" URL.*

There's just one little gimmick you may need to be aware of when constructing mailto: URLs. Some e-mail addresses—particularly UUnet addresses—use % symbols as subdividers, which are prohibited in URLs. A mailing list about the obscure musical instrument the Chapman Stick has the address:

```
stick%moliere@uunet.uu.net.
```

Just convert the "%" to "%25" and everything will be fine.

Archie & Finger Gateways

Archie and Finger are both standard UNIX services that were up and running decades before the Web was even a gleam in Tim Berners-Lee's eye. Archie searches FTP sites worldwide for keywords, and Finger returns details like who's currently logged in and who's read their mail when. Several sites offer gateways from HTTP to these services and, while not really legitimate as hyperlink destinations, they could be made to work as a gimmick.

For example, a search for information about "Java" could be automatically launched by:

```
<A HREF="http://hoohoo.ncsa.uiuc.edu/cgi-bin/
AA?query=java&type=Case+Insensitive+Substring+
Match&order=host&nice=Nicer&server=Internic&hits=10">
```

The best Finger gateway is at the University of Indiana. If you know somebody's e-mail address (in the form *user@host*) you can reach them by adding */host/user* to the Indiana URL. Find out who's logged on at *host* by simply adding */host*. For example, to find out if the President is paying attention to his e-mail, you might try:

```
<A HREF="http://www.cs.indiana.edu/finger/whitehouse.gov/
president">
```

Now for the disappointment—that one won't actually work, although *president@whitehouse.gov* is a legitimate e-mail address.

Very many sites, the White House among them, completely block access by Finger. It's not hard—all you have to do as sysadmin is fail to install the software that manages external Finger requests.

Inserting Special Linking Information in Your Page HEAD

Back in Chapter 1, when we introduced the <HEAD> tag, we cut straight to the chase, as it were, and focused almost exclusively on the all-important <TITLE> .... </TITLE> wrapper. We hand-wavingly noted that seven other elements find their natural home inside the document HEAD—and now it's time to deal with a couple of them, because they're important as linking information when you stand back and think of how your complete document fits into the overall scheme of things.

USING BASE URL

We talked earlier about the possibility of visitors coming to your Web site by various unforeseen means, such as through a link on another site or a search that turns up a secondary page on your site. There are perhaps other instances where, if you've been successful in posting something useful, your Web pages might be read out of context.

A few possibilities might be:

- A visitor downloads your page for reading or printing later, perhaps without preserving the original URL.
- A visitor uses a very modern browser with "enhanced page-saving," allowing download of all elements of the page as a body.
- You give permission for someone to post a document you've written on another site.
- A large company wants to post a document on several different computer locations, while the main resources remain on one site.

Relative links to other pages or resources posted on the original site might then be ineffective or lost entirely.

One way to ensure that your pages will never be "homeless" is to specify a "base URL" in the head information. URLs within the document that are in partial form will then be retrieved from the same location as the base URL.

BASE

The BASE element allows the URL of the document to be recorded in case the document is read out of context. BASE is only allowed within the HEAD of the document. The form is:

<BASE HREF="[complete URL]">

Partial URLs within the document will then be interpreted as on the same host and directory as the referring document.

Here's an example of an HTML page using this element:

```
<HTML>
<HEAD>
<BASE HREF="http://primus.com/docs/copolicy.html">
<TITLE>Doc Title</TITLE>
</HEAD>
<BODY>
....
<A HREF="hiring.html">Hiring Procedures</A>
```

...and so on. As you can see, "hiring.html" is a relative link that assumes that the file is on the same directory as this page. If the page is on a different site, the browser will then search for the file at:

```
http://primus.com/docs/hiring.html
```

Obviously, not every Web page needs this kind of insurance policy, but it's an extremely useful tool for an author if you do—in this case making it unnecessary to update the document on several different computers every time changes are made.

Relating Your Document Within Its Immediate Family

If (like us) you run a pretty compact HTML authoring shop, in which at least one person understands every possible ramification of every Web site the shop produces, you may never feel the need to set down the exact formal relationships between documents on a site, or embed details of how to get hold of the person responsible for updating the glossary (or whatever). Big corporations, however, create their own problems of size—and the extra housekeeping required by very big Web sites is one of them. Think of this, too—a medium-sized site may seem completely logical and clear to you right now, but what if a client comes back and wants changes made five years later?

The element used for internal housekeeping is LINK, with its attributes HREF, TITLE, REL, and REV. An unlimited number of LINK statements can be stacked up in the HEAD to define the document's place in the world as finely as you like. If this book were a Web site, this chapter might have a LINK to its Table of Contents as follows:

```
<LINK HREF="toc.htm" TITLE="Table of Contents" REV="ToC">
```

This indicates a *reverse* relationship (REV) to the T.O.C. The Contents page itself would have a series of *direct* relationships (REL) to its subsidiaries, like this:

```
<LINK HREF="ch3.htm" TITLE="Links, Links & More Links"
REL="chapter">
```

We're never likely to forget who was responsible for writing and editing this chapter, but in the messy corporate world where a Web site may have scores of authors and editors (at least half of whom have been downsized or outsourced by now, you may be sure), LINK allows them all to leave their snail trails through the site with statements like:

```
<LINK HREF="mailto:jonesh@huge.co" TITLE="Hugh Jones"
REV="author">
<LINK HREF="mailto:coltrane@huge.co" TITLE="Marcia Coltrane"
REV="editor">
```

LINK should always be accompanied by an HREF, to indicate the document or person it refers to, but the other attributes are optional. Interestingly, LINK is one of the original HTML 1.0 tags. It was originally defined as an element within the anchor tag, <A>, but that usage was never implemented. As a matter of fact, implementation of LINK as we just described it is slightly futuristic. LINK statements are obviously useful, but you have to display the source code to see them. One day Netscape will likely implement them fully, meaning there will be some magic button that will display the whole hierarchy of a site, as described by its LINKs.

Moving On

Links are so essential to the Web that in practice you'll probably use what you've learned in this chapter more than any other section of this book. You'll probably get the hang of it and have the essentials memorized pretty quickly. But as you go on to integrate your Web site with the huge resources available on the Web, you can refer back here for sound advice.

In the next chapter we'll go on to the second most essential topic of Web design: the business of making good images for the Web. First we'll look at how your computer makes and interprets pictures. Then we'll show you how to use this knowledge to put your best self forward visually on the Web.

4

All About Images

If links are the doors and hallways of your Web site, images are its interior decoration and its windows. Just like interior decoration, it's a topic on which everyone's got an opinion but about which the facts are sometimes hard to discern. In this chapter we'll tackle the subject of images on the Web head on, with a look first at how your computer makes and interprets pictures. Then we'll explain what this means for making good images on the Web.

The topics covered in this chapter include how to size and place images, how you can specify attributes that will fit your image naturally to the computer screen, and how to make text flow around images the way you want it to. We'll also discuss background and text colors and some nifty Web tricks like making transparent colors, interlaced Graphics Interchange Formats (GIFs), and progressive Joint Photographic Experts Group (JPEGs). Finally, we'll explain how to make clickable maps so you can create links within images.

THE TRUTH ABOUT COMPUTER VIDEO

Take a magnifying glass or a photographer's loupe sometime and peer closely at a white area on your color computer screen. If it's a loupe you may have to turn it around to get focus on the color mask (and if you can't be bothered with all that exercise, just take a look at Figure 4-1 for an "artist's impression" of what you should be seeing). See all those dots? Now you know that when you're looking at what you think is white, you're really looking at equal amounts of red, blue, and green. That's *additive color*, man....

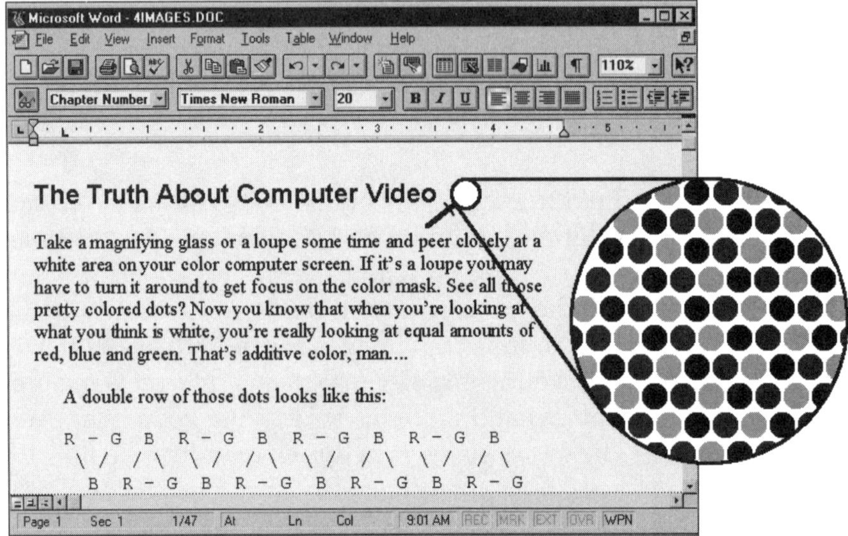

Figure 4-1: *Artist's impression of RGB color mask on a computer monitor. (You can see the color version on the Companion CD-ROM.)*

You could visualize a double row of those dots as a series of little RGB triangles like this:

```
R - G  B  R - G  B  R - G  B  R - G  B
 \ /  / \  \ /  / \  \ /  / \  \ /  / \
  B  R - G  B  R - G  B  R - G  B  R - G
```

What you've got then is a row of triangular dots whose apparent color can be controlled by varying the relative intensity of the R, the G, and the B.

If your monitor uses Trinitron color, you'll be seeing RGB bricks or stripes, but it's the same idea.

The "Argy Bee" System for Computer Colors

Color is created on computer screens by mixing appropriate degrees of red, blue, and green—RGB, or "argy bee" if you want to be whimsical about it. A computer picture is made up of rows and rows of tiny dots called *pixels,* and every pixel of an image can be analyzed as having from 0-255 degrees of Red, 0-255 of Green, and 0-255 of Blue. That adds up (or multiplies, actually) to 16,777,216 possible colors—probably enough for even the most demanding computer graphics enthusiast. Oh, by the way—a pixel is the smallest possible detail you can put in an image, but it isn't necessarily the smallest detail your screen can resolve. In other words, the relationship between a pixel and one of those triangular RGB dots depends on your system.

What's the implication of this for the storage of images as data files? At a superficial level, that's easy to calculate. You need to set aside 24 bits to store a number that could be anything between zero and 16,777,216. That's why a full-color image is often referred to as "24-bit color," or "true color." 24 bits equals 3 bytes, and therefore a computer image that's 600 pixels wide by 300 pixels high would make a data file 600 X 300 X 3 bytes, or a little over half a megabyte.

It's equally easy, of course, to calculate how many of such data files would fill up your hard drive and—even more to the point—how long it would take to download such a picture. It's because of these hard facts of life that there's a need to come up with some way of reducing the storage requirements of a computer image. And it's because so many brilliant people have worked on this problem for so long, and all of them think they have come up with the best "compression algorithm," that we see so many different image formats in use today.

THE COMPRESSION/QUALITY TRADE-OFF

One solution to the problem is to store information based not on the exact RGB value of each pixel, but on how each pixel differs from its neighbors. Some algorithms like this are "perfect," meaning that no color data is lost but some degree of compression is achieved. Others go for more compression and accept that some data will be lost—this is known as *lossy compression*.

Another, more radical, solution is some form of palette reduction—saying basically, "We'll just have to make do with fewer than 16 million colors." After all, most PC color systems can only display 256 colors anyway (although 24-bit "true color" is commonplace for Macs, and 16-bit "hi-color" is the latest rage in the PC world). If you take our 600 X 300-pixel image and make do with a reduced palette of only 256 colors, you'll then only need one byte per pixel (this is "8-bit color"), and the basic size of the file becomes a more manageable 180K. In many cases the reduction of palette by a factor of 65,000 is not nearly as devastating as you might think.

GIF OR JPEG?

The two data file formats that are most used in Web design, GIF and JPEG, represent almost the extremes of those two approaches to the problem of file size. JPEG, a format devised by a committee called the Joint Photographic Experts Group, goes for lossy compression. Furthermore, it lets the user choose how much trade-off of quality for storage space he or she wants. Using JPEG compression, most images can be compressed up to 20:1 without noticeable loss of quality; some can be compressed as much as 50:1, and if "preview quality" is acceptable 100:1 compression is possible.

The philosophy of GIF, the Graphics Interchange Format invented by CompuServe (and known as CompuServe format in some applications), is 8-bit color with a bit of compression and a gimmick. The gimmick is that, although each image only uses 256 colors, the color palette is customized *for that specific image*. Therefore, there are still 16 million colors to choose from, but you can only use 256 of them in any given picture. When you convert an image to GIF format, your software makes a decision about which

256 colors will render this particular image best, and arranges these in an index that is stored in the file header. Color #1 might be a shade of orange, color #2 royal blue, and so on. When it comes to rendering the image, it's literally like painting by numbers—pixel #12,220 is color #3, and so on. This scheme is known as *indexed color* as opposed to "true color."

The extra compression that's imposed on top of the indexed color scheme in GIFs is the LZW compression—that's the part that's caused a lot of controversy because of patent disputes. Basically, the original LZW work was done by Lempel, Zev, and Welch at the Sperry Corporation in the early 1980s and was legitimately patented. In 1986, Sperry merged with Unisys, which inherited the patent. A year later, CompuServe developed the GIF process using LZW compression. Everything seemed to be hunky-dory for several years, because CompuServe says it wasn't aware of the patent and Unisys says it wasn't aware of the GIF format. At the tail end of 1994, Unisys suddenly announced that it intended to defend its patent, causing consternation throughout the Web community.

With the situation now clarified, it's plain that, as mere users of the technology, we Web designers have no need to fear the midnight knock on the door by grim-faced, subpoena-wielding Unisys attorneys. If you wanted to develop a new GIF viewer, it might be a different story. However, the whole imbroglio has left many people with a bad attitude, and, added to the experts who thought GIF's days were numbered anyway for technical reasons, it has undoubtedly hastened the emergence of newer and better things.

Well, speaking of painting by numbers, take a look at Figures 4-2 and 4-3. They're our way of answering the eternal question, "What's the best format for Web images—GIF or JPEG?" The Union Jack in Figure 4-2 which, by the way, is 600 X 300 pixels, is an absolutely ideal image for the GIF format. Obviously, it suffers not at all from being restricted to 256 colors, since it would be perfectly content with just 4 (there's a thin black border, beside the red, white, and blue). It contains sharp lines, which the JPEG system is bad at. Finally, the big blocks of identically colored pixels are just what LZW compression loves best.

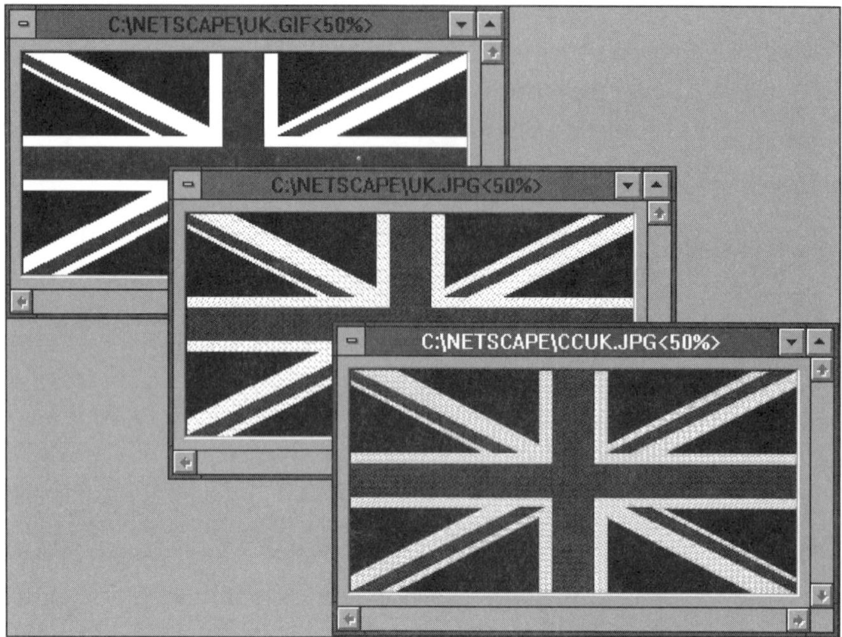

Figure 4-2: *Progressive deterioration as a GIF image is converted to JPEG and compressed. (You can see the color version on the Companion CD-ROM.)*

Figure 4-2 is intended to prove the point by showing the effect of taking the original GIF (the top left image), converting it to JPEG (middle image), and then highly compressing it. The resulting file sizes are:

GIF	6.7K
JPEG	121.0K
JPEG compressed	20.2K (27:1 compression)

The figure demonstrates very well JPEG's weakness with this type of image: The sharp lines are no longer sharp, and the white is progressively muddy. Actually, starting from an RGB value of 255,255,255 (pure white) in the GIF, the white converted to 244,250,243 (off-white) and then 240,240,192 (decidedly muddy).

Result: triumph for the GIF. Much smaller file, much better rendering. For sketches, line drawings, cartoons, pop art, posters, and icons, GIF is king.

Now look at Figure 4-3, a reproduction of a painting by the French impressionist Paul Gauguin. No sharp lines. No big blocks of color. Not the most demanding picture in terms of palette, but still requiring more than 256 colors for true repro. We made Figure 4-3 by converting the original JPEG to a GIF, capturing both images as they were seen in the Netscape content window, and then combining them. The JPEG is on the left, and the file size is 28K. The GIF (missing a few pixels) is on the right, and the file is nearly 100K.

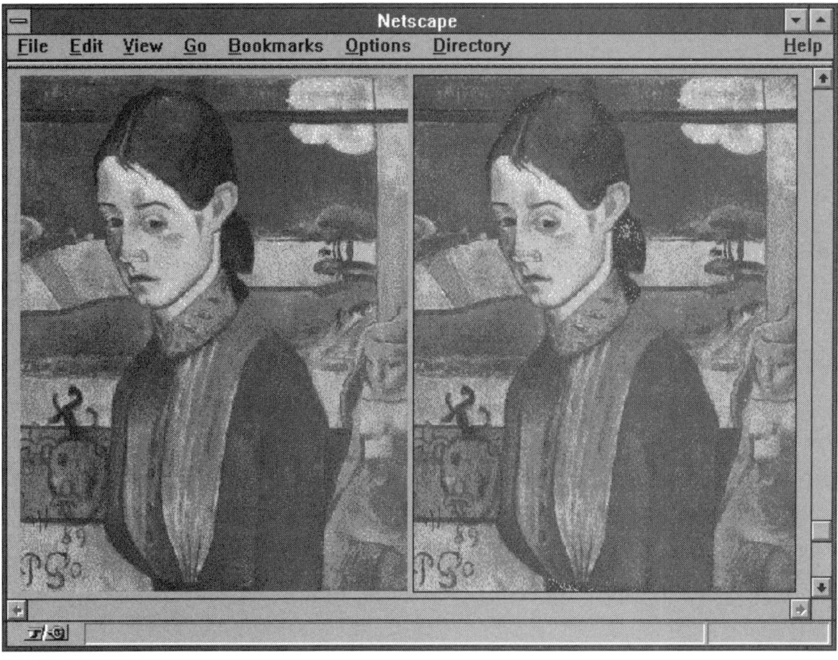

Figure 4-3: *Comparison of the JPEG and GIF treatment of fine art. (You can see the color version on the Companion CD-ROM.)*

Result: Game, set, and match to JPEG for this type of full-color or photographic image. As it happens, Gauguin's *Jeune fille de Bretagne* also takes very well to compression (perhaps it would cheer her up if she knew?). We were able to squeeze her down to 10K before she began to look kind of dirty, as well as depressed. Since the image is 295 X 383 pixels, the theoretical uncompressed file size would be 338.9k and so 10K represents better than 33:1 compression.

So here's our final answer to the Great GIF/JPEG Question: JPEG is Gauguin. GIF is Picasso.

AN IMAGE CHECKLIST

Here's a simple list of considerations you can use when deciding whether to use GIF or JPEG on a particular image:

- How many colors are there?
  Less than 16, you're probably better with GIF.
  More than 16, you *might* be better with JPEG, depending on other factors.
- Do colors shade or are there solid blocks of color?
  For solid color blocks, GIF is cleaner.
  For blending shades of color, JPEG does a better job.
- Do the images have sharp edges or are they "fuzzy" focus?
  Sharp edges usually are better in GIF (depending on surrounding color).
  Subtle images often look better in JPEG.
- How large will the final image be?
  Small images are often cleaner and sharper in GIF.
  Large images may benefit from JPEG compression.

However, most often the best solution is reached by experimentation. Try it both ways and see which format best achieves the look you want and compare file sizes. With a little experience, you'll soon acquire an eye for telling which format is best for a particular image.

THE INLINE PROBLEM

You might think JPEG, given its superior compression, would be the format of choice for full-color inline images, and the GIF format only used for line art, right? Well, the Web is definitely moving in that direction, but you will still see GIFs in situations where JPEG might be a better choice, and the reasons are complicated.

For one thing, only Netscape and a few other Web browsers support inline JPEGs (although their acceptance is growing), so if you use them they won't appear on many of your users' screens.

Also, the GIF format was first to offer some very interesting techniques, like interlacing and transparency, that we're going to be describing a few pages on. Not all of these techniques are possible for JPEG—yet. By the time they are, 24-bit color may be on the PC mass market, the GIF87a and GIF89a formats will be history, and the battle lines will be drawn over a brand new format, PNG.

The Color Palette Problem

Indexed color, as we said, works remarkably well considering the huge reduction in RGB color choices. If you're using an 8-bit computer color system, however, you will certainly see some pages that have the color trashed. This is because your monitor can only display 256 colors anyway, and it performs its own version of color indexing, known as *quantizing*. What this means is that you may end up with two GIF images on the same screen that have totally incompatible palettes—there's no way the quantizing algorithm can come up with 256 colors that will do justice to both, even if each image individually works well with its own palette.

There's another frequent source of disappointment when Web pages are viewed in their final form. Surprisingly few Web designers realize that, in 8-bit systems, Netscape Navigator reduces the palette from 256 to 216 colors—that's a combination of just six shades of red, six of green, and six of blue. Netscape refers to this color selection as a "color cube" because the 216-color palette can conveniently be represented as a three-dimensional color chart. If your inline GIF calls for a color that's not one of the 216 in the cube, Navigator will either pick the closest it has, or approximate your color by "dithering" two or more colors that *are* available (this is a user option). Obviously, therefore, if you're creating an icon from scratch you can achieve truer results by sticking to the 216-color cube. Find out more about this, and see the cube itself come to life, on Victor Engel's page:

http://www.onr.com/user/lights/netcol.html

TIP

For the Most Reliable Look of Your Page:
There's a way to make absolutely sure *that all your users are seeing the inline GIFs on your page as you intend. Here's how: Combine all the GIFs into one huge image. Make any palette adjustments you feel are necessary for the best overall look, using the Netscape 216-color cube if you want to be really fussy. Now save that palette and, one by one, open the individual images into your graphics editor, apply the global palette to them, and re-save them. (Adobe Photoshop has a "previous palette" option that is ideal for this purpose—and Mac users can do this with a highly sophisticated software application called a DeBabilizer).*

SIZING & PLACING INLINE IMAGES

It's been said with some justice that you're better off coming to Web publishing as a greenhorn—anybody who has plenty of experience in, say, magazine publishing or the graphical arts in general will have a harder time adapting to the Web environment than a newbie. Obviously that's a debatable point—but one very good illustration of the difficulty a magazine art director might have in adapting, for example, is the question of sizing and placing illustrations.

A standard magazine page is 8 $^1/_2$ X 11 inches, the same as ordinary letter-size paper. A margin of at least 9/16 inch is allowed all round, and frequently more in the "gutter"—meaning the left margin of a right-hand page and the right margin of a left-hand page. That leaves typically a 6 7/8-inch X 9 7/16-inch text space that is then subdivided into either three or two columns. The columns usually have 3/16-inch space between them, and so simple arithmetic defines the width of a column and the exact dimensions of a part of the page that can be sold to advertisers (see Figure 4-4). The standard size of a fractional-page ad, known in the trade as a "mechanical spec," varies very little from magazine to magazine. Everyone's life is a little easier that way. So an art director (or a production manager) can work from a thumbnail sketch of a page, figuring font styles and sizes in the secure knowledge that if the sums are correct the final page will end up looking right.

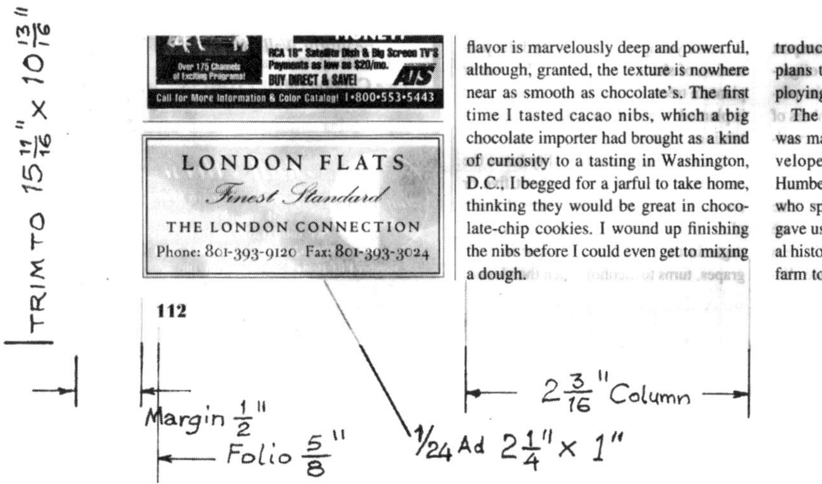

Figure 4-4: *Section of a magazine page, showing precise dimensions.*

A magazine professional transferring to Web design gets the same kind of shock an expert motorist does when he takes up flying. "Oh, no roads or signposts? OK." "Oh, we can move in three dimensions? Er... OK.... I guess." "Gosh, what was beside me a moment ago is now beneath me. Hmmmm...." On the Web, text can float in relation to pictures with almost that much freedom.

WHAT'S THE PAGE WIDTH?

When we hold a ruler up to the screen these words are being written on right now, the width is 9 ½ inches less ½ inch for the scroll bar, for a net page width of 9. But the monitor in our other office is ½ inch wider, and our neighbor has a laptop with a much smaller screen. No matter what the size of the monitor, we still see the same amount of content on the Netscape screen because we're all working in Windows with the same type of video. Obviously, then, it makes no sense at all to measure Web page width in inches or centimeters or shoe sizes or any other unit of linear measure (did you know that shoe sizes are based on the length of a barleycorn?). So what is the right way to think about the sizes of elements on our Web pages?

The answer is *resolution*. When you're presenting information on a computer screen, you should concern yourself with the pixel dimensions of your images, and how many of those pixels fit on the screen horizontally and vertically.

While a wide range of video resolutions are available to consumers, an overwhelming majority of monitors out there are the garden variety 640 X 480 VGA type. That means they have 640 pixels horizontally and 480 vertically. You won't go far wrong if you play the Web design game on a "playing field" of those dimensions, even if some players occasionally kick the ball into the parking lot.

Here's another useful guide: Horizontal resolution is much more important than vertical. Users expect to scroll vertically, but you'll irritate them if you force them to scroll horizontally to see everything on your page. In general, text on a page adjusts automatically to the width of the system it's being viewed on, but images do not. It's not good practice to put your images out in the "parking lot" beyond the 640-pixel boundary even if a minority of your users can see that far. Allowing for the scroll bar at the right edge, and the 10-

pixel left margin that Netscape imposes, a 605-pixel-wide picture will exactly stretch to the right-hand end of the content window. Six hundred pixels, allowing a little margin at the right end as well, is normally considered "100% of screen width," and the standard horizontal rule that you create with the <HR> tag is 600 pixels wide. It's worth bearing in mind, by the way, that the <HR> automatically adjusts for higher-resolution systems, whereas a fancy-colored bar, which is really an inline GIF, does not. (Stay tuned, however, for *Percentage Auto Scaling* later in this chapter.)

A Web page designer should never forget, though, that even in the PC world, screen resolutions of 720 X 512, 800 X 600, and 1024 X 768 are common for dedicated graphics setups. High-end Mac monitors are 832 X 624, and in the world of workstations 1280 X 1024 pixels is considered normal. And we're just talking about the *default* screen resolutions: Users are perfectly free to shrink their windows in both dimensions. So if you design to 600 pixels, very few of your users will find an image disappearing off the screen. Some, however, will find it occupying only half the screen width—and unless you specifically prohibit it, Netscape will use that "parking lot" for your text. Figure 4-5 is a particularly startling lesson in what can happen when a high-res system causes the elements of a page to fly apart.

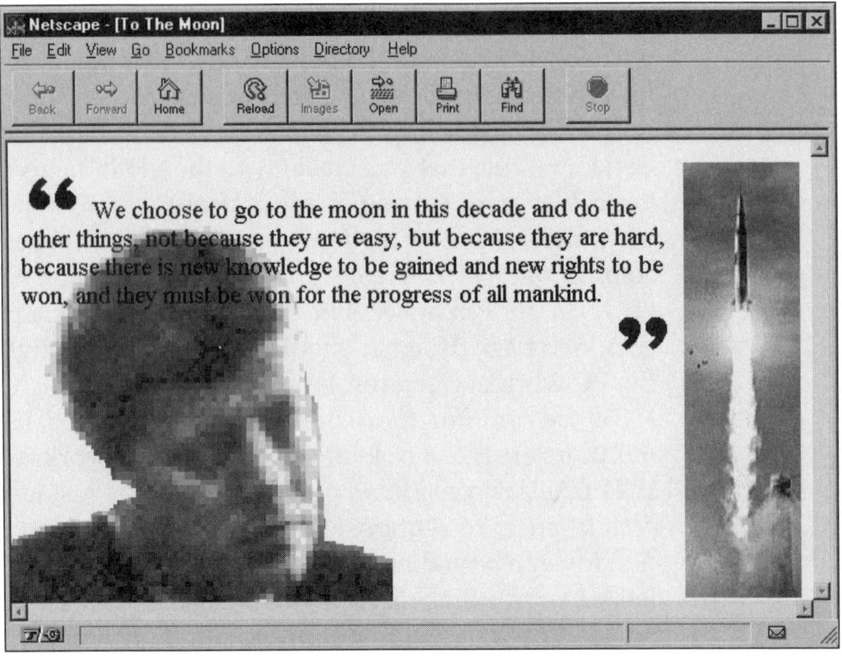

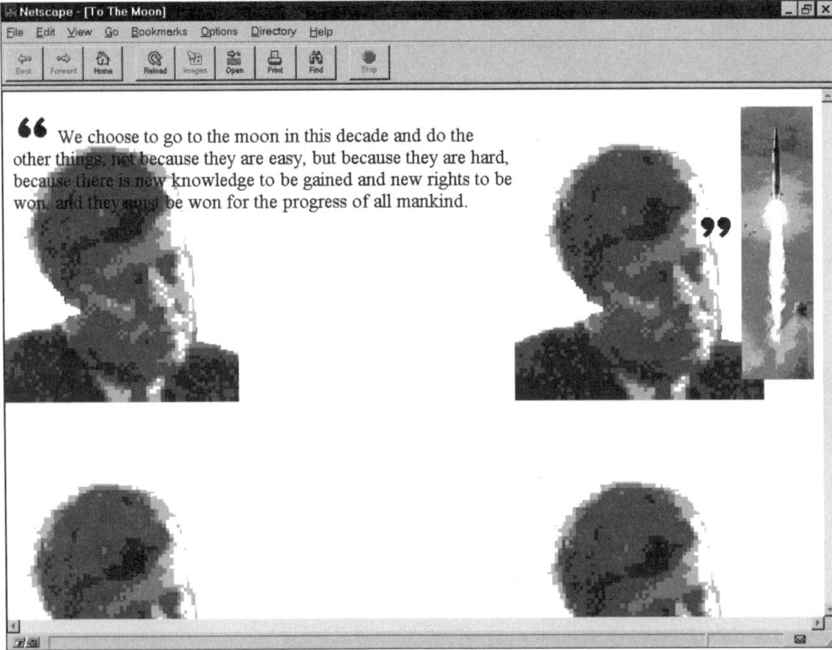

Figure 4-5: *A page designed for a screen at the standard 640 X 480 resolution looks very different when viewed at a screen resolution of 1024 X 768.*

A converse phenomenon can cause problems for users of low-end Macintosh computers. On those screens, the Netscape window defaults to a width of 480 pixels. It's very easy to stretch the window to 600, but of course not everyone does. Some Mac types have even suggested that 480 should be the *de facto* standard—and you will occasionally come across runty-looking pages that have been designed by these folks. We've been fairly vocal on the newsgroups and mailing lists arguing for a 600-pixel "standard." It's an interesting debate, and we look forward to continuing the (good-natured) battle into the future.

Sticking to Size

Not everyone is willing to accept the extreme flexibility of the Web as a design platform. A vocal minority of designers—they tend to be Macintosh enthusiasts, as far we can tell—insist that objects should retain their "natural" size when moved from one medium to another. Such people emphasize a different meaning of the term "resolution," namely the limiting resolution of a computer monitor, which is most often 72 dots per inch. These "sizists" maintain that all art should be scanned at 72 dpi and that there is no true Web image unless one image pixel exactly equals one screen dot. They sometimes seem to be saying that inflating or deflating an image breaks some fundamental rule of graphic arts—and that's nonsense. In the newspaper and magazine business, re-sizing artwork to suit page layout is an hourly occurrence.

One of the foremost proponents of the 72 dpi way of thinking, Walter Ian Kaye, even has a measuring scale on his home page marked off in thirty-seconds of an inch. "Use this in conjunction with a ruler ... to configure your video display," he requests. What he means is that his pages will only look "correct" if the video width is 640 dots at 72 dpi, or a bit under 9 inches. Note that *this is not the same thing as shrinking the Netscape frame to nine inches*. He wants you to actually fiddle with your monitor picture width and height controls. (His page is at http://www.natural-innovations.com/boo/measure.html).

We have a lot of respect for Kaye as a meticulous and inventive designer, but we felt we had to challenge him on this in an exchange that was partly conducted in private e-mail and partly on a professional e-mail list. "If I have a 12-point font on my display, I want it to be the same exact height as it is on a piece of paper," he wrote by way of explanation. By a fluke, in typography there are 72 points to an inch and so this lends support to those who see this monitor resolution as a "natural" resolution for computer graphics—and of course, Kaye is quite right when he points out that most of us are not seeing font sizes true on screen. We do have a couple of problems with this doctrinaire approach, however.

One is that there are too many other variables in the system for it to make sense most of the time—monitor size and viewing distance are two other important factors in the way we finally perceive graphics. The other is that it cannot possibly hold true for all cases. Not even Walter Ian Kaye, surely, would insist on viewing a Kandinsky reproduction on his Mac monitor in the size the artist originally created it.

One university's Department of Computer Design recently gave a student the task of measuring the dot pitch of every monitor the department owned. The reported results ranged from 53 to 111—proving that 72 dpi is not a standard to be trusted.

STANDARD SIZE ADS ON THE WEB?? OH NO!!!

The height of the Netscape content area is anywhere from 285 pixels to almost 400, depending on which version of Windows and which of the many possible combinations of toolbar, location window, and directory buttons the user chooses to see. 600x300 is gaining acceptance as the dimension of a "standard" full screen, since a panel that size would totally dominate the screen and be completely visible unless you're in Windows 3.1 with the maximum amount of clutter at the top of your screen. In case you hadn't already guessed, people with commercial minds have already begun to define standard ad sizes, just like the mechanical specs of the magazine world—600 X 100 for a "banner," 100 X (whatever) for a "border," and so on.

Just Plain Sensible Sizes & Positions

Figures 4-6 through 4-8 show pages that make use of several different image sizes.

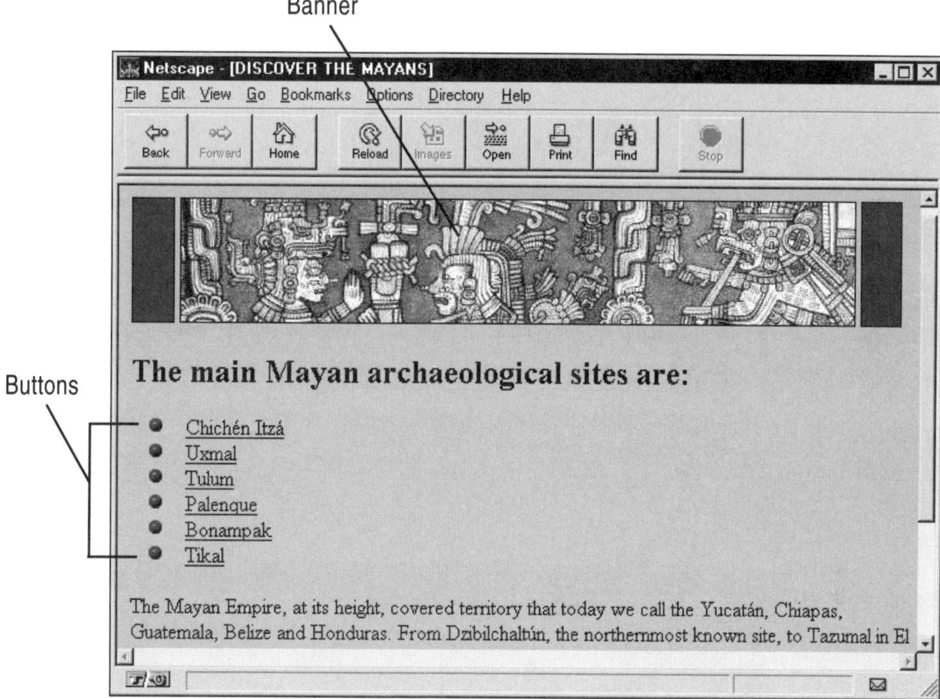

Figure 4-6: *One frame of an imaginary Web site about Mayan archaeology, showing various image sizes.*

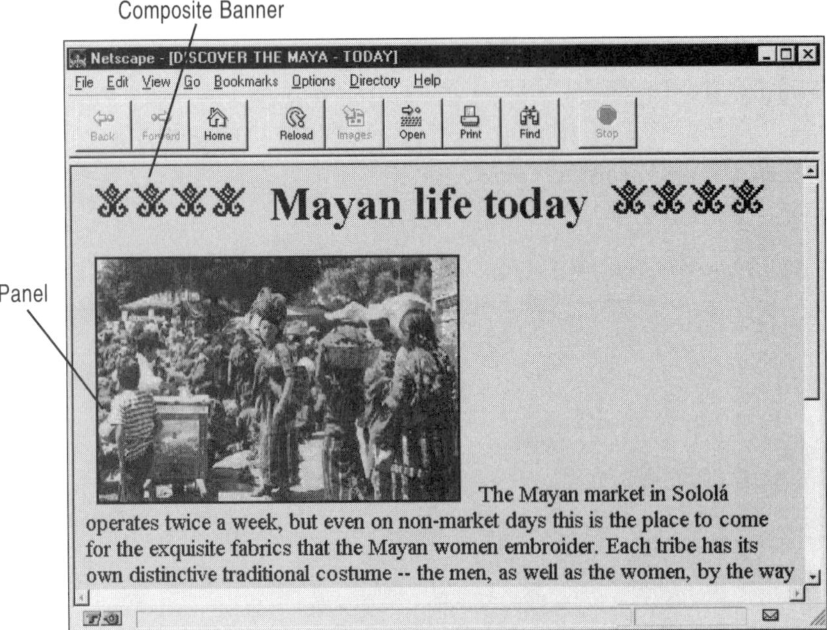

Figure 4-7: *Second Maya page, showing use of a composite banner and a panel-size image.*

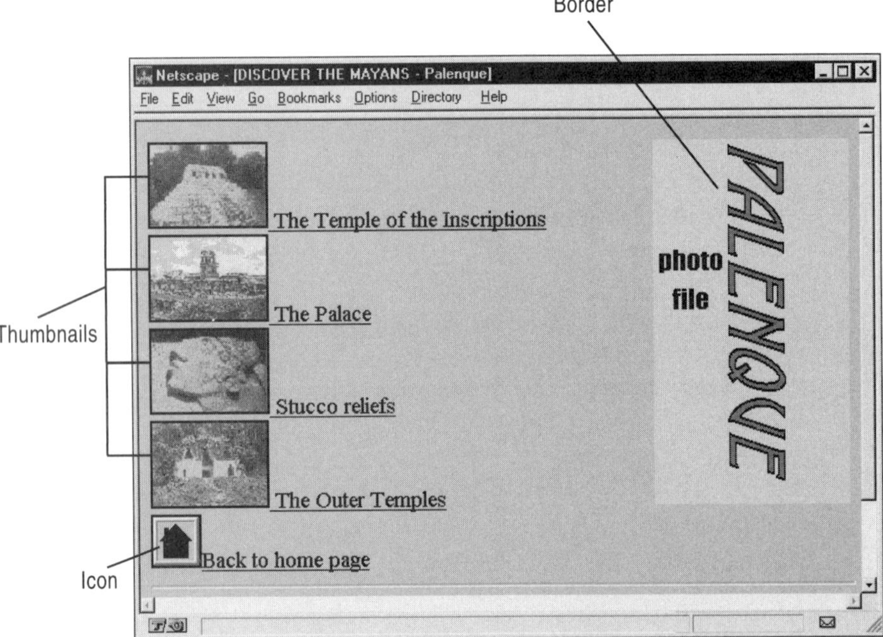

Figure 4-8: *Third Maya page, showing how other image sizes are used.*

In this book, we'll be using the following "unofficial" terms for the various sizes in common use.

BUTTON A very small inline picture, not more than 15 X 15 pixels, usually a round image with a transparent surround (see "Transparent Colors" later in this chapter). Its function is little more than to sit around being more decorative than a boring black blob in a standard bulleted list. Making a button "clickable" spoils it because the square outline then usually becomes visible.

BAR A decorative or stylistic horizontal rule. Usually 600 pixels wide and about 10 high.

ICON Usually square, not more than 40 X 40 pixels, and only two or three colors. Often used as something interesting to click on. Its content must be very simple so that it can make a visual impact at that size. Icons and buttons are *never* intended to be seen enlarged, and almost always have text to the right of them.

THUMBNAIL A small "reference" inline version of an external picture that is hyperlinked. A thumbnail is typically 50 X 50 pixels. It can be 8-bit color, and should invite the user to click on it to see the full-size version, or perhaps link to a page containing it. Sometimes referred to as a *preview* image.

PORTRAIT Usually 8-bit (or more) color, and about 100 to 150 pixels on its long side. An informative or decorative, but not lavish, picture that speaks for itself and does not need a hyperlinked version to provide more detail.

BANNER A decoration stretching the full width of the screen, but allowing plenty of space for text above or below it. Banners are usually 600 X 100 pixels, and are most effective when kept to few colors. Figure 4-7 shows a composite banner made up of a level 1 heading sandwiched between two pictures—this is dangerous practice, since the user can easily ruin the intended effect by changing the display font size. If you want that type of fancy header, better shoot the whole thing as a GIF banner, and repeat the text as the ALT attribute.

BORDER A decoration that (in theory) extends down the full height of the document, but allows plenty of space for text to left or right. A border can be as wide as 200 pixels, but determining its height is exactly like defining the length of "a piece of string," because the page designer cannot know the total height of the document as the user sees it. A front page border of 200 X 400 pixels is a safe compromise that guarantees that the border picture will bleed off the first "frame" of the document but allows it to disappear thereafter.

PANEL An inline picture that dominates one frame of a Web page. In other words, anything bigger than a portrait and all the way up to a full-screen picture.

Be Careful With Scan Quality

Occasionally you may be creating an image entirely on the computer, using Windows Paint (or Paintbrush) for some freehand airbrush work, perhaps. Or creating a street map from scratch, using Photoshop or Corel Draw!. But most of the time you'll be scanning existing artwork—or having it scanned by a digital photo service of some kind. The main danger here is too much quality. A photo service, used to scanning for publication, is liable to hand you a 1.4MB file in .TIFF format, scanned at 400 dpi and ending up several thousand pixels wide. By now you should realize that there's little point in producing anything over 600 pixels in width, and .TIFF files, pleasant though they may be, have very little application on the Web.

TIP

Don't Scan Too Fine:
Most scanners are adapted more for the desktop publishing industry than they are for the Web. The resolution of a scanner is measured in dots per inch (dpi), meaning how many pixels are resolved per inch of the original artwork. For desktop publishing, resolutions of several hundred dpi may be very appropriate. For professional magazine publishing, several thousand. However, scanning to fine resolution is a waste of time for the Web. If your artwork is the full 8-1/2 inches

wide, and you scan it at 400 dpi, you'll end up with an image 3,400 pixels wide and you're going to want to reduce it anyway. Far better to set the scan resolution to scan straight to your final image width. For example, if your artwork is 4 inches wide and you want to end up with a 600-pixel image, scan at 600÷4=150 dpi. This arithmetic is not Nobel prize stuff, and if you're lucky enough to have scanning equipment customized for Web work, rather than for print, it'll all be done for you anyway.

If you later change your mind and decide your image would look better at 550 pixels, it's obviously tempting to just re-size it in your graphics editor. That makes sense if you have to pay for scanning services, but if you own a scanner it is far better practice to go back and re-scan, this time at 550÷4=138 dpi.

Using the Image Tag

The HTML tag used to bring an image to the page is, of course "IMG"—and it has many possible attributes.

HTML Tag

<IMG>

Defines an image file to be inserted. The IMG tag has no corresponding </IMG>, since it cannot enclose anything except itself. However, its attributes are very important:

SRC="[path/name defining image file]"—Specifies the image to be inserted, in the form of a filename or full URL.

ALIGN="bottom/middle/top/left/right"—Specifies alignment of image in relation to the screen margins and/or text.

ALIGN="texttop/absmiddle/baseline/absbottom"—These are Netscape extensions to image alignment specifications.

WIDTH=w—Specifies the width of the image, in pixels.

HEIGHT=h—Specifies the height of the image in pixels.

UNITS="pixels/en"—Specifies units to be used in width and height specifications. This is an HTML 3.0-proposed attribute that is not recognized by most browsers including Netscape.

BORDER=b—Specifies a border of b pixels in width.

VSPACE=v—Specifies a clear vertical space (top and bottom of image) in pixels.

HSPACE=p (pixels)—Specifies a clear horizontal space (left and right of image) in pixels.

ALT="[text to display if user is not seeing images]"

ISMAP—Declares the image to be mappable. (Requires corresponding image map file at the server.)

USEMAP—Declares the image to be mappable by a client-side image map. The attribute #mapname references a <MAP> tag that heads the mapping code and is usually in the same HTML document as the USEMAP reference.

LOWSRC—Specifies a lower resolution image to be used until the full-size image (specified by SRC) can be downloaded.

SPECIFYING IMAGE FILES

This simply tells the user's client software where to go to get the image.
EXAMPLE: The red dots in Figure 4-6 are defined by

```
<IMG SRC="reddot.gif">
```

That very simple path/name definition works because in this case the image files are in the same directory as the HTML file that is referencing them. Many HTML authors separate text files and image files: they will have a master directory for the project—called, perhaps, MAYAWEB—then subdirectories one level down called TEXTS, IMAGES, AUDIO...and so forth. To reference an image in this type of structure, the code would be...

```
<IMG SRC="../images/reddot.gif">
```

...which means, "Back up one directory level, then change to the IMAGES directory, and there you should find reddot.gif." The forward slashes are NOT misprints—HTML uses UNIX-like punctuation in many cases. And speaking of UNIX, UNIX-like case sensitivity applies to path and filenames. Although...

```
<img src="reddot.gif">
```

...would be OK,...

```
<IMG SRC="REDDOT.GIF">
```

...would not find the right file (on most servers).

The pathway to the image file can be as complex as you like, even down to a fully qualified URL of another site, such as:

```
<IMG SRC="http://www.cs.mit.edu/~jovi/www/images/buttons/
reddot.gif">
```

The above code suggests going all the way to MIT and delving down four directory levels to find the same little red button that every HTML author has, which is the height of absurdity—but that type of SRC reference makes lots of sense if the image you wish to display is something like a weather map that somebody else updates frequently.

One final note about SRC: Path/name references will work perfectly well without being enclosed in double quotes. The reason everyone uses them is that they *are* required in the SGML convention, and some code parsers will insist upon them for that reason.

Aligning Text and Images

ALIGN specifies how the image will relate to text that accompanies it. The default is "bottom," which gives the effect shown by the text accompanying the Mayan Market portrait in Figure 4-7. As soon as the end of the screen is reached, text aligned "bottom" wraps underneath the picture.

Text aligned "top" and "middle" also runs for only one line before wrapping underneath the image, which really means these values are useful for captions only. Most people, we think, would find it hard to follow discursive text that started at the top of a picture then jumped beneath it after half a line.

Note that it's the baseline of the text that aligns to bottom and middle, but the top of the ascenders that aligns to the top of the image.

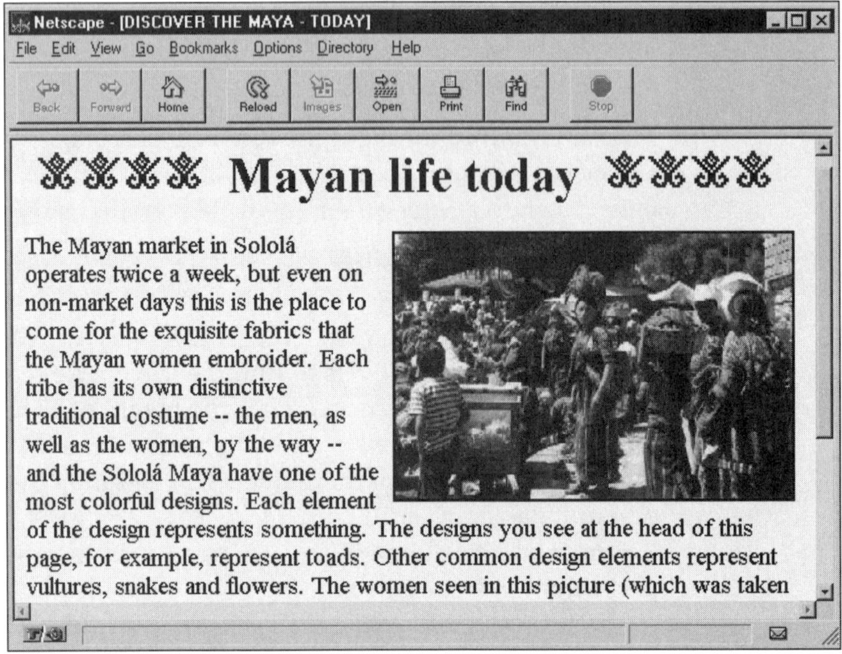

Figure 4-9A: *The same basic page as Figure 4-4, showing the effect of ALIGN RIGHT.*

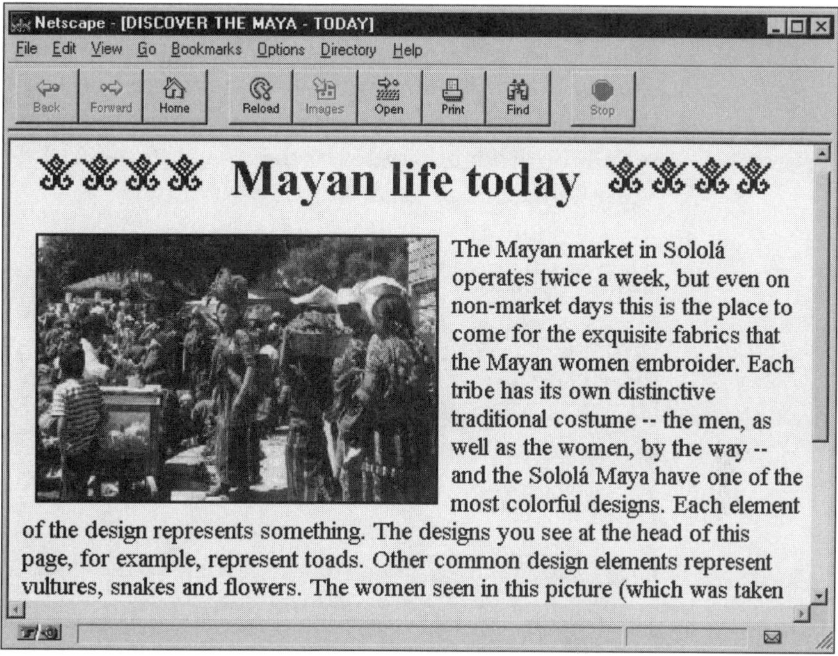

Figure 4-9B: *The same basic page as Figure 4-4, showing the effect of ALIGN LEFT.*

Up to HTML version 2.0, bottom/middle/top were the only possible values for the ALIGN attribute. It was probably the awkwardness of the ALIGN="top" effect that caused the Netscape people to jump the gun and implement the left and right values well before HTML 3.0 made them official. They were an immediate hit with HTML authors because they allowed what everyone instinctively knew ought to be possible—the ranging of blocks of text beside an image, as illustrated in Figure 4-9A where the ALIGN value is "right." Note that the lines of text are still left-justified, presenting their ragged ends to the picture. Purists hate that! You might choose to align the text right for a neater look—do this with <P ALIGN="right">, or better still <DIV ALIGN="right">.

With the Netscape Gold Editor you can choose the alignment graphically when you insert your image (see Figure 4-10). To change the alignment, right click on the image and choose Image Properties from the pop-up menu. Notice, in Figure 4-10, how we set all the other attributes of the image, too—ALT, HSPACE, VSPACE, and BORDER.

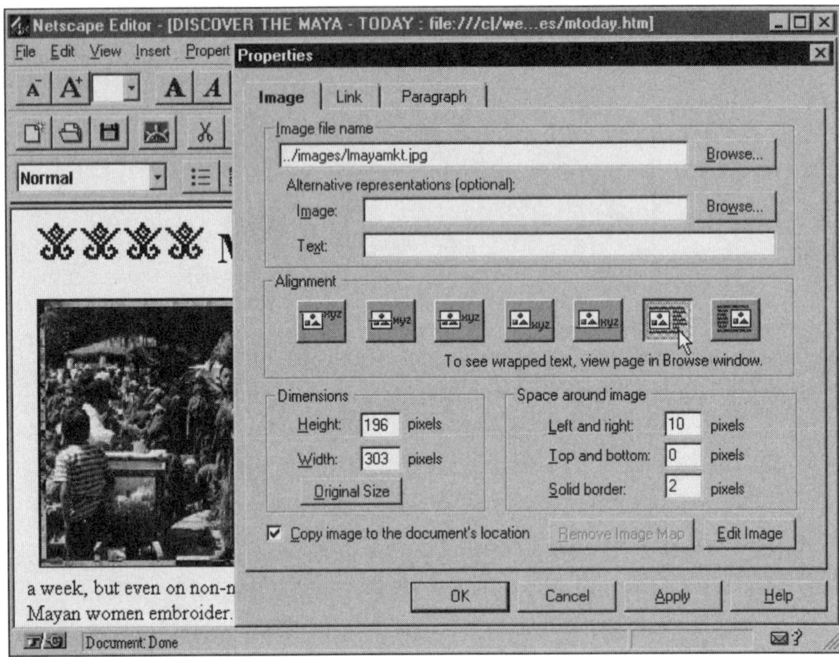

Figure 4-10: *Changing the image alignment attribute using the Netscape Gold editor.*

ALIGN="left" and ALIGN="right" technically have the effect of pushing the image to the left and right margins, respectively. But what's a margin, in the elastic world of computer graphics? If the image is the only one on the page, it simply means what you'd expect—the edge of the visible content window. But if there's already a picture at the margin, a second picture will simply stack up against it. This can be both a blessing and a curse, and we have more show-and-tell on this in Chapter 5, "Getting Stylish."

Extended Values of the ALIGN Attribute

Along with all of the other Netscape extensions to HTML 2.0 that were announced in early 1995, four (well, three really) refinements to the top/bottom/middle align values were announced. One picture is worth 1,000 words, so they say. By way of explanation of the new values, here's about 1,100 words-worth (Figure 4-11):

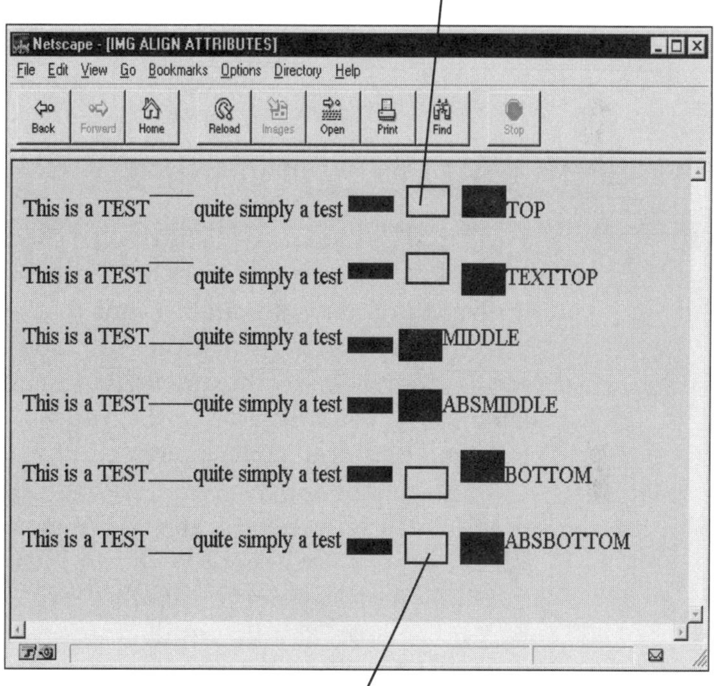

Figure 4-11: *Demonstration frame showing all the extended ALIGN values.*

TOP	The TOP of the image aligns to the TOP of the tallest object in the line to the image's left.
TEXTTOP	The TOP of the image aligns to the TOP of the text ASCENDERS (actually slightly above).

MIDDLE	The MIDDLE of the image aligns to the BASELINE of the text.
ABSMIDDLE	The MIDDLE of the image aligns to the MIDDLE of the text.
BOTTOM	The BOTTOM of the image aligns to the BASELINE of the text.
BASELINE	Same as BOTTOM.
ABSBOTTOM	The BOTTOM of the image aligns to the BOTTOM of the text descenders, OR the BOTTOM of the lowest object in the line to the image's left.

SPECIFYING IMAGE SIZE

The WIDTH and HEIGHT attributes specify the size of the image in pixels. One of its purposes is to speed up page loading, because it saves the client software the time it takes to calculate the image dimensions. When you use the Netscape Gold Editor to insert an image, the width and height attributes are automatically calculated for you and inserted in the code—a fine feature that saves time and cuts down the chances of error.

Guess what happens if you get one of the figures wrong? If you thought of a fairground distorting mirror, you weren't far wrong. What happens if you get *both* the width and height values wrong, but in the same proportion? Both 120 percent of what they should be, for instance? Yes, the result is an oversized picture that is not distorted (although it may get very pixillated if you go too far with this game). That's the idea behind an attribute that's been proposed for HTML 3.0—"UNITS=en". The idea is that you could specify an icon at a variable size, related to the size of the font that the user has selected—a process known as *auto scaling*. For example, the attributes WIDTH=8 HEIGHT=8 UNITS="en" would guarantee a square icon about twice the height of an uppercase letter, no matter what font size the user chose. This is a cute idea, and we hope Netscape implements it.

Note that in Figure 4-11 all of the solid black blocks, including the ones that look like em-dashes, are actually the same teensy-tiny GIF, only 802 bytes, consisting of a single pixel of black, but manipulated into three different shapes using the HEIGHT/ WIDTH attributes. The typographer Dave Siegel, in his "Tips for HTML Authors" page at http://www.best.com/~dsiegel/tips/, actually suggests making em-dashes by this method. We don't like that idea much personally, since we feel the color of an em-dash ought to match the color of the text on either side, and of course that cannot be guaranteed if you set the color of the em-dash in advance. Go ahead, though—feel free to use the technique to make colored blocks of any shape you want. Just realize that on browsers that don't recognize width and height attributes (and that's most of them), your pretty blocks will shrink right on back to one pixel.

The term *percentage auto scaling* refers to the use of a value for the WIDTH attribute that is a percentage of the current screen width. WIDTH=60% would convert to about 360 pixels under normal circumstances, but the image would shrink proportionally if the user shrank the screen. Perhaps more interesting, WIDTH=100% guarantees that those decorative bars that most Web designers like to use will stretch across the full width of the screen, even for people with 1280 X 1024 pixel video. HEIGHT=60% is interpreted as 60 percent of an average content window. This technique works very well with line art such as decorative rules and borders, but is fairly risky with full-color images. Image re-sizing, if it has to be done at all, is best done when the result is under your control.

Image Borders

Use of the BORDER attribute puts a border of the defined width in pixels all round the image. The color of the border will be the same as the text, whether as defined by the page author (see "Choosing Backgrounds & Text Colors" later this chapter) or overridden by the user's preference settings.

This can give an attractive effect, but it can also be confusing, since a colored border around an image is frequently taken to mean it is a hyperlink anchor. For that reason, it's good practice for both authors and users to choose very distinct colors for text and links. If the image in question *is* a link, the border will take on the link color and the thickness defined by BORDER=b (a link border is normally 2 pixels).

Note that BORDER=0 is a legitimate value, and it will have the effect of suppressing all image bordering, even when the image is a link. Use this when you don't want a colored border to destroy the look of your carefully composed image with a transparent background. The maximum thickness of a border is 127 pixels—and it looks pretty strange.

Making Space Around Images

Even before the advent of the ALIGN="left" and "right" values, it was noticeable that text tended to crowd images in a way that was not pleasing. One workaround was to tack neutral-colored borders onto inline images as a none-too-elegant way of holding the text off a bit. Now that wrapping text is more common, the HSPACE="h" and VSPACE="v" attributes are very useful. They specify that text—or another image—may not approach closer than h pixels horizontally and v pixels vertically. In Figure 4-9B the Mayan Market has the attribute HSPACE="10", and it's very beneficial to the look of the page. Note that the picture also offsets 10 pixels from the margin. If you want to create space on one side of an image only, a few nonbreaking spaces (c;) are a quick solution if you're separating images or you have only one line of text next to the image. For a larger block of text, you can use the "glass bricks trick" described later in this chapter or "Invisible Tables," in Chapter 5.

Providing Alternative Text With ALT

Back in Chapter 2, in the section "Document Checking," there's a list of all the HTML faults and peccadilloes that the Weblint HTML Validation service checks for. Among them is the question, "Do IMG elements have ALT text?" As a matter of fact, that's the *only* check that Weblint performs on IMG structures—and that's an indication of the importance of the attribute ALT="something for users to read if they are not displaying images." Don't forget that over 5 percent of your users may be seeing your work through the image-blind eyes of the Lynx browser, and when Lynx encounters an IMG tag without any ALT attribute, it places the marker "[IMAGE]" on the user's screen. The user's natural reaction is "Oh yeah? What am I missing here?" There are also those Web surfers in a hurry or those with slow modems who may prefer to run in images-off mode and take the option of loading only necessary images. They won't be able to tell the difference between a simple color rule or an image map unless you tell them so. Here are some suggestions for appropriate ALT text for various image types.

BUTTON	"o"
BAR	"HR" or "======================"
ICON	"ICON"
THUMBNAIL	"IMAGE LINK"
PORTRAIT	"Pic of [whatever]"
BANNER	"BANNER"
BORDER	"BORDER"
PANEL	"Pic of [whatever]"

TIP

While some attributes work equally well whether or not you put quotation marks around the attribute value, with others the quotation marks are essential. One example is HREF="..". ALT will generally work without the quotation marks, but not as you expect. If you write ALT=Tonya Harding's wedding, Lynx users will see only the first word, [Tonya]. It should be ALT="Tonya Harding's wedding."

Integrating Inline Images

For further tips on image placement, as for all aspects of Web design, DO learn from other people. When you see a page you think is successful, don't just say to yourself, "I wonder how they did that?" Check the source code and find out.

Here's a DON'T to match the DO. DON'T try to imitate magazine pages. It simply is not possible to design a Web page with the same rigid view of the relationship between text and pictures that a magazine art director has, and therefore it's foolish to attempt it. That does NOT mean, however, that you can't achieve some very pleasing effects on a Web page—particularly if you know some of the more advanced tricks we're about to describe.

Figure 4-12 shows the kind of trap an inexperienced Web designer can easily fall into. All it takes to throw off the designer's intent is for the user to set the font size on his or her browser one size bigger.

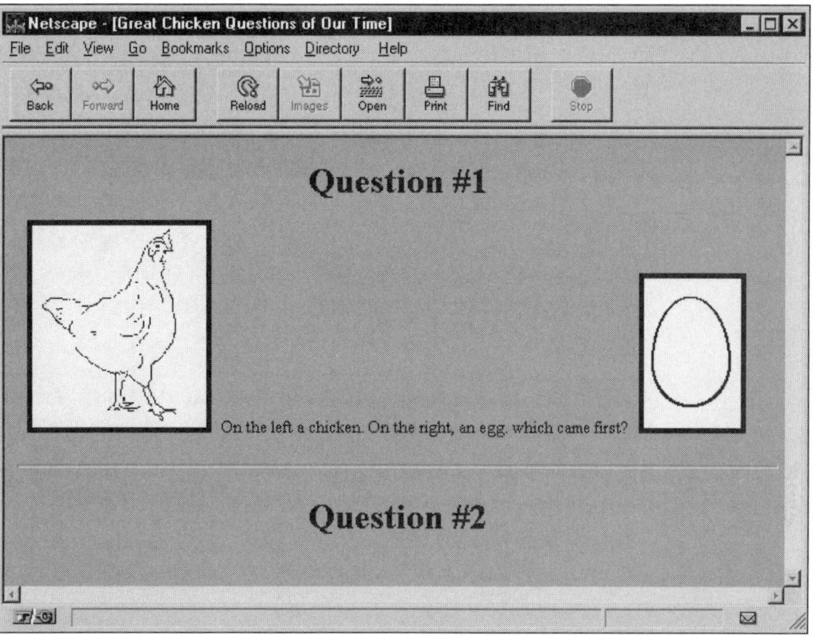

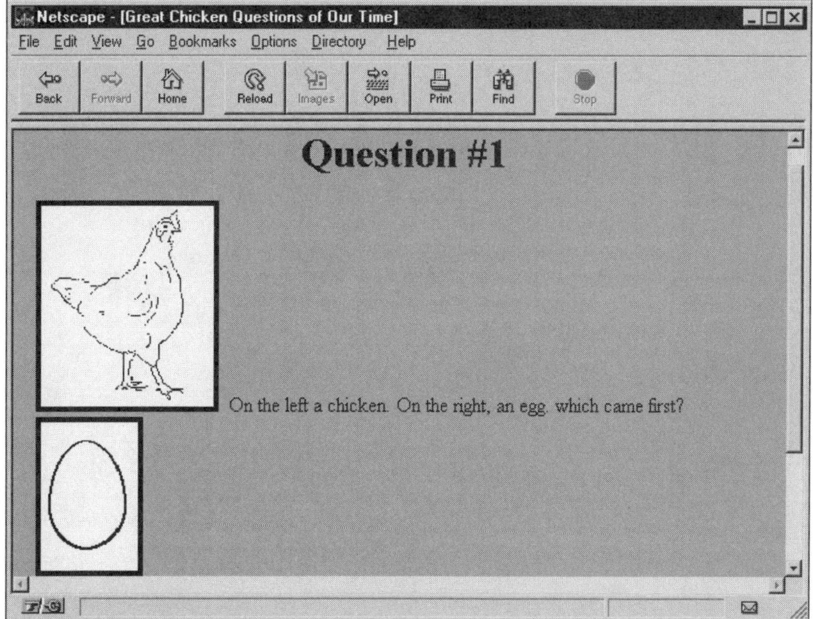

Figure 4-12: *Changing the font size from 10-point to 12-point upsets this design.*

Not all design professionals have taken kindly to the freedom the Web allows its users, and some who would like to take advantage of the Web distribution network simply don't have the resources or time to convert their regular format to HTML. For these there's the Portable Document Format (PDF), which allows the page to be displayed in its original format, or exactly as its designer intended. The New York Times is one organization that has taken advantage of this format for its online version (see Figure 4-13). The Acrobat Amber Reader can be obtained by FTP at: **http://www.adobe.com/Software/Acrobat**

Acrobat conversion software is also available from Adobe. If you have existing documents that you'd like to make available over a network or the Web and don't want to take the time to reformat them, you can convert them to PDF and post them and be sure that readers who have the Acrobat Reader will be able to view them.

Figure 4-13: *Part of the daily "NYTimesfax" seen by Adobe Acrobat, the foremost PDF application.*

But back to the options for integrating text with images using HTML. How do you make text flow effectively around images, when you can't be sure what screen size or font size your viewers will be using? There are in fact some successful techniques that are flexible enough to allow for viewer variation.

Text Flow

Figure 4-9B shows how immediately effective the ALIGN="left" attribute is in flowing accompanying text around a picture. Dead screen space is put to good use, and the user has less scrolling to do to get the information.

In Figure 4-14, various IMG attributes and formatting tags have been used to create complex text flow and planned empty spaces, for an overall effect.

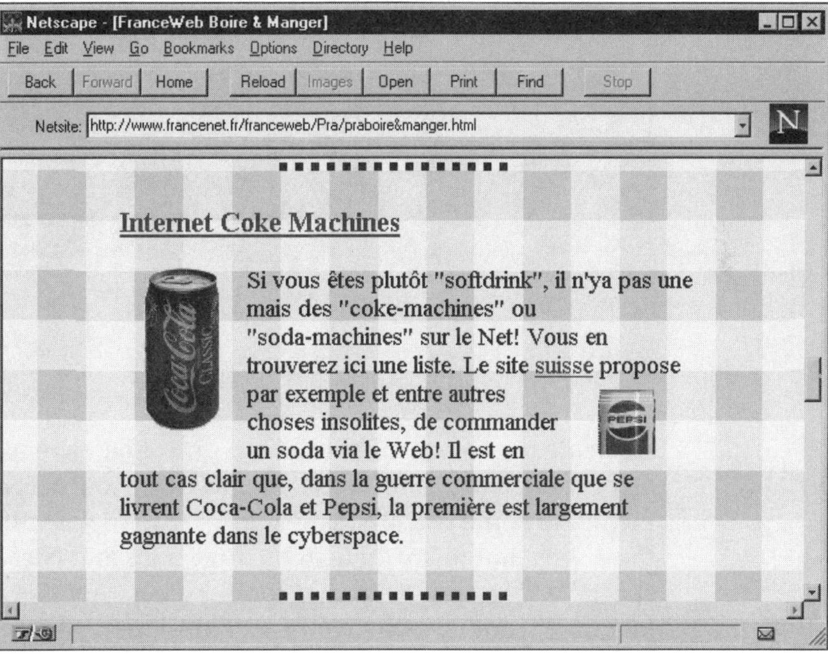

Figure 4-14: *More advanced text flow.*

This is just one section of a huge page about the delights of eating and drinking at "FranceWeb," and the design holds up quite well with changed font size (within reason!).

Figure 4-15, on the other hand, is a kind of in-joke, intended to make the point that you *cannot* flow text around the contour of a picture as you can on a magazine or brochure page.

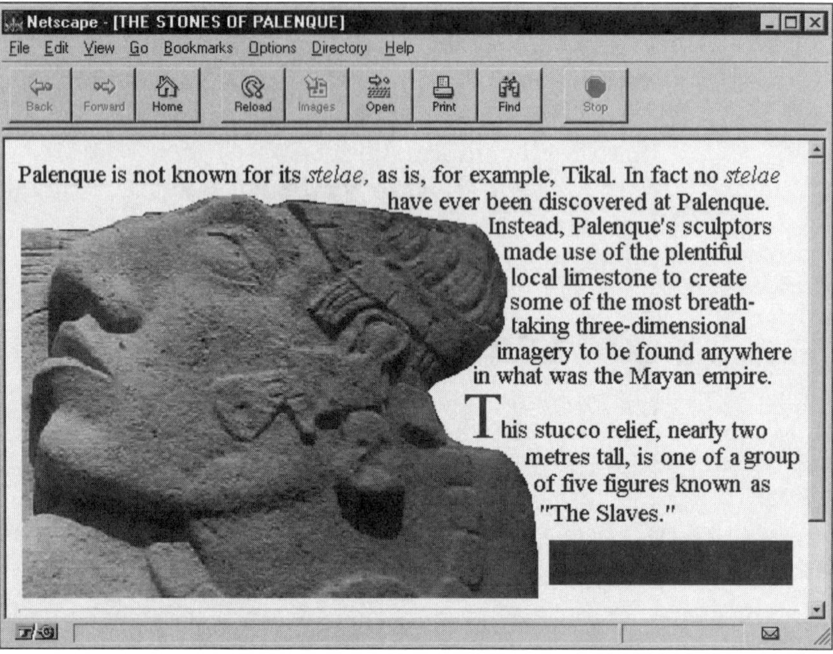

Figure 4-15: *Flow of text around an image contour—OR IS IT?*

To create this effect, all but the top line of lettering was actually incorporated as a part of the picture, so it's not text at all but a picture of some text. To make it appear to flow continuously from the only genuine line of text, the font sizes and backgrounds were specially matched. No prizes for guessing why this attractive looking layout is, in fact, poor Web design.

Drop Caps

The people who spend their lives debating the standards and practices of HTML (endlessly, it sometimes seems) have considered, and so far rejected, suggestions for some such tag as:

```
<P DROP LINES=4 BORDER=4>W</DROP>hilst I alone did call upon
thine aid,<BR>
My verse alone had all thy gentle grace;<BR>
But now my gracious numbers are decay'd<BR>
And my sick Muse doth give another place.<BR>
```

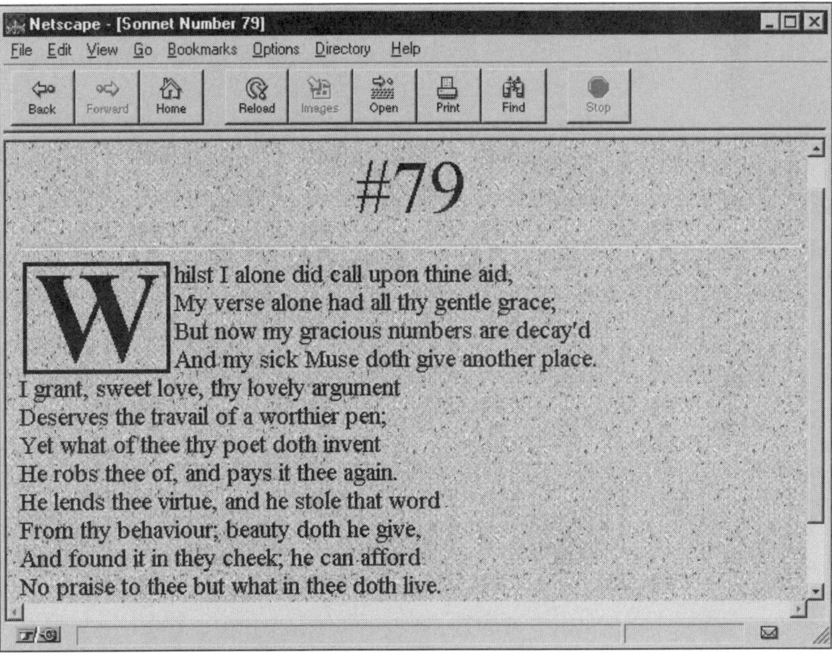

Figure 4-16: *Flow of text around a drop cap image.*

This pseudo-code is supposed to call for a drop-cap W four lines high, with a 4-pixel border, as depicted in Figure 4-16. Code of this type may one day be approved and implemented, although it now seems more likely you will be able to use a separate document called a *style sheet* (see Chapter 5) to define paragraph style, including drop-caps. Meanwhile, there's nothing to stop us from making an inline GIF of a large W and giving it the attributes ALIGN="left" HEIGHT=40 WIDTH=32 HSPACE=3 ALT="W". That is, in fact, exactly how Figure 4-16 was created.

MAKING INTERLACED GIFS

When the NCSA Mosaic Web browser was first released in 1993, it made many people suddenly understand the virtues of the Internet for the first time. It was so immediate, so flexible. For some time its users were blind to some pretty obvious faults. One of them was that the entire contents of a page had to be downloaded into cache before any of it was displayed. It may seem incredible now, but yes, folks, in those far-off days every GIF, every icon, every button had to be safely in the bag before you were given anything to look at.

When Netscape first came onto the scene in 1994, it went some way toward improving download with its concept of the multipass download, whereby the client grabs a bit of text, then a bit of image A, then a bit more text, then part of image B, and so on. As the page is on its way to the user there's always something happening, and most of the text comes up pretty quickly. That seemed good enough for a while, but the question of download time became such a major issue on the Web—designers wanting more and more complex pages, and users demanding faster and faster service—that a couple more steps have been taken along the road to solving this problem.

The first was support for a refinement of the GIF image format—the so-called "interlaced" GIF. This format, also a CompuServe invention, allows for the possibility of storing and displaying the lines non-sequentially. Instead of lines 1,2,3,4...n the image is displayed as follows:

First pass: ***Every 8th line starting at line 1***
Second pass: ***Every 8th line starting at line 9***
Third pass: ***Every 4th line starting at line 3***
Last pass: ***Every 2nd line starting at line 2***

The developers of the Netscape Navigator took advantage of this to display interlaced GIFs first in "venetian blind" mode and now in fully-interpolated mode. By "fully-interpolated" we mean that an entire image is displayed even if only partial information about its content is available. This leads to the brick wall type of effect illustrated in Figure 4-17. Interlacing actually *extends* the time needed to display an image by a small amount, but because it gives the user something to watch it seems quicker. Note that the first two passes combined only give the user a quarter of the total information in the image, so they are very quick.

Figure 4-17: *Progressive development of an interlaced image over the four passes.*

TIP

Peter Kaminsky, who offers the Internet community valuable services such as lists of ISPs, uses the interlacing sequence ingeniously in his logo at ***http://www.pdial.com.*** *The logo's background is mostly neutral colored, but every 8th line is blue. The first pass, therefore, develops a completely blue field, and subsequent passes fragment it more and more.*

If you want to interlace your own inline images, there are several affordable options. The image manipulation software LView Pro will interlace any GIF for you as it saves the image. Just choose the save GIFs Interlaced command from the Option menu.

LView Pro is available on the Companion CD-ROM or you can get it at:

ftp.ncsa.uiuc.edu/Web/Mosaic/Windows/viewers

16-bit: lviewp1c.zip
32-bit: lviewpro.zip

Another tool that will interlace your GIFs is a shareware application called WINGIF. It's available by FTP from:

gatekeeper.dec.com/pub/micro/msdos/win3/desktop/wingif14.zip

To make an interlaced GIF, load your image file into WINGIF, then save it, selecting a radio button and a check box in the File/Save dialog box to save it in the Interlaced GIF format.

A company called Visioneering Research Laboratory, Inc., of Las Cruces, New Mexico, offers an online service they call the Imaging Machine. As a way of promoting their advanced image manipulation services they will instantly carry out a variety of functions on your own GIF files, including interlacing by the ImageMagick process and also transparency, filtering, indexing, color compression, and much, much more. The only snag is that your GIF has to be on the Web already and have a URL. Enter the fully-qualified URL into the page at:

http://www.vrl.com:80/Imaging

If you work in UNIX, and you have UNIX image management tools, you can interlace a GIF using a switch on the ppmtogif utility. The command to interlace fishsoup.gif, creating ifishsoup.gif, would be:

```
cat fishsoup.gif | giftoppm | ppmtogif
-interlace >ifishsoup.gif
```

Other Forms of Image Interlacing

We mentioned a few pages back that the GIF image format had tricks up its sleeve that JPEG couldn't match, and that accounted for its popularity. Interlacing was one such exclusive trick—until progressive JPEGs came along.

Progressive JPEGs

If you remember, it's an important feature of the JPEG format that it allows wide latitude for trade-off of compression against image quality. JPEG's ability to derive a highly compressed—but poor quality—version of an image has recently been used to create a process that's claimed to be even more effective than GIF interlacing. In a so-called *progressive* JPEG, the very compressed version is loaded first, then better and better versions are loaded into the same screen space, gradually working up to the final image quality the author specified. The effect is like a very fuzzy picture coming gradually into focus, and it is indeed true that the "first pass" image displays very quickly. The processing time for subsequent passes is not trivial, but for those of us who depend on modems for our Net connection, processing time is swamped by transmission time so total load time is about the same as for a "baseline" JPEG. Amazingly, a progressive JPEG is generally a somewhat smaller file than its baseline equivalent.

Software for making progressive JPEGs is not very plentiful as we write this, neither are browsers capable of displaying progressives (Navigator versions 2.0b3 and later support them). We use a DOS command line application called JPEGTRAN for transforming our existing JPEGs, and CJPEG for converting a GIF

to a progressive JPEG. A complete software kit including both these utilities can be obtained from:
ftp://ftp.coast.net/SimTel/msdos/graphics

The file is JPEG6.ZIP for 16-bit, JPEG6386.ZIP for 32-bit.

Other software will undoubtedly be available soon. You should check the Netscape pages and other online resources for these.

PNG to the Rescue!

So GIF's days seem to be numbered, not so much because of the licensing controversy as because of its inherent restriction to 8-bit color. JPEG will never quite fill the gap, because it's lossy and it can never be made "transparent" (we're getting to that shortly). Isn't it time some genius thought up an image format specifically for the Web, with all the features Web designers look for?

Surprise, surprise—we weren't the first to have had this thought. The developers of the Portable Network Graphics (PNG) format claim, tongue in cheek, that its main advantage over GIF is that everyone knows how to pronounce it (it's "PING," whereas nobody truly knows whether GIF is pronounced "GIFF" or "JIFF."). More technically, its advantages are:

- Lossless compression up to 30%
- Up to 48-bit color, 16-bit grayscale
- Two-dimensional 7-pass interlacing
- Superior transparency declaration
- Error-checking

PNG was developed by a consortium of computer graphics enthusiasts, including a NASA group and a W3 group, as a direct response to the GIF patent controversy. CompuServe very shortly adopted it as their own preferred replacement for GIF, and effectively killed off the nascent GIF24 format. PNG's "home page" is:
http://quest.jpl.nasa.gov

Expect to see it incorporated into imaging software soon.

Temporary LOWSRC Images

Another, even more recent, bright idea of the Netscape developers to lend apparent speed to downloading is to recognize an IMG attribute that will display an entire temporary image on the first pass through the document. On subsequent passes the final high-resolution image will be progressively substituted, so that when the page is finished the low resolution image is no longer seen. The dimensions of both must be the same, because an area of the document is "reserved" by the low-resolution image and cannot be changed on a subsequent pass.

Low-source images are often used effectively to put up a black and white image that is then overlaid with a color one. A particularly crafty version of this is shown on the Companion CD-ROM in Figure 6-2. The crucial attribute here is LOWSRC, used as follows:

```
<IMG SRC="icons/windows.gif" WIDTH=428 HEIGHT=224
LOWSRC="icons/windows1.gif">
```

This technique is also often used to put a solid block of color into the space reserved for the final image. So long as the WIDTH and HEIGHT attributes are defined appropriately for the final image, a LOWSRC image which is just a tile of solid color can be any size you like, and so can be extremely quick-loading. It should be obvious, by the way, that LOWSRC does *not* speed up the appearance of an image. On the contrary!

TRANSPARENT COLORS

Take a look back at Figure 4-15. The *infamous* Figure 4-15, we might almost say. The reason the text contouring effect that we faked is impossible within the strict rules of HTML is that an inline image must have a rectangular shape. You can squeeze it and stretch it and venetian-blind it and brick-wall it, but it must be rectangular and text cannot trespass upon its perimeter.

Nobody, however, said it has to *look* rectangular. Imagine the lettering removed from Figure 4-15—that wouldn't strike you as a rectangular image, but it is. Better still, look at Figure 4-18A. Never mind how the pattern got there for the moment—we'll be coming to that in the next section. But surely *that's* not a rectangular image? Yep, it is—as Figure 4-18B shows, when you try to approach text to it. So what's going on here?

A

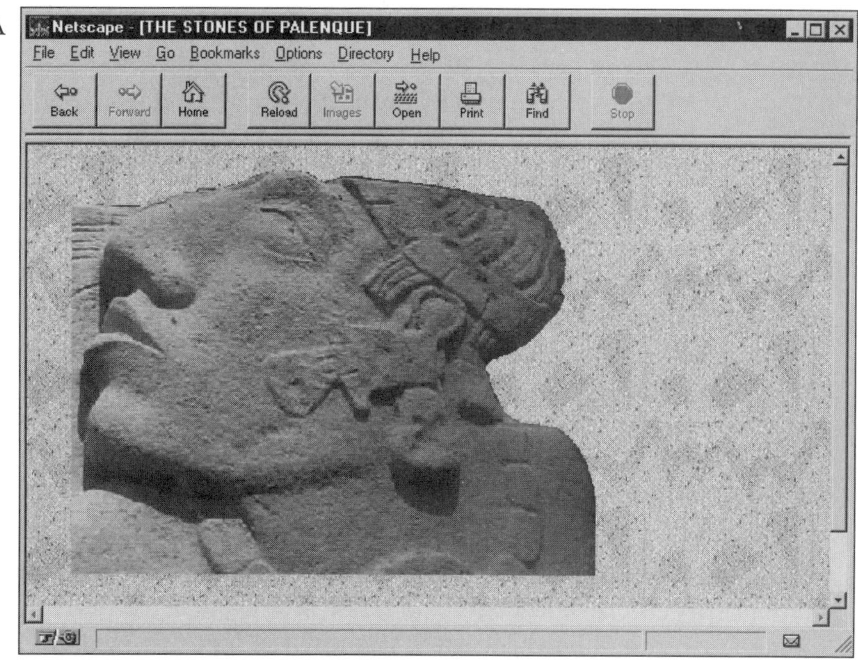

B

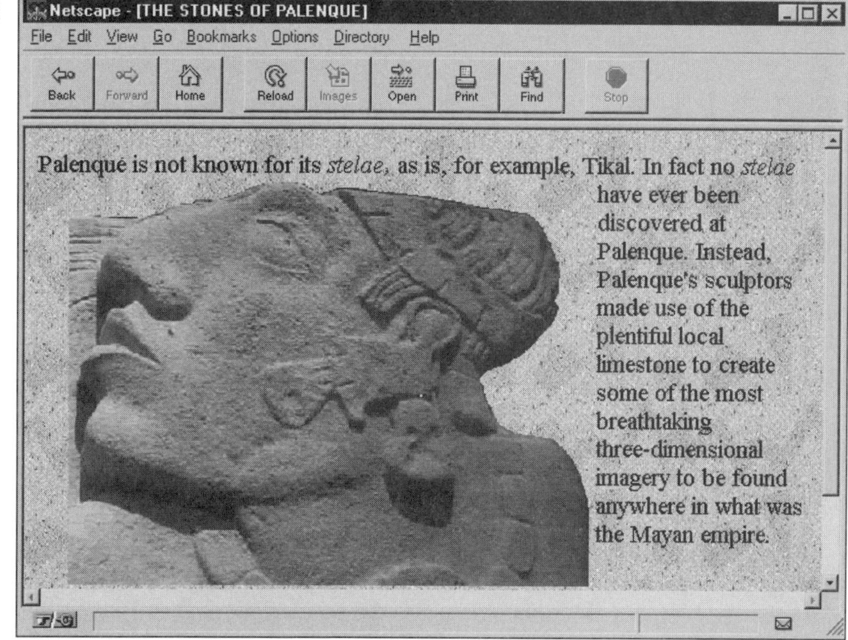

Figures 4-18 A&B: *Transparent image on a background, looking as though you can contour text to it—until you try.*

Chipping Away at an Image

The answer is that this is a *transparent* GIF—or, more accurately, a GIF in which one color has been declared transparent. This is a special feature of the GIF 89a format, and here's how it was done in detail.

First we scanned the photo to make a 400 X 300 pixel JPEG file (it is actually one we shot ourselves—not something we stole off the Web or out of a library book). Then we brought it into our favorite graphics editor, added some free space around it, and converted it to GIF format. Then we chipped away at the top and right-hand side of the image to "reveal" a pale gray background. We set this pale gray background color ourselves (RGB 240,240,240)—it's important to choose a color that is NOT present anywhere in the image itself, which was not at all hard in this case.

When we got bored with making pale gray pixels, we saved it and opened it up in LView Pro. Then we picked the menu choices Options/Background color, and located the palette representing our 240,240,240 gray, as shown in Figure 4-19. Behind the palette in that figure you can see the stone carving masked in black, which is how LView Pro lets you know when you've got the right color in the palette.

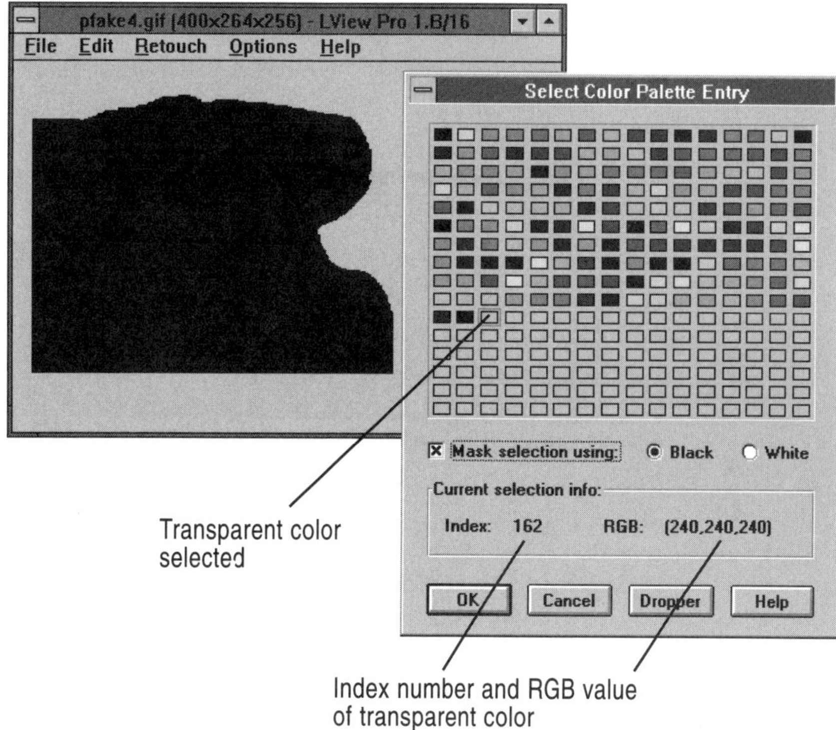

Figure 4-19: *Selecting a color to make transparent in LView Pro. Transparent color selected*

Finally, we exited via the menu option File/Save as..., and, using the "Save File As Type" pull-down provided, changed the image type from GIF 87a to GIF 89a. In the GIF 89a format, space is provided in the file header to declare one color transparent. It's referenced by an index number, rather than an RGB value (in this case it's Index 162, as you can also see in the figure), and the effect of it is that when Netscape displays the image, every time it comes to a pixel of that color it simply ignores it and displays nothing at all. Not pale gray—nothing. Images like the one shown in Figure 4-18 are sometimes called "floating images" because they seem to float on the background.

TIP

LView Pro is the easiest way to make transparent colors, but it's far from being the only way. Check the latest scoop on this topic on the transparency page at:

http://melmac.corp.harris.com/transparent_images.html

If you have a simple image, you needn't go to these lengths to create a transparent GIF. The balls that are often used instead of list bullets or other types of icons are common examples. In this case, the background is simply one solid color, usually white or black on which the image stands out. If you create your own icons, you'll want to make them transparent. This is how to do it in LView Pro (other image editors should have a similar procedure):

1. Choose Options/Background Color.
2. Select the color you want to make transparent from the palette.
3. Choose Mask color to mask everything in the picture but the color you've chosen to be transparent. (If your background color is white, you'll want the mask to be black, and vice versa.)
4. Choose OK. Then choose File/Save As, and select GIF89a format.

You won't see the effect of this in LView. View the file in Netscape Navigator to check that it worked as you intended.

CHROMA-KEY

Color transparency on the Web is analogous to chroma-keying in a TV studio. A chroma-key vision mixing circuit scans a foreground picture and, wherever it sees a pixel of a certain color, switches the output to the equivalent pixel of a background picture source. Both picture sources and the key color are controlled at the mixing desk, and that's how the weather map appears behind the weatherman (and in parts of his tie, if the keying color and the tie have not been chosen judiciously!).

The reason you must choose a color for transparency that's not used in the image itself is exactly the computer graphics equivalent of the problem of the weatherman's tie. The technology just does what it's told and makes no judgment about whether pixels properly belong to the foreground or background.

GLASS BRICKS TRICKS

Transparent colors were devised to make effects like Figure 4-18, but it wasn't long before some bright Web author wondered what mischief he or she could get up to with an *all*-transparent GIF. Quite a lot, as it turned out.

Many people who come from a background in typography to HTML authoring get annoyed by HTML's disdain for tabs and other methods of spacing text. (In HTML, all so-called "whitespace" is reduced to a single space character.) Once again, this is largely the reaction of people who wish that Web pages were magazine pages—but we confess to sometimes wishing we could indent text and space out pictures ourselves. Thanks to what we call "glass bricks," we can. Figure 4-20A shows a fairly attractive page in Netscape, and Figure 4-20B is the same page in Mosaic.

A

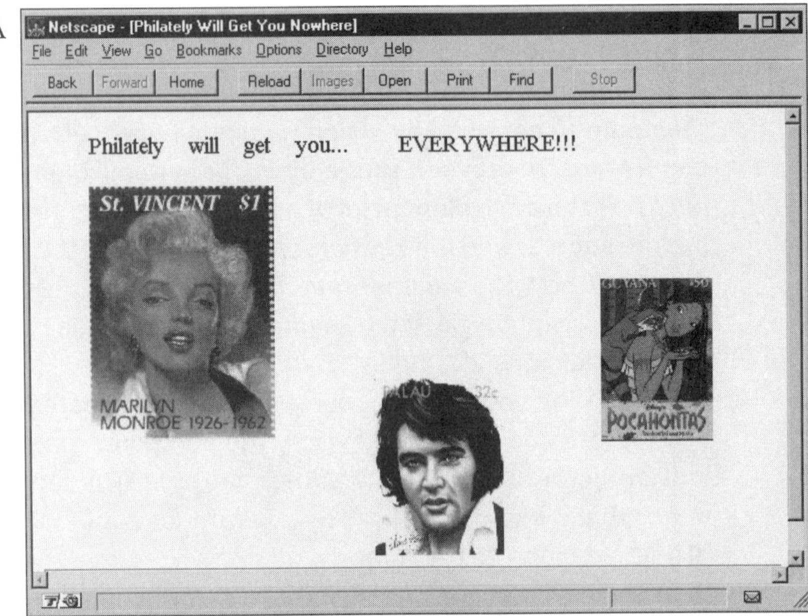

B

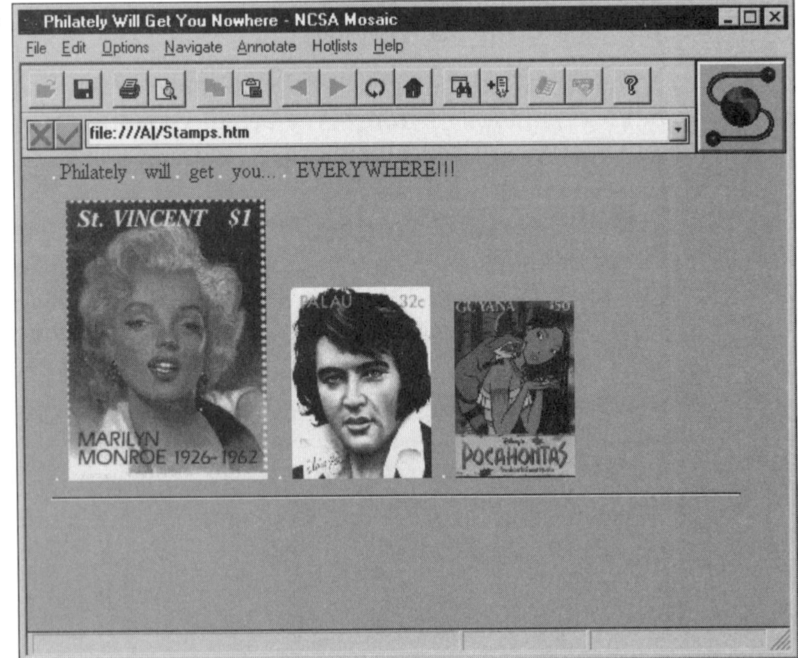

Figure 4-20 A&B: *Page laid out using "glass bricks," as seen by Netscape (top) and Mosaic (bottom).*

The Mosaic page not only reveals where the glass bricks are, but serves as a warning that Netscape page design is not always portable. The HTML code is:

```
<P><IMG SRC="gblock.gif" WIDTH=35 HEIGHT=2>
Philately<IMG SRC="gblock.gif" WIDTH=15 HEIGHT=2>
will<IMG SRC="gblock.gif" WIDTH=15 HEIGHT=2>
get<IMG SRC="gblock.gif" WIDTH=15 HEIGHT=2>
you...<IMG SRC="gblock.gif" WIDTH=35 HEIGHT=2>
EVERYWHERE!!!</P>
<IMG SRC="gblock.gif" WIDTH=35 HEIGHT=2>
<IMG SRC="marilyn.jpg">
<IMG SRC="gblock.gif" WIDTH=70 HEIGHT=2>
<FONT SIZE=7>
<IMG SRC="elvis.jpg" ALIGN="texttop"></FONT>
<IMG SRC="gblock.gif" WIDTH=70 HEIGHT=2>
<IMG SRC="poca.jpg" ALIGN="bottom">
```

The image "gblock.gif" is simply a 2- X 2-pixel white square with white being declared transparent—there's no need to make it any bigger, since the WIDTH and HEIGHT attributes allow you to "stretch" it to fit. However, since these attributes are not recognized by Mosaic, you could choose to make several " glass bricks" of different sizes to ensure it translates better to other browsers.

Choosing Backgrounds & Text Colors

It seems incredible already—and it's only been a matter of months—that there was a time when a Web page designer had no control over the color treatment of the page. Certain folks in the HTML community grumbled when Netscape implemented the coloring attributes, but there's no noticeable agitation now to return to the "good old days" before color specification. (See, however, the section "Style Sheets" in Chapter 5.) Note that the designer still has no *absolute* control over colors. The philosophy is, "Give the designer the ability to specify colors; give the user the ability to ignore the designer's intentions," which is probably correct.

Perhaps what the HTML purists found distasteful about Netscape's color elements was that they were introduced as attributes of the <BODY> tag, which was never intended to have attributes. Be that as it may, here's a complete list:

<BODY> color attributes:

BGCOLOR="#rrggbb"	Background color
TEXT="#rrggbb"	General text color
LINK="#rrggbb"	Link color
VLINK="#rrggbb"	Visited link color
ALINK="#rrggbb"	Active link color
BACKGROUND="foobar.gif"	Background image

The "#rrggbb" elements are strings of three hexadecimal numbers (see sidebar) defining the red, green, and blue components of the 24-bit color, respectively. Pure red is #ff0000, for example—and a fairly long list of designer colors with their #rrggbb equivalents is included as Appendix F of this book.

HEXADECIMAL NUMBERS

The hexadecimal numbering system is chosen for color definition strings because it relates more closely to the actual 24-bit color information, and all possible colors can be defined using six digits.

Hexadecimal simply means "base 16" as opposed to our everyday decimal, base 10, system. The first 16 numbers in the hexadecimal system are 1,2,3,4,5,6,7,8,9,A,B,C,D,E,F,10. The number FF is the same as decimal 255.

Here's an example of a complete color definition:

```
<BODY BGCOLOR="#00938f" TEXT="#000000" LINK="#ff4500"
VLINK="#912cee" ALINK="fff0f5">
```

That defines a page whose basic color treatment is black text on a "medium aquamarine" background. Links are in orange-red, visited links in purple, and active links in "lavender blush." The active link color is displayed only while the mouse button is actually depressed on the link, so it's usually just a quick flash of color.

Any color elements that are not defined as BODY attributes on a page simply default to the user's own settings—and the user can choose to override any of them by appropriate settings in Netscape's Fonts and Colors Preferences dialog box.

That also applies to the other BODY attribute, the BACKGROUND="foobar.gif" statement. This causes "foobar.gif" to appear as a background pattern for the whole page. If "foobar.gif" is not big enough to cover the page either in width or height, it is automatically repeated—or "tiled"—as many times as necessary. Figure 4-21 shows a well-executed and amusing example of the use of a background GIF.

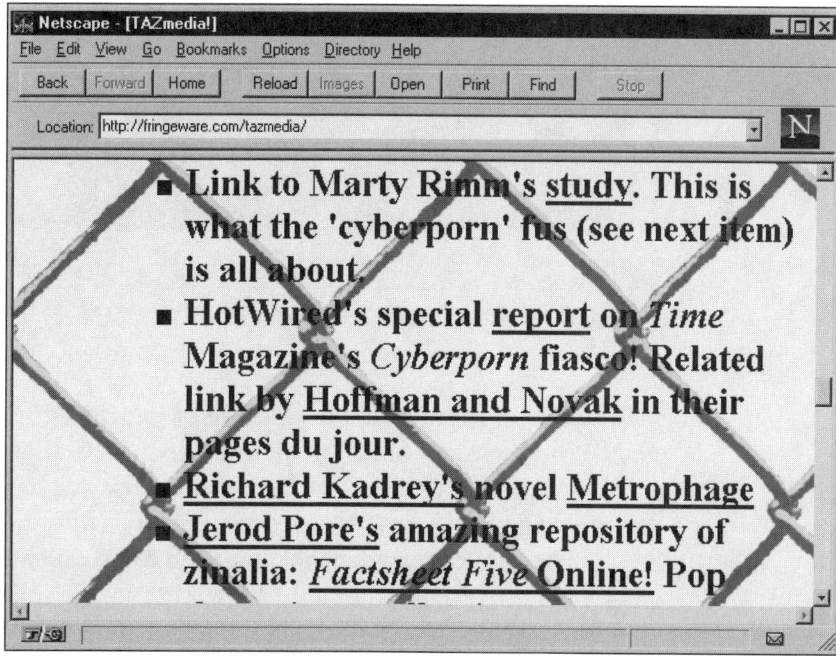

Figure 4-21: *The TAZMEDIA page: one image repeated endlessly as a background.*

Now It Can Be Told: This is how the background of Figure 4-18 was done. Now that that's no longer a secret we can put it together with some other techniques we've covered in this chapter to create a page that comes fairly close to the wrap-around text effect we were simulating in Figure 4-15, yet is legitimate HTML that makes sense to almost any browser. Here it is—Figure 4-22.

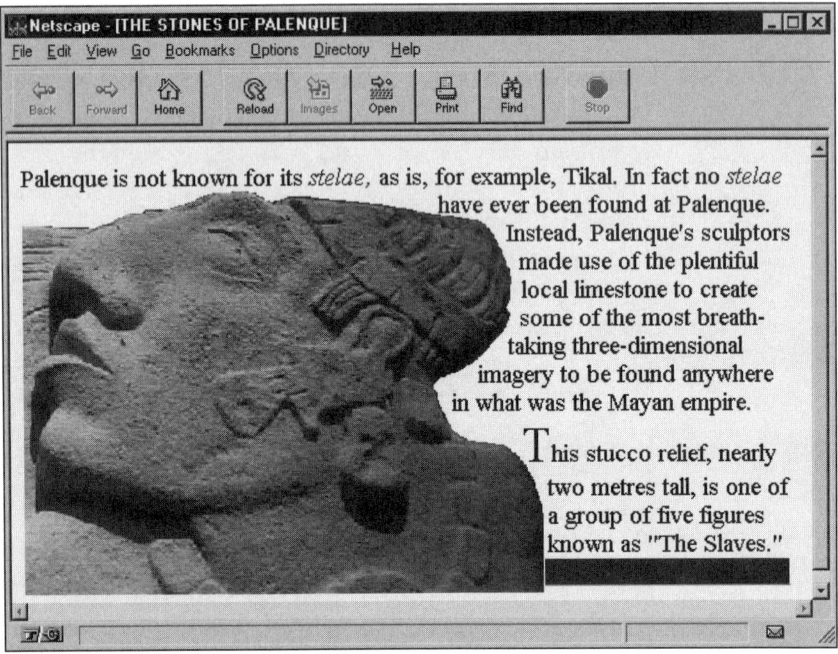

Figure 4-22: *A "legitimate" version of Figure 4-15.*

The chief (but not the only) crime of Figure 4-15 was, of course, that it put so much of its "text" into the picture that it would have been completely useless to a user who chose not to view images. Incorporating "decorative" text into a GIF is allowable for a header or anything that's short enough to be repeated as the ALT text, but Figure 4-15 went way beyond that. We call Figure 4-22 "legitimate" because its text really is text. The stone carving picture has gone into the background, and the text has been pushed over using a glass brick tailored for each line, so as to achieve something like the original contouring effect. We were careful to pad the background GIF with enough background so that it appears once only in all conditions we could think of. This technique is still, however, somewhat vulnerable to users' change of font size, and we would only use it for a special effect.

We can also use the BACKGROUND attribute to enhance Figure 4-8, the Palenque thumbnail page. Figure 4-23 shows a page with the statement <BODY BACKGROUND="psite.gif">

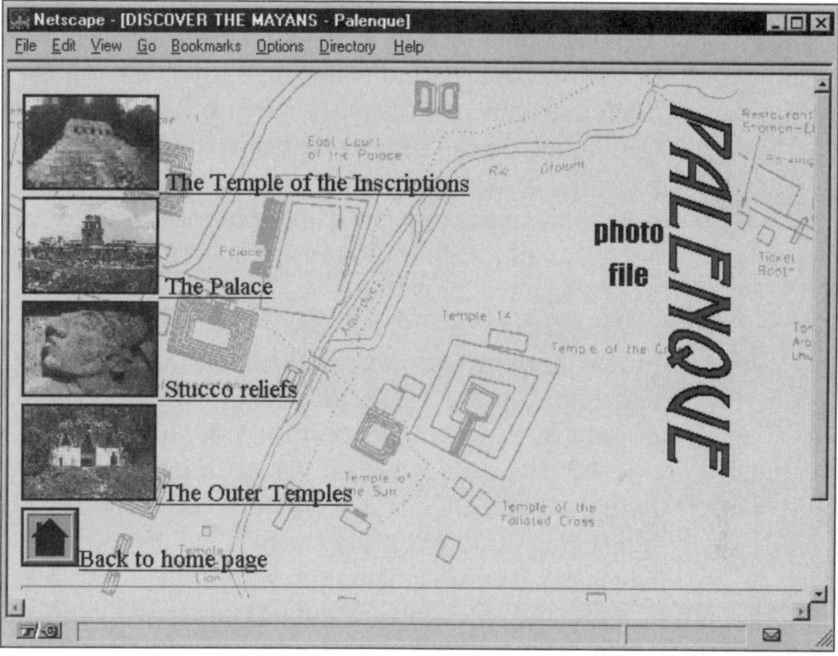

Figure 4-23: *The final version of Figure 4-8.*

The original page had too much empty space in the center, which we can now fill in with an evocative background. The border image is now also "floating."

TIP

The background of Figure 4-23 is an image of a guidebook map of the Palenque site. For this type of image, a "washed out" effect is desirable, so that the background doesn't tend to make the foreground unreadable.

If you have a graphics editor that allows you to decrease contrast and increase gamma, you'll find that to be very effective on the type of contrasty image we were dealing with here. For treating more complex images, edge softening may also be a good technique. NOTE: The technicalities of gamma correction are discussed briefly in the glossary, but you'll learn what you most need by trial and error anyway.

Background Color Slabs

Although the attribute BGCOLOR="#ffffff" is the "natural" way to define the background color of your page, some Web designers don't like using it because its texture is somewhat unreliable. Depending on the user's setup and the foreground content of the page, the background color can end up looking grainy (a frequent reason for this is that the background color is "dithered" because it's not available in the Netscape color cube. For the cleanest effect, stick to the six color levels 00,33,66,99,cc, and ff).

An alternative—which slows down page loading, but not much—is to provide a GIF which is simply a slab of plain color and specify it as BACKGROUND="slab.gif". The size of the slab doesn't really matter, since it is tiled into the entire background, but 50 X 50 pixels is a good bet. Yet another technique is to specify both a BGCOLOR *and* BACKGROUND="foo.gif". This has the interesting effect of letting the BGCOLOR show through at certain edges, notably at horizontal rules.

A background slab can even be arranged to create a "special effect" when a user arrives on your page. If the background GIF is 300 pixels high but only two pixels wide, and in an eye-catching color, it will create an effect exactly like a wipe edit in a movie as it tiles into the background two pixels at a time.

TIP

Netscape background "libraries" are now as common as icon libraries. Look around, and you'll find concrete, cork, pebbledash, spackle, chipboard, human skin... virtually anything. A generous assortment of background GIFs is also available on the Companion CD-ROM with this book.

The Basics of Image Enhancement

We already made passing reference to gamma correction, as a way of treating images to make them suitable for backgrounds. Gamma correction sounds scary enough (check the glossary for the real meaning), but it doesn't stop there. Among the processes offered by modern graphics editing software are resampling, despeckling, eroding, embossing, and mosaicing. You can posterize, solarize, or pinch deform, or....

No, we're not going to explain all of these image manipulations. Some of them are only available on really professional systems, and some create great effects but have little application on the Web. To be brutally honest, there are better books than this on the subject.

Sharpening and softening, however, are enhancement techniques that we use very regularly, and you don't have to pay top dollar for software that will do a good job of this. Virtually every photographic image that we used to make the illustrations for this book were sharpened to some degree, using either the Microsoft Image Manager or Paint Shop Pro. Sharpening, also known as *edge-enhancement*, simply passes the image file through an algorithm that looks for boundaries between colors. When it finds a boundary, it tries to decide what the principal colors are on each side of the boundary, and converts pixels of intermediate tone to one or other of the principals. The effect can be miraculous—it brought some of those Maya pictures to life in a wonderful way—but its success is obviously not guaranteed. Our advice is to try a little at a time. We often notice inline images on the Web that have been oversharpened, giving a metallic look that we don't much like.

If sharpening is so wonderful, why would you ever need to *soften* an image? "Jaggies" or "stair-steps," correctly known as *aliasing* are the answer. Unlike a photographic image, which benefits from sharpening, line art can look jagged at sloping or rounded edges unless the image is very big. That's because, on the Web, you only have a given resolution to work with, as we discussed at length earlier in this chapter.

To take an extreme case, think about representing a circle only eight pixels in diameter. There simply aren't enough pixels available to create a plausible-looking curve. The softening process, technically known as *anti-aliasing*, seeks out boundaries and actually adds pixels of intermediate tone to fool you into thinking you have more definition than you really have. Anti-aliasing is in the eye of the beholder—sometimes it makes an image merely look out of focus, sometimes it works really well. Figure 4-24 shows a "before and after" of one part of a company logo. The original was pure black and white, but some of the added pixels are actually colored—a legitimate technique that helps the deception.

Figure 4-24: *Part of a logo before (top) and after (bottom) anti-aliasing.*

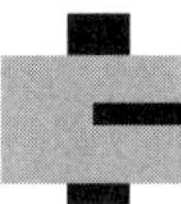

Creating Active Images

Any single image on a Web page that has hyperlinks to more than one destination is an *active image*. You must have seen plenty of these while cruising the Web—there's a good example on MCI's Gramercy Press site, shown in Figure 4-25.

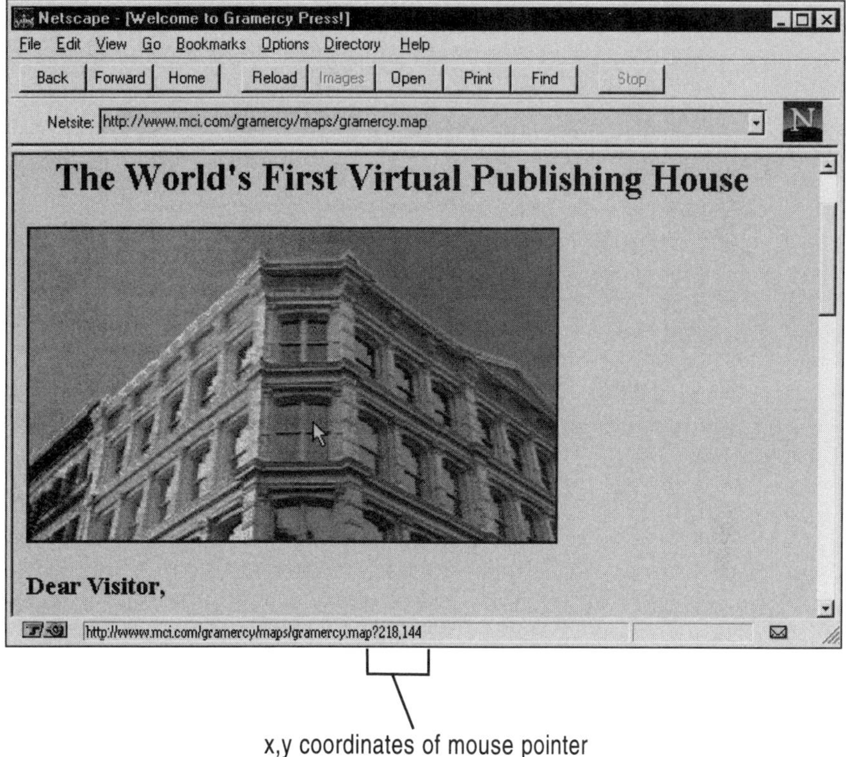

Figure 4-25: *Click on almost any window of the Gramercy Press building to begin eavesdropping....*

You may also have seen or heard these special images referred to as active maps, clickable maps, sensitive maps, or image maps. They're all intended to mean the same thing—although the term "image map" actually has a different meaning, as we shall soon discover. Even if you've never set one up yourself, it's a fairly safe bet that you've been tempted—perhaps put off by the complexity of the process and because you may have heard that only those with privileged access to the server could make these things happen.

Up until recently, it was indeed true that getting an active image to work correctly was both complicated and server-dependent. There was no way you could create an active image and make it do its thing (or things) using just your Web browser. With a "traditional" server-side system, the *image map* is a separate text file that defines the coordinates of your hotspots and their link destinations. You can create the image map at your desktop, but it can only work as interpreted by a UNIX/cgi-bin application called *imagemap* that comes as part of the server's software kit. So you can't test a server-side image map locally; you need the cooperation of your sysadmin to get it working, and what makes it even worse is that different flavors of Web server software have somewhat different requirements.

No wonder, therefore, that active images had a reputation for being difficult—and no wonder that the advent of client-side image mapping, which is available on Netscape Navigator 2.0 (or better), was greeted with enormous relief by the Web community. The client-side mapping conventions were actually devised in 1995 by James Seidman of Spyglass, Inc. for Spyglass's own proprietary browser. However, they were made public and quickly adopted by both Netscape for the Navigator and Microsoft for the Internet Explorer, and look likely to become HTML 3.0-approved markup. "Seidman mapping," as it's sometimes referred to, has taken all the terror out of image mapping, and it's now so common that we're going to describe this process as the primary way of activating an image. As always, however, we'll remind you at the end that using only a client-side map is a disservice to some of your users, and we'll tell you how to go about setting up a server-side map as well.

TIP

It must already be obvious that we're not going to get through this section of the book without recourse to words like "coordinate," "polygon," and "vertex." They're all in the glossary, but if this kind of talk is foul language so far as you're concerned, just skip it—active images are not your cup of tea.

Using Mapedit

The key to any type of image map is the x,y coordinates of the hotspots, measured in pixels from the top left corner of the image. It's perfectly possible to create an image map file "by hand," using just the coordinate information you could get from almost any graphics editor, but a shareware program called Mapedit, written by Thomas Boutell, makes the process of creating the image map remarkably easy. Mapedit is on the Companion CD-ROM accompanying this book—it was improved and fully adapted for Seidman mapping in late 1995.

Tip

For 32-bit systems, including Windows 95, a more sophisticated (and free!) image map editing program is available. It's called Map THIS!, by Todd C. Wilson, and it's available from ***http://galadriel.ecaetc.ohio-state.edu/tc/mt****.*

One advantage of "Map THIS!" is that it allows you to zoom in on your hotspots after you've created them, to make fine adjustments. Client-side mapping was introduced at version 1.20.0 in early 1996.

Defining the Image & Image Map

Step one is to create the image that you want to make active, or clickable. It can be either in GIF or JPEG format. Make a sketch or printout of it, and plan which areas you want to make into hotspots. We usually run a rough printout and outline each hotspot in a colored felt-tip pen, writing in the link destination in each case.

Step two is to make the HTML file that your active image is going to be a part of, including the image itself referenced simply by the <IMG SRC="....."> tag, plus any attributes you might need for page design reasons, such as VSPACE, HSPACE, and so on. It's a very good idea to include ALT="active image" as an attribute, and provide some alternative way for non-imaging users to access the link destinations you plan to use (for a very clever way of doing this, see the analysis of Figure 6-5 in Chapter 6). At this point, the HTML will be incomplete, but Mapedit is going to complete it for you.

Now, if you haven't already done so, install Mapedit and make it accessible from your Windows desktop. Fire it up and, from the menu bar, select File, then Open/Create.... You get the dialog box shown in Figure 4-26, which expects you to open up a two-part object to play with. Part One is the HTML file you just created, and Part Two is the image itself.

Enter the path and name of the HTML file in the upper box, either manually or by browse-and-click. Mapedit will now automatically (and very quickly) scan the file and present you with a second dialog box listing all the inline images, asking which of them you wish to activate. Just click on your choice and the rest of the dialog is done for you. The image appears in the main Mapedit window.

NOTE: The radio buttons inviting you to choose between NCSA and CERN map types are for server-side maps only. You don't need to make any selection at all for now.

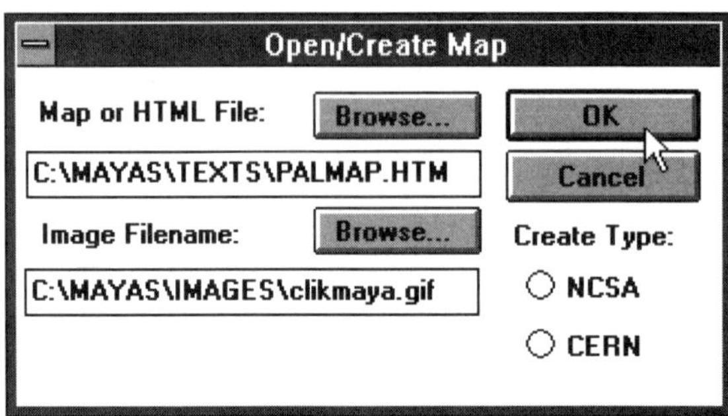

Figure 4-26: *Creating a new image map with Mapedit.*

Let's suppose we've created a single image that incorporates all four of those little thumbnail GIFs from Figure 4-8. The composite image is c:\mayas\images\clikmaya.gif, and we'll call the HTML file that includes it c:\mayas\texts\palmap.html.

Geometry Tools

Now for the fun part. Select the Tools menu item, and you'll see that the possible geometry tools are polygon, circle, and rectangle. For this example we would select "rectangle," then place our mouse cursor as accurately as possible at the top left corner of the small image of the Temple of the Inscriptions. We then click on the LEFT mouse button and drag the rectangle across to the lower right corner of the image. There's no need to hold the mouse button down as we do this, and the ESC key aborts the process. When satisfied that the rectangle is positioned accurately around the image, we click the RIGHT mouse button. This signals that we're ready to enter a link destination for this "hotspot" of our picture in the dialog box shown in Figure 4-27.

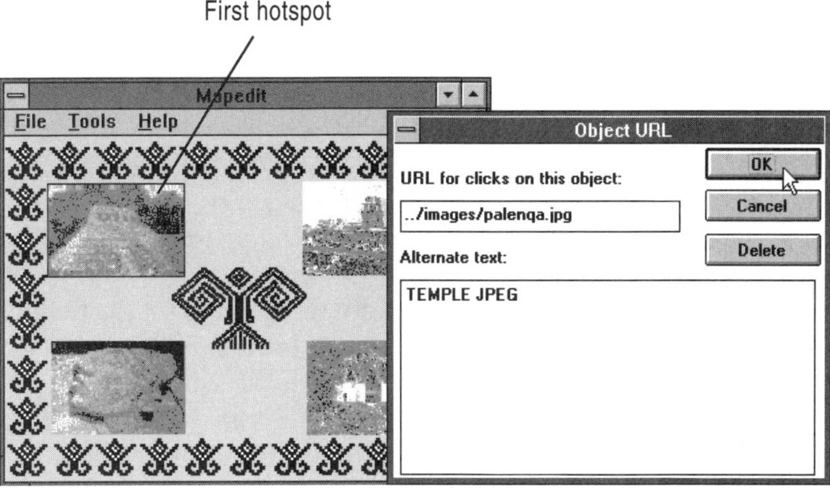

Figure 4-27: *Entering link information for one hotspot of an active image.*

Note that the pathway to the link destination is declared starting from the location of the image *map* file, not the image itself. Since we put "palmap.html" in the mayas/texts folder, a link to another local .HTM or .HTML file is direct, but a link to another image is relative—in this case we're entering "../images/temple.jpg" to link this thumbnail to the full-size JPEG of the temple in the images folder. This path relationship will be preserved when we finally post the set of files on the server.

For the Palenque example, we would repeat the process three more times for the other thumbnail hotspots. The other three link destinations don't necessarily need to be images—they can be anything up to the full URL of a document in New Delhi, if that's what you think is appropriate. There's no need to re-select Tools/Rectangle every time—the software assumes we're in this mode until we tell it differently. To create a circular hotspot (which isn't needed on this example), we would select the Circle tool and click the left mouse button in the dead center of the area we want to define. Now we'd drag the mouse pointer out in any direction until the circle looks right, and click the right mouse button.

By way of illustrating Mapedit's interesting and fun way of making a polygon hotspot, we're going to sensitize the pattern in the middle of our Palenque image, which happens to be the traditional embroidery pattern used by the Chiapas Indians to symbolize a vulture. We'll link it to a page about the Chiapas at the Science Museum in Minnesota (which is, in fact, where the pattern image came from in the first place).

Take the Tools/Polygon option. Now when you click the left mouse button for the first time, you'll set the first vertex of the polygon. Release the mouse button, and from then on an elastic line will stretch from the vertex to your cursor. You can pin this line down again at any other vertex with another brief click, and carry on. It doesn't matter where you start, but let's start at the far left corner and move northeasterly to the next corner, then southeast to the vulture's head, and so on round (see Figure 4-28). Unless you feel like getting very detailed around the vulture's talons, the outline can be completed in 15 vertices. Now, *don't attempt to complete the polygon by ending up at the exact same spot where you started.* Make your last left-button click at the base of the wing, then signal the end of the process with a right-button click.

Then enter the link destination in the same dialog box as the one we already depicted in Figure 4-28. Here are the 15 coordinates we ended up with:

```
124,115 149,93 161,103 174,92 187,102 198,92 226,115 205,135
186,119 186,140 202,153 150,153 164,140 162,121 146,136
```

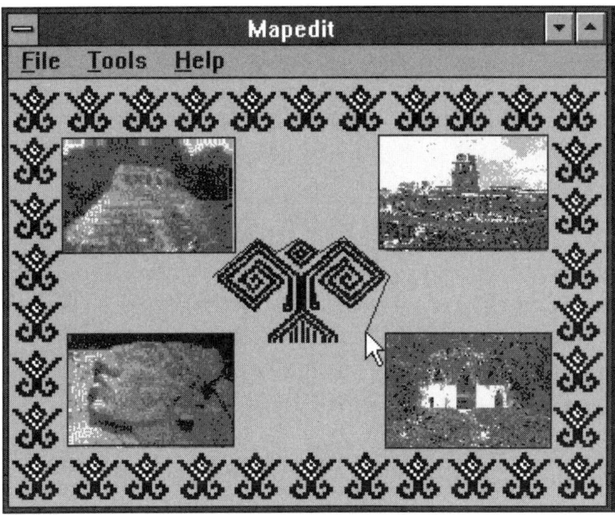

Figure 4-28: *Tracing round the vulture.*

We're sure you made your polygon perfectly—but let's pretend you were a little shaky your first time, and you can see some corner you'd like to improve by moving a vertex. Select Tools/Move and click anywhere in the polygon. Now any vertex point can be re-adjusted by dragging with the left mouse button. Cross-hairs appear in the center, and you can move the entire polygon bodily by clicking and dragging that spot. If you want to add new vertices—to refine that tricky bit around the vulture's feet, say—select Tools/Add Points and click briefly anywhere in the polygon as before. Your next click will create a fresh vertex. Tools/Remove Points does the reverse, of course.

DEFINING THE "COLD SPOTS"

If we wanted to be sloppy, we could now call the image map done because it already fulfills its main purpose, which is to associate five hyperlink destinations with four rectangular hot spots and one polygon. But what happens if the user clicks on the image outside one of the hotspots, in what we might call a "cold spot?" Nothing, in fact—but it's good practice to allow *something* useful to happen, even if it's only a page bearing the message, "No link here."

We'll imagine a page that will fulfill that task, and call it "coldspot.html." This is now known as the *default* link of the active image, and it's incorporated in the image map just like a hotspot. Staying in Mapedit, you can add this line by selecting "File/Edit Default URL." Finally, select Tools/Test+Edit and re-check all your hotspots by clicking on them. Mapedit will not actually follow the hyperlinks, but will "light up" the whole hot spot and display a dialog box confirming the link destination. Incidentally, note that the dialog box includes a Delete option that enables you to cancel a hot spot entirely. The default link does not provoke a dialog box.

LINKS FOR NON-GRAPHICAL USERS

One reason a default link is important is that some text-only browsers make that the only available link from the image. Quite recently, it's been proposed that whatever link is at the origin point (0,0) should be the one for text browsers to follow (Lynx is implementing this idea). That will often be the default link anyway—but if you want to be extra nice to Lynx users, include a line like:

<AREA SHAPE="rect" COORDS="0,0,1,1" ALT="ALL LINKS HERE" HREF="textlinx.html">

"textlinx.html", of course, is a little HTML document that you make up, making all the active image links available to your non-graphical users—which include the vision-impaired.

THE MAP MARKUP

Save the file—that's a *very* important step—and exit Mapedit. The job's now done—but before we rush off and see the result, let's lift the hood and peer inside the engine, as it were, of the image map. Take a look at the palmap.html file and you'll see that Mapedit has added, inside the <IMG SRC="../images/clikmaya.gif" ...> tag, the attribute USEMAP="#clikmaya." USEMAP takes the place of the "traditional" ISMAP attribute, and it's the definitive sign that this is a Seidman-type client-side active image. Mapedit has given the map itself the name #clikmaya, but the name could actually be anything.

So where is this map? Look down to the end of the palmap.html file. There it is, just above the </BODY> tag. Here's the version we ended up with:

```
<MAP NAME="clikmaya">
<AREA SHAPE="rect" ALT="TEMPLE JPEG" COORDS="32,34,134,100"
HREF="../images/palenqa.jpg">
<AREA SHAPE="rect" ALT="PALACE JPEG" COORDS="222,34,322,100"
HREF="../images/palenqc.jpg">
<AREA SHAPE="rect" ALT="SLAVES" COORDS="32,148,135,214"
HREF="slaves.html">
<AREA SHAPE="rect" ALT="OUTER TEMPLES"
COORDS="225,148,323,214" HREF="outlying.html">
<AREA SHAPE="polygon" ALT="CHIAPAS"
COORDS="124,116,148,94,160,104,174,92,187,
104,199,93,223,115,205,133,186,119,186,140,
201,153,201,153,151,154,163,140,163,140,163,
121,147,136,146,136" HREF="http://www.ties.k12.mn.us:80/~smm/
chiapas.html">
<AREA SHAPE="default" HREF="coldspot.html">
</MAP>
```

It's not too hard to figure out what's going on here, and for the sake of completeness, here's a reference to all the tags and attributes relating to image mapping. Use these to add your own "tricks of the trade" to what Mapedit supplies:

HTML Tag

USEMAP="mapref" — Attribute of an IMG tag that defines the image as a client-side active image. The format of "mapref" can either be "#infilemap", indicating that the map itself is in the same HTML document, or "maps.html#outfilemap" indicating the map whose name is "outfilemap" in the separate file "maps.html."

<MAP> .... </MAP> — Container tags for a client-side map.

NAME="mapref" — Mandatory attribute of <MAP>

<AREA> — One of an unlimited number of hotspot definition tags inside the <MAP> .... </MAP> container. There is no </AREA> containing tag.

Attributes of AREA are:

SHAPE="rect/circle/polygon/default"—If used, "default" must be the last-defined AREA

COORDS="x1,y1,x2,y2....."

For a rectangle, COORDS are left,top,right,bottom
For a circle, x(center),y(center),radius
For a polygon, successive x,y coordinates of vertices
[Total number of vertices limited only by the limit of 1024 characters in the attribute]

HREF="...url..."— Path to the hyperlink target of this AREA, relative to the directory of the HTML file containing the <MAP> definition, or a fully qualified URL link

ALT — Text that may be displayed by non-imaging browsers

NOHREF — Null attribute, meaning that the AREA leads nowhere

SERVER-SIDE MAPS

Mapedit is well capable of creating image map files that are interpreted by the server—indeed, it was originally created for that purpose. To create one, you'll need to make the background image and your sketch plan of how to link it as before, but you don't necessarily need to pre-code the HTML file that will include it. Instead, you'll need to be sure you're familiar with the directory structures at your server site, and find out whether the server software that will be managing your image map uses NCSA or CERN conventions. The CERN server is the original, and is more capable especially if security is an important issue. However, the NCSA type of server is much easier to configure and is better documented. Not surprisingly, NCSA servers are much more common. The Netscape server is NCSA-compatible, as is the highly popular Apache server for UNIX and virtually all the servers that you can set up on your own Windows 95/Windows NT machine. We'll assume, then, that NCSA is your game, but we'll note any important differences.

Choose a name for the image map file. This time, it's going to be a completely independent text file with the extension .MAP. Let's call it *mayaim.map.* Fire up Mapedit as before, then when you select File/Open/Create... and you're faced with the dialog box shown in Figure 4-26, select the NCSA radio button and enter mayaim.map in the top box. Put the path/filename of the background image *clikmaya.gif* in the lower box and hit "OK." Now, the process of creating hotspots and destinations is essentially the same as for the client-side mapping we already described. So far as the geometry goes, it's *precisely* the same. The difference is that the mapping definitions are sent to the separate file *mayaim.map,* they're in a slightly different format, and the pathways to local files you want to link to *must take into account the directory structure at your server site.* That last part is the only part that you really have to worry about—it's a matter of thinking about relative paths from the point of view of the server, rather than the map file. Here's the exact equivalent of the map we created before, as an NCSA image map assuming your user area is xusr:

```
default coldspot.html
#Temple comment
rect /~xusr/images/palenqa.jpg 32,34 134,100
#Palace comment
rect /~xusr/images/palenqc.jpg 222,34 322,100
rect /~xusr/texts/slaves.html 32,148 135,214
rect /~xusr/texts/outlying.html 225,148 323,214
```

```
poly http://www.ties.k12.mn.us:80/~smm/chiapas.html124,116
148,94 160,104 174,92 187,104 199,93 223,115 205,133 186,119
186,140 201,153 201,153 151,154 163,140 163,140 163,121
147,136 146,136
```

The other little difference in the mapping process is that the NCSA map allows comments, which you can place in the box provided in Mapedit's Object URL dialog box as you complete each hotspot (comments take the place of ALT text).

The CERN equivalent does not allow comments, and the first hotspot, in CERNese, would be:

```
rect (32,34) (134,100) /~xusr/images/palenqa.jpg
```

Also, a CERN circular hotspot, like a Seidman equivalent, is defined by its center and the radius. NCSA uses the center and any point on the circumference.

Linking Into A Server-side Map

As we already remarked, a BIG disadvantage of server-side image maps is that you can't test them locally. So having made the image map, you send it to the server site by whatever process you normally use to post your HTML files—FTP, carrier pigeon, or brown bag. It can sit in the texts subdirectory along with all your HTML stuff. Now comes the hard part.

You need to set things up so that, when a user clicks on the image, the coordinates of the clickspot are passed to your little file mayaim.map for comparison. The way to think about this is that mayaim.map is a rather special sort of hyperlink destination, and you mark it as special using the attribute ISMAP. So in the HTML file that you now have to create, part of the IMG tag is:

```
<A HREF="..[something]../mayaim.map"><IMG SRC="../images/
clikmaya.gif" ISMAP></A>
```

The missing [something] is, first, the reference to the cgi-bin program that will interpret the click coordinates, then the reference to *mayaim.map*, and the two pathways are run together. In an NCSA server, the program is *imagemap* (the CERN equivalent is *htimage*), and it's usually to be found at:

```
/usr/local/etc/httpd/cgi-bin/imagemap
```

The path to *mayaim.map* tacked on after the path to *imagemap* is called the *extra path* information. *mayaim.map* is probably at something like:

```
/usr/net/xusr/texts/mayaim.map
```

...which we've assumed may be found by the server shortcut:

```
/~xusr/texts/mayaim.map
```

Now, when the click coordinates arrive, they're processed at the "HTTPD" level of that structure, and the path to the processing program is the virtual path:

```
/cgi-bin/imagemap
```

...so taking that into account, and running the two halves of the path together, we end up with:

```
<A HREF="/cgi-bin/imagemap/~xusr/texts/mayaim.map"><IMG
SRC="../images/clikmaya.gif" ISMAP></A>
```

...which is the correct way to reference a server-side map.

TIP

Older versions of the NCSA server did things slightly differently. Instead of adding the extra path information so that imagemap *could locate the file it has to interpret,* mayaim.map, *both the map file and its location were given by an alias—simply* maya, *let's say. The HREF is then to /cgi-bin/imagemap/maya, and the alias is interpreted by a line in a special file called /usr/local/etc/httpd/conf/ imagemap.conf. The appropriate line, using our example, would be:*
maya: /~xusr/texts/mayaim.map
So if the instructions we gave earlier don't work, one possibility is that your site is using an out-of-date HTTPD (version 1.3 or earlier).

HAVING IT BOTH WAYS

We confidently predict the death of server-side image maps. Quite apart from the complexities of getting them to work, they obviously make the server work harder than do client-side maps, and so they're not good for site efficiency. They cannot permit the user to know in advance where a click might lead. And perhaps the most persuasive argument against them is that they invariably create aggravation for sysadmins! However, while we're waiting for the fat lady to sing, it's polite to let your users without client-side capable browsers enjoy your brilliant image mapping. For a site of any importance, we generally make image maps of both types—put one on the server, and one in the HTML file (which of course also ends up on the server). There's absolutely nothing to prevent us from calling it both ways, like this:

```
<A HREF="/cgi-bin/imagemap/~xusr/texts/mayaim.map"><IMG
SRC="../images/clikmaya.gif" USEMAP="#clikmaya" ISMAP
ALT="active image"></A>
```

A client-side capable browser, seeing that, will use the #clikmaya map information and ignore mayaim.map. A non-capable browser will do the opposite.

Moving On

In this chapter we've covered the basics of computer imaging and using color and images on your pages. So you should be well prepared to start experimenting on your own. But mastering the art of image making is a process you'll be refining for some time if you plan on doing a lot of work with Web pages.

Now we're ready to have some fun showing you the many ways you can add real style to your pages. We'll talk about using different font sizes and layout tricks and some of the fancier things you can do with Netscape extensions and proposed HTML 3.0 tags.

5 Getting Stylish

In the last chapter you should have picked up enough tips to start dressing up your Web pages with some stylish images. Groovy graphics, though, are just one way you can add impact to your Web pages. As you've no doubt noticed as you've cruised the Web, some Web authors have come up with some pretty creative ways to make their pages stand out. Novices are often bewildered as to how these effects are accomplished.

It's no accident that many of these same pages contain notices to the effect that "this page is designed for or looks best in Netscape." That's because Netscape has provided the most complete set of tools available for adding style components to your Web page. In this chapter we'll start learning how to use some of those Netscape extensions to add life and individuality to your pages. That includes varying font sizes and colors with the font attributes and using the table and list tags to solve spacing and layout problems. We'll also discuss the latest Netscape innovation: pages with frames. We hope this stimulates your creative juices to start turning out some of those great-looking pages yourself.

USING NETSCAPE EXTENSIONS

We've already covered some of the most popular Netscape extensions to HTML. The extended values of the IMG ALIGN attribute, the IMG WIDTH and HEIGHT attributes, the LOWSRC attribute, and the author-defined page backgrounds—all of these have had a dramatic effect on Web design, and all were originally Netscape-pioneered (although some are "official" HTML 3.0, and many have now been adopted by other browsers).

Likewise, we covered some Netscape extensions to the listing tags like <OL> back in Chapter 2, and Netscape-style tables and forms are dealt with in Chapters 7 and 9, "The World of Tables & Equations" and "Forms, Feedback & cgi-bin," respectively. In other words, Netscape extensions are discussed throughout this book.

Because this is a book about designing for Netscape, we need not be in the least shy about these "Netscapisms," but we will continue to remind you whenever we're discussing tags that are not universal. The best Web authors design pages that are coherent no matter which browser the user is running. We'll point out some workarounds you can use to ensure that your page is comprehensive to non-Netscape browsers as well. For those cases where there is no equivalent, we'll discuss how you can make different versions available to different browsers in Chapter 9. But for now, let's have some fun!

FONT FUN

Type style options point up the philosophical difference among HTML developers perhaps better than any other HTML development issue. In a design note issued along with the original HTML 1.0, it was stated:

> *"It is required that HTML be a common language between all platforms. This implies no device-specific markup, or anything which requires control over fonts or colors, for example."*

In spite of that strong statement, official HTML has always equivocated somewhat on type *style*, as opposed to font. "Font" refers to entire alphabet designs like Helvetica, Times Roman, and so forth, whereas "style" refers to italic, boldface, and so forth. *Physical* style tags such as <I>....</I> for italic and <B>....</B> for boldface were part of the original HTML as well as *logical* style tags like <EM>....</EM> and <STRONG>....</STRONG>. (If this is confusing to you, look back to Chapter 2, where we explain the difference.) It has always been emphasized by HTML experts that the logical styles are far preferable, since they give some indication of the intent of the author and leave it up to the browser to decide how to actually render the words. A browser or computer terminal that has no boldface display may have a problem when it comes across <B> because it can't tell what a suitable alternative might be. Despite the programmer's preference for logical styles, some physical style tags were included in HTML 1.0, and they've since been added to. HTML 3.0 has proposed adding <BIG> and <SMALL> as more general font size tags.

Netscape's approach is to place as much control as possible over page appearance—and that includes type appearance—in the hands of the author. The FONT tag is the one that does the job typographically.

HTML Tag

<FONT>....</FONT>

Any text between the FONT containers has its appearance influenced by the attributes of the FONT tag. The font tag has no meaning without at least one attribute. The attributes are:

SIZE=n where n is in the range 1 to 7, and specifies type size on an arbitrary scale. "Normal" is size 3.

SIZE=+x or -x Specifies a type size that is +x larger than, or -x smaller than, the default. The default is size 3 or as otherwise defined by <BASEFONT>.

COLOR="#rrggbb" The preferred color of text is defined with this attribute. The hexadecimal #rrggbb strings are made up in the same way as for BODY BGCOLOR (see Chapter 4).

<BASEFONT SIZE=n>

This tag, which appears within the <BODY>....</BODY> part of the document but *not* as an attribute to BODY itself, sets the default type size for the document on Netscape's arbitrary scale of 7. If inserted other than at the top of the document body, it only affects text from its insertion point on. If not specified, the default basefont size is 3.

<BLINK>....</BLINK>

Causes all enclosed text to blink.

The new <FONT> tag, used in conjunction with the old physical style tags, can exercise a good deal of control over type appearance. For example, the HTML code:

```
<I><TT><FONT SIZE=6>Mozilla lives!</FONT></TT></I>
```

should look something like:

Mozilla lives!

Figure 5-1 illustrates an attractive use of the <FONT> tag on the "Sarajevo Online" page. It's hard to see how anyone could object to that—although *not* hard to see why people don't much care for overuse of type size control

Like this!

This line is <FONT SIZE=5>.

The <BLINK> tags enclose the date.

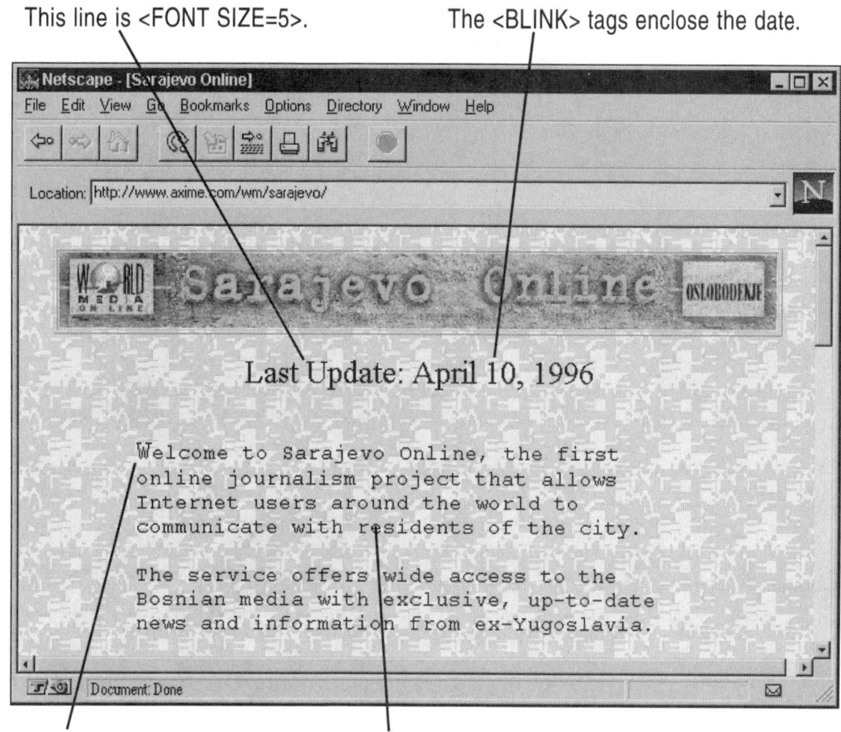

<TT> with <FONT SIZE=5> makes this large cap.

The text is <TT> with <FONT SIZE=4> enclosed in <BLOCKQUOTE> tags.

Figure 5-1: *A prizewinning Sarajevo page, with very tasteful use of the <FONT> tag.*

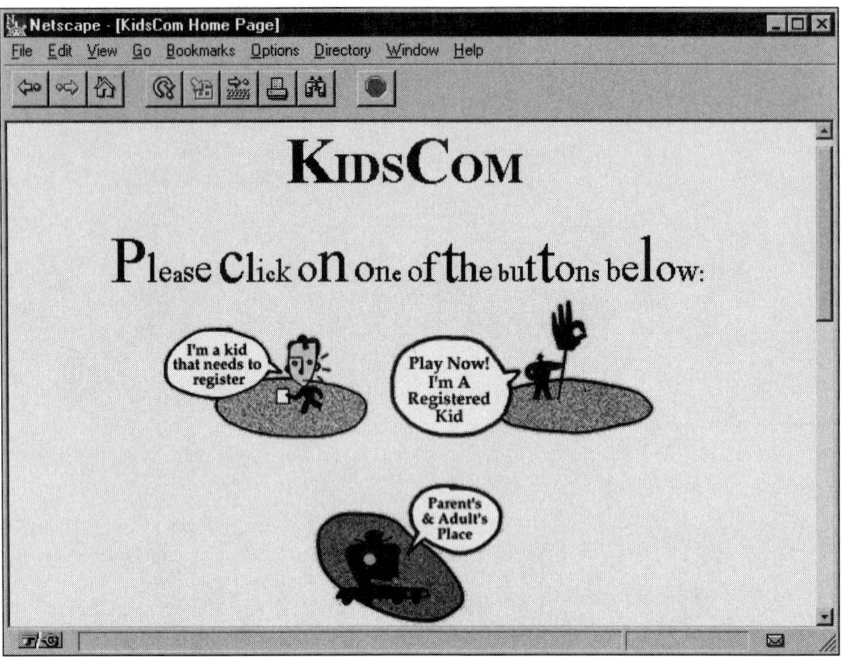

Figure 5-2: *This whimsical page is a typographical atrocity, but since it's for kids we'll forgive the authors.*

Both the Sarajevo page in Figure 5-1 and the kids' page in Figure 5-2 won **Planète D'or** prizes in 1995 from the French magazine *Planète Internet.*

VARYING RULE SIZES

In addition to the font variations, Netscape extensions allow you to vary the size of horizontal rules you may use for text divisions.The horizontal rule tag has extended attributes that allow you to use rules in more decorative ways. You can make short rules, long rules, fat rules, skinny rules, solid rules, and shaded rules. These can be very useful for adding a little style to your pages while using no extra bandwidth or download time.

HTML Tag

<HR>

The horizontal rule tag has Netscape-extended attributes:

WIDTH=n Sets the HR width (horizontally) in pixels (600 is standard on a 640 x 480 video system).

WIDTH=p% Sets the HR width as a percentage of page width. HR=100% ensures that the ruler will extend the width of the page, no matter what size the screen.

SIZE=n Sets the HR thickness in pixels (2 is standard).

ALIGN="left/right/center" Aligns a rule to the left or right margin or to the center of the page, as specified.

NOSHADE Specifies an "unmolded" HR style (a solid black line, instead of a shaded bar).

Controlling Text Layout

Other new Netscape tags allow you to control text breaks and alignment to control your layout more precisely. They include CENTER, NOBR, and WBR.

HTML Tag

<CENTER>....</CENTER>

Causes all enclosed text and/or graphics to be centered between current margins. Note: This is only one of several ways you can center items.

<NOBR>....</NOBR>

Causes all enclosed text to be treated as continuous, without breaking or wrapping at margins.

<WBR>

When used in a NOBR section of text, allows a break at that point. When used alone, it acts as a "soft" line break.

Many of the tags invented for font control purposes work perfectly well to control page layout more generally. Putting an inline image between <CENTER>.... </CENTER> tags does just what you'd expect—centers the image on the page.

CENTER is only one of several ways you can align text on a page. The ALIGN attribute can be used with the paragraph or heading tags to center text, but you may have noticed that this has a different meaning with the IMG tag, specifying not the placement of the image on the page, but the alignment of text next to it. You can use the CENTER tag around an image to center it on a page. There's yet another method, though.

HTML 3.0 prefers <DIV ALIGN=center> to the CENTER tag, and this has been incorporated into Netscape Navigator 2.0 to comply with that proposal. <DIV ALIGN=center> works with both text and images, as does the CENTER tag. But note that using the ALIGN attribute with the IMG tag will cancel out the effect. You have to resort to other methods if you want to both center an image *and* align text next to it. (See the section, "Invisible Tables" later in this chapter for one method.)

We'll discuss DIV later in this chapter in the section "Using HTML 3.0." You can use either tag in Netscape, as it suits you. But for now, note that while Netscape and a few other browsers now recognize <CENTER>, most browsers in the future are likely to conform to the HTML 3.0 standard and prefer DIV with the ALIGN attributes.

Using Tables as Page Layout Tools

One extension that has been used very inventively by Web stylists is the set of tags that were designed to create tables. We'll go into tables in much greater detail in Chapter 7, where there are many examples of real tables, with the kind of information one would normally want to put in them. We explain the full suite of table tags and attributes there. To use tables for layout or decorative purposes, you need only understand the elementary principles.

Decorative Tables

A very simple but common use of the table tag is to use it to draw a border of varying thickness around any picture—to frame it, as it were. For example, take a picture, any picture—let's take the pepper steak from Figure 3-3. Call it into your page like this:

```
<CENTER>
<TABLE BORDER=12>
     <TR><TD>
     <IMG SRC="bifstek.gif" ALT=[STEAK]> </TD></TR>
</TABLE>
</CENTER>
```

Here's what's being created: The <CENTER>.... </CENTER> tags center the whole picture on the page. The <TABLE>....</TABLE> tags declare a table—albeit a fake table in this instance. The <TR>.... </TR> tags say, "This is table row 1." Finally, the <TD>.... </TD> tags say, "This is the first cell of row 1, and it contains a picture." All that effort just to get the decorative border that goes around a table. In this case, we've asked for 12 pixels (BORDER=12) and Figure 5-3 is the result. Many people consider that quite stylish.

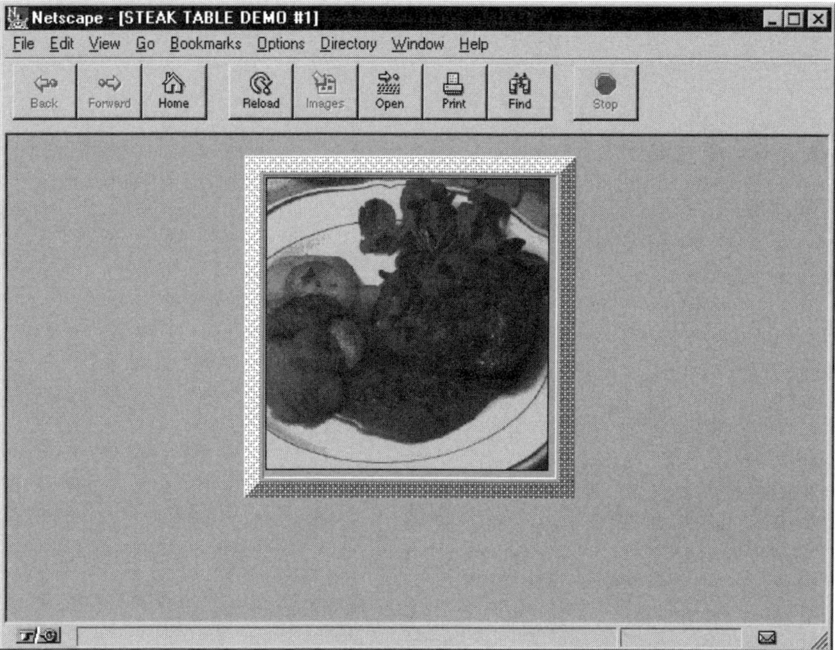

Figure 5-3: *Using simple TABLE tags to get a fancy border.*

If you're quick, you will have gotten the idea already. You create table rows with <TR> and cells with <TD>, which stands for Table Data. An *extremely* boring 2 X 2 table would look like this:

```
<TABLE>
     <TR><TD>CELL 1</TD><TD>CELL 2</TD></TR>
     <TR><TD>CELL 3</TD><TD>CELL 4</TD></TR>
</TABLE>
```

Let's do something a little more creative with our steak:

```
<CENTER>
<TABLE BORDER=2>
     <TH COLSPAN=3>Steak with green pepper sauce</TH>

            <TR><TD WIDTH=20><BR></TD>
               <TD><IMG SRC="bifstek.gif" ALT=[STEAK]></TD>
               <TD WIDTH=20><BR></TD></TR>
                        <TR><TD HEIGHT=20></TD></TR>
       </TABLE>
       </CENTER>
```

Now we've introduced another tag pair, <TH>.... </TH>, which means Table Header. That's what we need for the title of this table. Since we're about to create three columns, we indicate that we want this header to span all three by giving TH the attribute COLSPAN=3.

In the first table row we've defined three data cells. In the middle is the image, and on either side an empty cell that's there purely for decoration. We define it as being 20 pixels wide, and we put nothing in it except a <BR>. If there was nothing at all in the cell, it would look a bit different.

The only other row contains a single cell that is absolutely empty but defined as 20 pixels high. The overall effect is Figure 5-4—and now you should be able to spot the difference between a totally empty cell and a cell containing a <BR> tag. A cell that contains something (even if it's a non-visible character), will have a shaded, indented appearance, as opposed to a flat, or raised, appearance.

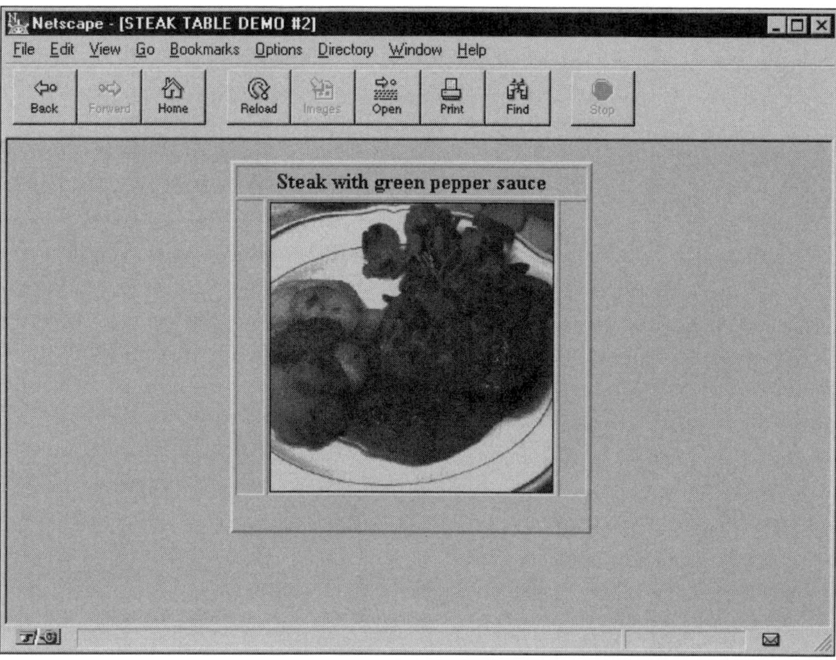

Figure 5-4: *Doing a bit more with table tags.*

By now you might have picked up the idea that using tables with empty cells of a specified size might be a good way to get things to go where you want them to on the page. If fact, that's just what a lot of Web page designers do. We'll leave the really involved stuff for Chapter 7, but for layout purposes all you need to understand right now is that each cell of a table can be sized with the attributes WIDTH and HEIGHT, and anything like an image can be positioned within the cell using the attributes ALIGN (horizontal) and VALIGN (vertical).

It follows, then, that you can use the table tags to divide up your screen and space out the page's elements more or less at will. To prove it, we're going to take the same problem that we solved with "glass bricks" in Figure 4-18 and solve it with a table. In Figure 5-5 we've deliberately coded it to leave the table borders in so that you can see what's going on, but if we had declared <TABLE BORDER=0>, they'd have disappeared and there would have been no way to tell how this was done—until you looked at the source. And speaking of the source, here it is:

```
<TABLE CELLPADDING=0 CELLSPACING=10 BORDER=1>
      <TH>Philately</TH>

      <TR><TD ROWSPAN=3 HEIGHT=250 VALIGN="top">
      <IMG SRC="marilyn.jpg" ALT="[Marilyn]"></TD>
      <TD WIDTH=150 ALIGN="center">will get you...</TD>
      <TD WIDTH=180></TD></TR>

      <TR><TD ROWSPAN=2 HEIGHT=250 ALIGN="right"
      VALIGN="bottom">
      <IMG SRC="elvis.jpg"ALT="[Elvis]"></TD>
      <TD ALIGN="center"><FONT SIZE=5>
      EVERYWHERE!!</FONT></TD></TR>

      <TR><TD WIDTH=220 HEIGHT=150 ALIGN="right" VALIGN="top">
      <IMG SRC="poca.jpg" ALT="[Pocahontas]">
      </TD></TR>
</TABLE>
```

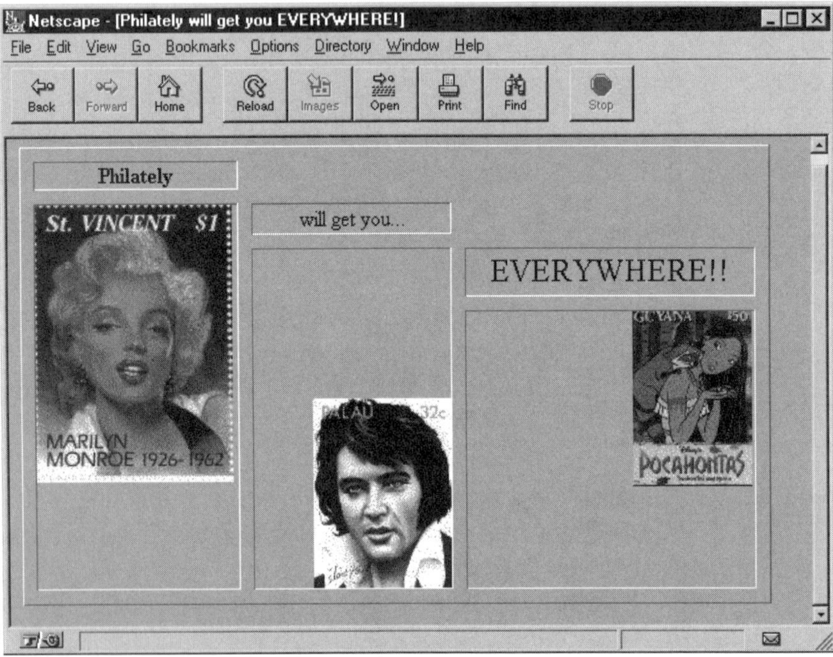

Figure 5-5: *Using more advanced table tags to lay out a whole page.*

Using this technique, our philately page looks pretty good in Mosaic, too.

TIP

Don't forget that some of the perfectly conventional HTML tags can be used to achieve very good layout effects if combined with good planning. BLOCKQUOTE and DL, nested if need be to increase their effect, can achieve a lot.

INVISIBLE TABLES

Many people coming to Web design from magazine or advertising backgrounds want to know how to create "white space" to make a more pleasing layout. In Chapter 4 we discussed one technique for doing this, the "glass bricks trick." This is useful, however, only if you know exactly how much space the material you're placing next to your glass brick will take up. An image will always align to the width of a "glass brick," but text could easily overflow the height. If you want to create white space next to a text block and want to allow for varying font and screen sizes used by different readers, an "invisible table" is a better option.

To dramatize the effect this can have, let's take a background image that contains a vertical stripe running down the left margin of a page (see Figure 5-6). This is actually a GIF only 20 pixels high and 1280 pixels wide (wide enough to cover the maximum screen width), which tiles in (repeating every 20 pixels) to cover the page. The blue border strip on the left is 150 pixels wide. Naturally we don't want the text to overwrite our pretty border. We'd really like our text to start a little beyond that. We'll start just with our basic two-celled table to get the placement right. Here's the basic code we begin with:

```
<BODY BACKGROUND="blustrip.gif" TEXT=#909090>

<TABLE BORDER=0 WIDTH=100%>
<TR>
<TD WIDTH=200><BR></TD>
```

```
<TD><FONT SIZE=7 COLOR=#ff0000>T</FONT><FONT SIZE=4>he Sea,
the Sand, the Sky</FONT>
</TD>
</TR>
</TABLE>
```

We've thrown in some fun font size and color changes to show you how creative you can be with this. You'll see what we're working toward in Figure 5-6.

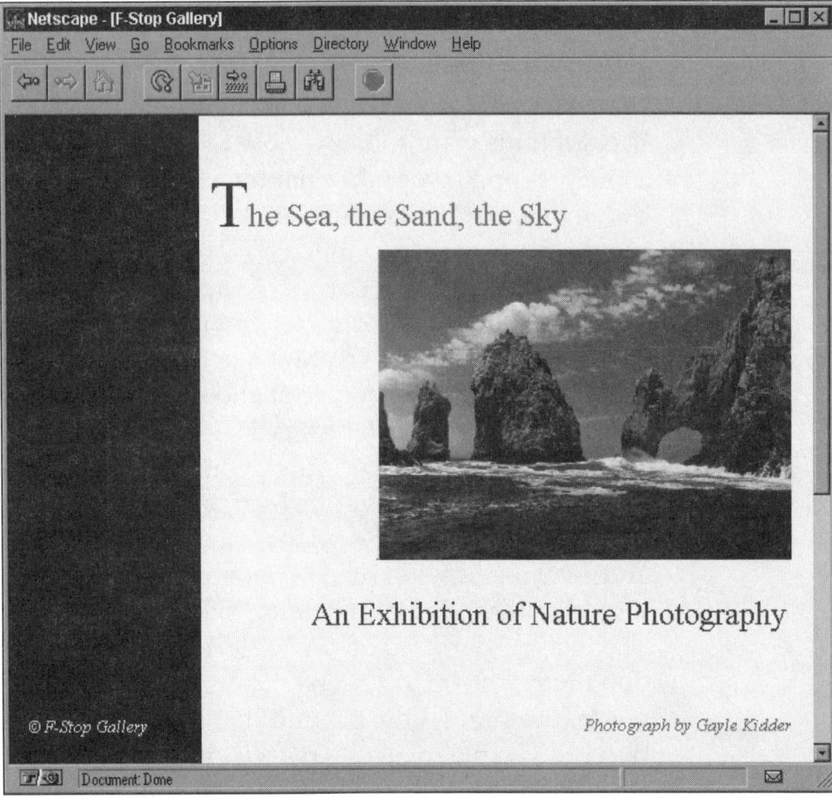

Figure 5-6: *A nice background GIF with a blue border stripe inspires a creative way to lay out a page using tables.*

Once we get the placement of the first line right, we're ready to start adding the rest of the elements. When you're trying to work out the dimensions of an invisible table for layout, it's useful to temporarily include the BORDER attribute in the table. Figure 5-7 shows how the borders can help you get your bearings during the design phase—you can see exactly what the dimensions of your cells are.

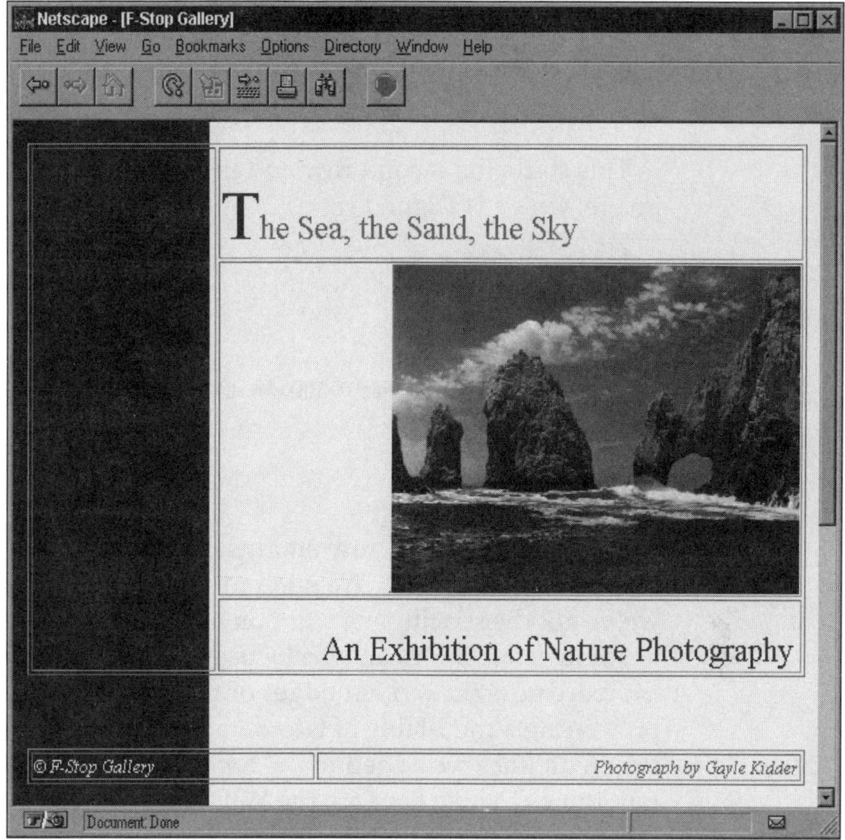

Figure 5-7: *With the BORDER attribute added to the table tag, we can see the borders of our invisible tables.*

When you've got it the way you want it, delete the BORDER attribute or set it to BORDER=0, and the lines will disappear.

To get the picture and the second line of text, we have to add some more cells to our table. The picture will occupy another cell on the right and the second title line will go in a third cell. Both of these will align right. The column that contains our blue strip on the left will span all three of these right hand data cells, so it will have to have a ROWSPAN=3 attribute added.

The rest of the code we come up with is:

```
<TR>
<TD align=right>
<IMG SRC="beach.jpg" ><BR>
</TD>
</TR>
```

This starts the second row and inserts the data cell for the image, which is aligned right.

```
<TR>
<TD align=right>
<P>
<BR>
<FONT SIZE=5 COLOR=#ff0000>An Exhibition of Nature
Photography</FONT>
</TD>
</TR>
```

This starts the third row and inserts the data cell for the title text, also aligned right. We end our table with </TABLE> and we've got the spacing we want on our page.

An invisible table can also be useful if you want to place text at the extreme right and left edges of the screen. For this you need only create a mini-table of two data cells. You can see this effect in the credit lines we added to the bottom of Figure 5-6. The important things to note here are the WIDTH=100% attribute in the table tag, which tells the table to scale to the available screen size, and the ALIGN attribute for the table data cells, which forces the text to the outer edges of the cells, and therefore the screen.

This is the code for the mini-table at the bottom of our exhibition page:

```
<TABLE BORDER WIDTH=100%>
<TR>
<TD ALIGN=LEFT><FONT SIZE=2 COLOR=#fefefe><I>&copy; F-Stop
Gallery</I></FONT></TD>
<TD ALIGN=RIGHT><FONT SIZE=2><I>Photograph by Ansel Adams
</I></FONT></TD>
</TR>
</TABLE>
```

Creating Columns With Invisible Tables

You can also use invisible tables to create columns of text, as shown on the HotWired page in Figure 5-8. In this case, it's useful to add the vertical alignment VALIGN=top attribute to your <TD> tag to assure that the initial lines of text start at the same line. (If the blocks of text are unequal, the taller block would define the cell height and the shorter block would be centered by default.) You can then space down to start your text block at any line you wish by using <PRE> ... </PRE> with any number of return characters in between.

Figure 5-8: *Use "invisible tables" to create columns of text like this.*

This HotWired page is a useful lesson in using tables for layout. Let's analyze what's happening on that page. The basic columnar layout is shown in Figure 5-9 below:

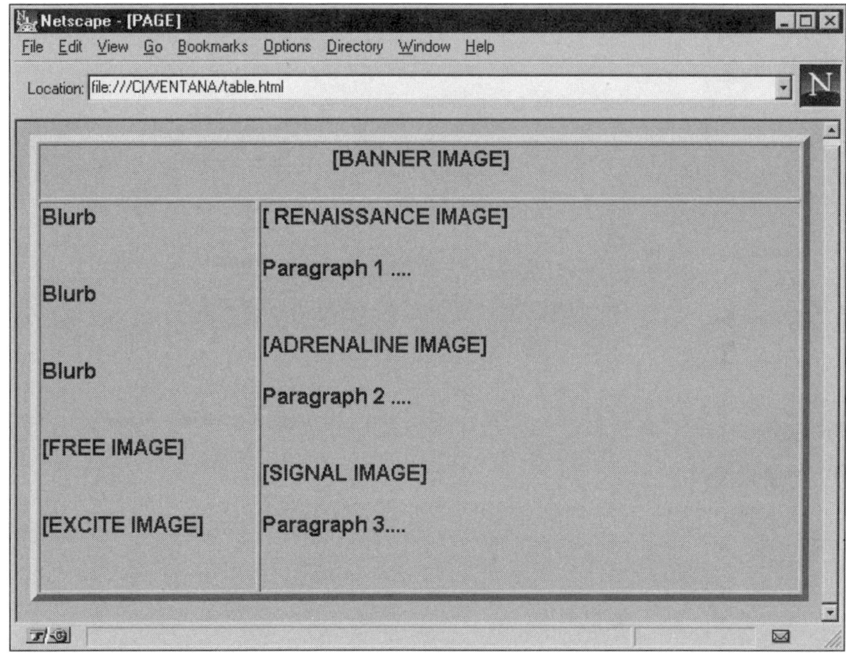

Figure 5-9: *The layout of Figure 5-8 revealed.*

Stripping the code down to the essentials, it looks like this:

```
<!-Begin table and top cell->
<TABLE BORDER WIDTH=100%>
<TR>
<TD COLSPAN=2>
<IMG SRC="banner.gif">
</TD>
</TR>

<!-First column->

<TR>
```

```
<TD WIDTH=28% VALIGN=top ALIGN=left>
<H4>
Blurb
Blurb
Blurb
</H4>
<IMG SRC="free.gif">
<IMG SRC="excite.gif">
</TD>

<!-Second column->

<TD VALIGN=top ALIGN=left>
<P><IMG SRC="renaissance.gif"><BR>
Paragraph 1 ....

<P><IMG SRC="adrenaline.gif"><BR>
Paragraph 2 ....

<P><IMG SRC="signal.gif"><BR>
Paragraph 3....

</TD>
</TR>
</TABLE>
```

We've included a percentage size attribute instead of a fixed number to the left column to make the page come out in the proportions we wanted, although there are other ways you could do this. (They used <PRE> followed by <H3> in order to break the lines exactly where they wanted, which allowed the line length to dictate the column width.)

TIP

Note the comment lines we put in to make clear the divisions in our code above. You can insert comment lines anywhere you like, by enclosing them in angle brackets and starting the comment with an exclamation point. The browser will then ignore them.

Workarounds for Non-Table Browsers

Now for the note of caution: Not all browsers recognize tables yet—although the most common ones do, and the rest will likely follow suit pretty soon. The table tag is one that everyone agrees is useful for serious as well as aesthetic purposes. If you're concerned about not leaving out any of your potential readers, there are various workarounds.

One favorite workaround of Web page designers is what we call "the empty nest." To accomplish roughly the same thing as shown in Figure 5-6, use a series of nested lists (see Chapter 2 for a full explanation of the list tags). For this purpose, the definition list <DL> is most useful, since it treats list items as blocks of text and does not place any bullets or numbers before the items.

We accomplished nearly the same layout effect as in Figure 5-6 with this code:

```
<DL>
<DL>
<DL>
<DL>
<DT></DT>
<DD>The Sea, the Sand, the Sky<BR>
  <DL>
  <DL>
  <DT></DT>
  <DD><IMG SRC="beach.jpg"></DD>
  <DT></DT>
  <DD>An Exhibition of Nature Photography</DD>
  </DL>
  </DL>
</DD>
</DL>
</DL>
</DL>
</DL>
```

Note that the definition term <DL> is an empty element here, whose only purpose is to create the indent we want, as is <DT> (the rules for a definition list require a <DT> tag even if there is nothing in it). You must also be careful to provide an end tag for every list start tag, or you'll find subsequent material on your page following the conventions of the still open tag. We also sacrificed our font variations in the above, as a browser that does not recognize tables is not liable to recognize font size and color changes either. But we could have left them in and they would just be ignored if not understood by the browser.

Columns are a different problem. The only other way of creating the columns shown in Figure 5-8 is to make a GIF of one of your text blocks. In the HotWired page, the left column with the "blurbs" or story sells could become a GIF. We don't really recommend this, though, because your layout would obviously be thrown off by any font or screen size differences used by a reader. And, if full text alignment is not recognized by the browser (as it still isn't in a number of browsers) you'd end up with only one line of text next to the GIF. <PRE> is of course an option, but if you chose to set up columns with preformatted text, you'd have to forego the images.

If you really want to use tables for those who can see them but don't want to leave out anyone, you can consider making two versions of your file, one with tables and one without. You can then use a cgi-bin script, which will send the viewer to the appropriate version based on the browser he or she has. This solution is also kinder to your potential visually impaired visitors (and yes, there are browsers for the blind!). See Chapter 9 for how to do this.

Using FRAMES

One drawback of tables for some uses is that they don't scale to different screen resolutions. That is, if your table is made to occupy a 640 X 480 screen nicely, it will still be 640 pixels wide when viewed on a screen only 480 pixels wide (a standard Macintosh Netscape window) or 1280 pixels wide (a full Sun workstation screen size). Enter Netscape's new frames feature—an advanced page-design capability that lets you create multiple, independently scrolling frames in a single page. If used correctly, frames scale to screen resolution automatically, and the user has some control over the frame boundaries.

FRAME Basics

Frames allow you, as a Web author, to divvy up the available space in the Netscape content area between two or more rectangular panes, put independent content in them, and address them as separate TARGETS. Typical uses of frames are:

- To hold one area static while the main part of the screen scrolls normally (the static part is sometimes referred to as a "ledge"). In Figure 5-10, this is the top frame that reads "History of Spaceflight."

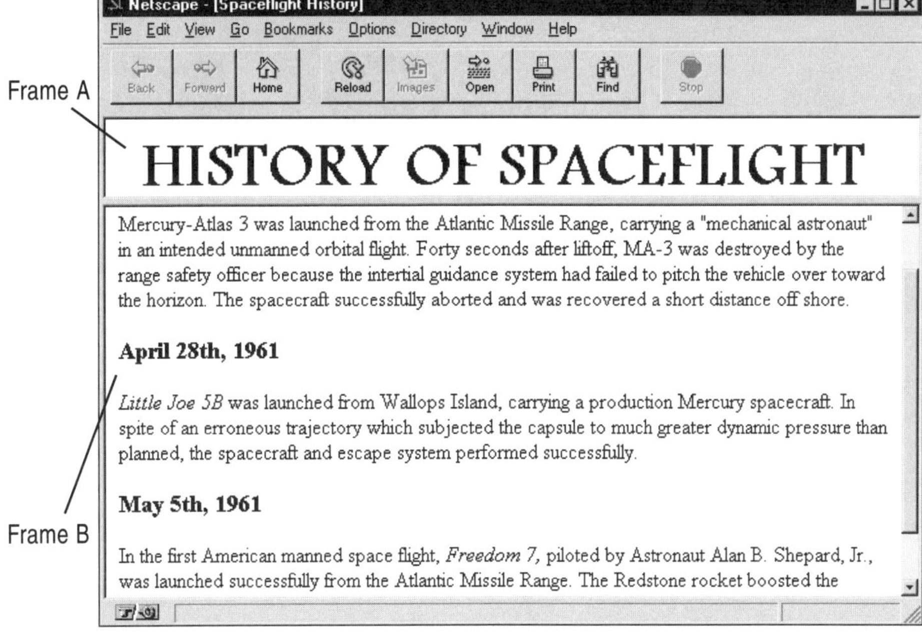

Figure 5-10: *Static "ledge" in Frame A surmounting a scrollable file in Frame B.*

- To keep a "Table of Contents" hyperlink list in a separate screen enclave, while the active part of the screen obeys the user's link requests. In Figure 5-11, this is the left frame that lists the space programs.

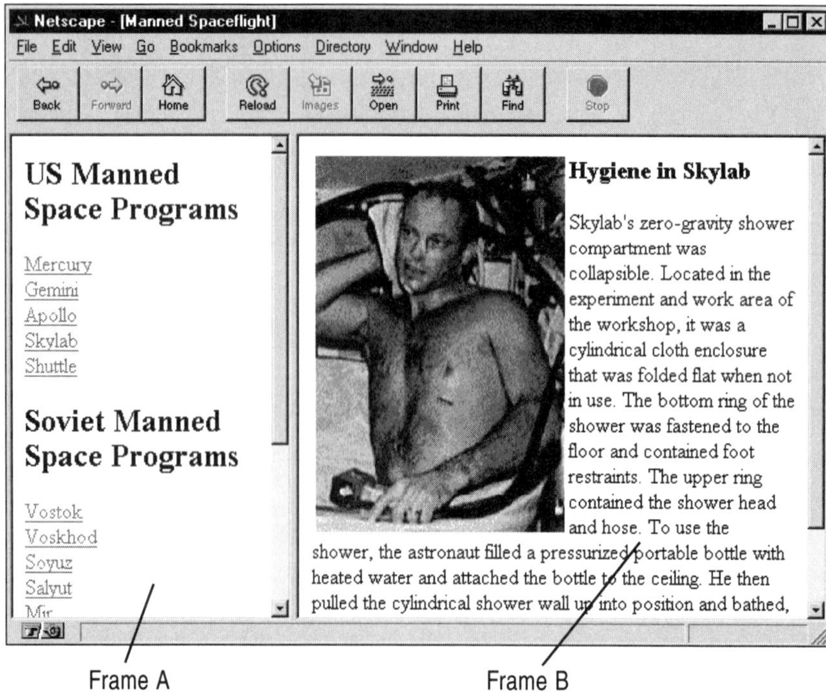

Figure 5-11: *Hyperlink list in Frame A controls display in Frame B.*

- To allow multi-dimensioned user choice. The display in Frame D might depend on user settings of Frames A, B, and C. See Figure 5-12.

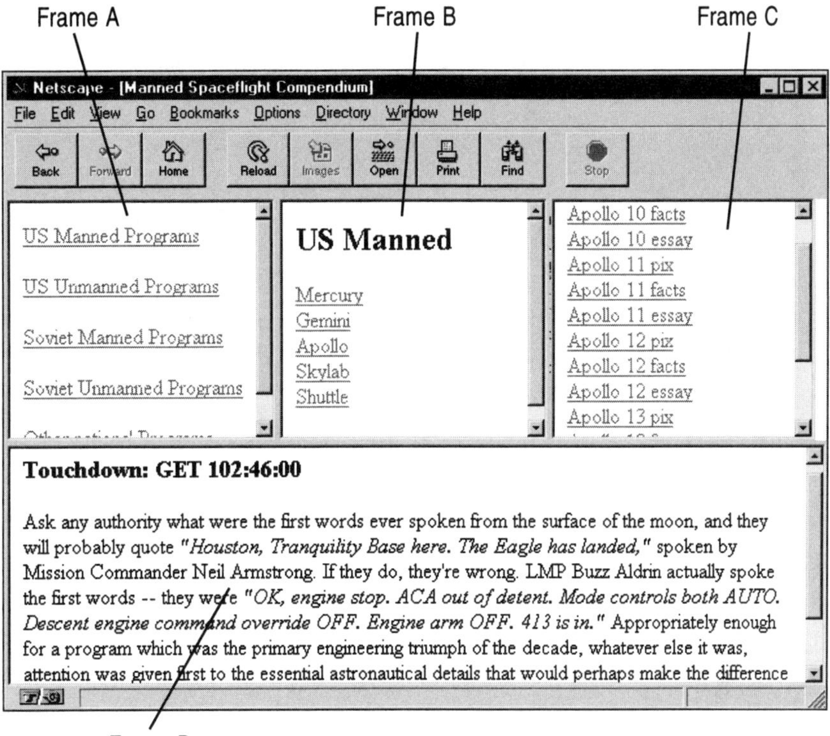

Figure 5-12: *User choice focuses from Frame A to B to C, producing final display in D.*

- Conversely, a user selection in Frame A might govern the display in two or more other panes—a static image in Frame B1 and a scrolling caption in Frame B2. See Figure 5-13.

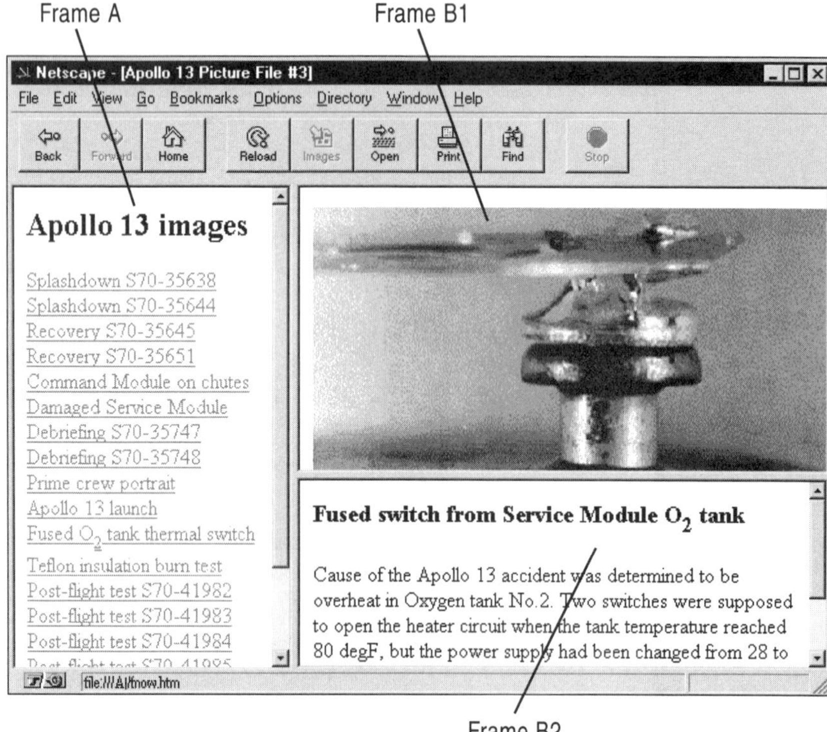

Figure 5-13: *User choice in Frame A produces a fixed image in Frame B1 plus a scrolling caption in Frame B2.*

- To reserve one screen area for form submission, and another for query results. See Figure 5-14.

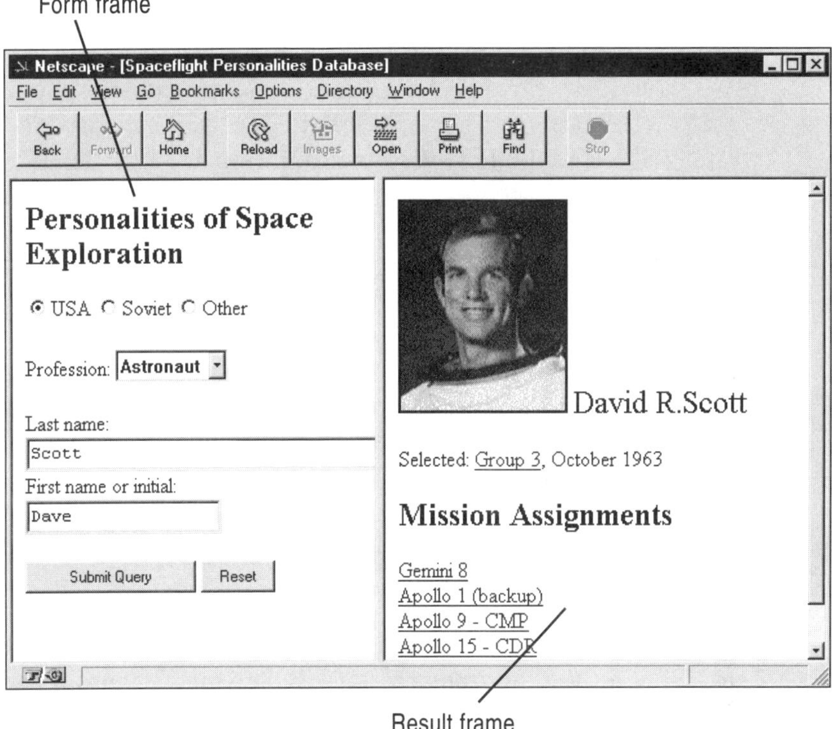

Figure 5-14: *Multiple-choice form produces display in a different frame.*

A frames document is rather special, in that it has no <BODY>....</BODY> container. Instead, it has a <FRAMESET> ....</FRAMESET> container wrapped around its principal content and, optionally, a <NOFRAMES> ....</NOFRAMES> container inside that which encloses alternative content for browsers that are not FRAMES-compliant. Use of NOFRAMES is *highly* recommended, since FRAMES is a Netscape invention and very few other browsers support it yet. FRAMES has, however, been submitted to the IETF for consideration as a standard.

HTML Tag

<FRAMESET>....</FRAMESET>

Replaces the <BODY>....</BODY> container of a normal HTML document and defines the document as a FRAMES page. Other <FRAMESET>....</FRAMESET> containers may be nested inside the first—typically to create a COLS subdivision of a frame that's already part of a ROWS frameset, or vice versa.

FRAMESET's attributes are:

ROWS="value,value,..."

COLS="value,value,..."—The ROWS and COLS "value lists" are comma-delimited lists of frame dimensions (vertical for ROWS, horizontal for COLS). See text for further explanation of value lists.

<FRAME>—Defines one FRAME in a FRAMESET. There is no </FRAME> tag. Attributes are:

NAME ="framename"—This optional attribute gives a name for the individual frame, which can then be referenced by a TARGET hyperlink from other frames in the document or from other documents.

SRC="[path/name of document that will define the content of this FRAME]"

SCROLLING="yes/no/auto"—Another optional attribute, defaulting to "auto." If SCROLLING="yes," scrollbars will be provided in the frame. If "no," they will not. If "auto," they will be present if Netscape decides they are needed.

MARGINWIDTH=m

MARGINHEIGHT=m—These attributes define the frame's margins in pixels. m cannot be zero. The default is "an appropriate margin."

NORESIZE—By default, a user may resize a frame by dragging its border to a new position. The NORESIZE attribute prevents this for the frame to which it applies.

<NOFRAMES>....</NOFRAMES>

Contains alternative content that will be seen by non-FRAMES browsers, and ignored by FRAMES browsers.

FRAMES Value Lists

The rows and columns value lists for a frameset can be expressed in several ways:

- **Percentage values.** Probably the most intuitive and useful expression. "80%,20%" divides the available space in a 4:1 ratio. If the sum of all terms in the value list does not come to 100% (i.e., someone screwed up), all terms are scaled up or down. For example, if instead of "80%,20%" someone entered "80%,40%" Netscape would effectively make it "67%,33%" since that would preserve the idea that the first bit is twice as big as the second bit. Netscape is said to be studying a version that will automatically send e-mail to the page author with the message "Learn arithmetic, you cretin." No, not really—we made that part up.
- **Arbitrary units.** Use asterisks as "wild cards" to represent "chunks." "4*,*" means "4 chunks then 1 chunk" and is exactly the same as "80%,20%." The supreme usefulness of a chunk is that it can also mean "whatever's left over" in combination with other units in the value list (a blessing for the mathematically-challenged). "65%,12%,*" would self-define a chunk as 23%. "100,*,100" would define the central row or column as whatever was still available after 100 pixels had been assigned to the frames on either side.

- **Absolute dimensions in pixels.** Although this might seem the most useful way of dimensioning frames, it's actually the most dangerous and not to be recommended. The problem is that, as we discussed in Chapter 4, there is no fixed width or height to a Web browser's content window. As an author you might satisfy yourself, for instance, that the exact effect you want is achieved by "COLS=406,112,87" but your gorgeous page will be distorted by users who shrink their overall Netscape windows, use different video resolution, use a different Web browser, or do all three. Nevertheless, it's understandable that you might want to fix the height of a frame that is only going to contain a banner GIF 55 pixels high. That's where the "chunk" concept really helps you out—"55,*" means "55 pixels, then whatever's left" and "55,2*,*" means "take 55 pixels off the top for my banner then divide what's left in a 2:1 ratio."

You should check over your frames text as follows: Within each FRAMESET there must be the same number of FRAMES or nested FRAMESETS as there are items in the frameset's value list. Here's the skeleton of one that's structurally correct:

```
<FRAMESET COLS="15%,85%">
      <FRAME.....>
      <FRAME.....>
</FRAMESET>
```

This is also correct:

```
<FRAMESET COLS="15%,15%,70%">
      <FRAME.....>
      <FRAME.....>
      <FRAMESET ROWS="*,*">
              <FRAME.....>
              <FRAME.....>
      </FRAMESET>
</FRAMESET>
```

This does not check out—there's a frame missing in the second frameset:

```
<FRAMESET ROWS="50,*,*">
     <FRAMESET COLS="3*,*,*">
            <FRAME.....>
            <FRAME.....>
     </FRAMESET>
     <FRAME.....>
     <FRAME.....>
</FRAMESET>
```

FRAMES Examples

Let's take a look at the code that created Figures 5-10 through 5-14, to help these concepts come alive.

Figure 5-10 is a straightforward example of a "ledge" graphic occupying part of the screen while the rest behaves normally. The FRAMESET here is:

```
<FRAMESET ROWS="68,*">
     <FRAME SRC="hos.gif" SCROLLING="NO" NORESIZE
     NAME=FRA>
     <FRAME SRC="hostext.htm" NAME=FRB>
</FRAMESET>
```

The value list "68,*" is a perfect example of reserving 68 pixels for the known height of the ledge and letting Frame B find its own size. Note the attribute NORESIZE for Frame A. By default, a user may resize a frame by dragging its border to a new position. The NORESIZE attribute prevents this for the frame to which it applies. It's not so important in this particular case, but this type of setup is often used to hold an advertising banner in place, and advertisers get upset if they discover it's possible to shrink their space to zero!

Figure 5-11 needs no NORESIZE, since it may be perfectly proper for the user to shrink the list of hyperlinks in Frame A once a link is made and the readable stuff is there in Frame B. Its FRAMESET is:

```
<FRAMESET COLS="35%,65%">
     <FRAME SRC="mstoc.htm" NAME=FRA>
     <FRAME SRC="mswait.htm" NAME=FRB>
</FRAMESET>
```

When this document is first loaded, no user choice has yet been made and therefore there's no logical content for Frame B. The file "mswait.htm" is a "wait file"—a place-holder which may be completely null or may have a brief label as its sole content. All hyperlinks in the file "mstoc.htm" are targeted to Frame B—here's an example:

```
<A HREF="skylab.htm" TARGET="FRB">Skylab</A>
```

The document shown in Figure 5-12 takes the concept of a hyperlink list controlling a different frame two steps further: Here the user gradually refines his choice of subject matter through hyperlink lists in Frames A, B, and C, ending with something worth reading (we hope!) in Frame D. The top frames are all active at once, so it's quite convenient for the user, but the downside is that there's not much space left over for Frame D. The hyperlinks in A are targeted to B, those in B are targeted to C, and so on. The nested FRAMESET is:

```
<FRAMESET ROWS="50%,50%">
     <FRAMESET COLS="*,*,*">
          <FRAME SRC="menu3a.htm" NAME=FRA>
          <FRAME SRC="wait3b.htm" NAME=FRB>
          <FRAME SRC="wait3c.htm" NAME=FRC>
     </FRAMESET>
     <FRAME SRC="wait3d.htm" NAME=FRD>
</FRAMESET>
```

Again, "wait files" act as placeholders until user choices are made.

The object of the document shown in Figure 5-13 is for a single hyperlink in Frame A to affect the display in two separate frames,

B (for images) and C (for captions). For this to work, two separate FRAMES files have to work together. First the screen is divided into A and B as follows:

```
<FRAMESET COLS="35%,65%">
      <FRAME SRC="a13menu.htm" NAME=FRA>
      <FRAME SRC="a13wait.htm" NAME=FRB>
</FRAMESET>
```

A hyperlink in "a13menu.htm" opens a file into Frame B which is itself a FRAMES file, subdividing B into B1 and B2 like so:

```
<FRAMESET ROWS="60%,40%">
      <FRAME SRC="fswitch.gif" SCROLLING=NO NAME=FRB1>
      <FRAME SRC="swtext.htm" NAME=FRB2>
</FRAMESET>
```

Note that scrolling has been turned off in Frame B1, where the pictures are directed, but the Frame may be resized by the user. Each picture/caption pair in this photo-library is free to divide Frame B in whatever way is most suitable. Some picture captions may fit comfortably within Frame B2—others, like the one illustrated, need to be scrollable.

Finally, Figure 5-14 manages a multi-dimensioned database rather neatly by allowing the user to set radio buttons and a pop-up menu in order to address the appropriate part of the database for the desired information display. When the completed form is submitted, the result appears in the other frame. Since we won't be dealing with forms until Chapter 9, the code for the Form Frame won't mean much—the point is that forms, as well as hypertext links, can be targeted.

Targeting FRAME Links

The links in the Result Frame in Figure 5-14 are of particular interest for another important element of frames. Here's one:

```
<A HREF="gemini8.htm" TARGET="_top">Gemini 8</A>
```

That target notation "_top" resolves a problem of frames documents—how do you get out once you're in? Any hyperlinks in a frame normally load their destination documents to the frame they occupy only, and this might be just what you want in many cases. But in linking to a page about the Gemini 8 mission we no longer care about the frames division of the current page. We'd like to open "gemini8.htm" into the whole content area. If we pick a new name as a target—"rosebud," or "Clytemnestra," say—Netscape will create a whole new window with that name for the destination document, with the frames document still present in the background. That might not be what we want, since it's sitting around consuming RAM when we may have no further use for it. The target "_top" is the solution, and it means "the TOP level window, before any framery began." You can also set, in the <HEAD> .... </HEAD> part of your document, the declaration <BASE TARGET="wname">, which means that all hyperlinks will be directed to "wname" unless otherwise specified.

A neat idea that we sometimes use is to give the user the option of expanding a frame to the top level. If, for example, we wanted to create the option of making the Skylab document from Figure 5-11 expand, we'd put in the following self-referential line:

```
<A HREF="skylab.htm" TARGET="_top">Expand this to full
screen</A>
```

After expansion to full screen, the Back button makes the display revert to its frames configuration, so that the user may make other choices.

Intermediate between "_top" and the current frame is the notation "_parent." This would load to the next level up in a cascade of FRAMES documents. For example, a hyperlink targeted to "_parent" in either Frame B1 or B2 of Figure 5-14 would load its destination document to the whole of Frame B, the "parent" frame, in other words.

Netscape FRAMES syntax also recognizes "_self", which is useful to override a BASE TARGET, if one is set, but otherwise simply achieves the default. The target "_blank" brings up a new unnamed window, essentially nothing that some much more poetic name like "Clytemnestra" would do.

TIP

The top-level document of a FRAMES set is the only one whose title is ever seen in the Title bar. The titles of subsidiary documents don't display, but you MUST give them some kind of title or they will not qualify as bona fide *HTML documents.*

Using HTML 3.0

A complete definition for HTML 3.0 is still not available as this book goes to press and in fact "HTML 3.0" no longer has any official meaning. We can only hope that it's released some time before all copies of this book have crumbled to dust!

The pattern for HTML 3.0 is fairly clear, however. A number of the proposed tags have the backing of a large enough consensus of participants—and such obvious utility—that Netscape has already implemented them, in anticipation of the next wave of Web evolution. In this section we'll discuss some of the new capabilities of HTML 3.0, including enhanced control over fonts, tabs, indentation, and footnotes, and support for text divisions and style sheets to aid in global style definition. Undoubtedly, many if not all of these features will re-emerge from the committees eventually.

Font Variations in HTML 3.0

The use of the <FONT> tag has remained controversial with the participants defining "official" HTML 3.0 because it is claimed that explicit control of type size is purely cosmetic and gives no information about document structure. Just as for the physical style tags like <I>, <B>, and<U>, however, the committee has allowed some tags that appear to be inconsistent with the stated philosophy. Here's the limited control you have over type if you want your pages to be readable by browsers that don't recognize the Netscape extensions:

HTML Tag

<BIG>....</BIG>

All enclosed text is bigger than normal.

<SMALL>....</SMALL>

All enclosed text is smaller than normal.

_{....}

Enclosed text is subscript.

^{....}

Enclosed text is superscript. <SUB> and <SUP> have ALIGN attributes when used within a <MATH> element.

<P ALIGN="left/right/center">

The default is "left"—normal left-justified text.
<P ALIGN="center"> is how HTML 3.0 wants you to center text between margins.

<P CLEAR="left/right/all">

Move down until the margin(s) is (are) clear or there is sufficient room before displaying. You may also specify a certain number of ens or pixels, such as CLEAR="40 pixels", meaning move down until 40 pixels are free. <P CLEAR> does not work in Netscape—use <BR CLEAR> instead at the point you want the margin cleared.

<P NOWRAP>

Turns off word wrapping for the paragraph. This does not work in Netscape Navigator.
Netscape uses the tag pair <NOBR> .... </NOBR>, which can contain any number of paragraphs or other text containers.
Another alternative is to replace spaces in a NOWRAP section with non-breaking spaces, signaled by

Many Web authors who want to cover the waterfront when using special tags will use both the Netscape version and the version (whether HTML 2.0 or 3.0) that will create the same effect in other browsers. For instance:

```
<CENTER>
<H1 ALIGN=center>Welcome to the Hotel California!</H1>
</CENTER>
```

This ensures that browsers that don't recognize <CENTER> but do recognize the ALIGN attribute in a heading tag will do the right thing, and vice versa. Netscape is equally happy with both, and doesn't mind the redundancy.

Correspondingly, you can use <BIG> along with a font size specification, as long as the <FONT> tag follows the <BIG> tag, like so:

```
<BIG><FONT SIZE=5>Text</FONT></BIG>
```

If the font size specification came first, like so:

```
<FONT SIZE=5><BIG>Text</BIG></FONT>
```

the effect would be to create a font size of 6, boosting the specified font size one more increment, since Netscape recognizes both tags as valid. It must be said, however, that the trend is for most newer browsers to recognize the font size specifications, so the <BIG> and <SMALL> tags may soon be obsolescent.

Document Divisions With <DIV>

There are times when it may be convenient to mark up certain sections of your text as a whole. Say you want the first several paragraphs of your text to be aligned right, as in Figure 5-15.

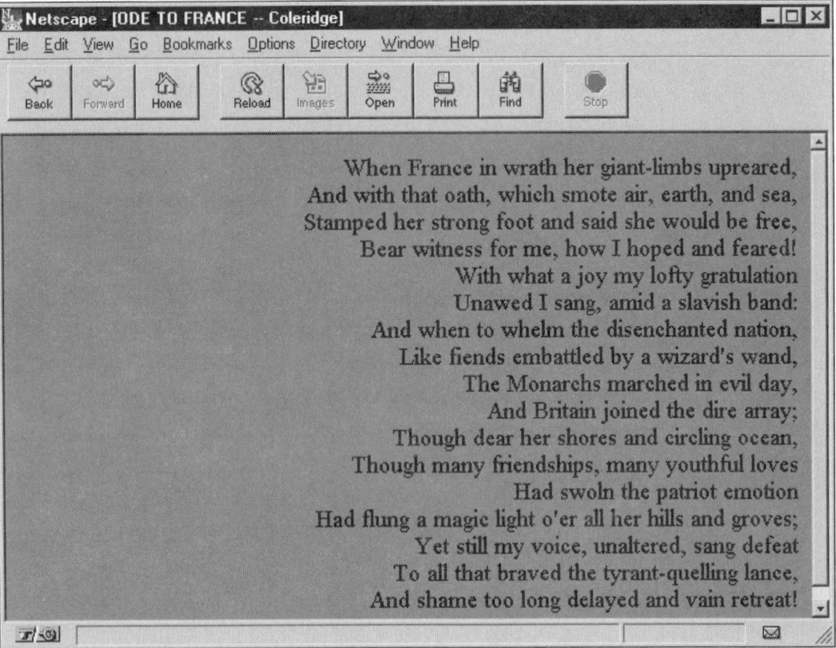

Figure 5-15: *All five stanzas of this poem can be formatted as a single DIV.*

The DIV tag is very useful for this. It tells the browser to treat everything within the tags in the same manner. DIV has the same attributes as the paragraph tag <P>, so instead of specifying the format for each paragraph, you can use the tag <DIV ALIGN="right">.

There are more sophisticated uses of the DIV tag that can be utilized with style sheets, such as designating all chapters to be formatted one way, appendices another way, and so forth. We'll say more about these when we discuss style sheets in the next section. But even without this level of detail, Netscape makes it easy to implement the division tag in elementary usage—and in fact it's the preferred alignment device used in Netscape Gold's Editor.

HTML Tag

<DIV> ... </DIV>

Designates a section of text to be treated as a whole for formatting or identification purposes, such as chapter, section, abstract, or appendix.

The <DIV> tag has the same attributes as <P>:

ALIGN="left/right/center"

CLEAR="left/right/all"

NOWRAP

In the context of style sheets, DIV may also have the attribute

CLASS=[Some general type of document section such as APPENDIX].

Style Sheets

As we've already hinted, the IETF and the W3 committees responsible for HTML 3.0 are not unaware of the clamor for more stylistic control of Web pages. As we've also hinted, although there are certain style elements that are considered totally heretical, there's little resistance to the idea of specifying style *as long as it's done in such a way as to be useful to all users.* Style sheets are, officially, the way to give document designers what they want while preserving the integrity of the actual HTML document.

Style sheets are not yet implemented as we write this, although they will certainly come into general use in some form during the lifetime of this book.

A style sheet is a series of statements, or "rules," of the form:

```
selector {property = value}
```

The *selector* is the element being lent the style: a header, a text class, a paragraph, a list, or a DIV, to name a few obvious ones. Not every element you could possibly think up is necessarily valid as a style selector.

The *property* is something about that selector that's variable—its color, its font, its spacing, and so forth; equivalent of an *attribute*.

The *value* is the chosen variable of the *property*. So the parallel between style sheet statements and HTML attributions such as <P ALIGN="center"> is rather close. Here's a statement that would define precisely how to treat level 1 headers in a Web document:

```
H1    {
      text-color = blue,
      font-family = helvetica,
      alt-font-family = arial,
      font-size = 12pt,
      font-leading = 2pt,
      font-weight = bold
      }
```

In that statement, the color "blue" is a bit vague, and the more precise hexadecimal #rrggbb color definitions already familiar to most Web authors seem certain to be allowed (perhaps along with other ways of saying "blue," such as "0 0 255").

Here's how a style sheet might very simply call for drop-cap paragraphs:

```
P     {
      text-effect = drop-cap
      }
```

For style sheets to work powerfully, every element in an HTML document should recognize a CLASS attribute, not just the DIVs. If and when style sheets are adopted as an official HTML standard, CLASS will be a valid attribute that can be applied to <P>, <H1>, <UL>, etc. The benefit of this is that you only have to define your formatting style once for it to be applied to every paragraph or heading or list—an obvious advantage in very large documents or a series of documents. For example, we might want to give particular formatting to certain paragraphs that are regarded as "key." In that case, the HTML would specify <P CLASS=key>, and the style sheet would include some such statement as:

```
P.key     {
          text-effect = drop-cap
          etc...
          }
```

An entire document can be styled by a rule such as:

```
HTML      {
          text-color = #ff0000
          }
```

Where Does the Style Sheet Belong?

By far the safest place for a style sheet is "some other place"—meaning that a style sheet should not, ideally, be contained within the document itself. That way various user interfaces could have the choice of applying the recommended style sheet, using a designated alternative, or ignoring the whole thing. If that's the case, the style sheet is a separate document referenced by a LINK of the type:

```
<LINK REL=STYLESHEET HREF="../styles/bklet.sty"
TITLE="Booklet">
```

...or perhaps a simpler form such as:

```
<LINK STYLE="../styles/bklet.sty">
```

This makes a style sheet into something extremely close to a word-processing template, such as the template Ventana provides for its authors to ensure that the words you are reading now come out as the book designer intends.

Some theorists of style favor allowing simple style instructions into the document itself. They would permit, for example:

```
<STYLE>P {text-color = "#00ff00"}</STYLE>
```

or even more locally...

```
<P STYLE="color:#00ff00">
```

In case of conflict between that and a style specified in a LINK stylesheet, the local STYLE takes precedence. As to why these same stylists deplore the simpler Netscape version:

```
<BODY text="#000000">
```

...don't ask us!

Another concept is to allow the "importation" of fragmentary style sheets as the need arises within a document, with code such as:

```
@import "../styles/bk023.sty"
```

The latest documentation (as we go to press) would allow the @import notation to bring in style specs from anywhere on the Web, by referring to a URL.

TABS & INDENTS

Here's another glorious example of a layout convention that was banned from early versions of HTML on the grounds that it had nothing to do with content, but is now creeping in again. Until the HTML 3.0 proposal, the only theoretical way to observe tab stops was to set the text as preformatted text using <PRE>... </PRE>, and even that was highly unreliable. Now TAB has been belatedly recognized as a legitimate part of document design.

HTML Tag

<TAB>

Controls the horizontal positioning of text in relation to either an embedded marker or a calculated indent.

ID="tabname" defines an embedded tab marker.

TO="tabname" causes the following text to set to the (previously defined) tabname.

INDENT=x causes a line to indent x ens.

ALIGN=left/center/right/decimal controls the relationship of the following text to the tab stop.

DP="." specifies the character that should be taken as the decimal point in a decimal tab. A period is the default in English language documents, but the LANG attribute of the document might change that to a comma, for example. An HTML author can choose any character to be used as a "decimal" column-alignment key.

A TAB ID can only be established by being set in a preceding line of text. For example, the code for Figure 5-16 is:

```
<FONT SIZE=5>WHEREAS</FONT> <TAB ID=tab1>the signatories to
this document desire to live in peace and<BR>
<TAB TO=tab1>harmony, the hundred years' war betwixt them
having
```

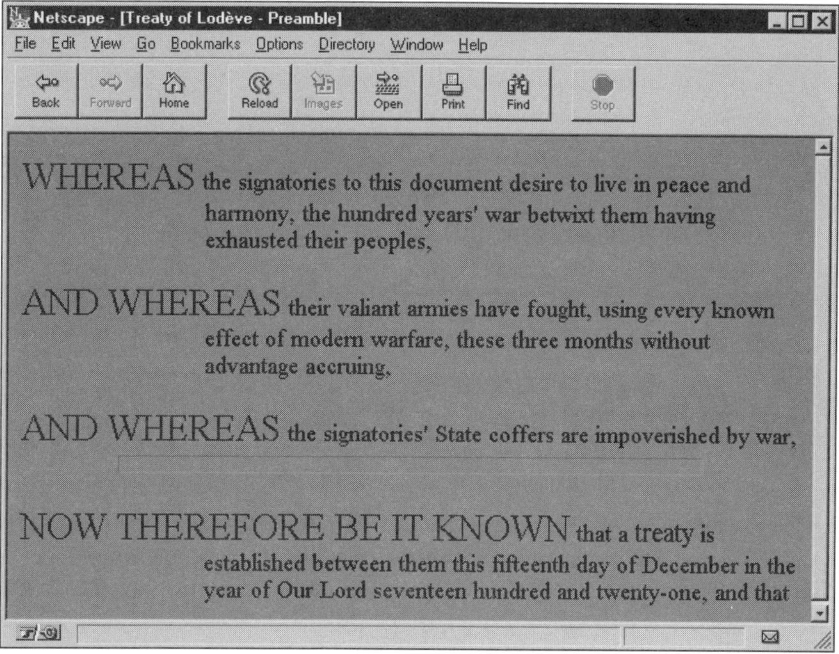

Figure 5-16: *Tabbing in relation to an embedded marker.*

Although no HTML element yet exists to define indent style for a whole paragraph (other than <BLOCKQUOTE>), this type of tabbing does suggest a way of creating a hanging indent, as shown in Figure 5-17. The "official" way of achieving this effect is with DIVs and style sheet statements, and it's definitely a better approach for documents like the one in the figure. If all dialogue can be defined by <DIV CLASS="dialog">, and all stage directions defined by <DIV CLASS="stgdirn">, two style sheet rules take care of 95 percent of the document's formatting.

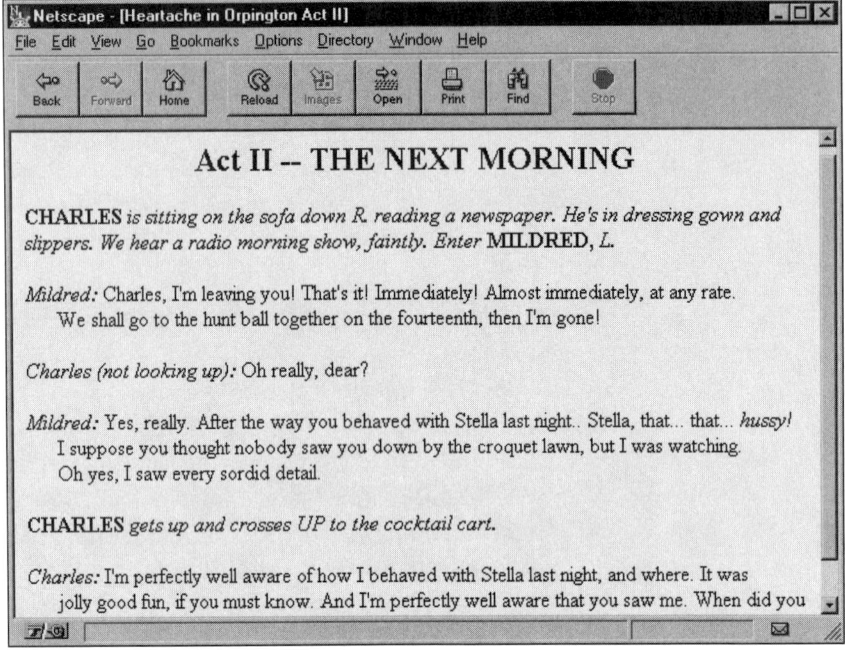

Figure 5-17: *Creating a hanging indent with TAB TO.*

The style of the paragraph you're reading right now is fairly standard for modern books—the first line is flush left and every other line is indented. We could achieve this effect in HTML with <TAB INDENT=4>. A double-indented paragraph is better done with <BLOCKQUOTE>.

Figure 5-18 is an illustration of the use of a "decimal" tab for non-decimal purposes. Here the page designer thought it would be good style to align all the e-mail addresses by their central @ symbols. So the tab stops were embedded in the double horizontal line, taking account of the length and placing of the addresses. Each e-mail address was then tabbed with the code:

```
<TAB TO="email" ALIGN=decimal DP=@>
```

It should be obvious that more conventional decimal tabbing, to line up columns of figures, is fairly straightforward.

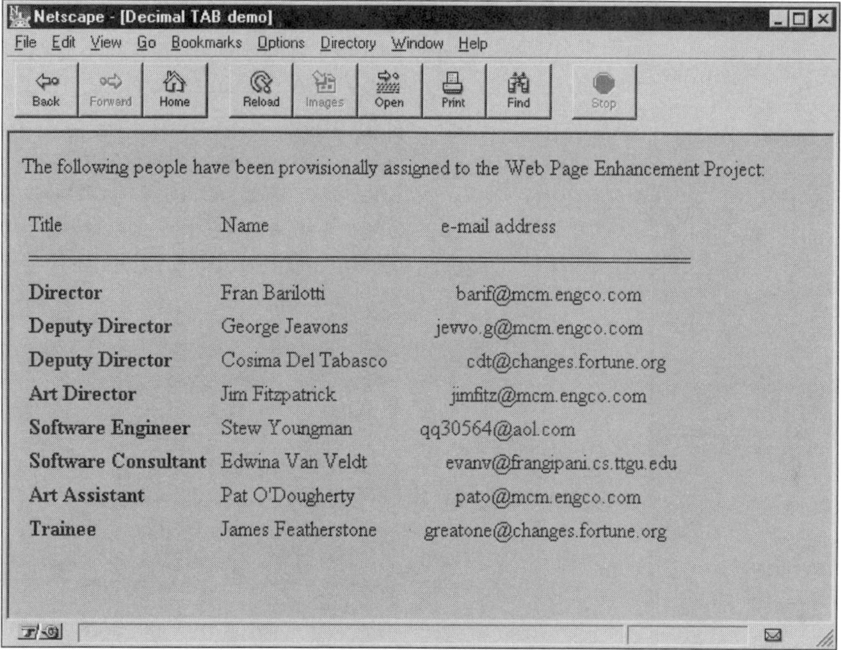

Figure 5-18: *Use of the DP attribute to align e-mail addresses by the @ symbol.*

Footnotes

Finally in this round-up of what's permitted by HTML 3.0 style-wise, check the groovy, pop-up explanatory note in Figure 5-19 (which admittedly we faked because the footnote tag is still in the realm of the theoretical). The phrase "Wooden O" was turned into a footnote anchor with the tags:

```
<A HREF="fn1">Wooden O</A>
```

...and the footnote itself supplied later like this:

```
<FN ID="fn1">This refers to the Globe Theatre of
Shakespeare's time, where <EM>Henry V</EM> would first have
been produced - built of wood in the shape of an O</FN>
```

While this use of footnotes in HTML would obviously be very useful, it has not yet been implemented, partly because the HTML committees are worrying about what they call "pop-up persistence"—meaning, how long should a pop-up stay popped up? Only while the user holds down the mouse button, for a timed duration (which we hate the idea of), or until the user does something else? Look for these philosophical discussions to come to an end, and for pop-up by FN to pop up in the near future.

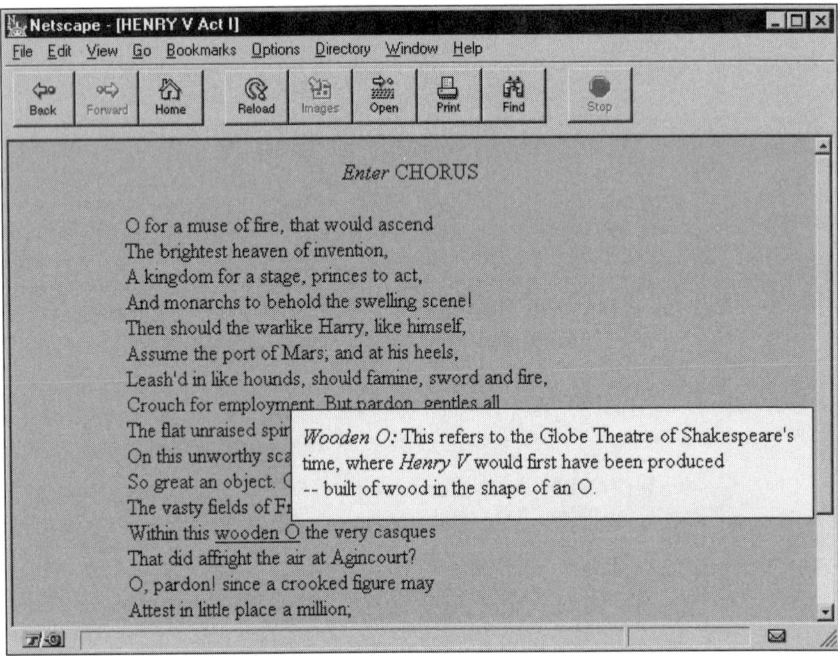

Figure 5-19: *A pop-up footnote.*

Standard Icons

Certain icons are in such common use all over the Web that they've really come to be accepted as an extension of the alphabet. The "folder" icon, for instance, or the "audio link" icon. The Web community is in favor of standardizing these and, instead of us all using disk space keeping GIF-format files of these icons, making them available as HTML entities or built-in IMG SRC libraries.

How standard is "standard?" Bert Bos, who was put in charge of developing standard icons for the WWW Consortium, wrote that the icons should come to be instantly recognizable by their design, but that no one specific pixel-by-pixel image should be "the one." He likens the situation to typography—we can all recognize the letter A, but the precise way in which an A is drawn on your computer screen is a factor of many things including the font size in use. So it should be, he writes, with the "standard" icons.

At this point, it will come as no surprise that two separate lists have emerged—one a proposal for HTML 3.0 (by Bert Bos) that is not yet implemented, and the other a Netscape built-in icon library that is implemented.

HTML Icons

A standard icon from the HTML 3.0 icon list may be evoked in one of two ways. The first way is by using the attribute "DINGBAT=" in conjunction with a header <H1> through <H5> or an unordered list, <UL>. For example, the code...

```
<P>The following movies are currently available:
<UL DINGBAT="film">
<LI>Barbell exercise
<LI>Jazz dance
<LI>Yoga sequence
<LI>Isometrics
</UL>
```

...produces the effect shown in Figure 5-20, with a standard FILM icon used as the bullet character of the list. In the case of headers, the dingbat is evoked the same way and appears to the left of whatever text you use as the header.

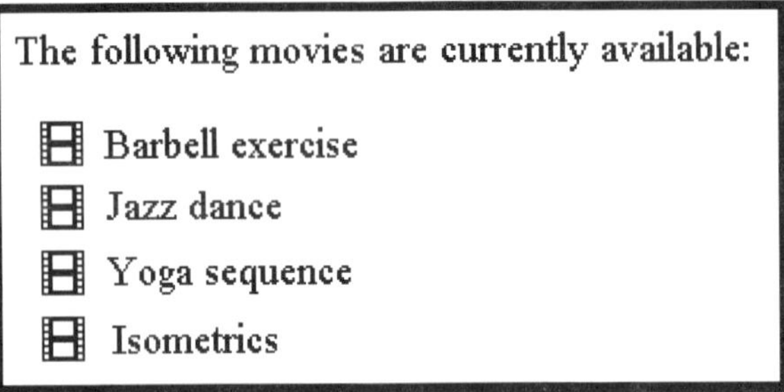

The following movies are currently available:
Barbell exercise
Jazz dance
Yoga sequence
Isometrics

Figure 5-20: *Dingbat list.*

The second way of evoking an HTML 3.0 standard icon is as an entity—the code *&film;* anywhere in your text would produce the icon on any compliant browser. For instance:

```
<H1>&film; Coming Soon</H1>
```

would insert a film icon next to the head "Coming Soon."

These are only proposed usages right now, and neither of these methods will work in the current version of Netscape Navigator, but they are likely to be implemented soon. So that you can test them out when they become available, a complete list of icons and the appropriate syntax for producing them is provided in Appendix G.

NETSCAPE ICONS

Netscape icons are built in to the browser software, and are the standard icons Netscape uses to display things like file menus and newsgroup lists. They cannot be evoked within the header or list tags as dingbats, as shown in Figure 5-20, but you can evoke them at any time—for the benefit of your Netscape users only—with the IMG tag, like so: <IMG SRC="internal-icontype-name">. (Since these are part of the Netscape software, you don't need to be online.) To make a standard Netscape folder icon appear before a heading, for instance, use:

```
<IMG SRC="internal-gopher-menu"><H1>Menu</H1>
```

To make them appear instead of list bullets on a list, you would have to use <DL> instead of <UL> for your list, like so:

```
<DL>
<DT><IMG SRC="internal-gopher-menu">List item 1</DT>
<DT><IMG SRC="internal-gopher-menu">List item 2</DT>
</DL>
```

Since these icons are specific to Netscape, you should supply an ALT reference for non-Netscape users. ALT=" * " or ALT="" are possible choices.

The list of Netscape icons is also in Appendix G.

Moving On

If you've surmised from this chapter that style in Web page design is one part artistic creativity and two parts technical mastery, you're not far wrong.

Now it's time for a little breather. In the next chapter we're going to take a look at some outstanding pages done by some very creative Web page designers. We'll analyze their pages to show how they solved some creative problems and how they added some original pizazz to their presentations. The chapter will also serve as an overview of the many different stylistic elements you can include in your pages. We hope you enjoy this visual treat as much as we do. Sit back and enjoy the show.

6

Design Tips: Learning From the Pros

As you've probably begun to surmise, good Web page design is a combination of both left and right brain activity. Visually oriented (or right-brained) people are liable to devote their energies to making high impact graphics for their Web sites. The analytically inclined left-brainers will be thinking about the many ways they can use the great referencing capability of hypertext to add multi-layered depth to their content. Really well-designed Web pages balance form and content so they complement each other—provided that the designers indeed have a message to get across. (There will always be those who use the Web purely as an art form, including one of our featured sites in this chapter, and we're not opposed to that.)

But in this chapter we're going to play to the right brain, in the firm belief that, no matter what your inclination, when you're trying to master a new skill, examples work best and a picture gets the point across fastest. With the help of some design wizards on the Web, we've assembled an outstanding cast of Web pages here, chosen because they're not just great to look at, but they all have something to teach about Web design techniques. We'll analyze the components of each page, so you can understand how these pages were put together. Then by following the examples and the references to other sections of the book, you'll be able to use these techniques yourself.

To appreciate these sites fully you should prepare to fire up your browser and go to the actual URL for each page that we give, so that you can see the full-color and (in some cases) live action components of these pages. Since these are cutting-edge designers, some of the pages are likely to have changed a little since our selections were made, but you'll no doubt find similar techniques and you're guaranteed to see something interesting. Color versions of the screen shots are also available for viewing on the CD-ROM (although action components will not be working, since these are proprietary elements).

In roughly easiest-to-hardest order, here they are:

TEXT AT ITS BEST

http://www.demon.co.uk/murderon/themenu/

Murder on the Menu (Figures 6-1 A & B) is a British theatre group specializing in audience participation mystery theatre productions for private parties or corporate entertainment. If their plots are as devilishly clever as this page, they can get away with anything.

The surprising thing about this page is that it is done with almost no fancy HTML tricks at all. The font sizes are achieved with header tags: <H1> for the large heads and <H3> for the body copy. A series of three nested <UL> tags, with cascading head tags for the list elements, creates the indented text toward the bottom of the page. The relevant section of the file is shown below:

```
<UL><IMG SRC="cork.gif" ALIGN=right alt="flying Champagne Cork">
<LI><H1>Whodunnit?</H1><br clear=right>
<A HREF="clist.html"><H3>murder in good company</H3></A>
      <UL>
      <LI><H1>Diversionary</H1>
      <IMG SRC="divert.gif" ALIGN=right
ALT="diversion sign">
<UL>
```

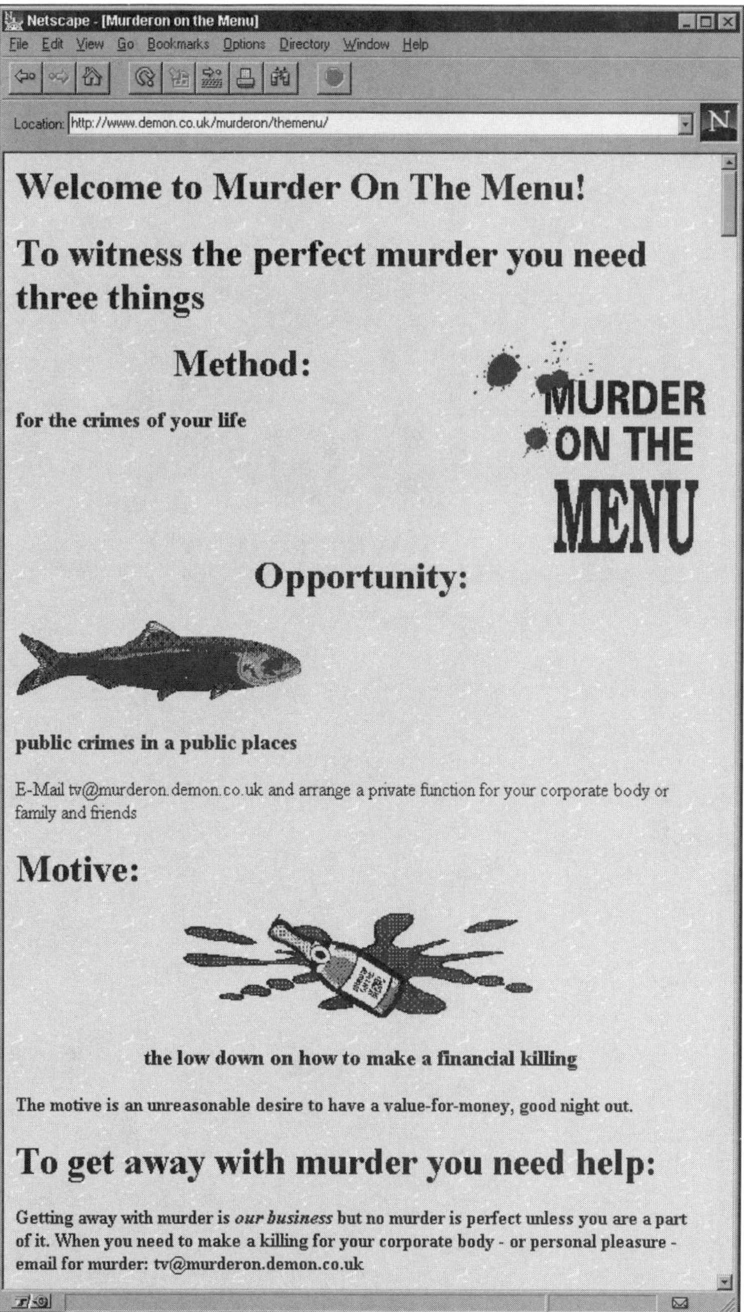

Figure 6-1A: *This British troupe may know some theatrical tricks, but it has a "no gimmicks" Web presence—the effects here are achieved purely with excellent "traditional" text and image management.*

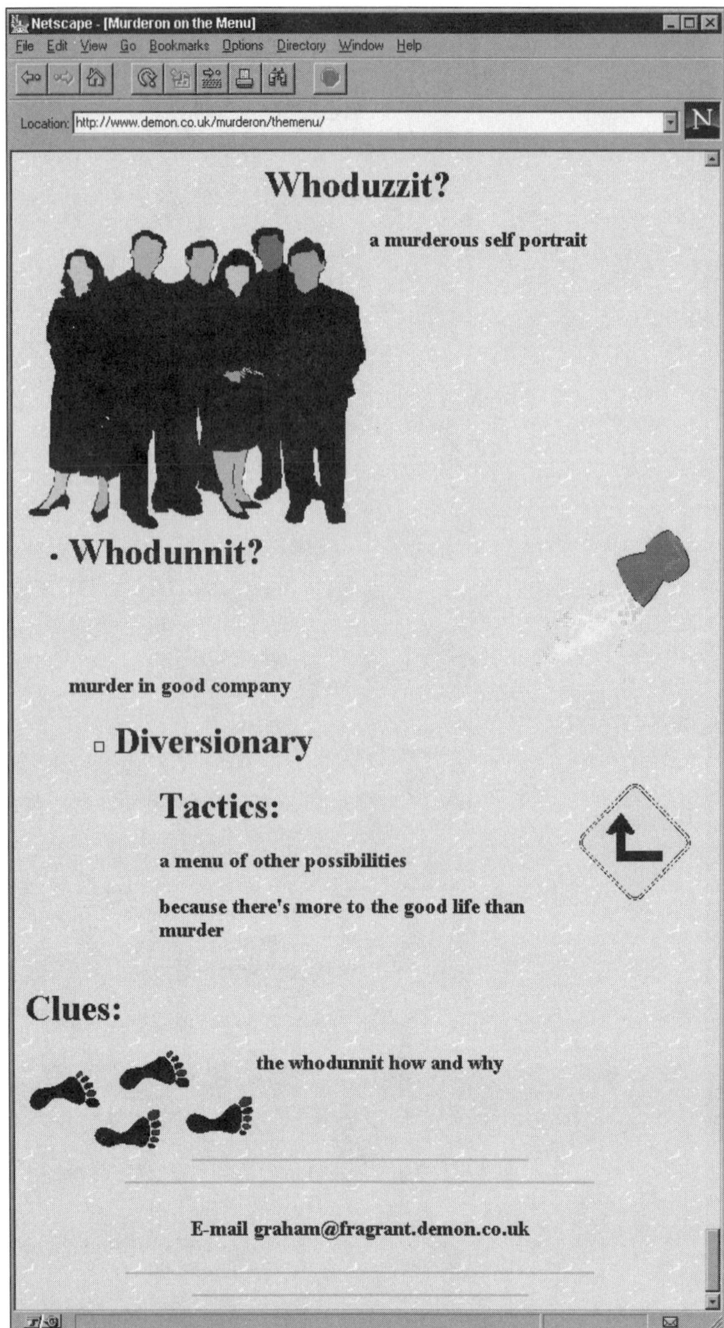

Figure 6-1B: *This page is a fine example of what you can accomplish using a few simple HTML tags.*

```
<H1>Tactics:</H1>
<A HREF="alsomenu.html"><H3>a menu of other possibilities
</H3></A>
<H3>because there's more to the good life than murder </H3>
</UL> </UL></UL>
```

The bonus to this page is that because it uses no fancy tags, it looks good in almost any browser. It even retains some impact when images are not loaded, or when seen in a text-only browser.

Captivating Color

http://www.berry-bros.co.uk/

This page for a wine dealer—surely a contender for "oldest-established business on the Web"—has been a favorite ever since Limitless Internet Consultants of London created it. Our nickname for it was "London Afternoon Gold," because we thought it represented a cityscape seen outside Berry Bros. windows in falling afternoon light. Now that Frank Wales, a partner in Limitless, has explained that this page is actually supposed to be looking *into* his client's window, we like it nonetheless. It's done with the use of a "low-source" black and white image, which loads quickly with the page text, followed by the interlaced imposition of the color version, complete with the pure gold of vintage wine.

This is the code that does the trick:

```
<IMG SRC="/icons/windows.gif" WIDTH=428 HEIGHT=224
LOWSRC="/icons/windows1.gif" ALT="">
```

The "windows1.gif" is the fast-loading monochrome picture, while "windows.gif" is the colored one that gradually replaces it.

They've used another easy trick to assure that the full effect comes through immediately. For the best and densest black, a small square black GIF is specified as a tiled-in background image. However, the background color is also defined as black (with BGCOLOR="#000000"). The background color loads first, then the GIF later (unnoticeable to a browser which already recognizes the background color). Other color components: text is white, links

Figure 6-2: *The Berry Bros. & Rudd Web site, consisting of over 500 documents in all, was a joint effort by three London companies. The front page, shown here, uses the IMG LOWSRC attribute, an interlaced color GIF, and excellent background management to achieve the dynamic color effect seen in three stages.*

cyan, visited links a slightly darker shade of cyan, active links flash red. This is the tag:

```
<BODY BGCOLOR="#000000" BACKGROUND="/icons/black.gif"
TEXT="#EEEEEE" LINK="#00FFFF" VLINK="#00BFBF"
ALINK="#FF0000">
```

On subsequent pages you can browse their various wine cellar wares and order a $3,000 bottle of 1945 Château Mouton-Rothschild, if you're so inclined. Actually, you can choose between $3,100, £2,000, or ¥320,000 because this site is "tri-monetary." It also serves up a different version if you come to it with a browser more primitive than Netscape 1.1. All those variations add up to make a 500-page site, a *tour de force* of Web design, and a great way of selling wine.

Limitless, whose full legal name is "Limitless Technical Dimensions Limited"—hmm, something very English about that—has plenty else in their portfolio to be proud of. Their home page is http://www.limitless.co.uk.

Great Graphics

http://www.telalink.net/~zoomst/

There are hundreds of variations on the standard bar GIF out there on the Web, but this one at a San Francisco site really caught our eye. Shiny pipe fittings enhance the idea of entering a piece of underground culture. This clever piece of *trompe l'oeil* is accomplished by the use of a transparent GIF imposed over a matching background GIF.

The two pieces of the puzzle are shown in Figures 6-3 A & B and the components on the facing page. The first piece is a GIF in the form of a wide stripe, with the vertical pipe section on the left edge. Designate this as a background GIF and it will tile in seamlessly down the page. If you try this technique yourself, the background GIF does not need to be large vertically, since it tiles to whatever height is required, but it should be sufficiently wide to account for a variety of screen sizes—1280 pixels will cover even the widest browser known to man.

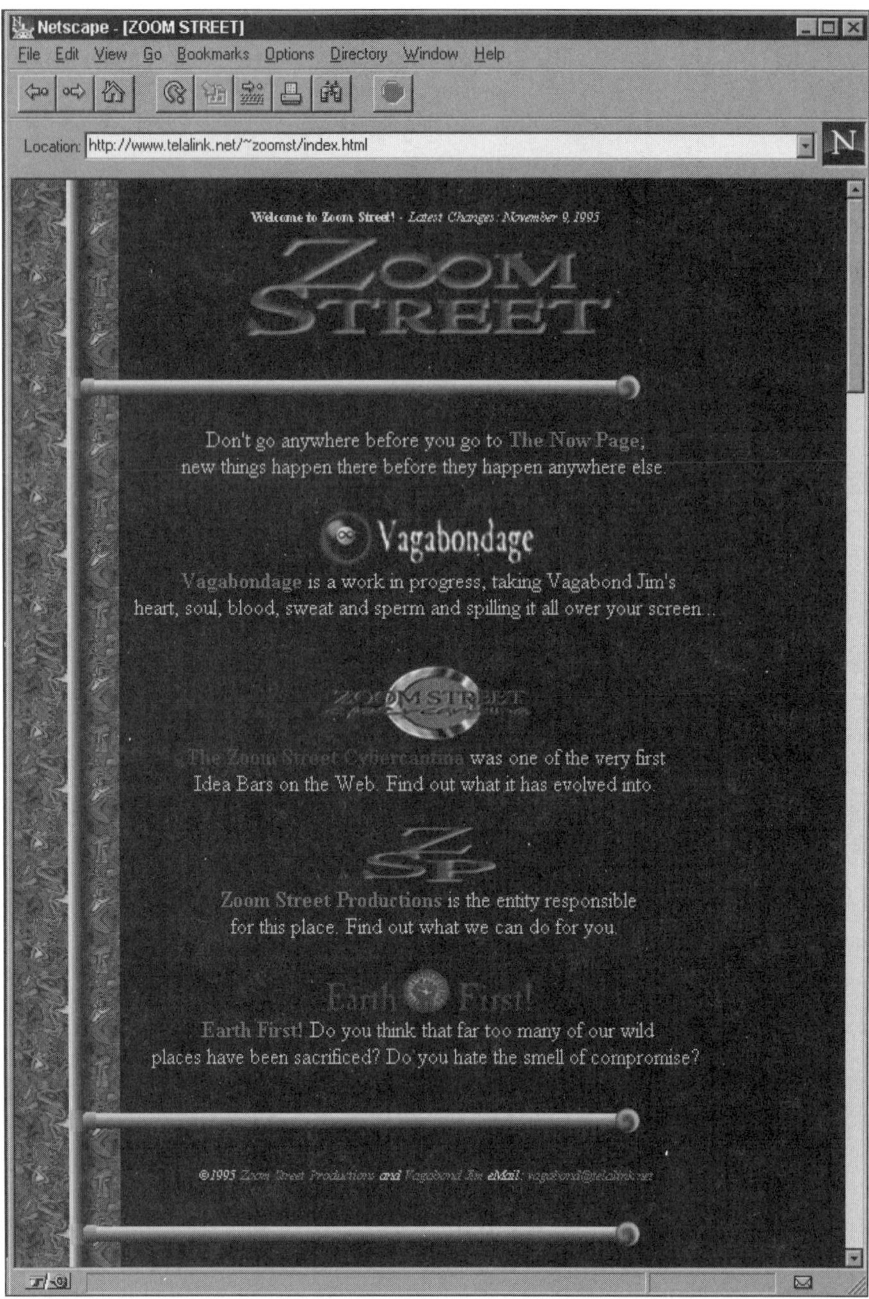

Figure 6-3A: *Absolute precision in matching foreground to background achieves a startling effect that many visitors to this page might not even notice. The vertical pipe is a background tile, and the horizontal text divider pipes both shown upper right are transparent foreground images.*

Figure 6-3B: *Check out the illusion of a tee-joint in this section of piping structure.*

Here's the code line that inserts it:

```
<BODY BACKGROUND="images/yellowbg.gif" BGCOLOR="#000000"
TEXT="#E5E5E5" LINK="#E48700" VLINK="#8E4300"
ALINK="#999999">
```

The horizontal pipe, inserted as a page separator, is a transparent GIF precisely calculated so that it joins the background at the right point and creates the illusion of a tee-joint in a piping structure. That's it, isolated in the lower half of Figure 6-3B. Here's the code, inserted each time the page separator is called for:

```
<IMG SRC="images/fullbar.gif">
```

The rest of the page is simple, if sassy, with centered text and a few elegant graphics to lead you on to your next chosen destination.

The Art of Client Pull

http://www.mcad.edu/home/faculty/szyhalski/Piotr3/

It's hard to enter Polish art student Piotr Szhalsinzki's Web site at the Minneapolis College of Art & Design without becoming drawn in and mesmerized by his mysterious images and high-quality graphic work. His meticulous sense of design carries over to precision in technical virtuosity, as he pushes the limits of HTML to see what he can achieve.

Although we could have chosen almost any of his pages to demonstrate something of interest, we've chosen his opening page for its stylish simplicity. As a metaphor for the artistic impulse, he

A

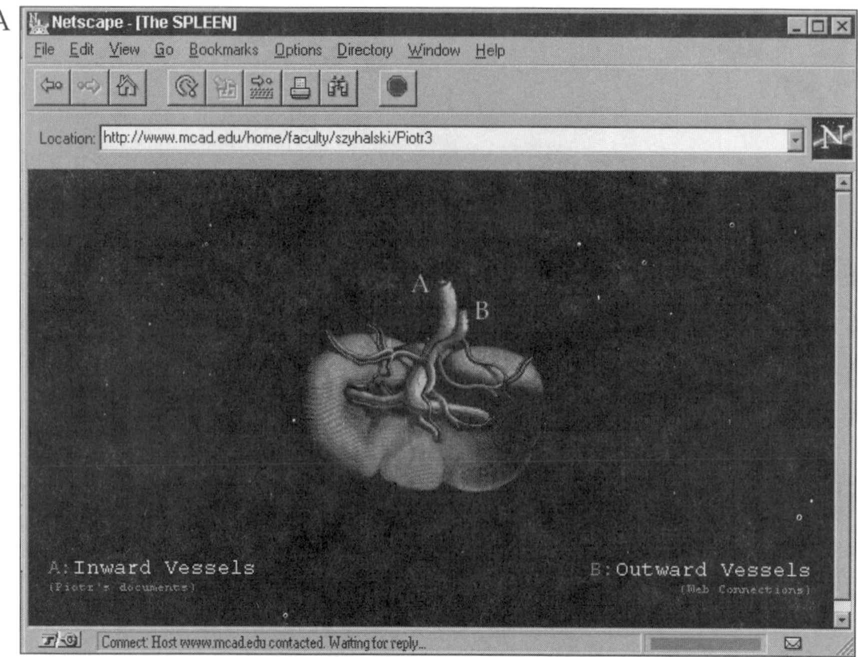

B

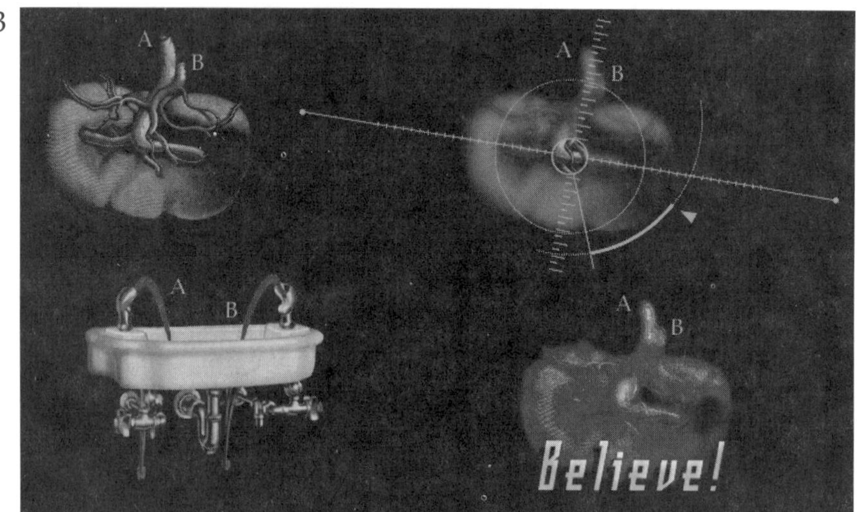

Figures 6-4A&B: *The technical story behind this beautiful page is fairly simple—it's a "client pull" animation. The artistic element is Piotr Szhalsinzki's tremendous flair for image production. All four of the images he uses on this front page are seen separately in the lower figure.*

uses the spleen, an organ whose purpose is somewhat mysterious and even, it's been said, unnecessary.

This opening page contains a series of continuously changing images that slowly evolve on your screen. This is accomplished with the "client pull" technique, discussed in Chapter 8. Although this looks tricky, it's actually very simply accomplished with one tag—the META tag with the HTTP-EQUIV="Refresh" attribute—inserted in the document head. Here it is, as Piotr uses it:

```
<META HTTP-EQUIV="Refresh" CONTENT="45; URL=Piotr4">
```

There are actually four pages labeled Piotr1, Piotr2, Piotr3, and Piotr4, each containing a different image. Each page gets this tag in the <HEAD> portion of the document, with the URL in the tag specifying the next in the series. This causes the next document in the series to be loaded automatically after 45 seconds. (As a page author, you can change the number to any length of time you wish.) The last reloads the first, so the cycle continues as long as one cares to watch.

To enhance the feeling of movement and evolution, each of the images is interlaced, so that something always seems to be evolving on your screen. This is one case where it's possibly even nicer to have an ordinary slow phone line rather than a high-speed Internet connection.

If you're curious about how he got the other components of the page (the links at the right and left bottom corners of the page) exactly where he wanted them, they are in a table with only two data cells (which we discussed in Chapter 5). The code:

```
<CENTER>
<TABLE WIDTH=100%>
<TR>
<TD ALIGN=left><PRE><FONT SIZE=4>A:<A HREF="spl/
Inward.html">Inward Vessels</A></FONT>
<FONT SIZE=2>(Piotr's documents)</FONT></PRE>
</TD>
<TD ALIGN=right><PRE><FONT SIZE=4>B:<A HREF="spl/
Outward.html">Outward Vessels</A></FONT>
<FONT SIZE=2>(Web Connections)</FONT></PRE>
</TD>
```

```
</TR>
</TABLE>
</CENTER>
```

Note that the WIDTH=100% attribute assures that the table will use the full screen size. In combination with the ALIGN left and right attributes for the two table data cells (<TD>), this assures that the elements will appear at the screen edges.

THE ALT TEXT TRICK

http://paradiso.itd.ge.cnr.it/tdpage/persone/borsisti/santi/santis.htm

At first glance—or even at second—you might not be able to tell what makes this page so special. Sure, it displays typical Italian panache, using some great graphics, but so what? The real trick to this page is hidden under the graphics, however. Santi Scimeca has come up with an ingenious way to provide alternative text for those browsing with images off. It's a variation on the "glass bricks trick" we discussed in Chapter 5.

This is the trick: Make a minuscule GIF of exactly 1 pixel—a screen dot, in other words. Make it white or black or choose the color to match your background. It doesn't matter, because you're going to save it as a transparent GIF. Now insert it into your file with the IMG tag and use the ALT attribute to supply text for a link destination. Put the BORDER=0 attribute in, too, to ensure that your dot does not get a teeny-weeny highlighted box around it to give away its location. Surround it all with an anchor tag (<A HREF>). Pop in as many of those as you need to take care of the links on your image map and presto! You've got alternative links that will appear only when the main image does not (see second frame of the figure on following page).

Here's the relevant code Santi used to accomplish this for the four links on his main image (the first line of code is the large active image):

```
<A HREF="tv.map"><IMG border=0 SRC="tv.gif" ISMAP>
</A><BR>
<A HREF="autobio.htm"><IMG border=0 SRC="dot.gif"
ALT="Autobiografia"></A>
```

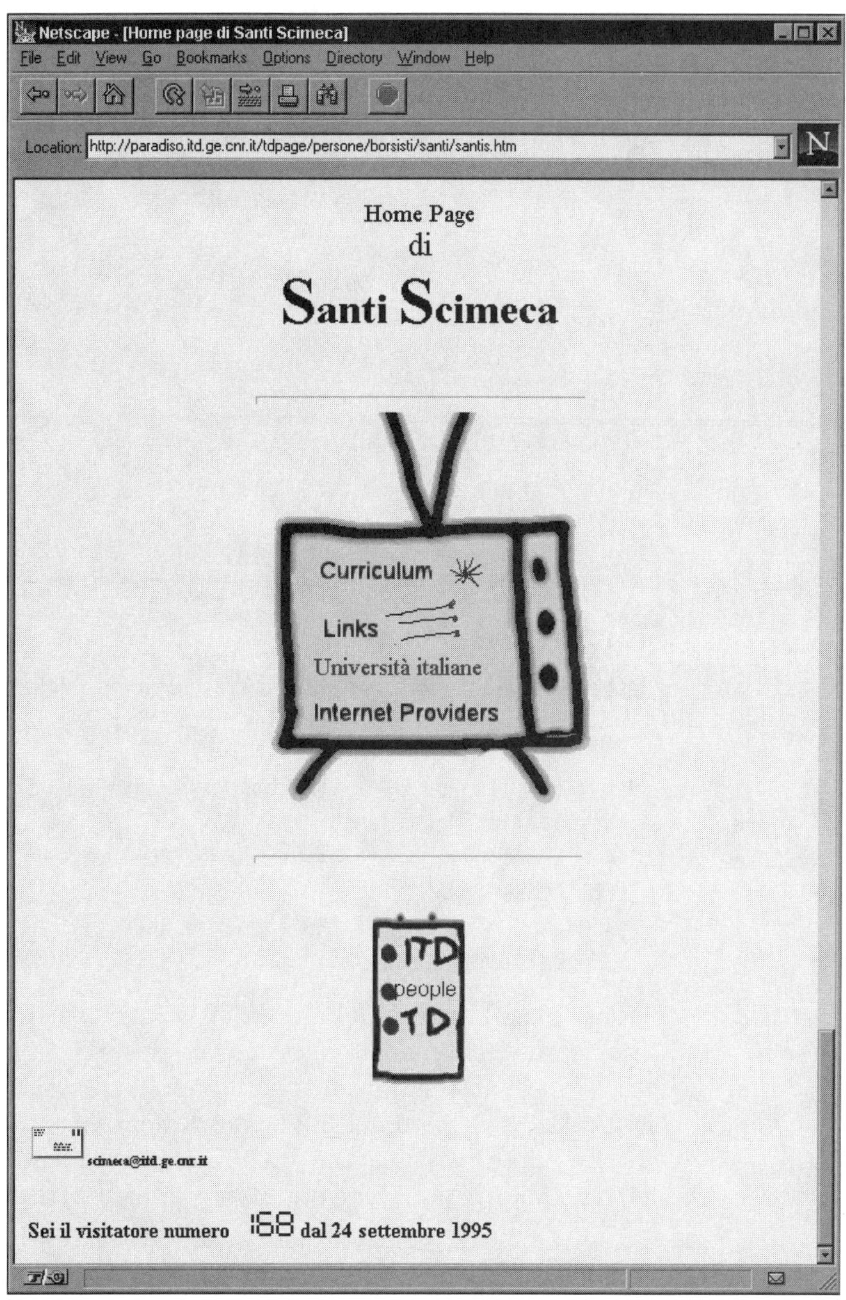

Figure 6-5A: *The main picture on Santi Scimeca's page is an active image with four outgoing hyperlinks. Turn images off, and the four links pop out of the background for you. The secret? The links are ALT text concealed behind tiny "glass bricks."*

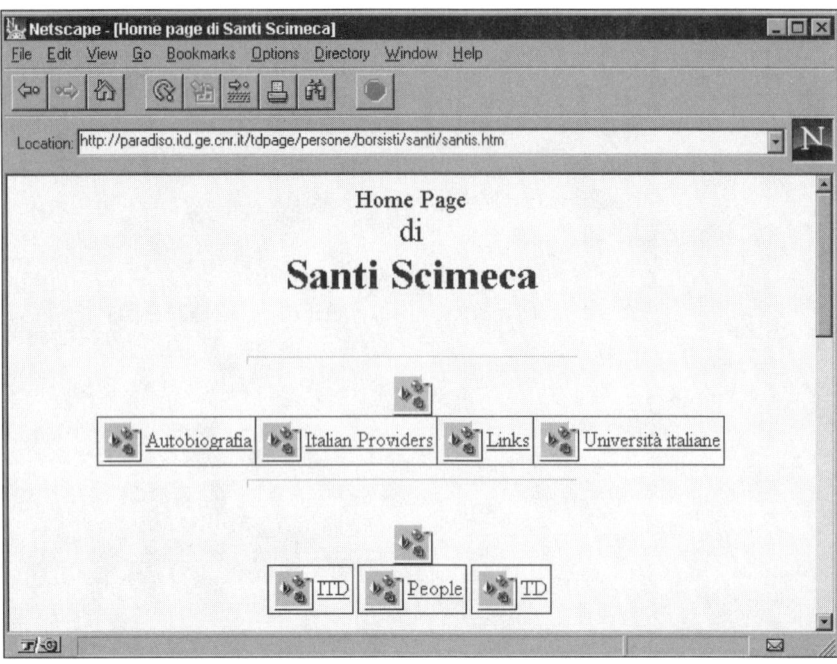

Figure 6-5B: This is an example of a Web page with "glass brick" links.

```
<A HREF="itaprov.htm"><IMG border=0 SRC="dot.gif"
ALT="Italian Providers"></A>
<A HREF="links.htm"><IMG border=0 SRC="dot.gif"
ALT="Links"></A>
<A HREF="univer.htm"><IMG border=0 SRC="dot.gif"
ALT="Università italiane"></A>
```

The "glass bricks with links" trick is particularly useful in this case because that main image is linked through an image map with several destinations that could not be designated with a single ALT text. Santi doesn't have to offend his great Italian graphic sense by displaying any unnecessary text on his page, but he's still taking care of the odd non-graphic Web browser.

Looking Good With Tables

http://www.discovery.com/

The Discovery Channel's Web site, which features online information about their programming, demonstrates an especially apt use of tables. What we really like about this page is that it all fits neatly on a standard 640 X 480 screen. (Okay, we had to get rid of the location window to get it all, but even without doing that everything important was visible.)

The table serves as a visually appealing introduction and a table of contents in one screen. It gives the appearance of being an image map, but in fact contains only linked images within each of the cells (the first and largest cell contains only the masthead). Stripping the coding bare, the essentials look like this:

```
<TABLE BORDER>
<TR>
<TD COLSPAN=3><IMG SRC="masthead.gif" BORDER=0></TD>
<TD ROWSPAN=3><IMG SRC="galapagos.gif" BORDER=0></TD>
<TR>
<TD COLSPAN=3><IMG SRC="date.gif" BORDER=0>
<TR>
<TD><IMG SRC="world.gif" BORDER=0></TD>
<TD><IMG SRC="onair.gif" BORDER=0></TD>
<TD><IMG SRC="tools.gif" BORDER=0></TD>
</TABLE>
```

In fact, it's a little more complicated than that, but not much. The date banner is actually generated by a cgi-bin script, so that it can be automatically updated without anyone having to attend to it. We'll be explaining cgi-bin in Chapter 9, but what it does in this case is retrieve the date and time from the host computer and display it—a simple "server-side includes" operation that's easy for anyone to do. And the right-hand column really contains another nested table, whose main purpose is to allow for different content to be easily dropped in on different days. The BORDER=0 attribute makes the table divisions transparent and also suppresses the box that would normally appear around a linked image. The coding for that long right data cell looks like this:

```
<TD ROWSPAN=3 VALIGN=top  WIDTH=150 ALIGN=top>
     <TABLE BORDER=0 CELLPADDING=0
     CELLSPACING=0>
            <TR>
            <TD ALIGN=left VALIGN=top WIDTH=150
            HEIGHT=322>
            <A HREF="nature.html">
            <IMG WIDTH=149 HEIGHT=256 BORDER=0
            SRC="onlinewingnov_30.gif"></A>
            <A HREF="../sponsor/">
            <IMG WIDTH=149 height=65 BORDER=0
            SRC="onlinewing.gif"></A>
            </TD>
            </TR>
     </TABLE>
</TD>
```

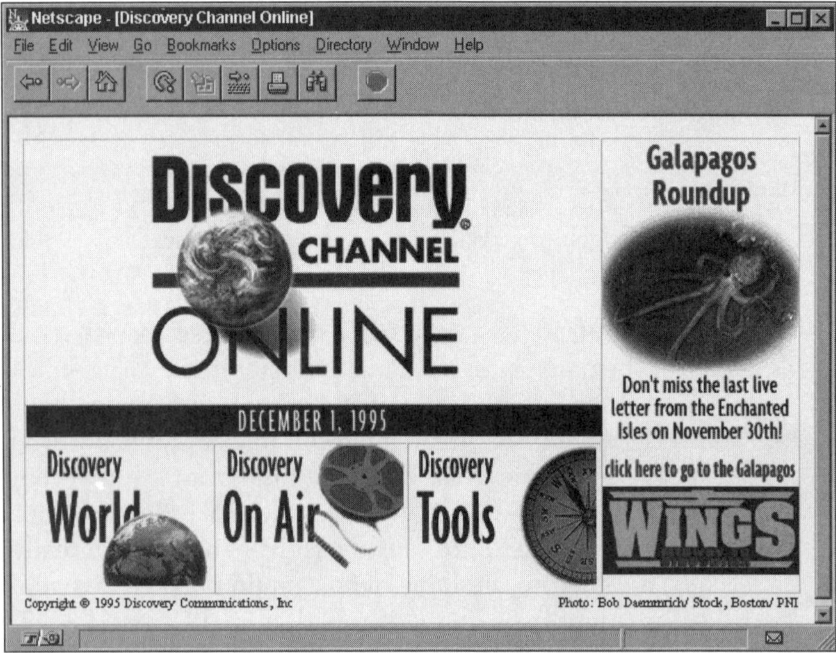

Figure 6-6: *This is a table within a table within a table, plus a cgi-bin script to display the date automatically. What's more, it changes every day!*

As you can see from the numbers above (just a few of those in the actual code), a lot of careful calculations had to be made for the size of images and data cells to make everything fit so well on the page, but the beautiful presentation makes it all worthwhile.

SMART SERVER PUSH

http://www.kidscom.com/

This very appealing and very simple page, which leads to an educational and games area for kids, contains an animated title of colorful letters which tumble into place. It's eye-grabbing and fun, and if you visit the site, you'll find yourself reloading the page several times just to see the effect all over again.

The title sequence is generated by a series of seven simple graphics, which load consecutively in the designated space. The actual cgi-bin script that's the engine of this gorgeous page is proprietary—but in Chapter 8, "Multimedia & the Web," we'll be introducing you to a public-domain animation script (written in the Perl language) that achieves the exact same effect.

Another simple trick here is the way the buttons are inserted for the four language versions. These are "fake GIFs" generated by the form tag—that is, not GIFs at all, but Netscape default graphics supplied when the FORM tag is used. The default wording on the button is "Submit" but you can change it to whatever you want using the VALUE attribute. If you don't have the time or resources to make your own buttons (or don't want to waste the bandwidth downloading GIFs), here's what you do:

```
<FORM ACTION="http://www.kidscom.com/index.html">
<A HREF="http://www.kidscom.com/english.html">
<INPUT TYPE="submit" VALUE="English">
</A></FORM>
```

The action line in this "form" is a dummy—it refers to the index page, but when the user clicks on one of the buttons no data is sent to that page (and that URL isn't even equipped to handle any). It's the conventional anchor tags (<A HREF>...</A>) that turn the buttons into hypertext links and do the real work here.

A

B

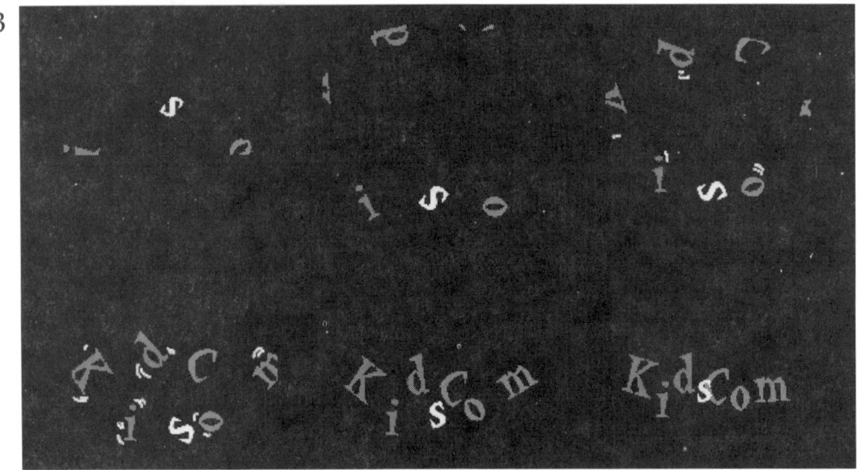

Figures 6-7A&B: *Server push is what drives this artful animation, which we show in six preliminary stages as well as in the final position. The select buttons are an interesting use of the FORM tags purely for decorative purposes..*

Notice that you can't control the size of the buttons, as that's dependent on the length of the text on them. A workaround might be to add nonbreaking spaces ( ) to make the text lines approximately equal.

A little-known secret: This page is the province of Internet guru Scott Yanoff, famous for his list of "Special Internet Connections," which just goes to show that even the pros are not averse to a quick dodge or two.

Database Wizardry

http://www.lonelyplanet.com/dest/dest.htm

Whenever we get a little bored staring at our computer and begin to think it's time to take a vacation, we like to visit this page. It provides a quick 10-minute daydream, where we can take a fantasy trip to anywhere in the world.

Lonely Planet is an Australian publishing company that produces some of our favorite travel guides—out-of-the-ordinary perspectives on some out-of-the-way places in the world. This simple but highly effective page allows you to choose any area of the world you want to know about, either from the large world map or through a searchable database. But the real fun is the "Mystery Tour." Take this option and you'll be instantly sent off to some random exotic destination, which you can read all about from their extensive collection of guide material.

There are three basic components to this page: an active image, a form which initiates a search, and a randomized cgi-bin script. We'll take them one at a time.

Making image maps like this is not as hard as it may seem. This one uses the ISMAP attribute in the IMG tag, which sends the server off to look for the file "world.map" to translate the click coordinates into link destinations. The line that makes it happen in this page is:

```
<A HREF="/maps/world.map">
<IMG SRC="wrlddest.gif" BORDER=0 ISMAP></A>
```

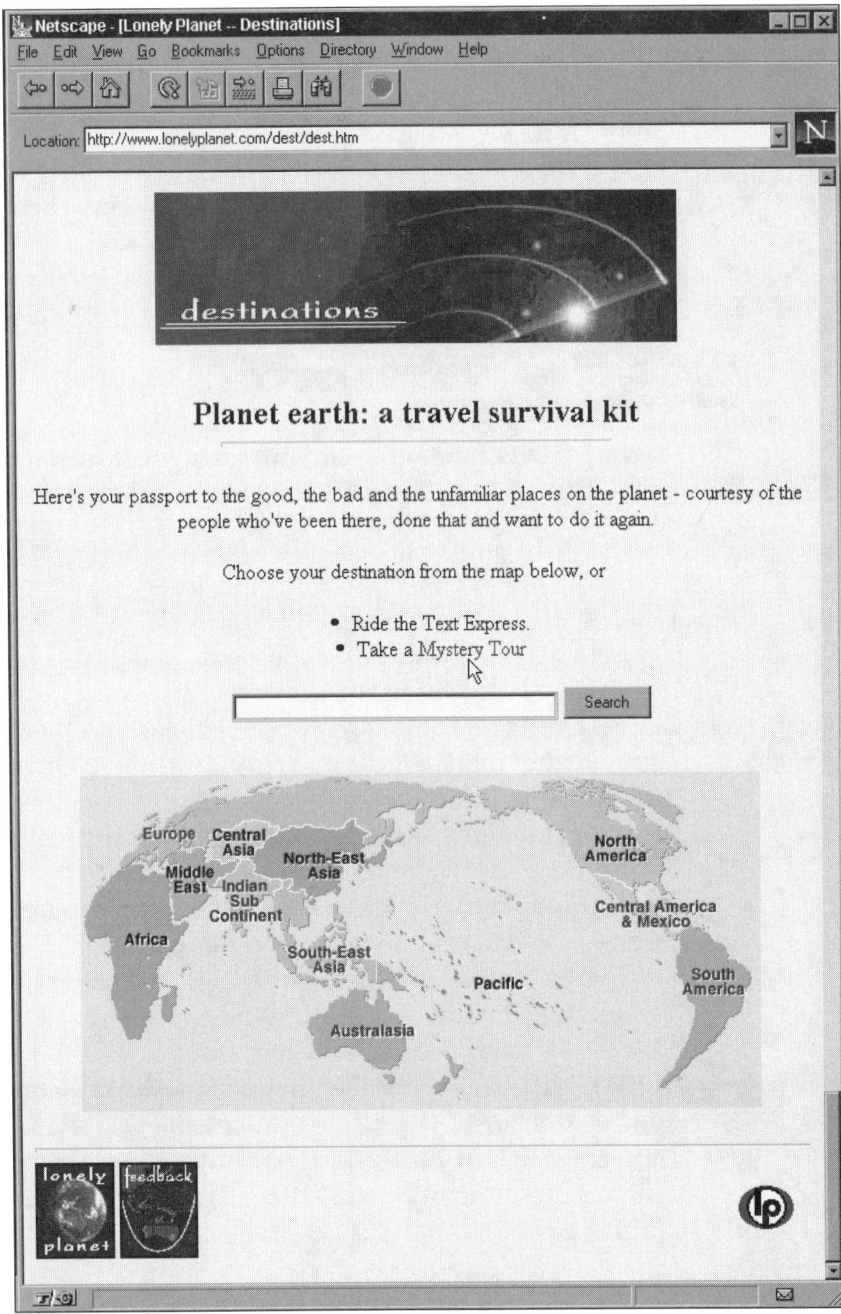

Figure 6-8A: *It won't come as a surprise that the world map here is an active image, leading to worldwide destinations. What is unique about this site is the database search and the hyperlink to a random destination.*

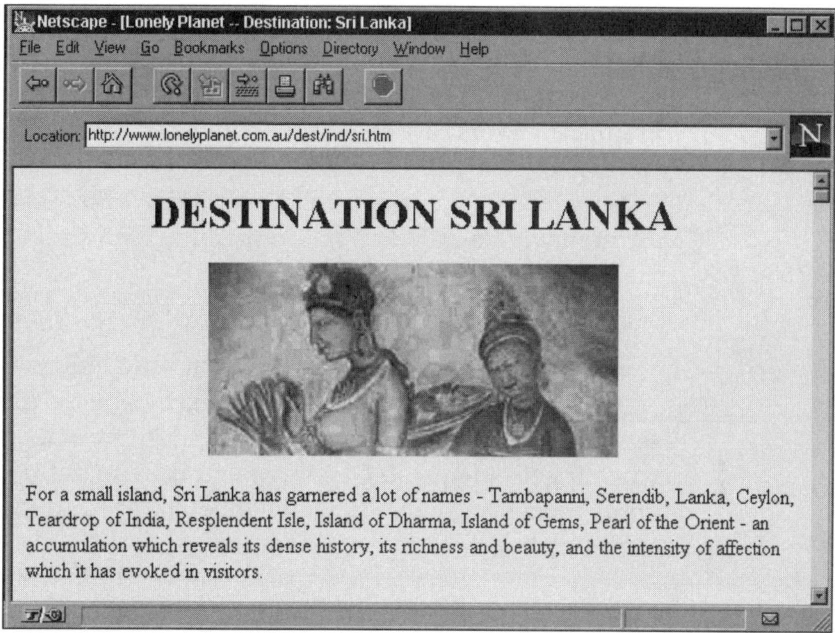

Figure 6-8B: *Destination Sri Lanka on the Lonely Planet Web page.*

This is called a server-side image map because it requires action from the server computer, through the direction of that little hidden file "world.map." But Netscape 2.0 also allows you to do client-side image maps, which are even easier to put together, and faster due to less demand on the server. Learn all about image maps of both kinds in Chapter 4. You can also use the tool Mapedit included on the CD-ROM in the back of the book to have your map sorted out in a trice.

The second component of this page is the mini-form—a one-entry window which initiates a keyword search. Inserting the form itself is simple. It's all done with this code:

```
<FORM METHOD=GET ACTION="/cgi-bin/ffwcgi.cgi/destindex">
<INPUT TYPE="text" NAME=key SIZE=30>
<INPUT TYPE="submit" NAME=go VALUE="Search">
</FORM>
```

The first line defines the path to the cgi-bin database manager "destindex" that will handle the user's query. The second line defines the entry window as a standard text field 30 characters wide, and the third line inserts the Submit button to begin the search. Chapter 9, "Forms, Feedback & cgi-bin" explains how to make forms and Chapter 10, "Databases, Web Servers & Search Engines," covers the technique of handing your users' form responses over to a searchable database.

Now for our favorite part: the Mystery Tour. This works through what's called a "randomized cgi-bin script." The line in the file looks like this:

```
Take a <A HREF="/cgi-bin/random.cgi">Mystery Tour</A>
```

The important part is, again, in that little hidden file "random.cgi." This contains a little executable script that tells the server to pick and send any file at random from its collection when it gets a request. Of course you have to define what "random" means and what the available files are, but that's not a terribly tall order.

OF FORMS & FRAMES!

http://www.ecola.com/news/frames/

When Netscape first announced its new FRAMES tags in version 2.0, a rash of frames pages began appearing everywhere like the measles. To be honest, most of them were more annoying than helpful. Personally, we think that there's got to be a good reason before you go mucking around reducing the size of people's screens and turning them into an imitation of one of those over-organized closets you see in home design catalogs.

Ecola, a Portland, Oregon, computer programming and Web design company, has found what we think is a very good use for frames, however, and has gone way beyond cool by embedding a form within a frames page. The reason this is so good is that you can search for something and get the results in one screen without ever losing the option to search again for something else if you don't find what you want. This page catalogs online publications of all kinds, and it's very useful for scanning through several databases quickly. The helpful instructions you get when you enter this site are:

1. Choose a category (top right frame).
2. Select viewing options (top left frame).
3. View results (bottom frame).

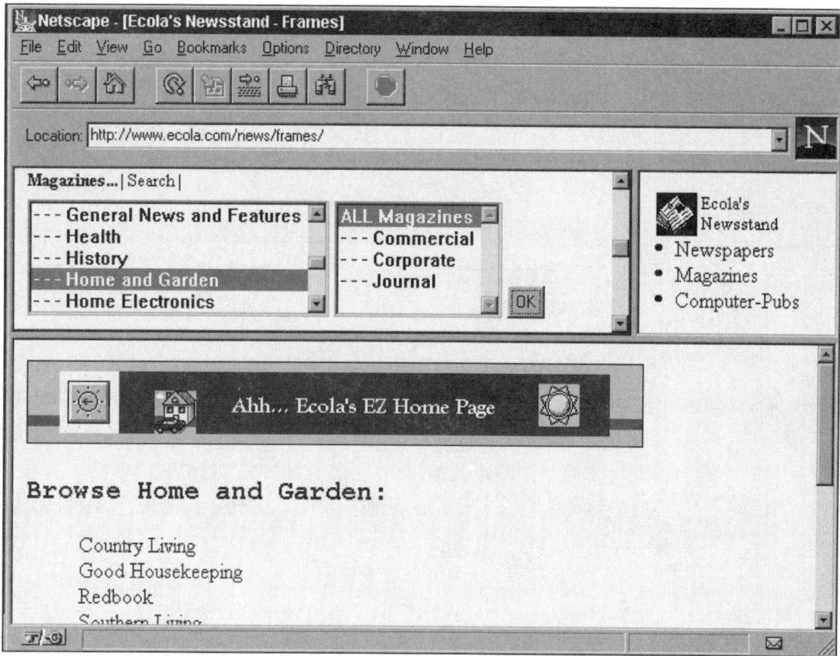

Figure 6-9: *To use this FRAMES page, you gradually refine your choice from the list at top right to the form at top left. A database search then provides a final list to select from in the lower frame. The Home Page banner space is for sale, if you're interested.*

Making a frames page is patently simple at first, but can get complicated as it begins to feel like you're opening a series of Russian boxes. You needn't do anything special to the files that go into your frames—they can be the same files you use in other non-frame contexts. You just create a frames page which defines how you want to split the screen and what file goes where initially.

This one is actually a two-level frames page. The first divides the frame into two horizontally, setting aside the top part (set at 128 pixels high) for search information and the bottom part (height undefined) for the content screen. The second splits the top section into two vertically, with the right side set to 160 pixels in width. The top left frame has been labeled "newsform," and the lower frame is "newscontent." These names are used to direct the flow of user-requested information to the right places. The coding to set this up is shown below:

```
<FRAMESET ROWS="128,*">
  <FRAMESET COLS="*,160">
            <FRAME SRC="inquire.htm#begin"
            NAME="newsform">
            <FRAME SRC="choices.htm">
  </FRAMESET>
     <FRAME SRC="info.htm" NAME="newscontent">
</FRAMESET>
```

Something many novice frames page writers don't know is that you need to add appropriate "target" attributes to the links within your regular pages in order to prevent Web readers from being trapped behind the bars of your frames as they wander away from your site. Learn about this in "Targeting Frame Links" in Chapter 5, where you'll also learn the other ins and outs of designing frames pages. Making forms and combining them with searchable databases is covered in Chapters 9 and 10.

JIVING WITH JAVA

http://www.cnet.com/

The designers of this page, the first of a very extensive site, set out with the goal of making it easy to update with new content on a daily basis. It includes a Java applet and a couple of active images. For these, the real magic is happening behind the scenes in the Java and cgi-bin scripts, although there's some pretty nice simple stuff too—like the triple combination

```
<FONT SIZE=5><TT><STRONG>
```

to achieve a strong, clean design.

As a tease for what's upcoming, here's the page code for the Java applet:

```
<applet code=News width=480 height=45>
<param name=image value=JAVA2/Javafield.short.gif>
<param name=fontsize value=12>
<param name=shiftleft value=2>
<param name=delay value=30>
<param name=scrollarea value="10 21 460 20">
<param name=url value=/Central/News/>
<param name=message value="Welcome to c|net: the computer
network.  Now the #1 computing site on the Net.  In the news
...  Industry Luminaries Back Cable Modem  ...  CMG May Sell
Lycos Shares to Public  ...  Student Drops Email Bomb on
University  ...  AT&T to Sell Intel PCs  ...  Maxis Offers
Free Theme Pack on New Site  ...  Division Demonstrates
Virtual Reality  ...  And  ...  check out the new c|net
radio.">
</applet>
```

The message that appears in the window is controlled by that last parameter, the "value" of "name=message." All they need to do to insert a new message is change that value in the HTML file. We'll be explaining some Java basics and how to use the parameters in Java applets in Chapter 8, "Multimedia & the Web."

Other changeable components include the central image, which links to the main feature and the four lines below it linking to different feature articles. They're all contained in five lines of code that can be easily replaced.

The "clickable buttons" on the page are active images (that we explained in detail in Chapter 4, "All About Images"). They take you respectively to a registration form page and a map of the site. The latter is a particularly nice feature to help you get where you want to go fast in this very rich site. You can see the site map in Figure 2-1 in Chapter 2.

If Santi Scimeca gets our first prize in the "be-nice-to-those-without-images" category, C|Net gets the second. Although not quite as ingenious as Scimeca, this designer has taken the trouble to accompany all the active images with generous ALT text such as "Links to contents, help and C|Net masthead."

This page may be beyond the skill of a beginner, but we believe in giving you something to reach for.

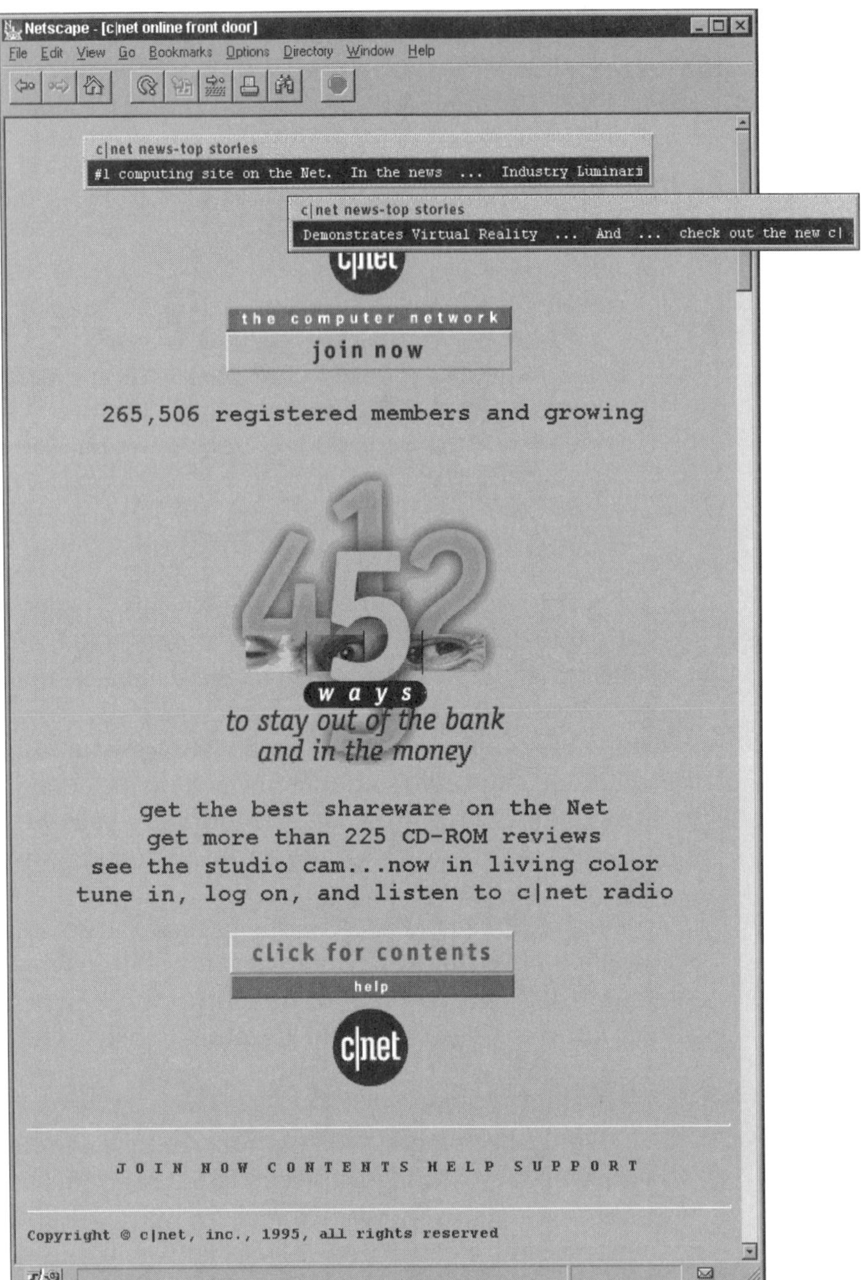

Figure 6-10: C | *Net uses a Java applet, some server push animation, and a "focus-pull" effect to make a smart page that's easily updated with new elements daily. [Reprinted with permission from c | net: the computer network, ©1996]*

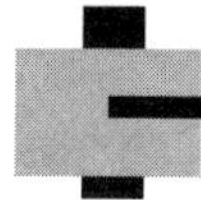

Multimedia Milieu

http://www.razorfish.com/

Razorfish is another site, like The Spleen, with a high intrigue quotient. You're not quite sure what this is all about when you wander into this site, but there's so much interesting going on you want to wait and look around awhile to see.

This page is never the same twice and is perpetually in motion. In fact, the entire page is generated by a Perl script and is actually index.cgi, not index.html (this switcheroo is permitted by the Apache HTTP server software). There are several things happening at once here. Watch the signature blue dot revolve, then dim and fade, then return again to bounce playfully around your screen. The Razorfish logo changes color, and focus pulls below the image reveal four different messages. The address on the lower right corner does another focus pull animation before settling down. You can play some music, RealAudio of course, while the screen does its dance for you.

The animations are done by means of AVI movie files put on a continuous loop. This is the source code for the blue dot:

```
<A HREF="/bluedot/"><IMG SRC="/bin/nph-newvid.cgi?LIST=/
bluedot/newblu.txt;loops=100;FR=200" ALT="the blue dot"
BORDER=0 DYNSRC="/avis/bluedot.AVI"
LOOP=INFINITE START=FILEOPEN></A>
```

Look hard? Let's break it down. There are two major components: the initial source file, which is a cgi-bin script that initiates the playing of the dynamic source file, which is the AVI movie file. The LOOP=INFINITE means, "Play this on a loop infinitely," and START=FILEOPEN means, "Start playing it when the file is opened." The most complicated bit is the initial source file line. It gives instructions for initiating the cgi-bin script, which is like the stage prompter whispering lines from behind the curtain. We explain the basics of including movie files in Chapter 8, and the cgi-bin mechanics in Chapter 9.

The line that inserts the RealAudio file is somewhat simpler. This is:

```
<A HREF="realaudio/st1.ram">
<IMG ALIGN=right SRC="images/ralogo.gif" BORDER=0></A>
```

As for making the RealAudio file: If you've got a sound card and a .WAV file you want to convert (or a microphone you can sing or play into to make one), you can do it yourself in about 10 minutes. Kick up the RealAudio Encoder, insert the file, and turn the crank. Well, okay, making a *good* audio file takes somewhat more care, but we'll tell you all about it in Chapter 8.

Figure 6-11: *Razorfish, designed at M.I.T., uses multimedia to achieve its stunning dynamic effects, including a plugged-in AVI movie and RealAudio for background music while you browse. The small insets show just a few of the intriguing things that happen to the blue dot and the Razorfish logo.*

Another thing to notice here: some interesting but very simple font type, size, and color changes. The Razorfish Web address and name in the middle third of the page between the two dotted lines (GIFs) is not a logo GIF, as one might expect, but a clever use of <PRE> combined with a large font size to create an oversized, monospaced typewriter-style (they could have used TT for this as well, but PRE allows them to space out the letters precisely as they wish). Tables are used in other parts of the page for placement (as we discuss in Chapter 5).

So what *is* Razorfish all about? It's a digital media design, development, and production company, of course.

Moving On

You've seen in this chapter that good Web page design doesn't necessarily mean high-tech solutions. Yet once you get a little experience, you'll discover there's a whole world beyond the flat screen where you can orchestrate a suite of interesting effects. That's what we'll talk about, as we move on to the still-evolving world of multimedia on the Web in Chapter 8, "Multimedia & the Web." But first, a lesson in some basic Web wizardry anyone can do without any special tools—making tables.

A special "thank you" to all the clever people whose work we featured (by permission) in this chapter.

7

The World of Tables & Equations

What are you to do with that big pile of material lying about your desk that you want to put in your Web page? That catalog, this list, that pile of numbers. There's really no other solution: Sometimes the best way of organizing your material and getting your point across is with a table. Whether you're compiling scientific data, presenting a catalog of items available to business customers, or just trying to make sense of a mass of information, tables can be a very useful and efficient way of presenting your material.

If numbers are really your thing, we'll also take a look in this chapter at some ways you can incorporate mathematical equations in your Web pages. Although math elements are still not defined for HTML, there are several solutions that math-oriented Web authors have come up with to take care of this need, and we'll tell you what they are.

Constructing Tables

Although you already got a glimpse of the things you can do with tables for layout purposes in Chapters 5 and 6, in this section we'll take a more formal approach to the complicated business of constructing tables. We'll lead you through the steps you need to turn that pile of papers into a tidy presentation.

TABLE BASICS

Unfortunately, the formal HTML standards for table implementation have lagged somewhat behind the practical need for them. Netscape stepped in to fill the void early on in version 1.1 and several other browsers have now followed suit. As the discussions over a formal HTML 3.0 standard have evolved, the table implementation has diverged slightly from Netscape's original. Interestingly enough, the differences aren't so much in the nitty-gritty details of defining table rows and columns as at the macro level. For example, should a table behave like a paragraph or like an image? Formal HTML says paragraph, Netscape says image; this matters in terms of how you position the table on the screen and particularly if you thought it might be nice to flow text around your table. Fortunately, standards are evolving in the direction of treating paragraphs and images about the same (the <P ALIGN="..."> attribution is a straw in the wind), so this aspect of the tables controversy may simply go away.

Fortunately, any differences in table implementation among browsers is slight, so the tables you create for Netscape should be readable by any other browser that currently recognizes tables.

In Chapter 5, we already saw several examples of how tables can be used to control page layout. Although we wouldn't go along with certain purists who would say that this is misuse, rather than use, of the TABLES tags, it was definitely rash of us to plunge right in to fairly complex tables with almost no groundwork. So we'll now make up for it with a more sober approach, starting with a second look at the *extremely boring* table we already introduced in Chapter 5:

```
<TABLE>
     <TR><TD>CELL 1</TD><TD>CELL 2</TD></TR>

     <TR><TD>CELL 3</TD><TD>CELL 4</TD></TR>
</TABLE>
```

A

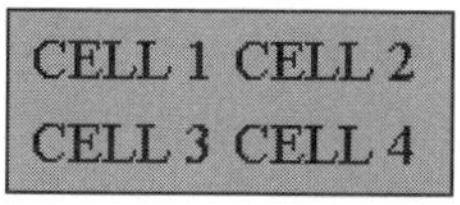

CELL 1	CELL 2
CELL 3	CELL 4

B

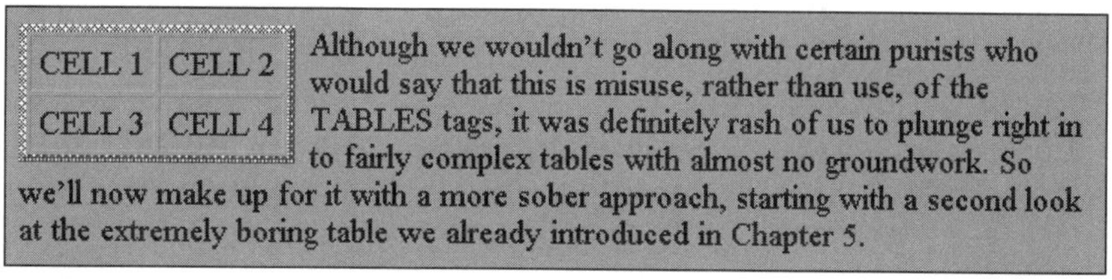

CELL 1	CELL 2
CELL 3	CELL 4

Although we wouldn't go along with certain purists who would say that this is misuse, rather than use, of the TABLES tags, it was definitely rash of us to plunge right in to fairly complex tables with almost no groundwork. So we'll now make up for it with a more sober approach, starting with a second look at the extremely boring table we already introduced in Chapter 5.

Figures 7-1A&B: *Two versions of the extremely boring table. The second demonstrates that you can wrap text around a table just as you can around an image.*

This time around, you get to admire this table, as Figure 7-1A. Surprised there aren't any borders? That's because we didn't ask for any, and the default is no borders. Change that first line of HTML to:

```
<TABLE BORDER=4 CELLPADDING=4>
```

...and we get not just 4-pixel borders, but a comfortable amount of CELLPADDING for the text to fit in. One more change to:

```
<TABLE BORDER=4 CELLPADDING=4 ALIGN=left>
```

...and we can prove that text can be permitted to flow around a Netscape-type table. Let's hear it for Figure 7-1B. But we're getting ahead of ourselves again. Here are the TABLES tags:

HTML Tag

<TABLE> .... </TABLE>

Main container for a table definition. Attributes are:

ALIGN="left/right"—Allows text to flow round the table, like a simplified form of the ALIGN attributes of <IMG>. If no ALIGN attribute is stated, the table is ranged left and text is not allowed alongside it.

BORDER—If this attribute is absent, borders and cell frames are unseen. A border thickness of 1, and cell frame thickness of 2 (pixels), is nevertheless present by default. If the BORDER attribute is added, these default boundaries become visible.

BORDER=p—Defines the thickness of the table border in pixels, and makes it visible. Does not affect the cell frame thickness. BORDER=p also implies a "standoff zone" p pixels wide for any wrapping text, analogous to the VSPACE attribute of images. BORDER=0 is legitimate, and removes the 1-pixel allowance as well as hiding the table grid.

CELLSPACING=p (default 2)—Defines the thickness of the cell frames, whether visible or not. CELLSPACING=0 is legitimate.

CELLPADDING=p (default 1)—Defines the closest approach cell content may make to its frames. CELLPADDING=0 is legitimate.

WIDTH=w or p%—Expresses the desired overall width of the table, either in absolute pixels or as a percentage of screen width between margins. In some cases desired width may be in conflict with width as calculated from the cumulative width requirements of cells in a table row. In such a case, cell widths take precedence.

HEIGHT=h or p%—Expresses the desired overall height of the table, either in absolute pixels or as a percentage of available screen height. The same conflict as with WIDTH may arise.

So that's six attributes that enable you to control the overall look and size of your table. Next come the basic tags for rows and cells.

HTML Tag

<TR> .... </TR>

Container for a table row. The number of rows in a table is absolutely defined by the number of <TR> tags. The </TR> container end tag is optional.

<TD> .... </TD>

Container for a table data cell. Not all rows have to have the same number of cells—the overall number of columns in a table will be the number of cells and COLSPANS in the longest row. Short rows are filled with blank cells at the right. A data cell can in principle contain any legitimate HTML element, including another (nested) table.

<TH> .... </TH>

Container for a table header cell. Header cells have their content rendered in boldface.

Attributes for <TR>, <TD>, and <TH> are:

ALIGN=left/center/right—Specifies the horizontal alignment of content within the cell(s), assuming there is room to move. Data cells default to left, header cells to center. ALIGN=decimal is a proposed HTML 3.0 option for decimal-alignment of columns of figures.

VALIGN=top/middle/bottom/baseline—Specifies the vertical alignment of content within the cell(s), assuming there is room to move. Defaults to middle.

Additional attributes for <TD> and <TH> are:

WIDTH=w or p%—Expresses the desired width of the cell, either in absolute pixels or as a percentage of the overall width of the table. In general this will affect all cells in the column to which this cell belongs, since a column cannot have variable width. If cells in a column have various different WIDTH requirements, the widest prevails.

HEIGHT=h or p%—Expresses the desired height of the cell, either in absolute pixels or as a percentage of the overall height of the table. In general this affects all cells in the row to which this cell belongs, since a row cannot have variable height. If cells in a row have various different HEIGHT requirements, the tallest prevails.

(NOTE: If a table data cell whose width and height are defined overflows—by the user setting an unexpectedly large font size, perhaps—desired width is preserved but height increases.)

COLSPAN=n—Specifies the number of columns of the table this cell stretches across. Normally used for a top header or sub-header.

ROWSPAN=n—Specifies the number of rows of the table this cell stretches down. Normally used for a side header.

NOWRAP—Inhibits text line wrapping within the cell. Line wrapping will be done by default to avoid having the table stretch beyond the screen margin or to conform to WIDTH attributes elsewhere.

<CAPTION> .... </CAPTION>

Container for the table's caption. If used, this is normally the first tag in a table and is a simple title. However, a CAPTION can in principle be any HTML element. The only attribute is ALIGN, which defaults to "top" but may be set to "bottom." A caption is always horizontally centered in relation to the table width, and line wrapping prevents a caption from overhanging either side if at all possible.

TIP

While tables may contain any elements normally allowed in the body of a document (paragraphs and lists, for example), all elements must be placed within one of the table container tags. A <P>, for instance, which is within the <TABLE>...</TABLE> tags, but not contained within a table head or table data cell will not be computed in the table layout and will be displayed at the beginning of your table.

BUILDING A TABLE OF SCIENCE DATA

We'll illustrate the construction of a basic table for presenting data by taking a little trip to the Southern hemisphere, where we'll follow in Darwin's footsteps and survey the unique array of animals on the Galapagos Islands. Figure 7-2 is our first attempt.

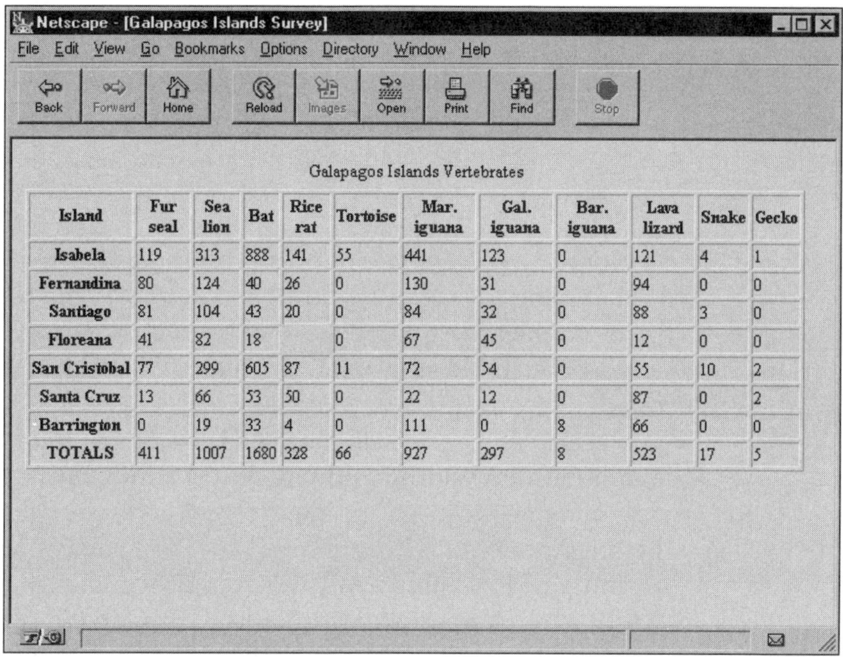

Galapagos Islands Vertebrates

Island	Fur seal	Sea lion	Bat	Rice rat	Tortoise	Mar. iguana	Gal. iguana	Bar. iguana	Lava lizard	Snake	Gecko
Isabela	119	313	888	141	55	441	123	0	121	4	1
Fernandina	80	124	40	26	0	130	31	0	94	0	0
Santiago	81	104	43	20	0	84	32	0	88	3	0
Floreana	41	82	18		0	67	45	0	12	0	0
San Cristobal	77	299	605	87	11	72	54	0	55	10	2
Santa Cruz	13	66	53	50	0	22	12	0	87	0	2
Barrington	0	19	33	4	0	111	0	8	66	0	0
TOTALS	411	1007	1680	328	66	927	297	8	523	17	5

Figure 7-2: *First attempt at the Galapagos table.*

The code, in part, is:

```
<TABLE BORDER>
<CAPTION>Galapagos Islands Vertebrates</CAPTION>
     <TR><TH>Island</TH><TH>Fur seal</TH>
     <TH>Sea lion</TH><TH>Bat</TH>
     <TH>Rice rat</TH><TH>Tortoise</TH>
     <TH>Mar. iguana</TH><TH>Gal. iguana</TH>
     <TH>Bar. iguana</TH><TH>Lava lizard</TH>
     <TH>Snake</TH><TH>Gecko</TH></TR>

     <TR><TH>Isabela</TH><TD>119</TD>
     <TD>313</TD><TD>888</TD><TD>141</TD>
     <TD>55</TD><TD>441</TD><TD>123</TD>
     <TD>0</TD><TD>121</TD><TD>4</TD>
     <TD>1</TD></TR>
     ....etc....
```

```
        <TR><TH>TOTALS</TH><TD>411</TD>
        <TD>1007</TD><TD>1680</TD><TD>328</TD>
        <TD>66</TD><TD>927</TD><TD>297</TD>
        <TD>8</TD><TD>523</TD><TD>17</TD>
        <TD>5</TD></TR>
    </TABLE>
```

Notice how Netscape figures everything out by word-wrapping and varying the column widths so that the whole table fits neatly between the screen margins. The calculation of table geometry when no WIDTH statements are included can get quite complicated—it's done *roughly* like this:

Netscape first scans all data cells, looking at their maximum and minimum width requirements. Maximums are given by assuming no word-wrapping except where an explicit <BR> tag has been inserted. The minimum width of any column is given by assuming all possible word-wrapping—it comes down to the width of the longest word or widest image in the column plus any allowance for CELLPADDING the author has called for. Don't forget, too, that the font size the *user* has set is an important factor in this calculation. These column widths are then added, and allowances made for BORDER and CELLSPACING requirements, to yield a maximum and minimum total width for the table. The table geometry is then decided as follows:

- If maximum width fits within screen margins, there's no constraint and all cells are allowed their maximum widths, with no word-wrap necessary.
- If the table overflows the screen margin even at minimum width, then the table has to be made horizontally scrollable and all minimum widths are given, using all word-wraps.
- If maximum width overflows, but minimum does not, then the total width of the table is set to precisely fit between margins. Column widths are assigned *pro rata,* favoring columns having more than one word.

The Galapagos table of Figure 7-2 fell into the latter category—"OK if squeezed," one might call it. All possible word wrapping has been done in the header row, but columns have not been pared down to minimum (note the spare space around several animals such as the iguanas). Also, "San Cristobal" in the leftmost column has not been wrapped—a desperation measure that the geometry algorithm would resort to if it had to, saving a few precious pixels.

The ingenuity of the algorithm that carries out these calculations is both a blessing and a curse—a blessing because the author is spared from tedious calculation in most cases, but a curse because for a mathematical table standardized columns are much more acceptable, and there's no simple way of declaring, "Make every column the same width, please."

Stage 2: Making a Table Look Right

So there are a few fixups we'd like to do on this table, starting with standardizing the column width. One of the Web designer's tricks we have up our sleeve is a set of pixel rulers to help out in situations like this. The horizontal ruler (see Figure 7-3) is simply a file called "hruler.gif," and it looks just like a school ruler except it's measured off in pixels.

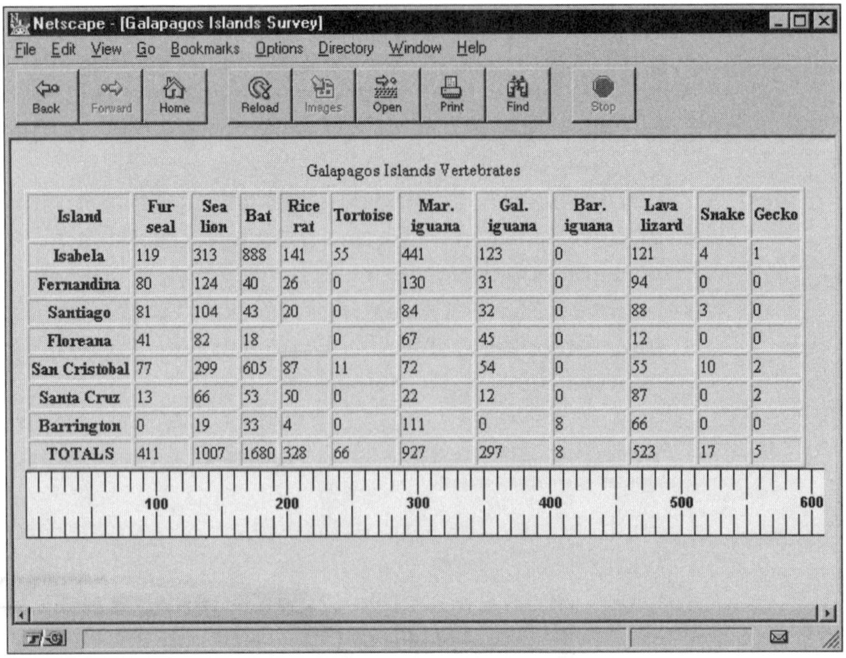

Galapagos Islands Vertebrates

Island	Fur seal	Sea lion	Bat	Rice rat	Tortoise	Mar. iguana	Gal. iguana	Bar. iguana	Lava lizard	Snake	Gecko
Isabela	119	313	888	141	55	441	123	0	121	4	1
Fernandina	80	124	40	26	0	130	31	0	94	0	0
Santiago	81	104	43	20	0	84	32	0	88	3	0
Floreana	41	82	18		0	67	45	0	12	0	0
San Cristobal	77	299	605	87	11	72	54	0	55	10	2
Santa Cruz	13	66	53	50	0	22	12	0	87	0	2
Barrington	0	19	33	4	0	111	0	8	66	0	0
TOTALS	411	1007	1680	328	66	927	297	8	523	17	5

Figure 7-3: *The Galapagos table with a pixel ruler brought in to assist.*

The ruler shows that the space available for the 11 species columns is 592 less the 82 for the left-hand column. So each column, to be even, should be 46 pixels, less 2 for the cellspacing, yielding 44. So here's a line of adjusted code:

```
<TR><TH>Island</TH>
<TH WIDTH=44>Fur seal</TH>
<TH WIDTH=44>Sea lion</TH>
<TH WIDTH=44>Bat</TH>
<TH WIDTH=44>Rice rat</TH>
<TH WIDTH=44>Gal. Tort.</TH>
<TH WIDTH=44>Mar. iguana</TH>
<TH WIDTH=44>Gal. iguana</TH>
<TH WIDTH=44>Bar. iguana</TH>
<TH WIDTH=44>Lava lizard</TH>
<TH WIDTH=44>Snake</TH>
<TH WIDTH=44>Gecko</TH></TR>
```

There's absolutely no need to define widths in any other table row: Since we know all other content in those columns is less than 44 pixels wide, this one line will suffice to set global column width. Notice we also abbreviated "Tortoise" to "Gal. tort." in the code, allowing this longest word to wrap (you can see the effect by looking forward to Figure 7-4).

Spanning Columns & Rows

The next fixup we'd like to do is to make a distinction between the mammals and the reptiles in the table. The first four animals, from Fur seal to Rice rat, are the mammals, then the seven from Tortoise to Gecko are the reptiles. So that suggests a new table row like this:

```
<TR><TH COLSPAN=4>Mammals</TH><TH COLSPAN=7>Reptiles</TH></TR>
```

That says that the "Mammals" header cell spans four columns, and the "Reptiles" cell spans seven. There's only one problem—the *total* number of columns should work out to 12, to include column 1 for the island names. One choice would be to put in a null cell at the beginning of the row, which would "blank off" the top left corner. Our preference, though, is to expand the cell containing the word "Island," and we do that by adding <TH ROWSPAN=2>Island</TH> at the start of that first row. Then the second row will take account of that ROWSPAN instruction and only expect 11 cells to make the whole row. You'll be seeing the result shortly.

Aligning Cell Content

Alignment of cell contents defaults to "left," which is fine for routine text or images. Mathematical strings, however, look horrid like that—they should always be ranged right so that they look like a proper column of figures ready to add up. Fortunately, to fix this up we don't need to declare an attribute for every single cell. The ALIGN=right attribute can be given to a <TR> row tag, and it's taken to apply to every cell in that row.

To set off the TOTALS row, we give it extra height by declaring just one of its cells HEIGHT=30, then declare VALIGN=bottom so as to separate the numbers somewhat from the rest of the table. A slightly more elaborate alternative might be to make a completely separate table out of the TOTALS row. Then it would be separated from the rest by whatever distance we chose, or we could interpose a horizontal rule. A simple solution might be to put the totals in bold.

Coping Gracefully With Empty Cells

Just one more little thing—the empty cell representing rice rats on Floreana. Perhaps the presence of rice rats on Floreana is unknown, or perhaps somebody lost the data, but at any rate this cell is empty rather than zero. However, if we simply declared the empty cell as <TD></TD>, the empty cell would have a "raised" look, which doesn't seem appropriate here. It's no good trying to put a space in—HTML doesn't recognize spaces. You can choose between two ways of getting this to look right: The cell can contain either a <BR> or a "non-breaking space" entity, written . Of the two we prefer <BR>, since more browsers recognize it.

Here's the final result, first in (partial) code:

```
<TABLE BORDER>
<CAPTION><H2>Galapagos Islands Vertebrates</H2></CAPTION>

    <TR><TH ROWSPAN=2>Island</TH>
    <TH COLSPAN=4>Mammals</TH>
    <TH COLSPAN=7>Reptiles</TH></TR>

    <TR><TH WIDTH=44>Fur seal</TH>
    <TH WIDTH=44>Sea lion</TH>
    <TH WIDTH=44>Bat</TH>
    <TH WIDTH=40>Rice rat</TH>
    <TH WIDTH=44>Gal. Tort.</TH>
    <TH WIDTH=44>Mar. iguana</TH>
```

```
    <TH WIDTH=44>Gal. iguana</TH>
    <TH WIDTH=44>Bar. iguana</TH>
    <TH WIDTH=44>Lava lizard</TH>
    <TH WIDTH=44>Snake</TH>
    <TH WIDTH=44>Gecko</TH></TR>

    <TR ALIGN=right><TH>Isabela</TH>
    <TD>119</TD><TD>313</TD><TD>888</TD>
    <TD>141</TD><TD>55</TD><TD>441</TD>
    <TD>123</TD><TD>0</TD><TD>121</TD>
    <TD>4</TD><TD>1</TD></TR>
...etc...
    <TR ALIGN=right><TH>Floreana</TH>
    <TD>41</TD><TD>82</TD><TD>18</TD>
    <TD><BR></TD><TD>0</TD><TD>67</TD>
    <TD>45</TD><TD>0</TD><TD>12</TD><TD>0</TD>
    <TD>0</TD></TR>
...etc...
    <TR ALIGN=right VALIGN=bottom>
    <TH HEIGHT=30>TOTALS</TH>
    <TD>411</TD><TD>1007</TD><TD>1680</TD>
    <TD>328</TD><TD>66</TD><TD>927</TD>
    <TD>297</TD><TD>8</TD><TD>523</TD>
    <TD>17</TD><TD>5</TD></TR>

</TABLE>
```

...and now as seen on the Netscape screen—Figure 7-4.

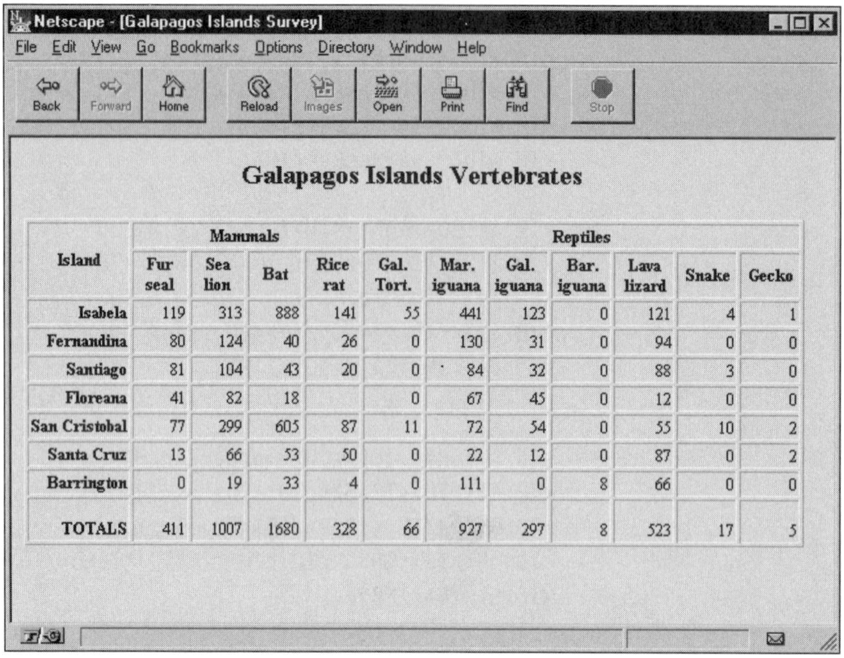

Netscape - [Galapagos Islands Survey]

Galapagos Islands Vertebrates

Island	Mammals				Reptiles						
	Fur seal	Sea lion	Bat	Rice rat	Gal. Tort.	Mar. iguana	Gal. iguana	Bar. iguana	Lava lizard	Snake	Gecko
Isabela	119	313	888	141	55	441	123	0	121	4	1
Fernandina	80	124	40	26	0	130	31	0	94	0	0
Santiago	81	104	43	20	0	84	32	0	88	3	0
Floreana	41	82	18		0	67	45	0	12	0	0
San Cristobal	77	299	605	87	11	72	54	0	55	10	2
Santa Cruz	13	66	53	50	0	22	12	0	87	0	2
Barrington	0	19	33	4	0	111	0	8	66	0	0
TOTALS	411	1007	1680	328	66	927	297	8	523	17	5

Figure 7-4: *The finished Galapagos table.*

ADDING IMAGES & LINKS TO TABLES

The rules of the tables game state that *any* element that would be a valid component of a document is also valid as table cell data. That means that you can put a TABLE inside a TABLE—as we saw on the impressive Discovery Channel site in Figure 6-6. You can put a list or a menu inside a TABLE, you can even put a <HR> inside a table (it simply makes the cell look as if it's been split in half). However, all elements must be inside a valid table data cell (either <TD> or <TH>).

Images and links are very common table components, and to illustrate the use of these, we're going to set up part of a vegetable gardener's planting chart. We start off getting hold of some veggie pictures (thank you, Sandra's Clip-Art Server, a useful Web site at Yale, now alas defunct) and reducing them all to the same size and shape. We use those as a pictorial left-hand column and then make columns for planting season, recommended planting depth and separation, time from planting to harvest, and additional info. We can crib all the data from a book we have lying around the office—in spite of what you might have heard, there *is* a planting season here in California!

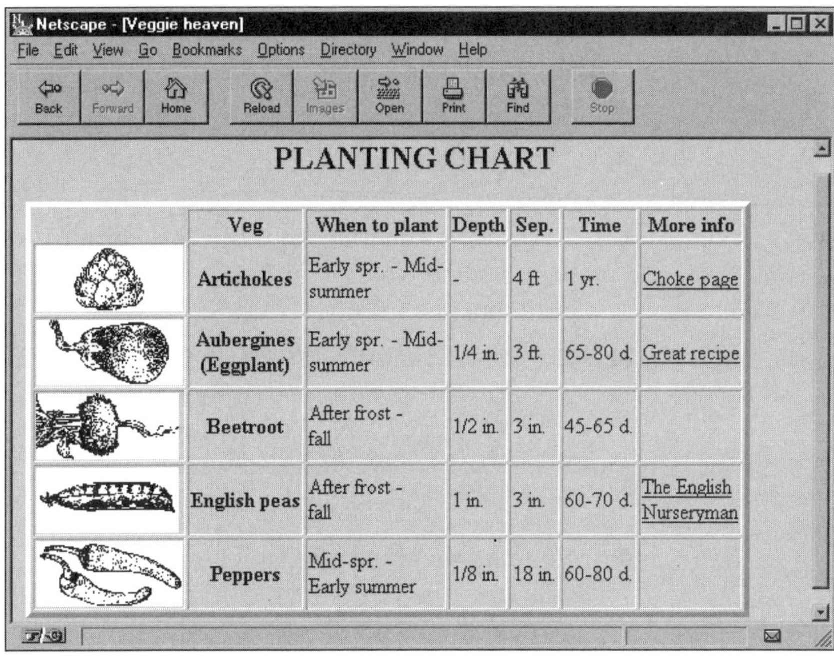

PLANTING CHART

	Veg	When to plant	Depth	Sep.	Time	More info
	Artichokes	Early spr. - Mid-summer	-	4 ft	1 yr.	Choke page
	Aubergines (Eggplant)	Early spr. - Mid-summer	1/4 in.	3 ft.	65-80 d.	Great recipe
	Beetroot	After frost - fall	1/2 in.	3 in.	45-65 d.	
	English peas	After frost - fall	1 in.	3 in.	60-70 d.	The English Nurseryman
	Peppers	Mid-spr. - Early summer	1/8 in.	18 in.	60-80 d.	

Figure 7-5: *First attempt at the planting chart.*

Figure 7-5 shows the first cut at this. In this case we opted for letting that top left cell stay blank, and we allowed Netscape to do all of the width calculations for us. Not too bad. Here's the Artichoke row in HTML, so you can see how extremely easy it is to make images and hyperlinks part of TABLE data.

```
<TR><TD><IMG SRC="artich.gif"></TD>
<TH>Artichokes</TH>
<TD>Early spr. - Mid-<BR>summer</TD>
<TD>-</TD><TD>4 ft</TD><TD>1 yr.</TD>
<TD><A HREF="http://www.fm.org/farming/plants/
chokes.html">Choke page</A></TD></TR>
```

We spent maybe two hours refining this, and kept a log of what we did:

- Spaced everything out a bit by adding CELLPADDING. After a bit of trial-and-error, we settled on 4 pixels.
- Set all the data rows to ALIGN=center. A great improvement.
- Merged the columns where the "Planting season" data was identical, using ROWSPAN=2. This then gave us extra space to...
- ...improve the rather cryptic wording of the Planting season data.
- Since there was nothing in the last column for the hot peppers, we went off and quickly ran up a "HOT!" GIF to put there just for fun.
- We noticed that the "18 in." in the Peppers/Separation cell was now being wrapped to two lines, and it looked pretty ugly. We added a NOWRAP attribute to that cell, forcing Netscape to go looking elsewhere for things to squeeze in order to fit the margins.
- Noticing that the veggie pictures no longer quite fit their cells (because of the CELLPADDING), we decided to make them all transparent, so that you can't tell what their actual dimensions are.
- Finally, we couldn't resist putting in a few unannounced links from the veggie pictures to weirdly appropriate places on the Web. We gave those images the attribute BORDER=0 so that the link border didn't give the game away.

Here it is, first in code...

```
<TABLE BORDER=4 CELLPADDING=4>
<CAPTION><H2>PLANTING CHART</H2></CAPTION>

<TR><TH></TH><TH>Veg</TH><TH>When to plant</TH>
<TH>Depth</TH><TH>Sep.</TH>
<TH>Time</TH><TH>More info</TH></TR>

<TR ALIGN=center><TD><IMG SRC="artich.gif"></TD>
```

```
<TH>Artichokes</TH>
<TD ROWSPAN=2>From early spring to mid-summer</TD>
<TD>-</TD><TD>4 ft</TD>
<TD>1 yr.</TD><TD><A HREF="http://www.fm.org/farming/plants/
chokes.html">Choke page</A></TD></TR>

<TR ALIGN=center><TD><A HREF="http://www.dur.ac.uk/~dgl3djb/
ukus.html#Aub"><IMG SRC="auberg.gif" BORDER=0></A>
</TD><TH>Aubergines<BR>
(Eggplant)</TH><TD>1/4 in.</TD><TD>3 ft.</TD>
<TD>65-80 d.</TD><TD><A HREF="ftp://ftp.gatekeeper.dec.com/
.2/recipes/meat/moussaka">Great recipe</A></TD></TR>

<TR ALIGN=center><TD><A HREF="http://www.mathcs.duq.edu/
~weigand/jk.html"><IMG SRC="beet.gif" BORDER=0></A>
</TD><TH>Beetroot</TH>
<TD ROWSPAN=2>Any time after the last frost, into fall</TD>
<TD>1/2 in.</TD><TD>3 in.</TD>
<TD>45-65 d.</TD><TD><BR></TD></TR>

<TR ALIGN=center><TD><IMG SRC="peas.gif"></TD>
<TH>English peas</TH>
<TD>1 in.</TD><TD>3 in.</TD>
<TD>60-70 d.</TD><TD><A HREF="ftp://ftp.demon.co.uk/pub/usr/
fodrules/plants.txt">The English<BR>Nurseryman</A></TD></TR>

<TR ALIGN=center><TD><IMG SRC="peppers.gif"></TD>
<TH>Peppers</TH>
<TD>Mid-spr. - early summer</TD><TD>1/8 in.</TD>
<TD NOWRAP>18 in.</TD>
<TD>60-80 d.</TD><TD><A HREF="http://www.nbn.com/
starving_artists/lotsa-hotsa/heat_scale.html"><IMG
SRC="redhot.gif" BORDER=0></A></TD></TR>

</TABLE>
```

...and now as seen by Netscape in Figure 7-6.

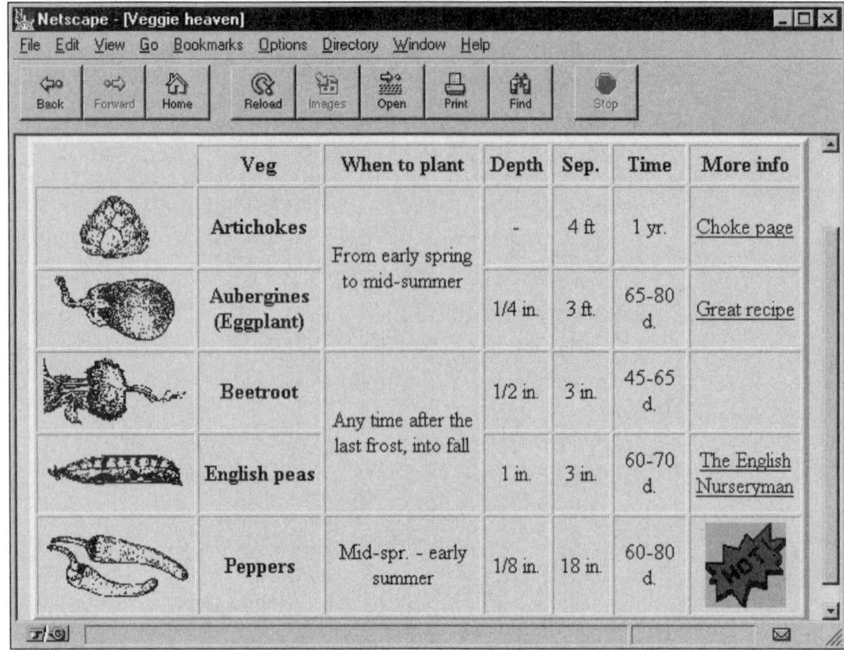

	Veg	When to plant	Depth	Sep.	Time	More info
	Artichokes	From early spring to mid-summer	-	4 ft	1 yr.	Choke page
	Aubergines (Eggplant)		1/4 in.	3 ft.	65-80 d.	Great recipe
	Beetroot	Any time after the last frost, into fall	1/2 in.	3 in.	45-65 d.	
	English peas		1 in.	3 in.	60-70 d.	The English Nurseryman
	Peppers	Mid-spr. - early summer	1/8 in.	18 in.	60-80 d.	HOT!

Figure 7-6: *The planting chart improved.*

ADDING FORM ELEMENTS

Another HTML element that's more and more frequently found within a TABLE is a FORM. This comes about partly because of the rush of business people who have discovered (or who *think* they've discovered) that the Web is a good way of selling merchandise. Selling means making users order things, and ordering things usually involves filling out forms.

So let's pretend that we're going into business with these veggies and turn our table into an order form (as well as changing the CAPTION to "ORDER FORM," we also change the document TITLE from "Veggie heaven" to "Veggie Heaven Inc."—naturally). We get rid of the columns for planting depth and separation—whaddya think this is? A charity? We've got money to make—and instead set up columns for the user to select from the many varieties of the veggie seeds we have in stock, and to place an order for

2 packets of Ruby Queen beet seeds or whatever. Make it 200—let's think big here. Now that we're commercial, we obviously have to have this week's special offer—we'll make that the beetroot, and we signal it with a little GIF that we "liberated" from our sysadmin's home page. In passing, that little decoration proved that, yes indeed, one table cell can contain a mixture of HTML elements.

The result's shown in Figure 7-7, and you'll be finding out in Chapter 9, "Forms, Feedback & cgi-bin," how to code those cute pop-up menu selectors.

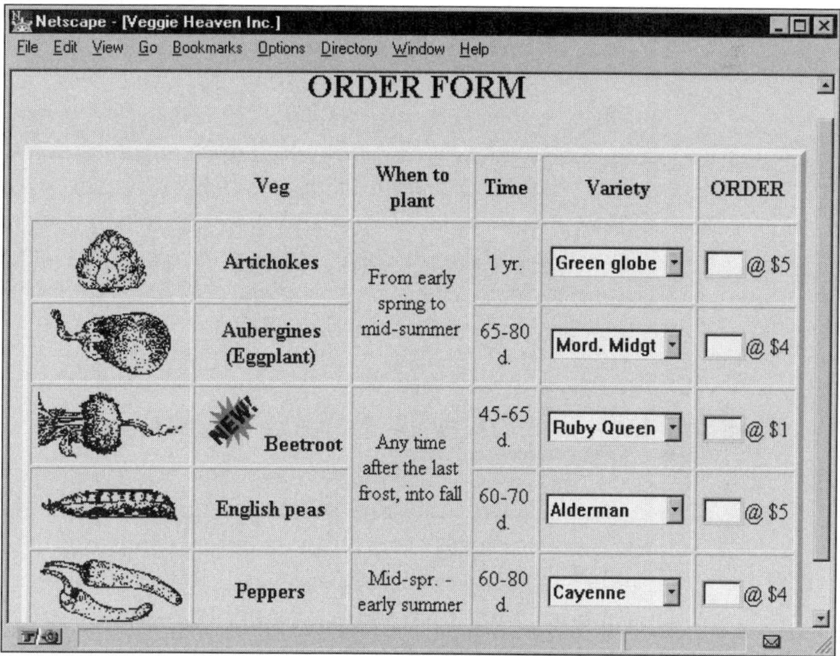

	Veg	When to plant	Time	Variety	ORDER
	Artichokes	From early spring to mid-summer	1 yr.	Green globe	@ $5
	Aubergines (Eggplant)		65-80 d.	Mord. Midgt	@ $4
	NEW! Beetroot	Any time after the last frost, into fall	45-65 d.	Ruby Queen	@ $1
	English peas		60-70 d.	Alderman	@ $5
	Peppers	Mid-spr. - early summer	60-80 d.	Cayenne	@ $4

Figure 7-7: *We're going into business!*

Hmmm, anyone can see that we're fakes at this commercial stuff. What sensible merchant would price things at $4 and $5, when everyone knows it should be $3.99 and $4.99? Never mind, we learned something from that exercise, and we hope you did too.

TIP

TABLES or FRAMES?
It might be worth flipping back to Chapter 5 at this point, to review the use of TABLES as page layout aids, and also to remind yourself of what FRAMES have to offer. For certain Web page designs, it's a close call whether TABLES or FRAMES are going to give you what you want as a designer.

Bear in mind the crucial difference—FRAMES auto-size to the user's screen resolution, and (in general) allow the user the freedom not only to scroll but also to shove your borders around. TABLES produce a result that's more rigidly defined, although a table that's squeezed somewhat to make it fit a 610-pixel content area may look a little different when allowed to relax into the wide open spaces of a Power Mac or a Sun Workstation. You can ensure that a TABLE fits the screen by declaring its WIDTH 100%, but there's no way at all to make the cells individually scroll or change their sizes.

The other main difference is in the behavior of links within the cells of your page. On a FRAMES page, a hyperlink can be targeted to any one of the individual frames, or to the parent or top level. TABLES links have no way of targeting one cell, so every hyperlink will lead to a "parent" (or full-screen) display.

EQUATIONS & MATH SYMBOLS

If you see a properly formed mathematical equation on a Web page right now, complete with Greek letters, divisions, and integrals as well as subscripts and superscripts, 10 to 1 it's a picture of the equation rather than the equation itself—unless, of course, this book has a longer lifetime than we (modestly) expect. Equations are the ugly daughter of HTML development, continually being put off because of ungainliness. In 1994 a confident-sounding proposal was issued by the W3 consortium, but the next year more pressing questions such as tables and style sheets occupied the HTML committees, and work on defining the math elements essentially came to a halt. Netscape independently implemented the <SUB> and <SUP> tags in late 1995 as a new feature of version 2.0.

All we can give here, then, is an informed guess as to how HTML math will eventually end up, so that one day we can all rejoice in including stuff like...

$$\psi = \int_{b}^{a} \frac{f(x)}{\Pi - x} \, dx$$

...in our Web pages. The presumed HTML for that equation would be...

```
<MATH>
&psi; =  <SUB>a</SUB><SUP>b<SUP>
&int;<BOX>f(x)<OVER>&PI; - x</BOX>dx
</MATH>
```

Here are some of the proposed math tags:

HTML Tag

$....$

Main container for a formula, or any markup that requires special symbols or math-style treatment.

<BOX> .... </BOX>

Container for an expression that will consist of a numerator followed by a denominator (may also have other functions).

<OVER>

Divider to separate the numerator from the denominator in a <BOX>.

_{....}

Subscript. May also be designated by a _ symbol on either side of the subscript character: _2_ is equivalent to ₂.

^{....}

Superscript. May also be designated by a ^ symbol on either side of the subscript character: ^2^ is equivalent to ².

<ABOVE> .... </ABOVE>

Container for any symbol or string that is to be drawn above the preceding expression.

<BELOW> .... </BELOW>

Container for any symbol or string that is to be drawn below the preceding expression.

The proposed math entities are:

Table Head		
VEC	→	Vector over symbol
BAR	¯	Bar over symbol
DOT	•	Dot over symbol
DDOT	¨	Double dot over symbol
HAT	^	Hat over symbol
TILDE	~	Tilde over symbol
SQRT	$^2\surd$	Square root symbol
ROOT	√	Root symbol
∫		Integral
&ldots;	...	3 dots on the baseline
&cdots;		3 dots in mid position
&vdots;		3 vertically aligned dots
&ddots;		3 diagonal dots (topL to bottomR)
&dotfill;		Array of dots in the symbol space
		Thin space
&sp;		En space
		Em space
&quad;		Double em space
α	α	
β	β	
γ	ϒ	
δ	δ	
ε	ε	
&vepsilon;	*(ε variant)*	
ζ	ζ	
η	η	
θ	θ	
&vtheta;	*(θ variant)*	
ι	ι	
κ	κ	
λ	λ	

(Continued)

μ	μ
ν	ν
ξ	ξ
ο	ο
π	π
ϖ	*(π variant)*
ρ	ρ
ϱ	*(ρ variant)*
σ	σ
&vsigma;	*(σ variant)*
τ	τ
υ	υ
φ	φ
ϕ	*(φ variant)*
χ	χ
ψ	ψ
ω	ω

Uppercase versions of all Greek letters will also be available (for instance, capital psi as &PSI;).

TIP

While waiting for implementation of the math side of HTML, all the above symbols and many more are available as transparent GIFs on the Web, courtesy of the University of Massachusetts Department of Astronomy. The URL is:
http://donald.phast.umass.edu/latex/tutorials/kicons.html

PICTURES OF EQUATIONS

We mentioned, back at the start of this section, the possibility that you might come across a "picture" of a mathematical equation on the Web. What did we mean by that? Simply that there are many specialized word-processing applications that create math according to their own conventions, and that an equation created by one of these can always be captured and brought into a Web page as an inline image. Figure 7-8 is a fine example of this genre—Gail

Bamber, who created a whole series of "equations from hell" for the San Diego Supercomputer Center, set them up using the Equations module of Microsoft Word, then imported them into Photoshop, increased their size to suit the standard Web-browser screen, and put them through an anti-aliasing process. The format she chose was GIF89a, interlaced:

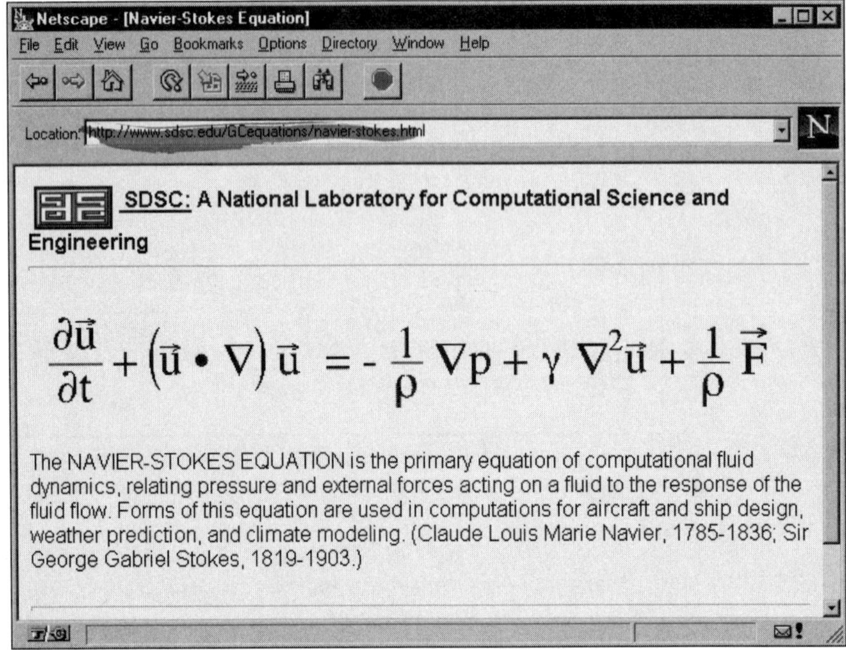

Figure 7-8: *The Navier-Stokes equation is one of a series of "Grand Challenges" put on the Web by the San Diego Supercomputer Center.*

Perhaps the most popular math display application is LaTeX, and its predecessor TeX. LaTeX is the *de facto* standard for exchanging documents in the math community, and in fact the underlying philosophy of the HTML tags that we listed above has quite a bit in common with LaTeX. Netscape recognizes LaTeX and TeX as helper applications, so files compiled with these programs can be read by anyone who has these programs by designating them in the Helpers preference panel of Netscape. It's possible a plug-in of LaTeX may come along in the future, so look for this if you plan on incorporating a lot of math work in your Web pages. Another solution might be the .PDF file format, for which the Adobe Acrobat Reader is available as a plug-in, as discussed in Chapter 4.

For more universal use in HTML files, there's an application called Latex2html that automatically converts a LaTeX equation into a GIF image. It was developed at the University of Leeds in England, and you can obtain it from:

ftp://ftp.tex.ac.uk/pub/archive/support/latex2html

The home page for LaTeX itself is:

http://www.tex.ac.uk/CTAN/latex/

LaTeX and TeX are the subject of the Usenet newsgroup **comp.text.tex**, and a FAQ file can be found at:

http://www.cis.ohio-state.edu/hypertext/faq/usenet/tex-faq/faq.html

Other Math Resources

It may well be that the vacuum caused by the HTML developers' loss of momentum on math will be filled by commerce—math on the Web, in other words, may be privatized. Already a company called Mathsoft is offering a mathematics-savvy Web browser called *Mathbrowser.* The software uses its own convention, called Mathcad, which can only read equations that it created itself. Figure 7-9 shows Mathcad setting about verifying the Bailey-Borwein-Plouffe procedure. Find out more about this 32-bit Windows application at:

http://www.mathsoft.com/browser

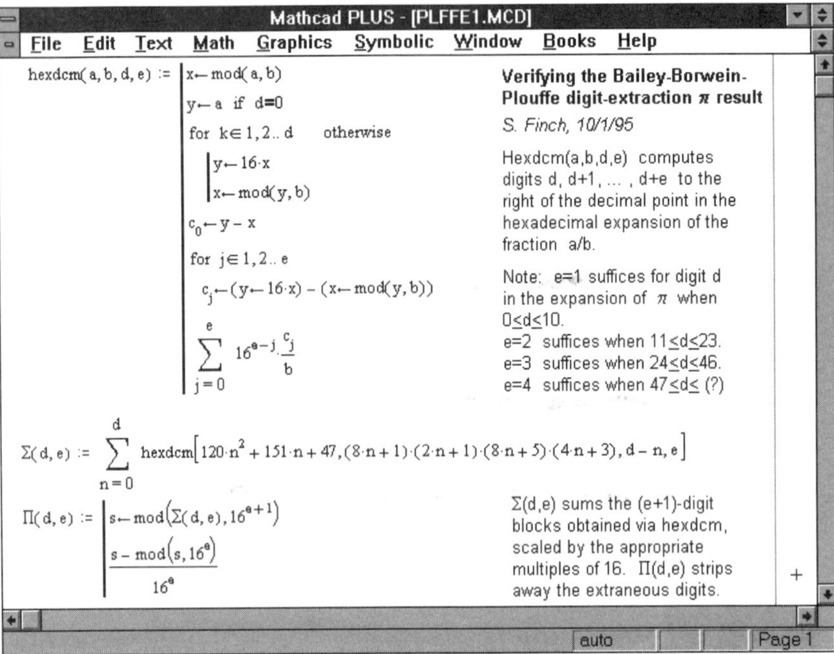

Figure 7-9: *Mathcad: Private enterprise tackles the equation problem.*

What's that? Oh, we assumed you knew... it's the latest way of expanding π (pi) to a zinjillion digits.

Finally, of the many indexes of math resources on the Net, we've picked two that will take you practically anywhere that math is the topic: the math departments of Florida State and Binghamton University, New York. Their URLs are:

http://euclid.math.fsu.edu/Science/Software.html
http://math.binghamton.edu/MATH/math/

...and *finally* finally, Yahoo has math. Of course it does—Yahoo has everything.

http://www.yahoo.com/Computers_and_Internet/Software/Mathematics/

Moving On

Next up is the material that's most difficult to illustrate in a book, but most attention-getting on the Web—page elements that walk and talk. In Chapter 8, "Multimedia & the Web," we'll be covering audio and video applications on the Web. We'll include so-called "streaming," which delivers its effect to the user in real time—multimedia, in other words, including applets and plug-ins and all the latest hot stuff to make your pages into moving TV screens.

Along the way we'll dip our toes into the water of cgi-bin scripting again, as we did for active images at the end of Chapter 4. This time around it'll be for a look at "server push" animation, which was a key feature of many of those excellent example pages we used in Chapter 6. We won't wade into cgi-bin scripting in earnest until Chapter 9, "Forms, Feedback & Cgi-bin," however.

8

Multimedia & the Web

To those familiar with the range of things one can do with CD-ROMs and home multimedia applications, the idea that you may be able to do things like play music or movies online may provoke a reaction like "Duh, so what's new?" We often get just this blasé reaction from a certain four-year-old Mac jockey (see Figure 8-9) who hangs around our house—and in fact, by the time he's grown up (or well before), the distinction between the television and the computer monitor, the cable and the telephone service, may be virtually non-existent.

Right now, though, we remain poised on the edge of a new communications revolution, in which multimedia applications on the Web are only beginning to play a significant part. What we're going to talk about in this chapter is the current state of the art in bringing multimedia to life on the Web. We'll explain how you can use existing software to insert sound and video files into Web documents, and how to set up "dynamic documents" that automatically load other files for animated effects. We'll take a look at the emerging use of virtual reality on the Web and the Virtual Reality Markup Language (VRML). Finally, we'll dip our toes into Java and show you how to insert Java "applets" in Web documents.

This is a chapter that is all too aware of its mortality. Take it as a starting point for exploring the types of things that we'll all be exploring together in the future.

Requirements and Options for Multimedia

Bringing true multimedia to the Web is a possibility that is exercising the minds of some of the best computer technologists and programmers today. It's whetting the appetites of industry moguls in Hollywood and making investors on Wall Street begin to salivate. Pretty impressive for something that's not really possible just yet.

The two things holding back the vision at the moment are the average capacity of the home computer and the capacity of a standard phone line—the last, and weakest link in the chain that brings the Internet to most desktops. The first may well be overcome in just a few years and the second is being circumvented even as we write, as cable companies enter the telephone company business and vice versa. But some major problems still remain to be worked out. If you intend to do a lot of intensive multimedia work, one thing you may want to check out is getting a high-speed connection. Just so you understand the parameters, we'll quickly review some high-speed options that are either currently available or on the frontier. However, don't think you need to go to these lengths just yet to use multimedia creatively on your Web site.

High-Speed Connection Options

Throughout this book we've been reminding you like a mantra to keep your files as small as possible to do the job. Once you decide to do multimedia on the Web, you'll find yourself highly frustrated and held back by this requirement. It's not our fault! Blame it on that dinky little plastic-coated wire that goes from the back of your modem to your phone jack, then snakes its way through your foundation and on out to the street to eventually join the computer that's part of that great Internet in the Sky.

But if speed is important to you—and if you do heavy-duty multimedia work it will be—you may have a few other options available to you, depending on where you work or where you live. These are the options to consider:

- Sign up for ISDN phone service.
- Get a cable modem to get Internet access through cable.
- Go directly into the Net with a big fat T1 line.

ISDN. Telephone companies in certain parts of the U.S. are already offering a new high-speed service called ISDN, for Integrated Services Digital Network. To take advantage of this, you must arrange with the phone company to have a special circuit card installed on your line. You then buy an ISDN modem to plug into your computer and subscribe to an Internet access service that is also wired for ISDN. When installed, the ISDN line is capable of carrying two channels that operate at 56 Kb per second plus an additional channel at 16 Kb per second. In practice this means that the same line can handle one ordinary speech circuit plus two data circuits, which can be combined into a single 128 Kb per second data channel. The great advantage of this is that you needn't be a big company to make ISDN work for you—it can be as easily installed into a private home, and although you'll be paying higher phone and access fees, it can be quite reasonable if you have a requirement for this kind of speed.

Cable Access. Cable companies are now working on a new high-speed connection technology called cable modems. With a cable modem, you bypass the phone company altogether and use the same cable technology that brings programs to your television set. The cable system has to be rewired for two-way traffic, but as of this writing several trials have been completed and it seems on the brink of being made more widely available. Customers will either purchase or rent a cable modem from their cable company, much like the box they may already have for their television set, but with two outlets, one for the TV and one for the cable modem that hooks up to their computer. The speed of a cable modem connection would depend on how many people were using the system at once, but they are capable of delivering information as fast as 4 MB per second, and in some cases as fast as 10 MB.

Direct to the Net. If you really crave access speed, you can do what the ISPs do and get a high-speed datalink at 1.5 MB per second (T1) or even 45 MB per second (T3). You'd order this from Sprint or AT&T, most likely, and a gang of cable-layers would disrupt traffic in your *quartier* for about a week. Either that or your house would take on the appearance of a radio telescope. The bill would be pretty staggering by most people's standards. But for a medium- to large-size business with a need for dedicated high-traffic computer lines, this can make a lot of sense.

What You Need to Create Multimedia

If all of the above options for high-speed connections are just pie-in-the-sky to you, don't despair. There are a number of great technologies on the Web frontier that circumvent the file-size-to-download-time problem, and we'll be discussing them later in this chapter. There are also some clever, relatively low-tech ways to make your Web site more animated.

First let's talk about your system requirements. The minimum system requirements to do the whole multimedia show—which includes not just accessing but creating full-scale real-time audio/video, are as follows:

- A 486DX with 66 MHz—but preferably a Pentium-based processor; the higher the clock speed the better, with at least 8 MB RAM (more for video).
- A 28.8 baud modem or better.
- A guaranteed good, clean, fast connection through your server.
- A 16-bit sound card for sound, and a video capture board for video.
- Lots of spare drive space—even temporary files consume massive amounts of storage in multimedia work.

Other useful tools include a microphone, video camera, cables for hooking up cassette players and/or cameras to your computer, and various bits of conversion software, which we'll discuss.

But again, if you can't meet all these requirements, don't despair. There are lots of things you can do to add multimedia effects to your Web pages and enjoy the results. And be assured that if you're preparing pages for general public consumption, most of your audience won't be equipped for special effects that are too demanding on their systems, either. The best advice we can offer is: Start simple. You can build up your arsenal of flashy effects and get more ambitious once you get familiar with what's possible and with what your system can handle.

We're going to approach this chapter with that principle in mind and go through some easy steps to introduce you to the various multimedia possibilities on the Web. Some of these delve into technical topics for which you're advised to go to other resources for a more thorough grounding, but we'll try to give you an idea of what's involved.

Sound & the Web

Producing sound files for the Web is probably the easiest multimedia task you can set for yourself. Since most computers come with sound cards and speakers these days, it's a safe bet that a large percentage of your Web audience will be able to access and enjoy the sound you produce.

Some common ways to use sound on a Web site are:

- A Welcome or Thank You message
- Background sound (perhaps loading automatically with the page)
- A music demo clip
- An audio recording of a radio show or commentary
- Fiction or poetry readings

The possibilities are limited only by your imagination—and possibly by your equipment. Fortunately, the latter is easy to overcome.

SOUND FORMATS

Your first major concern is to decide what format to use for your sound files. The output of a sound file on your computer is digital, as compared to the analog output of a conventional tape recorder. There are many different formats for digital files, some of them proprietary to certain computer platforms, and others in more general use.

Theoretically, any digital sound file can be transmitted over the Web. But each different file type requires a helper application to play it. For this reason, the types of sound formats used on the Web have settled down into a handful of types for which players are commonly available. The most common standard sound formats found on the Web are:

- Sun/NeXT audio or µlaw (with the extension .AU and sometimes .SND)
- Waveform sound (with the extension .WAV)
- Audio Interchange format (with the extension .AIFF)
- MIDI (Musical Instrument Digital Interface, with the extension .MIDI)—these are files created in electronic musical composition directly on the computer

Newer formats using advanced compression technology (more about these later) include:

- MPEG audio (with the extension .MP2)
- RealAudio (with the extension .RA for the sound file and .RAM or .RPM for "metafiles")
- Internet Wave audio (with the extension .VMF for the sound file and .VMD for the "metafile")

Deciding what format to use involves the kind of file you want to make (voice or music, mono or stereo), what software you have to create it, how large a file you want to handle, and what the anticipated playback device is.

In general you should try to keep your files as small as possible to deliver the quality you want. File size is directly affected by three things:

- The resolution expressed as bit-rate (8-bit or 16-bit)
- The channels used (mono or stereo)
- The sampling frequency (expressed in kilohertz)

An 8-bit mono file is fine for normal voice recording. However, this is generally insufficient for music recording. True music fidelity can only be achieved at 16-bit, so music will normally be recorded at 16-bit stereo (although the eventual ouput can be mono).

The sampling frequency will depend on both the source and the eventual purpose to which you put your recording. Music from a tape typically requires a sampling rate of 22 kHz. CD quality requires 44 kHz. The sacrifice you make for a higher-quality recording is file size. The higher the sampling rate, the more information in the file, therefore, the bigger the file. For example, a one-minute, 8-bit mono file sampled at 8 kHz would make a file of about 150k, while the same file recorded at 16-bit stereo with a 44.1 kHz rate may be 10 MB.

When producing sound files for the Web, you should bear in mind that not many of your Web visitors are likely to have state-of-the-art sound systems attached to their computers. So unless you're into a totally rad music scene, you should err on the side of caution and make your files with the minimum requirements to do the job.

Using Digital Sound Editors

Most sound cards come equipped with software to allow you to make digital sound files from analog input, through a microphone or other sound source such as a tape or CD. If you want to make your own sound files, the first thing you need to do is to check that you have input, output, and mic sockets on the back of your sound card. If so, you're in business. If you have an internal CD drive you'll be able to use that output, too, by just choosing that source through your software if your CD-ROM is properly cabled to the sound card. (Most computer bundles come this way. If yours is a special assembly or a mishmash of upgraded equipment, like ours, you can get a computer shop to fix this up for you.)

There are also a number of sound editors available as shareware on the Web, as well as a number of professional sound editors you can buy. Just as with image editors, the first major difference is in the number of different file types the sound editor can handle. The second is in the variety of special effects, and the third is in their ability to handle direct instrumental input. Unless you're seriously into music production, you won't need the most advanced sound editors and equipment (which can be very expensive indeed, but are worth it for professional-quality musical sound). If you plan to do more than one sound file, we recommend you get a good shareware sound editor that allows you to handle several different audio types and convert one to another. We've included two of these that are recommended for Windows on the Companion CD-ROM. You can also get information about them and updates online. They are:

CoolEdit

http://www.netzone.com/syntrillium

GoldWave

http://Web.cs.mun.ca/ ~chris3/goldwave

To find sound editors for a whole range of computer platforms, search the Yahoo directory at:

http://www.yahoo.com/Entertainment/Music/Genres/Computer_Generated/Music_Software/

Posting a Simple Audio File

You can take any file you have on hand or have made in a Web-compatible format and post it on your Web site. You need only provide a link to it so that readers can click to play or download it, depending on how they've set up their Web browser. Providing the link, via the anchor tag, is easy:

```
<A HREF="thefile.wav">The Beatles: Ob-La-Di Ob-La-Da</A>
```

Click on the link. If you've set up a helper application to deal with .WAV files, the file will download, and Netscape will launch the application and play it.You'll be back in the '60s with '90s technology (and unlike that old *White Album* in your closet, it won't warp and distort with time). It's considered polite, however, and useful to your audience to provide some information about the file along with the link. Make your link appear like so:

```
The Beatles: Ob-La-Di Ob-La-Da (456k .wav file)
```

and readers can determine whether they have the software to play it, whether they want to take the time to download it, and whether they'd like to play it immediately or save it to disk for later.
You can also provide your clip in a couple of different formats for people to choose between, such as:

```
The Beatles: Ob-La-Di Ob-La-Da (456k .wav file) or (392k
.aiff file)
```

Now for a word of caution: Taking pre-recorded music and converting it to digital sound on your computer is a very easy exercise to perform. But be careful how you use it! Music copyright issues are a lively battlefield on the Web right now. If you're just using it on your funky home page for family and friends ("My favorite song is..."), we doubt if anyone would notice or care. But if you were really going to take a Beatles recording and post it on a public Web site where it might be downloaded by others, you might get a nasty shock as a very large lawsuit arrives with a thunk on your doorstep.

If all you want to do is make a simple voice clip to insert in your page (like a "Welcome" message), your task is straightforward. In Figure 8-1, we're using Sound Blaster's WaveStudio, which came with our Sound Blaster16 card, to record a voice file to insert in a Web page. We bought an inexpensive microphone (all of $10) to plug into the mic socket on our sound card. For a voice file, we chose to record at 8-bit mono at 11 kHz sampling rate, which is the minimum specifications and perfectly adequate for the type of audio clip we have in mind in Figure 8-2.

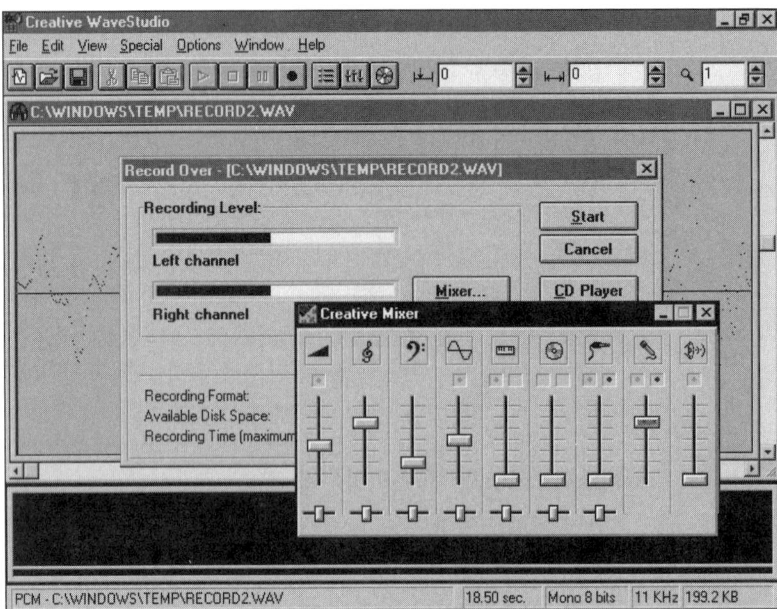

Figure 8-1: *Recording a simple audio file using the Sound Blaster editing software and a microphone.*

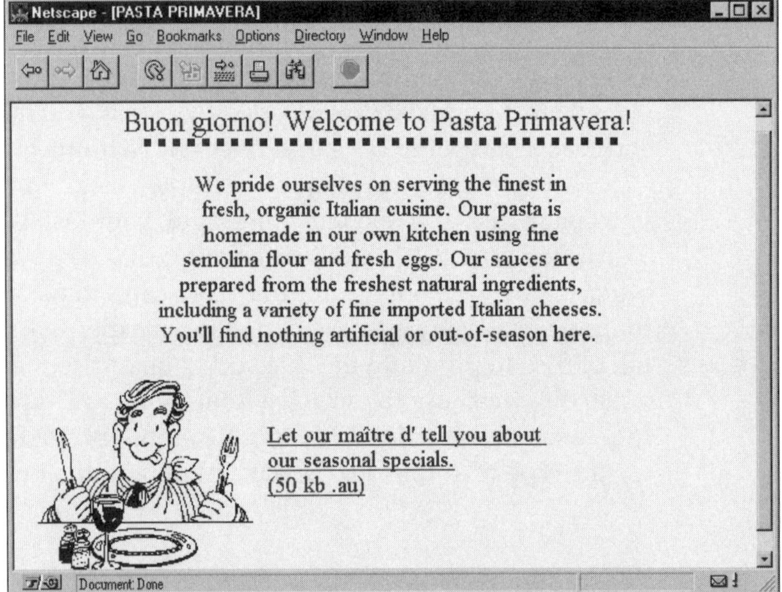

Figure 8-2: *A word from the maître d' adds a lively touch to this fictional restaurant's Web page.*

If you already have a voice clip on tape that you'd like to convert for use on your Web page, you can make a digital file using a tape recorder/player as the input device. Connect the output line on the tape player to the input line on the sound card with an audio cable. Cue up your tape where you want to start, then begin recording with your audio software and play your tape. It's advisable to make your initial digital recording in stereo and then convert it to mono—otherwise you'll only be receiving input from one channel.

You can also record a file from the CD player on your computer, if you have one, through the internal connection. Just choose that as the source of your file in your editing software. In Figure 8-1 you can see the CD Player option available to us in Sound Blaster's Creative WaveStudio. Again, your internal CD-ROM must be properly cabled to your sound card (see "Using Digital Sound Editors" above).

Music is created much the same way as vocal files, but for music files you will probably want a higher sampling rate for sound quality. (See the previous section on "Sound Formats.") If you've always dreamed of being a disk jockey, you'll be able to fulfill your fantasies as you discover the range of mixing effects you can make when you get used to your audio software.

Instant Gratification With Audio on Demand

The real up-and-coming development in audio on the Web is "real-time" audio, or audio on demand. This makes an end run around the whole issue of file size and download time as it applies to conventional sound files on the Web. It takes advantage of two innovations—first, file compression, and second, file buffering—to allow users to begin playing a file as soon as the first packet of information arrives. You needn't wait for the entire file to download—in fact, you never need to have the whole file on your computer, only the necessary packets as needed, so you don't take up valuable space on your computer.

Sounds great, hey? So what's the catch? The catch is that this is technology is still developing and the sound quality and reliability are not 100 percent. And not everyone has the software to play the files (the software is not yet available for all platforms), but its use is growing rapidly. In general, everything we said about requirements for state-of-the-art multimedia via the Web applies to real-time audio. The better your sound card, your computer capacity and your connection, the happier you'll be with the results. But developers of audio and video on demand are banking on the idea that we'll all have our computers up to warp speed in a few years, and they may be right.

A major advantage real-time audio offers is that it allows you to put very long-playing audio files on a Web site without taking up enormous chunks of storage space. A typical compression ratio for a real-time audio file can be as high as 44:1. This means an entire hour's broadcast can fit in a file of only 3.6MB.

There are a couple of competing formats for this developing audio compression technology, and it's a bettor's gamble who will pull ahead of the field in the next few years. Two current front-runners to keep your eye on are:

- RealAudio (Figure 8-3)
  http://www.realaudio.com/
- Internet Wave (Figure 8-4)
  http://vocaltec.com/iwave.htm

You can download the encoder for both of these formats along with the software to play them from these sites. While the technology is really impressive, making real-time audio files is easier than you may think. It's basically an insert-file, turn-the-crank operation. Most of the work is in properly preparing your sound file *before* you encode it. In the next section, we provide detailed procedures for creating and posting RealAudio files.

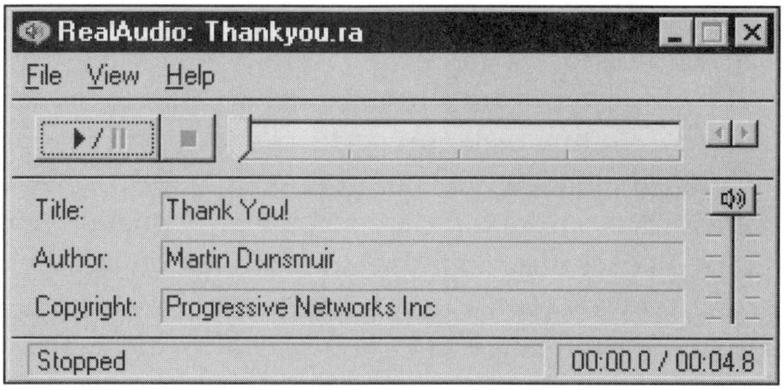

Figure 8-3: *The RealAudio Player.*

Figure 8-4: *The Internet Wave Player.*

Both your own browser and the server computer have to be configured to recognize the MIME types for these audio formats. The MIME types are what identify the files to the server and browser so that the appropriate software will be launched to handle them. You can configure your Netscape Navigator for new MIME types from the Helpers panel of General Preferences. Many plug-in packages like RealAudio will automatically configure your browser for the new file type when you install it. If you must do it yourself, you'll have to define three elements.

- The main MIME type: For RealAudio this is simply "audio"
- The MIME subtype: For RealAudio this "x-pn-realaudio"
- The file extensions: RA, RAM, and RPM for RealAudio

You'll also have to tell Netscape to launch RealAudio when it encounters a file of this type by clicking the Launch the Application button in the Action field and filling in the path to the application.

To work as intended, the server computer on which the files reside must be configured similarly and also have the RealAudio Server to dish up the files on request.

If you can't talk your sysadmin into installing the RealAudio Server, you can still use the file compression to shrink large audio files for transmission. Embed your audio on demand files in your Web pages the same as conventional sound files. When the link is chosen, the download will begin and after download, the player will be launched. This method allows you to take advantage of the file compression capability, but it does not take full advantage of the technology. In the next section, we'll explain how to properly embed the files so that the player will launch and the clip will begin to play immediately and "stream" as intended.

Also, since RealAudio is now available as a plug-in to Netscape, we'll show you the range of effects you can create in your Web pages using the RealAudio plug-in—and introduce a new HTML tag on the way. Bear in mind that the same techniques can be used with other plug-ins as they become available. Once you know how to use the RealAudio plug-in, you'll be prepared to understand and use some of the future multimedia applications that may be just a gleam in a programmer's eye at this writing.

Preparing and Encoding RealAudio Files

RealAudio works through its own server software that is installed on the host computer. You'll have to get your sysadmin to install this if it's not already on the system. If you're running your own Web server, you can get the server software from the RealAudio site along with the Player. The RealAudio Server works in conjunction with the Web server. When a user clicks on a RealAudio link, a "metafile"—a very small file containing the URL of the audio file—is accessed. This information is then sent via the RealAudio Player to the RealAudio Server, which then streams the audio file to the Player where it is buffered and then played. Providing the Server is installed on your host computer, there are then three components you need to produce RealAudio effects:

- The Web page that contains the reference to the file
- The metafile that references the RealAudio Server
- The audio file itself, in RealAudio format

Beginning at the end, the first thing you have to do is create and/or edit your source in its original format. The quality of the end file depends very much on the quality of the original input file. Satellite signals, Digital Audio Tapes (DATs), and compact discs (CDs) make the cleanest sound. For original recordings, you can use any input, including tiny condenser microphones, but the best results will come from using professional-quality microphones. Professional equipment yields professional results. Expect a certain amount of hiss and distortion from lower-end inputs.

Other recommendations from the RealAudio FAQ include:

- Use 16-bit not 8-bit files to encode from.
- If possible use a sampling rate of 22 kHz. The encoder will accept 8 kHz and 11 kHz, but 22 yields the best results.
- Set your input levels or recording levels correctly, so that the input approaches but does not exceed the maximum level.
- Use the full range of amplitude. You can adjust the range of an existing file using the Increase Amplitude or Normalize function on your sound editor. Set levels to about 95% of

maximum so that the loudest parts of the file approach but do not exceed the range (which would cause "clipping" and distortion).

Note that while we said above that 8-bit was fine for an ordinary voice recording in .AU or .WAV format, since the file will go through some compression for RealAudio, a 16-bit recording is recommended. Likewise, the recommendations about input levels and amplitude are aimed at creating the loudest possible files without distortion so that the Encoder will have the maximum amount of information to use in compression.

We'll illustrate the process by way of a little literary project we undertook to create a poetry corner on the Web. We found a great repository of audio clips, including readings of works by famous authors at the HarperAudio! site presented by the Internet Multicasting Service at:

http://town.hall.org/Archives/radio/IMS/HarperAudio/

We latched onto one of our favorites (flashbacks of long-ago late-night dorm sessions) and downloaded a file of poet Dylan Thomas reading his work in his booming Welsh baritone. The clip was 4.9MB bytes long and took quite a while to reach us (nearly two hours!). It was fun to listen to, but there was something lacking. We were interested in what we could do with just one of the poems on this clip to make it a more Web-friendly and immediate experience.

Figure 8-5 shows us bringing the clip into CoolEdit, a sound editor we find very friendly, and choosing the section of the file that contains the poem we're interested in. By a simple copy and paste operation we drop it into a new file, being careful to retain the original file format of 16-bit mono at 8 kHz. Even though a higher sampling rate, preferably 22 kHz, would be better, we're stuck with the original recording here, which we can't alter without distorting the sound. But there is one thing we can do to improve the output, and that's increase the amplitude of the original to the maximum in order to get a better quality RealAudio file. CoolEdit makes this easy by having a "Normalize" option on the Transform menu, which automatically chooses the maximum amplitude for the selection, without exceeding the maximum input level (which would create popping or "clipping" in the file). Figure 8-6 shows the new file (now 1.6mb) when we're ready to save it.

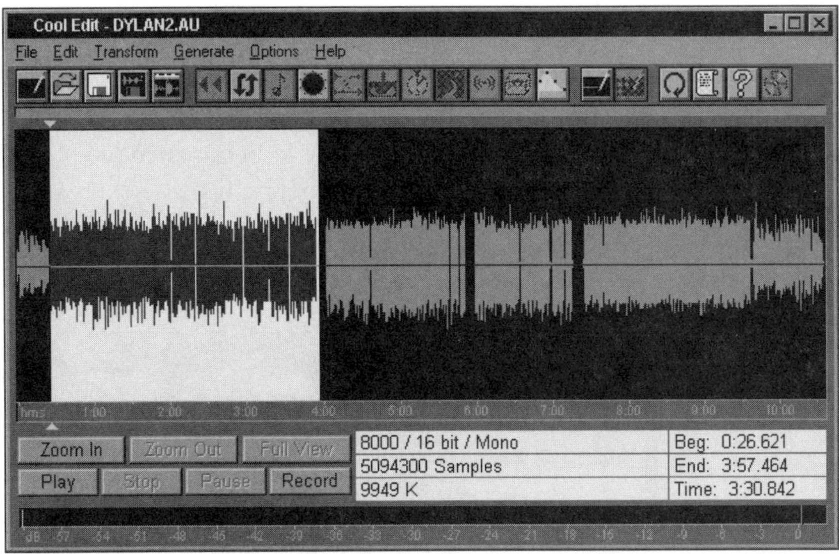

Figure 8-5: *CoolEdit lets you choose the section of the clip you want to use...*

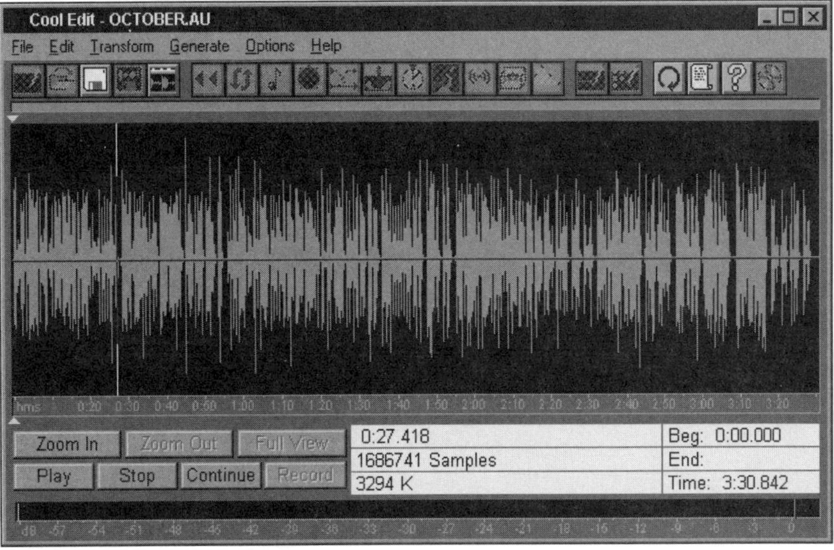

Figure 8-6: *...then drop it into a new file and edit it as necessary.*

Next, we'll start up the RealAudio Encoder and open the file. We have to be careful to choose the appropriate sampling rate to match the initial file, which is 8 kHz. If we chose a faster sampling rate, it would be like playing a tape at double-speed, and Dylan Thomas would end up sounding like Donald Duck. We'll input the Name/Author/Copyright information that will appear on the Player when the clip is played. That's almost all we have to worry about. Figure 8-7 shows the clip on its way to being encoded. The resultant audio file will have the name october.ra, the .RA extension being common to all RealAudio files. When it's done the original file of 1.6mb will make a 206k RealAudio file (an 8:1 compression rate).

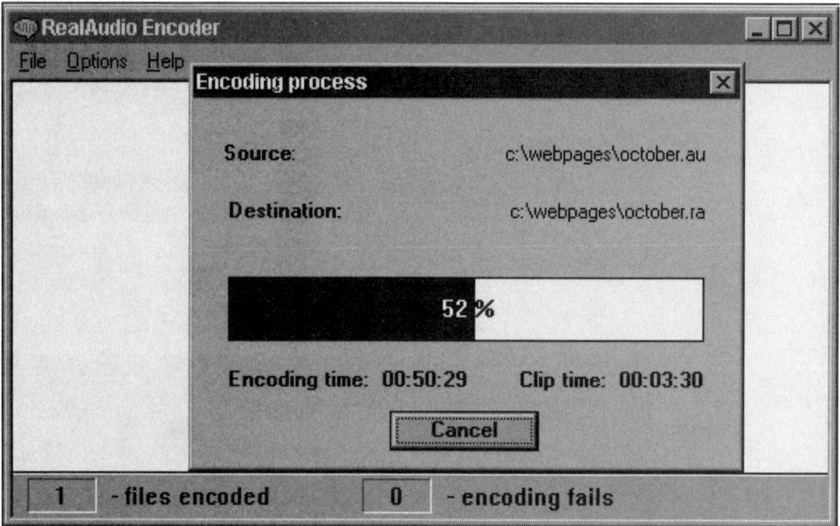

Figure 8-7: *The RealAudio Encoder on its way to creating a RealAudio file.*

Posting RealAudio Files

While that was doing its job, we created the Web page we wanted to put this audio file into—a straightforward job using just a few of the tricks we discussed in Chapter 4, "All About Images" (notably the "glass bricks trick" to make indents). Note, however, in Figure 8-8, that when we put in the link to the audio file, it is not to october.ra, but to october.ram. This is the metafile that will tell the RealAudio Server where to find the audio file itself. The next task, a simple one, is to make the october.ram file. We create a simple ASCII text file with one line in it, containing the URL of our audio file:

```
pnm://www.thegroup.net/october.ra
```

We save it as october.ram. Note: The metafile must have the same name as the audio file, but with the .RAM extension.

Now that we have our three pieces assembled we can post it on the Web site. It may be necessary, depending on how your server is configured, to post the audio (.RA) file itself in the directory that contains the RealAudio Server. You'll have to ascertain this by trial and error or by discussing with your systems administrator. When you've got it posted properly, you can click on the link and the RealAudio player will display and begin streaming the audio, as in Figure 8-8. The control panel allows you to control the volume, stop, pause, replay, or to choose any section of the clip to play.

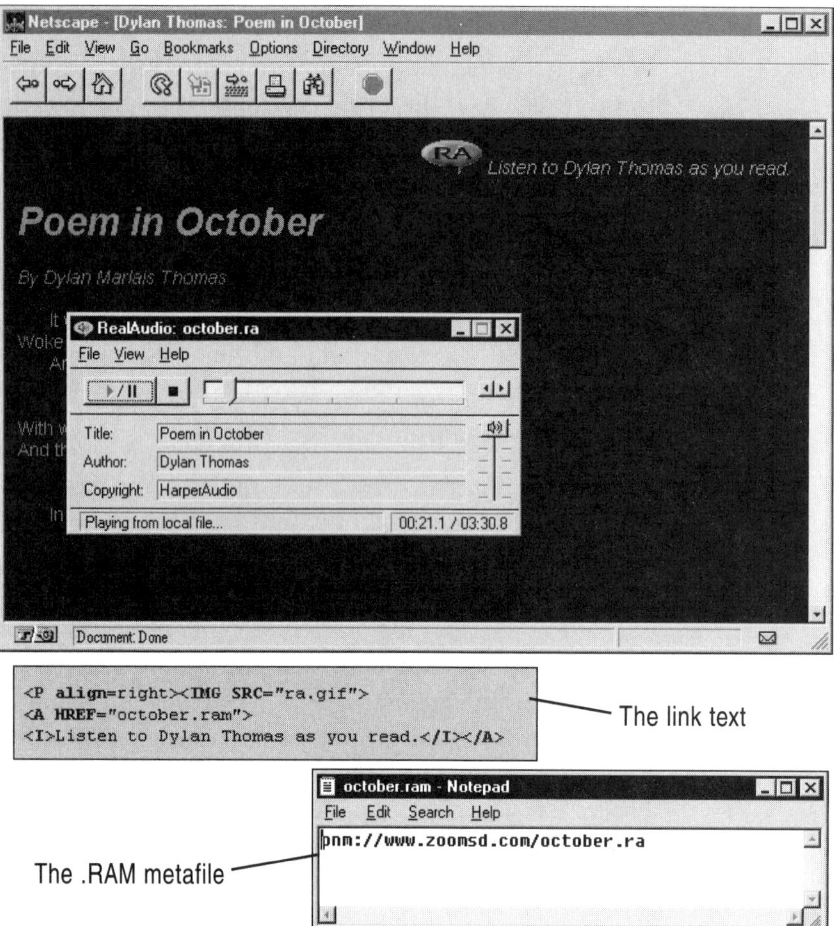

Figure 8-8: *The Dylan Thomas poetry page with the code for its RealAudio link and the metafile that acts as intermediary.*

Embedding RealAudio Controls

That's nice, but to tell you the truth there's something just a little annoying on this page about having the RealAudio Player come up and cover the text when we really want to read along. We'd prefer something more subtle and tasteful. Fortunately, the RealAudio 2.0 plug-in has just what we need.

Using the RealAudio plug-in, you can embed the whole player or just the controls you want in a page, and you can decide where you want it to appear on the page and just how big. To use the RealAudio plug-in you use the same components as above with just two differences:

- The EMBED tag is used in the referring HTML file instead of the anchor tag, and
- The metafile takes the .RPM extension instead of .RAM. The metafile is identical in all other respects—only the extension changes.

The simplest and most straightforward way to embed the RealAudio player in the page is a line like this in your HTML page:

```
<EMBED SRC="file.rpm" WIDTH=300 HEIGHT=135>
```

The result you see in Figure 8-9. In order for it to work, the .RPM file must exist (although it can be an empty file or a text file with just a few random characters in it for test purposes).

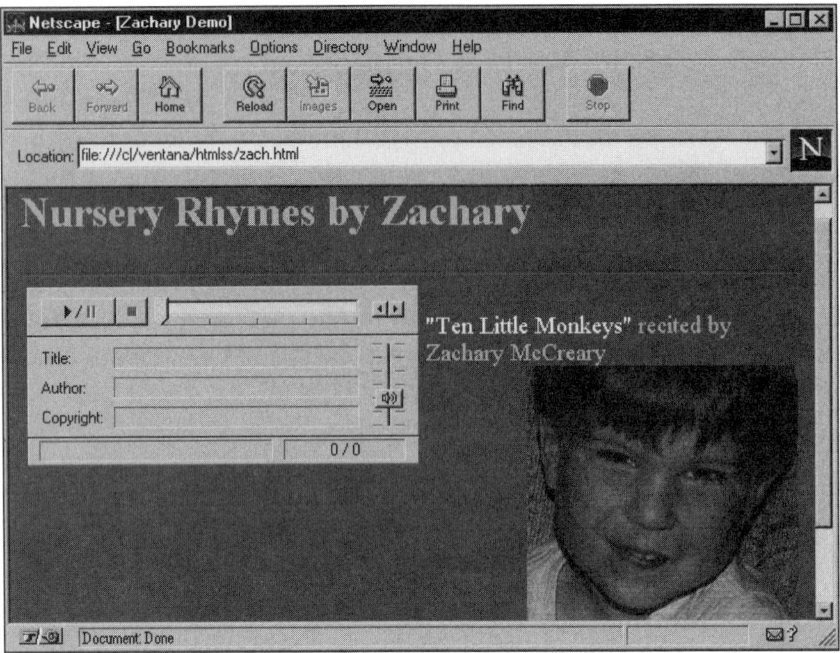

Figure 8-9: *The RealAudio Player embedded directly into a Web page using the RealAudio 2.0 plug-in.*

In this case, the EMBED tag requires both a WIDTH and HEIGHT attribute. The dimensions we gave it above allow for the full normal size of the player, but we can make this larger or smaller as we please and the player will adjust to fit as best it can.

HTML Tag

<EMBED>

Defines a container that allows the insertion of arbitrary objects directly into an HTML page. Embedded objects must be supported by application-specific plug-ins. Arbitrary attributes may be specified by those applications. The minimum required attribute is SRC. The end tag </EMBED> is not required in Netscape 2.0 but may be required by other browsers or in future versions.

SRC Specifies the URL source of the file to be embedded (either directly or via a metafile that contains the URL of the file).

WIDTH=w Specifies the width of the inserted object, in pixels or ens, or a percentage.

HEIGHT=h Specifies the height of the image in pixels or ens, or a percentage.

Other attributes common to the IMG tag that may be used include:

ALIGN="bottom/middle/top/left/right" Specifies alignment of image in relation to the screen margins and/or text

BORDER=b Specifies a border of b pixels in width. Default is no border.

HSPACE=p Specifies a clear horizontal space (left and right of image) in pixels

VSPACE=v Specifies a clear vertical space (top and bottom of image) in pixels

<NOEMBED>....</NOEMBED>

This tag pair may be used to specify alternate content for browsers that do not recognize the <EMBED> tag.

TIP

The EMBED tag may also be used to insert a text document of another type in an HTML file, such as a Word document. Providing the user has the appropriate viewer application set up as a helper application, the document will appear embedded within the Web page. (If you use EMBED this way, the document must reside on the server computer along with the HTML file to be viewable. It cannot be viewed locally.)

The RealAudio 2.0 plug-in has custom embed tag attributes that allow you to specify which types of controls you want to display, as well as a few other nifty options. In the case of our Dylan Thomas poetry page, we think just a discreet little play and pause button would be enough. So this is what we'll use to create the finished page you see in Figure 8-10.

```
<EMBED SRC="october.rpm" WIDTH=50 HEIGHT=25
CONTROLS=PlayButton>
```

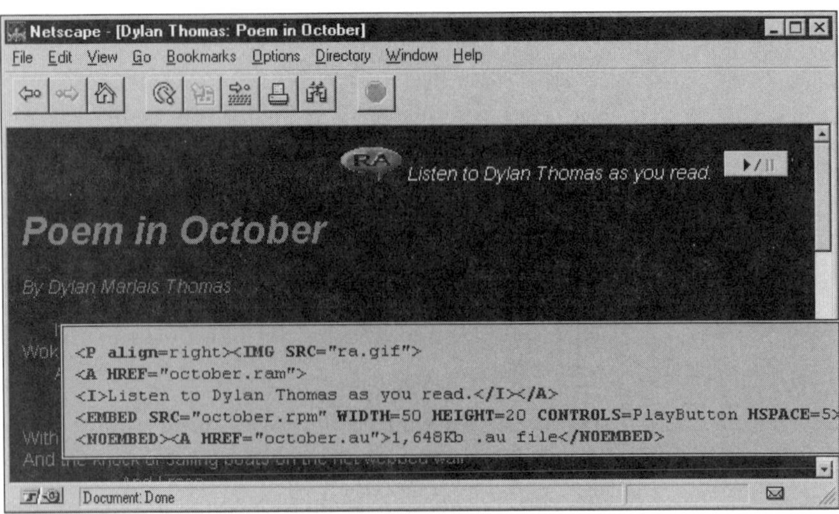

Figure 8-10: *The Play/Pause button controls are all we really need to make this page work like we want.*

TIP

Get the latest information on RealAudio development, FAQs and other information that will help you improve the quality of your files from the RealAudio Web site at:
http://www.realaudio.com/

RealAudio Custom EMBED Tag Attributes

The CONTROLS attribute tailors the display of the control elements for the RealAudio Player when embedded in a Web page. Custom attributes for the EMBED tag using the RealAudio plug-in include:

CONTROLS="All"—Default option embeds the entire Player control panel. Other values are:

- ControlPanel
- InfoVolumePanel
- InfoPanel
- StatusBar
- PlayButton
- StopButton
- VolumeSlider
- PositionSlider
- PositionField
- StatusField

AUTOSTART=TRUE—Tells the RealAudio to begin playing automatically when the page is loaded.

NOLABELS=TRUE—Causes the InfoPanel to appear without the Title:, Author:, and Copyright: labels appearing before the information. (May be useful for using languages other than English or to use these fields for other types of information.)

CONSOLE="_master" Links the plug-in to all others on the page, allowing you to specify one control panel (or section of a control panel) to display information for all audio clips on the page. You can also use this to include multiple components that work together as in the following example:

```
<EMBED SRC="sample1.rpm" WIDTH=30 HEIGHT=33
CONTROLS="PlayButton" CONSOLE="Clip1">
<EMBED SRC="empty1.rpm" WIDTH=300 HEIGHT=33
CONTROLS="PositionSlider" CONSOLE="Clip1">
```

USING INTERNET WAVE FILES

Internet Wave files, which use a different compression formula, work the same way as RealAudio. A metafile is necessary to transfer the request to the Internet Wave server. The Encoder automatically creates the metafile for you that takes the .VMD extension, while the audio files have the extension .VMF. As of this writing Internet Wave is not available as a Netscape plug-in—which means the player cannot be embedded in your pages, but it will start up when you click on a link to the Internet Wave metafile. You can get up-to-date information about Internet Wave on the home page at:

http://vocaltec.com/iwave.htm

MPEG AUDIO

The other type of compressed file format used for audio on the Web is the MPEG-1 layer-2 (.MP2) format. This is fast becoming a standard for quality compressed music files since there is less perceivable loss of sound quality in the compression process. This is because the audio compression scheme is based on psychoacoustic models of how we perceive sound. The extensive tests that went into creating this model have shown that you can simply throw away large parts of the sound wave information because the human ear simply can't hear them, and other parts can be selectively edited because they make little discernible difference.

For that reason MPEG (which stands for Motion Picture Experts Group) is the international standard for professional development in both computer audio and video, and is the format being used by Sony and Phillips, among others. If you intend to bring professional-quality audio to your Web site, you'll want to look into MPEG encoding.

MPEG audio files are most frequently offered as downloadable files in Web music archives, such as the Internet Underground Music Archive (http://www.iuma.com/). Recently, however, streaming technology has also been introduced to handle .MP2 files. Much of the excitement has been directed toward the live broadcast possibilities. By late 1995, a handful of live Web broadcasts of concerts in either audio alone or combined audio/video had been staged, with varying degrees of success.

One of the leaders in combined MPEG audio/video on the Web is Xing Technology, which has recently come up with a combined audio/video stream player, based on the MPEG standard, which we'll be discussing in the next section (look ahead to Figure 8-14). Xing offers both an inexpensive encoder and a player that you can get information about at:

http://www.xingtech.com/xingmpeg/index.html

For playing .MP2 sound files only, a free version of XingSound Player for Windows is available at:

ftp://ftp.iuma.com/audio_utils/mpeg_players/Windows/

Check the MPEG FAQ for a background in MPEG technology and progress at:

http://www.cs.tu-berlin.de/~phade/mpegfaq/

or:

http://www.crs4.it/~luigi/MPEG/

Animating the Web

Video and animations for the computer can be a very complex subject indeed. Basically, it helps to bear in mind that video is nothing more than a series of flashing pictures, just like the ones that Uncle Jack used to draw on the corner of a notepad for you when you were a kid. To ease into this subject, we'll start with the simplest kind of computer animations you can create using the Web protocol, which create a kind of slide show effect, and move on up to a review of the latest techniques for providing movies and live video feeds over the Web.

CLIENT PULL ANIMATIONS

The simplest and easiest kind of effect you can create to present a series of images on the Web, which you can do without any kind of special software or programming knowledge at all, is *client pull animations*. The term comes from the fact that the request for the next page is made by the user's browser (the client), albeit automatically by a command planted in the code of the Web page. It produces an effect something like a slide show, with pages loading consecutively.

In order to understand how client pull works, you need to know a little bit about how a server works when it receives a request and sends a response. When you click on a link on a Web page, you are actually activating your browser to send a request to a remote server housing the document you want. The request looks something like this:

```
GET /Tests/file.html HTTP/1.0
Accept: text/plain
Accept: application/x-html
Accept: application/html
Accept: text/html
Accept: audio/basic
Accept: audio/x-wav
...
User-Agent: Netscape 2.0b1 for Windows
```

You may recognize the above "Accept:" fields as the same things displayed in your Netscape Helper options panel. These are the "mime types" and "subtypes" your browser is configured to handle.

When the server receives the request, it processes it and returns the requested data preceded by a "response header," which contains information about the transaction that the browser can use. The response looks something like this:

```
HTTP/2.0 200 OK
Date: Tuesday, 15-Apr-96 23:59:50 GMT
Server: NCSA/1.3
MIME-version: 1.0
Content-type: text/html
Last-modified: Friday, 12-Apr-96 16:35:27 GMT
Content-length: 750

<HTML>
<HEAD>
…(and so on, the document itself)…
</HTML>
```

This information in the response header is information available for use by your browser or another program, such as a site counter or a search engine, or for inputting into a database. If you've cruised around the Web much, you've probably seen pages that pop up a personal welcome with your name (or Web alias) and tell you what browser you're using. These effects are created by so-called "server side includes" that utilize response header information, and we'll be telling you how to use them in the next chapter.

You can provide information to include in the response header when the server sends your documents using the META tag. This is a tag you'll never see unless you're poking around nosily in somebody's code, yet it pops up surprisingly often. In some respects META is kind of a catchall tag for any info you want to provide about a document that you can't do anyplace else. But it's also a convenient way of inputting info about the document into a database program, such as a search engine or library cataloging system.

HTML Tag

META

The META tag allows for including information about the document not defined by other elements. META information is included within the HEAD of the document. It must have at least the CONTENT attribute, with either HTTP-EQUIV or NAME to identify the type of action or data identifier to be associated with it.

NAME Specifies the name to be associated with the meta-information content, which must be understood by the browser or other program using it.

HTTP-EQUIV Can be used instead of the NAME attribute. META elements with this attribute are parsed by the server and converted into response header elements.

CONTENT Assigns the content to be associated with the META element.

The HTTP-EQUIV="Refresh" attribute is a Netscape extension (also recognized by a few other browsers) used with the META tag, which directs the server to automatically "refresh" this page with another after a specified time period. The complete tag you need to construct this looks like this:

```
<META HTTP-EQUIV="Refresh" CONTENT="3; URL=file.html">
```

The above line tells the browser to "refresh" this page after three seconds with the specified file, which may be a full or partial URL. It must be placed in the HEAD of your Web document. Obviously we can change the time lapse by changing the number in the CONTENT attribute. Bear in mind, though, that the number is somewhat approximate. The actual time it takes to get and load the next file will depend on the speed of the connection and how busy the server is, among other factors. It's not quite as reliable as the news flash that interrupts your favorite television series.

You can make a series of consecutively loading pages by embedding this command in the head of each document with the URL of the next document in the series. We used that to make the flashing billboard effect you see in Figure 8-11.

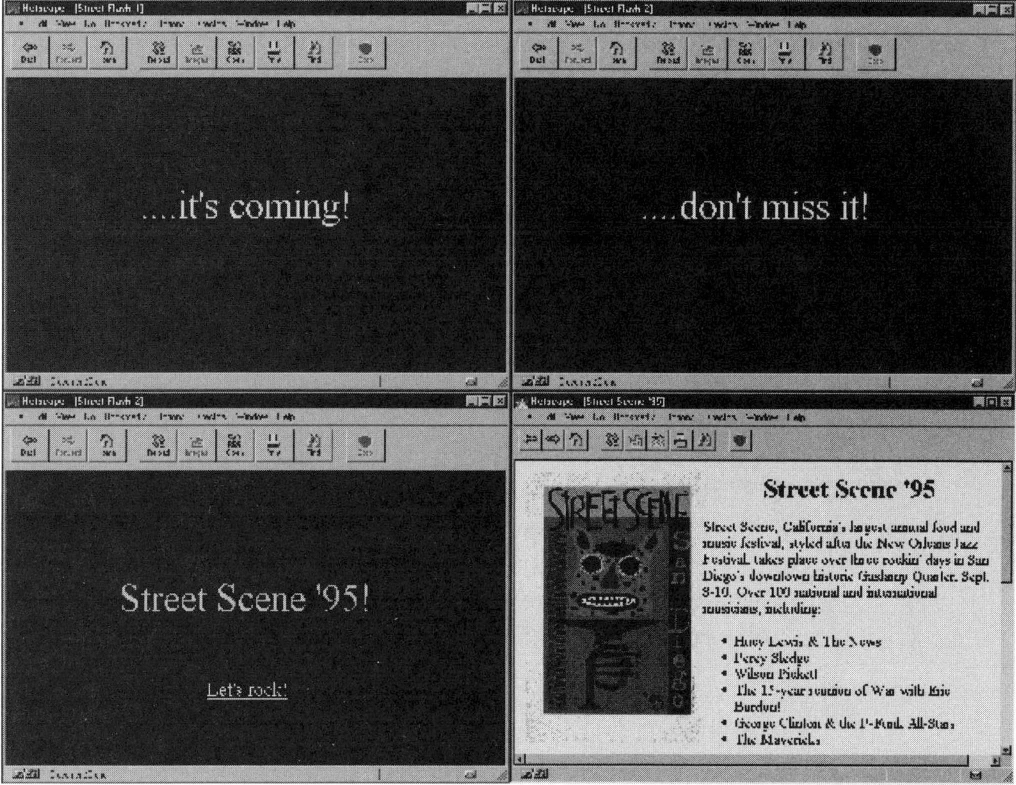

Figure 8-11: *In this client pull animation, each page automatically loads the next (starting clockwise from top left).*

SOME OTHER USES OF META

Obviously there are other uses you can make of the META tag. One common use is to enter keywords for a search engine to use. One example:

<META NAME="keyword" CONTENT="rhinoceros">

This might assure that a search engine looking for Web pages about rhinoceroses will find that page you did for the local zoo.

Another common use is to provide information about the currency of the page using the NAME= "Last-Modified" attribute. Searchers may be instructed to disregard any page whose "Last-Modified" date is too old to be of use—something that might be of use in a medical research database search, for instance.

SERVER PUSH ANIMATION

On the face of it, server push seems to be not a whole lot different from client pull—something changes as you look at a page. In reality, however, the two techniques are very different. Client pull can only work by re-loading the *entire* page. Server push operates on individual *elements* of a page—and since by far the most common application is animating a single inline image, we'll explain the process in those terms.

When you call an inline image into your page—a picture of a sheep, let's say—you write something like <IMG SRC="sheep.gif">. The file "sheep.gif" is brought into the viewer's screen preceded by a header that warns the browser software that it needs to be able to cope with this MIME-type: "Content-type: image/gif." (Actually, of course, a nongraphical browser *can't* cope and so skips immediately to the next task rather than attempt to display garbage.)

Every imaginable element of a Web site comes heralded by a MIME-type declaration (HTML files are "Content-type: text/html"), and Netscape responds in predictable ways to most of them. Here's an interesting one:

```
Content-type: multipart/x-mixed-
   replace;boundary="@@@@lambchop@@@@"
```

That's a Netscape invention specifically for server push, and what it says is "stand by to receive a multi-part message. You'll know when one part has finished and the next part is about to replace it by the cue line '—@@@@lambchop@@@@'. We'll let you know what the MIME-type of each part is, and it'll all be done when you see '—@@@@lambchop@@@@—'".

So now, if we want to send four animated frames of a sheep in rapid succession, we put the four frames in the same directory as all our other GIFs, and arrange to have them sent one after another into the browser. This is done with a binary file that will send 14 lines of code something like this:

```
Content-type: multipart/x-mixed
replace;boundary="@@@@lambchop@@@@"
-@@@@lambchop@@@@
Content-type: image/gif
<sheep.frame1.gif>
-@@@@lambchop@@@@
Content-type: image/gif
<sheep.frame2.gif>
-@@@@lambchop@@@@
Content-type: image/gif
<sheep.frame3.gif>
-@@@@lambchop@@@@
Content-type: image/gif
<sheep.frame4.gif>
-@@@@lambchop@@@@-
```

Behold, an animated sheep!

Well, not quite. The above 14 lines are "pseudo-code" intended to reveal the mechanics only, and would not actually work. A real server-push script would not look a whole lot different, though. In practice, it would be called sheep.cgi, because it would have to work through what's called the Common Gateway Interface between HTML and binary programs. It would be written in a computer language like Perl and run in the UNIX operating system. The reference to it in the HTML file would be not <IMG SRC="sheep.gif"> but <IMG SRC="sheep.cgi">.

Figure 8-12: *The magic of server push lets this sheep graze in your page by loading each image consecutively.*

In the next chapter we'll show you how to set up the user's area of a shell account for cgi-bin operations, and introduce the adventurous amongst you to the wonders of Perl. For right now, there's a little ready-made sheep-animating package on the Companion CD-ROM accompanying this book, and in the same folder is a README.TXT with explicit instructions for installing it. If successfully installed, you'll have not just *sheep.cgi* but also *sheep.html* and *sheep01.gif* through *sheep10.gif*. So you'll be able to bring not four but 10 frames of a sheep munching (actually one of the standard animation exercises from Corel Draw!) into a Web page. You should probably read the cgi-bin sections of our Chapter 9, "Forms, Feedback & cgi-bin," before attempting this. For much more about animations, check out Meng Weng Wong's Perl page at:

http://www.seas.upenn.edu/~mengwong/perlhtml.html

This is a great resource, including freebie helpers for animations of both the client-pull and server-push variety. The program *animate.pl*, which you can download and use, reads a list of GIFs from a separate list file that you create and server-pushes them into your page with user-definable pauses and loop-backs.

Just like client pull, server push can be arranged to keep going indefinitely—but endless server push is *not* a trick we recommend, since it's liable to keep on pushing and pushing, using server resources, even after the user has left your page far behind.

Combining Several GIFs Into One

Just as we were doing the final edits on this book, a new animation application for GIFs popped into view: the GIF Construction Set. For a simple GIF animation like the sheep above, it wins hands-down over server push. By incorporating all of the animation frames into one file that downloads as a piece, it takes the load off the server.

This is how it works: A GIF file usually consists of two blocks, a header and an image. However, the structure defined by the GIF89a specification allows for GIF files that contain multiple images and several additional block types.

To create the same sheep animation as we did with server push above, we created a new GIF file. Then we added our ten frames (each one in GIF89a format) using the Merge option on GIFCon. Then we inserted a Control block between each file. We modified each Control block with our own instructions by selecting the block and choosing the Edit option from the menu; in the resultant dialog box we were able to specify a delay in seconds between each frame. (See Figure 8-13.) We saved the file and loaded it into Netscape and tada! A perfectly smooth sheep animation in one GIF file of only 21 kb. Pretty nifty. Add a LOOP control block and you can make the sheep eat away happily all day.

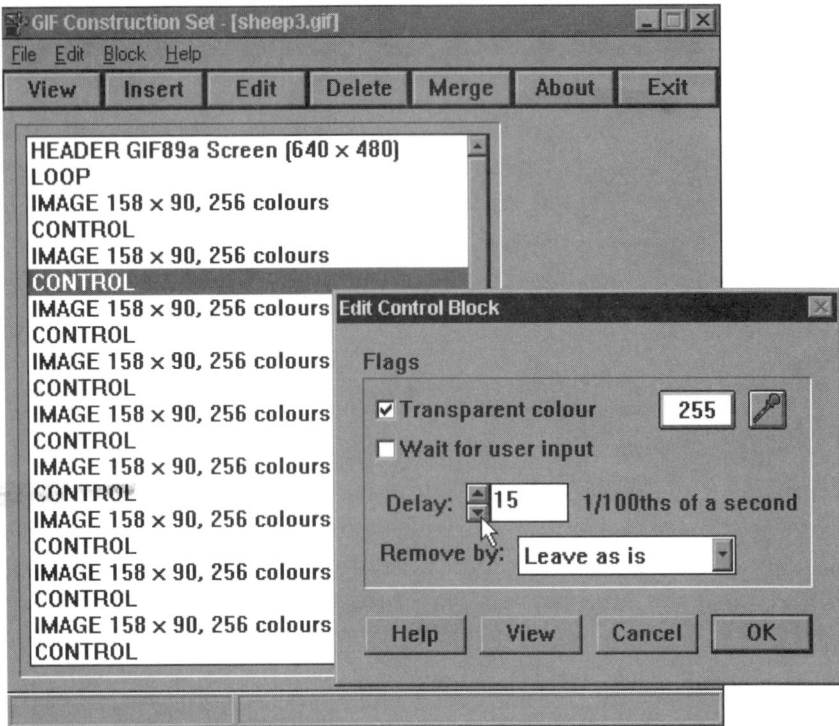

Figure 8-13: *Using the GIF Construction Set (GIFCon), you can combine several images into one and specify delay time between each image display to make an animation.*

Other things you can do with GIFCon are add text blocks to overlay an image without destroying the original image, and define image transparency.

You can get GIFCon from the Ontario company that originated it, Alchemy Mindworks, at:

http://www.mindworkshop.com/alchemy/gifcon.html

For information on how it all works and guidance in making your own animated GIFs, there's a good tutorial at:

http://member.aol.com/royalef/gifmake.htm

COMPUTER VIDEO: ON THE FRONTIER

Fortunately, on-Web movies don't come in such a bewildering variety of types as sound and image files. Unfortunately, they're a much more complex subject. Creating your own from scratch can be a daunting project, but there are nonetheless several ways you can bring the world of moving pictures to your screen via the Web.

But first a little background is in order. The professional broadcast quality video you see on your television differs from computer video in some crucial ways. Broadcast video (by the North American NTSC standard) is typically delivered at 30 frames per second with a quality of resolution that allows it to be viewed on a miniature watchband screen all the way up to a wall-size screen.

Another crucial element lies in the way those frames are presented. Each frame in a broadcast video is actually delivered in two passes or "fields," with the information in those fields interlaced, which gives a more fluid sense of movement. The amount of information a broadcast quality video with all the above specifications represents in digital form is about 30MB per second—obviously way beyond the capacity of the home PC.

Some sacrifices clearly have to be made to make videos that suit PC playing power. The first sacrifice is in frame rate. Most computer video (of the type usually used on CD-ROMs) has a frame rate of 12–15 frames per second, half that of broadcast video. The second is that they are non-interlaced, which means that the frames are each one pass of one image (which is why they are often called "animations," to distinguish them from conventional video). The third sacrifice is in size. A screen size of 320x240 pixels is the standard, and the even smaller standard of 160x120 is often used.

Finally, the information must be highly compressed. There are a number of compression algorithms available that accomplish this for video (Cinepak, TrueMotion-S, and Indeo are common choices). Any video you want to use on the Web is going to have to be compressed by one of these means. Each one has its advantages and disadvantages that affect final quality, but obviously something is going to be lost in that translation. Much of the information that is lost in compression is color palette information, though, not resolution—information that is unnecessary for viewing on the standard 256-color computer system.

VIDEO FILE FORMATS

The basic file formats you'll find on the Web are QuickTime, AVI, and MPEG. QuickTime, an Apple proprietary format originally developed for the Macintosh, is the most common type for combined audio/video. AVI, or video for Windows, is Microsoft's proprietary format. QuickTime players have now been available for Windows for some time, and there are players that easily convert AVI to QuickTime and vice versa, so the war of the McCoys and Hatfields has cooled somewhat on this front.

While MPEG is a standard for both audio and video, only recently have the two been combined in a single player for Web transmission. Most of the MPEG movies on the Web therefore do not have soundtracks. This will undoubtedly change soon, since MPEG compression provides a superior product at low bandwidth in the end—and now even offers the possibility of doing live broadcasts with real-time compression and decompression.

Watching one of these early trial broadcasts is a bit like witnessing the early days of television. (Take a look at the historic shot captured in Figure 8-14.) Frame rate varies but is invariably slow; sound quality is somewhat better. As cable modems move into the field, this will probably become an even more viable option.

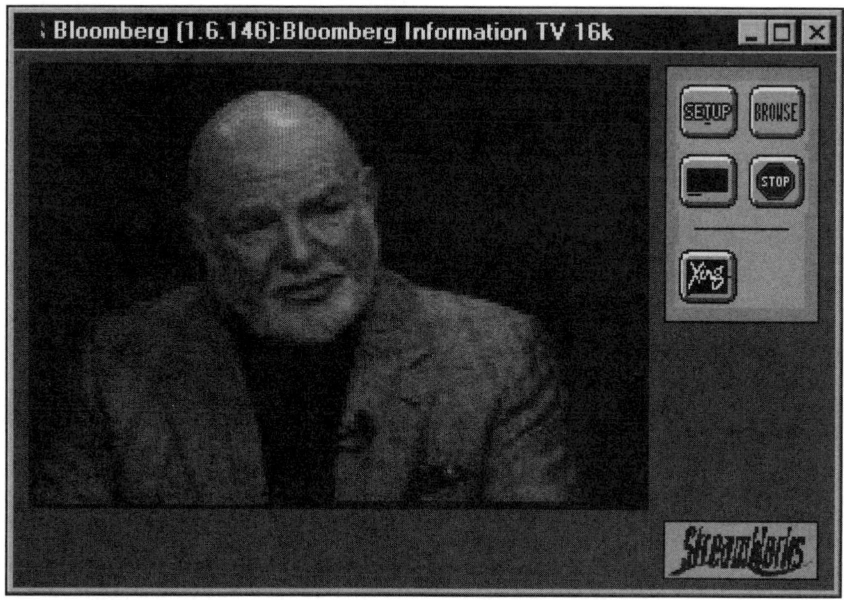

Figure 8-14: *The wave of the future: a live broadcast over the StreamWorks audio/video player captured in January of 1996.*

Converting Existing Video to Digital Format

If you have a videotape on hand that you want to put on your Web site—say a product demo—it's possible to get that converted into digital form for Web use through a service bureau. You should think about how you're going to use this first, though. If it's only for distribution over a local network and you've plenty of file space you may not care how big it is. But if it's for general Web distribution, you may want to edit it down to a reasonable size first. It's possible to do a lot with a VCR and a camcorder these days, if you're the do-it-yourself type, or you can have it done for you professionally for a fee.

So what kind of file size are we talking about? For the highest quality conversion (the type used on CD-ROM production), you can expect about 10MB per minute of video at 15 frames per second. If you want to sacrifice something on the quality end you can get this down to about 4 MB per minute at 12-15 frames per second. Any less would be pretty rough. Prices, of course, may vary, but one local company we checked with quoted $60 to $140 per minute, plus a setup fee of $250. The price and respective quality difference has to do with three things: the resolution, the frames per second, and the compression algorithm used.

If this is still way too big or expensive for you, you might consider still-frame captures from your videotape. This can be done for a reasonable fee, or you can do it yourself if you have a video capture board and compression software.

MAKING DIGITAL VIDEO

If your ambition is actually to make your own Web movies, you're going to need the biggest, fastest computer your money can buy—and lots of storage space. The basic requirements are a video capture board and video recording and editing software. Most video cards come bundled with editing packages, but quality can be highly variable. Also, you should be forewarned that setting up a video card can be a very complex operation.

Caveats aside, the process of digitizing video is called sampling, and it's similar to capturing audio. You can use a video recorder or a video camera as your source and cable it up to your video card. If you're working with U.S. television standard, you should be sure to select NTSC standard for your video, rather than PAL (which is used in Britain and other parts of the world and operates under a different line and frame standard). Capture the video raw or uncompressed if you plan to edit it. You can save it in compressed format later.

In most cases, you'll be capturing video in AVI format and converting it to QuickTime. You will not be able to save video in MPEG format in your usual video editor—if that's what you want you may have to get a service bureau to do it for you. Check with them first to see how they want you to save it. It will probably be in a format called YUV, which splits the file into three separate files, Y, U, and V, which the MPEG encoder uses to produce the MPEG file.

For do-it-yourself MPEG encoding, check out the XingMPEG Encoder. With this product you can directly compress digital files created using video capture cards, video editing software, and other popular multimedia tools. Get information at:

http://www.xingtech.com/

A good site to check for the details of digital moviemaking is the Homeport Hollywood site at:

http://www.el-dorado.ca.us/~homeport/

You'll find reviews and advice on all the latest hardware and software and lots of useful references.

Inserting Video in Web Pages

In general, movies can be inserted into your Web page using the anchor tag in your HTML page. Playing is usually external to the browser for one very good reason: Being large files, movies take quite a while to download, so the wise Web browser will always have files with movie extensions set to save rather than launch their movie player. Reference your movie files like so:

```
<A HREF="mylife.mov.">See the story of my life in live
action. (5.6 MB QuickTime movie)</A>
```

...and viewers can decide for themselves how (or if!) they want to handle it.

One of the best developments to come along in Netscape plug-ins lately, however, is players that allow you to preview movie clips by streaming in the clips while they're downloading. If you decide you don't want it after all, you won't have to waste the time downloading it.

For MPEG movies, you can get PreVU. The screen can be embedded in a Web page, so you can offer your viewers a quick preview of the movie you have to offer right on your page. Get information about PreVU at:

http://www.intervu.com/

For AVI movies, take a look at the CoolFusion stream player at:

http://www.iterated.com/coolfusn/download/cf-loadp.htm

For QuickTime, there's the ViewMovie QuickTime plug-in that supports viewing and embedding Apple QuickTime movies in Web pages. Info at:

http://www.well.com/~ivanski/download.html

To embed movies in your Web page, use the EMBED tag along with any custom attributes in the same way as we demonstrated with RealAudio.

VIRTUAL REALITY & VRML

Virtual Reality isn't exactly another medium, but another dimension. It lets you turn the flat plane of your computer monitor into a three-dimensional space (well, that is, if you're equipped with imagination). VRML not only creates the illusion of three dimensions, but also allows you to "walk" or "fly" around an object and observe it from all sides. Anyone who's ever played an arcade game or redesigned their kitchen with the aid of computer simulation should immediately know what we're talking about.

Very recently it's become possible to add virtual reality to the array of things you can do using the HTTP protocol of the World Wide Web. That's thanks to a very recent spin-off project of HTML called Virtual Reality Modeling Language (VRML).

There are several VRML browsers available on the Web. Netscape's own VRML plug-in is called Live3D. Originally called WebFX, it was developed by Paper Software and then acquired by Netscape. With the Live3D plug-in, VRML "worlds" display right within Netscape Navigator, so we're going to use that for our discussion here. (Since this is a fast-moving area of development, there may well be advances on this model by the time this book reaches you). If you don't already have Live3D, you can download it from:

http://home.netscape.com/comprod/products/navigator/live3d/download_live3d.html

In the installation process, Live3D automatically configures Netscape Navigator to recognize VRML files.

The Virtual Reality Modeling Language can be seen as a combination of basic high school geometry with elementary set theory. If it's been a long time since you thought about either of those subjects, don't worry. Like riding a bicycle, it should all come back to you. And the basic principles are all you need to keep in mind.

A VRML scene is called a *world*. There are three basic ways of viewing a VRML world, which basically represent the stages in the construction of its object. VRML objects (or nodes) start out life as *point clouds*, which look like miniature galaxies being born. A point cloud is simply the set of points that define the object's size and position in space. Connect the dots and you get a *wireframe*, which looks rather like a tinker toy construction. Wrap a surface around it and you get a *solid*. It takes less computer time to interpret and display a point cloud than a wireframe, and a wireframe is correspondingly faster to display than a solid. Therefore VRML browsers usually allow you to speed things up (or just have a look at the inner workings) by choosing to display point clouds or wireframes. (You can see that menu option revealed in Figure 8-15.)

So how do you use this in your Web pages? If you've downloaded Live3D and have it installed, you'll be ready to follow along in the simple VRML exercise we've designed to show you. This is an adaptation of a demonstration script by visionary VRML developer and pioneer Mark Pesce.

We're going to play God and create our own simple solar system. Remember that in the beginning was the word, so a VRML document, like HTML, is simply an ASCII text file, which takes the extension .WRL. Just use your favorite text editor and save your file as you go in ASCII format as solarsys.wrl.

Let's start by making a sun.

```
#VRML V.1.0 ascii
#Day 1: Create the Sun
Separator {
     Material {
           emissiveColor 1 1 0  #The Sun is yellow
     }
     Sphere {
           radius 10    #The sun is big
     }
}
```

That's all there is to it. If you save your file now and load it into Netscape, WebFX will launch and you'll see the sun rise on your new virtual world (see Figure 8-15).

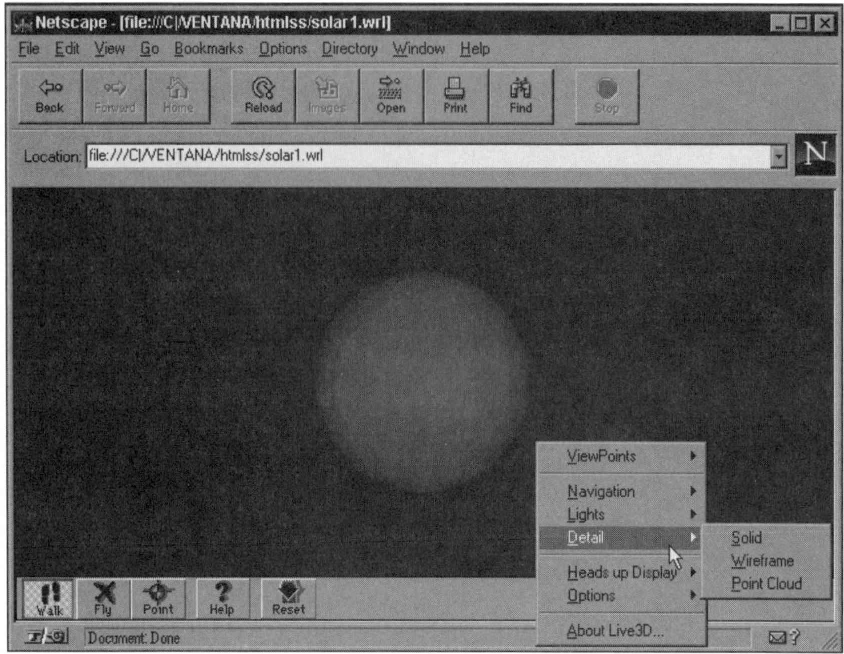

Figure 8-15: *Day 1 in our virtual world: The Sun rises.*

Let's analyze the few lines of code above. The first line is mandatory; it identifies the file as a VRML file so the browser will know what to do with it. The second line is for our information only. We'll use these comment lines liberally as we write our code, because it helps us identify easily the different parts of the file. Anything following a hash mark, up until the next return, is ignored by the browser (with the exception of that first line).

Note that the rest of the code contains three basic statements: Separator, Material, and Sphere. Each of these begins with an open bracket, contains some information, and then closes with a close bracket. "Separator" tells us this is a new element we're about to describe, and it encloses the next.two statements which will define our object. We gave the Sphere a radius of 10 and a Material to cover it.

We decided the sun should be yellow, which is defined in its red/green/blue components as 1 1 0. We chose to make it "emissive-Color" because this will approximate the way the Sun emits color. We could have chosen "diffuseColor" which would make a flat, even color surface. (We'll use that option for the Earth.)

Next we'll create the Earth. The Earth gets its own Separator, but since it is defined by its relation to the Sun, the specifications for the Earth will be contained within that first set of brackets for the Sun. As we go on it becomes clear that the Sun is the basic definition for the whole Solar System.

```
#VRML V.1.0 ascii
#Day 1: Create the Sun
Separator {
    Material {
          emissiveColor 1 1 0      #The Sun is yellow
    }
    Sphere {
          radius 10  #The sun is big
      }

    #Day 2: Create the Earth
          Separator {
              Transform {
                      translation 0 20 20 #Put it in space
                      }

              Material {
                      diffuseColor 0 0 1  #Make it blue
                      shininess 0.9       #Make it shiny
              }
              Sphere {
                      radius 2      #Make it smaller
              }
          }
}
```

Save that and load it into your browser and you now have an Earth revolving around your Sun. If you use the VRML navigation controls to move around, the objects will move in space but the Earth will maintain its proper distance from the Sun (Figure 8-16).

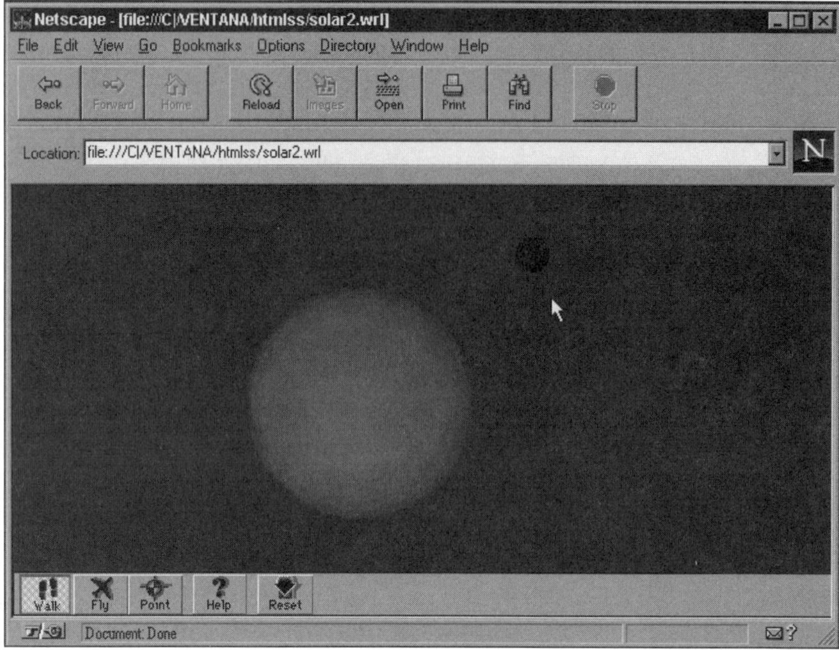

Figure 8-16: *Day 2: The Earth revolves around the Sun.*

You'll note a couple of extra things in the script for the Earth. First the Transform field, with "translation 0 20 20", which defines the location of the Earth in the x, y, and z planes in relation to the Sun. In the Material section we chose diffuseColor instead of emissiveColor, but we also added "shininess" as a property of the surface material. The Earth is largely water and reflects the Sun's light, so we thought that would be appropriate. The shininess factor can be anything from 0 (none) to 1 (max).

Note that we created a second indent level in the code for the Earth. All this indenting helps us be perfectly clear about the relationships of the statements and also helps us check that all the necessary closing brackets are there. (If your script doesn't work, the first thing you should look for is a missing bracket or one facing the wrong direction—it's a common mistake to make.) The format we're using is common practice in scripting languages, for obvious reasons of clarity.

Now it's time for a little romance. Let's put that old devil Moon up in the sky. The Moon is defined by its relationship to the Earth, and the Earth and the Moon are both contained by the Sun, so we'll create another sub-level for the Moon within the Earth's sphere.

```
#VRML V.1.0 ascii
#Day 1: Create the Sun
Separator {
    Material {
          emissiveColor 1 1 0      #The Sun is yellow
    }
    Sphere {
          radius 10  #The sun is big
    }

    #Day 2: Create the Earth
          Separator {
                Transform {
                      translation 0 20 20 #Put it in space
                }

                Material {
                      diffuseColor 0 0 1  #Make it blue
                      shininess 0.9       #Make it shiny
                }
                Sphere {
                      radius 2      #Make it smaller
                }

                      #Day 3: Create the Moon
                      Separator {
                              Transform {
                                      translation 4 4 0 #Put it
                                      in space
                              }
                              Material {
                                      diffuseColor 1 0 0   #Make
                                      it red
                                      shininess 0.3         #Make
                                                     it shine
                              }
```

```
                              Sphere {
                                    radius 1      #Make it tiny
                              }
                        }
               }
  }
```

If you closed all your brackets and spelled everything important correctly, when you load it into your browser you should have your solar system as in Figure 8-17. There are just a few things more we'd like to do to this before leaving you on your own to play with it. Since this is supposed to be about HTML not VRML, let's get back to what we can do linking this to other Web resources.

It would be kind of appropriate to link the Sun to a page about the weather. Just as with an image map, it's the essential geometric dimensions we need to make the Sun work as a link. They're all contained for us in the definition of the Sphere. Therefore, we wrap our link around the Sphere definition. We'll take just that section of code to show you how it's done:

```
DEF SUN WWWAnchor {
          name "http://www.nj.com/weather/
currcons.cgi?location=San+Diego"
            #link the sun to the weather page
          description "San Diego 5-day Weather Forecast"

                Sphere {
                radius 10    #Make a large sun
                }
}
```

In this case we've made the link to the five-day weather forecast for San Diego, which we can get from the New Jersey Online Weather service (home page: http://www.nj.com/weather/index.html). The "DEF SUN WWWAnchor" sets up the anchor, with brackets that surround the Sphere definition. The "name" element gives the link destination and the "description" element specifies the words to appear when the link is active. When you pass your cursor over the sun, the destination appears on the screen. If we had not supplied a "description" for the anchor, the

URL would appear, but since the link is to a database search, we thought it would be nicer to provide something a little less cryptic. The description line, with the text we want to appear in quotes, allows us to customize it with our own explanation of the link. Objects in a VRML scene can be linked not just to Web pages, but to other types of files as well, such as sound or movie files or another VRML world.

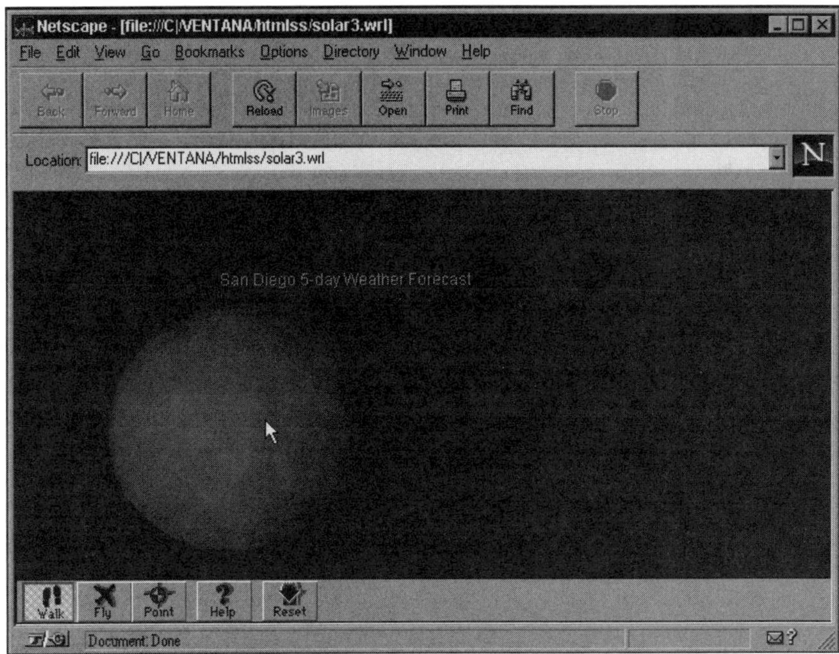

Figure 8-17: *Day 3: The Sun, the Earth, and the Moon. The Sun is hyperlinked to a weather page, whose destination appears on the screen. We've changed the light source on the menu to provide shading.*

Link an HTML page to a VRML page in the usual way with the anchor tag, like so:

```
<A HREF="solarysys.wrl">Enter my solar system.</A> (A virtual
reality world!)
```

Again, it's polite to let people know this is a link to a virtual reality site, so they'll know if they're equipped to handle it.

Well, as you can see, defining shapes like spheres, cubes, cones, and so on is easy. But you can imagine that more complicated shapes (like the Sphinx) would be a bit more difficult to construct. There's no reason to go reinventing the wheel every time you want some new shape, however. Fortunately, cooperation is the name of the game and there are libraries of VRML objects that you can access to find constructs that fit your needs or that you can build on. And there are lots of other levels of sophistication you can add to a virtual reality world, including different light sources to create more realistic shading (we did this as a simple menu option in Figure 8-17) and different camera positions to provide alternative perspectives on the scene. But we'll leave you to explore all that on your own.

For more information about VRML, visit the VRML Repository at the San Diego Supercomputer Center:

http://www.sdsc.edu/vrml/

The details of the VRML language are archived at:

http://www.w3.org/hypertext/WWW/MarkUp/VRML

JAVA

One of the more exciting developments on the Web recently is *Java*. You're probably heard a lot of the hype about this, but you can be forgiven if you're still scratching your head about what it means. Java provides a way of embedding mini-applications, appropriately called "applets," into an HTML file, so that different kinds of executable multimedia files, animations, or other applications can be brought to your desktop embedded in a Web document. When used well, Java scripts can also decrease the load on the server by doing the work formerly done by the server.

We can't possibly tell you all you need to know to begin programming in Java here. But what we can do is give you a taste for it and an idea about what's involved. If this gets you excited, you can take it from there.

It may surprise you that you don't really have to write a line of programming code to insert a Java applet in your HTML page. We're going to begin our simplified Java tutorial with a little exercise that shows you how you can use a Java applet we've provided on the Online Companion and alter it to your taste. Along the way you'll pick up enough basic understanding of Java to comprehend the way it all works and the ways you can use it.

A Simple Java Tutorial

Let's take a simple Java script called CrazyText. (The script, which was kindly provided to us by Patrick Taylor, can be found on this book's Online Companion.) Its purpose is to animate a short text message. The letters of the message dance and change into a rainbow of colors on your screen. We've attempted to capture this in our figures, but you'll have to imagine its full multi-hued action for now. The Java code for this is fairly short and simple, but we won't bother with that just yet. Let's just look at the HTML file that calls up the applet. Here it is:

```
<HEAD>
<TITLE>CrazyText</TITLE>
</HEAD>
<BODY>
<HR>
<APPLET CODE="CrazyText.class" WIDTH=150 HEIGHT=50>
<param name=text value="Java">
</APPLET>
<HR>
<A HREF="CrazyText.java">The source.</A>
</BODY>
</HTML>
```

The action is obviously all contained between the tags <APPLET> ... </APPLET>. The file that contains the binary code for the applet is called "CrazyText.class", therefore code="CrazyText.class". The size of the window in which the applet will be displayed is defined with the width and height attributes. The second line of the applet information clearly defines what kind of message will be displayed (in this case, text rather than image or something else) and what the text of that message is (the word "Java").

Take this file just as it is and load it into Netscape and chances are it'll do nothing at all. Hmmm.... What's missing? Well, first of all, this is not the code, it's just the file that *loads* the code. So unless you have that file called CrazyText.class for it to find, the browser can't do anything with it. The file called CrazyText.class is itself dependent on a whole set of Java files that defines the Java protocol and a lot of other basic things a Java applet needs to run.

So what do we have to do to make this work? Rummage around on the Online Companion and you'll find two files called CrazyText.class and CrazyText.java. Copy these files into the directory where you keep your HTML files. Now, load the file into Netscape Navigator, and voilà! Netscape finds the files it needs to run the applet. See Figure 8-18.

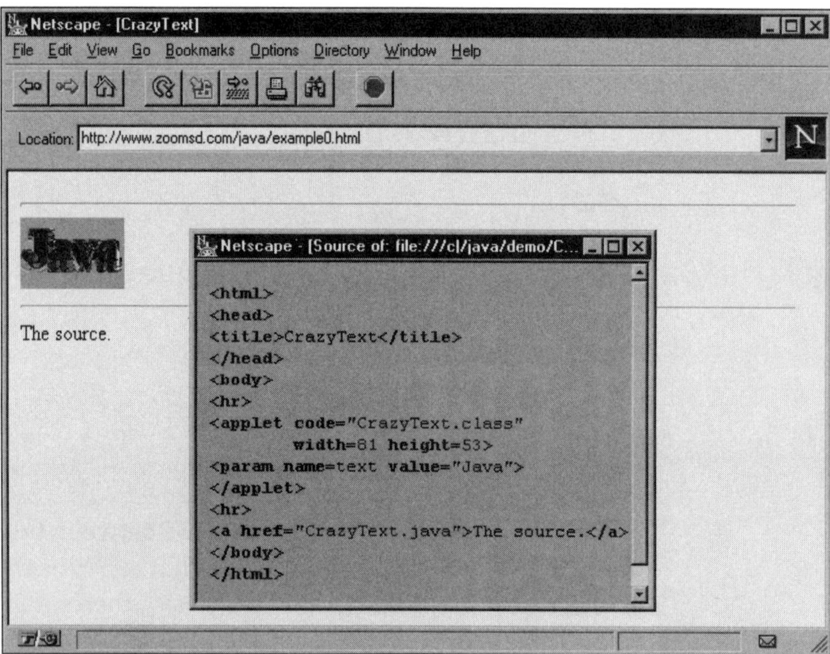

Figure 8-18: *The CrazyText applet running in Netscape.*

TIP

If you intend to post Java files on your Web site, first check to see if the server is Java-enabled. The administrator will have had to set up the basic configuration and Java protocol on the host machine. If your administrator tells you it is set up, then post the .JAVA and .CLASS files, along with the HTML file in which they're embedded, to your online directory. It's a good idea to make a separate subdirectory called Java off your main directory, so you'll have room to experiment with this.

Now, it only takes a little sporting sense to wonder if we couldn't change the message text. Let's try changing "Java" to something like "Happy Birthday." The result (which we assure you is quite colorful) is in Figure 8-19. The code, altered just a little, is below:

```
<TITLE>Happy Birthday</TITLE>
<HR>
<APPLET CODE="CrazyText.class"
        WIDTH=250 HEIGHT=50>
<param name=text value="Happy Birthday">
</APPLET>
<HR>
<A HREF="CrazyText.java">The source.</A>
```

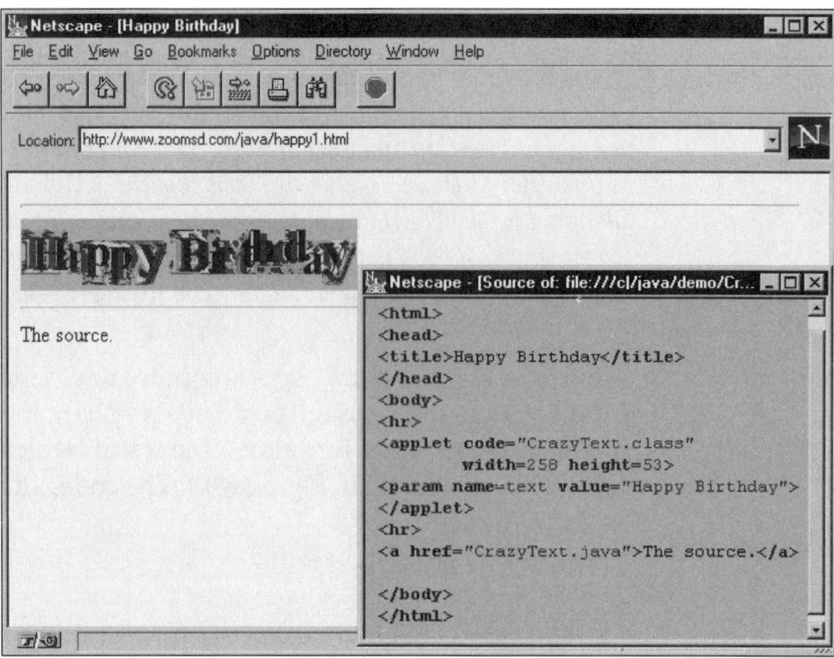

Figure 8-19: *We've changed the message on the CrazyText applet by changing the text parameter.*

Note that besides changing the "value" of the text message, we change the width of the message a little, to account for the fact that "Happy Birthday" is a bit longer than "Java." (This applet actually contains a very nifty feature: When you view it with the Java viewer that comes with the Java Developer's Kit, you can click on the image and it will tell you what size window it needs.) We also changed the title of the page to "Happy Birthday." But the source code is exactly the same. In other words, it's using the same original binary code file, just putting in a couple of different parameters we gave it. We didn't have to touch the source code at all.

About that source code.... You'll notice a link in the above page code to a file called "CrazyText.java" which is identified as the source. The applet doesn't really need this to run, since all the computer is interested in is CrazyText.class. That's because CrazyText.class is a binary file in machine-readable format—which means the computer can read it but we can't.

CrazyText.java is the human-readable file program file created by the author of this applet. Once the program was written, it had to be "compiled" with a Java compilation program to convert the programmer's instructions into binary, thus creating the .CLASS file. But if we want to see the source code that creates this applet, we have to look at the CrazyText.java file. So let's just take a peek at this now. After some basic comments by the author about what the applet does, we find these initial lines:

```
import java.awt.Graphics;
import java.awt.Font;
import java.awt.FontMetrics;
import java.awt.Event;
import java.awt.Color;

public class CrazyText extends java.applet.Applet implements
Runnable {

 // parameters
 String text = "Java"; // string to be displayed
 int delay = 100; // # of milliseconds between updates
 int delta = 5; // "craziness" factor: max pixel offset
 boolean clear = false; // should background be cleared on
update
 String fontName = "TimesRoman";
 int fontSize = 36;
 boolean fontBold = true;
 boolean fontItalic = false;
```

All of the initial lines beginning with "import" are the basic Java definitions upon which this program builds—the things CrazyText needed to find, either on the server or in the browser's files in order to operate. Then there's a necessary statement that this applet is an extension of the Java applet application.

After that we see a section called "parameters." Aha! We already know a little about parameters because we just used one to change our message text. If you look down through the list of parameters, you'll see that there are parameters for defining the font name, the font size, the frequency of the action, and the offset in pixels of the text as it changes location on the screen. Each of these parameters has a default value. Now think back to how we changed the text message above and you may infer, correctly, that it's possible to change all these parameters the same way we did the message. Try it. Here's one variation:

```
<APPLET CODE="CrazyText.class"
        WIDTH=250 HEIGHT=50>
<param name=text value="Happy Birthday">
<param name=fontName value="Arial">
<param name=fontSize value="48">
<param name=delay value="200">
<param name=delta value="10">
</APPLET>
```

In this variation, which you see in Figure 8-20, we decided to use Arial 48-point font. We slowed down the "frenzy level" of the applet by doubling the default delay value of 100. And just to see what happened, we changed the "craziness factor" to 10 from the default 5 (it made the whole image a tad larger as it bounces about).

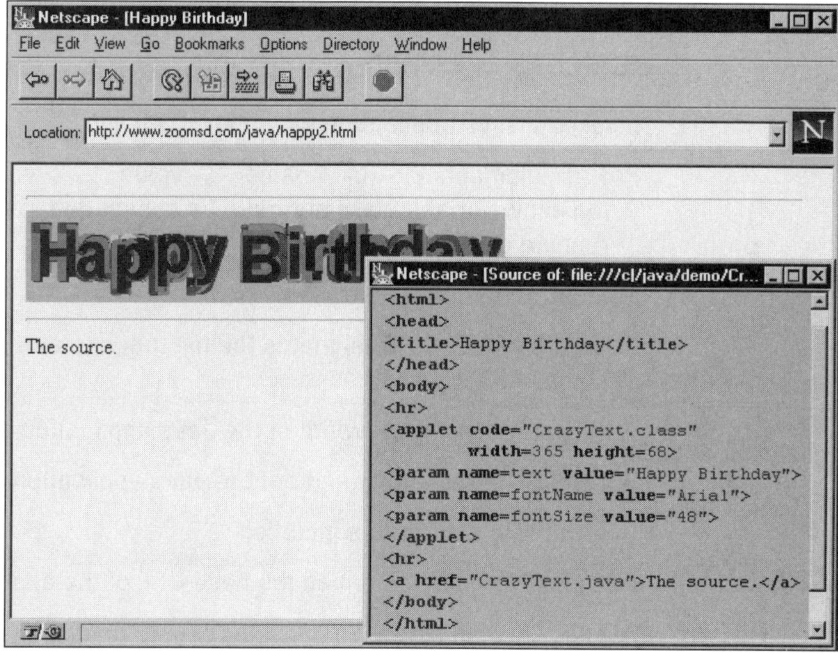

Figure 8-20: *The Happy Birthday applet customized with several new parameters.*

Notice that we didn't need to know anything about how to write the Java code ourselves in order to use this applet. We only had to interpret a couple of instructions in the code and understand what it needs to operate.

You can use this same technique with any publicly available Java applet, when the source code is available, and it's a very good place to start if you want to learn a little about it. As Java is so new on the Web, many Java programmers, in the spirit of learning from each other in cooperative development, have made applets like this available for public use. If you want to use an applet that you find, you'll need the .CLASS file for the applet for it to work, and the .JAVA file if you want to see all the parameters that you can change. You can write your own HTML file to embed it using the APPLET tag.

HTML Tag

<APPLET> ... </APPLET>

Invokes a Java application within an HTML file.

PARAM elements <PARAM name=".." value="..."> within the tag allow variable parameters to be substituted in the running of the applet.

Mandatory attributes are:

CODE="file.class" Designates the file that contains the compiled Applet subclass.

WIDTH=w The initial width of the Java application in pixels.

HEIGHT=h The initial height of the Java application in pixels.

Other possible attributes include:

CODEBASE="..." Specifies the base URL of the applet.

ALT="..." Specifies the character data to be displayed if the browser understands the APPLET tag but can't run it.

NAME="..." Specifies a name for the applet instance, which allows applets on the same page to reference each other.

ALIGN="bottom/middle/top/left/right" Specifies alignment of image in relation to the screen margins and/or text.

VSPACE=v Specifies a clear vertical space (top and bottom of image) in pixels.

HSPACE=p Specifies a clear horizontal space (left and right of image) in pixels.

TIP

If you alter anything in the .JAVA file for an applet, it needs to be compiled again to create a new .CLASS file to reflect your changes. For that, and to develop your own Java applets, you'll need the compiler that comes with the Java Developer's Kit or the new browser-based Java Workshop. Both are available from Sun Microsystems at: ***http://java.sun.com/***

We'll leave you on your own to design the birthday card to go with this.

JAVASCRIPT

JavaScript is a simplified form of the Java language that Netscape is developing in conjunction with Sun Microsystems to allow programmers to write scripts using the Java language without having to compile them into .CLASS files. If you've already done some programming before or are not adverse to learning a little, you may find this a useful tool.

JavaScripts are embedded directly into HTML pages. They can be made to respond to events, such as the user clicking a mouse or entering data into a form. For instance, if form input is invalid or incomplete, a JavaScript program can respond with an alert message. This is done without having to contact the server and execute a program off the server.

The down side is that because JavaScript does not depend on class files, they cannot build on previous classes and definitions. They're also not as susceptible to the kind of amateur tinkering with parameters we did with the CrazyText applet—although you can borrow them wholesale. Without getting into programming details, here's an example of a teeny weeny JavaScript you can embed in your Web page:

```
<center><p><script>document.write("The current time is
"+Date()+"<P>")</script>
```

Put that at the top of your document and load it into Netscape and you'll see a readout of the time, like so:

The current time is Fri Apr 05 16:50:14 1996

We'll start getting into a little programming in the next chapter, after which you may be better equipped to understand what's going on here. If you're interested in learning JavaScript you should start with the tutorials on Netscape's pages or go to Sun's Java pages at http://java.sun.com/. JavaScript is still in development, so the format is subject to change.

MOVING ON

We hope we've succeeded in taking the fear out of tackling multimedia in this chapter and sparked some new ideas to spice up your Web pages. Undoubtedly, as you develop a taste for this and learn to use multimedia files, you'll find lots more technical stuff to get immersed in to perfect your Web act.

In the next chapter we'll be tackling some more stuff that often looks more complicated than it is. We'll be talking about how to design forms for feedback from your Web visitors. In the process, we'll dive into a little programming basics so you'll be able to fulfill all your dreams of data collection and two-way communication with your Web site visitors.

9

Forms, Feedback & cgi-bin

Way, way back in Chapter 2, we advised you to hold off incorporating any code into your pages that you don't understand. But by now we hope you've learned enough to begin to understand the kinds of magic a little embedded code can do for you. It's time to take the gloves off.

It's probably been a while since you read Chapter 2, "Getting Down to Work" (it's certainly been a while since we *wrote* it!), so you may not remember the nine lines of code from the HalSoft validation service that we showed at the end of the chapter. To save the wear-and-tear of your flipping back seven chapters, here are those lines again:

```
<FORM ACTION="http://www.hal.com/hal-bin/html-check.pl"
METHOD="POST">
<INPUT NAME="recommended" VALUE="0" TYPE="hidden">
<INPUT NAME="level" VALUE="2" TYPE="hidden">
<INPUT NAME="input" VALUE="0" TYPE="hidden">
<INPUT NAME="esis" VALUE="0" TYPE="hidden">
<INPUT NAME="render" VALUE="0" TYPE="hidden">
<INPUT NAME="URLs" VALUE="YOUR URL HERE" TYPE="hidden">
<INPUT TYPE="submit" VALUE="Check my code">
</FORM>
```

The point of that code was that you could add it to one of your pages, and the result would be a little button like Figure 9-1. Click on it, and HalSoft would swing into action.

Figure 9-1: *HalSoft's form submit button.*

By the end of this chapter you'll understand not only what that simple bit of code does, but all about how to construct your own forms—and a great deal more about how you can turn your Web pages into a two-way info-bahn.

Encouraging User Feedback

One of the other topics we'll be getting to later in this chapter in the section, "Monitoring Access Using cgi-bin Scripts," is the Web equivalent of your Nielsen ratings. Since the Web is a computer artifact from the get-go, your "ratings" can be measured without having to recruit families all across the country, install special equipment in their homes, and swear them to secrecy. Information about who visits your site, where they came from and how long they stayed, is all logged in your server. Nothing comes more naturally to a computer than to store this easily obtained information.

What you will never find in that data store, of course, is information about what your users thought of your site. If you're curious about that (and who isn't?), you'll need to get the users to give you feedback—and with the use of forms, that can be very simple indeed.

Before we go slamming into the details of form creation, let's cheat a bit and work through a very quick exercise that you can do for yourself in a matter of minutes. The idea is to get you thinking "Hey—this form business is a piece of cake! Why didn't I try it before?" That way the "form newbies" will be encouraged, hopefully, to keep reading. Those who never had a problem with forms anyway can skip a couple of pages, feeling smug.

Strip those lines of HalSoft code above down to the bare bones, and you get:

```
<FORM ACTION=.... METHOD=....>
<INPUT NAME=.... VALUE=.... TYPE=....>
<INPUT NAME=.... VALUE=.... TYPE=....>
<INPUT NAME=.... VALUE=.... TYPE=....>
:
</FORM>
```

So, okay, there's a <FORM>....</FORM> container, inside which we have a series of INPUT lines, each of which has attributes NAME, VALUE, and TYPE. The FORM as a whole also has one attribute called ACTION and another called METHOD. Well, this is not, as they say, rocket science. An input TYPE is the kind of feedback you allow your users to send you, and the simplest is "text," meaning just a standard data field in which they can write something. The input NAME is whatever ID you decide to give to that input element so you can recognize it when you receive it, and the input VALUE is whatever the user actually enters. If you want a default value, such as "Great site, man!" you can declare that the input VALUE. Otherwise, the input has no VALUE until the user gives it one, so you just leave that attribute out. An "easy-as-pie" feedback form, therefore, would seem to be:

```
<P>So whaddya think of my page?
<FORM ACTION=.... METHOD=...>
<INPUT NAME="comment" TYPE="text">
</FORM>
```

When this form is "submitted"—by a user entering a comment and pressing the Enter key—data is sent as what's called a "name=value pair." The NAME of the only INPUT in this form is "comment," so if the user enters "I hate the puce color" that string will become the INPUT VALUE, and the entire data output of this form will be "comment=I+hate+the+puce+color." Note that, as nature abhors a vacuum, HTTP data streams abhor white space.

There's just one detail missing here—we haven't told this form what to *do* with the data. That's where the FORM ACTION comes in. We'll have a great deal to say about ACTION and METHOD later on, but for now just accept that one possible action is to use the mailto: protocol to send the data to your own e-mail inbox, and the METHOD needs to be set to "post" so that it goes off without having to be attached to anything. If your e-mail address happens to be "reader@ventana.books.com," a genuine, finished, working, feedback form is:

```
<P>So whaddya think of my page?
<FORM ACTION="mailto:reader@ventana.books.com" METHOD="post">
<INPUT NAME="comment" TYPE="text">
</FORM>
```

Your users' comments will pour into your mailbox with the sender field of the e-mail header correctly filled in with their names and e-mail addresses (or whatever story they told their Mail and News/Identity preference panels). The subject header will be "Form posted from Mozilla." Admittedly the message will be raw unprocessed name=value pairs, and the messages will have a curious MIME type, but they'll be perfectly understandable. Now what's so hard about that?

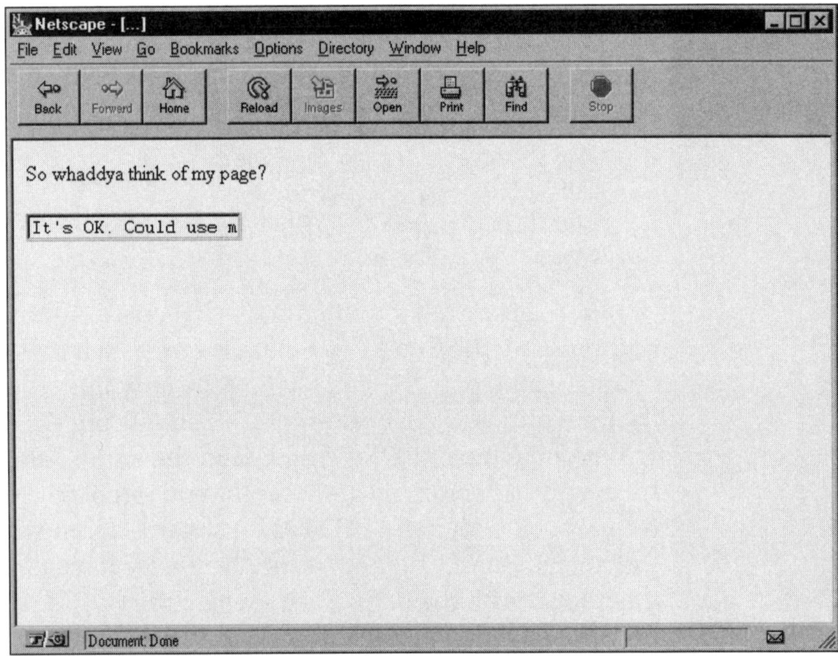

Figure 9-2: *The "easy-as-pie" basic form.*

That easy-as-pie form really does work—in Netscape. Better not rely on that style for all browsers, however. Later in this chapter we'll be indicating several ways in which this very crude form submission protocol can be improved.

Creating Forms

Backing up a bit, here's your handy reference to all the FORMS tags:

HTML Tag

<FORM> .... </FORM>

Container for a form. Can contain anything except another form, and is expected to contain at least one INPUT, SELECT, or TEXTAREA element. Attributes are:

ACTION="...url..." specifies the URL to which data output from the form is to be sent. A FORM *must* have an ACTION attribute, but it does not have to be a fully qualified URL. Forms frequently pass data to binary scripts in their immediate vicinity, referenced by relative path.

METHOD="GET/POST". GET (the default) sends data as a query string *?name1=value1&name2=value2&....etc.* appended to the ACTION URL. GET data appears on the server as the environment variable QUERY_STRING. Data sent by the POST method appears as "standard input" to the binary program handling it, and the length of the data stream is the environment variable CONTENT_LENGTH. POST is recommended *provided the server is configured to handle it.* More about this in the text of this chapter.

ENCTYPE="mime type/subtype" specifies the MIME-type of data to be sent by the POST method. It should be *application/x-www-form-urlencoded* (the default) or *multipart/form-data* for the special Netscape file upload form type. However, it can be whatever you decide—see later discussion.

Some other FORM attributes were proposed for HTML 3.0 but have not been implemented. Here are the details of that other important FORM tag.

HTML Tag

<INPUT>

Defines a field of the form, usually but not always user-accessible, that will normally contribute one name=value pair to the data output. There is no </INPUT> container. Attributes are:

NAME="name" is the author-defined label that will become the *name* component of a name=value pair. The *value* will generally be the user input to this element. Every INPUT *must* have a NAME, except for Submit and Reset buttons that don't actually send data.

VALUE="default value." Can be a pre-set value for the input element, overridable by the user. More often, there is no defined INPUT VALUE. The exception is input of type "radio", which *must* have a VALUE.

TYPE="input type." Every INPUT *must* have a TYPE.

Universally allowable INPUT types are "checkbox", "hidden", "image", "password", "radio", "reset", "submit," and "text". Other types are "file", for a Netscape file upload, "range", and "jot". These are all explained in the next section, together with their own attributes.

Meanwhile, here's the next exhibit in the FORMS gallery—the tag you need to create a pop-up list.

HTML Tag

<SELECT> .... </SELECT>

The select element is almost like a more complicated INPUT TYPE. It allows the user to create form data by selecting from an author-defined OPTION list. On Netscape, and pretty much all other browsers, the SELECT element appears as a pop-up list. Attributes are:

NAME="name" is the author-defined label that will be the *name* component of the name=value pair generated by the SELECT element. The *value* will be the OPTION selected at the time the form is submitted. Every SELECT *must* have a NAME.

SIZE=n is normally assumed to be 1, presenting one OPTION at a time in the pop-up menu format. If SIZE is other than 1, n OPTIONS are displayed at a time in a scroll box. If there are fewer than n defined OPTIONS, the scroll box will not only be non-scrolling but will also contain white space beneath the OPTION list.

MULTIPLE. If this attribute is set, the user may make more than one selection from the OPTION list, using the Windows standard Click-Ctrl-Click for non-contiguous items, Click-Shift-Click for a whole contiguous range. The data is sent as a set of name=value pairs, with NAME repeated for each of the selected VALUEs.

There are some other proposed attributes for SELECT—notably a SRC= "..." to enable an image to be displayed, with the OPTION list being a list of "hotspots."

<OPTION> item</OPTION>

Container for an item on the OPTION list. At least two of these elements are expected to be included within a <SELECT> container, to provide the list for the user. When a list item is selected, the "item" label is normally used as the value, or as one of the values, when the form is submitted. Attributes are:

SELECTED This attribute, if set for an item on the OPTION list, defines that item as the default value of the element. Write this as <OPTION SELECTED>item</OPTION>. In a MULTIPLE list, more than one item may be SELECTED.

VALUE="special value" If used, this makes the item pass this value to the data output instead of its own label.

An example of the use of OPTION VALUE is a multilingual form, where the output might be processed by the same binary program regardless of whether the form was submitted in English or Spanish, let's say. User choice from a list of months could be output as "01" whether "January" or "Enero" was what was actually picked.

Other attributes have been proposed for SELECT, including DISABLED for displaying a non-selectable, grayed-out item. And now we've arrived at the final tag that FORMS use—the free-form playground for your users to romp around in.

HTML Tag

<TEXTAREA> .... </TEXTAREA>

Container for a "free-form" scroll box in which the user may enter data longer than would be practicable in a text input element. Attributes are:

NAME="name" is the author-defined label that will be the *name* component of the name=value pair generated by the TEXTAREA. The *value* will be the user input. Every TEXTAREA *must* have a NAME.

COLS=c Defines the width of the TEXTAREA. Every TEXTAREA *must* have a COLS definition.

ROWS=r Defines the height of the TEXTAREA. Every TEXTAREA *must* have a ROWS definition.

WRAP=off/virtual/physical. A standard TEXTAREA has no word-wrap capability, and WRAP=off is still the default. However, Netscape allows WRAP=virtual, meaning that text wraps automatically on the user's screen but the line breaks are not sent in the data stream; and WRAP=physical, meaning that line breaks generated by auto-wrapping become part of the data stream (they will look like %0D%0A).

Other attributes proposed are ALIGN, DISABLED, ERROR.

NOTE: The TEXTAREA element has no meaningful VALUE attribute defining its default value. Instead, anything placed between the <TEXTAREA> .... </TEXTAREA> tags becomes the default text, and will become the VALUE if left undisturbed by the user.

All those definitions are, admittedly, quite a lot to swallow, so let's sum it all up in a way that lets you see the forest rather than a pile of trees. There are three principal styles for user input to a form:

- INPUT, which comes in at least eight types
- SELECT, which limits the user to a choice between a finite number of things
- And TEXTAREA, which is completely free-form.

Here's a bare-bones form using one of each:

```
<FORM ACTION="mailto:reader@ventana.books.com" METHOD="POST">

<INPUT NAME="usrname" TYPE="text">

<SELECT NAME="season">
     <OPTION>Spring</OPTION>
     <OPTION SELECTED>Summer</OPTION>
     <OPTION>Autumn</OPTION>
     <OPTION>Winter</OPTION>
</SELECT>

<TEXTAREA NAME="sonnet" COLS=66 ROWS=9>
</TEXTAREA>

</FORM>
```

This represents a form offering a simple text field for the user to enter his or her name, a pop-up selector to pick a favorite season—with Summer pre-selected—and a large area in which the user may compose and submit a sonnet. There it is, in Figure 9-3.

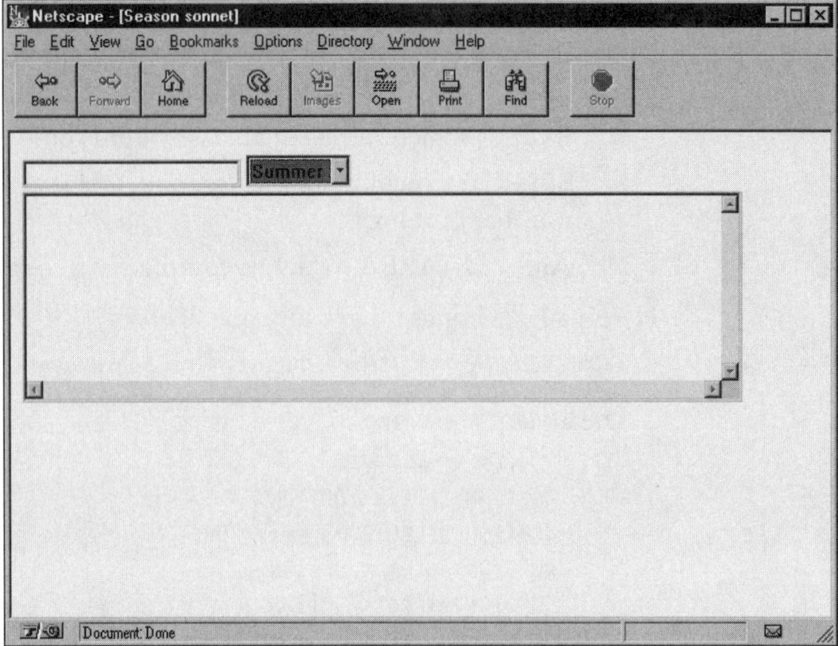

Figure 9-3: *The bare-bones sonnet form.*

That's fine as a reference to form structure, but we need to fix it up a bit to make it presentable. First we should add some ordinary text so the user has some idea what's expected, and then we should add a SUBMIT button. Up to now, we've been assuming that the form gets submitted when the user presses the Enter key. That's true for a single text input field, but it's very sloppy practice and it won't work at all if the user's last act is to compose a sonnet. When the user is in the TEXTAREA, Enter simply makes a line break.

One of the permitted INPUT TYPE elements is "submit", and that gives us what we need immediately. Here's a second attempt:

```
<H2>The Season Sonnet Sampler</H2>
<FORM ACTION="mailto:reader@ventana.books.com" METHOD=POST>

<P>Please enter your name:
<INPUT NAME="usrname" TYPE="text">

<P>Pick your favorite season:
```

```
<SELECT NAME="season">
     <OPTION>Spring</OPTION>
     <OPTION SELECTED>Summer</OPTION>
     <OPTION>Autumn</OPTION>
     <OPTION>Winter</OPTION>
</SELECT>

<P><TEXTAREA NAME="sonnet" COLS=66 ROWS=9>
Compose your sonnet in this space
</TEXTAREA>

<P><INPUT TYPE="submit">
</FORM>
```

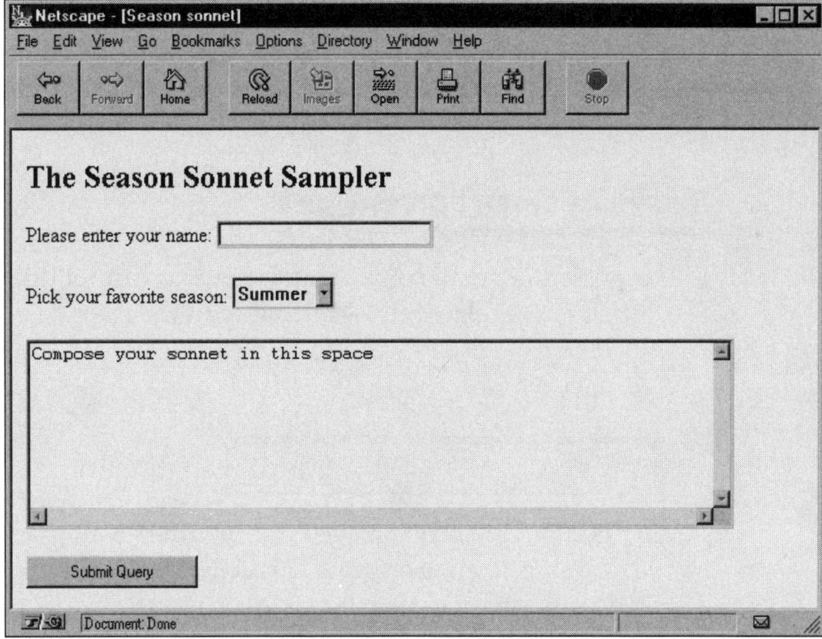

Figure 9-4: *A slightly more elaborate sonnet sampler.*

A plausible example of the data output from that form might be:

```
usrname=William+Browne&
season=Summer&
sonnet=There+is+no+season+such+delight+can+
```

```
bring+%0D%0A+As+summer,+autumn,+winter+and+
the+spring.
```

This would assume that the user had deleted the default text "Enter a sonnet in this space" before composing. It would also assume that our page had miraculously had a visitor from the 17th Century!

Tip

While you're developing a form, and you want to keep track of exactly what data output you are creating, change the ACTION to point to the local HTML file you're working on, and the METHOD to "GET". Then, when you submit the form, you will actually see the query string appear in the Netscape location window, attached to the URL. Example: <FORM ACTION="file:///C|/NETSCAPE/FORM2.HTM" METHOD="GET">

Form INPUT Types

Now for the details of what you can and cannot do with all those INPUT TYPE elements—starting with the two we've already met.

Text

INPUT TYPE="text", as we've seen, offers a simple rectangular box for free-form user input. VALUE is optional with this TYPE. By default, the onscreen box is 20 characters wide, but user input is unrestricted—the text line scrolls horizontally *ad infinitum.* It is highly desirable to place a restriction on this:

- The attribute MAXLENGTH=m restricts user input to m characters.
- The attribute SIZE=s makes an onscreen box s characters wide. If SIZE is less than MAXLENGTH, horizontal scroll is permitted up to a total of MAXLENGTH characters. Word-wrap is never possible in a text input box.

HTML 3.0 proposes the attribute for this and other FORM elements "DIR=ltr/rtl" to indicate left-to-right/right-to-left reading options, needed for some languages.

Submit Button

Submit Query

INPUT TYPE="submit", the other type we've already used, simply provides a way for the user to submit the form by clicking on a nice onscreen button bearing the words "Submit Query." However, it does not have to say that. The attribute VALUE="Whatever" causes "Whatever" to be the text on the Submit button.

A submit input-type with no NAME attribute creates no name=value pair of its own. It merely sends other name=value pairs on their way.

However, this type may be given a name, in which case it does create a name=value pair. Any number of Submit buttons with different names and/or values may be present in a form, creating a "pushbutton field" for instant user select (there's a mild example in Figure 9-7). In a sense, they act like glorified radio buttons, since only one of them could ever contribute to a given data stream.

Reset Button

Reset

INPUT TYPE="reset" places a Reset button on the screen. If the user clicks on it, it clears all form fields and resets all options to their initial values. It's considered polite to include a Reset button whenever there's a Submit button—almost always, in other words.

- VALUE is the only valid attribute for the "reset" input type. The attribute VALUE="Whatever" causes "Whatever" to be the text on the Reset button. "Oops," perhaps...

PASSWORD

INPUT TYPE="password" acts in every way like "text", including the limitations of SIZE and MAXLENGTH, but the screen echoes asterisks or some other character to prevent onlookers from seeing a secret password.

CHECKBOX

INPUT TYPE="checkbox" creates a checkbox onscreen that may default to checked or unchecked at the whim of the author. This type of INPUT has no VALUE: Uniquely, it sends the name=value pair "name=on" if checked at Submit time, and sends *no data at all* if unchecked. Important points are:

- Even though a checkbox has no VALUE, it must have a NAME.
- The attribute CHECKED causes the checkbox to appear checked by default. Write this <INPUT TYPE="checkbox" NAME="St. Felix" CHECKED>.
- A Reset by the user causes a checkbox to return to its original state.

RADIO BUTTONS

INPUT TYPE="radio" creates a radio button onscreen. Obviously, a single radio button is meaningless, although Netscape will create one if asked. Sets of radio buttons are declared as sets by having a NAME in common. Important points are:

- Every radio button *must* have a VALUE, and it is *that* which is passed as data together with the NAME that all radio buttons in the set have in common.

- The attribute CHECKED, given to one radio button in the set, defines which one will be selected by default. If more than one in a set is checked, the set will not function correctly. If none are checked by default, the set will send no data unless the user selects one.
- A Reset by the user will restore a set of radio buttons to its default condition.

Hidden

INPUT TYPE="hidden" is unique in that it accepts no user input—in fact, the user is not aware of its existence unless he examines the source code. Some uses for a hidden input are:

- To signal which of several Web pages that share the same processing program is submitting data (although that could also be determined from an environment variable, in general).
- To pass on an audit trail of previous transactions on a Web site. This would apply to forms that are created "on the fly" by a binary program in response to some previous feedback from the user. The hidden field might, for example, pass on the information that the user is ordering goods in a certain currency, or has already seen records 1-30 of a database (the HTTP protocol is "stateless"—meaning that this type of information is not normally preserved once a transaction is done).
- To convey information that the form's author has set semi-permanently, and which is of no interest to the user. The HalSoft code, with which we started this chapter, is a perfect example. The *level, input, esis, and render* fields are all parameters that you can set to control *HalSoft's* behavior. HalSoft therefore needs these in the data stream, but there is no point in displaying them onscreen. The only displayed part of the *HalSoft* code is the Submit button, whose VALUE is "Check my code".

IMAGE

INPUT TYPE="image" is another unique input style. It displays an inline image as specified by the author, and passes the x,y coordinates of the user's mouse pointer as he or she clicks on the image as data output. Important points are:

- The attribute SRC="some_pic.gif" specifies the image to be used. It must be in .GIF, .JPG, or .XBM format. Obviously, this attribute is required for an image-type input. "<INPUT TYPE="image" SRC="some-pic.gif">" is sufficient to define this input.
- The attribute ALIGN="top/middle/bottom/etc." aligns the image in relation to accompanying text, just as for any inline image (see Chapter 4, "All About Images," for details, particularly Figure 4-7).
- Mouse-clicking on the image submits the form immediately. Thus, an image-type input can function as a Submit button.
- Mouse pointer coordinates are measured in pixels from an origin at the top left corner of the image.
- Two separate name=value pairs are generated. An image whose NAME is "vote", clicked at 21,113, would send *vote.x=21&vote.y=113.* If the only true function of the image is to be a pretty Submit button, of course, this data will be ignored.

FILE

File to send: Browse...

INPUT TYPE="file" provides a way of transferring a data file from the user's computer to the server. The user sees a text input box for the file path/name, plus a Browse button to go find it. After a Browse operation, the selected file path/name appears in the text box. Important points are:

- File upload by this method WILL NOT WORK unless the form is declared as ENCTYPE="multipart/form-data" METHOD="POST".
- The attribute SIZE=s defines the width of the onscreen text box (20 characters by default). Some browsers accept SIZE="width,height" to create a box capable of accepting several file path/names for serial upload.
- The attribute MAXLENGTH=m sends data to the server about the maximum length of the file.
- The attribute VALUE is not required but may specify a default file path/name.
- For security reasons, the server is supposed to ask for confirmation before accepting upload of a default file.
- The NAME attribute is, as with all input types, required.

Jot

INPUT TYPE="jot" is the Netscape version of the proposed HTML 3.0 input type "scribble". It allows freehand drawing with the mouse pointer on top of an image.

The attribute SRC="some_pic.gif" specifies the image to be used as a jotting background. It must be in .GIF, .JPG, or .XBM format. Obviously, this attribute is required for a jot-type input.

Range

INPUT TYPE="range" is a proposed HTML 3.0 feature for numeric input. Some browsers will display this as a "slider" that is under the user's control. Important points are:

- The attributes MIN and MAX, both required for this input type, would specify the allowable limits of the input.
- VALUE defaults to the mean of MIN and MAX.

Neither "jot" nor "range" input types were implemented when this book went to press, but look for them in the future.

FORM EXAMPLES

Now let's see these form options in action. The Big Web Conference of 1996 needs some registration forms. Figure 9-5 shows the online form for participants, using four text inputs, two SELECT OPTION lists, two sets of checkboxes, one set of radio buttons, a TEXTAREA, and Submit/Clear buttons.

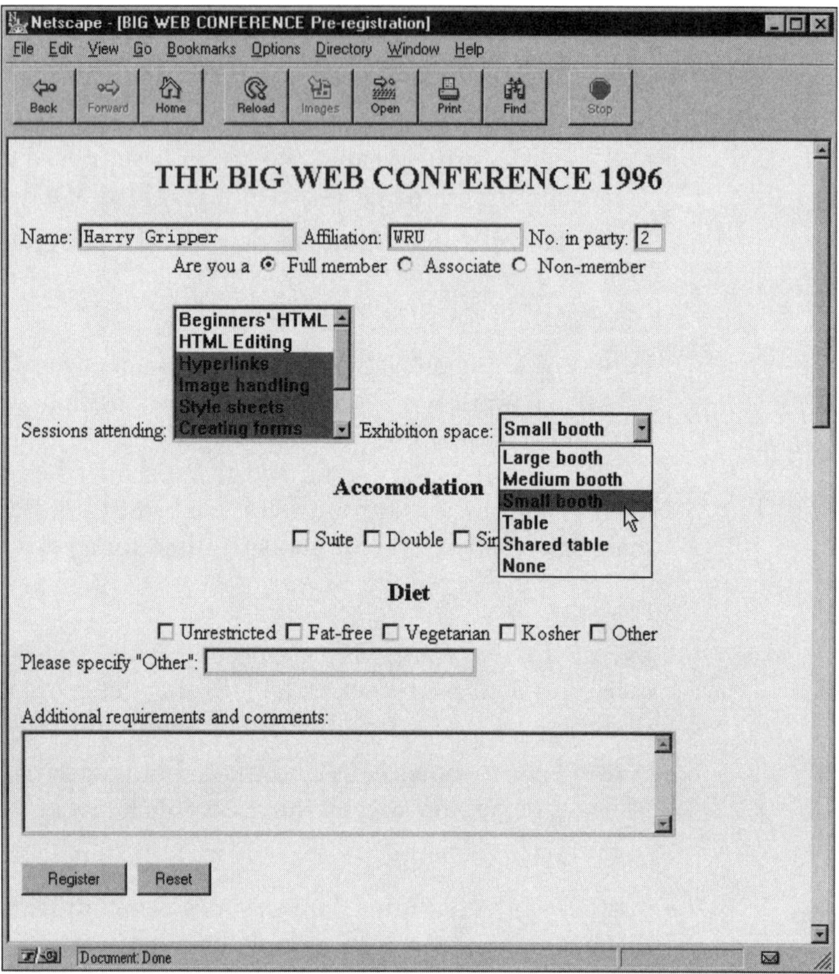

Figure 9-5: *A conference registration form.*

The FORM ACTION tag and the top two lines of the form are coded as follows:

```
<FORM ACTION="mailto:jquick@webconf.net" METHOD="POST">
<P>Name:
<INPUT NAME="My_name_is" TYPE="text" SIZE=20 MAXLENGTH=30>
Affiliation:
<INPUT NAME="My_affiliation" TYPE="text" SIZE=12
MAXLENGTH=12>
No. in party:
<INPUT NAME="Party" TYPE="text" SIZE=2 MAXLENGTH=2>
<CENTER>
Are you a <INPUT NAME="MEM" VALUE="full" TYPE="radio"
CHECKED> Full member <INPUT NAME="MEM" VALUE="assoc"
TYPE="radio"> Associate <INPUT NAME="MEM" VALUE="non"
TYPE="radio">Non-member
</CENTER>
```

Note that we've used very full NAME attributes, in order to make the reporting non-cryptic. The data from that form will begin "My_name_is=Harry+Gripper..." which is not hard to understand. The name field is kept to a SIZE of 20 for onscreen comfort, but the MAXLENGTH=30 allows some horizontal scrolling for anyone with a really long name.

The radio buttons all have the NAME attribute MEM. Since by definition only one can be selected, their joint output can only be MEM=full, MEM=assoc, or MEM=non. Again, the intention is to be non-cryptic. We busy conference organizers have enough to worry about without having to decode unfriendly computer data.

The remainder of the markup of this form is shown as Figure 9-6.

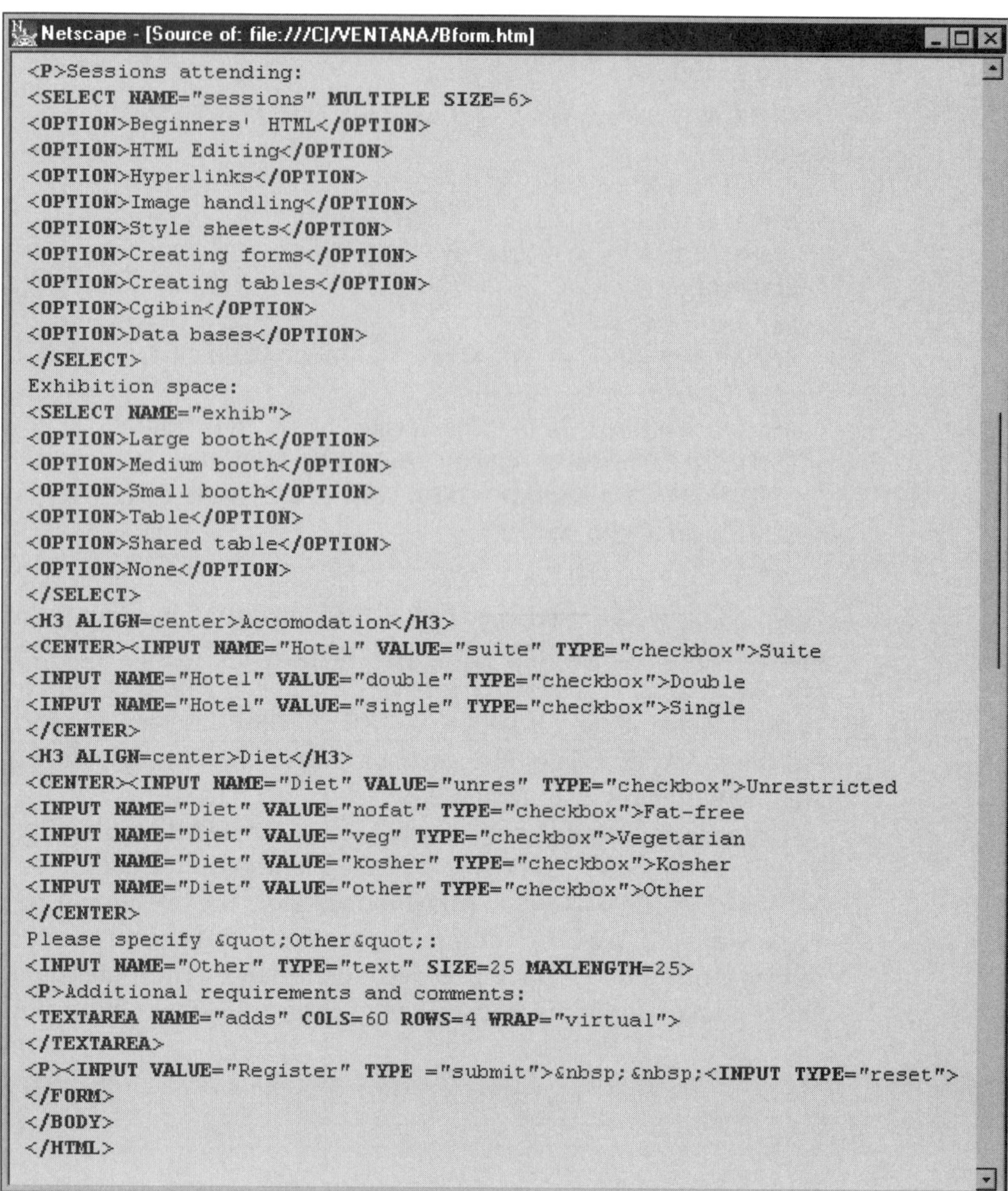
Netscape - [Source of: file:///C|/VENTANA/Bform.htm]

```
<P>Sessions attending:
<SELECT NAME="sessions" MULTIPLE SIZE=6>
<OPTION>Beginners' HTML</OPTION>
<OPTION>HTML Editing</OPTION>
<OPTION>Hyperlinks</OPTION>
<OPTION>Image handling</OPTION>
<OPTION>Style sheets</OPTION>
<OPTION>Creating forms</OPTION>
<OPTION>Creating tables</OPTION>
<OPTION>Cgibin</OPTION>
<OPTION>Data bases</OPTION>
</SELECT>
Exhibition space:
<SELECT NAME="exhib">
<OPTION>Large booth</OPTION>
<OPTION>Medium booth</OPTION>
<OPTION>Small booth</OPTION>
<OPTION>Table</OPTION>
<OPTION>Shared table</OPTION>
<OPTION>None</OPTION>
</SELECT>
<H3 ALIGN=center>Accomodation</H3>
<CENTER><INPUT NAME="Hotel" VALUE="suite" TYPE="checkbox">Suite
<INPUT NAME="Hotel" VALUE="double" TYPE="checkbox">Double
<INPUT NAME="Hotel" VALUE="single" TYPE="checkbox">Single
</CENTER>
<H3 ALIGN=center>Diet</H3>
<CENTER><INPUT NAME="Diet" VALUE="unres" TYPE="checkbox">Unrestricted
<INPUT NAME="Diet" VALUE="nofat" TYPE="checkbox">Fat-free
<INPUT NAME="Diet" VALUE="veg" TYPE="checkbox">Vegetarian
<INPUT NAME="Diet" VALUE="kosher" TYPE="checkbox">Kosher
<INPUT NAME="Diet" VALUE="other" TYPE="checkbox">Other
</CENTER>
Please specify &quot;Other&quot;:
<INPUT NAME="Other" TYPE="text" SIZE=25 MAXLENGTH=25>
<P>Additional requirements and comments:
<TEXTAREA NAME="adds" COLS=60 ROWS=4 WRAP="virtual">
</TEXTAREA>
<P><INPUT VALUE="Register" TYPE ="submit">  <INPUT TYPE="reset">
</FORM>
</BODY>
</HTML>
```

Figure 9-6: *Markup of the lower half of the registration form.*

We have a lot of expert speakers at this conference, and since the topic is HTML (very similar to the content of this book—now there's a coincidence) we can expect the speakers all to be very computer-savvy. In fact, we expect that they can all send us synopses of their seminar material. They'll be so perfect that we can drop them into the word processing file that will create the conference program with no editing. So we need an input of TYPE="file", and that commits us to ENCTYPE="multipart/form-data".

They've all been provided with a secret registration code, as an identity check, and we'd like this to be part of the form submitted data. However, since people may be looking over their shoulders, we make this field a TYPE="password" so that asterisks are echoed to screen.

Finally, they can all opt for one of four conference sessions, so we give them multiple Submit buttons to register that preference. The form and the markup are shown in Figures 9-7A & B.

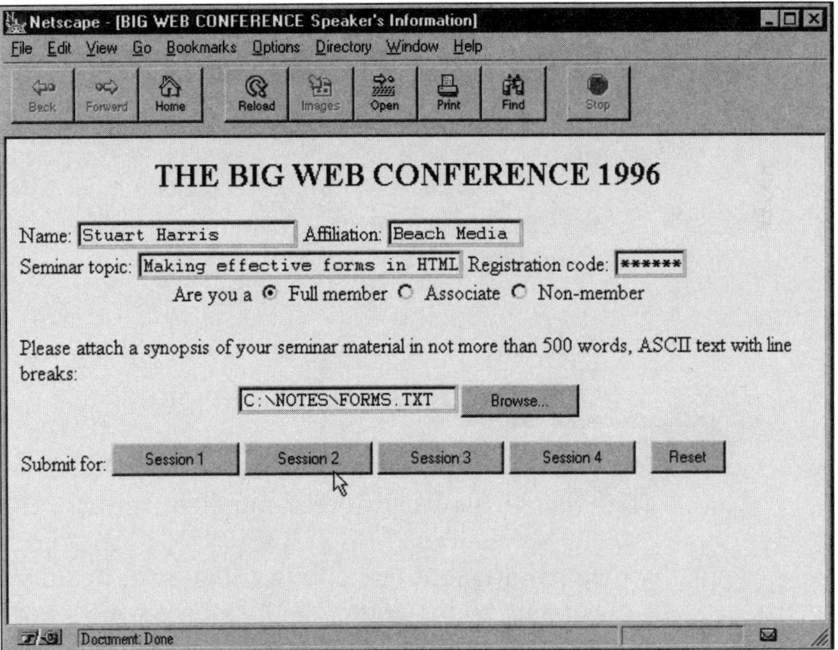

Figure 9-7A: *Conference speakers' registration form.*

Netscape - [Source of: file:///C|/VENTANA/Cform.htm]

```
<!doctype HTML public "-//W30//DTD W3 HTML 3.0//EN">
<HTML>
<HEAD>
<TITLE>BIG WEB CONFERENCE Speaker's Information</TITLE>
</HEAD>
<BODY>
<H2 ALIGN=center>THE BIG WEB CONFERENCE 1996</H2>
<FORM ACTION="mailto:jquick@webconf.net" METHOD="POST"
ENCTYPE="multipart/form-data">
<P>Name:
<INPUT NAME="My_name_is" TYPE="text" SIZE=20 MAXLENGTH=20>
Affiliation:
<INPUT NAME="My_affiliation" TYPE="text" SIZE=12 MAXLENGTH=12>
<BR>Seminar topic:
<INPUT NAME="My_topic_is" TYPE="text" SIZE=30 MAXLENGTH=30>
Registration code:
<INPUT NAME="code" TYPE="password" SIZE=6 MAXLENGTH=6>
<CENTER>Are you a <INPUT NAME="MEM" VALUE="full" TYPE="radio" CHECKED>
Full member <INPUT NAME="MEM" VALUE="assoc" TYPE="radio">
Associate <INPUT NAME="MEM" VALUE="non" TYPE="radio">
Non-member</CENTER>
<P>Please attach a synopsis of your seminar material in not more
than 500 words, ASCII text with line breaks:
<BR>
<CENTER><INPUT NAME="usrfile" TYPE="file"></CENTER>
<P>Submit for:
<INPUT NAME="1" VALUE="Session 1" TYPE ="submit">
<INPUT NAME="2" VALUE="Session 2" TYPE ="submit">
<INPUT NAME="3" VALUE="Session 3" TYPE ="submit">
<INPUT NAME="4" VALUE="Session 4" TYPE ="submit">
  <INPUT TYPE="reset">
</FORM>
</BODY>
</HTML>
```

Figure 9-7B: *Conference speakers' registrations, using the FILE Input Type and Multiple Submits.*

IMPROVING FORM DATA BY E-MAIL

We're going to move on shortly to some methods of transmitting form data that are considered more "legitimate" than the ACTION="mailto:..." METHOD="POST" routine, but first it's worth pointing out that a little attention to detail can improve the flow of data by this route. We'll assume you're using this simply to gather user feedback from your own pages—in other words, you're in control of both the sending and receiving end of things.

Figure 9-8 shows what you might typically see in your Netscape mail window when you receive feedback—not an immediately readable message at all!

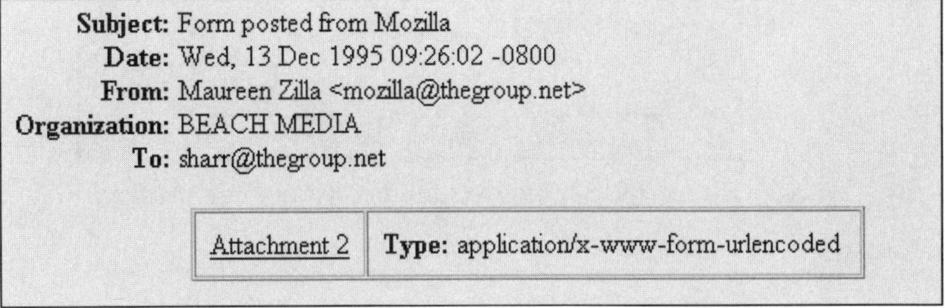

Subject: Form posted from Mozilla
Date: Wed, 13 Dec 1995 09:26:02 -0800
From: Maureen Zilla <mozilla@thegroup.net>
Organization: BEACH MEDIA
To: sharr@thegroup.net
Attachment 2
Type: application/x-www-form-urlencoded

Figure 9-8: *User feedback arriving via the "mailto:" pseudo-URL.*

The problem is with that MIME-type *"application/x-www-form-urlencoded."* The main function of a MIME-type header is to tell an e-mail manager what type of message this is, and indicate whether it's worth trying to display it as text or not. That's pretty sensible—after all, if somebody sent you a message whose MIME-type was *audio/x-wav,* you wouldn't want your e-mail manager to go trying to display it. It would probably give you a migraine just looking at all that trash.

If you remember, "application/x-www-form-urlencoded" is the default MIME-type of form data, and it's not a MIME-type that your e-mail manager knows about—unless you tell it how you want it handled. Well, just between you and us, you can do that the same way you tell Netscape how to handle any other MIME-type—in the Helpers preference panel under "Options/General Preferences." Press that "Create New Type" button (or Alt-N on the keyboard), and up pops a dialog box. Fill that out as per Figure 9-9, and OK it. Now you can decide what you want done with this, and one good option is to Launch an Application. Notepad, for instance, so that your user feedback name=value pairs will henceforth be sent straight to Notepad ready for editing, saving, or whatever.

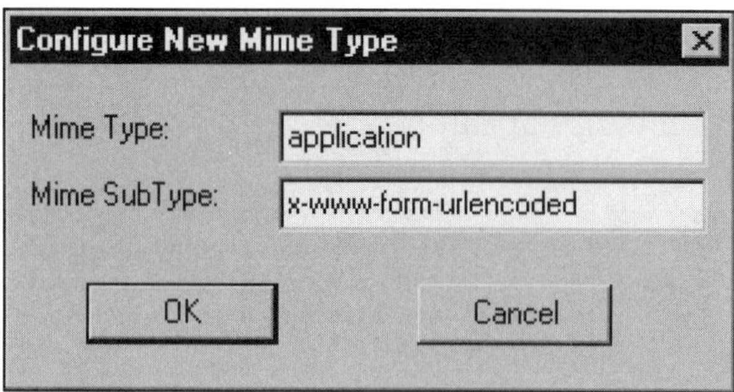

Figure 9-9: *Setting Netscape to cope with user feedback.*

So that's one way to make your feedback environment friendlier. Another is to insist that it be displayed as a genuine e-mail message. How do you do that? By making sure it arrives with the MIME-type "text/plain", just like any other straight message. Edit your HTML file so that the <FORM> tag is:

```
<FORM ACTION="mailto:..." METHOD="POST" ENCTYPE="text/plain">
```

According to the documentation, this is not supposed to be kosher—but it works, take it from us. Again, we're assuming that we're working in a controlled Netscape environment. These tricks are not portable.

Netscape itself, however, has provided a better bet than either of those options, if simply being able to see your feedback immediately is what matters most. This trick is using the MIME-type that Netscape invented for file transfer by form, *"multipart/form-data"*. What they don't tell you is that you're free to use this for *any* form output, not just files. Set your ENCTYPE to this and you're on easy street. The data arrives looking quite spiffy—see Figure 9-10.

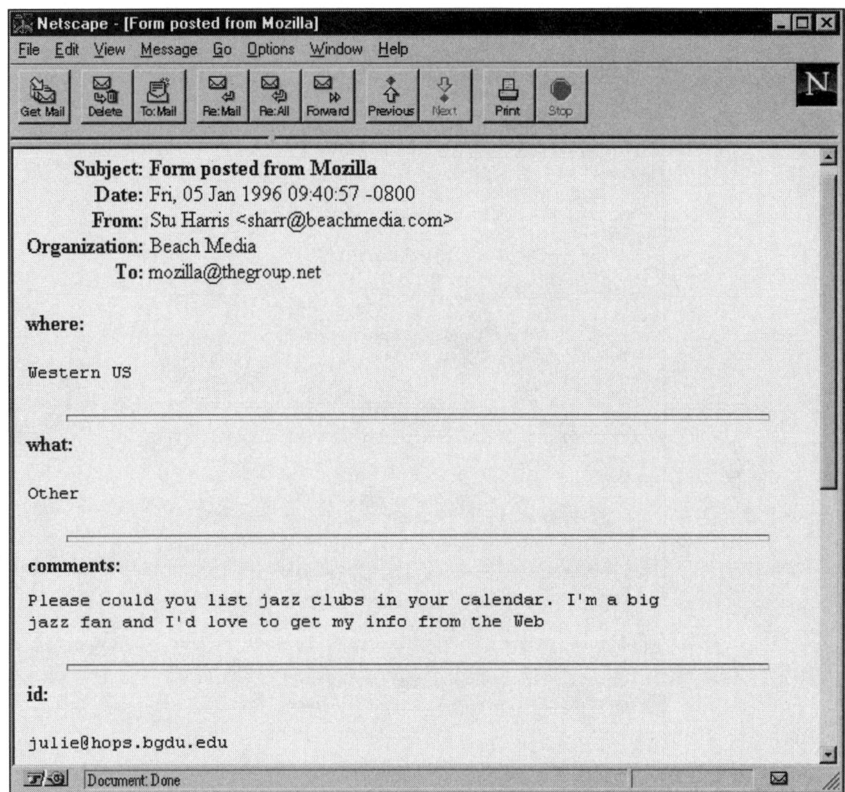

Figure 9-10: *Form data delivered by e-mail using ENCTYPE="multipart/form-data".*

Like all data with the *multipart* MIME-type, this stuff has embedded "boundaries" separating the parts of the document. The string that creates the boundary is defined in the header. Figure 9-11 shows what that same data really is—it's Netscape that interprets the boundaries as <HR>.

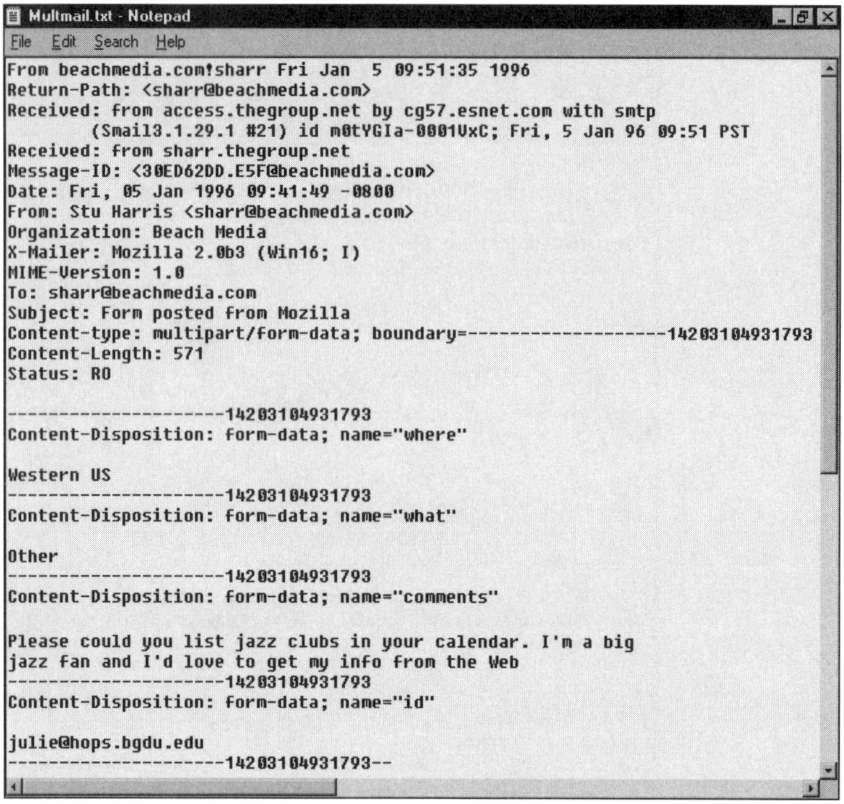

Multmail.txt - Notepad

File Edit Search Help

```
From beachmedia.com!sharr Fri Jan  5 09:51:35 1996
Return-Path: <sharr@beachmedia.com>
Received: from access.thegroup.net by cg57.esnet.com with smtp
        (Smail3.1.29.1 #21) id m0tYGIa-0001UxC; Fri, 5 Jan 96 09:51 PST
Received: from sharr.thegroup.net
Message-ID: <30ED62DD.E5F@beachmedia.com>
Date: Fri, 05 Jan 1996 09:41:49 -0800
From: Stu Harris <sharr@beachmedia.com>
Organization: Beach Media
X-Mailer: Mozilla 2.0b3 (Win16; I)
MIME-Version: 1.0
To: sharr@beachmedia.com
Subject: Form posted from Mozilla
Content-type: multipart/form-data; boundary=--------------------14203104931793
Content-Length: 571
Status: RO

---------------------14203104931793
Content-Disposition: form-data; name="where"

Western US
---------------------14203104931793
Content-Disposition: form-data; name="what"

Other
---------------------14203104931793
Content-Disposition: form-data; name="comments"

Please could you list jazz clubs in your calendar. I'm a big
jazz fan and I'd love to get my info from the Web
---------------------14203104931793
Content-Disposition: form-data; name="id"

julie@hops.bgdu.edu
---------------------14203104931793--
```

Figure 9-11: *The same document, without any fancy interpretation by Netscape.*

One final mailto: trick. Netscapes allows you to attach a query string to a mailto: URL. If the hyperlink that created the mail in Figure 9-10 had been written as **mailto:Mozilla@thegroup.net?subject=San%20Diego %20Events**, the subject line would have been amended appropriately.

WebForms

The best way of all to handle form output data is with a binary interface program of the cgi-bin variety. To implement one of them, you either have to learn a programming language such as perl or depend on a sysadmin who has plenty of time to do your programming for you. If neither of these is practical for you, you're pretty much stuck with the *mailto:* way of life—but that's not so bad, as we've already pointed out, unless you want to reach out beyond the Netscape community and/or do some really heavy database management.

Included on the Companion CD-ROM at the back of this book is an application called WebForms that's a lot of fun and has a unique angle on *mailto:* data gathering. WebForms is by Q&D Software Development of Chatham, NJ. Their Web site is at http://www.q-d.com, and the page /wflinks.htm has links to pages with interesting forms created by their users using WebForms.

WebForms has two main components—a Forms Generator and a Response Reader. Figures 9-12 and 9-13 show two stages in making a form in the Forms Generator. It's all modular construction: you make up all necessary INPUTS, SELECTS, and TEXTAREAS in any order, and add fragments of intervening text, images, and whatever (Figure 9-12 shows the composition of a SELECT list, which WebForms calls a List Box). Then to compose the form you bring all these elements together in a Controls List, and transfer them in the correct order to a Sequence List, making your finished form. That process is shown almost complete in Figure 9-13. The form is posted as <ACTION="mailto:...[yourself].." METHOD="POST">, so all responses accumulate on your mail server. So far, just a cute way of doing what we already learned to do.

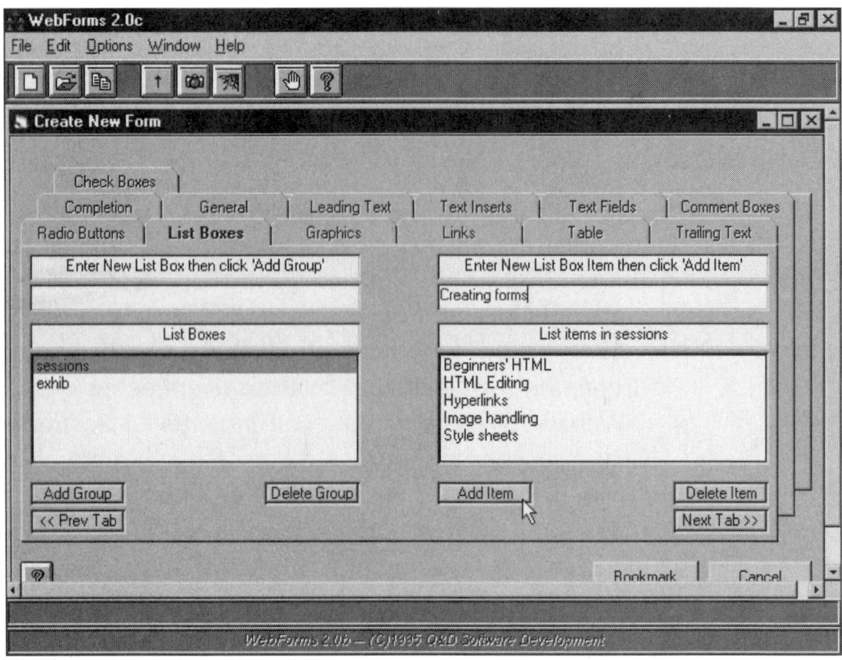

Figure 9-12: *Creating a List Box in WebForms.*

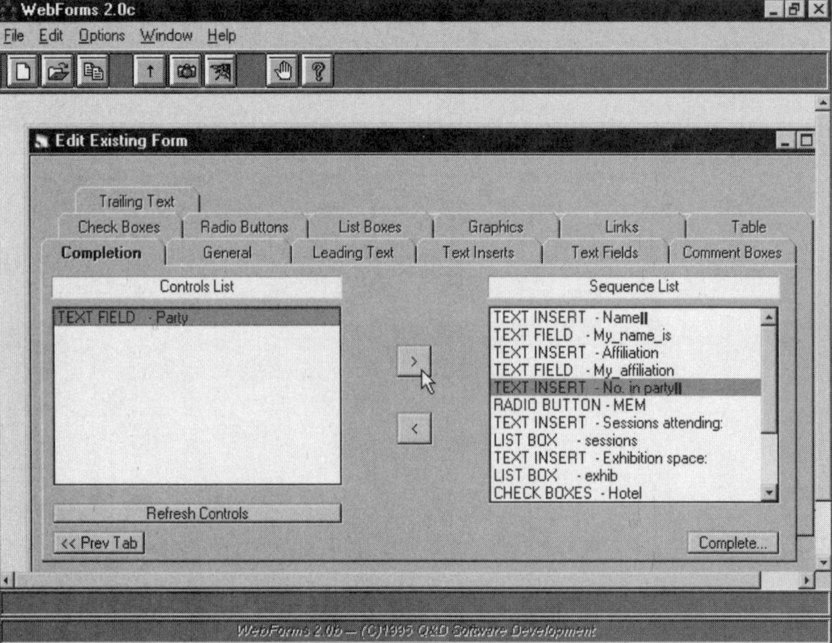

Figure 9-13: *Making the Sequence List.*

WebForms Grabs Responses From Your Mailbox

If you have a SLIP/PPP account, and a POP3 server for incoming mail, and you like WebForms enough to upgrade to the "Professional" version, you can take advantage of a great feature called "Direct Import" by the WebForms Response Reader. Let's say you've created a form called BIGFORM.HTM using WebForms, and now you want to check on what response you've had from your users. All you need to do is make your SLIP or PPP connection, launch the WebForms Response Reader, and select BIGFORM. The Reader software goes rummaging in your mail server, grabs the messages it knows are responses to BIGFORM, and tabulates them automatically. Figure 9-14 shows this process in action.

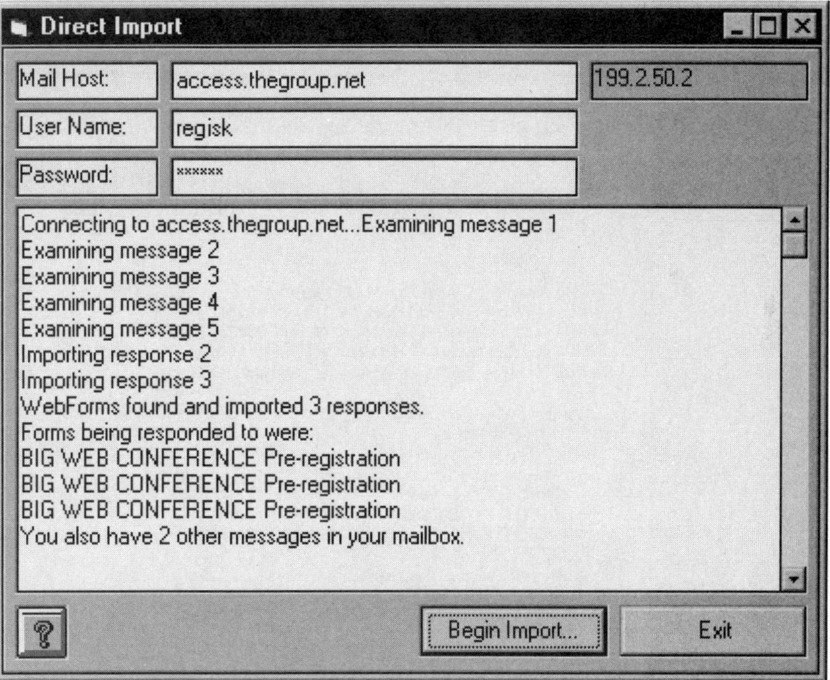

Figure 9-14: *Direct Response Import by WebForms.*

One snag—if you've already checked your mail, WebForms won't find it by this method because it'll be gone from the server. Netscape has a radio button in the Mail and News/Servers preference panel that allows you to opt for leaving your mail on the server even after you've downloaded it. This may or may not be functional—many sysadmins (ours included) head you off at the pass because they're fed up with packrats allowing 10 MB of junk mail to accumulate on their disk drives.

The fallback position is to save your form feedback messages to some specified subdirectory and let WebForms go rummaging for them there—they call this Indirect Import.

So how does WebForms know which messages are addressed to it, and whether they belong to BIGFORM or to NOTSOBIG? By not-so-secret hidden input fields, of course. Figure 9-15 shows, in WebForms' own HTML display window, code it created.

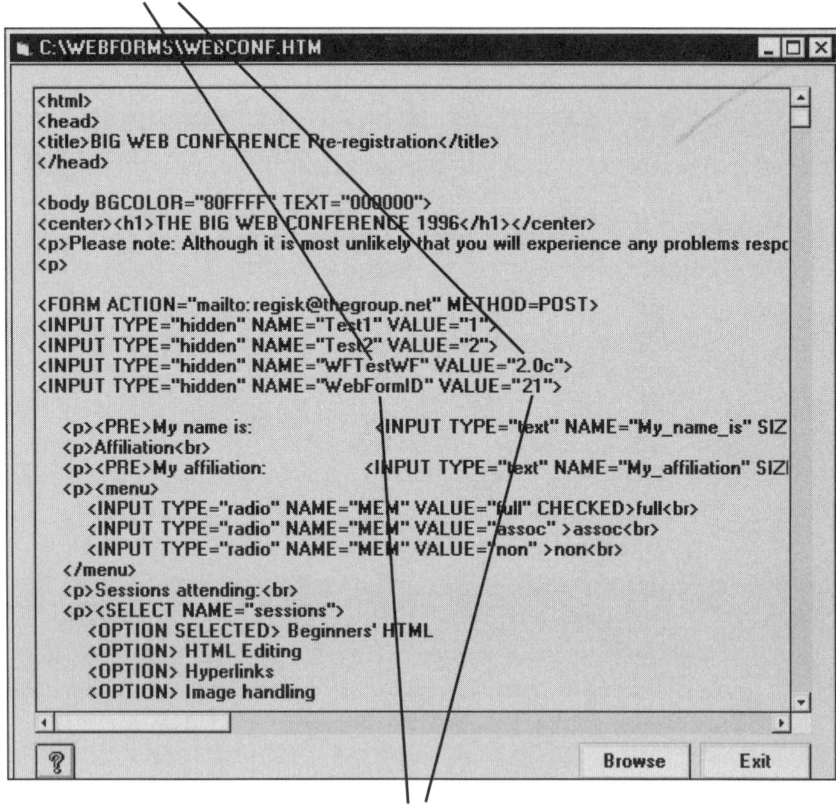

Figure 9-15: *WebForms marks its own data streams very simply.*

Managing Form Feedback With cgi-bin Scripts

It remains true that the majority of HTML servers use some variation of UNIX—the operating system of choice for Internet communications. And, as we already pointed out, the *mailto:* pseudo-protocol is just a kind of convenient cheat—query strings resulting from form submission are really supposed to be handled by binary programs running under UNIX, and often making use of built-in resources of the UNIX system that are in a totally different world from HTML. The convention that's been devised for HTML and UNIX binaries to talk to each other is the Common Gateway Interface, *cgi-bin*. Rather like a simultaneous translator at an international conference, cgi-bin is tucked away in a separate booth, creating nothing but understanding everything. It's into that booth we must now go—some of us, at least. Here's a quick test that might save you some frustration. How does the following make you feel?

```
#!/usr/local/bin/perl
if ($ENV{'REQUEST_METHOD'} eq "GET") {
   $in = $ENV{'QUERY_STRING'};
   }
   else {
   read(STDIN,$in,$ENV{'CONTENT_LENGTH'});
   }
```

If your reaction falls under the general heading of "NO WAY WILL I EVER UNDERSTAND THAT," you're going to be dependent on the kindness of sysadmins to handle your cgi-bin for you. The onward march of history may be your ally, too—as time goes on, many HTTP functions that used to be exclusively server-side are being duplicated by clever client-side code, image maps being the prime example of that trend. So don't fret about it: Just skip on over to the section "Subscription Services."

For the rest of you brave souls that are left, it's time to learn a new dance. Shall we perl?

GETTING SET UP FOR CGI-BIN

So you've decided that cgi-bin might be the way to go. Time to dust off that old UNIX shell account, read a few manpages, and clear out a few cobwebs. (Oh, looky here—so that's what happened to that e-mail message when my finger slipped as I was saving it two years ago!) The SLIP/PPP connection won't help you now—you're going to need to dial into the heart of the beast, and you'd better hope the beast is already pre-loaded with Perl.

Snoop around the directory structure of your site and familiarize yourself a bit with what's where. You might even ask your sysadmin for a guided tour. Here's the practical problem: cgi-bin scripts are normally expected to run from a special subdirectory on the server: /usr/local/etc/httpd/cgi-bin. You can examine the files in that subdirectory, but you can't edit them and you can't put your own files in there. You don't have "permissions" there (unless it's your own server—or your sysadmin's completely crazy). You're in a bind, because although most sysadmins will give due consideration to requests to transfer cgi files there, when you're in a debugging mode that's totally impractical. If you put in a call to a cgi-bin file in your own public_html directory, it will simply display itself rather than actually *doing* anything.

Your mission is to explain to your sysadmin that there *is* a way to run cgi-bin scripts from elsewhere, and that if he or she permits it, you will get on with your programming and stop whining. You will very likely meet resistance because, from a sysadmin's point of view, maverick cgi-bin stuff wandering around the computer unfettered represents a security risk. Be that as it may, the alternative is radically inconvenient.

The first essential is to modify the file that configures the server. It's called *srm.conf* (these instructions are for an NCSA-type server) and it resides in the httpd/conf subdirectory. The magic line that enables what you need is:

```
AddType application/x-httpd-cgi .cgi
```

In fact, that line's already there in *srm.conf*, but it's disabled with the comment symbol #. If you can just persuade your sysadmin to remove that #, you've won most of the battle right there. The other half of the battle is to make sure that the line

```
AllowOverride All
```

...is uncommented in the server's *access.conf* file. That permits the general restrictions on what users can do with the server to be overridden by a special permission file called *.HTACCESS*. So the next thing is to define a subdirectory under your personal control as one that's entitled to issue cgi-bin type commands. Make a subdirectory one level below the directory where you keep your HTML files, and call it /cgi-bin. Now create a file in it called *.HTACCESS*, with the following content:

```
Options ExecCGI
AddType application/x-httpd-cgi.cgi
```

Now, *as long as all your cgi-bin files have the .cgi extension*, they will work just as well as the "official" ones down there in /usr/local/etc/httpd/cgi-bin.

TIP

DO NOT create your personal cgi-bin directory on the same level as your HTML directory, so that references to it are "../cgi-bin/somefile.cgi". At some point somebody thought that was a security risk, so certain operations you might want to do are impossible with that path. Just another of those little facts that nobody will tell you but us....

cgi-bin Security

Those sysadmins who discourage their clients from using cgi-bin on security grounds are not crazy. In a commercial sense, they may be—because they lose business that way—but in a technical sense, they are merely being prudent. Here's the problem:

Sooner or later in your life as a cgi-bin hacker, you're going to want to implement a script that passes a user-generated string to UNIX command level and echoes the result back to the user. Your sysadmin is mortally afraid that you'll take a short cut, and create a form whose output is *echo=[user-generated-string].* That's when the mischievous user can enter:

%0Acat%20/etc/passwd

...and have the password file of your site dumped into his lap. Not good. It might help your case with your sysadmin if you can show that you are at least aware of the problem—and how to solve it (never allow a newline character like %0A through to command level). A good Web page to download as your security primer is:

http://www.cerf.net/~paulp/cgi-security/safe-cgi.txt

Reading and Using Form Data in CGI

Exchange of data between an HTML user interface and a cgi-bin program would be almost impossible without certain environment variables that respond to user activity and that can be read into a cgi routine. You pass these environment variables to a cgi routine using the operator $ENV{ }, with the variable you're interested in slipped in there between the braces. Here's a partial list of the environment variables that the NCSA server has to offer, as a cgi-bin program takes control:

SERVER_SOFTWARE	Type/Version of the server
SERVER_NAME	Host address of the server
GATEWAY_INTERFACE	cgi or other
SERVER_PROTOCOL	Protocol/Version

SERVER_PORT	Port number (usually 80)
REQUEST_METHOD	GET or POST
HTTP_USER_AGENT	Type of browser requesting
HTTP_REFERER	Address user came from
QUERY_STRING	Data from HTML interface
REMOTE_HOST	Requesting computer
REMOTE_ADDR	IP address of user
REMOTE_USER	Identity of user
CONTENT_TYPE	MIME type of data
CONTENT_LENGTH	Total bytes in data

Most NCSA servers have a little program in their main cgi-bin directory called "test-cgi" that simply echoes this list back to a requesting routine, with whatever values are currently in force. So one useful thing you can do is to create a form with attributes:

```
<FORM ACTION="/cgi-bin/test-cgi">
```

Now run the form, fill in some trial data, and submit it. You should see a readout of your name=value pairs as QUERY_STRING, and if it all looks as expected, things are going fine so far. Another thing you'd better hope your site has for you is a UNIX-based Web browser such as Lynx—that way you can get all this stuff working without leaving the shell. Use Lynx's cute little bookmark routines—*a* for Add, *v* for View—to save about a million keystrokes as you go back and forth debugging your program. If you really are a committed Windows/Netscape type, the alternative is to have a Telnet window running so you can click in there to hack code and click back to see the effect—but we recommend that you do your main Perl work at UNIX command level. It's actually the fastest connection you'll get, and that matters a lot.

Now we can take another look at that little Perl routine we teased earlier on. Here's that little fragment again, this time with lines numbered so that we can analyze it:

```
#!/usr/local/bin/perl
if ($ENV{'REQUEST_METHOD'} eq "GET") {      #2
   $in = $ENV{'QUERY_STRING'};              #3
}                                           #4
else {                                      #5
   read(STDIN,$in,$ENV{'CONTENT_LENGTH'}); #6
   }                                        #7
```

First, here's an important note about the programming language you'll use. When people talk about a "cgi-bin program" or a "cgi-bin script" (same thing), they don't mean "a script written in the cgi-bin language." That would be the same as thinking the translator in her sound-proof booth speaks "translator." Cgi-bin can be written in C, in C++, in many shell scripting languages, in *awk*, in *sed*, in Applescript, or in Perl. Line 1 of the above snippet simply declares that this is Perl. Why Perl? Good question, to which there are a few answers like portability and the fact that a Perl script is completely compiled before execution, so most screw-ups happen "off stage," so to speak. Another answer is personal preference, and another is that it's fashionable right now. By the way, /usr/local/bin is the path to Perl in many cases, but it might not be in yours. Verify this with the UNIX command *which perl*.

This fragment of code is, in case you hadn't guessed, nothing other than a routine to read a stream of name=value pairs from an HTML form into the string variable $in. In other words, the query string is given the label "$in" and is made accessible for manipulation. Line 2 tests the truth of the assertion that $ENV{'REQUEST_METHOD'} is "GET". If that's true, everything in the next set of braces is executed—very simple, $in is $ENV{'QUERY_STRING'} as per line 3. That's how GET does its thing, remember? Execution skips over the "else" instruction (line 5) and finds itself at the exit of the routine immediately. Mission accomplished.

If POST is the METHOD for this transaction, line 2 evaluates to false, so line 3 is not executed, and instead the name=value pairs will be available as <STDIN> and their data length will be $ENV{'CONTENT_LENGTH'}. Line 6 takes care of reading that in to $in, and we're all done.

There's a little slop in there, admittedly. We've made the gross assumption that if REQUEST_METHOD isn't GET it must be POST. Obvious to a layman, perhaps, but a trained programmer anticipates the possibility that REQUEST_METHOD one day turns up as 'GSQRRIT' or something, no matter how unlikely that may seem. As they say in the programming business, "GSQRRIT happens." So an error trap would be an excellent addition to that little routine, and we'll put that on the list of "Things We'll Do One Day."

Just note in passing that the branching structures are very C-like and that, as for C, all Perl statements end in a semi-colon, and that's about the limit of the Perl training *this* book will have to offer, other than by example. The only other pearls of Perl wisdom we have to offer are a list of the best Web pages, which you'll find printed in Appendix D and hyperlinked on this book's own Web page, and other Internet resources, coming right up...

Perl Resources

We don't claim to be ace Perl hackers, but we learned most of what we know from *Learning Perl*, by Randal Schwartz ("The Llama Book").

The Usenet groups to peruse are:

comp.lang.perl.announce
comp.lang.perl.misc
comp.lang.perl.tk
comp.infosystems.www.authoring.cgi

GET or POST?

It should be spectacularly obvious from the above that an interface program really doesn't care one way or another whether it gets fed its data snacks by POST or by GET. By the time you reach line eight of the program, it's ancient history. So, as an advanced Web author, which should you use?

It's tempting to just go with the flow and leave the default of GET, but here are a couple of reasons for considering POST:

- Never use GET for a form with a large TEXTAREA or any unlimited INPUT field. Any query string longer than 255 characters risks getting truncated in a UNIX environment.
- If security is an issue, use POST. POST sets off Netscape's security precautions, whereas GET does not.

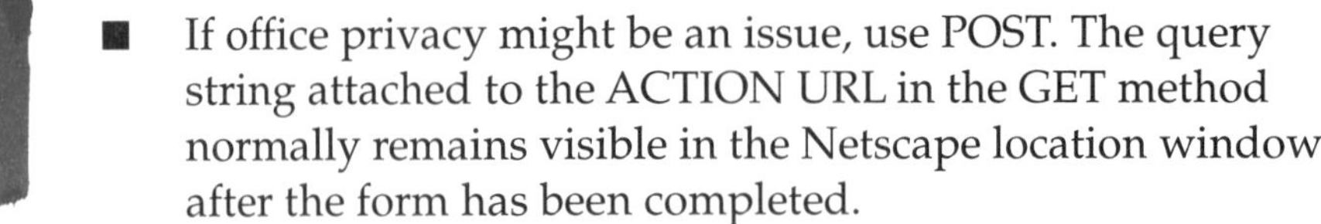

- If office privacy might be an issue, use POST. The query string attached to the ACTION URL in the GET method normally remains visible in the Netscape location window after the form has been completed.

Just to be fair, here's the "Let's hear it for GET" list:

- Not all servers support POST.
- If you really don't care about security, GET's lackadaisical attitude is an advantage, since you won't be alerting Netscape and making your users answer "Do you really want to do this?" questions.
- GET has a big advantage for queries that users might want to do repetitively—sending their location to a weather forecasting database, let's say. The entire ACTION URL including the query string can be bookmarked, and the whole process of filling out the form bypassed.
- GET has an irreplacable function as a modifying loopback. Normally, user choice can only be passed to the cgi-bin level by submitting a form, but with GET a hyperlink can work as well—you simply stick a query string on the end of the target of the link. In fact, there's nothing to stop you from putting a hyperlink in a cgi-bin-composed page that calls the page itself, but using fresh values. We use this technique when providing users with a way of requesting further data. Let's say we're building a script called *getfile.cgi* that accepts a keyword from a user, searches a data file, and displays the first 20 records in which the keyword appears. The initial query string might be "key=beaujolais&recnum=0" (see, we told you databases could be fun). At the end of the display, we can offer a further search with something like:

```
print "<A HREF=\"getfile.cgi?key=$key&recnum=20\">Next 20
records please</A>";
```

TIP

Whichever method you decide on, it's absolutely vital that you keep it consistent. If a cgi-bin script is expecting data by GET but receives it by POST instead, the effect will be to offer the user the entire cgi-bin file as a download—a potentially disastrous security gaffe. That's one reason why many Webmasters always use the "generic" subroutine (shown in the previous section) that will successfully read data whether it arrives by GET, POST, or Federal Express.

A Useful Perl Program

Here's *mailthanks*—a Perl program that reads form data to the variable $in (by the routine we already analyzed), then parses it by splitting $in into its individual name=value pairs, replacing the + signs with regular spaces and any special characters of the form %hex into something more conventional. It then mails a list of name=value pairs to the address given as $dest with a subject header $subj, and as a free bonus it adds the identity of the user who submitted the data.

Finally, the sub-routines *pagehead* and *pagetail* create a fresh HTML document with the string $title as its TITLE, and display the appreciative message $mest to the sender of the data. Note in particular the first line of the *pagehead* sub-routine, an *essential* signal to the server that we're creating HTML.

This little program is well worth having—it's far more powerful than using the *mailto:* protocol because the formatting of the data is totally under control and—even more important—it will work with virtually any browser, not just those that recognize *mailto:*. It's so worth having that we've included it on the Companion CD-ROM.

```
#!/usr/bin/perl
#=============== mailthanks.cgi ===========
#Retrieves and parses form data, mails data &
#displays thanks page
#-------- data -----------
$mest = "<H2>Thankyou</H2>\n<P>Your form output has been
recorded.";
```

```
$title = "We hear you!";
$dest = "sharr\@thegroup.net";
$subj = "Form Data";
#-------- code ----------
#:::: retrieve data by whatever method :::::

if ($ENV{'REQUEST_METHOD'} eq "GET") {
  $in = $ENV{'QUERY_STRING'};
  }
  else {
  read(STDIN,$in,$ENV{'CONTENT_LENGTH'});
}
#......... start a mail pipe ...............
open (M,"|mail -s '$subj' $dest");

#......... convert special chrs ............
$in =~ s/\+/ /g; #change the +s to spaces
$in =~ s/%([a-fA-F0-9][a-fA-F0-9])/pack("C",
             hex($1))/eg; #change %3F to ? e.g.

#........ make an array split on & ........
@in = split(/&/,$in);
foreach (@in) {
  ($nam, $val) = split(/=/);
  print M "$nam: $val\n"; #format mail
                            strings
}
print M "$ENV{'REMOTE_HOST'}\n"; # add userID
close (M);

#.......... now send the thanks page ........
&pagehead;
print $mest;
&pagetail;

#-------- sub-routines -------
sub pagehead {
  print "Content-type: text/html\n\n",
        "<HTML>\n<HEAD>\n",
        "<TITLE>$title</TITLE>\n",
        "</HEAD><BODY>\n";
}

sub pagetail {
```

```
    print "<HR>\n<ADDRESS>Beach Media Web Services, San
          Diego</ADDRESS>\n",
         "</BODY>\n</HTML>\n";
}
```

A Guest Book

It's fairly easy to see that *mailthanks* needs nothing other than cosmetics to turn it into a guest register. Figure 9-16 shows a guest register that uses *guestthanks* to send feedback from your guests by e-mail. Using this script, it'll be up to you whether to keep some permanent record of guest feedback by saving your e-mail to a data file called *guestbook.rec*. In the next chapter, we'll find out how to automate all that, and retrieve data from *guestbook.rec* into a Web page that all your visitors can browse.

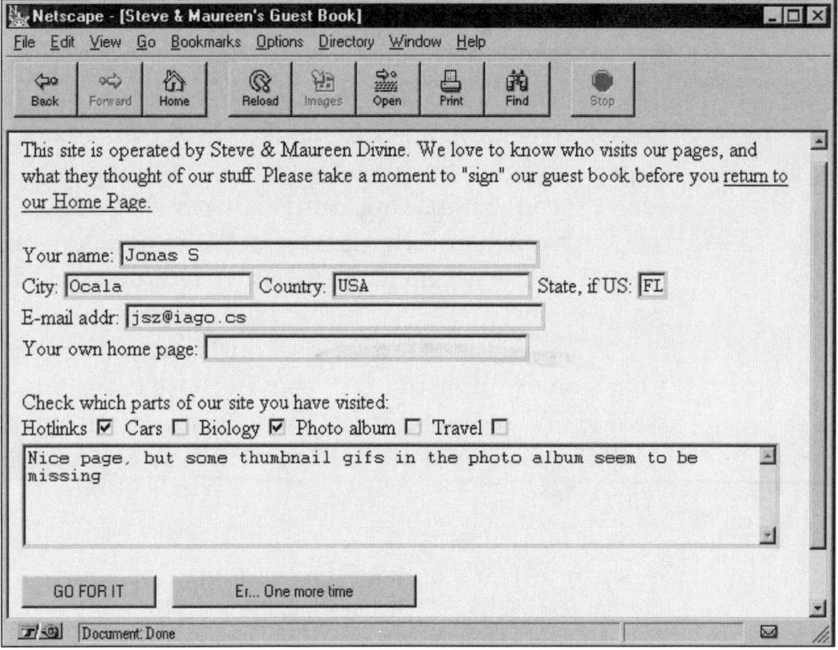

Figure 9-16: *Example of a guest register, using a cgi script that's almost identical to "mailthanks."*

As they say in the movies, "all characters in this guest register are fictional and any resemblance to real people living or dead is purely coincidental." Steve and Maureen Divine just sound to us like the kind of people who'd have a guest book on their site, and if there's a Jonas Szilard in Ocala all we can say is... "Hi, Jonas—thanks for the loan of your name."

CGI-BIN WITHOUT FORMS

The flexibility of cgi-bin form response scripts is virtually endless, and we've just sratched the surface of it here. In the next chapter we'll dig a little deeper and talk about the use of cgi-bin to manage databases. But cgi-bin can essentially do anything that a UNIX application can do, and not necessarily only because a user submitting a form tells it to.

SERVER-SIDE INCLUDES

Sticklers for Netiquette that we are, we really don't like serving up groovy Netscape 2.0-compliant code to consumers who aren't equipped for it. So whenever we do anything daring (and we don't mean just making words blink) we like to create alternative code for our non-Netscape users. We're not alone in this either—several of the excellent sites that we featured in Chapter 6 have the same policy.

"Branching on Mozilla" is a fairly simple cgi-bin exercise that's an example of other uses of those environment variables that HTTP servers put out there for our amusement. In this case, HTTP_USER_AGENT is the one to look at. Consider the following code:

```
#!/usr/bin/perl
#branch files on Mozilla
$brow = $ENV{'HTTP_USER_AGENT'};
print "Content-type: text/html\n\n";
if (index($brow,"Mozilla") != -1) {
  open (HTM, "../kewlpage.html");
}
```

```
else {
  open (HTM, "../dullpage.html");
}
while ($in = <HTM>) {
  print $in;
}
close (HTM);
```

That makes use of Perl's index( ) operator to scan the environment variable for the string "Mozilla." If the string isn't found, index( ) returns a value of -1. Line 5 uses that test to determine whether to open the "kewlpage" file or the "dullpage" file. Whichever is open is then dumped out, the Content-type header having been pre-sent at line 4. Again, not rocket science—but it works.

Here's an alternative approach called server redirection:

```
#!/usr/bin/perl
#branch redirect on Mozilla
$brow = $ENV{'HTTP_USER_AGENT'};
if (index($brow,"Mozilla") != -1) {
print "Location: http://www.yrhost.com/public_html/
    kewlpage.html\n\n";
}
else {
print "Location: http://www.yrhost.com/public_html/
    dullpage.html\n\n";
}
```

That code must be sent *without* any "Content-type" declaration, and it simply switches the user completely over to the appropriate URL.

Now for the really good news. You can easily set your directory up so that you can echo any of the HTTPD environment variables right into your HTML pages, without any cgi-bin activity whatsoever. Such echoed variables are known as *Server-Side Includes* (SSI). We already gave you a format for an .HTACCESS file for your cgi-bin directory—to play the "server-side include" game you need to create one for the directory where you keep your HTML files (probably public_html). Here's what this one contains:

```
Options Includes Indexes FollowSymLinks
AddType text/x-server-parsed-html .html
```

Now you can write lines like:

```
<P>Welcome, denizen of <!-#echo var="REMOTE_HOST" ->. How do
you like your <!-#echo var="HTTP_USER_AGENT" -> browser? And
what did you think of that last page you were looking at, <!-
#echo var="HTTP_REFERER" ->?
```

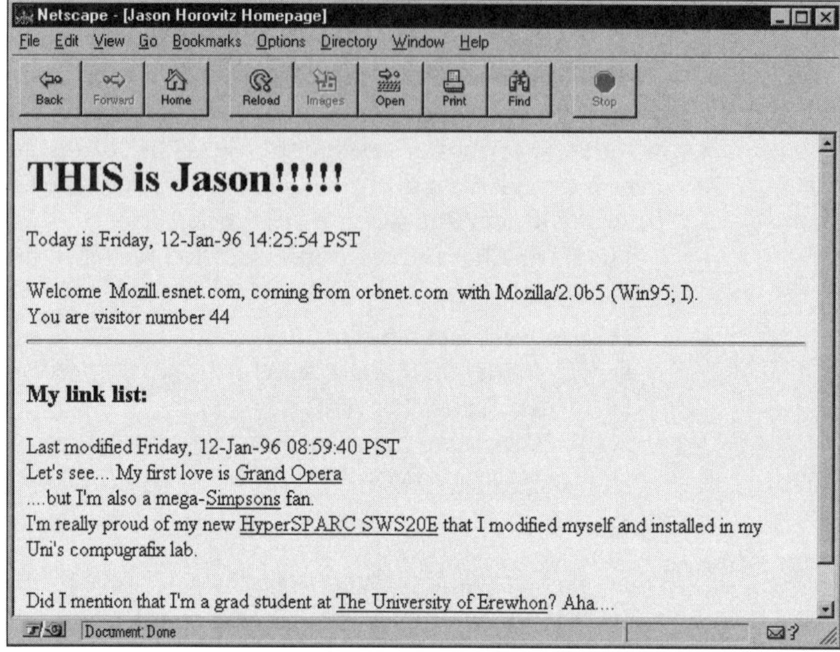

Figure 9-17: *A page that makes heavy use of server-side includes.*

TIP

In addition to all of the cgi environment variables you can invoke from the HTTPD server, so long as .HTACCESS is set up right you can use these, with <!— echo var=“.....” —>

DOCUMENT_NAME	*Name of the current HTML file*
DOCUMENT_URI	*Path to the current HTML file*
SCRIPT_NAME	*Name of the current binary*
DATE_LOCAL	*Local date and time*

DATE_GMT	*Universal date/time*
LAST_MODIFIED	*Date/time you last worked on the file*
PATH	*Current UNIX path setting*
SERVER_ADMIN	*E-mail address of sysadmin*

There's a slight downside to server-side includes that you should be aware of (just in case your sysadmin doesn't yell this at you!). In order for your server to act on them, it has to notice them. In other words, it has to look through your page and find them—*parse* the page, it's called. Now, that's not normal. Usually an HTTPD server simply serves, without regard to what it's serving. You turned on page-parsing with that line you put in *.HTACCESS*...

```
AddType text/x-server-parsed-html.html
```

But now, *every* file with the .HTML extension served from that directory has to be parsed, just in case it contains any SSI—and that's obviously liable to affect server performance, especially if the 400 users on this site are all SSI-hackers.

The official way to get around this is to declare a special class of SSI documents, with extensions .SHTML—it's a nuisance to have to train all visitors to your site to use that extension, but it's the considerate thing to do, and your sysadmin may insist on it. If he or she does, now you know why.

The Miracle of ExecCGI

If you add "ExecCGI" to that Options line in *.HTACCESS*, you can go one step further, and run a mini-script from your page. Let's say you don't much like the format of DATE_LOCAL or DATE_GMT, so you make your own Perl routine called *mydateserver.cgi*. You can invoke that with:

```
<P>Today's date is <!-#exec cgi="cgi-bin/mydateserver.cgi" ->
```

Now, so long as you haven't forgotten to add *print "Content-type: text/html\n\n";* to *mydateserver.cgi,* the routine's output will run right out there into the page.

In fact, the output of *any* cgi program can be arranged to feed into your page on the fly—and the implications of that are profound indeed, as we're about to see. Again, though, there's a down side you need to be aware of—and the objection to ExecCGI is more serious than that to SSIs because it reaches beyond the confines of your own site. When a user sends a request to your server for your page, the request always has at least one "header" stuck on the front. HTTP request headers typically contain information about what MIME-types the requesting browser can accept. They also provide the information about who they are and where they come from that passes through to those environment variables we've come to know and love.

Now, most sophisticated Web browsers (that's the software the remote user is running) try to be conservative with Internet bandwidth, and if the requested page is already in the user's cache, they like to say, in effect, "Don't bother with this if the page hasn't been modified since last Tuesday at 08:18:21 GMT." This is put in the form of a so-called *If-Modified-Since* request header—and if the answer is "no change" the server simply sends a response header 304 instead of clogging the Net with information the remote user already has in cache.

The problem with ExecCGI is that the server is in no position to guarantee no modifications to an included cgi-bin script, so the whole process is inhibited. Ninety-nine times out of 100, say the critics, the entire package (HTML page plus included cgi-bin scripts) is in fact unmodified but is sent anyway, thus wasting Internet bandwidth.

UNIX File Permissions

This seems a good moment to drop in some advice about file permissions. These are the restrictions that you place on who may read, write, or execute the files in your public_html and cgi-bin directories, and many a would-be UNIX hacker has torn his hair out trying to find a bug in a program that won't run, when in fact the only problem was permission.

Permission is given separately to three classes of people. First, the Owner (that's you). Second, users with the same GID (Group ID)—that's normally a sub-group of users of a UNIX machine like a college class, for instance. Third, world users—meaning just anybody. The file mode for a file for which everyone had permission to read, write, and execute looks like this:

-rwxrwxrwx

The important thing to understand is that your HTTP server is considered a world user, even if the software is sitting on the very same disk drive as your files. After all, it brings to your files users who are very literally from the world. So everybody needs permission to read all your files, and everybody needs permission to execute cgi files. You are the only person who needs permission to *write* the files. In other words, your normal HTML files should look like this:

-rw-r—r—   [644]

...and executables should look like this:

-rwxr-xr-x   [755]

Those numbers in brackets are the numbers you would use to get permissions set up right with a single *chmod* command . If you create executable files in a desktop PC and post them to a remote site by FTP, THEY WILL FAIL because the permissions will not be correct. Now you know.

MONITORING ACCESS USING CGI-BIN SCRIPTS

Perhaps the most immediately appealing implication of ExecCGI is that it opens up vistas of possibilities along the lines of an automated guest register. After all, if a Perl program can be arranged to run every time somebody visits your page, and if that program has instant access to those environment variables that tell so much, who needs a guest book form?

Well, let's not get carried away. We started this whole chapter with the observation that user logging will never tell you what your visitors actually thought of your page—for that, some kind of guest book is irreplaceable. However, ExecCGI can certainly be a powerful way of getting feedback from *all* your visitors, not just those who have the time and inclination to fill out your onscreen form.

VISIT COUNTERS

For a start, it's not hard to imagine how to count the "hits" on your page. Let's see now, we'd need a little baby data file that would store the magic number—we'll imagine that file as *hitstore*. Now we need a Perl routine that runs every time the page is accessed, gets the number out of the box called *hitstore*, increments it, prints it to the page, then pops it back in the box ready for next time. We could call the Perl routine *mycount.cgi*. Think we could manage that? Let's see...

```
#!/usr/bin/perl
#mycount.cgi....increments a counter and #outputs it to HTML
open (CC,"+<hitstore");     #open the box
$c = <CC>;                  #get out the number
++$c;                       #increment it
&htmlheader;                #get ready for HTML
print "$c\n";               #print the number
seek (CC,0,0);              #reset the box
```

```
print CC $c;                #put the number back
close (CC);                 #close the box

sub htmlheader {
  print "Content-type: text/html\n\n";
}
```

Well, what do you know?—it works! It's fairly amazing that you can do that in just eight lines of code (and a real Perl hacker could reduce that by one or two). But once you've gotten that far, you inevitably start coming up with a shopping list of refinements. You'd like to be able to exclude certain users from the routine, so you aren't counting your own visits or those of others in your "inner circle." You'd want a routine to insert commas every three digits so that 35731122 becomes readable (you should be so lucky). You might like the option of having the number written in ordinal form, like:

Welcome. You are the 3,302nd visitor.

...in which case the routine needs to know when to write "st" as opposed to "nd" or "rd" . Maybe even international variations like "me" "re" or "to"? How about aliasing several pages, so they all count together?

Obviously, we could spend quite a bit of time hacking away at this, but if we did we'd only be re-inventing a wheel that's running very smoothly on hundreds of thousands of Web pages already—it's the HTML Access Counter by WebTools. The UNIX module is included on the Companion CD-ROM. To install it, put it in your cgi-bin subdirectory (and, unless you're a sysadmin installing for an entire site, you'll need to change its name from *counter* to *counter.cgi*). Now enter the command:

```
perl counter.cgi -install
```

You should see:

```
Checking to make sure Perl is found properly...
Installing the counter...
        ...making counter executable
        ...making link from counter.cgi to
               counter-ord.cgi
        ...making link from counter.cgi to
               counterfiglet.cgi
        ...making link from counter.cgi to
               counterfiglet-ord.cgi
        ...making link from counter.cgi to
               counterbanner.cgi
        ...making link from counter.cgi to
               counterbanner-ord.cgi
...done!
```

Now you can verify that it's doing its job by entering *counter.cgi* on the UNIX command line. Every time you do that, it should return an incremented number. Now bring that number into your page with the line:

```
<!-#exec cgi="cgi-bin/counter.cgi" ->
```

See WebTools' Options Page for directions on how to turn on those advanced features with command line switches. You'll find that the number turns up on your page hyperlinked to the WebTools site. It's extremely easy to remove that link, but they ask you not to because it cuts down somewhat on the torrent of people posting to all the HTML newsgroups "How do I get a counter on my page?"

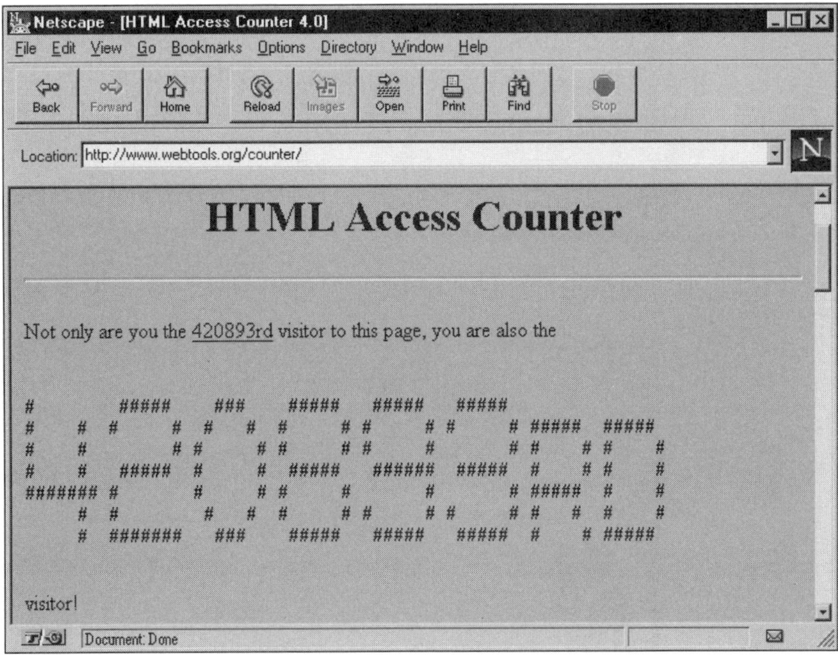

Figure 9-18: *The WebTools counter customized with "Figlet."*

The counter has one other great feature. It teams up with an application called *Figlet* that converts any letters or numbers to huge banner text in "ASCII Art" form. Figlet currently offers 126 different "fonts," one of which is shown on the WebTools page in Figure 9-18. This is quite a substantial installation that's really intended to serve an entire site rather than an individual user. Perhaps, therefore, you might encourage a sysadmin to do it, rather than undertake the C compilation and directory management alone. Figlet can be obtained from:

ftp.nicoh.com/pub/figlet/program/unix

The install module is available as .tar.Z (84 kb) or .UUE (117 kb), and unpacks to include a font subdirectory containing 16 fonts. Many other fonts are available from the fonts subdirectory at the same FTP site. Learn more about Figlet at:

http://st-www.cs.uiuc.edu/users/chai/figlet.html

To use WebTools/Figlet, substitute "counter.cgi" in your ExecCGI line with "counterfiglet.cgi font=fontname".

The WebTools page is simply

http://www.webtools.org/

THE MUQUIT COUNTER

Want to see a *really* cool hit counter? Take a look at Figure 9-19.

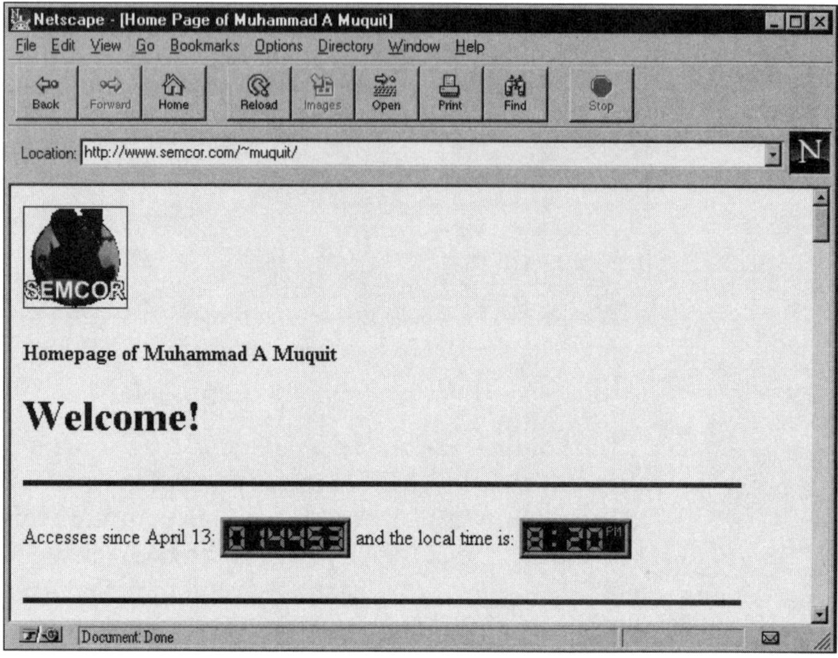

Figure 9-19: *The Muquit counter: one variation.*

That's the work of Muhammad Muquit, whose home page is at:

http://warm.semcor.com/~muquit/

How about this for the command line that invokes that very pretty Web *objet d'art?*

```
<IMG ALT="[COUNTER]"
SRC="cgi-bin/Count.cgi?ft=9|frgb=69;139;50
|tr=0|trbg=0;0;0|wxh=15;20|md=6|dd=C|st=1
|sh=1|df=count.dat">
```

Muquit has been generous with the customization options, to put it mildly. "ft" is the frame thickness in pixels, "frgb" is the frame color, "tr" is color transparency, "trgb" is the color to make transparent, "wxh" is the size of a digit, "md" is the number of digits to display, "dd" defines one of several styles for the numerals, "st" is the zero offset of the counter, "sh" is a hide-counter switch, and "df"—phew!—is the data file that holds the count number. Prior to version 2.0, every one of those options had to be overtly stated, or you'd get error messages (which had a beauty all their own, all framed and colored). Version 2.0 allows defaults, and also cuts down on the (very considerable) labor involved in unpacking, compiling, configuring, and installing the software.

The Muquit counter can relate to an unlimited number of data files, thus keeping count of an unlimited number of separate pages, each of which can set its own options. In other words, like Figlet, this is really a service for an entire server site, to be installed by an expert knowledgeable in the C language. We installed version 1.5 for ourselves, just to see how it went, and had to take three days off to give our brains a little rest.

So don't feel in the least guilty about getting your sysadmin to take on this task. Look at it this way—you're sharing this jewel with every user on the site rather than keeping it to yourself. The source code is a tar.gz file, available from:

ftp://warm.semcor.com/pub/muquit

Log Parsers

Well, it's easy to imagine the next step in ExecCGI-style feedback. The one where the Perl routine records all the environment variables relevant to your visitors and writes them out to a local data file.

Once again, however, consider whether you may be reinventing the wheel. In this case, the "wheel" is HTTPD's own access logs. If your page is called GreatPage.html, try this sometime at the UNIX prompt:

```
grep GreatPage /usr/local/etc/httpd/logs/access_log
```

...Aha! Every line from the log that contains the string "GreatPage." HTTPD access logs vary somewhat in what they record, but typically you get the URL of the visitor's site, the time of the hit, what files they looked at, and the number of bytes transferred. However, a standard log does not include HTTP_REFERER (where they came from) or record how long they stayed.

A routine that reads the access log and extracts from it the information that you want is known as a *log parser*, and there are many to choose from. We've included details of a few that parse logs of NCSA-type servers in the next section. As good as these programs are, the data you can derive from the HTTPD access log may not satisfy you, and may satisfy others even less. Certainly if your site has any commercial pretension, the advertising people will go crazy if they realize that it's possible to tell where your visitors came from and how long they stayed.

Even if you could not care less what advertising people think, you may have your own reasons for wanting more. In the next chapter, we'll present a parser that creates your own personal log, the way you want it.

SUBSCRIPTION SERVICES

At this point, readers who want nothing to do with Perl (and we know how they feel) may be rejoining us. Welcome back—the topic is how to get good information about all the visitors to your page, not just the minority that are going to enjoy filling out your feedback form or guest book. We've just been talking about how many, many people want to help us with this.

Yes, it's been clear for some time that there's a big demand for what the ad agency types call the "demographics" of a Web page, and a recognition that few authors are willing and able to do the necessary programming themselves. Some that are satisfying this demand are commercial, some are in it for the joy. One that's half and half, and also one of the very first in the business, is Internet Audit, known as *i-audit*. "Leave the counting to us!" is their motto.

i-audit arranges that every hit on your page is a hit on *their* page as well, so they can record all that information about your visitors for you. When you register with i-audit, they give you a piece of HTML with a code embedded in it, like this:

```
<A HREF="http://stats.internet-audit.com/cgi-bin/stats.exe/
qq55bv229">
<IMG BORDER=0 SRC="http://one.internet-audit.com/at/
qq55bv229.gif"></A>
```

You add that code to your page, and it produces a little inline GIF that originates at their site, not yours. Therefore, everyone who comes by your page with image-loading on has to hit the GIF with your personal code—qq55bv229—thus activating their user-recording software. The GIF is also a hyperlink to their *stats.exe* program which spits out the results when you click on it and enter a password (Figure 9-20 shows an example of a page audit). They offer daily, weekly, and monthly averages, and an extra "deluxe" version converts all this into the graphic form that advertising and sales departments drool over.

If you're interested in having your page stats done by i-audit, you can find out more at:

http://www.internet-audit.com.

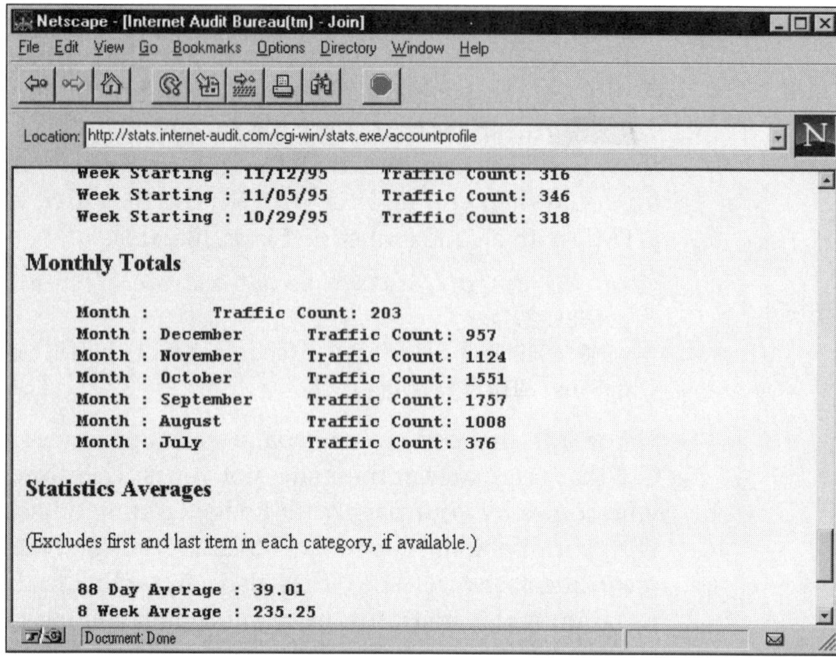

Figure 9-20: *Example of a Page Audit from i-Audit.*

Somewhat more comprehensive is FTPWebLog, written by Benjamin Franz for Net Images. This is freeware, because it borrows from the public domain package WWWSTAT written by Roy Fielding for the University of California. FTPWebLog is intended for an entire server site—and is shown in that role in Figure 9-21. It would really be overkill for a personal site. FTPWebLog's own site, where you can get information about downloading and installing it, is at:

http://www.netimages.com/~snowhare/utilities/ftpweblog

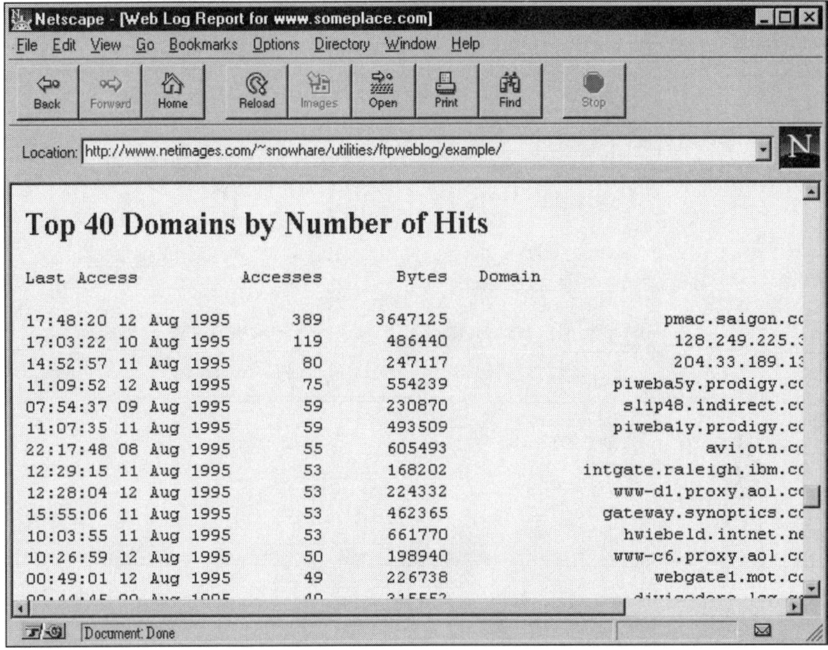

Figure 9-21: *One small corner of an FTPWebLog report.*

A very fine site stats package comes from the Old Country—from Cambridge University, in fact, where one of us was *nearly* educated. "Analog" is by Stephen Turner, and can be downloaded by FTP from:

ftp.statslab.cam.ac.uk/pub/users/sret1/analog

Figure 9-22 shows an example of an Analog report—again, just one small corner. The Web page that explains it all is at:

http://www.statslab.cam.ac.uk/~sret1/analog/

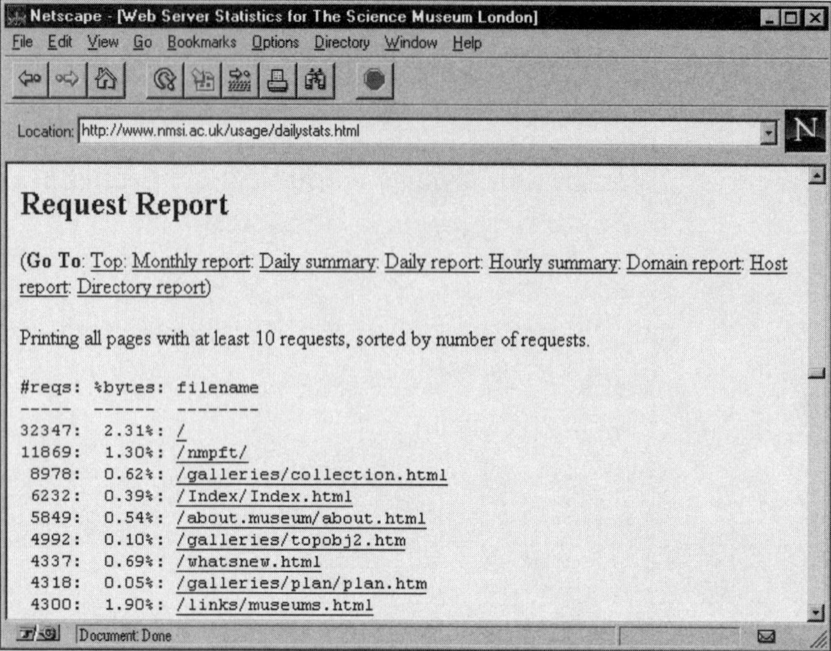

Figure 9-22: *Cambridge University's Analog reports the stats for the London Science Museum site.*

Finally, an example of the commercial end of this spectrum. At $695, Intersé Market Focus is not for the starving student, to be sure. It's a comprehensive package suitable for analyzing a collection of pages or an entire site, and it downloads its data into Word 6.0 documents, complete with histograms and pie charts (see Figure 9-23).

The Intersé people live in Sunnyvale, California. On their Web site, http://www.interse.com, you can see further examples of Market Focus, as well as some very nice pages they've done for clients.

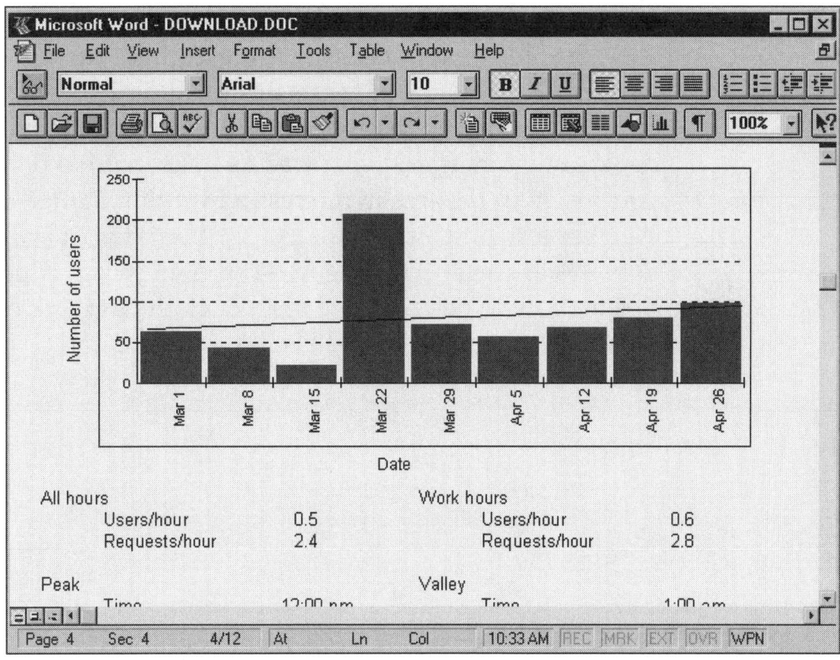

Figure 9-23: *Intersé Market Focus: sheer luxury for those who can afford it.*

NCSA itself does not provide a log parser to go with its server software, but it keeps tabs on what's available. Their useful descriptive list of more than 20 parsers, including WWWSTAT and Intersé Market Focus, is at:

http://union.ncsa.uiuc.edu/HyperNews/get/www/log-analyzers.html

MOVING ON

It's probably time, alas, to wave farewell to our Perl-incompatible readers. It's been good having you guys around, but the last chapter is basically alien territory for you.

By far, the most interesting thing you can do with your newly acquired knowledge of forms design and cgi-bin scripting is to collect information that's a bit more purposeful than a mere guest book, and store it in such a way as to keep it handy for you and your users to retrieve in interesting ways. Chapter 10, "Databases, Web Servers & Search Engines," is about that; it's also about firing your sysadmin and setting up your own server. Finally, it's a few tips on how to get your site visited. Come to think of it, even the Perl-haters would like that last bit. Stick around...

10

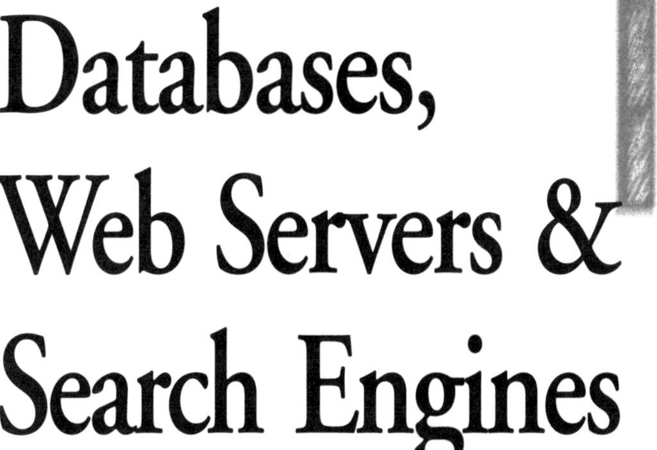

Databases, Web Servers & Search Engines

Does the word "database" make your eyes glaze over? Does it conjure up pasty-faced moles in windowless rooms reverberating with the white noise of fluorescent bulbs that need replacing? Hey, wake up and smell the coffee! What do you think all that material you gathered from the forms you cooked up in Chapter 9 is? Data!

In this chapter, we'll try to show you how you can do interesting things with the data you collect from forms and from your server. (Maybe we should call this "Databases for Fun & Profit.") We'll show you how to create your own logs to keep track of accesses to your site and how to pick out the information that's most important to you. We'll demonstrate how to turn form input data into useful readouts and searchable databases. If all that makes your brain hurt, we'll introduce some commercial products that are designed to make this task easier.

For the adventurous among you who like to take control themselves, we'll discuss how you can run your own Web server—a task that may be simpler than you think. As our final wrap-up, we'll discuss how to get your site into some of those important databases out there on the Web and let potential visitors know you're a part of cyberspace.

KEEPING DATA ON FILE

A few pages back we promised to get back to the guest book run by our imaginary couple, Steve and Maureen Divine, and add a bell here and a whistle there. Figure 10-1 shows an addition—just one line, reading "See what <A HREF="smgbook.html">others have written</A> if you like." Simple enough, and after all isn't it one of the pleasures of staying in small country hotels to thumb back through the guest register to entries like "We're really, really sorry about that bedspread."

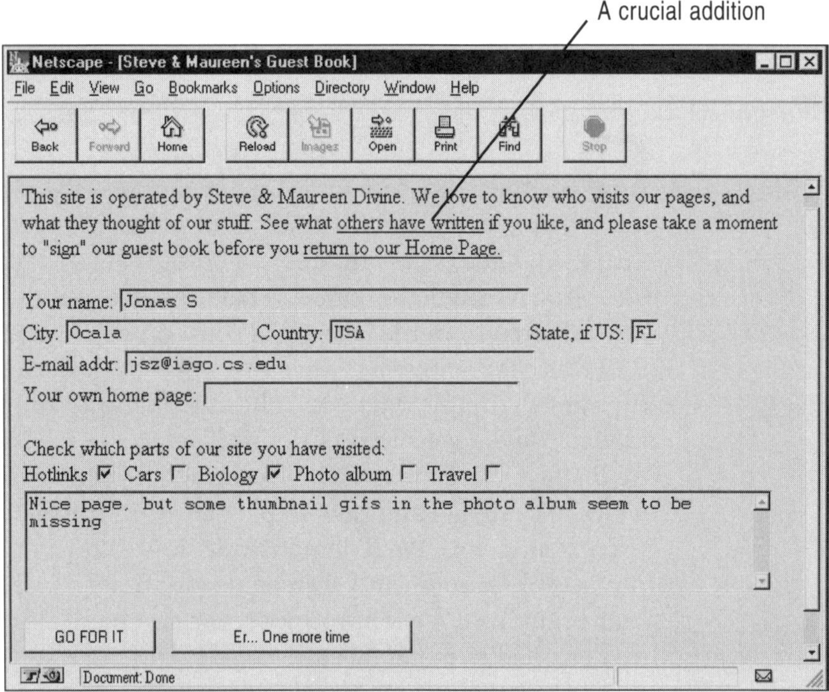

Figure 10-1: *The guest book improved.*

That simple addition, though, has non-simple implications for whoever's handling their cgi-bin stuff. The output of this form obviously now has to go not to a mail routine—or not *just* to a mail routine—but to some kind of semi-permanent store that everyone can retrieve and look at. This is elementary cgi-bin data management. Tell you what—we'll do it for Steve and Maureen, as a favor. We already have the file *newguest.html,* to manage guest input—now we'll need the following extra kit of parts:

- *guestbook.rec,* the basic data store
- *dobook.cgi,* to write new guest info to it
- *getbook.cgi,* to retrieve the entire file, and
- *smgbook.html,* to display the contents to our users.

Now, what features should we build into the system so that Steve and Maureen will really get satisfaction from seeing who visited their site? Some that might be desirable are:

- Automatic dating of entries
- Rejection of entries with no name field or other errors
- Display of the data with the most recent first

Let's assume that Steve and Maureen use a simple UNIX editor to take care of housekeeping jobs like cleaning up nuisance entries and making sure the data file doesn't grow too big. For the sake of clarity, let's also assume that they don't care to be alerted every time somebody creates a new entry in the "book," so we won't need a mail routine.

Here's a typical query string from newguest.html:

```
Name=Jonas+Szilard&City=Ocala&
Country=USA&State=FL&email=jsz%40iago.cs.ufl.edu&URL
=http%3A%2F%2Fwww.ufl.edu%2F%7Ejszil%2Fweb%2F&Links
=on&Pix=on&Comments=Nice+page,+but+some+thumbnail
+gifs+in+the+photo+album +seem+to+be+missing
```

There are many ways of playing this, but in the interest of keeping down the storage space required by *guestbook.rec,* we're going to have the routine *dobook.cgi* write new data to the file in its unparsed state. *dobook.cgi* will be responsible for adding today's date, putting the new entry at the head of the file, thanking those who contribute correctly, and chastising those who don't. We'll leave all the parsing and formatting to *getbook.cgi,* when the data is on its way out rather than on the way in.

Gathering the Data

For gathering the raw data, we know the form method will be POST, because that's what we wrote in the file *newguest.html*. So the generic data read-in that we used for the mailthanks program in Chapter 9 isn't needed, and *dobook.cgi* can be simpler in that respect. Here it is:

```
#!/usr/bin/perl
#dobook.cgi = reads data from newguest.html
#and inserts it as the first record in
#guestbook.rec
#-also responds to user appropriately
#---- data ------
$title = "Form response";
#---- code ------
read (STDIN,$in,$ENV{'CONTENT_LENGTH'});
$d = `date +"%I:%M %p %Z %d %b %y"`;
#the above line uses a shell command to read
#and format the date/time
chop($d);
&pagehead;
@nvp = split(/&/, $in); #split input into
#name=value pairs
($a, $name) = split(/=/, $nvp[0]); #split
#first name=value pair into $a and $name
$name =~ s/\+/ /g;
$name =~ s/%20/ /g;
if ($name) { #make sure user has entered a
#name
#--- respond to user -----
  print "Thankyou for your response, ",
        "$name.<BR>\n";
  print "Date: $d<BR>\n";
  print "<A HREF=\"../smgbook.html\">Read ",
       "the book</A> if you like, or return",
       "to our <A HREF=\"../index.html\">",
       "Home Page</A><BR>\n";
#--- now add to data file ---
  open (GBOOK,"+<guestbook.rec");
```

```
    @main = <GBOOK>; #read guestbook.rec to the
                     #@main array
    seek (GBOOK,0,0); #reset file
    print GBOOK "Date=$d&";
    print GBOOK "$in\n"; #print new record
    print GBOOK @main; #print old content
    close (GBOOK);
  }
  else {
    print "Sorry, we don't accept ",
         "anonymous entries.<BR>\n";
         "<A HREF=\"../newguest.html\">",
         "Return to Guest book form</A><BR>\n";
  }
  &pagetail;

  #-------- subroutines ------
  sub pagehead {
    print "Content-type: text/html\n\n",
          "<HTML>\n<HEAD>\n",
          "<TITLE>$title</TITLE>\n",
          "</HEAD><BODY>\n";
  }

  sub pagetail {
    print "<HR>\n<ADDRESS>Beach Media Web ",
          "Services, San Diego</ADDRESS>\n",
          "</BODY>\n</HTML>\n";
  }
```

Now here's smgbook.html, the small file that presents the guest register and thoughtfully provides some exits:

```
<HTML>
<HEAD><TITLE>Steve and Maureen's Guest Register</TITLE>
</HEAD>
<BODY>
<P>Return to <A HREF="index.html">Home Page</A> or
<A HREF="newguest.html">Guest book form</A>
<BR>Hi. Here it all is:
<P><!-#exec cgi="cgi-bin/getbook.cgi" ->
```

```
<P>Return to <A HREF="index.html">Home Page</A> or
<A HREF="newguest.html">Guest book form</A>
<ADDRESS>Beach Media Web Services</ADDRESS>
</BODY>
</HTML>
```

Parsing Your Guest Database Records

Obviously, the HTML file is just top-and-tailing, and it's the cgi-bin part that's doing 90% of the work here. Remembering that *getbook.cgi* has the task of doing all the formatting, and also that there are check boxes in the form, *getbook.cgi* is quite interesting. Checkboxes, unique among the form input types, send no data at all if they are unchecked.

```
#!/usr/bin/perl
#getbook.cgi reads query string from
#newguest.html and parses it to smgbook.html
#----- code ------
open (GBOOK,"guestbook.rec");
@in = <GBOOK>;
close GBOOK; #read data to @in array
print "Content-type: text/html\n\n";
foreach $in (@in) {
  @nvp = split(/&/, $in);
  foreach $nvp (@nvp) {
    ($nam, $val) = split(/=/,$nvp);
    $val =~ s/\+/ /g;
    $val =~ s/%([a-fA-F0-9][a-fA-F0-9])/
      pack("C", hex($1))/eg;
    $book{$nam} = $val;
  }
  print "On $book{'Date'}, $book{'Name'}",
       "from $book{'City'}, ";
  if ($book{'Country'} eq "USA") {
    print $book{'State'};
  }
  elsif ($book{'Country'} eq "US") {
```

```
    print $book{'State'};
  }
  else {
    print $book{'Country'};
  }
  print " visited this site.<BR>\n";
  print "e-mail: $book{'email'}";
  if ($book{'URL'}) {
    print " - Home page: ",
        "<A HREF=\"$book{'URL'}\">",
        "$book{'URL'}</A>";
    }
  print "<BR>\n";
  print "Pages visited: ";
  if ($book{'Links'}) {
    print "Hot-links ";
  }
  if ($book{'Cars'}) {
    print "Cars ";
  }
  if ($book{'Bio'}) {
    print "Biology ";
  }
  if ($book{'Pix'}) {
    print "Photo-album ";
  }
  if ($book{'Trav'}) {
    print "Travel";
  }
  print "<BR>\n";
  print "Comments:\n$book{'Comments'}<BR>\n";
  print "<HR>\n";
}
```

Figure 10-2 shows a part of this display. Obviously, once you've achieved the crucial task of creating the $book{ } array, formatting the screen display is a piece of cake. One subtlety we introduced here was to make the guests' own home page URLs, when they were provided, into hyperlinks (look closely at the lines containing $book{'URL'} to see how). There are plenty of other refinements we could get up to on behalf of "Steve and Maureen" but the point here is to keep the cgi-bin code as clear as possible.

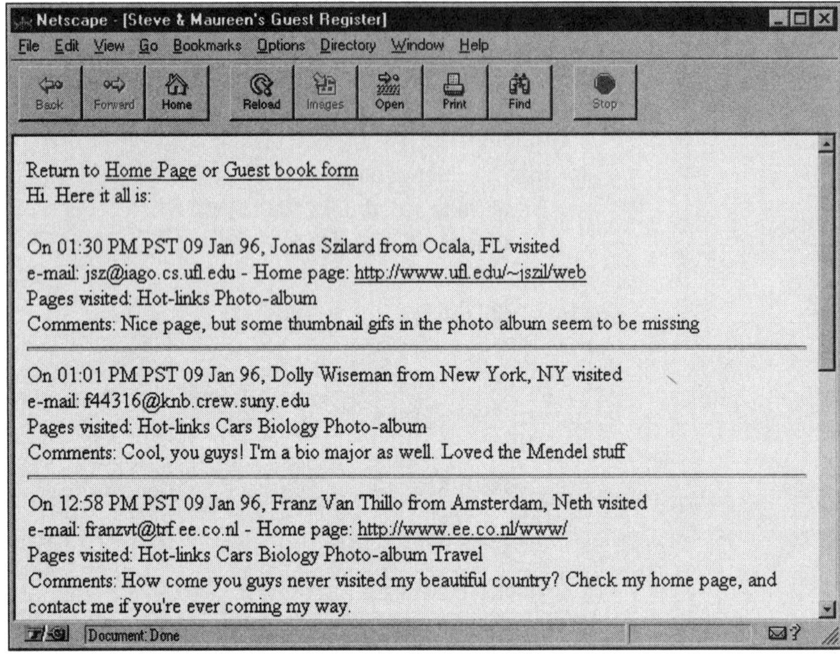

Figure 10-2: *Guest book data display by cgi-bin.*

The scripts presented here are our own work, and we give everyone permission to use them if they want. On the other hand, they aren't the best there is. There are several ready-made guest book "kits" available on the Web for free—Yahoo has a good listing. One very popular one that pops up all over the Web, and has many more user-selectable features than ours, is Matt Wright's work at:

http://worldwidemart.com/scripts/guestbook.shtml

ISINDEX: Making a Searchable Database

One of the very few HTML tags that has gone unmentioned so far in this book is <ISINDEX>. ISINDEX reminds us of the lonely and unpopular warthog tucked away in a gloomy cage at the back of a zoo we used to visit. While everyone was gasping at the antics of the really popular animals like gorillas and lions and gibbons, old warthog was curled up in the dirt trying to attract minimal attention. Just as the warthog was to be found in an out-of-the-way place, so ISINDEX properly belongs in the <HEAD> .... </HEAD> part of a document rather than in <BODY> .... </BODY>. However, ISINDEX is not proud, and will function even if misplaced.

As our friend the warthog looks like a cross between something useful like a pig and something noisy like a hyena, so ISINDEX is a bit like a cross between a simple form and a cgi-bin script to process a query string coming from that form.

ISINDEX turns any document into, in effect, a self-processing form. Add ISINDEX to any HTML document, and you'll find it displays "This is a searchable index. Enter search keywords:" followed by a standard-looking text input box. When you type something and press Enter, a query string is formed, but there's no need for any ACTION or METHOD or ENCTYPE as for a conventional form. Why? Because an ISINDEX document calls *itself* to parse and handle the query string. Since HTML files are not capable of parsing and interrogating databases, but cgi-bin scripts are well capable of doing those things *and* behaving as Web pages, ISINDEX documents are invariably written as binaries. Here's a kind of cartoon of an ISINDEX file in action:

```
Is a query string attached to me?
IF NO:  -Part A, input pass
  *Display the cue and input box.
  *Wait for user to type something and press Enter.
  *Attach user's input as a query string and
   call myself.
IF YES: -Part B, output pass
  *Process the query string according to
   whatever instructions my maker wrote.
```

```
*Display the result.
*Wait around.
```

That pastiche makes it look a bit as though Part A and Part B are equally important. In reality, however, Part A is just the warthog—the interesting animals are all in Part B. Once you comprehend the dual personality of an ISINDEX file, it's really very simple.

Gateways to Built-in UNIX Resources

In the "official" cgi-bin directory of most NCSA servers (/usr/local/etc/httpd/cgi-bin) you'll find little binary files called *finger, date,* and *calendar*. These are examples of ISINDEX documents that take advantage of the built-in UNIX processes of the same names. They're called *"gateways"* because they pass a user from the HTTP environment through to a UNIX executable.

Finding Things With FINGER

The gateways you'll find over in the server's territory are written (logically enough) as shell scripts. Since we're focusing on Perl in this book, here's a "translation" into Perl of the finger gateway:

```
#!/usr/bin/perl
#finger gateway
if ($#ARGV < 0) { #Part A--input pass
  $title = "Finger Gateway";
  &pagehead;
  print "<P>This is a UNIX finger gateway. ",
        "Enter user\@host or \@host.</P>\n";
  &pagetail;
}
else {   #Part B-------output pass
  $title = "Result of finger for $ARGV[0]";
  &pagehead;
  print "<P>";
  @fin = `finger $ARGV[0]`;
  print @fin;
```

```
  &pagetail;
}

#-------- subroutines -------
sub pagehead {
  print "Content-type: text/html\n\n\n",
        "<HTML>\n<HEAD>\n",
        "<TITLE>$title</TITLE>\n",
        "<ISINDEX></HEAD><BODY>\n";
}

sub pagetail {
  print "<HR>\n<ADDRESS>Beach Media Web Services, San Diego</
ADDRESS>\n",
        "</BODY>\n</HTML>\n";
}
```

So far as Perl is concerned, an attached query string is an "argument." The number of arguments is given by the expression $#ARGV. If there are none, $#ARGV evaluates to -1, and this is how that very first line of finger.cgi decides whether it's a warthog or a giraffe this time around.

TIP

There are pitfalls in using a Perl script to run a shell process like finger. The HTTPD server sets up its own PATH variable, which may make that process inaccessible. The finger.cgi *script actually fails to deliver the goods in one of the accounts we use, because the finger executable program is in the /usr/ucb directory. The answer in cases like this is to dictate whatever path suits you—but it's polite to restore it afterwards. In our case, these two lines need to be inserted before the call to finger:*

```
    $oldpath = $ENV{'PATH'};
$ENV{'PATH'} = "./:/usr/local/bin:/usr/ucb";
```

..and this line goes after the call:

```
    $ENV{'PATH'} = $oldpath;
```

FINDING OTHER THINGS WITH GREP

Another UNIX process much used by ISINDEX files is *grep*, the process that searches for strings in files. *grep* can get quite complicated, but a simple *grep* query is:

```
grep bra underwear.list
```

The result would be a readout of every line in *underwear.list* that contained the string *bra*—in this simple search, "embraceable" would be found as well as "brassière."

Suppose Steve and Maureen allowed their guest register file to grow very big—so big that manual searching became a chore. If they said to themselves one day, "I'm sure we had a visit from Robert Redford once—now when the heck was that?" here's an ISINDEX that would enable searching to happen right there on the Web, with the results shown in Figure 10-3:

```
#!/usr/bin/perl
#sg.cgi :ISINDEX search of "guestbook.rec"
if ($#ARGV < 0) { #Part A---input pass
  $title = "Guestbook Search";
  &pagehead; #-includes <ISINDEX>
  print "<P>Enter a name:</P>\n";
  &pagetail;
}
else { #Part B--------output pass
  $title = "Result of search for $ARGV[0]";
  &pagehead;
  print "<P>";
  $in = `grep -i $ARGV[0] guestbook.rec`;
  @nvp = split(/&/, $in);
#
#....etc. parse & display exactly as
#getbook.cgi
#
```

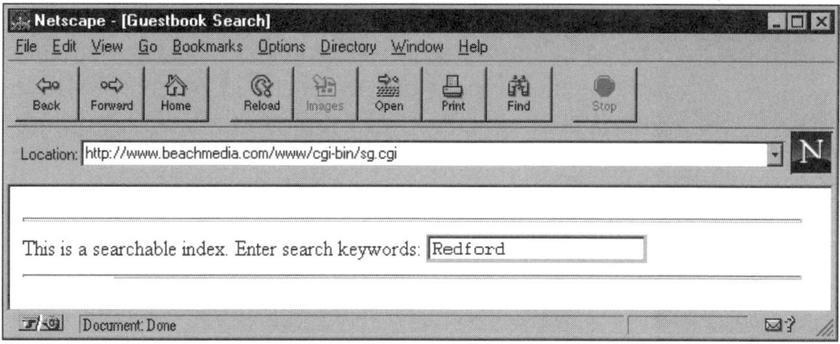

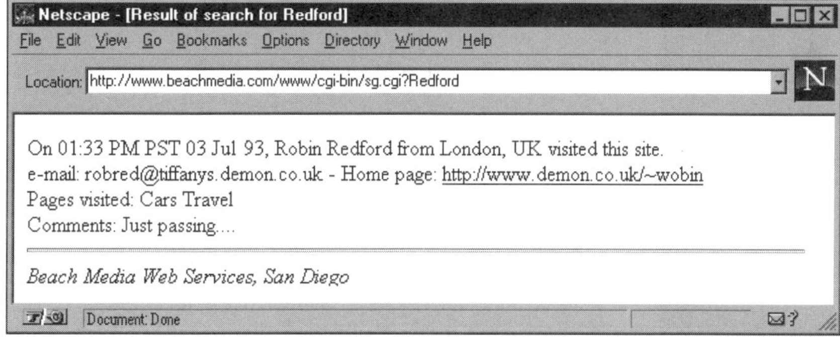

Figure 10-3: *Guest Book search by cgi-bin: Pity; it was Robin, not Robert.*

Database Creation and Display

The next step, naturally, is to cast off our dependence on built-in processes and go independent. We will cast off ISINDEX as well—truly the warthog of HTML tags, because it does nothing that a combination of an HTML form page and a decent cgi-bin script couldn't do much better. Begone, dull ISINDEX!

So here's where we fulfill the promise we made back in Chapter 9, "Forms, Feedback & cgi-bin," to actually create and display Web page visit logs the way we want them, rather than simply parsing the HTTPD access logs. We'll go even further and take you with us as we build a database from scratch.

First, though, look back at the two lists of environment variables in Chapter 9. You'll quickly come up with a list of over 20 things that any cgi-bin script called by an HTML page knows about the situation—and that isn't even a complete list.

REFINING THE SITE VISIT REPORT

blog.cgi is a script that writes some of these variables to a data file called *biglog*. Again, we're adopting the technique of writing basically raw data and leaving the fancy parsing stuff to the program that reads it back when asked. Since we already have plenty of well-debugged routines that deal with data in the form of name=value pairs, we're going to arrange for *blog.cgi* to write data in that exact same format. Here's a version that writes just six of the possible name=value pairs, and ignores our own visits:

```
#!/usr/bin/perl
#blog.cgi ::: writes page visit data
$host = $ENV{'REMOTE_HOST'};
print "Content-type: text/html\n\n";
if ($host ne "myhost.com") {
  open (OUT, ">>biglog");
  print OUT "host=$host\&";
  print OUT "date=$ENV{'DATE_LOCAL'}\&";
  print OUT "page=$ENV{'DOCUMENT_NAME'}\&";
  print OUT "IP=$ENV{'REMOTE_ADDR'}\&";
  print OUT "refer=$ENV{'HTTP_REFERER'}\&";
  print OUT "brows=$ENV{'HTTP_USER_AGENT'}\n";
  close (OUT);
}
```

Obviously, we could make *blog.cgi* keep going through all 22 environment variables, but we picked out those six partly because we have a special purpose in mind. We'd like to make those ad agency types happy by delivering reports stating where our visitors come from (in other words, which of our "back links" are the most effective), and how long they spend looking at our pages.

"Time on page" would be impossible to measure if the site was just one home page. A visitor's arrival time is known, but there is no such environment variable as EXIT_TIME. However, we're dealing here with a complex site consisting of 10 main pages plus a fairly complex multiple choice quiz, all of which is in two languages, for a total of nearly 80 HTML documents plus some 12 decorative GIFs. As a visitor wanders through the site, the time of arrival at page B can be assumed to be the exit time from page A, and so on through the cascade of pages until the only one that cannot finally be measured is the last one the visitor examines before he or she wanders off to the next Web goodie.

The *blog.cgi* script we already introduced is called by all 80 of the documents on the site, and the duty of *logparse.cgi* is to analyze the resulting log, looking for blocks of records with the same $host. Each block can be assumed, then, to represent one "site visit," and the time-on-page data can all be calculated with the exception of the last page in any visit block.

The approach we chose for *logparse.cgi* was to first scan through the entire data file and compile all the data into the two-dimensional array $plog{'variable_name', 'record_number'}. On the way through, the $date field—which looks like "Tuesday, 02-Jan-1996 14:33:19 PDT"—is separated out into the subfields $day, $dt and the all-important $tim.

If the 'host' field is found to be the same as that field in the previous record, this record's time becomes $now, the previous record's time becomes $was, and the subroutine "&subtime" returns the difference between them, which is then stored as the variable $read for the earlier of the two records.

Not much is left to do for the second pass through the data, other than formatting and making it clear which records are considered to belong to a "visit." Here's the code, and Figure 10-4 shows a screen's worth of our massaged data.

```
#!/usr/bin/perl
#logparse.cgi reads biglog and
#parses it as called by getlog.html
format STDOUT =
@<<<<<<<<<<<<<<<<<<<<<<<<<<<< @<<<<<<<<<<<<<<  @<<<<<
@<<<<<<<<<  @<<<<<<<<<
$host,$page,$date,$tim,$read
.
format STDOUT_TOP =
```

```
Visitor                          Page             Date    Arr
time   Time on pg
==============================================================
.
open (LOG,"biglog");
@in = <LOG>;
close LOG;
print "Content-type: text/html\n\n";
foreach $in (@in) {
  @nvp = split(/&/, $in);
  foreach $nvp (@nvp) {
    ($nam, $val) = split(/=/,$nvp);
    $plog{$nam,$tot} = $val;
    $plog{'read',$tot} = "";
    if ($nam eq "date") {
      ($plog{'day',$tot},$plog{'dt',$tot},
        $plog{'tim',$tot},$plog{'zone',$tot})
        = split(/ /,$val);
      if ($plog{'host',$tot} eq
        $plog{'host',$tot-1}) {
      $now = $plog{'tim',$tot}; $was =
        $plog{'tim',$tot-1};
      $plog{'read',$tot-1} = &subtime
      }
      elsif ($plog{'host',$tot} eq
        $plog{'host',$tot-2}) {
      $now = $plog{'tim',$tot}; $was =
        $plog{'tim',$tot-2};
      $plog{'read',$tot-2} = &subtime
      }
    } #---end 'date' nvp
  } #---end nvp
  ++$tot;
} #----end log line
foreach $x (1 .. $tot) {
  $host = $plog{'host',$x};
  $date = substr($plog{'dt',$x},0,6);
```

```
  if ($host eq $plog{'host',$x-1}) {
    $host = "";$date = "";
  }
  $tim=$plog{'tim',$x};$read=$plog{'read',$x};
  $page = $plog{'page',$x};
  write;
  if ($plog{'host',$x} ne $plog{'host',$x+1}) {
    print
"=====================================================================\n";
  }
}

sub subtime {
  ($nowh, $nowm, $nows) = split(/:/,$now);
  ($wash, $wasm, $wass) = split(/:/,$was);
  if ($nowh < $wash) {
    $nowh +=24;
  }
  if ($nowm < $wasm) {
    $nowm +=60; $nowh -=1;
  }
  if ($nows < $wass) {
    $nows +=60; $nowm -=1;
  }
  $readh = ($nowh - $wash);
  $readm = ($nowm - $wasm);
  $reads = ($nows - $wass);
  if ($readh < 10) { ($readh = "0$readh") }
  if ($readm < 10) { ($readm = "0$readm") }
  if ($reads < 10) { ($reads = "0$reads") }
  return "$readh:$readm:$reads";
}
```

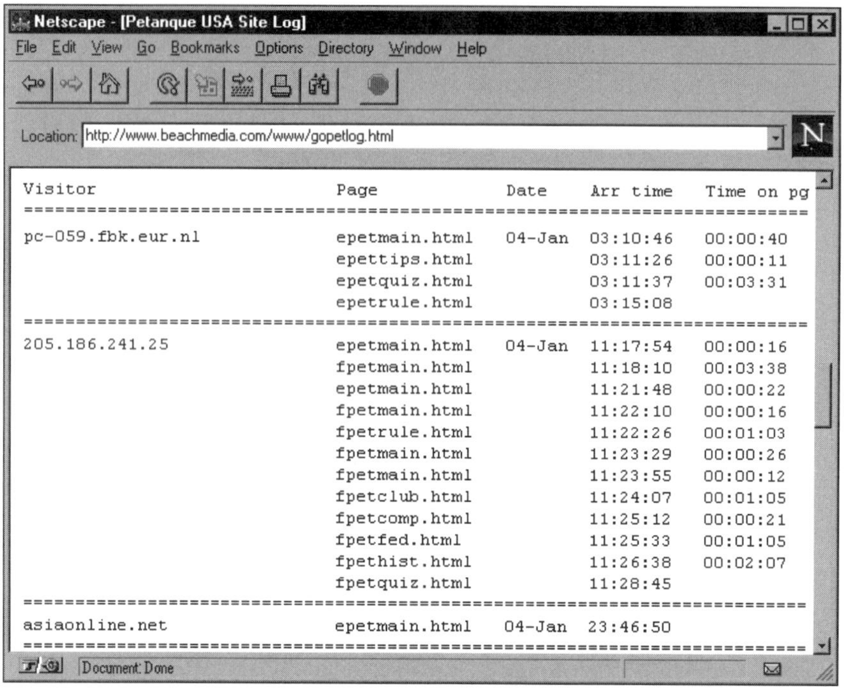
Netscape - [Petanque USA Site Log]
File Edit View Go Bookmarks Options Directory Window Help
Location: http://www.beachmedia.com/www/gopetlog.html
Visitor Page Date Arr time Time on pg
pc-059.fbk.eur.nl epetmain.html 04-Jan 03:10:46 00:00:40
epettips.html 03:11:26 00:00:11
epetquiz.html 03:11:37 00:03:31
epetrule.html 03:15:08
205.186.241.25 epetmain.html 04-Jan 11:17:54 00:00:16
fpetmain.html 11:18:10 00:03:38
epetmain.html 11:21:48 00:00:22
fpetmain.html 11:22:10 00:00:16
fpetrule.html 11:22:26 00:01:03
fpetmain.html 11:23:29 00:00:26
fpetmain.html 11:23:55 00:00:12
fpetclub.html 11:24:07 00:01:05
fpetcomp.html 11:25:12 00:00:21
fpetfed.html 11:25:33 00:01:05
fpethist.html 11:26:38 00:02:07
fpetquiz.html 11:28:45
asiaonline.net epetmain.html 04-Jan 23:46:50
Document: Done

Figure 10-4: *Site visits as reported by blog.cgi and logparse.cgi.*

It must be obvious—we sincerely hope—that if we were willing to let the display overflow horizontally it would be child's play to add information about where each visitor came from and what browser software is in use. In fact, the whole point of the *blog.cgi/ logparse.cgi* partnership is that they can be considered generic, and can be adapted to provide whatever reporting format makes you and your sponsors happy. The only caveat is to reset the *biglog* data file on a regular basis—on a busy site, *biglog* will soon become *hugelog* and then *enormouslog*, and reporting will slow down noticeably.

COLLECTING BUTTERFLIES ON THE WEB

Once a year, in the fall, millions of Monarch butterflies from all over the USA and Canada head south, like their human counterparts the snowbirds, to winter in Florida and Mexico. They reproduce in early spring, and the next generation then remigrates north in a resplendently colorful flittering flight of fancy.

Figure 10-5.

This phenomenon is fairly well-known for inspiring various Latin American novelists of the Magical Realism school into flights of fancy of their own. It's less well known that lepidopterists study it with a passion bordering on mania—it's the most spectacular butterfly migration in the world, and that fact that individual Monarchs will often fly thousands of miles to return to the very same spot where their grandparents wintered is definitely interesting.

The fringe of this phenomenon brushes past us here in California, and once in a while we'll contribute our ha'penny's worth to science by reporting to our friendly neighborhood lepidopterists that they're swarming on the Torrey Pines in our front yard (the butterflies, not the lepidopterists). If we throw in some scientificky sounding data like vanishing bearings and ambient temperature they're always ridiculously grateful.

There's plenty of information about Monarchs on the Web, but the Web isn't being used to actually gather data on their peregrinations. Very wisely, since there are far too many pranksters around to make any Web-gathered data reliable. However, using our authors' license, we're going to pretend that the world is more perfect than it really is, and use totally faked-up Monarch migration data as an exercise in developing a searchable database on a Web site.

RECORD GATHERING

Figure 10-6 shows the form we developed so that users all across the migration area could report their observations. Thirty-one data fields—more than enough for an exercise like this, but if we were doing this for real we would probably allow for even more.

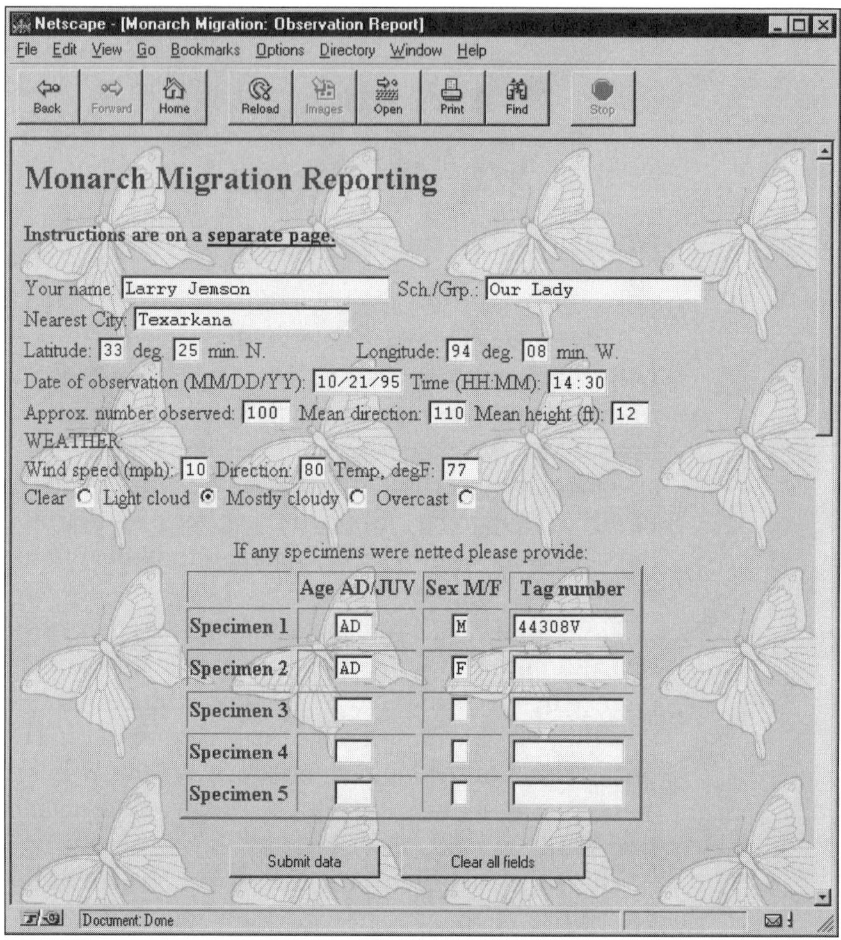

Figure 10-6: *The observation report form.*

The form, BUTTERF.HTML, sends its data by POST to the data manager *domon.cgi*, some of whose features will be familiar by now:

```
#!/usr/bin/perl
#domon.cgi reads POST query string from
#butterf.html and stores in monarch.rec
$title = "Monarch Observation data - Form
   response";
read (STDIN,$in,$ENV{'CONTENT_LENGTH'});
&pagehead;
$e{'sysdate'} = `date +"%I:%M %p %Z %d %b
   %y"`;
@nvp = split(/&/, $in);
foreach $nvp (@nvp) {
  ($nam, $val) = split(/=/,$nvp);
  $val =~ s/\+/ /g;
  $val =~ s/%([a-fA-F0-9][a-fA-F0-9])/
     pack("C", hex($1))/eg;
  $e{$nam} = $val;
}
if ($e{'name'}) {
  print "Thankyou for your response,
      $e{'name'}.<BR>\n",
  "Date: $e{'sysdate'}<BR>\n",
  "return to the
     <A HREF=\"../butterf.html\">Data Entry
     Form</A><BR>\n",
  "or go to the
     <A HREF=\"../mquery.html\">Database
     query</A><BR>\n";
  open (BUTT,">>monarch.rec") || die
     "Can't open file monarch.rec";
  print BUTT
pack("A22A30A30A30A3A2A3A2A8A5A6A3A3A2A2A3AA3AA15A3AA15A3AA15A3AA15A3AA15",
$e{'sysdate'}, $e{'name'}, $e{'grp'}, $e{'city'},
$e{'latdeg'}, $e{'latmin'},
$e{'londeg'}, $e{'lonmin'}, $e{'date'}, $e{'time'},
$e{'num'}, $e{'vanb'},$e{'alt'}, $e{'wvel'}, $e{'wdir'},
$e{'temp'}, $e{'cloud'}, $e{'age1'}, $e{'sex1'}, $e{'tag1'},
$e{'age2'}, $e{'sex2'}, $e{'tag2'}, $e{'age3'}, $e{'sex3'},
$e{'tag3'}, $e{'age4'}, $e{'sex4'}, $e{'tag4'}, $e{'age5'},
$e{'sex5'}, $e{'tag5'});
```

```
    print BUTT "\n";
    close BUTT;
  }
  else {
    print "Sorry, we can't accept anonymous
      entries.<BR>\n",
    "<A HREF=\"../butter.html\">Return to data
      entry form</A><BR>\n";
  }
  &pagetail;

  #-------- subroutines -------
  #....[the usual]
```

The first half of domon.cgi is just the familiar process of splitting out the name=value pairs into an array, and adding a 32nd data field—the system date/time. When it comes to database management in Perl, there's an easy way and a hard way—we chose the "sort-of-easy" way, which is to write to a conventional data file "monarch.rec" in such a way that the width of each field in each record is absolutely predictable. The sum of the widths of all 32 of our fields is 250—add one for a newline character, and that makes 251. Fixed-width databases may lack elegance, but they make it very easy to pull the variables back out again and they allow for virtual keying, since it's childishly easy to figure out where you need to go using the seek( ) operator to retrieve record number 112, let's say.

We achieve this simple file architecture using the pack ( ) operator. That long parenthesis following "pack", that looks as if it might be a message from the KGB, simply says "Field widths for the upcoming data are 22,30,30,30,3....etc.

MAKING USE OF THE DATA

When it comes to handling database queries, we need to be just a bit subtle. We'd like to give the user a free choice of which fields to display, so that the resulting readout doesn't get ridiculously wide. We also want to allow for some kind of simple search criterion, such as "all records from latitudes greater than 42ºN" or "all records entered by Paul Martinez." That's pretty easy—all it takes is one text field for the search criterion and a suite of 32 check boxes to turn on and off field reporting. MQUERY.HTML is shown in Figure 10-7.

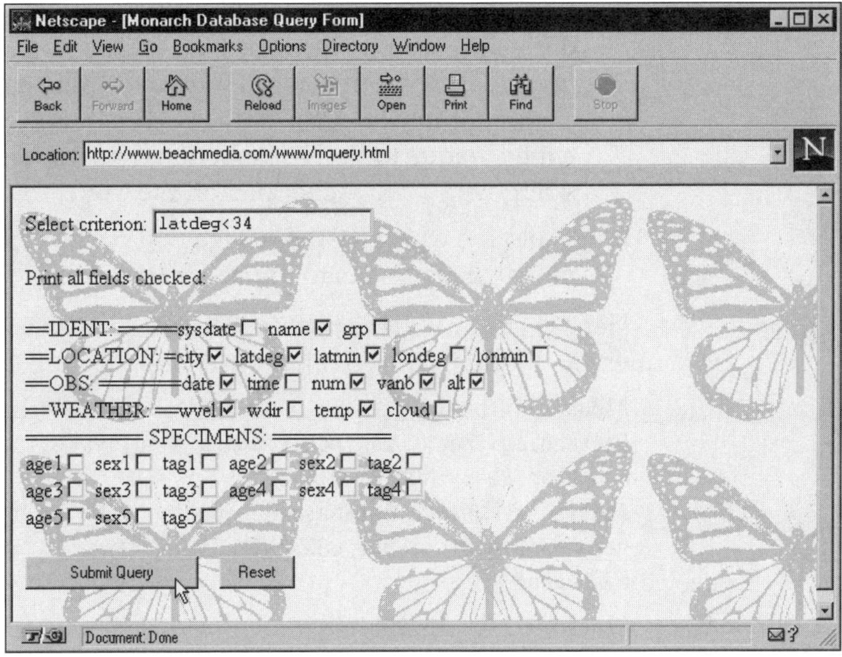

Figure 10-7: *The Monarch Database Query Form.*

We've got two things going for us here. The first is that, this being a scientific enterprise, we can trust our users to enter search criteria like "latdeg<34" and we don't have to spend energy constructing subroutines to interpret the vernacular of ordinary mortals. The other is that, when it comes to formatting and lining up the data, Netscsape's TABLE routines basically do the job for us. Here are a few tricky little points:

- Criteria like "latdeg<34" are fine for math, but when it comes to displaying them every > must be converted to > and every < to <
- Since each record is evaluated to see whether it passes the search criterion, what happens if there is no criterion? If the

user wants to see certain fields of *all* records, in other words? We use an old database dodge here—setting the criterion to "2>1" which is guaranteed to evaluate to true. Every darn time.

- It's no good depending on the old "split /=/" routine to derive the search criterion, since it may well contain a *bona fide* equal sign of its own. The name=value pair may come across, for instance, as "crit=cloud==4". So we use a different technique to derive $subcrit, which is the name=value string with "crit=" chopped off the front.
- The same weird KGB message that packed the data file monarch.rec serves to unpack it again.

Here's getmon.cgi, the routine that interprets a user database query and formats the result as a Netscape TABLE (Figure 2-8):

```
#!/usr/bin/perl
#getmon.cgi reads monarch.rec and displays
#data as RQ by MQUERY.HTML
$title = "Monarch Database Readout";
read (STDIN,$in,$ENV{'CONTENT_LENGTH'});
&pagehead;

$thead = "<TR ALIGN=left>";

@nvp = split(/&/, $in);
foreach $nvp (@nvp) {
  $nvp =~ s/%([a-fA-F0-9][a-fA-F0-9])/
      pack("C", hex($1))/eg;
  ($nam, $val) = split(/=/,$nvp);
  $val =~ s/\+/ /g;
  $e{$nam} = $val;
  if ($nam ne "crit") {
      $thead .= "<TH>$nam"; #add $nam to TABLE
                             #HEADER row
  }
}
$subcrit =
  substr($nvp[0],(index($nvp[0],"=")+1),31);
$test = "\$" . $subcrit;
if ($subcrit eq "") {
```

```
  $test = "2>1";
} #No search criterion, so set $test to
#an expression that always evaluates true
$subcrit =~ s/\</&lt;/g; #convert < > chars
$subcrit =~ s/\>/&gt;/g; #to HTML entities
print "Your search criterion was $subcrit
   <P>\n";
print "<TABLE BORDER=4>$thead";
open (BUTT,"monarch.rec");
while ($rec = <BUTT>) {
($sysdate, $name, $grp, $city, $latdeg, $latmin, $londeg,
$lonmin, $date,$time, $num, $vanb, $alt, $wvel, $wdir, $temp,
$cloud, $age1, $sex1, $tag1,$age2, $sex2, $tag2, $age3,
$sex3, $tag3, $age4, $sex4, $tag4, $age5, $sex5, $tag5) =
unpack("A22A30A30A30A3A2A3A2A8A5A6A3A3A2A2A3AA3AA15A3AA15A3AA15A3AA15A3AA15",
$rec);
  if (eval $test) {
    print "\n<TR>"; #This rec passes $test so
                    #start a new TABLE ROW
    if ($e{'sysdate'} eq "on") { print
       "<TD>$sysdate  ";
    }
    if ($e{'name'} eq "on") { print
       "<TD>$name  ";
    }

#....and so on through 29 other fields to..

    if ($e{'tag5'} eq "on") { print
       "<TD>$tag5  ";
    }
  }
}
close BUTT;
print "\n</TABLE>\n";
&pagetail;

#-------- subroutines -------
sub pagehead {
```

```
  print "Content-type: text/html\n\n\n",
        "<HTML>\n<HEAD>\n",
        "<TITLE>$title</TITLE>\n",
        "</HEAD><BODY>\n",
        "<H2>RESULT OF YOUR QUERY OF THE
   MONARCH MIGRATION DATABASE:</H2>\n";
}

sub pagetail {
  print "<HR>\n<ADDRESS>Beach Media Web Services, San Diego</
ADDRESS>\n",
        "</BODY>\n</HTML>\n";
}
```

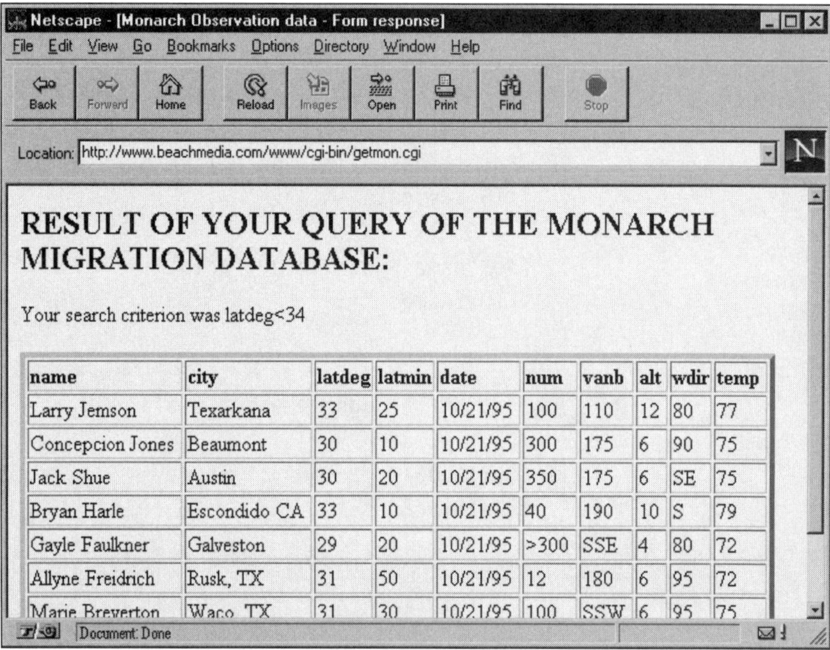

RESULT OF YOUR QUERY OF THE MONARCH MIGRATION DATABASE:

Your search criterion was latdeg<34

name	city	latdeg	latmin	date	num	vanb	alt	wdir	temp
Larry Jemson	Texarkana	33	25	10/21/95	100	110	12	80	77
Concepcion Jones	Beaumont	30	10	10/21/95	300	175	6	90	75
Jack Shue	Austin	30	20	10/21/95	350	175	6	SE	75
Bryan Harle	Escondido CA	33	10	10/21/95	40	190	10	S	79
Gayle Faulkner	Galveston	29	20	10/21/95	>300	SSE	4	80	72
Allyne Freidrich	Rusk, TX	31	50	10/21/95	12	180	6	95	72
Marie Breverton	Waco, TX	31	30	10/21/95	100	SSW	6	95	75

Figure 10-8: *A Monarch Database query fulfilled.*

Somehow we doubt that the "official" Monarch data-gatherers will be beating a path to our door asking for our help. *getmon.cgi* is useful as a demonstration of how cgi-bin can answer a specific need for data reading. Let's face it, though, it's not very user-friendly—and we could all think of immediate improvements. Multiple search criteria, for instance, with Boolean relationships. Before we knew where we were, we'd be devising a routine that responded to queries like:

```
SELECT name grp date num alt
  FROM monarch.rec
  WHERE num>20
    AND latdeg>42
```

....and there's another perfectly fine wheel we would have re-invented.

Commercial Database Integration

Anybody who has had any serious contact with the world of databases will recognize the fanciful query we just displayed as Structured Query Language (SQL, pronounced *SEQUEL*).

SQL is not, in fact, a "commercial" database language but an ANSI/ISO standard (it has in common with HTML the fact that its standards are royally disregarded by its most influential users). Part of its appeal is that it's designed for easy embedding within programs written in many different languages for many different platforms, precisely so that programmers don't constantly have to re-invent the wheel when it comes time to give their users an interface to the underlying data. SQL is, therefore, ubiquitous, not always visible, and flexible enough to cope with all but the most mightily complex relational database management.

Web-SQL Options

To bring the power of SQL to your cgi-bin setup, all you really need is a UNIX-compatible SQL package.

For gSQL, which was specifically designed for this precise purpose, you need look no further than NCSA. gSQL is written in C, but the SQL instructions are passed in *proc* files, which aren't too hard to get used to. The code, and the documentation, are at:

ftp://ftp.ncsa.uiuc.edu/Web/tools/gsql/starthere.html

Under the heading of "commercial," Microsoft markets an SQL server, and very nice it is, too, at over $1200. Can it be linked to Web page queries via cgi-bin? Absolutely.

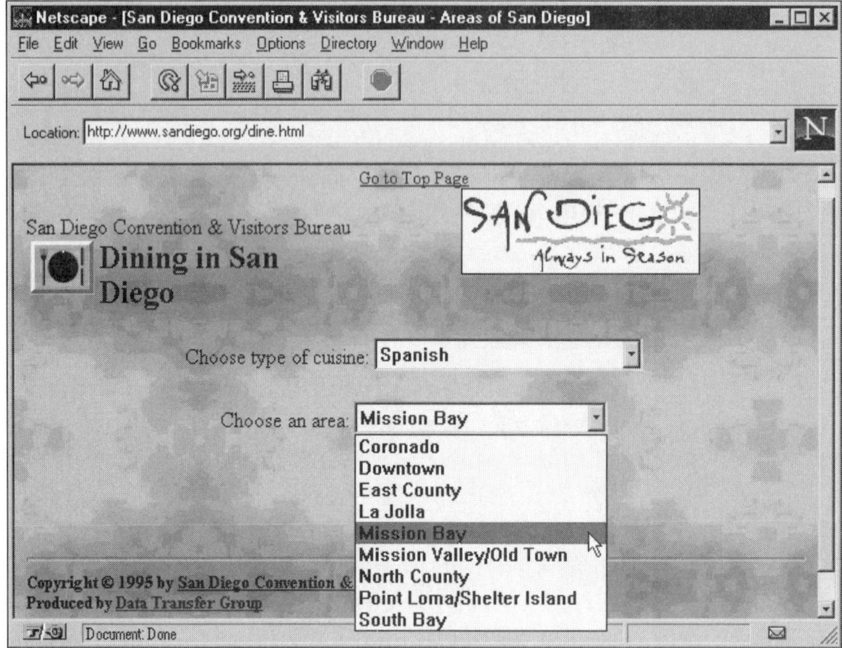

Figure 10-9: *Data Transfer Group's HTTP/mSQL link providing San Diego ConVis info.*

Figure 10-9 shows an implementation of the link from Web to Microsoft SQL by our own sysadmin, Mark Burgess. The requirement was to provide user-friendly lookup of our fine city's facilities on behalf of the San Diego Convention and Visitors' Bureau (ConVis). This particular section is Restaurants—there are also sections on Hotels, Arts/Events, Transport, Shopping, and Mexico. All of them get over the problem of query formatting by giving users of the database a range of options as their primary query method, but some free-form name searching is also allowed.

The whole thing, including the HTTP server, runs on a PC using Windows NT. On the Web server end, a cgi-bin program takes the user's request from the onscreen form shown in Figure

10-9 and reprocesses it into what's called an IDC file. The IDC file contains a SQL query and a format template for the response. The Internet server, running Microsoft SQL, accepts the query and formats the response. Then it's over to the cgi interface again to put an HTML wrapper on the response so that the user sees it as an ordinary Web page.

TIP

*If you're thinking of visiting San Diego, Mark's database at **http://www.sandiego.org** is well worth consulting. So is our own take on local happenings, at **http://www.zoomsd.com/**. Although the addresses are aliased to look different, the machines are just a few feet apart. Since we aren't SQL gurus, our database engine is 100% tailor-made perl, and certain privileged users are allocated passwords allowing them to add database records (concert dates, for example).*

Also under the heading of commercial, a company called Aegis has a product called FoxWeb that, they claim, can be installed with no knowledge of cgi-bin at all. It interfaces with FoxPro (how did you guess?), and its cost is $250 per server installation. Check it out at:

http://www.foxweb.com/

Perl/Database Language Options

We said earlier that one of the virtues of SQL was that it loves to be embedded in other languages. So how about our own cgi-bin language of choice, Perl? Again—absolutely. One example is the msql-Perl adapter at:

http://www.law.washington.edu/~madsen/manpage/Msql.html

Another excellent example of the Perl/SQL marriage is WDB, invented by the European Southern Observatory to keep track of their telescope bookings and made available to the Perl community via the Web page at:

http://arch-http.hq.eso.org/bfrasmus/wdb/intro.html

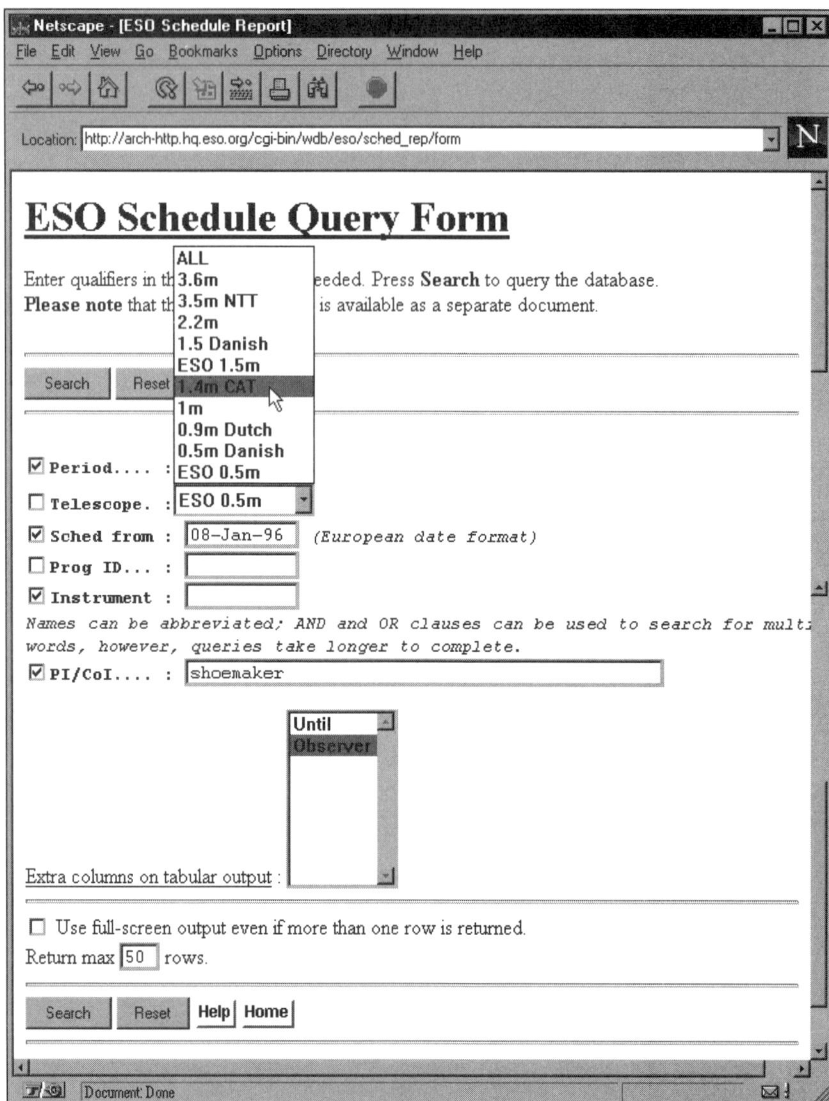

Figure 10-10: *Complex user inquiries can be handled by the WDB Perl/SQL combo.*

Other well-known database "languages" that have been allied to Perl include Sybase (sybperl), Oracle (oraperl), and dBase (dbperl). Just about every Perl-compatible database can be found at either or both of these two FTP sites:

ftp.demon.co.uk/pub/perl/db/

ftp.uu.net/archive/pub/database/perl-interfaces

Using Databases & Scripts for Automated Page Makeup

Databases can really come in handy when you have a lot of Web pages that get updated on a regular basis. You're soon liable to get tired of redoing every page every time you need to do an update. Your work can be made a lot easier if you can turn the content of your pages into database format. Some questions to ask yourself are:

- Are there clearly definable, repetitive items that can be turned into database "fields"?
- Can you define an order in which to assemble these items?
- Are there consistent elements that appear on your Web pages, or variable elements that can be substituted depending on content?

If the answers to the above are yes, you may be able to automate page makeup using either a custom-designed Perl program or a commercial package. You can use more or less the same techniques discussed in the section on retrieving the monarch butterfly data. If you don't want to do it yourself you have two options. First, outline what you want carefully, design the way you want the output to look, then take a nice plate of cookies to the programmer down the hall. Or use one of the commercial packages for automated page makeup that are just coming on the market.

Another Refuge for the Perlophobes

Quite a few "Netrepreneurs" are doing their best to cash in on the (substantial) population who would like to manage Web/database operations but feel cgi-bin is beyond them. Like "Webforms," which we covered briefly in Chapter 9, "Forms, Feedback & cgi-bin" these packages make use of hidden form fields to pass instructions to an all-purpose cgi-bin program. Sometimes the data processing is done at the vendor's own site, which slows things down somewhat—but this is not always the case. Perhaps the most popular strap-on database manager is *Cold Fusion,* which has a SQL database lurking beneath the surface. Figure 10-11 shows a physician search database "powered by Cold Fusion." Here's the URL:

http://www.allaire.com/

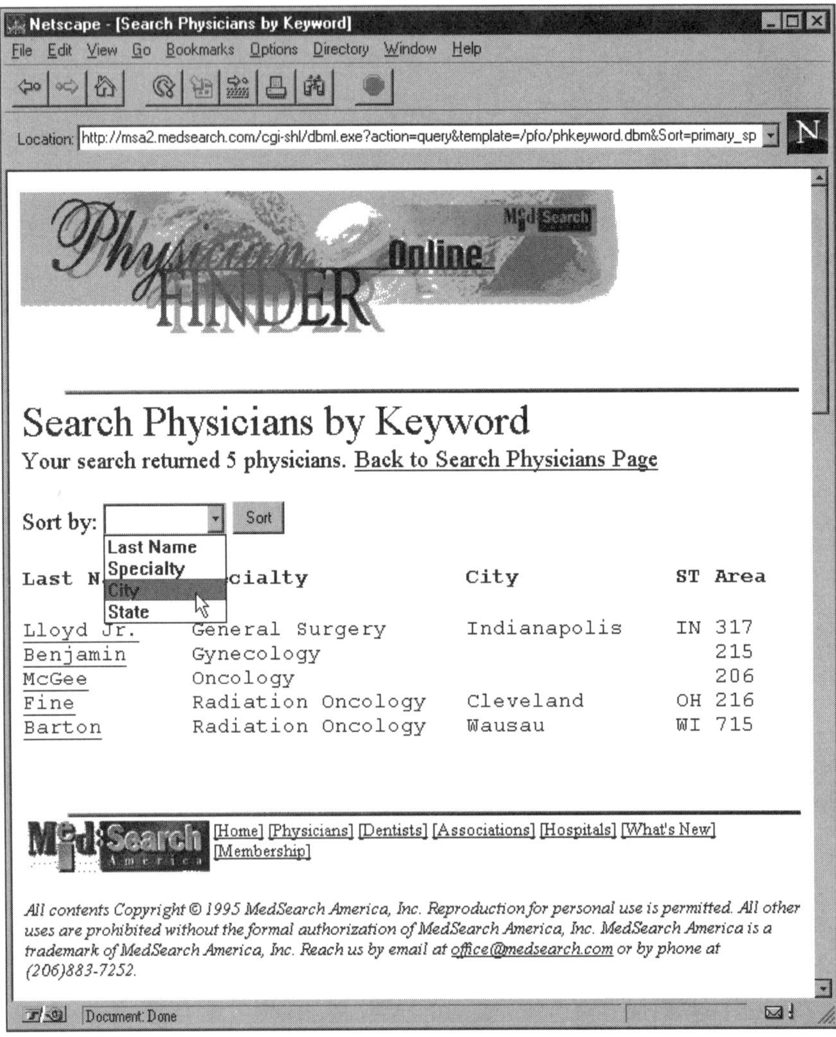

Figure 10-11: *Physician database at MedSearch America, Inc., run by "Cold Fusion."*

Taking Control With Your Own Server

If you've actually got through this whole course so far, including writing your own cgi-bin scripts, we wouldn't blame you if you were feeling a little bit cocky by now. In fact, you may have just the chutzpah it takes to run your own server.

"Who me? You mean a *Webmaster*?" Yeah, you. It's not as difficult as it might seem. Even if all you have is a dial-up connection to the Internet, you can run your own server right off your desktop. Of course there are a few caveats:

- Your server will only be operative as long as you maintain an open connection with your access provider. This means if you want 24-hour access you need to have a dedicated phone line and be willing to pay for it.
- Although this can be a perfectly safe operation, you should probably learn a little bit about security before allowing the world access to your computer.
- A local server running under Windows is an excellent resource for checking the performance of pages you're developing, including server-side operations. However, if your intention is to transfer it all to a permanent UNIX site, there's no guarantee that everything will work exactly the same.

Contrary to common assumptions, though, it doesn't take a supercomputer with 10 gigabytes of storage space to run a Web server. You can run your own server right off your little 486 or Pentium with about 16mb of RAM. Including the server software, it can take as little as 5 to 10mb of disk space. It goes without saying that the faster your computer, the better your server will perform.

Since we're firm believers in demystifying all the hocus-pocus that goes on in the back room of the computer shop, we're going to show you the guts of a server right here. We chose the O'Reilly Personal Website to install on our machine, because it's designed to run on Windows 95 and they offer an easy-to-install 60-day trial package. This server, designed exclusively for personal use, only allows a maximum of two users at a time. We originally installed it and had it running in less than 30 minutes—honest.

Figures 10-12 through 10-15 show four of the dozen or so setup panels that run our Web server. The kind of information you see here will be common to all Web servers. The domain name of our access provider is the most important item. Then we specify a working directory where our Web information will be stored (Figure 10-12).

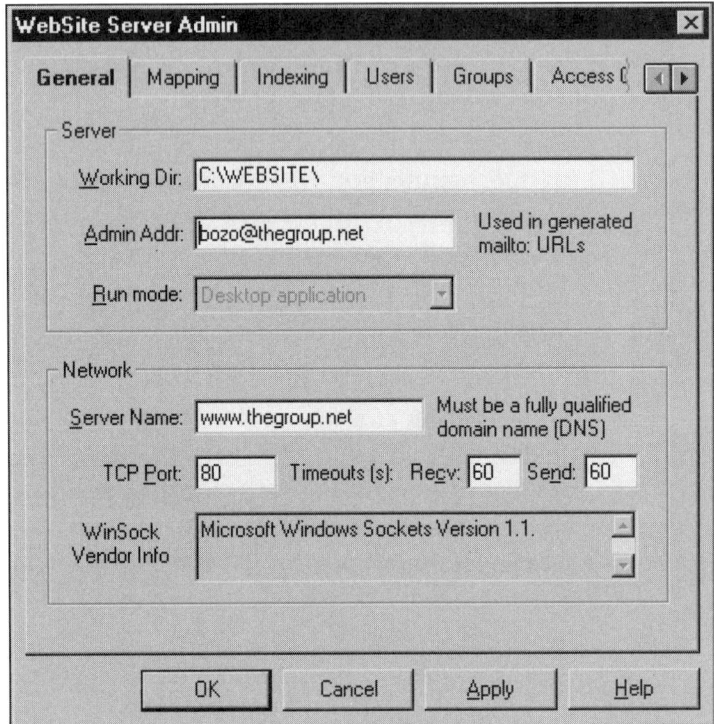

Figure 10-12: *Some principal information about our Web server includes the domain name of our access provider.*

The working directory becomes our root directory. If we define it carefully, visitors will be prohibited from browsing the rest of our computer system, or even seeing the structure. We also need to tell the server where to find other kinds of documents, like cgi-bin scripts (Figure 10-13).

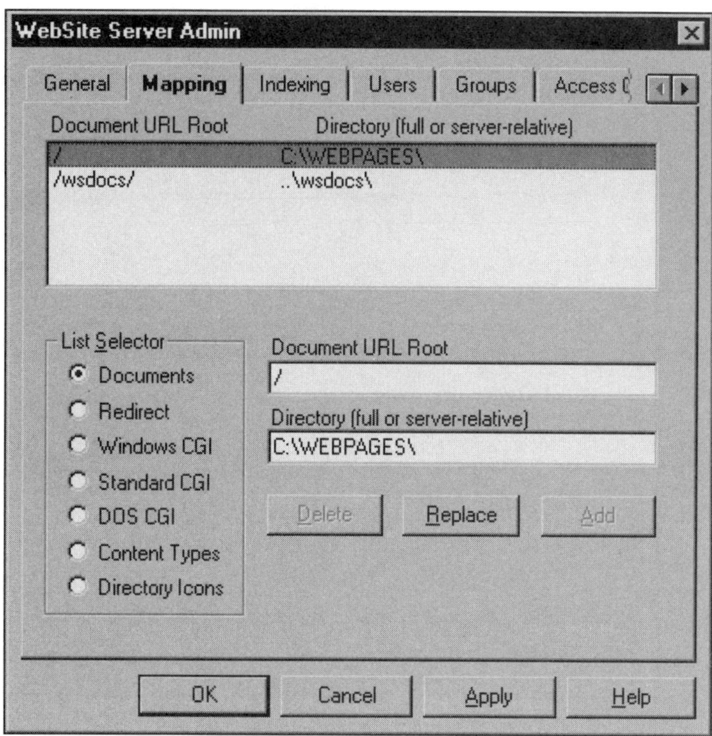

Figure 10-13: *Here we specify the root directory that Web visitors will be allowed to enter.*

You can set up user accounts with passwords if you want to allow restricted access (Figure 10-14). You'll also have to set up an administrator's account so that only an authorized individual can change server settings.

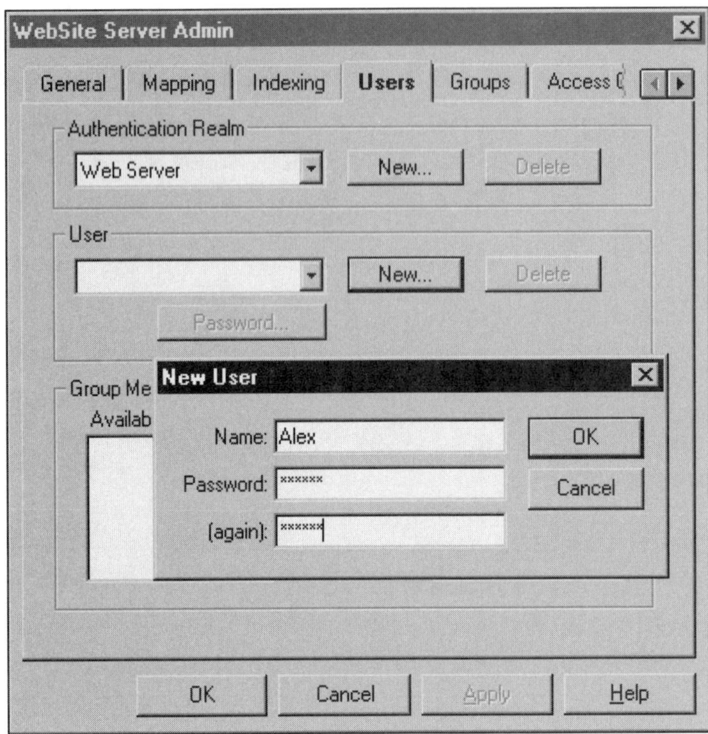

Figure 10-14: *We can set up user accounts here.*

Define the kinds of documents the server is liable to encounter by specifiying MIME types (Figure 10-15).

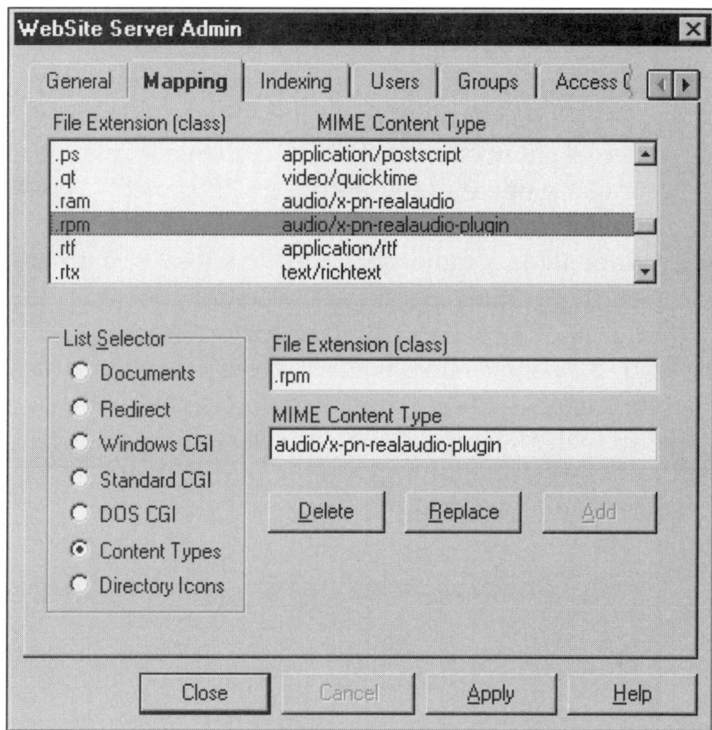

Figure 10-15: *This panel allows us to add MIME types for new applications.*

So what are the advantages of running your own server? For one, you can try out all your cgi-bin scripts and install your own special applications. (As you can see in the setup we're doing in Figure 10-15, we used it to test our RealAudio setup and files, without having to bother our sysadmin a dozen times a day.) For small business, research or educational use, you can use it to share documents and information with colleagues anywhere in the world. Just turn on your server and let them know you're active. The URL of the server, from other people's point of view, will be http:// followed by the IP address assigned to you for normal SLIP/PPP connections. You'll be able to tell from your access logs whether the job was accomplished. And it can all be perfectly safe and private—after all, nobody can reach you unless they know you're there and what your IP address is. You decide what directories they access and what files are available (as per Figure 10-13).

A Web server running on a LAN can be used even without the Internet connection to share documents across the network (the popular name for this setup is an "Intranet"). A wide variety of server software packages are available for both personal and professional (or commercial) use. Netscape's Commercial Server and Communications Server are two very good ones for business use. Netscape's new FastTrack Server for Windows NT (which was just out in a beta version as this book went to press) also provides an inexpensive solution for small businesses, with a seamless integration with Netscape and Netscape Gold's Editor. See Figure 10-16 for a preview look. You can get information about this and their full-scale server from Netscape's home page.

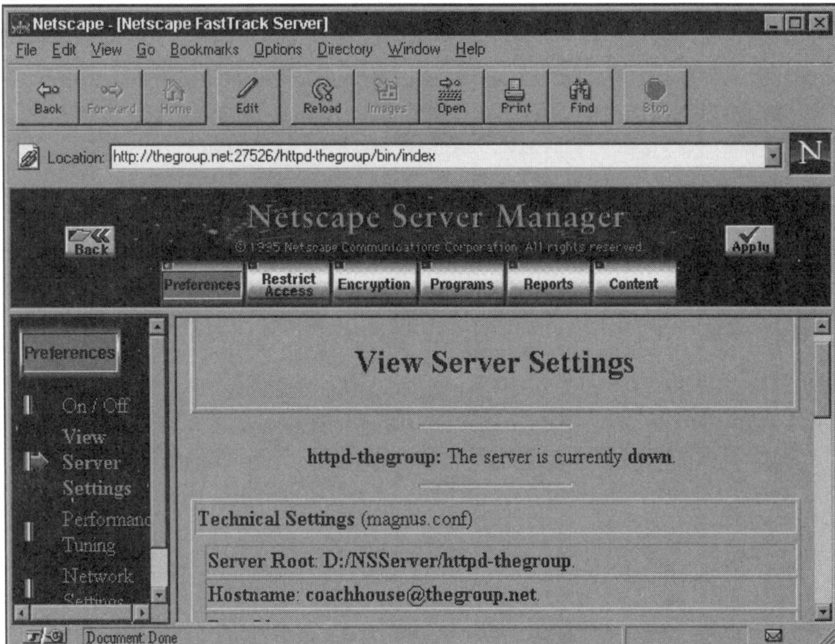

Figure 10-16: *Netscape's FastTrack Server is an inexpensive Web server package designed for small businesses on a budget.*

Several other server packages are available on the Internet, a number of them free, including the popular NCSA server, if you're the do-it-yourself type.

Publicizing Your Web Page

Building a Web site is not quite like building a baseball stadium. While the idea that "if you build it, the people will come" may work in baseball, on the Web you could easily end up more like that lonely warthog in the back corner of the zoo if you don't make some effort to let people know you're there.

So how do you get people to visit your Web site? The Number 1 way, at the heart of the Web itself, is incoming links, sometimes called "back-links."

Thinking about how to get people to visit your site, the question to ask is "How do people find Web pages, anyway?" The answer is, in probable order of importance:

- Topic searchers like Yahoo, WebCrawler, Lycos, and AltaVista.
- Magazines and periodicals
- Books like this one
- Usenet newsgroups and FAQs

If your site is really just a personal "home page" with information about your music CD collection and your son's amazing prowess at soccer, you're practically out of luck on all of these prime highways into your page. We can guarantee—personally—that magazine and book authors pay zero attention, these days, to exhortations to "check out my kewl new page." Most readers of the Usenet **comp.infosystems.www.*** newsgroup set would have about the same reaction, unless you can persuade them that there's something *truly* innovative to look at. A better approach with that crowd is to ask advice about a problem you're having — "Can anyone tell me why my inline JPEG is coming out all muddy?"—then everyone will go and have a look just to feel superior. That kind of thing goes down well on certain IRC channels, as well, where many people are hanging around waiting for something to happen.

As the proud owner of a really *personal* home page, your only hope of international fame is the Nerd World index, at:

http://challenge.tiac.net/users/dstein/nw163.html

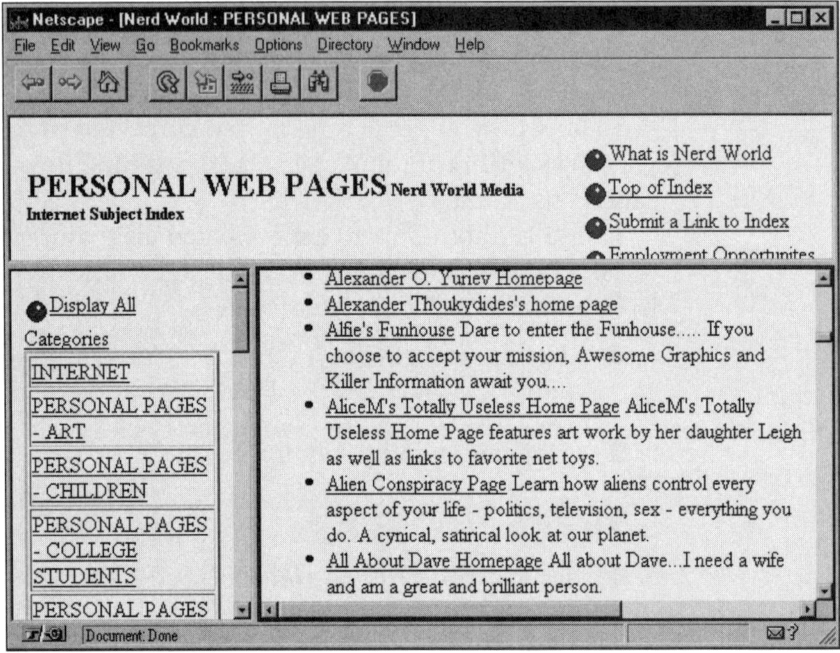

Figure 10-17: *One small part of the Nerd World index of personal home pages.*

We can't say how you qualify for inclusion in this index, but judging by its content, the tests are not exactly rigorous. It's kind of cute actually, and a pleasant way to spend a rainy day, but last we looked it was a Big Honking Page at around 450kb, and loading it took most of the only rainy day *we've* had in months. They're obviously going to have to do something about that—probably have by now.

If, on the other hand, you have a site on a topic of legitimate public interest, many of the topic indexes and searchers will list it for you—although some of them are so snowed under with requests that it could take a while. Save yourself an afternoon's Web cruising and get all your requests in at once with:

http://www.submit-it.com

Submit It!, maintained by Scott Banister, is your one-stop shop for 14 Web indexes and searchers, including Yahoo, The WebCrawler, The Starting Point, Lycos, Infoseek, Harvest, Apollo, the Whole Internet Catalog, and Nerd World (see Figure 10-18). We recommend, however, that you visit each of these searchers yourself first so that you get an idea how to tailor your information to fit in with their individual approaches.

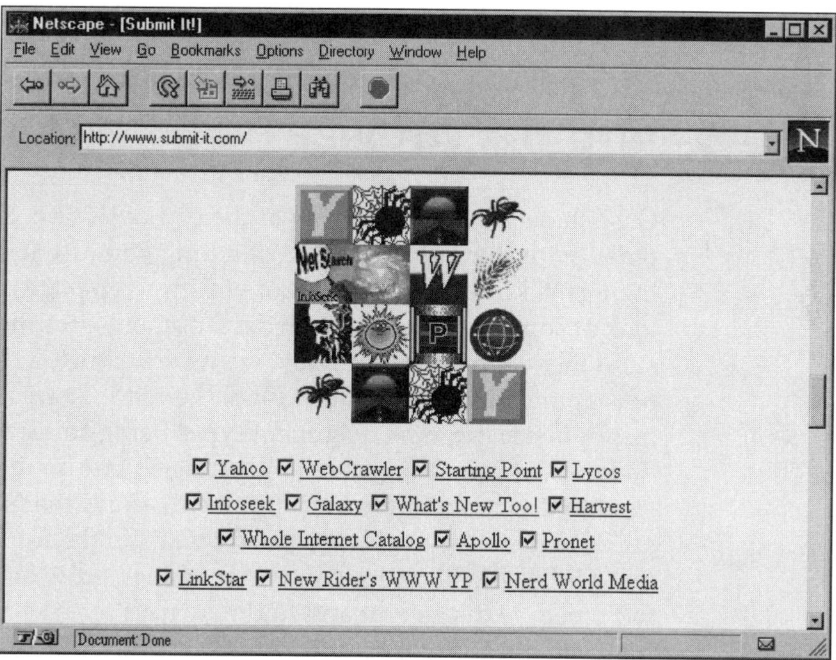

Figure 10-18: *Just check off the searchers on which you want to add your listing.*

As a supplement to the searchers, or as your last desperate hope if they ignore you, it's worth devoting some serious time to Web cruising, looking for sites and people that have enough in common with you that they might consider a back-link. The best approach is to first put in a forward link to them, then send e-mail saying "I hope you don't mind but I've linked to you. Please take a look at my page and see if you think a back link might be appropriate, blah blah..."

When you run out of ideas about whose arm to twist next, take a look at your access logs. See what kind of people are finding you, and where they're coming from. Who knows? Your page might have appeal to some offbeat set that never would have occurred to you...

TIP

You can get a readout of your backlinks at the AltaVista index. Enter "link:" followed by your URL. AltaVista is at:

http://www.altavista.digital.com

INTO THE FUTURE

Gosh, here we are all the way at the end of this book we set out to write, with the ambitious goal of telling you just about everything there is to know about the art of writing Web pages. We just took a look at some our favorite Web development sites this morning and suddenly we realize that while we were writing, a dozen or more new applications have come down the road. There are new plug-ins for Netscape, new document types being squeezed into the Web picture, and things are happening so fast on the multimedia front that we can barely keep up. We're afraid that's the way it's going to be for several years now. What's in the future, we wonder. The Web will undoubtedly continue to grow as more and more people discover it and find new uses for it.

As we discuss this prospect with our peer group, both face-to-face and on the Net, it amuses us to notice how everybody projects personal hopes into the future of the Web. A pal who's crazy about 3-D graphics confidently predicts that VR will take over everything. A colleague who's a C++ hacker thinks plug-in applications will make HTML obsolete, and a businesswoman we know simply sees the next frontier for capitalism to conquer. For ourselves, we'll just continue to enjoy the freedom to be creative in an international forum as we have since we first set finger on the Net.

We hope that one day all of us, you readers as well as we authors, will be proud of the fact that we were part of the first developmental wave. We hope, too, that some of you will be among the pioneers who forge new paths in the Webspace of tomorrow with Web applications that will enrich the lives of all of us.

If in the process of writing this book we've managed to pass on to you a tenth of the spirit of cooperation that we find on the Web every day, we'll be happy. But now it's time to send you on your way with your own dreams.

Good-bye and good luck. See you in the future.

Appendix A
About the Online Companion

Information is power! The Netscape Press Online Companion is all you need to be connected to the best Internet information and Netscape resources. It aids you with understanding the Internet and Netscape's role in the technology.

You can access the special Web site for purchasers of Netscape Press products at http://www.netscapepress.com/. Some of the valuable features of this special site include information on other Netscape Press titles, Netscape news, and Navigate!, the magazine for Netscape Press.

Navigate! is the official electronic publication of Netscape Press. Netscape Press is a joint effort between Ventana and Netscape Communications Corp., and serves as the publishing arm of Netscape. Navigate! is a monthly online publication that offers a wide range of articles and reviews aimed at Netscape users. Navigate! will also feature interviews with industry icons and experts, as well as articles excerpted from upcoming Netscape Press titles.

The *Official HTML Publishing for Netscape* Online Companion also links you to the Netscape Press catalog, where you will find useful press and jacket infomation on a variety of Netscape Press offerings. Plus, you have access to a wide selection of exciting new releases and coming attractions. In addition, the catalog allows you to order online the books you want without leaving home.

The Online Companion represents Netscape Press' ongoing commitment to offering the most dynamic and exciting products possible. And soon netscapepress.com will be adding more services, including more multimedia supplements, searchable indexes, and sections of the book reproduced and hyperlinked to the Internet resources they reference.

Free voice technical support is offered but is limited to installation-related issues; this free support is available for 30 days from the date you register your copy of the book. After the initial 30 days and for non-installation-related questions, please send all technical support questions via Internet e-mail to help@vmedia.com. Our technical support staff will research your question and respond promptly via e-mail.

Appendix B

About the Companion CD-ROM

The CD-ROM included with your copy of the *Official HTML for Netscape* book contains a wealth of valuable software, including the following:

- Adobe Acrobat Reader
- Cool Edit
- Counter
- LView Pro
- Mapedit
- Paint Shop Pro
- RTFtoHTML
- Web Forms
- WebWhacker
- WinZip

Installing the CD-ROM is simple. If you are running Windows 95, insert the CD into the CD-ROM drive and choose Run from the Start menu. Then double-click the viewer.exe icon. You'll see a welcome screen that introduces the CD.

If you are running Windows 3.11, insert the CD in your CD-ROM drive and with Windows running, select File, Run from the Program Manager. Then type D:\VIEWER (where D: is your CD-ROM drive) in the command-line box and press Enter. You'll see a menu screen offering several choices.

After the initial introduction, a menu screen appears. You can choose Netscape Press, CD Contents, Image Library, or Hot Picks. Click on a choice.

If you click on the Netscape Press option, you can read about Ventana or get further information about Netscape Press. Click on the item you want to know more about.

If you click on CD Contents, a list of the software that appears on the CD is displayed. Click on one of the folders to get further information about the program or utility. At the bottom of the description box, you can choose to view the README file or install the program to your hard drive.

The Image Library option displays the images that are available from the CD. You can click on the buttons at the bottom of the display to view backgrounds, icons, or images. Press Ctrl-Click to increase the view of the image. To scroll through the images, use the scroll arrows that appear on either side of the display box.

Choosing the Hot Picks option displays a list of other Netscape Press titles. Click on a book cover to read a brief description of each book.

Appendix C
HTML Tags

This list includes most of the HTML tags and attributes in common usage. Some HTML 3.0 tags that may not be generally supported are included, as they may be recognized by some browsers or expected to be instituted soon. This is *not* a complete set of all known HTML tags. A more complete, up-to-date HTML reference can be found at:

http://www.sandia.gov/sci_compute/elements.html

* *Designates Netscape extensions*
** *Designates HTML 3.0 proposed tags*

Structural Elements

<HTML>....</HTML>	Defines an HTML document
<HEAD>....</HEAD>	Document header
<TITLE>....</TITLE>	Document title
<BODY>....</BODY>	Document body
*BACKGROUND="any.gif"	
*BGCOLOR="#rrggbb"	
*TEXT="#rrggbb"	
*LINK="#rrggbb"	
*VLINK="#rrggbb"	
*ALINK="#rrggbb"	

**<BANNER>	
<DIV>	
ALIGN=	left, center, right, justify
NOWRAP	
CLEAR=	left, right, all

HEAD ELEMENTS

Note: These elements can occur only with the HEAD of a document.

<BASE>
<ISINDEX>
<LINK>
REL
REV
HREF
<META>
NAME
CONTENT
HTTP-EQUIV
** <STYLE>

BLOCK ELEMENTS

<H1> ... </H1>	Heading (values 1 to 6)
ALIGN=	left, center, right
NOWRAP	
**CLEAR=	left, right, all
**SEQNUM	
**SKIP	
**DINGBAT	
**SRC	
<ADDRESS>....</ADDRESS>	Address info section
**CLEAR=	left, right, all
NOWRAP	
<PRE>....</PRE>	Pre-formatted text

<BLOCKQUOTE>....</BLOCKQUOTE>	Citation (usually indented)
**<BQ>	Same as <BLOCKQUOTE> in HTML3.0
NOWRAP	
**CLEAR=	left, right, all
<HR>	Horizontal rule
*SIZE=n	
*WIDTH=	n or n%
*ALIGN=	left, right, center
*NOSHADE	
**CLEAR	
**SRC	
<P>	
ALIGN=	left, center, right, justify
**CLEAR=	left, right, all
NOWRAP	
**<NOTE> .... </NOTE>	
CLASS	Proposed classes: NOTE, CAUTION, WARNING
SRC	
**<FN> .... </FN>	Footnote (to be rendered as pop-up)
ID	
DIR	

List Elements

<UL> ... </UL>	Unordered (bulleted) list
*TYPE=disc, circle, square	
CLEAR	
PLAIN	
SRC	
**DINGBAT	
WRAP=	vert, horiz
COMPACT	

<OL> ... </OL>	Ordered (numbered) list
*TYPE=1, A, a, I, i	Designates numbers, upper or lower-case letters, upper or lowercase Roman numerals
*START=n	Initial letter or numeral for sequence
**SEQNUM	Same as START in HTML3.0
CLEAR	
CONTINUE	
COMPACT	
<LH>	List header (use for UL, OL, and DL)
<LI> .... </LI>	List item
*TYPE=	Changes current list type A/a/I/i for OL or disc/circle/square for UL
*VALUE	Changes current sequential number or alphabetic order value
<DL>....</DL>	Definition list
CLEAR	
COMPACT	
<DT>	Definition term
<DD>	Definition
<DIR> .... </DIR>	Directory list
<MENU> .... </MENU>	Menu list

Hypertext Anchors

<A >	Hypertext anchor
HREF	Defines document link by filename, bookmark, URL, or id
NAME	
SHAPE	default circle x, y, r rect x, y, w, h polygon x1, y1, x2, y2, ...
TITLE	
REV	
REL	

Lines & Spacing

 	Line break
CLEAR	
*<NOBR>	No line break
**<NOWRAP>	Same as <NOBR>
*<WBR>	Insert line or word break here as needed (soft break)
**<TAB>	
INDENT	
TO	
ALIGN=	left, center, right, decimal
DP	
*<CENTER>	

Images & Embedded Applications

<IMG>	Inline image
SRC	
ALIGN=	top, middle, bottom, left, right Netscape additions: texttop, absmiddle, baseline, absbottom
WIDTH	
HEIGHT	
UNITS= ens or pixels	
*BORDER	
VSPACE	
HSPACE	
ALT	
ISMAP	
LOWSRC	
<EMBED> .... </EMBED>	
SRC	
WIDTH	
HEIGHT	
attribute_1	
attribute_2	
<NOEMBED>...</NOEMBED>	

<APPLET>....</APPLET>	
CODE	
WIDTH	
HEIGHT	
CODEBASE	
NAME	
ALIGN	
VSPACE	
HSPACE	
*<SCRIPT>....</SCRIPT>	JavaScript
CODE	
WIDTH	
HEIGHT	
CODEBASE	
NAME	
ALIGN	
VSPACE	
HSPACE	

Informational Styles

<CITE>....</CITE>	Citation (usually italic)
<CODE>....</CODE>	Computer code (usually monospaced)
<EM>....</EM>	Emphasis (usually italics)
<KBD>....</KBD>	Keyboard input
<SAMP>....</SAMP>	Literal text
<STRONG>....</STRONG>	Emphasis (usually boldface)
<VAR>....</VAR>	Variable name (usually italic)
<DFN>	
<Q>	
<LANG>	
<AU>	

<PERSON>
<ACRONYM>
<ABBREV>
<INS>
<DEL>

Physical Font Styles

<B>....</B>	Boldface
<I>....</I>	Italic
<TT>....</TT>	Teletype (monospaced font)
<U>	Underline
<S>	Strikethrough
<BIG>	Big print
<SMALL>	Small print
<SUB>	Subscript
<SUP>	Superscript
* <FONT SIZE=n>	n=1to 7, default = 3.
* <BASEFONT SIZE=n>	n=1to 7, default = 3.

Form Elements

<FORM>....</FORM>	Interactive form section
ACTION	
METHOD	
ENCTYPE	
<INPUT>	Form field
TYPE	
VALUE	
<TEXTAREA>	Large form field
WRAP	off/virtual/physical
<SELECT>	List of options for a form field
<OPTION>	Item in a SELECT list

TABLES

<TABLE>

BORDER	
*BORDER=x	Border thickness
CLEAR=	left, right, all
NOFLOW	
ALIGN=	bleedleft, left, center, right, bleedright, justify (Horizontal alignment of table, not its elements)
COLSPEC	Specifies width and alignment of columns
UNITS	
DP	Specifies character to use for decimal point (dp=",")
WIDTH	
NOWRAP	

<CAPTION>

<TR>

ALIGN

<TH>

COLSPAN

ROWSPAN

ALIGN= left, right, center (default), justify

<TD>

ALIGN

**Math Elements

Note: ALL Math elements are proposed only, and not generally supported.

<MATH>
  BOX
<BOX>
<SUB>
<SUP>
<ABOVE>
<BELOW>
<VEC>
<BAR>
<DOT>
<DDOT>
<HAT>
<TILDE>
<SQRT>
< ROOT>
<ARRAY>
<TEXT>
<B>
<T>
<BT>

Appendix D
HTML Online References

All of these references are available as active hyperlinks on this book's own home page:

http://www.netscapepress.com

HTML References

The World Wide Web Initiative: The Project
Mother of all WWW Consortium home pages. From here you can link to anything worth reading online on the subject of HTML.

http://www.w3.org/hypertext/WWW/

HTML: Working and Background Materials

http://www.w3.org/hypertext/WWW/MarkUp/MarkUp.html

HTML Current Concerns
This is the page for the very latest news—including a form submit area where you can register to be put on a mailing list.

http://www.w3.org/hypertext/WWW/MarkUp/Activity

HTML3 Draft Spec
The now-expired IETF draft of HTML 3.0, by Dave Raggett of the Hewlett-Packard Research Labs in Bristol, UK.

http://www.hpl.hp.co.uk/people/dsr/html3/CoverPage.html

HTML Style Sheets
WWW Consortium's explanation of style sheets, with an abundance of links to other pages.

http://www.w3.org/hypertext/WWW/Style/

Cascading Style Sheets: A Draft Specification
The front-running style sheet idea, by Håkon Lie.

http://www.w3.org/pub/WWW/Style/css/

HTML Reference Manual
A comprehensive reference to all HTML tags and attributes recognized by any browser, maintained by Michael Hannah of Sandia National Laboratories.

http://www.sandia.gov/sci_compute/html_ref.html

Ian Graham's HTML DTD Complete Reference
Hierarchical tag reference maintained by the author of "HTML Sourcebook."

http://www.hprc.utoronto.ca/HTMLdocs/HTML_Spec/html.html

HTML 3.0 DTD
Another tag hierarchy, from Hal Software Systems.

http://www.halsoft.com:80/sgml/html-3.0/DTD-HOME.html

Netscape Tables
Netscape's own reference to the tables tags, with examples.

http://home.netscape.com/assist/net_sites/tables.html

HTML 3.0 Examples
A good general page by Michael Johnson of the Relay Web Traveler.

http://mordor.relay.com/Traveler/examples.html

Abigail
Abigail, the pseudonym of a Dutch computer programmer, is one of the foremost defenders of "formal" HTML against trendy modification by browser manufacturers. Her site contains many thought-provoking pages, including the "Abigail's Dream" piece we reprinted in Chapter 1.

http://www.edbo.com/abigail/

Acrobat and the Web
Everything about Adobe Acrobat and the Portable Document Format, as described briefly in Chapter 4. Download your Acrobat plug-in here.

http://www.adobe.com/Acrobat/AcrobatWWW.html

HTML Developers' References

The Web Masters' Page
A cornucopia of Web info in more than 30 sections, covering practically everything this book covers, by Bob Allison.

http://gagme.wwa.com/~boba/masters1.html

The Web Developer's Virtual Library
Tutorials, demos, book reviews, and jobs are just four of the main sections in this amazing Web resource. A search engine will even search the archives of all the professional WWW newsgroups and mailing lists for your keyword.

http://www.stars.com/

Web Documentation/Resources
A fine collection of up-to-date documents and links, by Robert Lentz of Northwestern University.

http://www.astro.nwu.edu/html-www/html-docs.html

LIST of low-cost Web space services
Independently maintained register of services such as graphic design, scanning, and virtual hosting, by Alex Chapman, BudgetWeb.

http://digiserve.com/mercer/lowcost/

Arena Trial Browser
The WWW Consortium maintains its own UNIX-compatible browser, "Arena," as a test-bed for the latest ideas such as style sheets. This is Arena's home page, including downloadables and source code.

http://www.w3.org/hypertext/WWW/Arena/

Browser Caps (browser benchmark tests)
A "semi-official" page of tests, to see how your browser displays certain standardized markup.

http://objarts.com/bc/

WWW Viewer Test Page
Another tester, at Lawrence Livermore National Laboratory, including standard hypermedia downloads like audio and video files.

http://www-dsed.llnl.gov/documents/WWWtest.html

InterNIC Registration Service
Help Desk for domain name/IP address registration

http://rs.internic.net/rs-internic.html

Real-time Audio/Video

TrueSpeech

http://www.dspg.com/internet.htm

RealAudio Home Page

http://www.realaudio.com/

Internet Wave

http://vocaltec.com/iwave.htm

Xing Technology Corporation

http://www.xingtech.com/streams/index.html

VDOLive: Real-time Internet Video

http://www.vdolive.com/

RealAudio Encoder
This page is described in Chapter 8.

http://download.realaudio.com/encoderdload/encoder.win32.html

LIVE RealAudio Events Directory
Directory of RealAudio events that are online RIGHT NOW. Updated every five minutes.

http://www.realaudio.com/live/index.html

Some StreamWorks Media Servers in the United States and Abroad
This page contains a list of Streamworks servers and their IP addresses.

http://www.xingtech.com/streams/info/streamwk-sites.html

Authoring with the RealAudio Plug-in for Netscape

http://www.realaudio.com/products/ra2.0/plug_ins/

JAVA

Java
The original Java home page at Sun Microsystems.

http://java.sun.com

Java Mirror Sites

http://java.sun.com/mirrors.html

Gamelan Java Demos

Hyperlinked directory of Java applets and effects, by Earthweb.

http://www.gamelan.com

MULTIMEDIA

Homeport Hollywood

This is an unashamedly commercial site—they have wares to sell, including unedited versions of movies on CD-ROM for you to practice editing on. The company really is run by Hollywood pros, though, and the site has oodles of tips on movie-making.

http://www.el-dorado.ca.us/~homeport/

Welcome to Macromedia!

Macromedia Inc. brings its multimedia expertise to the Web. Among their "cool tools" are Shockwave and Director.

http://www.macromedia.com/

QuickTime Movie & Music Archive

http://quicktime.apple.com/archive.html

Guide to Film and Video Resources on the Internet

Part of the excellent SILS project at the University of Michigan, this comprehensive document by Lisa R. Wood will help anyone developing an interest in Web multimedia.

http://http2.sils.umich.edu/Public/fvl/film.html

Malcolm's Guide to Server PushPull & CGI Animation

Malcolm Humes covers here the same territory as we did in Chapter 8, with hyperlinks to other resources.

http://www.emf.net/~mal/animate.html

PowerWeb
A great resource on Web movies—MPEG archive and FAQ.
http://www.powerweb.de/

IUMA, Welcome to IUMA
The Interact Underground Music Archive.
http://www.iuma.com/

Services

WebTechs HTML Validation Service
A reminder of the code-checking service we covered in Chapter 2.
http://www.webtechs.com/html-val-svc/

WebLint
Another code validation service.
http://www.unipress.com/web-lint

No Shit
Another code validation service.
http://emile.math.ucsb.edu:8000/~boldt/NoShit/

Submit It!
Multiple submission of your site to the searchers.
http://www.submit-it.com/

Pointers To Pointers
Like Submit It!, this site lets you fill in one central form of info about your site, then check any or all of about 50 checkboxes to submit it to the searchers for inclusion.
http://www.homecom.com/global/pointers.html

FAQ: How to Announce Your New Web Site
Epage is a commercial Web service offering classified ads ("Let your mouse do the walking" is their motto). This extremely useful FAQ lists most of the searchers and directories with brief descriptions, helping you decide which of them are a MUST for you.

http://ep.com/faq/webannounce.html

Internet Audit Bureau
Web page logging service; described in Chapter 9.

http://www.internet-audit.com/

Internet Writers Guild
This site is another cornucopia of excellent links and FAQs for HTML authors. You don't have to join the Guild to access most of it, but check their prospectus—there are advantages.

http://www.hwg.org/

The Copyright Web Site
Worried about copyright on your creations? Guilty about using other poeple's? Benedict O'Mahoney lays it on the line here.

http://www.benedict.com/

Internet Security
The security section of Global Network Navigator's "GNN Select" list. FAQs and links on encryption, etc.

http://gnn.com/wic/wics/internet.secur.html

The URL-minder: Your Own Personal Web Robot
Register your favorite pages on this service, and Netmind will send you e-mail whenever one of them changes.

http://www.netmind.com/URL-minder/URL-minder.html

IMAGING

The Imaging Machine
Online image manipulation service offered by Visioneering Research; described in Chapter 4.

http://www.vrl.com/Imaging/

Background Colors Page
An almost indispensable page for trying out combinations of background, text, and links colors. Recently re-made with FRAMES.

http://www.infi.net/wwwimages/colorindex.html

Grahames Graphic Source
One of the very best sources of free graphics, buttons, and bars.

http://www.computan.on.ca/~grahame/graphics.html

Interactive Graphics Generation Page
A marvelous playground at Kansas State lets you make your own icons and buttons by specifying all elements of them.

http://www.eece.ksu.edu/IGR/intro.html

Netscape Color Cube
Informative page on Netscape color processes, maintained by Victor Engel.

http://www.onr.com/user/lights/netcol.html

Netscape Color Guide
Interactive color selection site that lets you feed in the RGB numbers and see the result immediately.

http://www.vmedia.com/alternate/vvc/onlcomp/hpiw/rgb.html

Graphical Information Map Tutorial

http://wintermute.ncsa.uiuc.edu:8080/map-tutorial/image-maps.html

VRML

Dimensional Graphics

A Web design company that's on the forefront of VRML.

http://tcc.iz.net/dgraphix/indexhtml.html

Virtual Reality Modelling Language (VRML) Forum

An unofficial watering-hole for VR enthusiasts, hosted by Wired Magazine.

http://vrml.wired.com/

VRML Virtual Reality Modeling Language

Official intro to VRML from the WWW Consortium.

http://www.w3.org/hypertext/WWW/MarkUp/VRML/

VRML Repository

VR links and FAQs by the San Diego Supercomputer Center.

http://www.sdsc.edu/vrml/

CGI AND PERL

cgi-FAQ

http://www.best.com/~hedlund/cgi-faq/faq.html

Perl-FAQ

http://www.cis.ohio-state.edu/hypertext/faq/usenet/perl-faq/module-list/faq.html

Steven Brenner's form handling—sample scripts
http://www.bio.cam.ac.uk/web/form.html

Perl manpages
http://www-cgi.cs.cmu.edu/cgi-bin/perl-man

Book by Larry Wall
http://www.cis.ufl.edu/cgi-bin/plindex

Tom Christiansen's page
http://www.perl.com/

Mooncrow's CGI/PERL Source Page
http://www.halcyon.com/mooncrow/cgi.htm

CGI specification
http://www.ast.cam.ac.uk/~drtr/cgi-spec.html

Web Stuff-cgi
http://meyer.fys.ku.dk/~zqex/c.cgi?cgi#Cgimain

Matt's Script Archive
http://worldwidemart.com/scripts/

Appendix E
Special Symbols in HTML

HTML allows an extended set of symbols, which is based on the International Standards Organization's *Latin-1* set—basically the lower half of the table you see when you use Word 6.0's menu option Insert/Symbol.

Two different formats are recognized. All accented letters plus a few special symbols may be represented as *entities*. These are fairly easy to remember; for example, é for é is intuitive once you get the feel for it. A larger set of symbols is represented by numeric *character references*, which are far from intuitive and are not much used if an entity is also available for the symbol needed.

Char.	Entity	Numeric	Description
†		†	Dagger
‡		‡	Double dagger
ˆ		ˆ	Circumflex accent
‰		‰	Salinity sign
Š		Š	Uppercase S, haček
Œ		Œ	Uppercase OE diphthong
™		™	Trademark symbol
š		š	Lowercase s, haček

Char.	Entity	Numeric	Description
œ		œ	Lowercase oe diphthong
Ÿ		Ÿ	Uppercase Y, umlaut
¡		¡	Inverted exclamation mark
¢		¢	Cent sign
£		£	Pound sterling
¤		¤	General currency sign
¥		¥	Japanese yen
¦		¦	Broken vertical bar
§		§	Section sign
¨		¨	Umlaut (diaeresis)
©	©	©	Copyright symbol
ª		ª	Feminine ordinal
«		«	Left angle quote, guillemet left
¬		¬	Not sign
-			Soft hyphen
®	®	®	Registered trademark
¯		¯	Macron accent
°		°	Degree
±		±	Plus or minus
²		²	Superscript two
³		³	Superscript three
´		´	Acute accent
µ		µ	Micro sign (Greek mu)
¶		¶	Paragraph sign
·		·	Middle dot
¸		¸	Cedilla
¹		¹	Superscript one
º		º	Masculine ordinal
»		»	Right angle quote, guillemet right
¼		¼	Fraction one-fourth
½		½	Fraction one-half
¾		¾	Fraction three-fourths
¿		¿	Inverted question mark
À	À	À	Uppercase A, grave accent
Á	Á	Á	Uppercase A, acute accent
Â	Â	Â	Uppercase A, circumflex accent
Ã	Ã	Ã	Uppercase A, tilde
Ä	Ä	Ä	Uppercase A, umlaut
Å	Å	Å	Uppercase A, ring
Æ	&Aelig;	Æ	Uppercase AE, diphthong (ligature)

Char.	Entity	Numeric	Description
Ç	Ç	Ç	Uppercase C, cedilla
È	È	È	Uppercase E, grave accent
É	É	É	Uppercase E, acute accent
Ê	Ê	Ê	Uppercase E, circumflex accent
Ë	Ë	Ë	Uppercase E, umlaut
Ì	Ì	Ì	Uppercase I, grave accent
Í	Í	Í	Uppercase I, acute accent
Î	Î	Î	Uppercase I, circumflex accent
Ï	Ï	Ï	Uppercase I, umlaut
Đ	Ð	Ð	Uppercase ETH, Icelandic
Ñ	Ñ	Ñ	Uppercase N, tilde
Ò	Ò	Ò	Uppercase O, grave accent
Ó	Ó	Ó	Uppercase O, acute accent
Ô	Ô	Ô	Uppercase O, circumflex accent
Õ	Õ	Õ	Uppercase O, tilde
Ö	Ö	Ö	Uppercase O, umlaut
×		×	Multiply sign
Ø	Ø	Ø	Uppercase O, slash
Ù	Ù	Ù	Uppercase U, grave accent
Ú	Ú	Ú	Uppercase U, acute accent
Û	Û	Û	Uppercase U, circumflex accent
Ü	Ü	Ü	Uppercase U, umlaut
Ý	Ý	Ý	Uppercase Y, acute accent
Þ	Þ	Þ	Uppercase THORN, Icelandic
ß	ß	ß	Lowercase sharp s, German (sz ligature)
à	à	á	Lowercase a, grave accent
á	á	á	Lowercase a, acute accent
â	â	â	Lowercase a, circumflex accent
ã	ã	ã	Lowercase a, tilde
ä	ä	ä	Lowercase a, umlaut
å	å	å	Lowercase a, ring
æ	æ	æ	Lowercase ae diphthong (ligature)
ç	ç	ç	Lowercase c, cedilla
è	è	è	Lowercase e, grave accent
é	é	é	Lowercase e, acute accent
ê	ê	ê	Lowercase e, circumflex accent
ë	ë	ë	Lowercase e, umlaut
ì	ì	ì	Lowercase i, grave accent
í	í	í	Lowercase i, acute accent

Char.	Entity	Numeric	Description
î	î	î	Lowercase i, circumflex accent
ï	ï	ï	Lowercase i, umlaut
ð	ð	ð	Lowercase eth, Icelandic
ñ	ñ	ñ	Lowercase n, tilde
ò	ò	ò	Lowercase o, grave accent
ó	ó	ó	Lowercase o, acute accent
ô	ô	ô	Lowercase o, circumflex accent
õ	õ	õ	Lowercase o, tilde
ö	ö	ö	Lowercase o, umlaut
÷		÷	Division sign
ø	ø	ø	Lowercase o, slash
ù	ù	ù	Lowercase u, grave accent
ú	ú	ú	Lowercase u, acute accent
û	û	û	Lowercase u, circumflex accent
ü	ü	ü	Lowercase u, umlaut
ý	ý	ý	Lowercase y, acute accent
þ	þ	þ	Lowercase thorn, Icelandic
ÿ	ÿ	ÿ	Lowercase y, umlaut
			Nonbreaking space

In addition to the extended characters, four keyboard characters have special meanings in HTML and therefore need to be encoded as entities if the intention is to display them literally.

Char.	Entity	Numeric	Description
<	<	<	Less than sign
>	>	>	Greater than sign
&	&	&	Ampersand
“	"	"	Double quote sign

Mathematical and Greek symbol entities are listed in Chapter 7, "The World of Tables & Equations."

Appendix F

Interpreting Color Strings

On the Web, colors are specified by their red/green/blue components. Each component color may be present in any intensity from 0 to 255. Hexadecimal numbers (see Glossary) are convenient for specifying color components, because the 0–255 range in decimal becomes 00–ff in hexadecimal, requiring only two digits. Thus, in this convention, #000000 is pure black and #ffffff is pure white.

This partial list suggests which colors are created by some #rrggbb strings in between those two extremes. These strings may be used to specify Web page colors—for example, in the HTML code <BODY BGCOLOR="#5f929e"> to make a cadet blue background.

Color	#rrggbb
alice blue	#f0f8ff
antique white	#faebd7
antique white1	#ffefdb
antique white2	#eedfcc
antique white3	#cdc0b0
antique white4	#8b8378
aquamarine	#32bfc1
aquamarine1	#7fffd4
aquamarine2	#76eec6
aquamarine3	#66cdaa
aquamarine4	#458b74
azure1	#f0ffff
azure2	#e0eeee
azure3	#c1cdcd
azure4	#838b8b
beige	#f5f5dc
bisque1	#ffe4c4
bisque2	#eed5b7
bisque3	#cdb79e
bisque4	#8b7d6b
blanched almond	#ffebcd
blue1	#0000ff
blue2	#0000ee
blue3	#0000cd
blue4	#00008b
blue-violet	#8a2be2
brown	#a52a2a
brown1	#ff4040
brown2	#ee3b3b

Color	#rrggbb
brown3	#cd3333
brown4	#8b2323
burlywood	#deb887
burlywood1	#ffd39b
burlywood2	#eec591
burlywood3	#cdaa7d
burlywood4	#8b7355
cadet blue	#5f929e
cadet blue1	#98f5ff
cadet blue2	#8ee5ee
cadet blue3	#7ac5cd
cadet blue4	#53868b
chartreuse1	#7fff00
chartreuse2	#76ee00
chartreuse3	#66cd00
chartreuse4	#458b00
chocolate	#d2691e
chocolate1	#ff7f24
chocolate2	#ee7621
chocolate3	#cd661d
chocolate4	#8b4513
coral1	#ff7256
coral2	#ee6a50
coral3	#cd5b45
coral4	#8b3e2f
cornflower blue	#222298
cornsilk1	#fff8dc
cornsilk2	#eee8cd
cornsilk3	#cdc8b1
cornsilk4	#8b8878
cyan1	#00ffff
cyan2	#00eeee
cyan3	#00cdcd
cyan4	#008b8b
dark	#bdb76b
dark goldenrod	#b8860b
dark goldenrod1	#ffb90f
dark goldenrod2	#eead0e
dark goldenrod3	#cd950c
dark goldenrod4	#8b6508
dark green	#00562d
dark khaki	#bdb76b
dark nessy	#de00a5
dark olivegreen	#55562f
dark olivegreen1	#caff70
dark olivegreen2	#bcee68
dark olivegreen3	#a2cd5a
dark olivegreen4	#6e8b3d
dark orange	#ff8c00
dark orange1	#ff7f00
dark orange2	#ee7600
dark orange3	#cd6600
dark orange4	#8b4500
dark orchid	#8b208b
dark orchid1	#bf3eff
dark orchid2	#b23aee
dark orchid3	#9a32cd
dark orchid4	#68228b
dark salmon	#e9967a
dark seagreen	#8fbc8f
dark seagreen1	#c1ffc1
dark seagreen2	#b4eeb4
dark seagreen3	#9bcd9b
dark seagreen4	#698b69
dark slate blue	#384b66
dark slate gray	#2f4f4f
dark slate gray1	#97ffff
dark slate gray2	#8deeee
dark slate gray3	#79cdcd
dark slate gray4	#528b8b
dark turquoise	#00a6a6
dark violet	#9400d3
deep pink1	#ff1493
deep pink2	#ee1289
deep pink3	#cd1076
deep pink4	#8b0a50
deep skyblue1	#00bfff
deep skyblue2	#00b2ee
deep skyblue3	#009acd
deep skyblue4	#00688b
dodger blue1	#1e90ff

Color	#rrggbb
dodger blue2	#1c86ee
dodger blue3	#1874cd
dodger blue4	#104e8b
firebrick	#8e2323
firebrick1	#ff3030
firebrick2	#ee2c2c
firebrick3	#cd2626
firebrick4	#8b1a1a
floral white	#fffaf0
forest green	#509f69
gainsboro	#dcdcdc
ghost white	#f8f8ff
gold	#daaa00
gold1	#ffd700
gold2	#eec900
gold3	#cdad00
gold4	#8b7500
goldenrod	#efdf84
goldenrod1	#ffc125
goldenrod2	#eeb422
goldenrod3	#cd9b1d
goldenrod4	#8b6914
gray	**
green1	#00ff00
green2	#00ee00
green3	#00cd00
green4	#008b00
green-yellow	#adff2f
honeydew1	#f0fff0
honeydew2	#e0eee0
honeydew3	#c1cdc1
honeydew4	#838b83
hot pink	#ff69b4
hot pink1	#ff6eb4
hot pink2	#ee6aa7
hot pink3	#cd6090
hot pink4	#8b3a62
indian red	#6b3939
indian red1	#ff6a6a
indian red2	#ee6363
indian red3	#cd5555
indian red4	#8b3a3a
ivory1	#fffff0
ivory2	#eeeee0
ivory3	#cdcdc1
ivory4	#8b8b83
khaki	#b3b37e
khaki1	#fff68f
khaki2	#eee685
khaki3	#cdc673
khaki4	#8b864e
lavender	#e6e6fa
lavender blush1	#fff0f5
lavender blush2	#eee0e5
lavender blush3	#cdc1c5
lavender blush4	#8b8386
lawn green	#7cfc00
lemon chiffon1	#fffacd
lemon chiffon2	#eee9bf
lemon chiffon3	#cdc9a5
lemon chiffon4	#8b8970
light	#f08080
light blue	#b0e2ff
light blue1	#bfefff
light blue2	#b2dfee
light blue3	#9ac0cd
light blue4	#68838b
light coral	#f08080
light cyan1	#e0ffff
light cyan2	#d1eeee
light cyan3	#b4cdcd
light cyan4	#7a8b8b
light goldenrod	#eedd82
light goldenrod1	#ffec8b
light goldenrod2	#eedc82

** Any string defining equal red/green/blue components produces a gray. Thus, there are 254 gray levels available, from #010101 (one shade lighter than black) to #fefefe (one shade darker than white).

Color	#rrggbb
light goldenrod3	#cdbe70
light goldenrod4	#8b814c
light goldenrod-yellow	#fafad2
light nessy	#ff80d2
light pink	#ffb6c1
light pink1	#ffaeb9
light pink2	#eea2ad
light pink3	#cd8c95
light pink4	#8b5f65
light salmon1	#ffa07a
light salmon2	#ee9572
light salmon3	#cd8162
light salmon4	#8b5742
light seagreen	#20b2aa
light sky blue	#87cefa
light sky blue1	#b0e2ff
light sky blue2	#a4d3ee
light sky blue3	#8db6cd
light sky blue4	#607b8b
light slate blue	#8470ff
light slate gray	#778899
light steel blue	#7c98d3
light steel blue1	#cae1ff
light steel blue2	#bcd2ee
light steel blue3	#a2b5cd
light steel blue4	#6e7b8b
light yellow1	#ffffe0
light yellow2	#eeeed1
light yellow3	#cdcdb4
light yellow4	#8b8b7a
lime green	#00af14
linen	#faf0e6
magenta1	#ff00ff
magenta2	#ee00ee
magenta3	#cd00cd
magenta4	#8b008b
maroon	#8f0052
maroon1	#ff34b3
maroon2	#ee30a7
maroon3	#cd2990
maroon4	#8b1c62
medium	#d1c166
medium aquamarine	#00938f
medium blue	#3232cc
medium forest green	#32814b
medium goldenrod	#d1c166
medium orchid	#bd52bd
medium orchid1	#e066ff
medium orchid2	#d15fee
medium orchid3	#b452cd
medium orchid4	#7a378b
medium purple	#9370db
medium purple1	#ab82ff
medium purple2	#9f79ee
medium purple3	#8968cd
medium purple4	#5d478b
medium sea green	#347766
medium slate blue	#6a6a8d
medium spring green	#238e23
medium turquoise	#00d2d2
medium violet-red	#d52079
midnight blue	#2f2f64
mint cream	#f5fffa
misty rose1	#ffe4e1
misty rose2	#eed5d2
misty rose3	#cdb7b5
misty rose4	#8b7d7b
moccasin	#ffe4b5
navajo white1	#ffdead
navajo white2	#eecfa1
navajo white3	#cdb38b
navajo white4	#8b795e
navy blue	#232375
nessy	#ff42d2
old lace	#fdf5e6
olive drab	#6b8e23
olive drab1	#c0ff3e

Color	#rrggbb
olive drab2	#b3ee3a
olive drab3	#9acd32
olive drab4	#698b22
orange1	#ffa500
orange2	#ee9a00
orange3	#cd8500
orange4	#8b5a00
orange-red1	#ff4500
orange-red2	#ee4000
orange-red3	#cd3700
orange-red4	#8b2500
orchid	#ef84ef
orchid1	#ff83fa
orchid2	#ee7ae9
orchid3	#cd69c9
orchid4	#8b4789
pale	#73de78
pale goldenrod	#eee8aa
pale green	#73de78
pale green1	#9aff9a
pale green2	#90ee90
pale green3	#7ccd7c
pale green4	#548b54
pale turquoise	#afeeee
pale turquoise1	#bbffff
pale turquoise2	#aeeeee
pale turquoise3	#96cdcd
pale turquoise4	#668b8b
pale violet-red	#db7093
pale violet-red1	#ff82ab
pale violet-red2	#ee799f
pale violet-red3	#cd6889
pale violet-red4	#8b475d
papaya	#ffefd5
peach puff1	#ffdab9
peach puff2	#eecbad
peach puff3	#cdaf95
peach puff4	#8b7765
peru	#cd853f
pink1	#ffb5c5
pink2	#eea9b8
pink3	#cd919e
pink4	#8b636c
plum	#c5489b
plum1	#ffbbff
plum2	#eeaeee
plum3	#cd96cd
plum4	#8b668b
powder blue	#b0e0e6
purple	#a020f0
purple1	#9b30ff
purple2	#912cee
purple3	#7d26cd
purple4	#551a8b
red1	#ff0000
red2	#ee0000
red3	#cd0000
red4	#8b0000
rosy brown	#bc8f8f
rosy brown1	#ffc1c1
rosy brown2	#eeb4b4
rosy brown3	#cd9b9b
rosy brown4	#8b6969
royal blue	#4169e1
royal blue1	#4876ff
royal blue2	#436eee
royal blue3	#3a5fcd
royal blue4	#27408b
saddle brown	#8b4513
salmon	#e9967a
salmon1	#ff8c69
salmon2	#ee8262
salmon3	#cd7054
salmon4	#8b4c39
sandy brown	#f4a460
sea green	#529584
sea green1	#54ff9f
sea green2	#4eee94
sea green3	#43cd80
sea green4	#2e8b57
seashell1	#fff5ee

Color	#rrggbb
seashell2	#eee5de
seashell3	#cdc5bf
seashell4	#8b8682
sienna	#96522d
sienna1	#ff8247
sienna2	#ee7942
sienna3	#cd6839
sienna4	#8b4726
sky blue	#729fff
sky blue1	#87ceff
sky blue2	#7ec0ee
sky blue3	#4a708b
slate blue	#7e88ab
slate blue1	#836fff
slate blue2	#7a67ee
slate blue3	#6959cd
slate blue4	#473c8b
slate gray	#708090
slate gray1	#c6e2ff
slate gray2	#b9d3ee
slate gray3	#9fb6cd
slate gray4	#6c7b8b
snow1	#fffafa
snow2	#eee9e9
snow3	#cdc9c9
snow4	#8b8989
spring green	#41ac41
spring green1	#00ff7f
spring green2	#00ee76
spring green3	#00cd66
spring green4	#008b45
steel blue	#5470aa
steel blue1	#63b8ff
steel blue2	#5cacee
steel blue3	#4f94cd
steel blue4	#36648b
tan	#deb887
tan1	#ffa54f
tan2	#ee9a49
tan3	#cd853f
tan4	#8b5a2b
thistle	#d8bfd8
thistle1	#ffe1ff
thistle2	#eed2ee
thistle3	#cdb5cd
thistle4	#8b7b8b
tomato1	#ff6347
tomato2	#ee5c42
tomato3	#cd4f39
tomato4	#8b3626
transparent	#000001
turquoise	#19ccdf
turquoise1	#00f5ff
turquoise2	#00e5ee
turquoise3	#00c5cd
turquoise4	#00868b
violet	#9c3ece
violet-red	#f33e96
violet-red1	#ff3e96
violet-red2	#ee3a8c
violet-red3	#cd3278
violetred4	#8b2252
wheat	#f5deb3
wheat1	#ffe7ba
wheat2	#eed8ae
wheat3	#cdba96
wheat4	#8b7e66
white smoke	#f5f5f5
yellow1	#ffff00
yellow2	#eeee00
yellow3	#cdcd00
yellow4	#8b8b00
yellow-green	#32d838

Appendix G
Standard Icons

HTML Standard Icons

These may be invoked either by the attribute DINGBAT in conjunction with <Hn> or <UL>, or by using the official icon names listed here in the form of an entity reference—e.g. &audio; for the standard audio icon.

More information on this, and an example, are at the end of Chapter 5, and definitions are at **http://www.w3.org/pub/WWW/TR/WD-wwwicn-960108** (or superseding Working Document).

clock

compressed.document

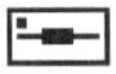

disk.drive

diskette

display

document

fax

filing.cabinet

film

fixed.disk

folder

form

ftp

glossary

gopher

home

image

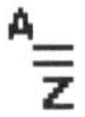

index

keyboard

mail

mail.in

mail.out

map

mouse

network

new

next

notebook

parent

play.fast.forward

play.fast.reverse

play.pause

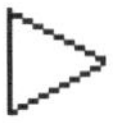

play.start

play.stop

previous

printer

sadsmiley

smiley

stop

summary

NETSCAPE STANDARD ICONS

This icon set is built in to the browser software. Invoke the icons as <IMG SRC="internal-iconname"> whether you are online or not.

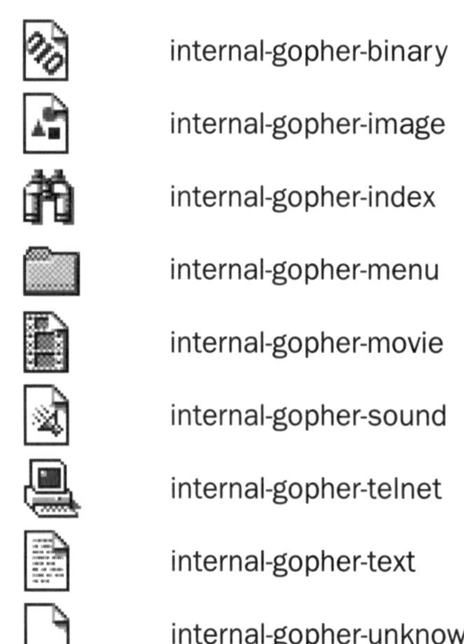

 internal-icon-baddata

 internal-icon-delayed

 internal-icon-embed

 internal-icon-insecure

 internal-icon-notfound

internal-news-catchup-group

internal-news-catchup-thread

internal-news-followup

internal-news-followup-and-reply

internal-news-go-to-newsrc

 internal-news-newsgroup

 internal-news-newsgroups

 internal-news-next-article

 internal-news-next-article-gray

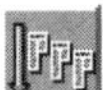 internal-news-next-thread

 internal-news-next-thread-gray

internal-news-post

 internal-news-prev-article

 internal-news-prev-article-gray

 internal-news-prev-thread

 internal-news-prev-thread-gray

internal-news-reply

internal-news-rtn-to-group

internal-news-show-all-articles

internal-news-show-unread-articles

internal-news-subscribe

internal-news-unsubscribe

Glossary

Alias A nickname used, for example, in e-mail managers so that you can enter "fred" and your e-mail manager knows you mean "edf556@froward.cursci.com".

Algorithm A mathematical analysis of a task to be carried out by computer programming. The algorithm is not the program *per se,* but it is the proof that a proposed programming strategy will work.

Analog Continuously variable, as for example a conventional audio output that at any instant can have any value between zero and a few volts, and can accurately be graphed as a waveform. In contrast, at any instant a digital signal can only have the values 0 or 1.

Anchor In hypertext, the object that is highlighted and "clickable." It may be a word, a phrase, or an inline image.

Anonymous FTP An FTP service that serves any user, not just users having accounts at the site. Anonymous FTP generally permits downloading of all files, but uploading only into a directory called "/incoming."

Applet A "miniature application"—an enhancement to a Web page done by embedding a completely foreign type of program in the page.

Archie A keyword search service that searches the directory and file titles of all FTP sites that are indexed.

Array In computer programming, a set of strings that are interrelated and may be addressed as a group, or by suffixing the array name, as "$names[23]" meaning the 23rd member of the $names array.

ASCII (American Standard Code for Information Interchange) An agreed-upon coding of letters, numbers, and symbols developed for teletype data exchange. An ASCII file is one that makes use of only the first 128 ASCII symbols—the "printable" symbols you see on your keyboard, basically, plus the essential control characters. The advantage of ASCII files is that one bit per byte is always available for purposes such as error-checking.

Attribute Qualifying property of an HTML tag. For example, ALIGN is an attribute of IMG that qualifies its position in relation to text. Attributes are usually optional.

.AU The "Sun Audio" format for audio data files. Extremely popular on the Web because of its portability between operating systems.

.AVI A combined video/audio compressed file format.

Backbone The connections between the primary computers in a network. Stub networks branch off the backbone.

Back link Hyperlink that links *into* a page, as opposed to a normal hyperlink that takes the user away from the page.

Bandwidth Used (somewhat inaccurately) to express the maximum possible throughput of a data link in bits per second. A so-called T1 line has a bandwidth of 1.544 Mbps. A 28.8k baud modem has a nominal bandwidth of 0.0288 Mbps.

Beta (release) software Software that is not considered finished enough to market, but is released so that the general public (or a selected population) can participate in the development process by trying it out and reporting bugs. So called because *alpha* debugging is done before any public release. Netscape Communications Corp. has a general policy of releasing several betas before each commercial version—often these are designed to "self-destruct" after a period of time judged adequate for all bugs to be discovered.

Binary A numbering system used in computing that has two as its base. A binary file, as opposed to an ASCII file, makes use of 256 symbols and so does not keep a bit free for error-checking—hence the error-checking file transfer protocols that are essential for successful binary file transmission.

Bleed In page layout, extension of artwork to the extreme edge of the page, allowing no margin. Adopted in Web design to mean an image that flows outside what is assumed to be the user's content area.

Bookmark A Web address in the form of a URL that a user keeps a record of in order to be able to return to it easily.

Boolean operator Same as a logical operator [AND, OR, NOR, XOR, NOT]. Used on the Web to define search keywords with precision. A search for California AND wine would give a different result from California NOT wine.

Bullet In graphic art, a small typographical symbol used to draw attention to the items in a list.

Cache 1. An area of RAM set aside to hold data or instructions that would normally be read from disk, in order to speed up access to it. 2 In network operation, an area of disk set aside to hold data that would normally be read from the Net, for the same reason. Netscape makes use of both types of cache.

CD-I Compact Disk-Interactive: Hardware system allowing interactive use of the data on a CD-ROM disk rather similar to Web page interaction, but much faster and more multimedia-capable.

CD-ROM Compact disk formatted to act as data storage for a PC. The "ROM" part (Read-Only Memory) is a reminder that, just like a music CD, information from it is read to you, but you can't write new information to it.

cgi-bin The Common Gateway Interface through which binary files and HTML files communicate. The expression "a cgi-bin program" is used as though cgi-bin were a computer language, which it is not (see Chapter 9).

Checkbox Very small active area in a form or a dialog box that has only two states, checked and unchecked. Toggles between the two states with mouse clicks.

Client pull A very simple type of Web "animation" in which a series of pages is loaded in succession, governed by concealed coding in the headers of the HTML files.

Client/server software An arrangement of computers, very common in Internet systems, whereby a small system called the client makes use of the data management services of a much larger computer, the server. Netscape Navigator is a client/server system, with the client running on your machine taking advantage of the far greater processing power of the server at a remote site.

Clipboard In Windows applications, a part of computer memory used as temporary storage for any text, picture, or object that the user places there using "Edit/Copy" or "Edit/Cut" (or keyboard equivalents). The object remains on the clipboard until replaced or until the end of the Windows session. The purpose is to enable the object to be re-inserted using "Edit/Paste" or Ctrl-V into a different position or to a completely different Windows application. The contents of the clipboard can be seen at any time using the Windows Clipboard Viewer.

Content window The portion of the Netscape screen in which actual page content is seen, as opposed to the control and information portions.

Coordinates [x,y coordinates] A set of measurements that define the position of a point in however many dimensions are in use. As used in Web graphics, the x,y coordinates of a point on an image are the horizontal and vertical distances from a point of origin at the top left corner of the image, measured in pixels.

Cropping Cutting off unwanted borders from a photograph or other artwork so as to correct framing errors or bring out a detail. In computer graphics, done with a "crop-box" drawn across the artwork with the mouse.

Cyberspace Fanciful term coined by William Gibson in the novel *Neuromancer* to describe the sum total of computer-accessible information in the world.

Database Orderly collection of information in a computer file or files, which can be manipulated and displayed in useful ways by a DBMS (DataBase Management System). The essence of a database is that it is practically unintelligible in its raw state.

Demographics As used by the advertising industry, a breakdown of the types of people that are attracted by a medium—ages, incomes, genders, etc. As the industry develops an interest in the Web, it is bringing pseudo-science like demographics with it.

Dial-up account The type of Internet access account that is connected only when a modem connection is established, as distinct from a direct permanent connection. Often used to refer to a shell account as opposed to a SLIP or PPP-type access, even though SLIP/PPP accounts are mostly also established by dialup.

Digital Applied to computer data, especially when it is in transit between one system and another, to mean "either on or off—no intermediate value." By contrast, an analog data stream is continuously variable between its minimum and maximum values.

Direct connection In the Internet context, a hard-wired connection between a computer and the Internet, giving the computer an IP address and the ability to function as a Web site. By contrast, a dial-up connection is only made when needed.

Directory Logical division of a computer data storage device such as a disk drive so as to group files in a way that makes sense to the user. All Jane's memos in the C:\JANE\MEMOS directory, to take a simple example. See also Folder.

Dithering In a computer image, juxtaposition of two or more differently-colored pixels, with the intent of creating the subjective impression of a color that cannot actually be represented, because of palette limitations.

DNS (Domain Name Server) Software that converts host names to IP addresses and searches for them.

Drag-and-drop Mouse operation, allowing the user to click on a screen icon and, by holding down the mouse button, move it (or a "shadow" of it) to another part of the screen. When the mouse button is released, some appropriate event happens such as copying a file to a new location or application.

Ethernet A high-speed LAN system using bus topology that's highly suitable for connection to the Internet.

.EXE file extension In DOS, denotes an "executable" file that will run if its name is simply entered at the DOS prompt (with or without the .EXE). Files that are executable in Windows frequently have the extension .EXE also.

External image An image that may be accessed by a hypertext link from an HTML page, but is not automatically displayed when the page loads, as is an inline image.

FAQ (Frequently Asked Questions) Pronounced FAK, shorthand for an information file about some system. In Usenet newsgroups, you should always read any FAQs you can find because if you ask a question that's already covered in the FAQ you are likely to be "flamed" (see below).

Field In a database, one coherent part of a record, such as the name field of a name/address/title/ID personnel record.

Finger Originally a UNIX command requesting information about another registered UNIX account-holder. Now available to Netscape by courtesy of Finger "gateways."

Flame A deliberately abusive message in e-mail or Usenet post.

Flow chart Visual aid used by computer programmers to sketch the overall logic of a complex program.

Folder Logical grouping of files in disk storage. The term was familiar to Macintosh users, but not to DOS/Windows users, until Windows 95. Windows 95 uses the "folder" convention extensively in its file structure displays, to indicate a group of files having something in common, but the older DOS "directory" structure still exists.

FTP (File Transfer Protocol) One of the original protocols on the Internet, which allows for very efficient transfer of entire data files between computers but discourages interactive browsing.

Gamma In the RGB color system used for computer monitors, all variations in intensity of the primary colors are brought about by variations in electrical voltage. The relationship between voltage and the degree of perceived color on the monitor (luminance) is non-linear, and is the exponent of the arithmetical equation that relates them. Gamma correction is, strictly speaking, an electronic manipulation that restores linearity between color assigned to a pixel and actual pixel luminance. It's more commonly used to refer to the process used in computer graphics to correct for mismatch between the original and the electronic version, either bringing computer art closer to what is "expected," or deliberately introducing color distortion to achieve a desired effect. Since gamma correction only affects the shape of a curve that has fixed points at either end, it has no effect on color intensities that are zero or maximum, only on the mid-ranges.

.GIF (Graphics Interchange Format) One of many formats for computerized images, designed to be highly transportable between computer systems. Ideal for line art, and very frequently used for inline images in Web pages. See Chapter 4 for more discussion of the .GIF format.

Gopher An Internet search-and-display application that reduces all Internet resource "trees" to onscreen menus.

Grayed Most Windows applications, Netscape included, have an extensive choice of toolbar buttons and menu options. However, not all of these options may be actually available at any given moment. (The "paste" option is not available when nothing is on the clipboard, for example.) Rather than eliminate these options altogether, software designers arrange to display them in a pale color rather than sharp and contrasted. They are then said to be "grayed out."

Helper applications Applications that cooperate with Netscape and other Web browsers to perform functions that Netscape itself is not programmed to perform, such as viewing video files.

Hexadecimal An arithmetical system, used in computer programming, that has 16 as the base instead of 10. The first sixteen numbers in hex are 1,2,3,4,5,6,7,8,9,A,B,C,D,E,F,10.

Home page 1. Whatever page you designate (in the General/ Appearance preference panel) as the Web page you want Netscape to load at startup. 2. A personal page you control and refer other people to. 3. The "entry page" of a multipage Web site.

Host A computer whose primary function is facilitating communications.

Hotlist A personal list of favorite Web addresses, organized so that it creates hypertext links to the addresses. Same as a **bookmark** list.

HTML (HyperText Markup Language) A convention for inserting "tags" into a text file that Web browsers like Netscape can interpret to display or link to hypermedia. HTML files usually have the extension .HTML or .HTM.

HTTP (HyperText Transfer Protocol) Advanced protocol developed for the exchange of hypertext documents across the Internet, with destinations of all internal and external hyperlinks included.

Hypermedia Media such as video and audio, which go beyond what was thought (not so very long ago!) to be the realm of personal computer display.

Hypertext System of interactive text linking allowing the reader to choose any path through the sum total of available text.

Icon 1. On a Windows desktop, a small image representing a dormant application or program group that can be brought to life by double-clicking. 2. In a Web page, a small image that may or may not be a hyperlink to some other resource.

Inline image On a Web page, an image to be loaded along with the page text (although inlines can be suppressed by a Netscape user to speed up page loading).

Interlacing 1. In computer graphics, download of an image in several passes, so that an approximate view of the whole image is delivered quickly, rather than one slice of the finished image. 2. In broadcast video, delivery of each frame in two separate fields, field 1 being lines 1,3,5... and so on of the frame, and field two being the interlaced even-numbered lines. A computer monitor is almost never interlaced.

Internet A network of computer networks stretching across the world, linking computers of many different types. No one organization has control of the Internet or jurisdiction over it.

IP address An Internet machine address formatted with numbers rather than a host name. An IP address may also contain a port number, separated from the host address by a colon.

ISDN (Integrated Services Digital Network) Local telephone switching system that allows a single phone line to carry several high-speed data circuits as well as a voice line on a high-speed timeshare basis.

ISP Internet Service Provider.

Java A system invented by Sun Microsystems, now embedded in Netscape, enabling dynamic objects called "applets" to be transmitted through HTTP server-client links. Animated pictures are an example. *Hot Java* is separate client software designed specifically to display Java applets.

.JPEG or .JPG (Joint Photographic Experts Group) A modern image file format allowing for a choice of three levels of file compression, with progressive trade-off of image quality. JPEGs are ideal for photographic art, as opposed to line art that compresses better in .GIF format. See Chapter 4 for further discussion.

Key In a database, a field in each record (put there for that sole purpose, if need be) that is guaranteed to be unique in every record, and is used for systematic searching.

LAN (Local Area Network) Group of computers and peripherals that are interlinked to share resources in a restricted area, typically an office building. Although Netscape was designed for the World Wide Web, its nifty hyperlink features make it very suitable for operation within a LAN.

Link In the World Wide Web context, short for "hypertext link," meaning a path a user may follow that connects one part of a document to another part of the same document, a different document, or some other resource.

Lynx Name of a text-only World Wide Web browser, available for UNIX, Linux, DOS, and a few other operating systems.

Macro Sequence of instructions to a computer that, for the convenience of the user, can be issued with one simple command alias, such as a control keystroke.

Mail server A computer whose primary function is e-mail management for a group of subscribers.

Manpage Explanatory text file ("manual page") available to UNIX users to remind them of UNIX command syntax.

Metafile Small data file whose sole purpose is to pass on information about another file—its address, format, length, etc.

MIME (Multipurpose Internet Mail Extensions) A set of agreed-upon formats enabling binary files to be sent as e-mail or attached to e-mail. "MIME types" have come to mean hypermedia formats in general, even when not communicated by e-mail. WWW browsers such as the Navigator depend upon MIME type declarations, tacked on as headers to incoming data, to decide how to deal with the data.

Mirror site A subsidiary FTP site that has the same content as the main site that it reflects. Used to take the load off sites so popular that they are frequently inaccessible because of congestion.

Mixing In audio operations, the creative act of taking several audio sources and dynamically adjusting their levels to make a single smooth recording that includes all of them.

Mosaic A World Wide Web graphical browser, forerunner of Netscape Navigator.

Mozilla Pet name the software authors gave to Netscape Navigator during development, which has survived as the name of the green monster who decorates many of the Netscape information pages, and also as the browser description reported by the HTTP_USER_AGENT environment variable.

.MPEG or .MPG (Motion Picture Experts Group) Modern standard format for compression and storage of video hypermedia files.

NCSA (National Center for Supercomputing Applications) A U.S. Government center at the University of Illinois. NCSA developed the Mosaic Web browser and other Internet interfaces.

Netscapism Affectionate sobriquet for an HTML tag or attribute that is only interpreted by the Netscape browser. More correctly known as a *Netscape extension.*

NEWSRC file Data file that keeps a record of which newsgroups a user is subscribed to, and which articles have already been read.

Newsreader Software whose function is to interact with Usenet newsgroups, providing services such as subscription, display, follow-up, print, download, and so on.

NNTP (Network News Transport Protocol) The protocol used by the Usenet newsgroups to disseminate bulletins.

NTSC Acronym for the RGB color TV standard used throughout North America. Cynical European engineers, who think their luminance/chrominance system is better, say it stands for "Never Twice the Same Color," but actually it's "National Technical Standards Committee."

Packet-switching A system, used extensively throughout the Internet, for handling messages based upon the breakdown of a message into standardized packets, each of which is independently routed to the addressee.

Pane Sub-section of a Window. For example, the Netscape mail window has three panes: the folder pane, the mail pane, and the message pane. The boundaries between panes can be moved by the user.

Parent/child Technically, the relationship between a master process in UNIX and a sub-process spawned by the parent. Adopted by Netscape as a way of referring to the relationship of FRAMES on Web pages, which can be nested down to many levels.

Parse In data management, to examine byte by byte in order to extract certain expected patterns, such as filenames, dates, etc.

Path A complete instruction defining where in a computer's directory structure a certain file is located. A path may be indicated from the root, such as, "C:\WINDOWS\WINAPPS\GAMES, or relative to the current subdirectory. "..\WINAPPS\ACCOUNTS" means "starting from here, go up one level than back down to WINAPPS\ACCOUNTS".

.PDF (Portable Document Format) A convention that imports a completely formatted document to a user's screen, including all fonts, colors, and illustrations exactly like a magazine page. At the present time, only the application Adobe Acrobat can read and display .PDF files on the Web.

PERL (Practical Extraction and Report Language) A modern computer language whose features make it very suitable for cgi-bin tasks.

Permissions A UNIX file may be designated as readable and/or writable and/or executable. The designation is made independently for the file's owner, for other users on the same system, and for users from outside. The total designation is known as the file's permissions.

POP (Post Office Protocol) mail An e-mail system that establishes your primary mailbox in your own desktop computer rather than at your access provider's site. POP mail is the usual protocol for incoming mail, while SMTP is used for outgoing.

PPP (Point-to-Point Protocol) A convention for transmitting packet-switched data over long-distance networks.

Properties window Pop-up window displaying hidden information about some object selected with the mouse. Properties windows usually, but not always, allow the user to edit the information.

Proxy A device used to access the Internet around a "firewall" put up to ensure security in a large system.

QuickTime A combined compressed video/audio format, invented for Macintosh multimedia systems but now also available for DOS/Windows.

Radio buttons Small buttons that appear in sets on a computer interface screen, allowing the user to select one only from a range of choices. Like the select buttons on a car radio, selecting one automatically de-selects all others in the set.

RAM (Random-Access Memory) The part of a computer's memory that is available for loading user-selected software and data.

Record In a database, one complete entry—usually consisting of several fields.

ROM (Read-Only Memory) The part of a computer's memory that contains manufacturer's instructions, not available for the user.

Search engine Keyword searching algorithm or complete software package including search algorithms.

Server The server half of a client/server pair: the computer that handles the primary data management tasks on behalf of its clients.

Server push Simple Web animation technique by which an image called into a Web page is not actually an image but a cgi-bin script that loads a series of images.

SGML (Standard Generalized Markup Language) The forerunner of HTML, still used for many documents on the Web, particularly reference works. Embedded "tags" similar to HTML tags describe the format of the document so that it can be displayed "across platforms," meaning on any computer system.

Shell 1. A simple, usually menu-driven, interface that shields a computer user from the complexities of operating systems such as UNIX. Hence a common type of Internet connection, known as a "UNIX shell account," can be operated efficiently with extremely limited actual knowledge of UNIX. 2. A type of simple computer language using UNIX commands and conditional structures to make an executable file.

.SIG file A short text file that you habitually use as your personal sign-off or signature at the end of e-mail and/or Usenet postings. Netscape and other Internet applications make it possible for your .SIG to be appended to outgoing messages automatically.

SLIP (Serial Line Internet Protocol) A convention for transmitting packet-switched data.

SMTP (Simple Mail Transfer Protocol) The usual protocol for outgoing Internet e-mail.

Socket One of a series of memory addresses in a computer reserved for data exchange with a TCP/IP stack.

Source document In the World Wide Web, the raw ASCII text file that an HTML author creates, as distinct from a Web page that is the representation of a source document in hypertext.

Storyboard Visual aid used in pre-production of movies (especially for commercials, when the concept has to be explained to many non-technical people) that lays out the visual treatment as a series of sketch panels accompanied by plot notes. Now also used by meticulous Web authors for site planning (especially when they need to explain the concept to inexperienced colleagues or clients).

Stack In the context of TCP/IP, the ordered series of protocols and packet drivers required to interface a desktop computer with the Internet.

String In computerese, any sequence of characters. "Desktop/412" is a string. So is "µ668_counter‰". Basically, any variable used by a computer that cannot necessarily be evaluated numerically is a string.

Style sheet Text file that defines the stylistic elements of a series of HTML files, such as fonts, colors, and so on. "Official" HTML much prefers this way of defining Web style rather than by the use of tags such as <FONT> and attributes such as BGCOLOR. A style sheet may be referenced by an unlimited number of HTML files.

Tag Name given to the code strings embedded in HTML documents, such as <H1>, that control the formatting and display of documents on the Web.

TCP/IP (Transmission Control Protocol/Internet Protocol) Shorthand for the most common packet-switching protocols used on the Internet.

Telnet A software system that establishes a connection between two computers for the purpose of character-based data exchange. Unlike FTP, Telnet is interactive and, as commonly used, makes a desktop computer behave as though it were the workstation of a much larger computer.

.TIFF or .TIF (Tagged Image File Format) A standard format for storing bitmapped image files. A .TIFF file is uncompressed (and therefore generally large) and can contain many images.

Toolbar Area of a computer application screen used in conjunction with a mouse pointer to perform various functions by clicking. The active areas of a toolbar are usually drawn to look like pushbuttons, and often have different "in" and "out" renderings.

Trumpet Winsock A popular Winsock package (TCP/IP stack) designed by Peter Tattam of the University of Tasmania. (See also **Winsock**.)

UNIX The operating system of choice for computers dedicated to the Internet. UNIX is inherently suited to network operations.

URL (Universal Resource Locator) An address that completely defines a resource of the World Wide Web. A URL has four elements:

- The service—HTTP or FTP or a few others.
- The host—the computer that handles the resource.
- The port number (often not necessary because it defaults according to the service requested).
- The path and filename of the resource.

Format of a URL is service://host:port/path.

Usenet A worldwide network exchanging news bulletins grouped under subject categories called "newsgroups." Most newsgroups are open, and anyone may contribute. Netscape has its own built-in newsreader for interacting with Usenet. (See also Newsreader.)

Veronica An online keyword searcher for the Gopher.

Vertex (plural Vertices) Point of intersection of two adjacent sides of a polygon.

VRML (Virtual Reality Markup Language, or Modeling Language) "Virtual Reality" is the term used for three-dimensional multimedia computer effects which, if sensed through special viewers, can give the user the feeling of being in a virtual world. As applied to the Web, VR is like an applet introducing 3D effects, and VRML is the set of conventions by which an author composes and defines an effect.

WAIS (Wide Area Information Service) A database service of the Internet allowing structured searching for keyword combinations. WAIS supplies a measure of how well documents it finds match your keywords in the form of a "relevance score," with a score of 1000 being a perfect match.

.WAV A standard format for storing hypermedia audio files, common in DOS/Windows systems and not as portable as the .AU format.

Web Short for the World Wide Web.

Web browser User interface to the Web. Netscape is a graphical Web browser.

WebCrawler Software that searches the Web (or, more commonly, a database *derived* from the Web) for keywords input by a user.

Web page Coherent document that is readable by a Web browser. A Web page may vary in complexity all the way from a simple piece of text enclosed by the HTML tags <PRE>....</PRE>, meaning "pre-formatted," to a densely coded HTML file giving the user access to many types of hypermedia.

Web server A server computer equipped to offer World Wide Web access to its clients using HTTP.

Web spider A type of keyword search software.

Webmaster Person at a Web server site who is qualified to administer all Web resources at that site.

Winsock Short for Windows Sockets: the interface between your Windows version of any local Internet software (including Netscape) and the Internet, using the TCP/IP protocols.

Wireframe Approximate rendering of a 3-D object in Virtual Reality, which is nothing but its main vertices joined up by straight lines.

World Wide Web Arrangement of Internet-accessible resources, including hypertext and hypermedia, addressed by URLs.

Wrapping Creating artificial, and temporary, line breaks in text in order to confine it within the viewing width actually available.

WYSIWYG (What You See Is What You Get) Used as an adjective to describe a word processor whose screen display is the same as the final printed result. Also applied to HTML editors whose screen display looks like the intended appearance of a Web page.

Zine Any online magazine.

Index

A

B

C

H

I

J

K

L

N

O

P

Q

R

S

T

U

V

W

X

Y

Z

Explore the Internet

Internet Business 500

$29.95, 488 pages, illustrated, part #: 287-9

This authoritative list of the most useful, most valuable online resources for business is also the most current list, linked to a regularly updated *Online Companion* on the Internet. The companion CD-ROM features the latest version of *Netscape Navigator*, plus a hyperlinked version of the entire text of the book.

Walking the World Wide Web, Second Edition

$39.95, 800 pages, illustrated, part #: 298-4

More than 30% new, this book now features 500 listings and an extensive index of servers, expanded and arranged by subject. This groundbreaking bestseller includes a CD-ROM enhanced with Ventana's WebWalker technology; updated online components that make it the richest resource available for Web travelers; and the latest version of Netscape Navigator along with a full hyperlinked version of the text.

Quicken 5 on the Internet

$24.95, 472 pages, illustrated, part #: 448-0

Get your finances under control with *Quicken 5 on the Internet*. Quicken 5 helps make banker's hours a thing of the past—by incorporating Internet access and linking you directly to institutions that see a future in 24-hour services. *Quicken 5 on the Internet* provides complete guidelines to Quicken to aid your offline mastery and help you take advantage of online opportunities.

HTML Publishing on the Internet for Windows 

HTML Publishing on the Internet for Macintosh 

$49.95, 512 pages, illustrated
Windows part #: 229-1, Macintosh part #: 228-3

Successful publishing for the Internet requires an understanding of "nonlinear" presentation as well as specialized software. Both are here. Learn how HTML builds the hot links that let readers choose their own paths—and how to use effective design to drive your message for them. The enclosed CD-ROM includes Netscape Navigator, HoTMetaL LITE, graphic viewer, templates conversion software and more!

The Web Server Book

$49.95, 680 pages, illustrated, part #: 234-8

The cornerstone of Internet publishing is a set of UNIX tools, which transform a computer into a "server" that can be accessed by networked "clients." This step-by-step in-depth guide to the tools also features a look at key issues—including content development, services and security. The companion CD-ROM contains Linux™, Netscape Navigator™, ready-to-run server software and more.

The Windows NT Web Server Book

$49.95, 500 pages, illustrated, part #: 342-5

A complete toolkit for providing services on the Internet using the Windows NT operating system. This how-to guide includes adding the necessary World Wide Web server software, comparison of the major Windows NT server packages for the Web, becoming a global product provider and more! The CD-ROM features a hyperlinked, searchable copy of the book, plus ready-to-run server software, support programs, scripts, forms, utilities and demos.

Books marked with this logo include a free Internet *Online Companion*™, featuring archives of free utilities plus a software archive and links to other Internet resources.

Web Pages Enhanced

Shockwave!

$49.95, 350 pages, illustrated, part #:441-3

Breathe new life into your Web pages with Macromedia Shockwave. Ventana's Shockwave! teaches how to enliven and animate your Web sites with online movies. Beginning with step-by-step exercises and examples, and ending with in-depth excursions into the use of Shockwave Lingo extensions, Shockwave! is a must-buy for both novices and experienced Director developers. Plus, tap into current Macromedia resources on the Internet with Ventana's *Online Companion*.

Java Programming for the Internet

$49.95, 500 pages, illustrated, part #: 355-7

Create dynamic, interactive Internet applications with Java Programming for the Internet. Expand the scope of your online development with this comprehensive, step-by-step guide to creating Java applets. Includes four real-world, start-to-finish tutorials. The CD-ROM has all the programs, samples and applets from the book, plus shareware. Continual updates on Ventana's *Online Companion* will keep this information on the cutting edge.

Exploring Moving Worlds

$19.99, 300 pages, illustrated, part #:467-7

Moving Worlds—a newly accepted standard that uses Java and JavaScript for animating objects in three dimensions—is billed as the next-generation implementation of VRML. Exploring Moving Worlds includes an overview of the Moving Worlds standard, detailed specifications on design and architecture, and software examples to help advanced Web developers create live content, animation and full motion on the Web.

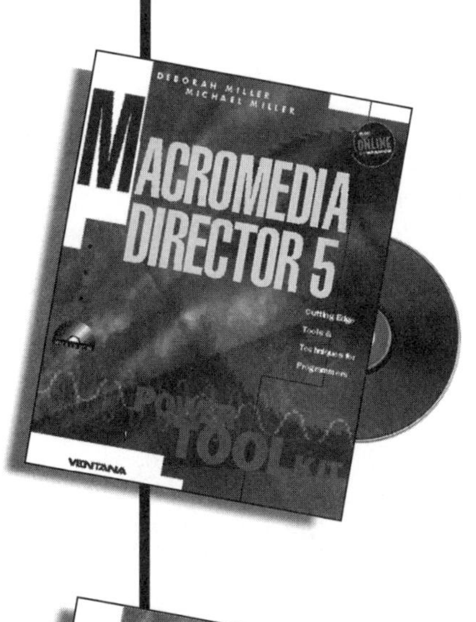

Macromedia Director 5 Power Toolkit 

$49.95, 800 pages, illustrated, part #: 289-5

Macromedia Director 5 Power Toolkit views the industry's hottest multimedia authoring environment from the inside out. Features tools, tips and professional tricks for producing power-packed projects for CD-ROM and Internet distribution. Dozens of exercises detail the principles behind successful multimedia presentations and the steps to achieve professional results. The companion CD-ROM includes utilities, sample presentations, animations, scripts and files.

Internet Power Toolkit

$49.95, 800 pages, illustrated, part #: 329-8

Plunge deeper into cyberspace with *Internet Power Toolkit,* the advanced guide to Internet tools, techniques and possibilities. Channel its array of Internet utilities and advice into increased productivity and profitability on the Internet. The CD-ROM features an extensive set of TCP/IP tools including Web USENET, e-mail, IRC, MUD and MOO, and more.

The 10 Secrets for Web Success

$19.95, 350 pages, illustrated, part #: 370-0

Create a winning Web site—by discovering what the visionaries behind some of the hottest sites on the Web know instinctively. Meet the people behind Yahoo, IUMA, Word and more, and learn the 10 key principles that set their sites apart from the masses. Discover a whole new way of thinking that will inspire and enhance your own efforts as a Web publisher.

Books marked with this logo include a free Internet *Online Companion*™, featuring archives of free utilities plus a software archive and links to other Internet resources.

To order any Ventana title, complete this order form and mail or fax it to us, with payment, for quick shipment.

TITLE	PART #	QTY	PRICE	TOTAL

SHIPPING

For all standard orders, please ADD $4.50/first book, $1.35/each additional.
For software kit orders, ADD $6.50/first kit, $2.00/each additional.
For "two-day air," ADD $8.25/first book, $2.25/each additional.
For "two-day air" on the kits, ADD $10.50/first kit, $4.00/each additional.
For orders to Canada, ADD $6.50/book.
For orders sent C.O.D., ADD $4.50 to your shipping rate.
North Carolina residents must ADD 6% sales tax.
International orders require additional shipping charges.

Subtotal = $ ______________
Shipping = $ ______________
Total = $ ______________

Name ______________________________
E-mail ______________________________ Daytime phone ______________________________
Company ______________________________
Address (No PO Box) ______________________________
City ______________________________ State __________ Zip __________
Payment enclosed ___VISA ___MC ___ Acc't # ______________________________ Exp. date __________
Signature ______________________________ Exact name on card ______________________________

Mail to: Ventana • PO Box 13964 • Research Triangle Park, NC 27709-3964 ☎ 800/743-5369 • Fax 919/544-9472

Check your local bookstore or software retailer for these and other bestselling titles, or call toll free:

800/743-5369